943.0007

014847

GERMANY TURNS EASTWARDS

Michael Burleigh is the author of seven well-received books including *Death and Deliverance, The Racial State* and *The Third Reich: A New History*, which won the Samuel Johnson Prize for non-fiction in 2001.

THOMAS HALL'S SCHOOL LIBRARY

WITHDRAWN 12/5/23

D1341080

Also by Michael Burleigh

Prussian Society and the German Order

Death and Deliverance:
'Euthanasia' in Germany 1900–1945

The Racial State:
Germany 1933–1945

Confronting the Nazi Past:
New Debates on Modern German History (ed.)

Ethics and Extermination:
Reflections on Nazi Genocide

The Third Reich:
A New History

014847

MICHAEL BURLEIGH

GERMANY TURNS EASTWARDS

A STUDY OF *OSTFORSCHUNG* IN THE THIRD REICH

PAN BOOKS

First published 1988 by Cambridge University Press

This edition published 2002 by Pan Books
an imprint of Pan Macmillan Ltd
Pan Macmillan, 20 New Wharf Road, London N1 9RR
Basingstoke and Oxford
Associated companies throughout the world
www.panmacmillan.com

ISBN 0 330 48840 6

Copyright © Michael Burleigh 1988

The right of Michael Burleigh to be identified as the
author of this work has been asserted by him in accordance
with the Copyright, Designs and Patents Act 1988.

All rights reserved. No part of this publication may be
reproduced, stored in or introduced into a retrieval system, or
transmitted, in any form, or by any means (electronic, mechanical,
photocopying, recording or otherwise) without the prior written
permission of the publisher. Any person who does any unauthorized
act in relation to this publication may be liable to criminal
prosecution and civil claims for damages.

3 5 7 9 8 6 4 2

A CIP catalogue record for this book is available from
the British Library.

Typeset by SetSystems Ltd, Saffron Walden, Essex
Printed and bound in Great Britain by
Mackays of Chatham plc, Chatham, Kent

This book is sold subject to the condition that it shall not,
by way of trade or otherwise, be lent, re-sold, hired out,
or otherwise circulated without the publisher's prior consent
in any form of binding or cover other than that in which
it is published and without a similar condition including this
condition being imposed on the subsequent purchaser.

for Jeremy, Henrietta,
Philippa and Paul

CONTENTS

LIST OF TABLES

ACKNOWLEDGEMENTS

The archivists and librarians of the Berlin Document Center; Bundesarchiv, Koblenz; Geheime Staatsarchiv, West Berlin; German Historical Institute, London; J. G. Herder-Institut, Marburg; Hessische Staatsarchiv, Marburg; Uniwersytet Jagielloński Archiwum and Biblioteka Jagiellońska, Cracow; and the Wiener Library, London have my gratitude for their assistance with technical questions.

The written record was supplemented by a series of interviews with Drs E. O. Kossmann and Johannes Papritz in Marburg. The latter also put important material at my unlimited disposal. Professor Henryk Batowski kindly shared his memories of the 'Sonderaktion Krakau' in November 1939.

Rolf Huhn, Albrecht Kannegiesser, Prof. A. Mania, Dr Allan Merson and Dr R. Mühle of Rostock University supplied material that would otherwise have been unobtainable. Mechthild Rössler shared many references and her unrivalled knowledge of geographers in the Third Reich. Antje and Dietz von Beulwitz provided ideal surroundings in which to finish the book in Berlin.

My special thanks must go to Prof. Wolfgang Wippermann whose work suggested my own, and who has been the main source of encouragement, criticism and advice. I would also like to thank Eric Christiansen for his comments on earlier drafts and other kindnesses.

I am profoundly grateful to the British Academy and New College, Oxford for grants and research fellowships which made this project possible. The Chairman of the Modern History faculty in Oxford also responded readily to a belated request for assistance in going to Poland.

Michael Burleigh
Oxford, July 1987

I am glad that Pan Macmillan has decided to keep this book in print, especially since its subject matter is currently the object of intense scholarly interest in Germany. I have made some minor corrections to the original text.

MB
London, October 2001

PART ONE

INTRODUCTION

German perceptions of eastern Europe were inevitably influenced by the fact that from the late eighteenth century Germans governed Poles. Power over a part complicated perceptions of the whole. Since the Poles were also Slavs, and because people thought in terms of ethnic totalities, the notions used to rationalize Prussian rule in Poland were potentially and actually transferable to the Slavs in general. Despite brief periods, as in the 1830s, when Polish exiles from the revolt against reactionary Russia became the cynosure of German liberal enthusiasm, the Prussian solution of the German national question eventually resulted in liberal subscription to most of the concepts which made up Prussian governmental orthodoxy concerning Poland and the Poles.[1]

By the middle of the nineteenth century a series of concepts, of varying intellectual provenance, described German relations with the Slavic East. In a sense they ran deeper than, say, the community of diplomatic purpose vis-à-vis Poland between reactionary Prussia and Russia. These concepts were ultimately a means of justifying Prussian–German rule over a refractory Polish minority. They had little substantive historical reality, but owed much to subjective prejudice, incomprehension, and not least the need to rationalize Prussian rule.

The cynical partitioning of Poland in the late eighteenth century by a monarchical consortium was partly justified by the notion that Poland suffered from a unique form of 'mismanagement'. Although the concept *polnische Wirtschaft* was probably coined by Georg Forster (1754–94) – who died a republican outlaw – it also served to express a monarchical, moralizing, critique of an aristocratic republicanism that was the antithesis of the enlightened absolutism of the Sparta of the North.[2] Ever contemptuous of 'that imbecile crowd whose names end in -ki', Frederick the Great delivered the classic Prussian judgement on Poland and the Poles

That kingdom is caught in eternal anarchy. Conflicting interests separate all the magnate families. They put their own advantage above the public good and unite among themselves only to consider cruel and atrocious means of oppressing their serfs, whom they treat like cattle. The Poles are vain and haughty when favoured by fortune, abject in defeat, capable of the greatest baseness when money is to be gained … but after getting it, they throw it out of the window. Frivolous, they have neither judgement nor firm opinion … In this kingdom, reason has become the vassal of women, they intrigue and decide about everything, while their men worship the bottle.[3]

The corollary of the notion that Poland had a uniquely chaotic constitution, *polonia confusione regitur*, which *inter alia* August Wilhelm Schlegel (1767–1845) translated into a *general* governmental incapability of the Slavs, was that the Germans had an historical mission to bring order, civilization and government to Poland in particular and the East as a whole.[4] Romantic–conservative historians, and their successors in the ascendant *Kleindeutsch* school, also reappraised phenomena like the conquest of Prussia by German Knights, which had appalled thinkers like Herder. Many acts of pious barbarity were excused in terms of secular, cultural improvement.[5] The idea that the Germans were 'bearers of culture' (*Kulturträger*) was axiomatic to a wide range of historians, novelists and theorists including Marx and Engels.[6] A few examples will demonstrate what they meant. In *Soll und Haben*, the Silesian historical novelist Gustav Freytag (1816–95) described the foundation of a town called Rosmin. Before the Germans arrived, Rosmin was virtually in a state of nature, with Slav peasants living under 'filthy straw rooves', and their master 'haughtily in his wooden palace'. German traders – bearing luxury goods – purchased the right to stay. '*In the woods around*', whence by an act of authorial legerdemain the Slavs had been transposed, the latter related 'with wonder' how the men speaking a foreign tongue had erected fine buildings and introduced a monetary economy.

In this way Rosmin arose, like many German towns on ancient Slav soil. They remained what they were from the beginning – the markets of the great plains, places where Polish crops were exchanged for the products of German industriousness, the knots of a firm net which the Germans laid over the Slavs, artful knots in which numerous strands ran together, and through which the humble labourer was bound to other people with education, freedom and a civilised state.[7]

Freytag's friend and life-long correspondent, Heinrich von Treitschke (1834–96), gave these relations a particularly aggressive accent in the service of 'germanizing' Prussia's Polish minority. In his 1862 essay *Das deutsche Ordensland Preussen* he sought to convey 'to the mind of a South German boy an intimation of the most stupendous and fruitful occurrence of the later Middle Ages – the northward and eastward rush of the German spirit and the formidable activities of our people as conquerors, teacher, discipliner of its neighbour'.[8] Equally evident was a retreat into the irrational, and the application of social–Darwinian concepts of race; 'spells' rose from the 'blood-drenched ground' while, 'in the unhappy clash between races, inspired by fierce mutual emnity, the blood-stained savagery of a quick war of annihilation is more humane, less revolting, than the specious clemency of sloth which keeps the vanquished in a state of brute beasts'.[9]

Relations between Germans and Slavs were gradually hypostatized in terms of a West/East 'cultural gradient' (*Kulturgefälle*) declining from the 'civilized' West towards the 'uncivilized' East.[10] Since the German 'cultural mission' appeared to be a recurring – not to say continuous – historical phenomenon, it was a short step to the idea that the Germans were uniquely 'driven' towards the East. The notion of a timeless German *Drang nach Osten* had gained sufficient purchase by the 1860s for the Polish historian Karol Szajnocha to write, 'What the Germans of today call in self-justification the drive to the East said to be dictated by destiny, was and is in fact a drive in all directions wherever rapaciousness has dared and succeeded to force its way through.'[11] The flight from the discrete, human, and contingent reached its most eloquent nadir when the Nazi publicist Adalbert Forstreuter wrote that German migration eastwards, 'reminds one precisely of the birds, a phenomenon that may well have climatic origins, but which would not have assumed so clear a form if an original impulse had not been present in the souls of the birds'.[12] Metaphors borrowed from the biological–organic realm were also employed to describe movements of peoples in the past and present. The medieval *Ordensstaat*, for example, became a 'bulwark', 'dam' or 'dyke' holding back the 'wildly agitated, restless Slav and semi-Slav flood'[13] or 'the growing Slav ethnic flood',[14] metaphors which ultimately reflected present anxieties about an unassimilable Polish minority, augmented by influxes of migrant workers to the factories of the Ruhr or the east Elbian estates of the Junkers.

After 1918 the concepts considered above became intertwined with the intention of radically revising the frontiers created by Versailles. According to Karl Hampe, the Germans should resume the '*Zug nach dem Osten*' which had been broken off in the Middle Ages.[15] Where professional historians led, turning the sources into 'weapons' for the 'struggle for national existence', others were not slow to follow.[16] History lent an air of apparent familiarity to chill, ahistorical, racial reality. The Germans should once again set out on 'the march of the Teutonic Knights of old' towards Russia.[17] Ethnic–biological survival dictated that the Germans took up 'where we broke off six hundred years ago'.[18] But as Hitler's descriptions of Russia made plain, the familiar has the deceptive quality of the comforting elements in a nightmare. They gave way to something uncontrollable.

> ... the organisation of a Russian state formation was not the result of the political abilities of the Slavs in Russia, but only a wonder ful example of the state-forming efficiency of the German element in an inferior race ... Lower nations led by Germanic organisers and overlords have more than once grown to be mighty state formations and have endured as long as the racial nucleus of the creative state race maintained itself. For centuries Russia drew nourishment from the German nucleus of its upper leading strata. Today it can be regarded as almost totally exterminated and extinguished. It has been replaced by the Jew ... He himself is no element of organisation, but a ferment of decomposition ... And the end of Jewish rule in Russia will also be the end of Russia as a state.[19]

History was merely a prophylactic for a view of life governed by the criteria of race, and the primal carnage of foxes and farmyard rats. Anyone or anything in history could be appropriated or rejected in the service of the new. For example, 'germanising' the East 'in the old sense', through education, legislative coercion, and economic discrimination was no longer the guiding intention; it was necessary 'to make sure that only people of true German blood dwell in the East'.[20] This was meant literally. Having conquered the East, the erstwhile *Kulturträger* rapidly shed their load. In September 1942 Himmler addressed a group of senior SS leaders at Hegewald (Žitomir) in the USSR. He passed from the matter of explaining fierce Soviet resistance in terms of aberrant, German blood coursing through the veins of 'an Attila, Genghiz Khan, Tamburlaine (or) a Stalin' and the necessity of stemming 'potentially dangerous life', to his and his Führer's vision of the future.

We are not bringing these people civilisation. I can only repeat to you word for word what the Führer wishes. It will be enough if (1) the children learn to read the traffic signs so that they do not run under vehicles (2) if they learn their 2 × 2 so they can count up to 25, and (3) if they can write their own names; no more is necessary.[21]

The concepts briefly outlined here influenced the terms of professional academic studies of the East. This is a history of the internal and external pressures which kept an academic discipline on a fundamentally false course leading to total instrumentalization under the Nazi regime. Of course, any academic discipline consists of different schools or possibilities for developments to be otherwise. This work tries to show why a school which was incapable of construing its subject autonomously, heterogeneously, or beyond a germanocentric perspective, gained the ascendancy over genuine attempts to work in another direction. The experts did not challenge existing stereotypes and misconceptions; they worked within their boundaries and reified them through empirical 'evidence'. Dissident voices were silenced by authoritarian scholar-managers who policed the politics of their subordinates without government prompting. Anti-democratic professional structures served at once to perpetuate misconceptions and to facilitate government control. The politicians and bureaucrats had the measure of academic power-brokers. As the Nazis discovered, deference to existing hierarchies and proprieties achieved more than radical confrontation. This is not a history of a radicalized and opportunistic 'lunatic' fringe but of a section of the established, educated élite. The advent of a regime bent upon drastic territorial revisions in the East presented an opportunity to translate the labours of the study into present political fact. The *Ostforscher* voluntarily and enthusiastically put their knowledge at the disposal of the Nazi regime, rapidly disowning their conservative political backgrounds, and taking on board as many aspects of Nazi racial dogma as were consistent with their own (limited) notions of scholarly propriety. For example, before 1933, Hermann Aubin had DNVP sympathies. By 1937 he was described as being 'positive towards National Socialism', or indeed *nationalsozialistisch zuverlässig*.[22] In September 1939 he wrote:

We must make use of our experience, which we have developed over many long years of effort. Scholarship cannot simply wait until it is called upon, but must make itself heard.[23]

A few months later he was lecturing in front of Hans Frank in occupied Cracow. No one asked these scholars to put their knowledge at the service of the government: they did so willingly and enthusiastically. There was virtually no 'resistance', and what has been described as such turns out, on closer inspection, to have been the result of political miscalculation, a naïve unawareness of the priority of ideology over scholarly exactitude or, more simply, a matter of being outmanoeuvred by more practised political operators. While there was almost no 'resistance', there was much willing legitimization of the status quo as the fulfilment of the past, or provision of a scientific basis for government policy in the occupied East. While it is doubtful whether any of the scholars considered here influenced major geo-political decisions, ethnic-political policy was another matter. That is why, despite the exigencies of wartime, the subject enjoyed continuous institutional expansion, generous funding, and the large-scale exemption of its personnel from military service. Exponents of the view that academics were without influence have to explain why hardheaded SS managers thought and acted otherwise. Rightly or wrongly the latter recognized that the domination of conquered populations, and all that went with it, could be achieved through research institutes in Berlin or Breslau, as well as on the snows of Russia or in the gas chambers of Auschwitz. As scholarly experts on the East, the *Ostforscher* had a distinctive contribution to make to the accurate 'data base' – the statistical and cartographical location of persons – upon which *all* aspects of Nazi policy in the East, as elsewhere, ultimately rested. Deportations, resettlements, repatriations, and mass murder were not sudden visitations from on high, requiring the adoption of some commensurate inscrutable, quasi-religious, meta-language, but the result of the exact, modern, 'scientific' encompassing of persons with card indexes, card-sorting machines, charts, graphs, maps and diagrams.[24] All that an individual was, or was going to be allowed to be, could be precisely expressed through cards and index tabs. The existing methods and preoccupations of German *Ostforschung* dovetailed usefully with Nazi policy. That was why the subject received generous funding.

This work is therefore largely a study of the relations between academics and the Nazi regime.[25] Self-exculpation, and the workings of academic clientage, have ensured that until recently this subject has been neglected in West Germany. By contrast, in East Germany and to a lesser extent in Poland, the subject has been studied, and often studied well, for its ideological and political effect. Yesterday's Nazi professor is the prominent public figure of today. The post-war product of the *Ostforscher* themselves – obituaries, autobiographical essays and reminiscences, and a few unsatisfactory ventures into disciplinary history – has its own problems. Scholars are born, attend this or that university, write books and articles, serve in the army, suffer grievously under Soviets and Poles, and then die. They do not turn their pens to the production of propaganda in politicized institutions, aid and abet obsessive racists, sift and sort conquered populations, or slide effortlessly into the ranks of the SS. In fact that was what they did do. By unlocking received categories concerning degrees of involvement, and by restoring some of the scholars' absent associates, it becomes clear that relations between the temples of learning and those at the sharp, operative, edge of the Third Reich were multiple and fluid. In other words, scholars are part of their social and political milieu and not aggregates of learned books and papers. This is, of course, no novel wisdom.

So this is a study of the deficit side of intellectual endeavour, of the politicization and instrumentalization of a scholarly discipline under the Nazi regime. It is concerned with why an academic discipline, that was often progressive in narrow, methodological terms, pursued a path which led into the impenetrable thickets of biological racism. It commences with a brief outline of the formation of the subject, its institutional bases, and principal schools of thought. The decision to concentrate largely upon one institution in Berlin is partly a reflection of an inadequate documentary base for institutions elsewhere, partly a consequence of the fact that the *Publikationsstelle* in Dahlem was a command post for all the rest. It was the crucial link between government ministries in Berlin and institutes further afield. The *Publikationsstelle* and North-East German Research Community were also directly involved in the creation of the main research institute in the occupied East: the Institut für deutsche Ostarbeit in Cracow. Although the former lost control over the latter, parentage is reflected through the device of beginning the history of the IdO in the previous chapter. The final chapter is both an epilogue, and a discussion of the political function of *Ostforschung* in West and, negatively, East Germany since 1945. Notwithstanding generous funding, the present-day West German institutes are outlying appendages to the heterogeneous study of Eastern Europe and the USSR in the universities.

With so vast a spatial and chronological field as that encompassed under the rubric *Ostforschung*, certain regions are better represented here than others. The concentration upon Czechoslovakia, Poland and western Russia reflects the relative importance of these areas within the subject. Much more could usefully have been said about the Baltic states or south-eastern Europe, although it is doubtful whether this would alter the overall picture. The occasional reference to Transylvanian Saxons or Swabians in the Banat merely serves to remind the reader of the geographical scope and ethnic limitations of the subject. In attempting to capture the multiple levels of intellectual activity, some chronological overlap has been necessary. The emphasis upon biographical detail and connections reflects a conviction that, in this case, an autonomous history of ideas, or internal disciplinary history, renders the subject far more harmless than it actually was.

Scholars are sometimes notoriously sensitive to criticism of their work, and quick to condemn whatever questions their own assumptions or sense of self-importance. At no point here has it been the intention to denounce either the living or the dead. However, it is important to bear in mind the unreflective and unselfconscious ways in which some of the academic experts discussed here took it upon themselves to order the lives of people whose concern was the more prosaic one of survival. The easy disassociation of expertise from its human consequences, quite apart from any 'professional' ethical considerations, in Germany then, and anywhere now, is not something to be regarded with either equanimity or scholarly detachment.

014847

THOMAS TALLIS SCHOOL LIBRARY

1. THE RISE OF A PROFESSION: CLASSICAL
OSTEUROPAFORSCHUNG 1902–33

i. Schiemann and Hoetzsch

Although a professorship in Russian history had existed at the university of Dorpat since the early nineteenth century, and Slavonic studies had been taught at Breslau since 1842, the origins of the interdisciplinary study of eastern Europe and Russia are conventionally associated with the founding of the *Seminar für osteuropäische Geschichte und Landeskunde* at Berlin in 1902.[1] The first director of the Seminar was the Baltic publicist and historian Theodor Schiemann (1847–1921). Leaving Reval in 1887, to evade the consequences of 'russification', Schiemann was taken up in Berlin by the elderly Treitschke, who expedited Schiemann's *Habilitation*.[2] Next, Schiemann marshalled prominent Baltic aristocrats to work upon the Foreign Office and *Kultusministerium*, in the interests of his own academic career.[3] Meanwhile he lectured at the university, from September 1888 at the Academy of War, and worked as an archivist in the Geheime Staatsarchiv. The Academy of War brought contacts with senior officers – Waldersee, Schlieffen, Manteuffel and Litzmann; through the archives he met Sybel, Meinecke and Reinhold Koser.[4] Schiemann's knowledge of Russia, and his high-level contacts, resulted in regular work for the *Allgemeine Zeitung* from 1889, and the *Kreuzzeitung* from 1892. A felicitous combination of his own ambitions, and the desire of the Foreign Office to promote Russian studies through someone they could rely upon, eventually resulted in Schiemann's elevation to an extraordinary professorship in eastern European history on 16 April 1892.[5] The very low attendance figures at his lectures confirm the impression that high-level wire-pulling, as opposed to either his own abilities or any consumer demand for his subject, lay behind the appointment.[6]

From his new position Schiemann essayed plays for the further expansion of the subject, plans which included his own promotion to an *Ordinariat*.[7] His faculty colleagues were dubious about his scholarly record, journalistic involvements, and fearful of losing their monopoly of historical studies, but any objections from this corner were futile, since Schiemann enjoyed the goodwill of Wilhelm II.[8] A deliberately provocative anti-Polish lecture on 6 December 1901 – 'If he were a Pole, he would hide his face' – resulted in stormy scenes, cries of *Polen raus!* and the deportation of the Polish students involved, but served to confirm Schiemann's public image as an 'upright German'.[9] On 30 June 1902 he was appointed director of the new Seminar and, after four more years of intrigue, he became an *Ordinarius*.[10]

From 1905 the seminar held in the Behrenstrasse 70 was attended by an average of twenty-five persons. By 1910 the library consisted of 2,425 volumes, including most of the important source collections for the advanced study of Russian history.[11] In addition to encouraging the acquisition of Slavonic languages through classes by native lecturers, the emphasis was upon the history, contemporary geography and political economy of eastern Europe. Although Russian studies were most prominent, the terms of reference covered the rest of eastern Europe. This disciplinary and regional synthesis was determinative for all subsequent foundations in the field of *Ostforschung*.[12] The foundation, in Vienna in 1907, of an *Institut für osteuropäische Geschichte* under Joseph Constantin Jireček (1854–1918) and Hans Uebersberger (1877–1962), enabled Schiemann to make comparisons with the Viennese competition, and hence to lobby for the further expansion of his seminar.[13] In 1912 he approached the *Kultusministerium* in order to create an extraordinary chair for his co-editor of the 'Zeitschrift für osteuropäische Geschichte' (1910–1914), Otto Hoetzsch. Although the Berlin faculty wanted a chair in west European history, and sought to check Schiemann by making the terms of appointment so high that only Uebersberger could fit the bill, the latter's reluctance to leave Vienna, and support for Hoetzsch in the Prussian House of Deputies, resulted in Hoetzsch's appointment on 1 November 1913.[14]

Born in Leipzig on 14 February 1876, Hoetzsch studied in Leipzig under Karl Lamprecht and Friedrich Ratzel, and in Berlin under Otto Hintze. Hoetzsch combined his studies with a career as a conservative political agitator. A leading member of the Pan-German, anti-Semitic 'Kyffhäuser-Verband der Vereine deutscher Studenten', Hoetzsch was active by the turn of the century in the Pan-German and Navy Leagues and the Eastern Marches Association.[15] A member of Schiemann's seminar since its inception, the thirty-year-old Hoetzsch was appointed professor of history at the Prussian Royal Academy in Posen on 1 October 1906.[16] In addition to his lectures to the teachers and bureaucrats who attended classes at this outpost of German *Kultur*, Hoetzsch was much in demand as a public speaker. In 1907 he was elected chairman of the Posen branch of the Eastern Marches Association, and two years later a member of the national committee.[17] In this capacity he lent his developing reputation to demands for a realization of Bismarck's settlement plans, brushing aside any objections based upon humanity, principle or constitutional propriety, to compulsory purchase or expropriation of the Poles.[18]

Hoetzsch's distinctive views on Russia increasingly brought him into conflict with 'the publicist ambassador of the Baltic Provinces'.[19] Schiemann's conception of Russia was heavily coloured by the problems that he and other Baltic Germans had faced under the regime of Alexander III.[20] Russia was the antithesis of Schiemann's repatriate's enthusiasm for the Prussian–German state. In Russia there was no respect or instinctive sympathy for the rule of law. A corrupt and self-serving bureaucracy abused a people who were congenitally disorganized and in whom over-indulgence in alcohol rapidly summoned 'the beast' to the surface.[21] Dynamic elements came from outside – whether in the form of the Romanovs or German railway officials – to a people habituated to mindless obedience by centuries of Tatar lordship. Any cohesion in this polyglot structure was provided by the failing bonds of Tsarist absolutism.[22] Schiemann's principal achievement was to disseminate the idea that the Russian 'colossus', feared since the defeat of Napoleon, had feet of clay. This was a dangerous and self-interested perspective, as was apparent to Maximilian Harden writing in 1896: 'The Balts who are active in the German press under the protective cover of anonymity have done much damage and have more than once brought us close to war. War for what? Primarily for the benefit of individual Baltic barons . . .'[23]

Hoetzsch substituted pragmatism for Schiemann's prejudice. Beginning with the assumption that both Prussia and Russia had a community of interest in perpetuating the partition of Poland, Hoetzsch carried the community of interest onto the global stage. He argued that Russia was both Germany's natural ally against British imperialism, and a modernizing economy in need of German capital.[24] This geo-political and economic predisposition towards Russia was reinforced by what he saw at first hand of the country and its people.

Before 1914, he made about ten trips to Russia and was well-versed in the Russian authors that Schiemann regarded as symptoms of national decline.[25] He subscribed to a form of relativism which accepted that each people had its own future and potential for development.[26] Russia's development would involve 'reconciliation' between Tsarist absolutism and constitutionality – he had high hopes of the Third Duma – and the ultimate triumph of capitalism.[27] In the case of non-Russian nationalities, Hoetzsch saw their future, conveniently enough, in terms of the advantages they derived from their historical association with the Russian state. Since Germany's future depended upon a strong, reformist, and modernizing Russia, Hoetzsch's relativist sympathies did not extend to separatist tendencies in the Ukraine or, of course, to the national aspirations of the Poles. But there was much here, including optimism, a wide perspective, and an awareness of the social and economic forces at work in Russia, that differed from Schiemann's pessimistic and prejudiced perceptions of the 'Russian threat'.[28]

Fundamental differences of opinion were inevitably bound up with more prosaic animosities. Coolness between mentor and protégé developed into outright hostility, as Hoetzsch tried to step into shoes that Schiemann had not yet vacated. He took over Schiemann's lectures, and – while Schiemann was in England in April 1914 – his Wednesday column in the conservative *Kreuzzeitung*.[29] The foundation on 6 October 1913 of the Deutsche Gesellschaft zum Studium Russlands hastened the personal break. Following a study visit to Russia by 108 academics and administrators in 1912, the political economist Max Sering entrusted Hoetzsch with the elaboration of a memorandum concerning a society to promote the study of Russian history and society in Germany.[30] Employing unfavourable comparisons with the state of knowledge in England and France, Hoetzsch envisaged a politically neutral association designed to study the past, present and future military and economic potential of Germany's eastern neighbour. The work of the society included lectures by foreign and German scholars, raising funds to support academic work, study trips, translations, and the fostering of contacts between scholars and businessmen trading with Russia.[31] The steering committee included Auhagen, Goetz, Hoetzsch, Sering and Schiemann.[32] The latter joined without any great conviction. Following the lead of his friends in the Foreign Ministry, who cold-shouldered Hoetzsch's plans from the start, Schiemann took the earliest opportunity to disassociate himself from the Society, on the grounds that 'it did not correspond to either our interests or the policies pursued by our government'.[33] Soon Schiemann would endeavour to block Hoetzsch's succession to his *Ordinariat*. Ironically enough, in his unscrupulous efforts to nominate his own successor, Schiemann spoke snobbishly of Hoetzsch's journalistic involvements. This was precisely the question mark that had been put beside his own name almost fifteen years before.[34]

Schiemann and Hoetzsch entered the lists in the broader academic debate about German war aims. Ultimately, Schiemann saw the war in terms of ethnic conflict.

> Against the contrary, in part consciously falsified claims, of the so-called experts on Russia [he meant Hoetzsch], one cannot argue sharply enough that the most dangerous and bitter enemy of the German Reich *and Germandom in general*, is to be found in the *Russian people*, as was already apparent to the Baltic Germans fifty years ago.[35]

Given Russia's allegedly considerable powers of demographic recovery, the present war would not be the last. The invasion of the three Baltic provinces, which Schiemann advocated, would be a major blow against the Russian 'colossus', and could be regarded as an act of liberation on behalf of the oppressed. His reaction to the creation of the Polish Congress Kingdom demonstrated that 'liberation' was firmly subordinated to strategic advantage in the struggle with the arch-enemy. 'We did not go to war in order to liberate Poland, rather we have liberated the Poles in order to protect the most endangered part of our frontier, and we have created an independent Poland because we want to have a friendly people as our neighbour.'[36]

While Schiemann acted as a middleman between the Baltic German nobility and Wilhelm II in their common desire to wring the greatest advantage from the confusion that engulfed Russia, Hoetzsch elaborated his own war aims, at some distance, it should be said, from practical decision making. Hoetzsch enjoyed protection from the conservative Count Westarp: Schiemann had influence with the Kaiser.[37] Hoetzsch was the main academic advocate of an 'eastern orientation' in German policy during the First World War. Hoetzsch's long-term aim was the creation of a continental bloc consisting of the Central Powers, the Balkans, Turkey and Russia as a counterweight to the 'napoleonic' 'world despotism' of the Anglo-Saxons.[38] There was no fundamental conflict of interest between Germany and Russia (which for two centuries had had good dynastic and economic relations) and no grounds for presupposing immutable hostility between the two peoples.

> Naturally in relations between two powerful states there are always possibilities of conflict and friction. But these were not important or fundamental in the relations between these states with one another. Rather these relations were conducted by both sides in the knowledge that actually, to use the hackneyed but appropriate slogan, political points of friction between Germany and Russia did not and do not exist.[39]

It was also erroneous to believe that the sentiments, aired in the pages of *Novoe Vremya* by segments of the germanophobe intelligentsia, were identical with the views of a population that was largely illiterate.[40] One could hear vituperative talk about 'the damned dutchmen' (*sic*!) in an English 'public bar', but, Hoetzsch claimed, outside the Panslavist Petersburg intelligentsia, such sentiments were rare in Russia.[41] Dismissive of the wilder strategic speculations of some of his academic colleagues – *Kannegiesserei* ('ale-house politics') – Hoetzsch was equally scathing about Liberals and Social Democrats who justified war in terms of interfering in internal Russian political affairs, and Conservatives who had fantasies of dissolving the Russian state into a congeries of nationalities.[42] The latter were busily cutting the bear's skin before he was down and out, with all the insouciance of someone 'picking apart the leaves of an artichoke'.[43] The hegemony of Greater Russia represented six centuries of evolution in that direction, and was no more accidental than the hegemony of Vienna or Berlin.[44] He reserved his greatest contempt for the Baltic historical lobby, with their various pseudo-historical rationalizations of the political situation

> We do not see that judgements about the German-Russian conflict are in any way furthered by talk of an essentially asiatic state that has to be thrown back behind its asiatic frontiers, or of a colossus on feet of clay, or, usually without adequate historical knowledge, of the significance of the Tatar lordship and the Tatar element.[45]

Although Hoetzsch may have been 'against the stream' in his attitudes to Russia, his views on Poland were conventional. On 26 September 1917 he wrote, 'Three quarters of humanity can be in favour of a free and independent Poland, we in Prussia and Germany cannot be ... The national aims of the Germans and Poles are irreconcilable.'[46] Like the 352 professors who signed the *Intellektuelleneingabe* in July 1915, Hoetzsch subscribed to the view that Germany should take advantage of the military situation by annexing and settling a belt of territory to guarantee its strategic and ethnic survival and, of course, its stock of strategic resources.[47] Since the conduct of German troops meant that the Poles were cool towards the 'German war' and efforts to use them against the Russians, only traditional anti-Polish policies remained.[48] Traditional policies, involving almost casual steps into constitutional illegality, were justified in terms of demographic pressure and, increasingly, with reference to the future 'health' of the German *Volk*.[49] New settlement lands in the East would contribute to the 'physical, moral, and spiritual health' of the nation.[50] The authors of settlement and resettlement plans – for example Professor Waterstrad, *Oberpräsident* Batocki, and the professional bureaucrat Schwerin – were ominously casual in overriding 'cosmopolitan legal sensitivities' or 'individual cases of hardness'.[51] In the interests of creating a demographic 'well-spring' for Germany, Schwerin actively advocated the 'replanting' of whole villages of Poles in a Polish 'protected state', and the repatriation of the Volga Germans to take their place. He also hoped that the Jews would leave 'of their own accord' for Morocco, Palestine or Asia.[52] If the Russians, despite their poor administration, could transfer hundreds of thousands of persons at will, so could the Germans.[53] As Imanuel Geiss has cogently argued, these plans, and the justifications that accompanied them, bear considerable verisimilitude to what the Nazis would do later.[54]

Hoetzsch's plans for annexations were couched in terms of the need for 'security' and 'settlement lands'. In 1914 he argued that Germany should secure the fortress line Osowiec, Lomza and Ostrolenka, a considerable part of Kurland and the west Polish *Gouvernements*.[55] These territories were to constitute a 'reservoir' for future 'displacements'(!) of population – he spoke of 'one to two million heads' – and were to be outside the legal orbit of the Reich. The native German nobility was to form 'a sort of colonial administration'.[56] Although in more precise plans in June 1915 he rejected the idea of tampering with the existing agrarian structure, his minimal demands nonetheless involved the annexation of some 50,000 sq km of territory.[57] As his advocacy of the annexation of Belgium, or of unlimited submarine warfare and aerial bombardment against England confirms, there were limits to Hoetzsch's much-vaunted detached and pragmatic rationality.[58]

His conservative, russophile, views resulted in a bitter public clash with the Tübingen medieval historian Johannes Haller (1865–1949).

In 1917 Haller published a pamphlet entitled 'The Russian Threat in the German House' in his fellow Balt Paul Rohrbach's series 'The Russian Menace'. Neither man ever visited Russia. The 'old, unbroken Tatardom, animal in cruelty and greed' – he meant the Russians – was abroad again. Haller identified attempts to correct the notion of immutable 'Tatardom' with treason.

> Whoever tries to shout down the sentries in a besieged town who warn of the proximity of the foe, is helping the enemy whether he wants to or not. Whoever denies the Russian threat is himself a threat, the Russian threat in the German house.[59]

Convinced of the regenerative value of war as a means of merging the individual with the state, Haller was too politically unaware to combat Hoetzsch with rational arguments.[60] Hence he suggested, mendaciously, that 'Otto Adolfowitzsch' receive psychiatric treatment.[61] Inevitably, by the time Hoetzsch's career lay in ruins, Johannes Haller was paraphrasing the *Iliad* to describe the warming rays of the National Socialist dawn.[62]

ii. A parting of the ways: the institutional and conceptual foundations of *Ostforschung*

During the First World War studies concerned with eastern Europe underwent considerable institutional expansion. On the eve of war, the Hamburg *Kolonialinstitut* responded to Max Sering's call for intensified study of Russia, by creating a chair in Russian history and civilization. The first professor was one of Schiemann's pupils, Richard Salomon (1884–1966), although the date of his appointment – 1 August 1914 – meant that his professional acquaintance with Russia began in the armed forces.[63] The *Institut für Weltwirtschaft* (1913–) in Kiel served as a model for the *Institut für ostdeutsche Wirtschaft* which was opened in Königsberg on 18 May 1916. Financed by capital raised through the *Vereinigung für ostdeutsche Wirtschaft*, the institute became a regular part of the university on 21 May 1918.[64] Housed eventually at Mitteltragheim 31, the institute was concerned with the study of the economy of 'the German East' and economic relations with neighbouring countries. Given the poor level of local administrative expertise, and the problem of how to allocate resources to repair local war-time damage to the economy, the institute had an applied aspect that went beyond studies of the smoked herring trade between Danzig and Königsberg.[65]

The post-war role of the Albertus university, as a 'citadel of the German spirit in East Prussia' in the 'struggle to maintain Germandom in the East', was emphasized in prospectuses for would-be students.[66] Generous reductions in the price of railway and steamer tickets brought the adventurous to a small university of about 3,000 students, set in an alluring countryside. It was presumably a good place for study, since apart from the Palästra Albertina and a zoological museum generously stocked with Mediterranean fish, there was little in the way of distraction.[67]

The tasks of the institute were defined as being:

a) Study of the foundations and conditions for development of the economic life of the eastern provinces
b) Tracing economic relations with neighbouring foreign countries
c) Employment of the results for academic training, for the administration and economic practice.[68]

Although the emphasis in Königsberg was firmly upon applied economic studies, the approach adopted, necessary language skills, and the technical apparatus that sustained the whole were interdisciplinary. There were nine departments, for 'agrarian politics'; 'agriculture'; 'trade and industry'; 'financial studies'; 'social policy'; 'business management'; 'economic history'; 'Russian and eastern European economy', and an archive for economic affairs.[69] The library and archive were catalogued according to subject and the following regions:

1) East Prussia, Danzig, Memel
2) Poland
3) the Baltic States, Lithuania, Latvia, Estonia, Finland
4) Russia and the Ukraine.

Inevitably, the rapid expansion of 1916–18 gave way to a period of stagnation. The academic staff was scaled down and the local housing department disturbed the studious calm by billeting a sailor's family – *mit lebhaft schreienden Kindern* – in the building.[70] Recovery was associated with the appointment of Fritz Mann to the directorship in May 1922, and with the harnessing of research to what were by then the specific problems of an isolated and stagnating economy.[71] By the mid 1920s a period of renewed expansion ensued, with the establishment of outlying branches in Riga for the study of Russia.[72]

Mann outlined the parameters of scholarship and politics. The institute existed to 'diagnose' economies, and to outline the consequences of policy options: 'economic political objectives must never be the task of research that strives for the highest objectivity'.[73]

The *Osteuropa-Institut* Breslau was founded by Adolf Weber in the summer of 1918 and was designed to assist the more thorough exploitation of those areas left behind by the Treaty of Brest-Litovsk.[74] It was a matter of quickly making up for pre-war ignorance of Congress Poland, White Russia, Lithuania, the Ukraine and occupied Serbia.[75] In line with plans to concentrate the study of particular regions on the adjacent German universities, the university of Breslau began courses in the summer of 1918 on the political history and ethnography of eastern Europe, subjects which were soon augmented by ecclesiastical history, literature, geography, economics and law. The relative dearth of suitable textbooks in these areas resulted in calls for a research institute. In the summer of 1918 Weber raised money from heavy industry in the Rhineland and Upper Silesia – although one suspects that textbooks were not on the minds of those in that quarter – and from 'private' individuals who happened to be the Governor-General of Warsaw and Field Marshal von Eichhorn in faraway Kiev.[76] The result was a research institute consisting of eight sections including eastern European law, economics, agriculture, mining, industry, geography, religious, and literary-linguistic studies and a technical apparatus.[77] While war-time priorities ensured that certain departments did not develop beyond the paper they were written on, the mining department went immediately into top gear. It collected information upon the coal and steel industries of eastern Europe on behalf of the Main Mining Office in Breslau, and produced studies of the coal, iron, copper, and gold reserves of Russia.[78] The institute's research was cut to suit the interests of its industrial and military benefactors.

The interdisciplinary approach institutionalized in Königsberg and Breslau was given an explicitly germanocentric focus by one of the main Weimar foundations. If the earlier institutes were concerned with the study of the economies and societies of eastern Europe as autonomous objects of research, the Leipzig *Stiftung für deutsche Volks- und Kulturbodenforschung* was concerned exclusively with the Germans in eastern Europe.[79] Founded in 1926 at the behest of the Interior Ministry, the *Stiftung* was concerned with the interdisciplinary study of the consequences for Germany of the frontier created by

Versailles. The institute's name reflected the considerable influence that ethnocentric geo-political and cultural-geographical concepts were to have upon *Ostforschung* thereafter. Indeed a case could be argued that from this moment onwards, the various disciplines working in the field were doing little more than supplying the detailed evidence to substantiate the political claims represented by these concepts.

The concepts were explained in detail by Albrecht Penck, the professor of geography at Berlin, in his contribution to *Volk unter Völkern* published by the *Deutsche Schutzbund für das Grenz- und Auslanddeutschtum* in 1926.[80] By *Volksboden* Penck understood those areas settled by Germans, where one could hear German spoken and see the results of German industriousness.[81] Only two-thirds of this area – of some 606,000 sq kms – were within the present frontiers of the German Reich, for some ten states, including Poland, Czechoslovakia, and Hungary, had seized parts of this German ethnic territory.[82] Beyond the *Volksboden* lay yet further German *Kulturboden*.

> The German *Volksboden* is accompanied by a characteristic German *Kulturboden*, which is different from the neighbouring areas of culture. It is characterised by an extremely careful form of cultivation, which does not grind to a halt when it encounters difficulties.[83]

In the East, this *Kulturboden* was a matter of subjective perception and was practically limitless. After all, one could 'see' it.

> Certainly it is not hard to distinguish in [the province of] Posen between the tidy German and the frequently wretched Polish villages, but intensive German soil cultivation and the good roads and paths that go with it, extend up to the Russian border. This was the great frontier of civilisation that German soldiers were so aware of as they marched eastwards. It is so vivid that one can observe it oneself from the train. The plain stone houses cease to appear in the villages. Cultivation becomes less diligent and the woods are obviously badly managed.[84]

Subjective perception was objectified by pointing to harvest yields, sanitation, architectural styles, order and street-lighting.[85] But these matters were the proof of a higher truth. The cultural frontier had nothing to do with geography or climate – let alone history or politics – because similar German achievements could be observed in the jungles of Brazil, or in the proximity of the frozen wastes of the far North.[86]

> The German cultural landscape does not result from the interaction of
> various natural causes, but is the work of people with definite natural
> abilities, who change nature according to their wills.[87]

This triumph of the will was evident in pre-history and had been
resumed by medieval colonists of the East.[88] Common effort had
integrated a people divided by geography, religion, education and class
in one purpose. The will was individual and collective.[89] This embodiment of the German people *as* achievement was a powerful mobilizing
ideology:

> When the young are taught from childhood about the civilising tasks
> carried out by our people, when in their maturity they are informed
> about the German *Kulturboden*, when this is thoroughly studied at the
> universities, investigated by scholars, and held aloft by the whole, then
> a feeling of strength will develop in the nation, which will not merely
> be intoxicated with its '*gloire*' or by cries of 'Hurra', but anchored in
> the soul of the nation.[90]

A striking black map showed both *Volks-* and *Kulturboden* spilling
across the present frontiers at most points of the compass, and a
series of ethnic exclaves scattered like bursts of shrapnel towards the
Russian frontier.[91] The other contributors chronicled the cultural
achievements and endangered ethnicity of exclaves like the Transylvanian 'Saxons'. The latter were now cut off from the German 'core
area' by two or three customs frontiers and interminably inefficient
railway systems.[92] Some 230,000 'Saxons' – they were mostly from
Rhineland–Franconia – existed cheek by jowl with one and a half
million Rumanians, about a million Magyars and 100,000 gypsies. In
every respect, Professor Fritz Jaeger argued, the 'Saxons' were 'cultur-
ally superior' to their neighbours. Cultural superiority meant that 'in a
certain sense' the 'Saxons' were a *Herrenvolk*.[93] Their architectural
styles, industrial activity, agricultural techniques and schools clearly
set them apart from the 'foreign substructure' of Rumanian shepherds,
domestic servants and factory workers, and the gypsy penumbra
squatting on the outskirts of their villages and towns.[94] The Rumanian
rate of reproduction meant that the 'Saxons' were facing *Volkstod*.
This demographic problem was compounded by the Rumanian government's policy of compulsory purchase of larger properties, the nation-
alization of industry and natural gas, and the withdrawal of subsidies
for confessional schools.[95]

The concepts of *Volks-* and *Kulturboden* gave cohesion to the various contributions to Wilhelm Volz's *Der ostdeutsche Volksboden* which appeared in 1926. Volz, himself the director of the *Stiftung*, gave the concepts historical depth:

> The soil has been teutonic-German *Volksboden* for 3,000 years; as far as the Vistula. In the 6th and 7th centuries after Christ the Slavs pushed outwards from their eastern homelands and into the ancient German land as far as the Elbe and Saale – admittedly only for a few hundred years. Already in the 10th century the German resettlement began. Higher German '*Kultur*' triumphed over primitive Slavdom; the Germans wrested massive areas of new settlement land from the primeval forest – admittedly many drops of Slav and German blood flowed, but in general, it was a great triumph for civilisation, and the greater part of the (in any case) not numerically strong Slavs went slowly but surely into Germandom . . .

Volz had little time for the ethnic pretensions of intermediary nationalities

> the Kashubians and Masurians, the Upper Silesians and Sorbs are German in culture, members of the German nation, Germans, even though the ancient idioms are not yet extinguished; their ethnic will and ethnic consciousness is German – they 'have gladly demonstrated that again and again. Race does not determine ethnicity – is the Sorb physically different from the Saxon? The '*wasserpolnisch*' speaking Upper Silesian [different] from the German speaker? – but the will and consciousness of ethnicity. Therefore the problems in the East are quite different from those in the West: the language frontier is not the ethnic frontier! The eastern German '*Volksboden*' encompasses the peripheral intermediate peoples of the German nation.[96]

In addition to this ominous negation of the separateness of intermediary groups, *Der Ostdeutsche Volksboden* was significant in another respect. It must surely have been one of the earliest instances whereby prehistorians (Wolfgang LaBaume), Slavists (Max Vasmer), geographers (Volz and Otto Schlüter) and historians (Rudolf Kötzschke, Robert Holzmann, Christian Krollmann, Erich Keyser, Harry Gollub and Manfred Laubert), the last six representing several provincial historiographical schools, brought their respective approaches to bear upon common themes. The regular conferences organized by the Leipzig *Stiftung* served to give the work of individuals unity of purpose.[97]

In terms of the range of problems dealt with *Der ostdeutsche*

Volksboden was a significant landmark in the development of *Ostforschung*, away from the course pursued by students of eastern Europe and Russia like Hoetzsch.

Most of the issues that exercised German *Ostforschung* for the next twenty years were essayed in this book. Scholarship, as several of the contributors made clear, was a means of substantiating 'rights'. Research on all aspects of the German colonization of the East would strengthen belief in the indivisibility of the German people and hence in 'their sacred right' to 'those parts of our people delivered into foreign sway'.[98] Study of the exact limits of German or Slav settlement would 'uncover the historical roots of German rights to the homeland in the East'.[99] The ramifications of these studies transcended 'the purely academic', for under the circumstances created by Versailles, it was not a matter of indifference whether the Germans had been in the East a thousand years before the Slavs, or whether medieval German migrants were the harbingers of a higher civilization or mere 'guests' and 'strangers'.[100]

These political considerations narrowed the terms of enquiry. The remoter the object of enquiry: the more strident the speculation. Wolfgang LaBaume dispatched any connection between a 'Lusatian civilisation' and the Slavs as being the work of 'hairsplitting Polish prehistorians' bent upon claiming eastern Germany as 'primeval' Slav land.[101] By contrast, he had no difficulty in arguing that since the early Iron Age (800–600 BC)

> the whole of eastern Germany up to the Oder in the West and the greater part of the present Republic of Poland formed from then onwards is, as the germanic character of the finds enables us to recognise, germanic, and in particular eastern germanic territory.[102]

German monks and peasants who migrated eastwards from the tenth century onwards were the bailiffs of civilization come to eject the squatters of history from lands 'which had been germanic lands for many centuries, and long before a Slav set foot there'.[103] The question of the 'original homeland' of the Slavs therefore assumed considerable importance. The professional Slavist, Max Vasmer, attempted to locate their *Urheimat* on the middle Dniepr in order to refute the idea that eastern Germany belonged to it too[104]. The cultural achievements of the medieval migrations provided a second line of defence around the speculative meditations of the pre-historians. Rejecting the idea that the population east of the Elbe consisted of Slavs 'covered with an exterior German veneer', Hans Witte argued that the triumph of German *Kultur* – 'evident' in the effective extinction of the Sorbs in Mecklenburg – had resulted in the creation of 'German soil' which in turn created 'German right'.[105] The influence of the concepts *Volks-* and *Kulturboden* was most evident in the contributions of the distinguished Leipzig historian, Rudolf Kötzschke (1867–1949), whose work in many respects anticipated that of Hermann Aubin.[106] The twin concepts served to establish the extent and character of German and Slav settlement in the East, which in turn was proof of 'right to the *Heimat*'.[107] The Germans who 'resettled' ancient germanic lands, fashioned the country through their 'superior' agricultural techniques, field systems, regular villages, uniform building styles, and purposiveness in shaping an orderly environment.[108] The Slavs merely existed in an environment that they could not master; the more developed Germans *shaped* that environment – and the term *Raum* is notoriously difficult to render meaningful in English – and by doing so made it 'their own'. Transformation brought proprietorship. Emptiness was filled with order.[109]

In addition to 'proving' the quintessential German character of large tracts of the East, while negating Slavic influences and Slav 'remnants' within Germany itself, the *Ostforscher* carried the battle onto Polish ground. While most of the chapters in *Der ostdeutsche Volksboden* were designed to demonstrate the historical homogeneity of the German presence in the East, two of the authors were at pains to cast doubt on the ethnic cohesion of the Polish neighbour. Harry Gollub argued that the Masurians – whose ancestors had been recruited from the duchy of Masovia by the German Knights to settle a particularly intractable part of south-east Prussia after the German colonization had peaked – were an essentially germanized people in a Polish guise.[110] They were Protestant, saw themselves as being *Prussaks* and not *Polaks*, spoke a language that knew no infinitives but which modified German verbs (*erbuje* = *ich erbe* = I inherit), and finally, who despite the efforts of Polish-backed agitators in the 'Masurian People's Party', had voted overwhelmingly (97.5 per cent), for Germany in the referendum of 1920.[111] If inner conviction determined nationality, then the Masurians were 'an indivisible part of the German nation'.[112] Although it was impossible to claim that the Kashubians in East Pomerania and West Prussia were Germans, strenuous efforts were made to delimit them, historically and linguistically, from the Poles. Here historians were on safer ground, since the area between the Oder and Vistula had once been inhabited by 'Pomeranians', whose rulers managed to fend off Polish aggression until the twelfth century.

This fundament of political identity survived in the form of the Rashubian 'language', which bore many of the marks of a Pomeranian language once separate from Polish.[113] Although Polish scholars argued that Kashubian was a Polish dialect, and not a separate (though related) language, there is little doubt that despite their loss of political identity, the Kashubians considered themselves to be 'other than' the Poles – or, one should add – Germans. Although their sense of being Kashubian endured, their wider identities were pragmatic. Polish lordship after 1466 brought enserfment; Prussian rule freed the Kashubian peasants and opened up careers for the petty nobility. The Prussian bureaucracy managed to squander Kashubian goodwill by identifying 'Polish' with 'Roman Catholic' and by subjecting the Kashubians to anti-Polish legislation. Initial enthusiasm for the Polish Republic was in turn dampened by the arrival of Galician bureaucrats bent upon introducing the Kashubians to civilization.[114] Although the author of the chapter did not make much of Kashubian separatist politics, he was worrying a nerve that had profound implications for the homogeneity of the Polish state. This was again paradigmatic for future developments in the subject.

iii. A subject transformed, 1925–35

By the mid 1920s two parallel tendencies, each with their own institutional and organizational base, were apparent in multi-disciplinary studies of eastern Europe. On the one hand, *Ostforschung*, in which the emphasis was upon pre- and medieval history because of the utility of these disciplines in the fight for Germandom. On the other, *Osteuropaforschung*, in which the societies and political systems of eastern Europe and the USSR were regarded as autonomous objects of research, and in which the various disciplines congregated at the contemporary end of the chronological spectrum. From time to time representatives of either tendency would emerge in the opposite camp.[115] Both trends stood in a functional relationship to government: broadly speaking, the first supplied long-range historical arguments with which to challenge the Poles, the other provided contemporary analysis of the Soviet Union. Which tendency would expand, contract, stagnate or be subsumed by the other was both a political question and a matter of the presence of ideas and problems which were easily functionalized. Although in the end the Nazis resolved these questions in favour of the discipline that most approximated their own ideological and political concerns (and in which Nazi activists and their conservative sympathizers occupied all key positions), in the 1920s the issue was still open. As we shall see, if relations between *Osteuropaforschung* and regime resulted in a grinding clash, *Ostforschung* fitted relatively smoothly into the machinery of Party and State.

Although Hoetzsch was an inveterate anti-Communist, and initially supported the idea of intervention in Russia by the Entente and Germany, his enthusiasm for Russian–German understanding survived the Revolution.[116] As a DNVP Reichstag deputy for Leipzig (1920–30), member of that party's foreign affairs committee, founder member of the *Deutsche Stiftung*, parliamentary spokesman on the budget of the Foreign Ministry, and Reichstag representative on the committee of the *Notgemeinschaft für deutsche Wissenschaft*, Hoetzsch had influence at the interstices of politics and academic life.[117] An admirer of the English Tories, who thought that the SPD should be recognized as a *Staatspartei*, Hoetzsch had fundamental reservations about the capacity of Weimar democracy to restore Germany to the position of a *Machtstaat*, but rejected attempts to alter the status quo by force.[118] For Hoetzsch, the way out from the 'misery' of Versailles lay through closer association with the other 'pariah' nation, with which he was in instinctive sympathy.[119] He pressed for an active foreign policy towards the USSR rather than anticipation of a regime 'that suits us and the rest of the world'.[120]

In September 1923 Hoetzsch made his first visit to the Soviet Union. Although the Communist Party reminded him of a religious order, and he lamented the disappearance of the 'old cultured class', no one tried to show him Potemkin villages, and the children seemed better fed than those in Germany.[121] With the more dire imaginings of the Western press dispelled by first-hand experience, Hoetzsch set about establishing and formalizing scholarly contacts. He worked successfully together with the retired bureaucrat Schmidt-Ott in the revived *Deutsche Gesellschaft zum Studium Osteuropas*, and was involved in the foundation of the Westphal Committee in 1923 to promote contacts between German and Soviet scholars. The committee members included Einstein, von Laue, Planck, Harnack, Wilamowitz-Moellendorf, Eduard Meyer and Werner Sombart.[122] Two years later, Hoetzsch reactivated plans for a journal designed 'to serve knowledge

and the evaluation of eastern Europe in the present'.[123] The result was
Osteuropa: Zeitschrift für die gesamten Fragen des europäischen Ostens
which was (and once again is) one of the most intellectually substantial
periodicals in the field of contemporary affairs. The journal has been
sensitively analysed by Fritz Epstein, Gerd Voigt and Jutta Unser – in
itself testimony of a sort to Hoetzsch's massive achievement.[124]

While *Osteuropa* was effectively Hoetzsch's 'own' periodical – he
was responsible for 23 per cent of the content of the first issue – other
regular contributors included Otto Auhagen, Arthur Luther and the
editorial secretary Hans Jonas. Although it is not necessary to refute
Nazi charges that these men were 'salon bolsheviks', something should
be said about the limits of their enthusiasm for Russia. Auhagen was
an expert on the Soviet economy, whose career included diplomatic
postings in St Petersburg (1900–6) and Moscow (1927–30), and the
directorship of the *Osteuropa-Institut* in Breslau.[125] His sojourn in
the Moscow embassy ended abruptly, after an article in *Osteuropa*
examining the plight of German peasants who had decamped from
Siberia to the capital, in the vain expectation of being granted permission to emigrate.[126] Auhagen's article contributed to their eventual
success; he was declared *persona non grata*. Within the *Deutsche Gesellschaft* Auhagen acted as a brake upon Hoetzsch's more relentless enthusiasm. Through Schmidt-Ott he endeavoured to 'manage' the visits of
Soviet scholars. In 1925, for example, he cautioned Schmidt-Ott against
allowing Eugen Varga to address any group larger than a small circle
of experts, lest Varga make too great an impression upon the young
'and others not equipped with the necessary powers of critical judgement'.

> We should not take our eyes off the efforts of the Russian government
> to kindle communist Revolution in Germany as well. Although at the
> moment one might regard the threat as being limited, it is surely not
> desirable that a respected German society (albeit unwittingly), assists
> the propagandistic aims of Russia.[127]

The borders between concern and censorship – and we can all think of
more local examples of this phenomenon – were fluid.

Russian exiles, particularly those involved in the *Russische wissenschaftliche Institut*, which Hoetzsch had helped to establish, and
Soviet authors, were represented in the pages of the journal.[128] If Luna-
carsky painted too rosy a view of the conditions for scholars in the
USSR, Luther appended a report that made analogies with the state of

affairs under Peter the Great.[129] The journal also covered the German–Soviet scholarly conferences, which were organized under the aegis of the *Deutsche Gesellschaft*, in the wake of the 200th anniversary celebrations of the Russian Academy of Sciences in September 1925. The natural scientists met in Berlin from 19–25 June 1927; the historians between 7–14 July 1928; and from 7–14 January Moscow hosted a week of German technology.[130]

The Russian historical week was carefully prepared and has been minutely reconstructed by a scholar working under the auspices of Eduard Winter. The Soviet guests, including Pokrovsky, Adoratsky, Egorov and Platanov, were warmly welcomed by Hoetzsch, who nonetheless attacked historical materialism and held up the example of Herder.[131] The Soviet scholars gave some twelve lectures on subjects ranging from the agrarian reforms of Stolypin to the military councils of Oliver Cromwell. Between the lectures, the visitors traipsed around the Geheime Staatsarchiv, the Reichsarchiv and Sanssouci.[132] As we will see, the goodwill created during the conference resulted in agreements on archival policy and on the publication in Germany of Russian documents on the origins of the First World War.[133]

The end of this honeymoon came gradually as the political shadows lengthened. The slow transformation of *Osteuropa* illustrates that distinctive combination of pressure from without, and compromise within, that conspired to destroy German academic life. It became risky to say anything positive about the Soviet Union. In 1932 Hoetzsch's protégé Klaus Mehnert gave a lecture about his recent visit to Russia. His talk ended abruptly when SA men in the audience broke up their chairs and threw the pieces at the lecturer.[134] Hoetzsch, whom the US diplomat Dodds noted was keen to conform for fear of losing his job, tried to live down his image as a 'salon bolshevik'. A paragraph was belatedly inserted in an article that appeared in November 1933. It used terms like *Ostraum*, 'intellectual mobilisation', 'struggle for the East', 'scholarly weapons', and referred approvingly to a programmatic article in *Volk und Reich* by one of the younger exponents of *Ostforschung*, Wolfgang Kohte.[135] Hoetzsch was trying to hitch his coat to the future.

Even though *Osteuropa* would continue to study eastern Europe – though the reorientation towards Poland is unmistakable – the editors now felt obliged to declare that they were with the German minorities abroad in the spirit.[136] The elliptical promises, delivered behind closed doors in the Foreign Ministry, followed. Hoetzsch indicated that

Osteuropa might be 'harmonised' if not actually 'coordinated with' the regime.[137] With the imminent presence of NSDAP figures on the editorial board and the committee of the *Deutsche Gesellschaft*, Hoetzsch gradually withdrew from effective involvement in the journal he had created. His successor, Klaus Mehnert, decided by 1934 that as 'a man of Rapallo' the time had come to leave for a post as a foreign correspondent in Moscow. Two years later, German newspapers were told to stop taking his stories.[138] His successor, Werner Markert, was an SA member who subscribed to the view that scholarship was a form of 'struggle'. His first programmatic statement in *Osteuropa* struck the appropriate postures. Markert quoted the Führer to underline the point that there was no room for grey: 'every German who goes abroad is either an emigre or a National Socialist, i.e. today every individual is the bearer of the total political will of the nation'.[139] Claiming that creeping authoritarianism and fascism in Central and Eastern Europe needed expert study, Markert attacked the cosmopolitan character of his own journal. As in the case of Walter Frank, Hans Reinerth and all the other spokesmen of the academic radical right, one needed an entrenched 'establishment' for purposes of self-definition and self-aggrandizement. *Osteuropaforschung* had been in the hands of 'cosmopolitan emigres' for too long. Most of them worked 'as if they were sitting in old Moscow, Warsaw or Prague'.

It was 'an international, secret science'; Markert intended to bring it back on the rails of German academic life, by coordinating research with German political interests. Whatever the individual scholar studied was a matter of 'indifference', *provided* he or she integrated the work into *German history*, asked the questions from a *German* perspective, and acted with a sense of *political responsibility*.[140] This meant the end of *Osteuropa* as a respected forum for international scholarship.

Hoetzsch was pushed from his professorship in May 1935 for continuing to supervise a Polish Jew writing a doctoral thesis on Jews in the Soviet Union. The thesis, that the position of Soviet Jewry was unenviable, was in contradiction with the view that the Soviet Union was a 'Jewish state'.[141] Hoetzsch's place was taken by the Austrian Nazi Hans Uebersberger, from the *Osteuropa-Institut* in Breslau. In 1940 Uebersberger chronicled his past political history in a letter to the Ministry of Education, designed to refute charges that he was having an extra-marital affair with his assistant, Dr Hedwig Fleischhacker. From 1918–21 he had co-edited the *Wiener Mittag*, 'which conducted, in the sharpest form, the struggle for the *Anschluss* and against the Habsburgs, Jewdom and socialism. I was also renowned as a champion of the cleansing of the university of Jewish professors and the exclusion of Jewish lecturers, a struggle which I also successfully carried out, in conjunction with the likeminded, in my own faculty.' In 1918, Uebersberger had founded with members of the conservative Deutsche Klub a 'secret, militant Aryan organisation' to combat the growing *Verjudung* of Vienna. Organized according to the cell principle, it was

> above all the task of the members in their official capacities to exclude every influence of Jewdom, and only to appoint indubitable Aryans, and those not related to Jews, to offices and important functions in the state, as well as only to patronise Aryan business people. At the same time a cadaster of houses in Vienna in Jewish possession or occupation was drawn up, and further, an address book of Aryan firms was put together.[142]

The way was eventually clear for *Osteuropa* to be endorsed as essential reading by *Der Stürmer* and for contributions from the leading academic anti-Semite Peter-Heinz Seraphim.[143] *Ostforschung* had penetrated, absorbed and neutered one of the main bastions of *Osteuropaforschung*. It was not so much a matter of *Osteuropa* being radically transformed, but rather that it was no longer what it once was.

From the mid 1930s Hoetzsch retired into brooding silence in his house in the Bendlerstrasse. Several of his best pupils and close associates had to choose between emigration or persecution. Richard Salomon's chair at Hamburg was 'cut' even though it was funded by private sources: there were funds in abundance for a new chair in military studies. When the Hamburg Gestapo began looking for evidence to link the study of Russia with Communist involvements, Salomon left for the USA.[144] Further Jewish scholars, like Hoetzsch's assistant Leo Loewenson and Fritz Epstein, fled to Britain and North America.[145] One of the few *Osteuropaforscher* who was a Communist, Georg Sacke (1901–45), stayed.

Sacke had had to work his way through Leipzig university as a builder's labourer.[146] From the mid 1920s he gave classes on Russian and the USSR to workers and the unemployed. Although his academic work showed considerable promise in the application of Marxist analysis to eighteenth-century Russian absolutism, and was encouraged by Hoetzsch, Sacke's academic career was over before it started.[147] A faculty that could dispense with the services of Walter Goetz, Alfred Doren and Sigmund Hellmann (who died in Theresienstadt) could painlessly eject the politically dubious. On 1 April 1933 Sacke heard from Professors Hans Freyer and Friedrich Braun that:

> I have to inform you that as from today you are removed from your position as an academic assistant in the eastern European department ... since Professor Gerullis, as the representative of the committee for the reformation of higher education, has informed me that your Marxist interpretation of historical problems and your positive attitude towards the Soviet Union have made your further employment in the Institute appear untenable.[148]

To dismiss someone on these grounds, and in this political context, was to throw them to the wolves. The Gestapo arrested him in December 1934. There was a trial in November 1935 – his citizenship was revoked that summer – and Sacke was acquitted. His SPD co-accused died in concentration camps.[149] Denied permission to re-enter the institute, but dogged by its hostile references, Sacke was unemployed for seven years. The Hitler–Stalin pact brought temporary respite: a post at the Weltwirtschaftsinstitut in Hamburg. He was finally rearrested on 15 August 1944 and delivered into 'protective custody'. He corrected the spelling errors in the Gestapo's account of his interrogation – *Mir macht das nichts aus, aber Ihnen?* – and refused to act as an interpreter during executions at Neuengamme concentration camp.[150] When Neuengamme was cleared in March 1945, Sacke was one of those inmates moved to Lübeck for a voyage on ships that the SS intended to sink. He collapsed during embarkation and was either kicked or shot to death a few minutes later.

While Hoetzsch's circle were scattered abroad or, as in this case, spun into the undertow of the concentration camps, the *Ostforscher* manoeuvred to centre stage. Using other institutional routes, they established new academic empires. Ideological coincidence and political utility favoured expansion, but expansion at the price of being willingly, and enthusiastically, functionalized by the regime. Paradoxically, the dominant figures were not thrusting, young opportunists – the Walter Franks steadily lost their nuisance value – but well-placed members of the German academic establishment, with backgrounds of solid, scholarly, achievement. At the centre of the institutional coordination of *Ostforschung* was a crucial institution, the last of the Weimar foundations, from which central vantage point it is possible to survey the field as a whole. The Publikationsstelle-Dahlem was to become a command post for the scholarly censors facing towards the East. The commander was Albert Brackmann.

PART TWO

2. ENTER THE GENERAL

i. *Ein deutschbewusster nationaler Mann*

When a journalist from the *Hannoverschen Kurier* interviewed Professor Albert Brackmann, in July 1941, he was struck by the septuagenarian's taut, disciplined figure and bright, piercing eyes.[1] It was the year of Brackmann's seventieth birthday. The interview with the editor from his native town – printed around another piece illustrated with a photograph of a burning Soviet tank – being one of a number of occasions in 1941 on which Brackmann was called upon to review a life rich in achievement. A life soothed now with honours and recognition from on high. The Führer had bestowed the *Adlerschild* of the German Reich upon 'the deserving researcher of German history', and congratulatory telegrams arrived from Göring, Frick, Ribbentrop, and a host of academic dignitaries acclaiming 'the worthy *Führer* of *Ostforschung*'.[2] The replies were dispatched a few days later:

> My Führer,
> May I express my deepest gratitude for the bestowal upon me of the *Adlerschild* of the German Reich. It will act as an incentive to the septuagenarian to continue on his present course, and to maintain *Ostforschung*, which has been entrusted to his charge, ready for when it is needed for the struggle for the reconstruction of Europe being prepared under your leadership.[3]
> Heil my Führer!

And to Frick:

> It is a great pleasure for me that my own and my colleagues' work for the German East has not been without success and has gained the recognition of the political authorities of the Reich. It seems to us that the work is now more necessary than ever. Therefore we are arming ourselves for the future and we hope to be ready when the Reich needs us.[4]

Those too preoccupied to acknowledge this significant moment were later reminded of their duty through presentation copies of Brackmann's two-volume *Festschrift*. *Obersturmführer* Worninghoff of the *Reichsführer*-SS's personal staff indicated that the book had been well received in the Prinz-Albrecht-Strasse, while from the corner of a foreign field, SS-*Obergruppenführer* and General of the Waffen-SS Karl Wolff let it be known that 'he was overjoyed at the consideration shown to him and would read the book, which he thought very good and rich in content, in his spare time'.[5]

Brackmann was born in Hannover on 24 June 1871. The father's side consisted of pastors and scholars, while his mother hailed from the industrial dynasty of the Egestorffs. Following family tradition, Brackmann initially studied theology, but then switched to history at Tübingen, Leipzig and Göttingen. Specializing in the editing of sources on relations between medieval Emperors and Popes, Brackmann joined the staff of the MGH at 27 and became an *Extraordinarius* in Paul Kehr's *Institut für Historische Hilfswissenschaften* at Marburg in 1905. Brackmann was called to the chair of medieval history at Königsberg in 1913. There he increasingly devoted his time to the history of the Germans in the East. He had his first direct experience of war and became involved in nationalist politics. Later Brackmann regarded the transfer to Königsberg as a major turning point in his life.[6] Since he was declared unfit for military service, Brackmann spent the war working in hospitals, helping refugees, and writing tracts, reports, and articles for the *Königsberger Allgemeine Zeitung* about the Russian invasion of East Prussia and, subsequently, pieces refuting Article 92 of the Treaty of Versailles.[7] In one of these tracts, written in about 1917, he described the roads swamped with displaced persons, unattended livestock in the fields, the charred buildings and refugees huddled despondently around camp fires. The glance of a medieval chronicler would have alighted upon acts of sacrilege committed by pagan invaders; Brackmann's eyes focused upon the wanton destruction of the sacred objects of the present – sets of lead soldiers smashed to pieces or the eyes of the Kaiser bayoneted from his portraits. Elsewhere, the dead were unceremoniously tipped from their lead resting places; peasants were shot in reprisal for attacks on Russian troops and some 366 women 'suffered the greatest deprivation'.[8] After two years in Marburg, Brackmann succeeded Dietrich Schäfer in 1922 as professor in Berlin. He retained an honorary chair there after becoming, in personal union, General Director of the Prussian State

Archives and First Director of the Geheime Staatsarchiv in October 1929, and commissary leader of the Imperial Archives in 1935. Although not an archivist by training, his appointment represented the continuation of a tradition begun by Sybel, whereby the archives would be led by eminent scholars able to promote historical research by their staff.[9] Along the way, Brackmann accumulated several honours: membership of the learned society of Göttingen (3 July 1925), co-editorship of the *Historische Zeitschrift* (1928–35), membership of the Prussian (22 February 1930), German (24 June 1933) and Bavarian (21 May 1939) academies and a place on the central directorate of the MGH.[10] He also had access to high places, a ramified network of academic and administrative contacts, and a regiment of grateful former pupils.

Active in nationalist politics during the First World War, and the man the *Reichswehr* could rely upon to recommend history books for officer training, Brackmann belonged to the DVP from 1919 to 1925 and the DNVP thereafter; he also supported veterans' associations, the Eastern Marches Association from 1926 and, to put it no higher, the Dahlem group of the NSDAP was in touch with him in 1933 concerning possible donations to their funds.[11] Like the majority of conservative historians, of whom it was once said that 'they easily lose the ability to move their heads because of their always looking backwards, so that if any movement at all is possible, only movement to the right remains', Brackmann was not well-disposed towards the Weimar constitution.[12] Thanking Professor Otto Becker in September 1931 for an article on 'the Weimar Constitution and National Development', Brackmann remarked that:

> You were especially voicing my innermost thoughts when you dissociate yourself so decisively from parliamentarism in its present guise. Whoever can observe the deleterious effects of factionalism from so closely as we can here in the centre, must in fact reach the conclusion that this system is rotten. I always think this could be remedied more constructively by the introduction of a Senate with a restricted membership, somewhat along Roman lines, or better still in the form of the Venetian Council of Ten, but I agree wholeheartedly with you that such changes can only be achieved by means of strengthening the ruling elements, i.e. in this case, the constitutional position of the Reichspräsident.[13]

Although his head invariably turned upwards for solace in difficult times, there were limits beyond which he would not stray until power conferred the semblance of respectability, and respectability required loyalty to those at the helm of State. This caution irritated the committed. An NSDAP report noted:

> Brackmann's field of interest is in the area of medieval German history and in particular German relations with the East. In this area he is recognised as the best among German historians.
>
> Brackmann is a very controversial figure. Without doubt he is very ambitious and power-hungry, on the other hand helpful and kind when one accommodates him. Politically, all in all, he is rejected by the Party, however acknowledged academically. He is not a National Socialist, and he will never become one, rather he has always been a German-conscious national man.[14]

ii. Cerberus of the *Archivstrasse* and the Polish 'onrush'

Brackmann directed his far-flung archival patrimony from the office of the First Director on the second floor of the Geheime Staatsarchiv. Modelled upon late-eighteenth-century buildings in Potsdam, today the Geheime Staatsarchiv stands incongruously in a long row of undistinguished houses. The Prussian eagle above the entrance extends its stony wings towards a field containing American radio masts. The building was the product of an optimistic, expansionary era in the history of the Prussian archival administration. Before the First World War, plans were made to shift the archive away from the noise, soot and structural damage caused by underground trains in the centre of Berlin. A comparatively cheap site opposite the Dahlem Domäne became attractive, once access to the centre and farther suburbs had been secured by the construction of the rail-line Dahlem Dorf-Podbielskiallee.[15] Building work began in April 1915, but ground to a halt because of wartime labour and materials shortages. In May 1920 the covers were removed from the rusting steel frames, and work recommenced on a less elaborate structure whose furnishings reflected post-war austerity; the offices of Brackmann and the Second Director had carpets, their staff had to make do with linoleum.[16] The building was opened by Otto Braun on 26 March 1924.

As the personal choice of Braun, Brackmann could afford to negotiate conditions for his own appointment. Under Sybel, Koser, and Kehr there had been a steady, tightening professionalization of the qualifications for admission to the archival service. However, the latter was still reliant upon volunteers and the available course in Marburg lacked both unity and a common sense of purpose among the lecturers.[17] In 1929 Brackmann secured an extra 25,000 RM for the creation of an in-house *Institut für Archivwissenschaft*, modelled upon French and Austrian exemplars, which would train historians and archivists for work on major publications like the MGH or *Germania Pontificia*. Occupying rooms 43, 44, and 49 on the top floor of the Geheime Staatsarchiv, IfA was opened on 1 May 1930. It was to be 'a nursery for state and private archivists and a teaching and research institute for younger historians'.[18] Organizationally, Brackmann tried to keep his nursery apart from the universities (which supplied lecturers), and the archival administration (which afforded the postgraduate students practical experience), by running research projects which were funded by the *Kultusministerium*. The middle way was eventually abandoned because most of the students wished to become archivists rather than university teachers and an exam-oriented professional training gained the upper hand.[19]

The archive in Dahlem also housed the records recovered from and concerning the lost eastern provinces. In March 1929 Second Director Melle Klinkenborg commissioned Johannes Papritz, who had returned from a two-year period in Danzig equipped with a working knowledge of Polish, to build a department within the archive for the records of the province Grenzmark Posen-Westpreussen formed from the remains of lost territories after 21 July 1922.[20] The object was to preserve, at least within the bowels of the Geheime Staatsarchiv, the names, traditions and administrative apparatus as 'the archival embodiment of German claims to the lost territory'.[21] Since Papritz had considerable organizational talents, Department I spawned a collection point in Schneidemühl and a regional 'association for the fostering of consciousness of the homeland and the importance of its historical record'.[22] Following Klinkenborg's death in March 1930, Brackmann appointed his Hannoverian compatriot Adolf Brennecke as Second Director but the relationship that increasingly mattered within the archive was that of the General-Director and the promising young man in charge of Department I.

These two developments – the training of archivists and historians in IfA and attempts to use the historical record to support revisionist claims in the East – eventually coalesced with Brackmann's third preoccupation; how to exclude from the archives anyone likely to produce work that did not endorse the status quo. For he ran the

Prussian archives as if they were a series of fortresses besieged by the enemy without and the enemy within. The Soviets were the first to be sent packing. Following the normalization of German–Soviet relations after 1922, the Soviet archival administration approached their Prussian colleagues to obtain technical publications to aid in the construction of their own archival system. During the 1920s a number of scholars from the Marx-Engels Institute (MEI) went to western Europe to study the history of the labour movement: V. P. Polonsky to Dresden to study Bakunin in 1848 and Boris Nikolaevsky to work on Marx and Engels. These scholarly contacts – which were reciprocal – resulted in the archival agreement of 15 July 1928, signed by Pokrovsky and Paul Kehr in the wake of the Berlin 'Russian Historical Week', and a wider agreement of 4 December 1929 (Brackmann missed the meeting), which encompassed the MEI, central archives in Moscow, and the Imperial Archive in Potsdam.[23] Essentially, these agreements regulated the exchange of official publications, information about holdings, photography and mutual bidding arrangements to fight off competition at auctions. The good-will represented by the treaties did not survive the first year of Brackmann's period in office. Reviewing his own achievements in 1937, he noted how 'fortunate' it had been that Soviet scholars working in Germany in exchange with Germans working on the correspondence of Wilhelm I and the Tsar, had relayed police records to a Magdeburg Communist party newspaper enabling Brackmann to abrogate the treaties.[24] He was also largely instrumental in banning the radical young historian Eckart Kehr from the archives on the grounds of technical incompetence in his editing of Prussian financial records.[25]

The threat from Poland required a response of a qualitatively higher order. On 15 July 1931 seventeen men gathered in the great conference chamber of the Prussian Ministry of State to listen to Brackmann's plans to deal with the 'onrush' of Polish visitors to the archives. The composition of the meeting suggested which way the sails were about to be set. University professors (Laubert, Hoetzsch and Vasmer) were in a minority of three. There were four bureaucrats representing the Foreign Office and Prussian Ministry of State. However, the largest contingent consisted of nine directors of Prussian archives, with Papritz – sitting proudly in Otto Braun's vacant chair – there to take the minutes. It was a sort of meeting at Telgte for Prussian archivists, although conflict rather than irenicism was on their minds, with Max Hein from Königsberg, Dersch from Breslau, Randt from Stettin and

Brennecke from the Archivstrasse. Brackmann was in control from start to finish.

He began by setting the cup of ambition firmly to one side:

> He had not called the conference together to found a new academic organisation or to initiate a political counterattack against the Poles. It should merely advise how a certain unity could be achieved in the academic handling of Polish questions. The Minister President himself had not taken the initiative, but had commissioned the Prussian archival administration to do so.[26]

Dark clouds were gathering from the East. The Baltic Institute, founded in Toruń in August 1925 and another recently established in Danzig, were purveying a type of politicized scholarship – he called it 'applied science' – designed to give a fundament of historical legitimacy to Polish claims in the Baltic and Pomerania.[27] These institutes had close connections with the Polish Western Marches Association, the Liga Morska i Kolonjalna and with the Polish government. The Prussian archives were well-placed to appreciate the strength of this Polish 'intellectual offensive'. Polish scholars were receiving generous research grants, or periods of extended paid leave, to seek out materials in the Prussian archives to discredit Prussian administration of the eastern provinces. Acting closely with the Foreign Office – through whom Polish user applications went – the archives had adumbrated a few stratagems to combat the Polish 'onrush' to the sources. Papritz had been assembling evidence of non-cooperation experienced by German historians working in Poland to legitimize retaliatory action. The study produced the shocking statistic that for every German working in Poland, there were four Poles studying in German archives.[28] Apart from a chronological limit of 1880, the archives could claim that the documents requested were being edited for official publications. This would enable them to quarantine sensitive material 'without drawing upon oneself the charge of illiberality' and not seeming to act as if there was something to hide.[29]

But a more positive response was needed. Surveying the existing institutes concerned with the East, Brackmann thought that they were too physically dispersed, often duplicated work, were russo- rather than germanocentric, and were not subject to any overall control. The universities were not much better. They had neglected the teaching of Polish (it was better to put Hoetzsch and his colleagues on the defensive from the start), a task that could be taken over by the

Prussian archives with their fund of language experts from the eastern provinces. IfA should train 'a staff of historians' by running language classes and courses on Polish history. The result would be 'a properly armed, broad, defensive front to oppose the Poles'.[30] Evidently stung by Brackmann's manifest contempt for the achievements of himself and his colleagues, Hoetzsch tried to question the seriousness of the threat from Poland, endeavoured to cling on to primary language instruction, and queried Brackmann's attempts to regulate *Ostforschung* by pushing German–Polish archival relations into the centre ground. Brackmann was unimpressed. Using a familiar form of irrelevant analogy, he decried the absence of a chair in Polish history when funds were evidently there, he darkly averred, for professorships in Iranian or 'negro languages'.[31] But he conceded the responsibility of universities for primary language studies, adding that if students came to him well prepared, all the better, but he would retrain them if they were not. He then ranged his guns towards other competitors in the field. Aided by Laubert from Breslau, Brackmann took the *Osteuropa-Institut*'s translation of Egorov's history of the colonization of medieval Mecklenburg – it had carried a red marker rather than a full, critical introduction to warn the susceptible of its contents – to impugn the academic competence of the Breslau and Königsberg institutes. The discussion reverted to the problem of whether the ban on Soviet scholars should be extended to the Poles. Recke from Danzig suggested,

> The front against the Poles must be kept labile. It would be very advantageous however, to have a documentation centre, which kept a card index on the personalities in question. The archives concerned could then easily keep themselves informed from there.[32]

Brackmann seized the moment by advocating a central information service which would also coordinate current projects and dissertations on eastern subjects. This proposal met with the approval of Windecker from the Foreign Office and Weichmann from the Ministry of State, whose finance department thought it tidier if the share of the 20 million RMs *Ostfonds* to be allocated to these schemes ran through the orderly mechanisms of the archival bureaucracy. At the end of the meeting, Brackmann could afford to be pleased.

With support from Otto Braun, who was sufficiently impressed with Brackmann's image of the archives as 'inundated with politically motivated Polish user applications' to instruct the Interior Ministry (it needed no encouragement) to devote 'particular attention' to the financing of these projects, Brackmann turned ideas into organizational structures.[33] IfA would shortly commence classes on Polish history. From April 1932 Polish-speaking archivists would receive leave to work in Poland. A card index dealing with Polish works on the German eastern provinces would be opened in Department I of the Geheime Staatsarchiv. Reviving pre-war plans, Brackmann initiated a number of source publications whose effect would be to show Prussian administration in Poland in a positive light.[34] With simultaneous lobbying of the *Reichskanzlei* by such figures as the chairman of the historical commission for Silesia, designed to pressurize the Prussian Finance Ministry, Brackmann's proposals were discussed by representatives of the Interior Ministry, Eastern and German departments of the Foreign Office on 11 December 1931. Although they were not prepared to license every proposal, they approved the plans for source editions as a way of demonstrating 'what the Prussians did in these lands to raise the level of *Kultur*'. They also shared Brackmann's reluctance to leave the scholarly counterattack in the hands of university academics. Their reasoning suggests that they were well aware of the advantages of dealing with Brackmann:

> the new service, closely connected with General-Director Brackmann and the state archives, has the advantage that the work can be carried out under a certain political control.[35]

This view was endorsed by the representative of the Foreign Office's Germandom department who stressed that:

> a unification of the activities of research institutes throughout Germany was desirable, and also a form of monitoring so that no publication appears that does not lie in Germany's interests.[36]

Brackmann's driving ambition, in other words, could be used to achieve the sort of coordination that both the Interior and Foreign Ministries had already brought about in the wider field of subsidizing a continued German presence in the lost territories.[37]

The problem of how to distinguish what was being planned from the sort of work carried out by the Polish institutes was the theme of a final meeting in the Prussian Ministry of State on 25 February 1932. Observing that university professors behaved 'as if the fact did not exist that a new state has been created on our eastern frontiers', Braun stressed that it was not a question of subordinating, as the Poles did,

scholarship to politics, but rather – and the distinction was fine –
'that scholarship can supply the politicians with the material from
which they can draw their conclusions'.[38] Ever solicitous in obliging
the wishes of authority, Brackmann volunteered that Department I
of the Geheime Staatsarchiv had established a card index on Polish
scholarship and that each source publication – whose contents 'would
be determined by the demands of the present' – would contain a
summary and selection of the most important documents, to enable
the nation's political masters to orientate themselves at their own
convenience. Dammann from the RMdI concluded by offering a
provisional 40,000 RMs for the new *Zentrale für die Ostforschung*
which, he added, 'must be formed from the archival administration
and the interested ministries'. Otto Braun's observation that the work
should be purely scholarly in character was already belied by the fact
that the archival administration was to be a front organization for the
research requirements of the RuPMdI and the Foreign Office.

iii. 'Our firm'

A memorandum produced sometime in 1932 described the tasks of
the *Publikationsfonds* – as it was called until Brackmann changed
'our firm's' name to *Publikationsstelle* in late March 1933[39] – and
more extensive plans for the organization of *Ostforschung* as a whole.
So far the 'PuFo' consisted of a library on Polish history and a card
index with 12,000 items on the Polish literature, cross-referenced to
critical German reviews, as well as material on the Polish institutes,
conferences and individual scholars.[40] There were also seventeen
young historians being trained in IfA. While these developments
would bear fruit in the long term – ten years was mentioned – in
the form of official source publications, and a team of specialists
responsible for particular areas of interest, a rapid response was
needed. Given the shortage of skilled German personnel within the
archival service, it would be necessary 'to strengthen the weak
German front' by commissioning work through grants to scholars
outside the service, thus compensating for the absence of career
opportunities for academic *Ostforscher*.[41] Both the outside work and
that of the existing institutes could be coordinated by emulating the
Pomerelian Meetings of the Poles which brought together institute
personnel, professors, amateur historians and representatives of the

government.[42] They could meet secretly under the aegis of existing scholarly conferences.

The time it would take before the source publications came on stream could be bridged in a variety of ways. Collected essays – along the lines of the 1931 *Deutsche Staatenbildung und deutsche Kultur im Preussenlande*,[43] could be produced more rapidly than monographs. There was also a need for a journal which would deal largely with Polish history; the existing *Zeitschrift für osteuropäische Geschichte* neglected Poland, and the organs of the eastern regional historical associations had other priorities. But in order to respond in kind to Polish scholarly claims, it was necessary to be able to read the work and, as was too evident, few German historians could do so. The problem of publishing translations was that this inadvertently guaranteed Polish scholarship a wider, European audience – the *Osteuropa-Institut*'s translation of Egorov being the example to be avoided. One solution would be to produce typed translations – thus circumventing copyright – which could be circulated 'to a closed circle of German authorities and interested individuals'.[44] The *Deutsche Stiftung* had already commissioned the Geheime Staatsarchiv's Dr Anton Loessner to do this, and the PuFo was about to experiment with a Polish biography of Boleslaw Chobry. This could be extended to cover the Polish daily Press. In essentials, the PuSte had taken shape.

The publications work of the Geheime Staatsarchiv began with a grant of 10,000 RMs from the RMdI in 1931. The earliest financial accounts are virtually the only written source for the first year of its activity. Very small amounts were spent on administrative costs which suggests considerable reliance upon overtime by archivists in the pay of the Prussian archival administration. The largest budgetary items were respectively 4,304 and 4,838 RMs for a Polish library and the stipends of five researchers.[45] These included Dr Sergei Jakobson, editing Prussian ambassadorial reports from eighteenth-century Warsaw (2,711 RMs), Dr Erich Maschke writing a *Cultural History of Germandom in Poland* (900 RMs) and small sums for Dr Anneliese Schwarz for a *History of the Prussian Administration of West Prussia 1786–1808*. The quadrupling of the RMdI subsidy in 1932 enabled the PuSte to expand both the library and the number of researchers. In that year some 11,229 RMs were spent on books, including several major sets; a 28-volume Polish bibliography, 22 volumes of the *Scriptores rerum polonicarum* and the complete run of the *Kwartalnik Historyczny*.[46] The card index had swollen to

25,000 items. Some 500 RMs were expended upon Polish newspapers for the incipient translation service run by Loessner and two assistants. Early customers included the Gestapo, who wrote in October 1933 requesting a copy of an article in the *Kurjer Poznanski* and information on its Russian author,[47] and the BDO's weekly *Ostland* which, by July 1933, was taking 60–70 per cent of its material from the PuSte.[48] The number of stipendiaries had grown to twelve, including IfA graduates like Wolfgang Kohte, supernumerary employees of the Geheime Staatsarchiv like Jakobson and Schwarz, but also a faint penumbra of scholars employed elsewhere. These included the university lecturer Erich Maschke and the archivist Kurt Forstreuter, both of whom worked in Königsberg.[49] By July 1933 the first signs of a coherent subdivision of labour were in evidence. Jakobson and Schwarz were involved in editorial work whose effect would be to present Prussian involvement in Poland in a positive light. Loessner's translation service had processed some 256 items since February, including the minutes of the third Pomerelian Meeting. The PuSte was also subsidizing work by Harry Gollub, Forstreuter, Maschke and Theodor Schieder in Königsberg. Preparations were underway for the forthcoming International Historical Congress to be held, auspiciously, in Warsaw in August 1933. What did the work involve and who was doing it?

The politicization of even the most harmless-sounding scholarly pursuits can be demonstrated by looking closely at the work of Helmut Lüpke who received PuSte grants totalling 2,025 RMs between October 1932 and July 1933.[50] In April 1933 Lüpke produced a report on his research to date. He had taken over earlier work by a Dr Goldfriedrich on Polish attempts to reach the Baltic sea – the chronological range was indeterminate – but had rapidly reduced this to a study of the Netze fortress Zantoch. Since the charred stones were currently being excavated by a team led by Wilhelm Unversagt, Lüpke was trying to re-create the part played by the fortress in relations between Poles and Pomeranians by merging written and unwritten evidence. He had read most of the available sources and secondary literature generating endless cards as he went along – and was now working through the map collection of the GStA and Berlin *Staatsbibliothek*. He wanted to do further research in Königsberg, and was planning to write the history of all the Netze fortresses.[51]

Despite his demonstrable assiduity, Lüpke felt that a little contemporary relevance would not go amiss:

The ultimate goal and objective of this work, is to prove that the castle of Zantoch and with it the other Netze-Warthe fortresses, were originally Pomeranian constructions and settlements, and that they fell victim to the expansionist efforts of Poland but were always reconquered by their heroic Pomeranian defenders. It therefore has to do with showing the struggle for freedom of the Pomeranian peoples against a Polish annexationist and expansionary policy, in so far as the struggle took place on the strategic Warthe-Netze line.[52]

Put more succinctly in the PuSte overview, Lüpke's project was designed to show the hereditary enmity of Pomerania and Poland 'in order to take away the Poles' right to pose as advocates for their Slavic brothers'.[53] Since no research report would be complete without whetting the appetite for work yet to be done, Lüpke essayed the desirability of a synthesis on the whole German eastern colonization. This would demonstrate the pacific nature of the process by stressing that the initiative behind this 'unheard of cultural progression' came from Slav rulers and landlords. This was partially correct. However, his conclusion exemplifies the slide from disinterested academic enquiry into the substantiation of the claims of the moment:

If the fact that peaceful expansion and higher civilisation is in itself already the best propaganda for Germany, we should consider that Polish scholars have for some time not restricted themselves to the defence of Pomerelia, but have gone openly onto the attack with propaganda to support their political claims to East Prussia, Silesia and the lands up to and beyond the Oder ... That is why it seems to me to be of vital importance to refute their theses and beyond that, to simultaneously strongly represent the German cultural claim to West Prussia, the whole of Silesia and at least a large part of Posen.[54]

German historians – Lüpke was going to remedy this defect – should be ashamed that there was no overall study of 'the greatest deed of the German people in the Middle Ages'.

Kurt Forstreuter was a *Staatsarchivrat* working under Max Hein in Königsberg. Hein released him from his editorial work on the PUB and the PuSte held out the incentive of either 100 RMs for two or three hours' extra work on a *History of German Kulturpolitik* in Lithuania, or a lump sum when he had finished it.[55] The object of the book was to demonstrate that 'Prussian Lithuania' was a German *Kulturraum* into which Lithuanian culture 'had flowed and ebbed away again'. In other words, 'Lithuaniandom' was transient and superficial; below lay centuries of older and higher German history.[56] Unlike Forstreuter, Erich Maschke (1900–82) did not enjoy the relative economic security of a position with the archival service. Born in Berlin, Maschke developed an interest in history through his experiences with the Kreuzberg youth group *Volk vom Eichhof* which organized visits to Schinkel's *Neue Wache* or the tomb of Kleist, as well as the usual camping trips. Although he initially followed family tradition by studying medicine, Maschke abandoned this in favour of history and in 1925 moved with three friends to Königsberg. There, near the spits, dark lakes and endless woods, the young men found a model for their own aspirations in the German Knights. They called their journal *Der Weisse Ritter* and regarded the Knights as 'an association of men who sought to realise a heightened form of human existence'.[57] Maschke wanted to work on the Knights for his doctoral thesis. This was eventually published in 1928; a study of the conversion of the pagan Prussians to Christianity. Recommended to Max Hein, Maschke initially began work editing medieval Prussian charters but managed to get a junior university post in 1929. As a young scholar of promise and with an historiographical essay on Johannes Voigt behind him, Maschke was invited to contribute to the volume *Deutsche Staatenbildung und deutsche Kultur im Preussenlande*, whose title was an accurate reflection of the two main preoccupations of this branch of studies. Contributing an historiographical review, and liberated in this context from the tedium of footnotes, Maschke accorded Treitschke's 1862 essay lavish praise. It combined a sense of 'a masculine, state-oriented will' with a dramatic style that had resulted in 'a masterpiece of historical literature that had not been superseded'. While his concluding observation that although modern source-critical methods had stabilized the wilder flights of Romantic historians, a new era was dawning in which under pressure of national necessity 'weapons would be forged from the sources' for 'the struggle for existence', was conditioned by the widespread need to refute Polish claims, it also signalled a formal departure from disinterested scholarly activity.[58]

Despite his respectable scholarly output, Maschke and his wife were in difficult straits on a university stipend of 61 RMs per month.[59] Hope appeared across the horizon when in 1931 Papritz wrote asking for an account of his experiences working in the Polish archives for the report on how German visitors were treated. Maschke sent a report – on the whole the Poles had been obliging and had even spoken German – but followed this with a letter to Brackmann about the possibility of a grant. By May 1932 he was receiving 300 RMs per month (tax free and exclusive of any other income) from the PuSte for work on German 'subjective national and cultural identity' in medieval Poland.[60] By 1934 he wanted a travel grant of 300 RMs in order to work in the Polish archives for two or three weeks. But there was a problem about the wording of the application to the Polish authorities. It was a question of either 'Studies on the History of Germandom' or 'Studies on the Social and Economic History of Poland'. The latter had the advantage, he thought, of being related to his *Habilitations* work on an aspect of papal taxation in Poland.[61] Brackmann thought the first title 'too obvious' and it might draw attention to the PuSte's activities. It would be best, however, to give the Poles some indication of where his interests lay. By late March Maschke had found the appropriate wording: 'Structural Changes in the Demographic Structure of Poland under the Influence of German Law', under which loose, pseudo-scientific camouflage he would publish something to satisfy the Poles. His real work could appear as 'a supplement'.[62] In the summer of 1934 Maschke spent a week in Toruń and a fortnight in Warsaw. The Polish archivists were again obliging. Although he lacked the necessary permission secured through the German embassy, to work in Poznań, the Poles offered to speed an application through the Ministry of Culture in Warsaw. Maschke was reluctant. It might set a precedent for Polish scholars working in Germany and upset, as we will see, a finely wrought mechanism for obstructing their applications to use the archives.[63]

iv. The VIIth International Historical Congress in Warsaw, August 1933

In addition to the work of individual researchers, the PuSte staff were involved in larger collective enterprises. The decision, taken at the VIth International Historical Congress in Oslo in August 1928, to hold the next meeting in Warsaw in August 1933 was a major opportunity for the PuSte to demonstrate its usefulness (and as it turned out, ideological flexibility) to its political masters. The formal German preparations – or in other words the activities recorded in the *Historische Zeitschrift* – were discussed at a meeting of German historians in Göttingen in August 1932. Since the Warsaw Congress was going to concentrate upon east European history this meant 'recognising the fact that German historical scholarship had principally to direct its attention to where the questions of national existence lie in the present'.[64] With some fifteen sections – on, for example, legal, economic, art, and demographic history – and as many international study groups – on bibliography or iconography – requiring representation, it was decided to concentrate the German forces in the medieval and modern political history sections. The *älteren Fachgenossen* would set the tone.[65]

Since not all of the German delegates could be expected to be *au courant* with contentious issues dividing German and Polish scholars, the PuSte produced a Vademecum for the German delegates to steer them through the reefs of Polish tendentiousness. This consisted of a series of imaginary – though not improbable – dialogues between 'a Pole' and 'a German' on a variety of disputed issues. These began in the mists of deep time, with arguments over who had been responsible for the Lusatian Bronze Age civilization. The hypothetical Pole argued that eastern Germany was originally inhabited by Slavs who were merely submerged during the early Iron Age under a transient, immigrant German ruling class. Once the Germans had moved on in the period of the migrations, the Slavs resurfaced. In other words, there had been no Slav migrations – they were there all the time like a field under temporary flood. The German, bristling with learned citations from Gustav Kossinna, Wolfgang La Baume, and Max Vasmer, argued against any identity between this 'Illyrian' civilization and the Slavs. The latter (their original home was gently removed to faraway Kiev) had merely strayed into a lordless land vacated by Germanic tribes a thousand years after the Lusatian/Illyrian civilization had passed into the night of archaeological inscrutability.[66]

Another likely area of controversy would be whether or not the German Knights had slaughtered 10,000 Polish citizens in Danzig in 1308 in order to gain the city for themselves. The German argued that the town was overwhelmingly German in composition and that the inhabitants of the suburban villages were 'not Poles but Pomerelians and non-Slav Prussians'. Moreover massacring so many in Danzig in 1308 would be difficult with a total population of between 1,500 and 2,000. Aware of the uses of an infallible ally in Catholic Poland, the German pointed out that the Pope had twice exonerated the Knights from these allegations in 1310 and 1320. Following the customary tussle over the ethnic identity of Copernicus and Veit Stoss, the Vademecum addressed itself to more contemporary issues. The Pole argued 'that it was not justifiable to accuse modern Poland of imperialist tendencies because of its new frontiers: this is proved, for example, by the fact that its present frontiers lay way behind those of 1772'. The German thought that this merely 'proved' that Poland's political frontiers in 1772 had far outstripped any legitimate *ethnic* borders. In 1772 and by these criteria, Poland was three times, and in the seventeenth century five or six times, as large as it had any right to have been. In modern Poland, the Poles themselves constituted more than half the population in only 55 per cent of the territory encompassed by their frontiers.

The ethnic composition of Poland led ineluctably to the 'Kashubian Question'. As far as the Pole was concerned: 'the Kashubian nationality does not exist. The Kashubians and Masurians are simply Poles'. Only German dialect researchers, spurred on by German political interests, saw diversity where there was none. If the same methods were to be applied to the German language, one could split Germany into a hundred dialectical groupings and, by extension, into a hundred separate peoples.[67] Acknowledging the political sensitivity of the issue, the German nonetheless maintained that Kashubian was not a Polish dialect but a form of Pomeranian that had once been the lingua franca between the Vistula and Oder, Baltic and Warthe-Netze, and which had been progressively 'polonized' following Polish conquest of the region. Finally, lest the talk at Warsaw became topical, the German scholars came armed with the intricacies of coal-dumping. The Pole argued that Polish exports were considerable enough to warrant two major harbours. It was unthinkable that a state with thirty million people should funnel its exports through one, German, port. Ingeniously, the German replied that with the accession of the mines of Upper Silesia, and in order to avert mass unemployment, the Poles were obliged to heavily subsidize rail transports of coal to the ports. Subsidies to the railways of 177 million złoty between October 1929 and October 1932 proved the folly of separating Upper Silesia from 'its natural market in Germany'. Moreover the wages of east Upper Silesian miners compared unfavourably at 8 złoty a day with their German colleagues in west Upper Silesia earning 12.70 złoty a day, and this reduction in purchasing power was destroying the economy of the region. Because of this artificial price support, domestic coal consumers were paying more than export customers in Germany.[68]

However, a more durable response at Warsaw was needed than a typescript vade mecum. In November 1932 Brackmann informed his colleagues that the leader of the *Deutsche Stiftung*, Krahmer-

Möllenberg, had suggested a pre-emptive strike in the form of a book
to be entitled *Germany, Poland's Archenemy?* or, *Germany and
Poland*, designed to refute the notion of inevitable enmity between the
two nations. With the approval of the Foreign and Interior ministries,
the task was to be allocated to a young historian. Sensing a job for the
experienced hand, Brackmann thought it would be more appropriate
if the book consisted of short essays by leading German historians, as
a response to the Franco-Polish *La Pologne et la Baltique*. The book
was to be 'a declaration by German historians, which certainly will
not defuse the situation, but which would not be without a certain
political significance'.[69]

The project's political significance was not lost either upon the
Foreign or Interior ministries. The former attached great importance
to the English and French versions, while the latter was prepared to
cover the costs of the German publication, provided the publishers
would keep the shop price at the low figure of 3.50 RM.[70] The book
was the subject of a conference in the Prussian Ministry of State on 8
February 1933 attended by Krahmer-Möllenberg, Brackmann, representatives of the interested ministries and the Reichskommissar for
Osthilfe. They stressed that the book should not consist of individual
polemics, but should 'handle the controversial questions from a universal, historical standpoint'. The two most interested ministries would
each contribute subsidies of 5,000 RMs towards the costs of the
book.[71] A few days later, the publishers Oldenbourg agreed to produce
three editions, 5,000 in German and 1,000 each in French and English,
with a shop price of 4.80 RMs – 3 RMs to the ministries – and two
free copies for each contributor.[72]

As with many similar enterprises, the prospective contributors
were mostly in the dark about what exactly was required of them.
Gerhard Ritter, whose lack of Polish meant ignorance of the Polish
'propaganda literature', plaintively insisted 'I must first of all know
about the offensive against which I should direct myself'.[73] His offer
to cover the Prussian administration after the third Partition did not
fire Brackmann's imagination: 'as far as I am concerned', he wrote,
'the period belongs to the most miserable chapters in Polish administrative history: shady deals, corruption, land speculation, sloppiness in
every direction. Shall we give that on a plate to the Poles?'[74] But there
were other difficulties. The non-polemical tone required by the editors
led to much soulsearching by the hardened warriors in the Königsberg
archives. Max Hein expostulated that:

I can only conceive of an historical mission of East Prussia in the sense that this advanced post of Germandom represents a vital expansion of German *Lebensraum* and the German sphere of political influence, and that only Germans, and not the Poles, have a right to the area acquired through German blood and German effort. However, that does not seem to me to correspond with the intentions of the book.[75]

A. O. Meyer was also having trouble adhering to the standards of scholarly politesse in his essay on Silesia. 'How should one', he asked, 'write unpolemically about the terrible act of sadism experienced through the tearing apart of Upper Silesia?'[76] Those working on the more lightweight aspects of the subject had to bow to the political priorities of the book. Professor W. Drost, who was to contribute an art historical essay, was told that 'with reference to the political aim of the book, the account of artistic developments seemed the most easily dispensable'.[77] The contributors were also subjected to various kinds of editorial criticism. This could be conventional – Aubin (whose prose tends to pseudo-metaphysical obfuscation at the best of times) had to unmix his 'lee of the culture stream'[78] – or a matter of political 'clarification'. Rothfels in Königsberg was informed by Brackmann that the sentence 'They [the Poles] first of all upset the sense of Prussian statehood among the West Prussian Kashubians and Upper Silesians' might be 'expressed more cautiously' in the form 'This led . . . undoubtedly to a crisis of conscience'. Rothfels had also written of 'the amputation of Soldau'. Taking few chances, Brackmann noted 'that one generally only speaks of amputation in the case of a limb that has become diseased. Aren't you also of the opinion that one could better use the word "cession"?'[79] On the same page Rothfels had used the phrase 'confessed Polish as their mother-tongue', which indicated a degree of (unwanted) commitment among the Kashubians. A formulation substituting 'declared' for 'confessed' might leave the right air of doubt in the readers' minds.[80] Some contributors were rather more obliging. A. O. Mayer gave Brackmann *carte blanche* to alter his work should the Foreign Office object to any of it. He sent along a list of alternative sentences, adding 'hopefully these concessions will satisfy the Foreign Office'.[81] But Brackmann was a cautious man too. As the book took shape, he sent the title page and list of contents to Krieg in the Propaganda Ministry and to Gerullis in the Prussian Ministry of Science, Arts and Education for their opinions. Gerullis regretted the presence of Hoetzsch and the lack of Laubert, but as the book was being paid for by other ministries, saw no point 'in our ministry

exercising any censorship activity'.[82] Brackmann reported to his co-
editor Brandi that he had begun to detect a certain indisposition in
'NSDAP circles' to their choice of contributors and had called a
meeting in the Prussian Ministry of State 'to feel which way the wind
is blowing'.[83]

Eventually, *Deutschland und Polen* appeared in early August
1933.[84] One hundred and twenty review copies were dispatched to
inter alia the *NS-Monatshefte*, *Deutscher Lebensraum*, *Die Ostmark*,
Der Stahlhelm, *Der Angriff* and the BDO's *Ostland*. Forty-nine copies
went gratis to government officials, including one for Hindenburg and
another to Hitler. A letter accompanied the Führer's copy:

> Most highly esteemed Herr Reichskanzler!
>
> In this collective volume, which I permit myself to send to you,
> 19 German historians have taken the opportunity to set the German
> point of view against the false accounts of German–Polish relations
> from the side of the French and Poles. As the preface shows, we have
> endeavoured to write as objectively and calmly as was possible but at
> the same time to express our opinions clearly and unequivocally. We
> believe we have acted in accordance with the words that you delivered
> on relations between the German and Polish peoples in your speech of
> 17 May of this year which set the direction for our course. We ask
> you, most respected Herr Reichskanzler, to accept this work, which
> was supported by the Imperial and Prussian ministries, as an external
> sign of our gratitude for the intelligent and success-promising way in
> which you too have tackled these most difficult questions of our
> internal and foreign policy.
>
> On behalf of the contributors,
> Professor Dr Brackmann[85]

On 12 August 1933 Regierungsrat Dr Meerwald informed Brackmann that 'the Herr Reichskanzler received the book with pleasure
and would like me to convey his most lasting thanks for the consideration shown to him'.[86] Hitler's Reichstag speech of 17 May was an
attempt to defuse a diplomatic situation that had steadily deteriorated
since the electoral successes of the NSDAP in February and March
appeared, in Polish eyes, to open the sluice gates for the revisionist
demands of the powerful eastern lobby. Convinced that Hitler would
support revisionism by force, and worried by aggressive headlines and
the noisy, terroristic appearance of the SA in Silesia, Danzig and East
Prussia, Piłsudski reinforced his troops on the Westerplatte and in the
vicinity of Toruń-Danzig.[87] A preventative war seemed imminent. That

it did not occur was the result of the reluctance of Poland's allies to become involved in a venture whose first movements had already been condemned by the League of Nations. Hitler began to extricate himself from this situation during a conversation with the Polish ambassador Wysocki on 2 May 1933: the frontiers with Poland were a bone of contention dropped between Poland and Germany by the allies, he respected Poland as a reality and hoped that their respective interests could be discussed dispassionately.[88] The speech of 17 May, in which Hitler averred that 'we respect the national rights of other lands too and would like, from the bottom of our hearts, to live with them in peace and freedom' was also aimed at a Polish audience.[89] A similarly reassuring tone was kept up after the German departure from the League of Nations on 19 October 1933 reawakened Polish fears and Polish plans for a preemptive war. On 24 October he tried to reassure the Poles with his speech 'There are Germans in Europe, there are Poles in Europe', while in November he stressed a community of interest in combating Soviet communism:

> The Chancellor declared that acts of aggression contradict his policy and that a war would be a catastrophe for everyone. Any war could only bring communism to Europe which would be a terrible danger. However Poland is an outpost against Asia. The Chancellor took up the thought that every possibility of war must be excluded from German–Polish relations whereby he remarked, that these thoughts could be given the form of a treaty.[90]

Two and a half months later, on 26 January 1934 Foreign Ministers Beck and Neurath signed the German–Polish non-aggression pact.

Brackmann's *Deutschland und Polen* was an attempt to bring history into line with the course heralded on 17 May. In the preface he and Brandi set aside the polemics of the recent past – although a glancing blow at a recent Franco–Polish publication was irresistible – in favour of a more conciliatory tone:

> In the pages that follow we will consciously avoid speaking, in connection with historical phenomena . . . of *injustice* and *droit*, of a *rêve ambitieux* of nations, or employing other value judgements of publicistic writing, because the historian is not a judge of the past nor a law maker for the future, but a servant of the truth, who as such, is duty-bound, by birth to his own people, but also to those bound to him in spatial or cultural community as neighbours, and to the well-being of humanity as a whole. We want to remember here that it is the task

of the historian; to critically resolve error, to expose partiality and to avoid it oneself, but nonetheless, to always keep the universal-historical perspective in the sense of Leopold von Ranke, before one's eyes.[91]

As the contents of the book demonstrate, it was difficult to revise the prejudices of many decades overnight. Wilhelm Unversagt – adopting a 'swinging pendulum' as a metaphor for the 'series of great conflicts between East and West' – rapidly dispensed with any connection between Bronze-Age Lusatian 'Illyrians' and a Slav *Urheimat*.[92] However, he saw no incongruity in explaining the resistance encountered by Saxon conquerors at the hands of West Slav tribes in terms of the latter's infusion of 'nordic blood' from the remnants of the migrant German barbarians.[93] His own excavations of the fortresses between the Oder and Elbe and north of the Warthe were producing evidence of considerable Pomeranian, Liutizen and Sorbian resistance to the expansionist Polish state. He was unimpressed, indeed almost offended, by the low level of the latter's civilization:

> The excavations in Oppeln and Zantoch give an impressive picture of how it looked in the East before the German colonisation. The domestic and defensive buildings were constructed in the most primitive block-technique, with open-hearth fires inside the houses, from thick layers of compressed manure. The smell, that even today wafts upwards from these ruins, conveys an all too clear image of the cultural conditions of those times. When one recalls that such houses appear in the residences of Slav princes, and at a time when the imposing romanesque churches were built on the Rhine and in central Germany, which even today arouse our highest admiration, one can understand what the culturally superior germanic West had to give to the primitive Slavic East.[94]

Hermann Aubin detected a 'cultural gradient' running from South and West towards the North and East. Charlemagne had been the first to clearly recognize 'the Western task of civilising the sub-germanic zone'. There could be no peace in medieval Europe 'so long as the lower-placed neighbours did not draw close to the *Kulturniveau* of the Germans'.[95] Brackmann, favouring a more lyrical approach than Aubin's cultural morphologizing, set the same scene:

> While the Slav peoples of Europe, including the Russians, still lay in a deep intellectual slumber, the monk Widukind wrote his Saxon history in the monastery of Corvey on the Weser, the nun Hroswitha in the abbey of Gandesheim her song to Otto the Great and her classical

dramas, and in Merseburg Bruno of Querfurt his life of St Adalbert and bishop Thietmar his chronicle ... Where then could one find in Poland cultural centres like Corvey or Gandersheim or Magdeburg – not to speak of the centres of ancient civilisation on the Rhine? Gnesen and Posen were settlements of the most primitive type.[96]

So did Max Hein:

As in the year 1000 it was again the Germans, and moreover Germans summoned by Poland, who sought to realise the christianisation and germanisation of the Prussians and their addition to the German *Lebensraum* and to the German, and at the same time, West European, *Kulturkreis*. The Prussian undertaking of the German Order is, on the one hand, the fulfilment of the great German cultural mission in the East, and on the other, the expansion of the all too narrow *Lebensraum* in the old Reich.[97]

And finally Walter Recke:

This land [West Prussia], whose civilisation and population were German, which voluntarily chose the overlordship of the King of Poland, and in which *Polentum* first found entrance as it was made a part of the Polish state by force, was recovered for Germandom by Frederick the Great through the so-called First Partition of Poland. That was the monstrous crime that was allegedly atoned for at Versailles in 1919 by the creation of the Corridor.[98]

So the essays went on, with Max Hein losing his sense of chronology – the Second Treaty of Thorn in 1466 became 'the *Thorner Diktat*' – and Hermann Oncken trying to ingratiate himself with an English readership by referring to Germany's *Irland-Ulster*.[99] The contributors took pains to ensure that Poland remained land-locked: 'the Poles are a continental race, their state became a continental state',[100] 'it may be that residual Germans settled on the coast served as maritime teachers for the Slav races',[101] or 'the Poles are – as their name indicates – the inhabitants of the fields, they are ... an inland people (Landrats), with all the characteristics of their continental situation'.[102] They were also loath, as their adoption of 'structural' or 'structural-ethical' forms of explanation reveals, to see human agency at work in the Partitions of Poland. Aubin detected a 'power-gradient', conveniently occupying the same morphological zone as his 'cultural gradient', separating 'the forward-striding German territorial state' from the 'hyper-trophic, *weitergebildeten*, dualistic *Ständestaat*' of Poland.[103] The gap between the 'power and level of organisation' of the former explained the demise of the latter. Brackmann, straying now from the paths of judicial impartiality established in the preface, preferred the wages of win:

> Instead of building their state in the directions in which Casimir had taken – in peace with the German neighbour and with the help of his *Kultur*, whose superiority no one had honoured more than the last Piast, the Jagiellonians and their successors pursued an unbounded expansionary policy towards the East and West and finally, also towards the North and surrendered one position after another inside the country on behalf of unachievable goals, until their sovereignty became a matter of appearance and their Polish country a plaything for the stronger powers. Seldom in the history of the nations has the false imperialist policy of a country avenged itself as in the history of Poland, and today still it has an after-effect because it does not enable the Polish people to rest, but rather drives them to realise political goals from the past which once brought about their downfall. The medieval history of Poland is a warning of the most serious kind – for Poland itself, for its neighbours and for the continent of Europe.[104]

The VIIth International Congress opened in Warsaw on Monday 21 August 1933 with a reception for the delegates, Polish dignitaries and the diplomatic corps. The German contingent, including four PuSte employees (their fares were paid by the Foreign Office), stayed at the residence of ambassador Moltke. This arrangement did not cover German Jews whom the leader of the German contingent, Brandi, insisted 'we tolerate only as a separate group'.[105] In the following week Kehr spoke on the problems of editing papal charters, Aubin on the penetration of the ancient world by Teutons and Arabs, Schramm on coronation *Ordines* and Brackmann on a caesura in medieval history around 1100. Breakfast and tea-time were taken up with special sessions on such matters as the history of science. The conference ended, as it had begun, with a grand reception in the royal castle at which the delegates could sport their decorations, before adjourning to Cracow for another round of Polish hospitality.[106] The German view of the proceedings was one of cautious optimism. Brandi noted that while the academic product was not startling, the reawakened interest in Slav history was positive. Wolfgang Kohte from the PuSte commended the hospitality of the Poles although he felt duty bound to add that behind the curtain of glittering receptions lay 'the poverty of the proletarian quarters of the Polish big cities'. However he also noted the difficulty experienced by a younger generation of German academics in communicating to foreign scholars the 'fundamental concepts' of race and linguistic families that they were employing in their work. But he agreed with Brandi that 'scholars have the task of being not only standard-bearers but also the physicians of their peoples'.[107]

Any goodwill created at Warsaw was rapidly destroyed by the appearance of *Deutschland und Polen*. In December 1933 Dölger in Munich sent Brackmann a copy of a letter he had received from Oskar Halecki in Warsaw saying that 'the positive atmosphere of the Congress had, on account of the book, slipped into a particularly tricky phase'.[108] The *Gazeta Warsawska* said that the book represented 'overt disrespect for and systematic disparagement of the cultural achievement of Poland's past and an assault on the West of Poland'.[109] The reviewer in *Wiedza i Zycie* thought that very few of the contributors had managed to achieve scholarly objectivity as opposed to 'National Socialist tendentiousness'.[110] This view was evidently shared by the Polish customs. In April 1934 Brackmann informed the Congress organizer Marcel Handelsmann that the book was being confiscated under laws governing the importation of 'products and materials that expressed mockery or offended against religious, national or moral sentiment'. He had it reliably, from the *Deutsche Rundschau* in Bromberg, that not only his book, but the Führer's *Mein Kampf* were on an index of undesirable literature.[111] The existence of a ban on the book was confirmed by Maschke who tried to take the work into Poland in June. It was eventually lifted in January 1936.[112]

The final budget for *Deutschland und Polen* of 11,196 RMs included 2,620 RMs for four translators.[113] The translations reached their French and English audience either officially – in late September Windecker of the Foreign Office asked Papritz for 150 free copies – or in one instance, through the good offices of young German scholars working abroad.[114] Richard Drögereit, an archivist in Hannover, had worked on the English version. In February 1935 he wrote to Brackmann seeking a reference to the Deputy Keeper of the British Museum. Having heard that 'the Marienburg and the German *Ordensland* have a great impact on the Anglo-Saxons', Drögereit wanted to produce an edition of sources on relations between England and Prussia in the Middle Ages. He thought he might also find a home for a few free copies of Brackmann's book which he offered 'to distribute to a few – English professors or historical institutes as unobtrusive propaganda'.[115] He thought of presenting a copy to UCL 'as a book that I had come across, in order to avoid the impression of official propaganda'.[116] Brackmann sent him four copies 'for the eventuality that you can win friends in England for our scholarly viewpoint'.[117]

v. *Ostforschung* and the effects of the Hitler–Piłsudski Pact

The first cycle of institutional development closely connected with the PuSte can be concluded with the founding of the *Nordost-Deutsche Forschungsgemeinschaft* (NODFG) on 19 December 1933 at the former *Herrenhaus* in the Leipzigerstrasse in Berlin. The idea of coordinating the work of individuals and institutions studying ethnic Germandom was not new and mirrors the political pressures towards homogenization brought to bear by government upon associations concerned with the East or, for that matter, upon the societies and organizations of the German minority in Poland.[118] In 1921 the RMdI founded the Leipzig-based *Stiftung für deutsche Volks- und Kultur-bodenforschung* which was designed to coordinate the efforts of those working on the German *Volksboden*, i.e. areas overwhelmingly settled by Germans, and German *Kulturboden*, i.e. areas inhabited by other peoples but in which the German cultural influence was dominant.[119] The *Stiftung* ran biannual conferences to bring together historians and geographers working in the field. Since, as we have seen, the RMdI and Foreign Office were not reluctant to encourage minor academic empire-builders as a means of cementing their own influence, the RMdI responded positively to a suggestion by the *Stiftung*'s director Volz that his organization should be the base for a new *Zentralstelle für Ostforschung*. Although this was founded in 1928, methodological quarrels between the *Stiftung*'s leaders, and embezzlement of its funds by Volz, resulted in the dissolution of both *Stiftung* and *Zentralstelle* in 1931.[120]

Following this fiasco, and with plans for the PuSte well underway, the RMdI and Foreign Office decided upon a regionalist solution. Instead of a *Zentralstelle*, there would be a series of regional research communities, which would exchange results and information and pursue broadly similar objectives.[121] The task of forming the communities was assigned to the VDA leader Steinacher. By October 1933 he had assembled the *Alpenländische Forschungsgemeinschaft* to cover Switzerland and the Tirol; the *Sudostdeutsche Forschungsgemeinschaft* for Hungary and South and East Czechoslovakia, the *Westdeutsche Forschungsgemeinschaft* for France, Luxembourg, and the Belgian and

Dutch borders and the *Überseedeutsche Forschungsgemeinschaft* for the Germans overseas.[122]

At the *Herrenhaus* meeting Brackmann announced the founding of a *Nordost-Deutsche Forschungsgemeinschaft* as a 'combative association' designed to coordinate the efforts of those working on the Northeast. Since Hitler had outlined 'a clear, purposive *Ostpolitik*' there were no obstacles to the implementation of old plans. Aamann from the ALFG sketched the developments since the failure of the Leipzig *Stiftung* and the aims and structure to be emulated. Although the methods to be adopted should be scholarly, 'the objective is political in the broadest and best sense'.[123] The NODFG should consist of an overall leader and a number of chiefs of subregional sections. Steinacher insisted that the leaders should be nominated rather than elected. Costs were to be kept minimal and meetings 'should never take on the character of popular assemblies'. Brackmann suggested that meetings should be held in small towns, for security reasons, and to enable German academics from Poland to attend without compromising themselves.

There was something approaching a debate over the extent of the region to be covered. Ziesemer insisted upon the inclusion of the Volga Germans, Aubin argued for a unified approach to Silesia and Hoetzsch tried to exclude Scandinavia. Others argued in favour of a more flexible stance. Erich Maschke thought that current political interests should be as decisive as hard and fast regional boundaries, while Steinacher argued in favour of an expansive approach that went beyond the German–Polish borders to tackle Poland itself. As he put it, the task of these 'shock-troops of ethnic German effort in the North East' was 'to forge offensive and defensive intellectual weapons for Germandom'.[124]

On the following day the chairman of the *Volksdeutschen Rat* (which was subordinate to Rudolf Hess), Professor Haushöfer, nominated Brackmann, Aubin and Recke as members of the NODFG ruling committee and the young lecturer from Königsberg, Theodor Oberländer, as its executive officer. The rest of the proceedings were occupied with reports of work in progress. Brackmann reported on the PuSte, and Recke on the *Ostland Institut*'s work 'at the front'. Almost in passing, Brackmann mentioned 'that in agreement with the RMdI a number of tasks have been assigned to German academics *in* Poland'.[125] The first fruits of subsidizing scholarly subversion in another country were heard in the afternoon. Franz Doubek from

Wilna stressed the need for an atlas showing German dialects in Poland, a task that required haste 'on national grounds because of the rapid, almost daily disappearance of the stock of dialects'. Walther Kuhn from Bielitz mentioned the talents of a young German historian called Kurt Lück, and of the need 'to understand and support' the culture of the ethnic Germans in Volhynia who, although 50 per cent illiterate, revealed 'a remarkable strength and capacity for reproduction'. Following reports from absent friends in Poland, the gathering eventually decamped to the Eastern exhibition of the BDO and a convivial evening in the spiritual Mecca of the *volksdeutsche* movement, the *Volksdeutsche Klub*.

The BDO's exhibition *Der Osten- das deutschen Schickalsland*, timed to catch the Christmas shoppers, provided Brackmann and his colleagues with an opportunity to foster a connection with an organization that had swallowed most of the eastern lobby groups and which had plans to coordinate academic research on the East. Founded in the wake of the 'Day of the German East', on 27 May 1933, the BDO absorbed the *Ostmarkenverein, Heimatbund Ostpreussen, Jungpreussische Bewegung* and the *Reichsbund der Schlesier* and many more, taking over their regional organizations and subjecting the whole to Franz Lüdtke the leader of the main section, 'the German East', in the foreign affairs office of the *Reichsleitung* of the NSDAP.[126] It was emphasized that the BDO was not going to be another sentimental gathering place where 'a couple of brave citizens get together over *Eisbein* and *Sauerkohl* to exchange old memories from the beloved homeland' but a movement 'that will be grasped by the people and which will seize them too'.[127] Organizationally, the BDO consisted of a federal leader and committee and seven regional branches. It stood under the protection of Wilhelm Kube, the *Oberpräsident* of Berlin and Brandenburg. The BDO's firm commitment to educational issues – it wanted compulsory courses on eastern questions and had its own department for higher education and research – ensured that the organization as a whole quickly became the subject of a PuSte report. The report of July 1933 was particularly concerned about the BDO's Department 6 (it had nine offices) for scholarship and research. While there was nothing amiss in the BDO's plans to lobby for a concentration of spending on eastern political studies, there was at least food for thought in the notion 'that scholarship must adjust itself to the problems of the state'. The appointment of *Oberarchivrat* Volkmann to manage Department 6 did not augur well for *Ostforschung* either.

He knew nothing about the subject and had not heard of most of the institutes which were to come under his department's control.[128] This last development was described by Brackmann in a letter to Fritz Rörig in July 1933 as a dangerous attempt to coordinate the whole of *Ostforschung* so that nothing could be published 'without the agreement of the BDO'.[129] Hence Brackmann took the earliest opportunity to forge a connection with this threatening organization.

On 1 November Brackmann, Aubin, Papritz and Laubert met the BDO's leaders to discuss what they could contribute to the historical sections of the planned exhibition. Designed to cover an indeterminate 'East' from the Stone Age to the present, the exhibition was to be divided into four sections. Brackmann secured the sub-section, 'the course of history', for himself. Given the developing German–Polish thaw, the exhibition organizers required some caution: 'in the Führer's view claims should only be raised on what was acquired by our cultural achievements. We will never draw people to us by force who do not love us, far less through the blood of those we love.' The aims of the exhibition and 'the thoughts of the National Socialist leadership' were to be conveyed through films and lunchtime and evening lectures. Brackmann not only organized part of the show but also reviewed it. Knowledge of the historical past was vital for 'the understanding between both nations that the Führer has inaugurated'. The exhibition was supposed to introduce the layman to 'the cultural achievement that the German people performed there in the East'. Inevitably, the emphasis was severely germanocentric. Describing the section on the 'civilising' work of German townsmen, Brackmann singled out a map of Konitz which epitomized 'how German blood streamed towards the east'; Konitz, he went on, 'founded in accordance with German law, by Culmic law, laid out on a German town plan, as it still reveals today, and only colonised with German blood which streamed endlessly out of the homelands, precisely at the time when Konitz belonged to Poland' and so forth.[130]

The implications for *Ostforschung* of the Non-Aggression Pact were high on the agenda of the NODFG conference held at Kahlberg between 6 and 10 August 1934. Seventy-four *Ostforscher* gathered in conditions of some secrecy – Brackmann banned waiters from the room – at this remote location on the Frische Nehrung. Brackmann posed the crucial question: 'Germany has entered into a new era of peaceful relations with Poland on account of the Pact of 26 January and it is necessary to establish how far scholarship should take into account the political situation.'[131] On the 7th he read out a discussion paper entitled 'Frontier Studies and the Ten Year Pact' by *Regierungspräsident* Budding from Marienwerder. There was to be no beating of swords into ploughshares. Since the Poles had not decelerated their academic propaganda, Budding argued that it would be both a betrayal of the German minority in Poland, and a renunciation of German rights, if German scholars were to suddenly change course. There could be a change of tone:

> Polemics and revisionist demands must drop out of sight and government agencies should not be in evidence. Organisation and forms of expression are to be changed. Accounts must be objective . . . Cooperation between Germany and Poland is to be stressed everywhere. The spirit of frontier work is still necessary and possible on the basis of the ten year pact.[132]

The resulting discussion concerned tone rather than content. Papritz argued for a more moderate use of language and the adoption of French 'Courtoisie' to palliate the Polish Press, but the work should not be influenced by the Pact. Laubert and Maschke were opposed to any change in tone on the grounds that this would compromise scholarly criteria of right and wrong. Maschke insisted 'we should not turn our view of history into rubble on account of this or that political consideration. No renunciation of writings, work of publishing'.[133] Theodor Oberländer, who, like Hitler, thought that treaties affecting the East 'were only conditionally sacrosanct', argued that they should continue as usual 'so that after ten years we have everything ready that we could need in any given circumstances'. Arguments about tone struck Tiedje from the RMdI as irrelevant. The crucial matter was that scholarship 'must remain in touch with the state. Not the form or type of research but its thrust must stand in agreement with the state'. Whatever the public face of German–Polish relations, the irons of *Ostforschung* were going to stay firmly in the fire.[134]

As if to confirm these larger deliberations, the specialist speakers described work of a distinctly uncompromising nature. Oberländer, chairman of the BDO from 19 October 1934, addressed the conference on rural overpopulation in Poland. Starting from the observation that if there was a 'cultural gradient' from West to East, there was a 'birthrate gradient' running in the opposite direction, Oberländer outlined the distribution of unviable, dwarf agricultural holdings in Poland. Under 'the cultural circumstances of the moment', he vaguely averred,

'Poland has eight million inhabitants too many'. In the resulting discussion, Uebersberger from Breslau sought to introduce some historical differentiation:

> In Prussian Poland the relations are otherwise. Judaisation has disappeared, the Poles have learned from the Prussian state. In Congress Poland rural reform was carried out in the Russian interest against the Polish landlords. Judaisation persists; in 1910 75% of all urban communities in Congress Poland had a Jewish majority.

Following further contributions on Silesia – including the first ominous mention of the racial studies of Professor Otto Reche in Leipzig – the convivial part of the proceedings commenced. They cruised by motorboat across the Haff to Buchwalde, visited Frauenburg to call to mind the great astronomer, and Elbing to cast a baleful eye over the frontier. At Neudeck the party observed a few minutes silence in the park to commemorate the passing of the Field Marshal and President. A bus took them to Weissenberg for a last thought-provoking glimpse of 'the impossible frontier arrangements of 1920'.[135]

3. WATCH IN THE EAST

i. Papritz's 'rare birds': personnel, pay and politics

The day to day business of the NODFG was conducted from the offices of the PuSte whose staff dealt with correspondence, administered its finances, and organized NODFG conferences. The NODFG annual report for 1938–9 remarked that the PuSte's base in Berlin had the advantage of being near the ministries and NSDAP offices 'with whom the closest working relations exist'.[1] The growth of the PuSte-NODFG apparatus gradually became burdensome for the host institution, the Geheime Staatsarchiv, particularly after Brackmann's premature retirement in 1936 and his replacement by Zipfel who had no pronounced interest in *Ostforschung*.[2] It was not just a matter of archivists having to work overtime in the PuSte, but also a question of space. In 1936 the PuSte had a library with 5,500 books, and another 3,500 from the OMV lying unpacked in the cellars, some 30,000 cards, and a duplicating machine that generated about 20,000 sheets of translated press extracts a week.[3] The attic floor had had to be converted early in 1935 into rooms for the translation service, library, and deputy administrator Kohte, but other staff had to work in a library belonging to the Geheime Staatsarchiv, or next door in Brackmann's villa. Papritz was ensconced on the ground floor which involved a two-minute climb to confer with Kohte.[4] Although the 14 academic staff, 7 administrative employees and 2 technicians were thus dispersed throughout the building, the only formal connection with the host establishment was that Papritz and Kohte were archivists, and the First Director did the formal hiring and firing of staff.[5] In order to become independent of the archive, the PuSte needed somewhere in Dahlem with at least 27 rooms, the formal release of Papritz and Kohte from their duties in the archive, and regular salaries for researchers if the PuSte was not to become 'a sort of academic transit camp or a temporary abode for the needy'.[6] In September 1938 the PuSte rented Gelfertstrasse 11 at a cost of 16,000 RMs per annum. The retired General-Director received a salary of 3,600 RMs to supplement his pension and Papritz was put on a regular salary of 7,240 RMs p.a., Kohte 4,800 RMs.[7]

Papritz was largely responsible for recruitment.[8] The language requirements for a post with the PuSte virtually ensured that the personnel would consist of 'rare birds' rather than the more conventional products of the academic mill. Papritz himself was born in Berlin-Charlottenburg in April 1898. He attended the Kaiserin Augusta Gymnasium before seeing active military service on both fronts in the First World War. After this experience, he resumed his studies in Berlin (1919–21), Jena (1921), and Berlin (1921–3) where he was particularly impressed by Dietrich Schäfer, Rudolf Häpke and Michael Tangl. He was awarded a doctorate in November 1922 for a thesis on the Stettin salt-trading dynasty of Loitz.

Papritz studied to be an archivist and, in 1927, after two years at the Geheime Staatsarchiv, was posted to Danzig. In March 1929 he returned to the Archivstrasse to run Department I.[9] He marched, so to speak, with the Stahlhelm into the SA and, he claims, through an over-obliging SA-*Scharführer*, into the NSDAP in 1937.[10]

The men and women that Papritz recruited – and a biographical approach that generalizes over fourteen years is adopted here – came to Germany either to further their education, or because endemic nationality conflict (or religious/racial persecution), in their place of origin had stymied their careers. They were mostly 'of a certain age' and had been living a peripatetic, hand-to-mouth existence on a succession of grants and temporary jobs for a little too long. The gaps between posts became lengthier, the prospect of a particularly atomized form of proletarianization greater, and domestic strain and an increasing touchiness neared the surface. The PuSte held out the prospect of regular pay, a chance to start a family, colleagues instead of the crepuscular silence of the archives, and an opportunity to use the skills that circumstances had given them. In the world at large they were nobodies, within the PuSte they became somebodies. During the fourteen years of its existence, the PuSte developed its own ethos based upon polite, Prussian correctness; its own hierarchy, enmities and allegiances; and the usual forms of ritualized jollification through circularized witticisms and office parties. Inevitably, the PuSte also mirrored that remarkable political comformity that has often been seen as one of the characteristics of academic life at the time.[11]

Sergei Jakobson, whom we have already encountered, was an early 'rare bird'. Born in Moscow in 1901, Jakobson studied at the universities of Hamburg and Berlin from 1919–25. He had a formidable roll-call of distinguished teachers including Brackmann, Hoetzsch, Marcks, Meinecke, Stählin and Tangl.[12] Although employed by a publishing firm, Jakobson had not abandoned all hope of academic preferment. In October 1931 he wrote to Brackmann to discover whether his talents could be used in the editorial work beginning in the Geheime Staatsarchiv. There was clearly a lot at stake for him. 'Time moves on', he wrote, 'one gets older and apart from material concerns, one has the great psychological worry of having missed the boat.'[13] The PuSte gave him a grant from 1 January 1932.[14] By July 1933 he had one work, on Prussian relations with Danzig between 1636 and 1703, ready for the press, while simultaneously editing ambassadorial reports from eighteenth-century Warsaw, whose effect would be to present a less intentionalist version of Prussian involvement in the Partitions of Poland.[15] Despite his Russian origins, Jakobson was a proud 'Prussian citizen'. He was naturalized in March 1930.[16] However, by October 1933, following the 'Laws for the Restoration of the Professional Civil Service', Jakobson was corresponding with his erstwhile colleagues on PuSte notepaper from an address in London NW11. In a particularly unpleasant example of retrospective self-justification, the PuSte outlined the circumstances that had led them to employ a Russian Jew to work on Prussian history. After the First World War there had been a shortage of linguistically competent German scholars capable of training young historians for the intellectual repulse of the Poles. Jakobson was talented, knew the right languages, and came highly recommended – one name was conspicuous by its absence – by Meinecke, Marcks and Stählin. The PuSte had employed him, *faute de mieux* so to speak, but at least his two immediate colleagues were NSDAP members.[17] In line with instructions from Brackmann, strenuous efforts had been made from the stars 'to keep Jakobson as a Jew, as far from the foreground as possible, and in particular we discussed how one could avoid beginning the publications series with one of his works'.[18]

Another early recruit, and victim of enforced political conformity, was Dr Anneliese Schwarz. In September 1931 Brackmann hired her to work on sources from the era of the Polish Partitions in Department I of the Geheime Staatsarchiv.[19] Schwarz was born in West Prussia in 1907. She lost her customs-officer father at Tannenberg seven years later. After studying in Greifswald, Berlin, Königsberg and

Graz, Schwarz gained a doctorate in July 1931.[20] Brackmann, who had a high regard for her work on the Swabian colonization of West Prussia, secured her a grant through the *Notgemeinschaft für Deutsche Wissenschaft* of 150 RMs per month.[21] However in April 1933 the political police, shortly to become the Gestapo, confidentially informed him that they had searched Schwarz's flat, and her mother's home in Stettin, fearing that she might be a communist agent.[22] The police search of her one-room flat yielded a poor trawl: some index cards in Polish (she was allowed to take work home), two Intourist brochures, a membership card for the *League Against Colonial Repression and Imperialism* and her Chinese friend Bing-Nan Wang.[23] During the resulting interrogation, the police tried to make her confess to being a KPD functionary, and to associate herself with people of whom she clearly had no knowledge. She said the charges were false. Bing-Nan Wang, the twenty-eight-year-old Chinese, was from the university of Shensi and was attending, quite legitimately, various lectures on post-war German politics and relations in the Pacific.[24] With the usual catholicity of suspicion, the police tried to implicate him in the recent smashing of the windows of two Japanese restaurants.

Although both Schwarz and the Chinese were released, Papritz preempted the police threat to sack her through the RMdI by contacting the *Notgemeinschaft* to terminate her grant.[25] Brackmann had this measure underway in April 1933. Writing to the President of the *Notgemeinschaft*, Schmidt-Ott, he noted:

I have been confidentially informed by the police headquarters in Berlin that accusations of communist activities have been made against Dr Schwarz. Since the evidence appeared to be confirmed, a house-search was carried out the day before yesterday. This did not produce any incriminating material although that could be because Schwarz's mother, who lives in Stettin, may have informed her by letter a few days before, that the police had conducted a search of her home on account of her daughter. Earlier police surveillance has shown that Dr Schwarz, the daughter of a captain who fell at Tannenberg, is living permanently with a Chinese student. During the search she described him as her fiancé. I leave it respectfully to Your Excellency's discretion to decide whether Miss Schwarz, against whom communist activity is not definitively proven, is, on account of the above circumstances [which replaced *on account of her cohabitation with a Chinese student* in the first draft] worthy of further support from the *Notgemeinschaft*.[26]

On 14 April 1933 Brackmann banned Schwarz from the Geheime Staatsarchiv and a month later the *Notgemeinschaft* terminated her grant.[27] By September 1934 Schwarz was working as a journalist.[28] Brackmann believed in running a tight ship.

The PuSte's librarian Harald Cosack also arrived by a circuitous route and like Schwarz was subjected to Brackmann's anti-communist preoccupation. In Cosack's case this was probably more accurate – he worked for the communist underground – although he never joined the KPD, but joined the SED in the summer of 1946.[29] Born in Pernau (Estonia) in December 1880, Cosack studied in Dorpat and Reval before working as a German teacher in Taschkent in Russian Central Asia. In 1908 he and his family moved to Berlin where he read history, philosophy and slavonic languages. Unfit for military service, Cosack worked from 1915 as chief of the Russian department of the Oriental Institute, which produced translations and briefings for *inter alia* the Foreign Office. After 1917 he worked for a Red Cross home before moving in 1923 to the *Osteuropa-Institut* in Berslau. There he produced bibliographies and taught Russian, until some obscure tensions resulted in his being sacked. He was unemployed from October 1931 until January 1934.[30] Already over fifty, Cosack was interviewed by Papritz for a post with the PuSte and was taken on despite not being an NSDAP adherent.[31]

Within ten months Cosack was in deep trouble on account of what he subsequently described as the rise of Nazi *Spitzeltätigkeit* within the PuSte. For a week in December 1934 an in-house hearing took place under the chairmanship of Papritz and at the instigation of Brackmann, to determine whether Cosack was a communist or not. He was certainly unaware of the constraints upon free expression under an authoritarian regime. During a walk with a Swedish colleague Cosack had apparently tried to justify what the colleague referred to as 'Bolshevik and Jewish acts of murderousness'.[32] The Swede's political credo consisted of 'not shrinking from putting a bullet through the ribs of anyone who stood up for bolshevism', and of boasting of his part in the assassination of Swedish communists.[33] Others testified that Cosack had shocked sibling recruits by mocking their attempts to blend in with their surroundings through the Hitler salute, by responding 'I am not called Hitler, and why hail?'[34] This witness was asked whether Cosack's seditious utterances were 'conversational' or was there 'a certain tendency?'. 'Tendency', he replied. On the second day the parameters of Cosack's '*Tendenz*' were explored more thoroughly.

He had said that if Germany were to be 'sovietised' it would acquire colonies in Siberia. Every Soviet worker had his own four-room home and could sub-let; they could bask regularly in the Crimean sunshine, and cleaners could avail themselves of the utilities of the Lenin Library in their off-duty hours. He had also been contemptuous of the 'childish beliefs' of his Christian colleagues, and thought that the Soviets were correct in persecuting the Christian churches. Those of his colleagues with aristocratic pretensions fared no better. He had told the Baron Wrewsky, who had relatives in Russia, that 'all the Tsars were a pack of degenerates' (*ein ganz verworfenes Pack waren*), and he had aggravated others by reading aloud extracts from Polish newspapers. Most dangerously, Cosack had described the Nazi race laws as 'a crime against humanity' and the Protocols of Zion as *ein Phantasieprodukt*.[35]

Those who spoke on his behalf reflected the inverted moral universe of Nazi Germany as much as his accusers. Bellée testified that Cosack had been sacked in Breslau because of his 'anti-Semitic opinions'. Since this did not chime with Cosack's views on the Nazi race laws, the witness added that Cosack's anti-Semitism was 'personal' and not something he thought should be a subject of state policy.[36] Anton Loessner stressed that Cosack had always been careful when the Swede, 'whom none of us regards as entirely normal', had been present. As for the accused, he said that although he had grown up feeling contempt towards the Slavs, the tenacity of Russian resistance in the First World War and after had led him to revise his opinions. He had merely said to his Christian colleague, 'For God's sake I don't want to rob you of your childhood beliefs.'[37] The Swedish assassin could only see 'red clouds that gobbled their way into people's lungs'. No, Cosack was no communist. From 'the moment when Germany's way was clear and purposive after 30 January 1933, I conducted myself loyally towards this state and have continued to do so'. To establish whether this loyalty extended to Cosack's reading habits, Papritz wrote to the Prussian *Staatsbibliothek* for a list of the books Cosack had recently borrowed. The order coupons for P. J. Ljascenko's *Jstorija russkogo narodnogo chozjajstra* (Moscow 1930) dutifully came back.[38]

Given the objectives of the PuSte, those recruits who hailed from Poland were subjected to informal security checks. Eugen Oskar Kossmann 1904–) came from Ruda Bugay. He attended the *Lodzer Deutsches Gymnasium* (LDG), which had been founded in 1906.[39] After reading geography in Tübingen, Cracow, and Vienna (1922–5),

Kossmann went to Warsaw to acquire the licence to teach in German schools in Poland. In September 1928 he became a geography teacher at his old school.[40] After four years, and in the wake of an unsuccessful libel action fought by the staff against a German-language Polish newspaper that had claimed that the LDG was a breeding ground of German nationalism and militarism, Kossmann was summarily dismissed by the Polish authorities.[41] Although unemployed for nine months thereafter, Kossmann came into contact with the circle around Alfred Lattermann in Poznań.[42] Brackmann spotted him at the Danzig meeting of the NODFG in December 1934.[43]

Kossmann's appearance and background warranted a degree of caution before any firm commitments were made. Brackmann contacted Professor Meynen of the VDA, who had been consulted by the publishers, Justus Perthes, about Kossmann's urban geography of Łódź. Meynen said that Kossmann was 'a dark type', but not a Jew, however the question was 'how one is to assess his character, whether only the misfortune that he has experienced at the hands of the Poles has driven him into our arms'.[44] Plans to employ him at the Gymnasium in Marienwerder were dropped after the ubiquitous Krahmer-Möllenberg (with assistance from the German consulate in Łódź) reported that Kossmann was 'a problematic character' who could be employed in a purely German setting, but who had to be kept apart from Poles. He did not belong in 'a national battle zone' like Marienwerder.[45] Residual worries about Kossmann's political connections in Łódź were cleared up after discreet enquiries by Brackmann to the thoroughly reliable Nazi historian Kurt Lück.[46] Eventually, in August 1936, Kossmann took his oath of allegiance and began receiving a PuSte grant of 250 RMs per month for work on German settlements in central Poland.[47] Since his language skills (he could speak Polish and Russian and read Czech) rendered him indispensable, he was assigned the tasks of observing anti-German publications and the workings of the German–Polish Press Agreement, with responsibility for monitoring the Polish Academy of Sciences, the Wilna Institute and the Historical Association in L'vov.[48] In April 1938 he was put on a regular salary of 443.51 RMs per month.[49] His appearance periodically still caused problems.[50] Like Kossmann, Franz Doubek came to the PuSte following friction with the local authorities. Born in Graz in March 1903, Doubek worked as a *Lektor* at the university of Wilna between October 1927 and March 1934. He joined the Austrian NSDAP on 1 August 1932 and, via the SA, the SS in 1939. Doubek came to Brackmann's notice through the offices of Lattermann and by attending the NODFG conferences.[51] Doubek and his wife were living in not particularly genteel poverty on an income of 250 złoty a month. Overwork, trying to prove the origins of German settlers in Poland through research on their dialects, was ruining his health. As Lattermann remarked 'at least I do not have to worry in my work of whether I will have anything to eat tomorrow'.[52] The job in Wilna brought tension of another kind. In December 1932 his first-year language class was interrupted by a student who raced into the lecture theatre and collapsed. Doubek tried to conceal the student and confronted his pursuers with a revolver.[53]

The move from Wilna was overdue. Assured by Lattermann that Doubek 'conformed to the conditions of employment for civil servants in force today' – it was better to broach the unpalatable euphemistically – Brackmann set about finding Doubek a post.[54] He received Doubek at his villa in November 1933. A job with the Danzig Society for the Study of Poland and a NODFG grant of 2,500 RMs followed in October 1934.[55] The work involved producing a dialectological atlas of Poland with the aid of questionnaires, recordings and the PuSte's cartographic collection.

Regardless of from which point of the compass they came, the recruits shared jarring experiences in the background. Horst Ost and his parents had been driven out of Essen by the French following his father's participation in disturbances in the Ruhr. As a fifteen-year-old, Ost was sent by the VDA to stay with a German farming family in Estonia 'to acquaint him with the conditions of the Germans abroad'.[56] He studied chemistry, biology and geography in Berlin and Greifswald but his interests slowly moved towards history. Like many of his colleagues, the certainties of postgraduate research gave way to a succession of temporary posts; as an assistant at the Geological Institute in Berlin, a lectureship at the Central Pedagogical Institute and as a part-time NSDAP lecturer. His father, too, a retired and much decorated army officer and head of a school, was by then also involved in local NSDAP educational activity.[57] Ost joined the Party on 1 April 1933. In 1934 he managed to get a four-month *Notgemeinschaft* grant for archival work in Poznań, Bydgoszcz and Warsaw to study the colonization of West Prussia. This appealed to the PuSte which awarded him a monthly grant from 1 June 1937. As Brackmann explained to the Foreign Office, Ost's work on the German population of the region 'would lead to irrefutable proof against

Polish claims to these territories, of German civilisation of these lands'.[58] Ost was also given responsibility for East and West Prussia, Pomerania and Brandenburg, the Kashubian Question and monitoring the Baltic Institute in Gdynia.[59] A final fugitive from afar was the Baron Dr Kurt von Maydell, who hailed from Maidell (Harrien) in Estonia. Born in 1902, Maydell was educated in Dorpat and Reval. Following the interruption of his education in the First World War, and subsequent service in the *Deutsche Schutzbund* and the *Schüler-bataillon* of the Baltic Regiment, Maydell resumed his studies in architecture at the TU in Munich and the universities of Riga and Prague.[60] Having abandoned architecture in favour of history, Maydell was awarded a doctorate in 1936 for a thesis on the diffusion of German law in Little Poland in the Middle Ages. He financed his studies through an SODFG research grant for a project on the Sudetenland. In October 1937 at the suggestion of Aubin and Wittram, Maydell wrote to Brackmann seeking support for a study of the Baltic–Polish problem. His SODFG grant was going to evaporate on New Year's Day 1938.[61] From 1 February 1938 Maydell received a PuSte stipend of 200 RMs per month. This was not a princely sum for a thirty-five-year-old who wanted to get married.[62]

Table 1 shows the academic backgrounds, language skills, areas of special responsibility (including the monitoring of rival Polish institutions), political affiliations and salaries of the PuSte staff in 1936–7.[63]

The PuSte and NODFG derived their funds from two separate ministries: the RMdI and the Foreign Office. Two or three times a year funds were transferred from the RMdI into the account 'Dammann-Brackmann' with the *Reichskredit-Gesellschaft*, and from the Foreign Office into an account with the Prussian *Staatsbank*.[64] This dual ministerial funding can be traced back to the struggle that took place in the early 1920s over ministerial competence in the German eastern provinces after Versailles. The Foreign Office regarded attempts by the RMdI to usurp areas of foreign policy on the basis of 'historical' administrative arrangements with the utmost hostility; the RuPMdI thought that the best way to maintain claims to the lost territories was to continue to regard them as an aspect of internal affairs. In January 1923 they agreed to divide their responsibilities so that the RMdI was responsible for the 'cultivation of Germandom' within the Reich frontiers, the Foreign Office for Germandom beyond the borders of 1914. The agreement recognized that although the Foreign Office had primary responsibility in the 'new abroad', the RMdI had a special interest in the territories lost after 1918 too.[65] Table 2 shows the sums received by the PuSte and NODFG from the two ministries.[66]

Leaving aside the larger problem of how these resources were spent, the main categories of expenditure for the PuSte[67] and NODFG[68] in 1936–7 were as shown in Table 3.

In view of the significance that *Ostforscher* then and subsequently (not to speak of their modern critics) attached to their work, it is worth bearing in mind that the largest sum received by the PuSte at the height of its activities in 1941 (415,000 RMs) was slightly more than the credit made available to one ailing West Prussian estate from the *Osthilfe* funds in the 1920s.[69] If scholarship had its price, the price was not very much. The following parts of the present chapter will examine more closely how these funds were spent and the nature of the work carried out in Dahlem before the onset of the Second World War.

ii. On a card darkly: the double life of Polish scholars

The PuSte kept thousands of cards to monitor the activities of the Polish institutes, scholarship and scholars. In November 1936[70] there were about 73,000 cards in the following sub-sections:

a) bibliography on German–Polish questions	40,000
b) information on Polish academics and politicians	12,000
c) Lithuania	4,000
d) Latvia	5,000
e) Estonia	3,000
f) Czechoslovakia	9,000
g) concordance of Polish terms for German placenames, waterways, physical features, and official German placenames.	
Total	**73,000**

Occasionally, someone stumbled upon the card index by accident or design. In April 1933 an archivist from Breslau, called Swientek, strayed from the classrooms of IfA and alighted upon the cards. He was reminded of his oath of silence regarding the PuSte, and was told 'you yourself will recognise that my request to treat the matter confidentially also lies in your own best interests'.[71] For in addition to helping German scholars orientate themselves in a foreign literature,

Table 1. The staff of the Publikationsstelle in 1936–7

Name	Subjects studied at university	Languages: read	speak	Responsibilities	'Jomsburg'	Political affiliation	Pay
Papritz, J.	history, German studies, archival studies	Polish	none	administration	co-editor	SA, NSDAP (1937–)	6120 RMs (1937)
Kohte, W.	history, economics, archival studies IfA	Czech	Polish	Czechoslovakia, administration, art history	economic history, Poznań	SA (1933?–)	4800 RMs (1937)
Koppe, W.	history	Danish?	Swedish?	Schleswig-Holstein, Baltic region, Baltic Institute (Riga)	co-editor	SA, NSDAP (21.4.1936)	3600 RMs
Conze, W.	history, economics	Russian	Polish	Baltic, East Prussia	NE Poland	SA (22.4.1936)	3000 RMs (1937)
Kossmann, E.	geography, *Volkskunde*	Russian	Polish	Polish Academy of Sciences, Historical Society L'vov, Wilna Institute	geography, central Poland, Polish law/ constitutional history		5800 RMs (1938)
Doubek, F.	German, *Volkskunde* demography	Czech Sorbian	Polish	Germandom in Poland, cartography, Polish Minorities Institute	cartography, statistics, minorities	NSDAP (1.8.32) SA (1.7.36) SS (1939)	6043 RMs
Loessner, A.	history, German	Polish Czech Sorbian	Russian Polish	translations militaria modern Polish history, Piłsudski Institute	naval military	NSBO (26.4.33) DAF (1.1.35)	7247 RMs
Cosack, H.	history, Slavonic studies	Polish Czech	Russian	library, bibliography	libraries	DAF (1.2.34)	4256 RMs

Name	Field	Language	Language	Task	Topic	Affiliation	Salary
Ost, H.	chemistry, biology, geography	n/a	n/a	East and West Prussia, Danzig, Gdynia, Kashubians, Pomerania, Grenzmark, Brandenburg, Polish cards, Baltic Institute	none	NSDAP (1.4.33) SA (15.8.33)	n/a
Schaeder, H.	history, Slavonic studies	Polish	n/a	n/a	obituaries, Polish history 1772–1815	n/a	n/a
Sappok, G.	n/a	Polish	n/a	Silesia, Saxony, Sorbs, Polish cards, Silesian Institute, Katowice, Silesian Committee of Polish Academy of Sciences	n/a	SA (5.7.33)	3000 RMs
Klostermann	history, Slavonic studies	Polish Czech	Russian	Press translation photo archive	Polish history 1895–1914, Austria, Russia, foreign policy		2400 RMs
Hassinger, H.	history	n/a	n/a	Baltic cards, Wilna institute	Polish history 1500–1772	SA (November 1933–5)	n/a n/a
Morré, F.	history, IfA	n/a	n/a	West Prussia	Pomerania		3000 RMs
Hahn	history, geography, archival studies	Polish	n/a	Poles in exile, Silesia, Saxony, Liga Morska	exile Poles, Colonies		1200 RMs
Busse, M.	n/a	n/a	n/a	accountant	n/a	DAF/NSV	3267 RMs
Schröter, I.	n/a	n/a	n/a	filing	n/a	DAF/NSV	2146 RMs
Rudloff	n/a	n/a	n/a	typist	n/a	DAF	1528 RMs
Pieta, S.		Polish	n/a	Polish press	n/a	DAF	2430 RMs
Ziemsen	n/a	Czech	n/a	Czech/Baltic press	n/a	DAF/NSV	n/a
Roy, I.	n/a	n/a	n/a	Press translation	n/a	DAF	2531 RMs

Table 2. PuSte and NODFG income from RMdI and Foreign Office, 1931–44

Year	PuSte RMdI	PuSte F.O.	NODFG RMdI	NODFG F.O.	
1931	10,000	2,000	—	—	
1932	40,000	—	—	—	
1933	50,000	—	—	2,500	
1934	47,000	—	37,000	20,000	
1935	50,000	—	5,000	20,000	
				+20,000*	
1936	61,000	—	25,000	25,000	
1937	72,000	—	30,000	30,000	
1938	96,000	—	32,500	32,500	
1939	n/a	n/a	n/a	n/a	
1940	129,430	—	15,651	34,980	
1941	415,590	—	—	39,260	
1942	398,700	—	—	32,000	
1943	344,000	—	—	38,000	RSHA
1944	396,300	—	—	38,200	RMs

* Carried over from 1934.

Table 3. Main categories of expenditure of PuSte and NODFG (in RMs)

PuSte (1936)		NODFG (1937)	
academic salaries	26,020	clerical salaries	4,950
clerical salaries	10,400	equipment	250
technicians' wages	760	post, telephone, etc.	1,200
post, telephone, etc.	7,270	books	1,200
library	4,500	conferences	9,000
travel	500	travel	1,000
publications subsidies	1,000	subsidies for scholars in	
press translations	850	Poland, Estonia, Latvia, Czechoslovakia	41,500
Total (RMs)	51,300	Total (RMs)	59,100

the main purpose of the cards was to enable the Prussian archivists to inform themselves about the politics of those seeking permission to work in the archives. For reasons of convenience, the cards were worked up into a multi-volume A–Z containing all relevant correspondence concerning individual Polish scholars.

The road to the archives was circuitous and fraught with obstacles for the Poles concerned. In the autumn of 1930 Karol Górski, from the university of Warsaw, applied through the Polish embassy in Berlin for permission to work (on the history of Pomerania between 1453 and 1466) in the archives of Königsberg. In October 1930 his application was forwarded by the embassy to the German Foreign Office and, via the archival administration in the Prussian Ministry of State, to the Geheime Staatsarchiv. The PuSte prepared a report of Górski for Brackmann. Since the card index had little to reveal (Górski was young), they approached their colleagues in Poznań for assistance. Górski had spoken at the third Pomerelian Conference, lectured on Polish literature, and was a member of 'the Society of Friends of Historical Research' in Poznań. The PuSte report remarked that while the 'fiction' of access to the archives was to be maintained, 'rejection (of an application) will always be dependent upon the political views of the applicant as well as his subject'.[72] Consequently, by June 1933 Górski's application remained unanswered. Since he was enjoining the Polish archives to take retaliatory action an answer seemed expedient. It might take the form of claiming that the Königsberg archivists were working on the same materials.[73]

Over the following years, the PuSte built up further reports on Górski's work. An article in the National Democratic *Kurjer Poznański* to the effect that the German Knights were poor examples of a higher civilization because few of them could mutter the Lord's Prayer let alone read or write, did not improve his chances. An 'anti-German' scholar should not be allowed near the archives of the Order 'which for us is a national legacy'.[74] He did manage to work in Königsberg in 1935 – the PuSte allowed for the change in political climate[75] – but under strained conditions. In a report for Hein in 1938, Kurt Forstreuter recalled the unwelcome visitor in the summer of 1935:

> Every item that was given to him was subsequently checked to see whether it really pertained to his subject ... Without doubt Górski belongs to the most anti-German foreign historians. Under the circumstances, I regard it as questionable to give Górski permission to work

in the archives again. However, it is to be feared that in the event of rejection, he will step up, whenever possible, his attacks against the archival administration.[76]

The cards could also be used to establish the identity of possible foreign contributors to German journals. In March 1936 Prof. Hans Uebersberger contacted the PuSte for information on a Professor Przybyłowski. Cosack produced a small dossier.[77] A month later Uebersberger sent a list of sixty possible Polish contributors whom he wanted to write for his new *Jahrbuch für Geschichte Osteuropas*.[78] The PuSte split the list into three parts and gave numbers 1–20 to Hahn, 21–40 to Buttkus and 41–60 to Werner Conze. The object was to mark the names with the following symbols:

$$+ \quad = \text{ suitable}$$
$$? \quad = \text{ reservations}$$
$$- \quad = \text{ unsuitable}$$
$$V \quad = \text{ inadequate information}$$
$$\text{----} = \text{ no information}$$

The results were:

$$+ \quad = 22$$
$$? \quad = 9$$
$$- \quad = 11$$
$$V \quad = 12$$
$$\text{----} = 6$$

The criteria adopted for unsuitability included hostility towards Germany, involvement with or membership of the Baltic and Silesian institutes, or racial/political dubiety. The library director, Stefan Bodmiak, was apostrophized as 'a keen champion of Polish maritime notions at the Pomerelian meetings'; Oskar Halecki, as 'a chief spokesman of Polish historical–political propaganda in Western Europe, clerical sympathies' and, Professor W. Abraham, as 'aryan?, member of Academy of Sciences and vice-president of L'vov Scientific Society, work on Polish ecclesiastical history'.[79]

The cards contained the answers to many mysteries. In February 1938 Theodor Schieder enquired whether it was permissible to correspond with a Professor Zygmunt Lempicki in Warsaw.[80] In February 1939 Uebersberger wanted to know if the cards had 'information on the racial background and political views of the lecturer Wojciech

Hejnosz' who had offered him an article on 'The Question of Serfdom and Slavery among the West Slavs'.[81] The PuSte replied that they had nothing directly on Hejnosz but that 'his name is not on a list of Jewish, or lecturers of Jewish descent, at Polish universities and we have not as yet traced any anti-German views in his work on legal history'.[82]

The cards (and an ability to use *Who's Who*) were also used to compile a report for the Foreign Office and RMdI on Cambridge University Press in September 1937. The report dealt with CUP's projected two-volume *History of Poland* which was a belated English response to the Warsaw Congress. The report noted that 'Poland is deploying its best forces in this unique opportunity to represent their views in a publication that will be distributed throughout the world. It is . . . self evident for every Polish historian that he is not just a pure scholar but also a propagandist and herald of Polish political views'. The instigators of the project were Poles 'active' in England, Halecki and Dyboski, who had teamed up with Reddaway, Temperley and Sir Henry Penson. The PuSte staff unravelled the tangled skeins of the English academic–military–intelligence Establishment. Penson was described as being the chief of the War Trade Intelligence Department in the First World War, and chief of intelligence at Versailles; Temperley was a former staff officer in the Dardanelles, and a contributor to the Paris Peace Conference. His brother (Arthur Cecil) was a senior War Ministry official and, since 1925, military representative to the League of Nations. Information on the Canadian, Professor William Rose, who since 1935 held the chair in Polish civilization at the Institute for Slavonic Studies in London, extended to his holidays in Cracow and Łódź. The Roman Catholic Monica Gardiner had been recruited by Halecki.[83]

The information on which the card entries were based came from oral sources too. In April 1937 Krahmer-Möllenberg reported to the Foreign Office, RMdI and PuSte information he had received from someone in the audience of a lecture given by Professor Zygmunt Wojciechowski, a National Democrat, which appeared to favour Polish expansion towards the north and west. However, in the course of his lecture Wojciechowski had also said that:

> the anti-Bolshevik policy of Hitler has certain common features with the universal, Christian policy of Otto the Great. Just as since Otto I and Otto III the expansionary direction taken by the German Reich

was directed from the East to the South, which saved the integrity of the Polish state, so too through the, to a certain extent, anti-Russian policy of present day Germany, a great danger for Poland has been averted.[84]

German scholars in Danzig, Poznań or Silesia were also invaluable sources of information. In August 1939 Zipfel informed the PuSte that the archives in Danzig had drawn his attention to the July number of *Wiadomości Literackie* in which eighteen Polish authors had expressed hostile opinions towards the Reich and the status of Danzig. He wanted their names 'in order to decide correspondingly about any subsequent applications to use the archives'.[85] Karl Sczodrok of the Upper Silesian Geographical Institute in Opole was the eyes and ears of the PuSte in Silesia.[86] He monitored the activities of the Silesian Institute in Katowice,[87] and work on Silesia carried out further afield in the Biblioteka Polska in Paris.[88] His reports went, *inter alia*, to Aubin, the PuSte, RMdI, Ministry of Propaganda and Breslau Offices of the Hitler Youth, BDO and VDA.[89] The subjects covered by Sczodrok encompassed most areas of life in Silesia in the 1930s: employment of the profits of the Bank Słowianski in Germany to subsidize Polish schools in Prussia;[90] thirty Jews working voluntarily on Polish farms to win over the peasants before the 'Aryan rural labour detachments' arrived. Sczodrok sent Brackmann the names of the peasants concerned and how many Jews they had employed.[91] Polish anthropologists who had been examining naked schoolchildren in eastern Upper Silesia until the Wojewod terminated their obscure pursuits;[92] news, too, of a Professor Stojanowski, who had been lecturing on the results of his racial tests on 456 conscripts at the Silesian Institute. This report was a little confused as Sczodrok's informant did not have a sound mastery of Polish anthropological terms.[93] Sometimes Sczodrok ventured a few suggestions of his own. He recommended books for translation into German and, given keen Polish interest in racial studies, was anxious that political restraints on similar work in Germany should be lifted to make possible the publication of the Freiherr von Eichstedt's anthropometric work in Upper Silesia.[94] Although Aubin was also particularly enthusiastic about Eichstedt's 'methodology' – which entailed measuring and photographing 1,500–2,000 persons – whose results, he suggested, could adorn Eugen Fischer's *Deutsche Rassenkunde*,[95] Essen in the RMdI consulted the NODFG's racial expert Otto Reche (who thought

Eichstedt's methods were *gefährlich*) and turned the project down.[96] Brackmann consoled Eichstedt with the thought that *he* had done his best to help but, 'as scholars we must naturally do as we are told, and racial studies within frontier research are not politically desirable at the moment'.[97]

The PuSte was also engaged in constant translation work through the use of stenographic typists. In 1936, for example, the PuSte translated a total of 1,425 items from foreign newspapers. These included 480 items from Polish newspapers, 85 Czech, 85 Sorbian, 150 Lithuanian, 165 Latvian and 145 Estonian items.[98] They also regularly translated extracts from *Isvestia* and *Pravda* as well as Soviet academic journals. The cost of the Polish Press translations was borne by the RMdI; that of the others by the Foreign Office. These translations were confidential and were circulated to government and NSDAP offices. According to Brackmann, 'the press extracts have, I can say without any exaggeration, won an extraordinary significance in the defensive efforts of German scholarship and government'.[99] Part of their significance was made explicit in a letter from Vollert of the RMdI to Papritz dated 12 August 1938. The RMdI was particularly interested in extracts 'that contain hateful attacks against Germany which contravene the spirit of the Press Agreement between the two countries'.[100]

In addition to the Press translations, the PuSte produced confidential translations of foreign books and scholarly articles. In 1936, for example, they had finished translating some 73 Polish and 9 Czech books as well as 90 communiqués from the Polish institutes in Toruń and Katowice.[101] Although much of this work was carried out in the PuSte, they also farmed out the translating to the young and needy. Since the translations were confidential, the PuSte sent lists of potential translators – drawn from members of the NS-*Studentenschaft* studying Slavonic languages – to Dr Werner Best of the Gestapo whose agents then approached the students concerned. This, according to Best, ensured that the PuSte got 'absolutely trustworthy persons'.[102]

The notion, aired recently by some of those involved, that these translations were marked 'Confidential' in order to make possible the circulation among scholars of works somehow disapproved of by the Nazi regime is difficult to reconcile with what was being translated – paeans to Hitler and attempts to range Piłsudski alongside Mussolini and the Führer – and is belied by the obvious question that if this was the case, why bother to make the books more accessible even through confidential translation? The titles included Germantas, *Communism – Accident for Humanity* (Kowno 1938); *The Report and Programme of the Baltic Institute in Toruń* (1935); Jan Czechanowski, *Anthropological Traces of the Goths in Poland* (L'vov 1934), and his *Racial Structure of Silesia in the Light of Polish and German Researches* (Katowice 1936); Karol Górski, *Hans von Baysen in the Light of the Documents* (Poznań 1937); Ludwig Korwin, *Polish Nobles of Jewish Extraction* (Cracow 1935); Alfons Krysinski, *Developing Trends in the Demography of Poland with respect to Nationality and Confessionality in the Post War Period* (Warsaw 1931), and his *Nationality Structure of the Polish Towns* (Warsaw 1937); Adam Kunciewicz (ed.), *General Plans of Polish Towns* (Warsaw 1929); Mateusz Mieses, *Christian Poles of Jewish Origin* (2 vols.) (Warsaw 1939); Ludwig Musiol, *Germanised Placenames in Silesia* (1936); Piotr Ponisz, *The Jewish Question in Poland from a National and Catholic Standpoint* (Czestochowa 1938); Kazimierz Smogorzewski, *Elements of the National Socialist World View* (1935); Bozena Stelmachowska, *The Kaschubei and the Poles* (n.d.); Karol Stojanowski, *Craniological Types in Great Poland* (Poznań 1935); Janusz Urbach, *The Role of the Jews in Poland's Struggle for Independence* (1938); *The Second Meeting of the Poles Abroad* (1934); *Report on the Activities of the Maritime and Colonial League* (Warsaw 1935); *Report of Ceremonial Session of the Polish Academy of Sciences on 16 June 1937 and 19 June 1938* (1937–8); and *Art and Science in the State Budget 1935–1938* (1938).[103]

iii. Scholarly subversion in inter-war Poland: Kuhn and Lück, Kauder and Lattermann

Under the terms of the Treaty of Versailles, 90 per cent of the former Prussian province of Posen, with some 670,000 German speakers, and 66 per cent of the province of West Prussia (Pomerelia), with 412,000 German speakers, became part of Poland.[104] Before the First World War the Prussian state maintained the German element in these territories with economic subsidies and discriminatory legislation designed to weaken the Polish presence. After 1919 the roles were reversed.[105] The German minority (in 1921 it accounted for 3.9 per cent of the population)[106] was exposed to the chill winds of economic boycott, withdrawal or over-zealous enforcement of the 'protection' of the law, and attempts by the Polish state to weaken their economic base, ethnic schools and cultural associations. These efforts to force either assimilation or emigration were designed to remove any justification for future revisions of Poland's frontiers. If there was no substantial German minority, there would be no frontier problem.[107]

Some two-thirds of the 1,100,000 Germans in Poznania and West Prussia moved to Germany between 1918–22. The largest losses were from the towns. While in 1910, 42 per cent of the inhabitants of Poznań, 77.5 per cent of the population of Bydgoszcz, or 85 per cent of the inhabitants of Gruziądz were German, by 1931 the Germans accounted for respectively 2 per cent, 8.5 per cent and 7.5 per cent of the population in these places. The flight of government officials, businessmen, teachers and craftsmen meant that the hard core of the German minority was left on the land.[108] As the Polish government began to address itself in earnest, in the early 1920s, to legislative measures designed to redistribute the balance of rural property in the two provinces away from the German landowners, successive Weimar governments, regardless of their political persuasion, were faced with the choice of either accepting the flight of the German minority, which entailed compensation payments and the problem of assimilating a population permeated with a frontier psychosis, or of keeping the Germans where they were. Since the latter were living proof of the need to revise the frontiers, this was the policy pursued.

This policy had other serious advantages. In view of the strength of the Reichsmark against the złoty it would be cheap, and it obviated the snowball effect latent in compensation payments to refugees which might encourage more to follow in their footsteps.[109] However, financial support could not appear to come directly from the German authorities. To this end, the Foreign Office and RMdI, as the (rival) competent ministries, created front organizations, the *Deutsche Stiftung* and *Konkordia Literarische Gesellschaft mbH* (1920), and a 'brass-plate' bank called the *Hollandsche Buitenlands Bank* in the Hague, to launder government and private capital through a neutral country to subsidize the Germans in Poland.[110] Given the social predispositions of the Foreign Office and the *Deutsche Stiftung*'s administrator Krahmer-Möllenberg, and the ease with which the larger landowners could visit Berlin to exploit their political connections while stressing their own patriotism, indispensability and impecunity, the lion's share of the credit funds went to them. In 1925, for example, the objections of the Finance Ministry were overcome by the Foreign

Office to provide an initial 3,000,000 RMs and, three years later, a further 5,000,000 RMs for the ailing estates of the Prince Pless in eastern Upper Silesia, on the grounds that the fall of Pless would mean the collapse of an oasis of Germandom in the region. Some 400,000 RMs were also made available to support the uneconomic estates of the nephew of Bethmann-Hollweg at Runowo in West Prussia.[111] The east Elbian aristocracy, sapped of economic initiative by decades of government support, were adept at prising open the taxpayers' purse.

In addition to this primary assistance for impecunious aristocrats, further sums were expended to maintain ethnic consciousness among the dwindling German minority through private German-language schools; an apparently independent Press – the *Konkordia Literarische Gesellschaft* covered its financial wires by maintaining the party political allegiances of the newspapers it effectively owned – and a host of cultural associations.[112] In due course, the NODFG took over responsibility for subsidizing the numerous German historical associations, societies, journals and individual scholars.[113] As the breakdown of the 1937 budget (see p. 80) showed, most of the funds made available to the NODFG were relayed to German scholars in eastern Europe. Table 4 shows the sums allocated to the various regions between 1933 and 1938.[114]

Complex procedures were used to transfer funds to Poland. One method was for the NODFG to settle debts owed by ethnic Germans in the Reich, who in turn would pay the grants locally.[115] However, the usual procedure was for the PuSte to contact the Office for Exchange Control in Berlin for permission to send cheques, issued by Papritz, to the German consulates in Poland which made the final payments.[116]

Table 4. Sums allocated by NODFG between 1933 and 1938 (in RMs)

	1933	1934	1935	1936	1937	1938
Germany	—	2150	351	786	—	—
Danzig	—	326	200	—	—	—
Poland	2500	7733	10469	14582	11921	10311
Baltic	—	4900	—	—	—	7903
Estonia	—	309	2310	4623	7130	7420
Latvia	—	—	3300	8120	10495	8099
Czechoslovakia	—	1200	3300	7671	6407	1304
Total (in RMs)	2500	16618	19930	35782	35953	35037

In 1938 matters were complicated by the insistence of the Office for Exchange Control that payments should be made from the stock of złoty frozen in the Deutsche Bank branch in Breslau. This was dangerous as the Polish authorities insisted on knowing the purpose and origin of the payments.[117] The Deutsche Bank was told that on no account was the NODFG to be named in the transaction. In the end, the money was transferred in the name of the Foreign Office to the consulates in Katowice and Poznań under the general rubric 'transfer for running costs'.[118] In keeping with the conspiratorial manner that the *Ostforscher* liked to adopt, the NODFG made use of more irregular routes. In 1937 the PuSte's deputy administrator, Kohte, was apprehended by Czech customs officers on his way to a conference in Leipe. In his briefcase they found a credit note for 4,000 Kr. 'which appeared to be slightly at variance with my military leave pass for the 7th. to the 15th. July'. On the way to the police station he aroused further suspicion by trying to destroy shorthand notes in Italian and Rumanian. After a night of discomfort in a cell Kohte was interrogated about his frequent visits to Czechoslovakia. After sixteen hours of questioning, in which the matter of importing nearly 10,000 RMs in March was raised, the police fingerprinted and photographed him and put down *osidlovači a narodnostuí rozurotveni* (propagator of ethnic nationalism) as his occupation on his file. Kohte thought it was time to acquire a fresh passport.[119]

The crucial link in the chain from the Foreign Office, NODFG, banks and consulates to individual scholars in Poland were the offices of the *Historische Gesellschaft für die Provinz Posen* (1885–), which issued a journal called the *Deutsche Wissenschaftliche Zeitschrift für Polen* (1923–), and the *Deutsche Kulturbund für die Wojwodschaft Schlesien*, with a journal called *Schaffen and Schauen* (1924–).[120] Both enterprises were one-man bands, the former run by Hermann Rauschning until 1926, and thereafter by Alfred Lattermann (1904–45), a former member of the Freikorps Grenzschutz, the *Silesian Kulturbund* by Viktor Kauder.[121] Through their journals (and in Kauder's case a network of 560 rural libraries in Silesia) both had contacts throughout the German academic scene in Poland. As the men responsible for submitting research and budgetary proposals to the NODFG in Berlin, Lattermann and Kauder were the brokers of academic patronage for a wider penumbra of young scholars in Poland.[122]

Although the largest items within the budgetary sub-section for Poland were subsidies towards the publishing costs of the *DWZP* and

Schaffen und Schauen, from 1934 onwards there were annual requests for funds for scholars like Walter Kuhn and Kurt Lück, who were both to be constant beneficiaries of the NODFG. In 1934 Kauder sought 500 RMs for Kuhn, whereas Lattermann suggested putting Lück in the way of a job, and the task of re-working Erich Schmidt's *Das Deutschtum im Lande Posen* (1904).[123] Since this was a group that believed in self-help, Kuhn had also been singing Lück's praises at the opening session of the NODFG in Berlin.[124]

If Kauder and Lattermann were organizers and prolific reviewers of other people's books, Lück and Kuhn were indefatigable researchers. Although their work reflects their different academic backgrounds, they both operated in the grey zone where scholarship (which they both had) and political activism merge. This distinction would probably have been meaningless to them. Both were intoxicated by the idea of politically engaged scholarship and both – they dealt with Brackmann – were bereft of wider counsels, or any form of criticism, to dampen down their respective enthusiasms.

Lück was born in Kolmar in August 1900. As an eighteen-year-old, he was wounded in the defence of Posen. After studying Slavonic languages at Breslau he was employed in the offices of the German delegation to the Sejm while simultaneously organizing the Association of German University Teachers in Poland. In 1926 he moved to the small Volhynian town of Łuck where, supported by business interests in Poznań, he founded the *Kredit Lutzk* to provide low-interest loans for the local German farmers.[125] His doctoral thesis, which traces the effects of nineteenth-century Polish politics upon the changing stereotypes of peasants, Jews and noblemen deployed in nineteenth-century Polish novels, was published in 1926. Like much of his work it reveals a mechanical talent for digesting book after book, and an ability to camouflage his own antipathies beneath those of the authors he refers to.[126] He was an adept at the blow through a third party. In 1928 he had his first experience of a Polish prison as a German candidate for the Sejm.

The demise of the Leipzig *Deutsche Stiftung* which had kept him afloat with a small grant left him in dire straits. His own martyr mentality did not help. In September 1931 Lattermann informed Brackmann that Lück had sold his furniture 'to Lutzker Jews ... whereby he was naturally taken to the cleaners and will only be secure for a little while longer'. A grant of 200–250 RMs a month might keep him bobbing above debt, depression and marital breakdown for a little longer.[127] In March 1932 Brackmann reported that he had recommended Lück to the *Notgemeinschaft* and had been in touch with the RMdI about the possibility of a grant.[128] He allotted Lück the task of re-working Schmidt's book and in January 1934 began subsidizing Lück on a regular basis.[129] The latter drove himself frenetically in search of 'epoch-making new discoveries'.[130] In May 1933 Lattermann reported that Lück had been confined to bed for a month with nervous exhaustion after completing his *Deutschtum in Cholmer und Lubliner Land*, and needed a break in the mountains before tackling his next project.[131] Emboldened by funds already received, Lück approached Brackmann directly in May 1934 for 4,000 RMs for an expanded version of his *Deutsche Aufbaukräfte*. Brackmann observed that 'together with the work of Kuhn [your book] supplies the evidence for what Germans in Poland have achieved in scholarship' and offered him 2,000 RMs.[132] Not all of the money he received came from the Foreign Office. By 1938 he was receiving, via the NODFG, about 600 RMs a year from the Ministry of Propaganda for whom he observed the Polish literature.[133]

Lattermann and Kauder thought that Walter Kuhn was also particularly cut out for a life of scholarly endeavour.[134] His work was recommended by Hassinger of the SODFG, and Kuhn did not miss the opportunity to stress his own achievements at the opening session of the NODFG, permitting himself the minor indulgence of referring to work written under the pseudonym Andreas Mückler (a chronicler from Bielitz), as well as work published under his own name.[135] In 1934 the NODFG gave him 500 RMs.[136] Kuhn came from the Upper Silesian textile town of Bielitz (Bielsko Biała), which lies south-west of Auschwitz, in the foothills of the Beskiden. Most of the inhabitants of Bielitz (87 per cent) and of the surrounding villages were German.[137] His father was the Professor of Mechanics at the local trade school and was, Kuhn averred, 'Pan-German right down to his knees'.[138] As an eleven-year-old, Kuhn showed an early interest in nationality conflict by distributing cornflowers to German youths defending a bridge over the Biała against Polish boys celebrating the assassination of the Archduke Ferdinand.[139] He went to the TH in Graz to study electrical engineering, but was more interested in the classes on *Volkskunde* at the university. During a vacation Kuhn and three friends from the *Wandervogel* formed a study group for *Heimatkunde*. Kauder managed to publish the first fruits of their labours, a book on the gilds of Bielitz in 1924.[140] Together, as we shall see, they also visited the

German villages in Volhynia. After qualifying as an engineer in 1927, Kuhn managed to get grants to attend the universities of Tübingen and Vienna. In 1931 a further book on the German linguistic exclaves of eastern Poland was accepted as a doctorate.[141] The prospect of a post with the DAI in Stuttgart fell through in 1932 and, after some twenty semesters of study, Kuhn returned home a disappointed man. The only relief from Bielitz was afforded by coach trips to Czechoslovakia organized by the SODFG. In November 1932 he got a job as an academic assistant with Kauder's *Deutsche Kulturbund*. Through Kauder he came to the notice of the NODFG which paid him 4,200 RMs and further sums for field work in 1934.[142]

Kuhn's work concerned German linguistic exclaves in Galicia and Volhynia. He was interested in the differences between medieval settlements and those formed between the sixteenth and nineteenth centuries. The former, in which assimilation and mixed marriages with the surrounding Slavs had occurred, showed signs of contraction. The latter, and the resort to biology rather than chronology is symptomatic of the times, revealed a 'biological' strength based upon the 'selection' of the most vigorous elements from the older settlements. The peasants in the more recent colonies did not intermarry with the Slavs, were more mobile and, despite being largely uneducated, considered themselves to be superior to the Poles and Ukrainians, and were therefore less susceptible to 'de-Germanisation'.[143]

The linguistic exclave that most fascinated Kuhn lay in the western Ukraine between the upper reaches of the Bug, and Žitomir and Kiev towards the East. The population of Volhynia consisted of 70 per cent Ukrainian '*Mushiks*', living in conditions of abject poverty after centuries of servitude; 17 per cent Poles, including most of the landowners; 10.5 per cent Jews concentrated in the towns of Łuck, Wladimir Wołynski, Rozyszcze and Dubno; 1.5 per cent Czechs; 1.7 per cent or 50,000 Germans.[144] The latter were settlers enticed from Congress Poland by the biblically effusive propaganda of the Polish landowners, or refugees from overpopulated villages and repressive circumstances following the collapse of the 1863 risings. They received about 8 hectares of land on renegotiable leaseholds and had to make do with low-level mud huts until the land became cultivable. This consisted of sand, swamps and woods. Winters were long and harsh and even in 1939 the nearest roads and railways were a long way off.[145]

Despite large-scale migration to South America, Canada, Siberia and the Baltic from the 1890s, by 1914 the German population had swollen to about 200,000 in 550 closely packed settlements. Although many of the men joined the armies of the Tsars, and were dispatched to the Turkish front, the advance of Mackensen's troops reactivated Russian plans for their immediate resettlement. The Volhynian Germans were marched off to the Volga or Siberia. After the collapse of the Tsarist regime, some 50,000 returned to their villages. Many of these had been smashed by war; the land was chiselled with entrenchments, the *Mushiks* had occupied their vacant homes and worse, they had to accept their lands on extremely harsh terms in a Polish state bent upon weakening the German minority.[146]

In August 1926 Kuhn and eleven friends, dressed in the uniform of the *Wandervogel* – windcheaters, shorts and rucksacks – wandered eagerly through this pocket of rural desolation at the behest of the Galician German activist Heinz Heckel. Armed with questionnaires rather than understanding, the twelve decided to make their task more manageable by concentrating on the villages bounded by the triangle Łuck, Wladimir and Rozyszcze and formed three groups to gain maximum coverage. In addition to the usual materials needed by statisticians, the twelve sought information on communal politics, access to libraries, use of folk costume and so forth.[147] They also combed the registers of the Lutheran clergy with whom they stayed, and sat reverentially at the feet of wizened peasants who recounted the history of the first German settlements.[148] The object of the exercise was:

> to transform the instinctive feeling of superiority and pride towards the surrounding peoples that characterises the colonists into a true national consciousness that is not based solely upon feelings, but also upon the knowledge of the strength and beauty of the German *Volkstum*. That is the fundamental task of national education in the eastern lands.[149]

Reading between the lines of this scholarly odyssey, a natural divergence becomes apparent between the concerns of the young visitors – who saw themselves as 'bearers of civilisation' – and their interview subjects.[150] Whereas the former were alive to the slightest shimmer of ethnic consciousness, the peasants wanted to talk about the terms of their leases; old wives' remedies or, on a higher plane, the ghost of the avaricious nobleman Trebinski and his guilt-ridden land-surveyor who wanted to make amends in the after life for defrauding the peasants. As they argued 'Here is the pole!', 'No, the pole goes here!' the peasants could hear the rattle of measuring chains in the dead of night.[151] As far as one old woman was concerned, Kuhn and his colleagues might have been from the moon: 'Ach', she said, 'you're the men from the League of Nations.' Assured that they were not she insisted, 'But the twelve men from the League of Nations wear the same clothes as you.'[152] Instead of revealing much interest or sympathy for Germany – of which they had slight knowledge – many of the peasants bitterly recalled being treated on a par with Russian prisoners of war and being called 'Russians' by their German captors.[153] Nor were they interested in the Lutheran faith. They stayed away from the 'Temples of Baal' and preferred to send their offspring to the Ukrainian schools rather than to the 'worldly' German establishments. Sectarianism was on the ascendant. Those who had been evicted from their homes (and photographs taken by Lück show them cooking in holes in the ground where the walls of their homes had been wrenched away) were even less interested in Kuhn's group. The smooth, enthusiastic faces of the scholars contrast unfavourably with those of the tired and grimy men and women they were studying.

After three weeks in Volhynia, Kuhn contacted the leader of the German delegation to the Sejm, Eugen Naumann, and then published newspaper articles on the fading ethnic consciousness of the Volhynian Germans. Rauschning set aside a double issue of his *Deutsche Blätter* for their findings. Inevitably, one of the first to take action was Kurt Lück, who, after a field trip of his own in September 1926, decided to take up residence in Łuck. He photographed the hovels of the dispossessed and reported on the main deficiencies in the region:

> This must be said with all sharpness: Germandom is not up to the competitive struggle that is beginning and will lose more and more ground unless it takes up a self-conscious stand against these dangers and is supported vigorously in this by the other German areas in Poland.[154]

He thought that the Germans should acquire their own land, which would break the demoralizing cycle of renewable, exorbitant leases, eviction and the steady drift of landless men to the towns. In order to bypass ruinous local credit sources, Lück founded the *Kredit Lutzk* in 1926, with funds from the German communal bank in Poznań, to enable the peasants to purchase their own land.[155] He also initiated studies of his own, that reflect his own literary training, designed to help along the Volhynian Germans' 'self-conscious stand'.

He attempted to purify their language of loan-words from Polish and Russian. They said *sud* instead of 'court', *Podatken* for 'taxes', *Gromad* for 'village assembly', *Urzond* for 'office' or *perejest* instead of 'railway-crossing'. Regular contact with other languages and isolation from sources of correct grammar also resulted in incorrect sentence constructions like *er hat drei Jahre alt* or *wir sind schon nach dem Mittag* instead of *er ist drei Jahr alt* or *wir haben schon Mittag gegessen*. He was also engaged in a race against time to recover and set down folk songs and dances, as well as peasant jokes, proverbs and riddles.[156]

Lück's efforts in the 1930s were devoted to his *Deutsche Aufbaukräfte in der Entwicklung Polens* (1934), and *Der Mythos vom Deutschen in der polnischen Volksüberlieferung und Literatur* (1938). In the preface to *Deutsche Aufbaukräfte*, Viktor Kauder described the series in which Lück's books appeared, as consisting of 'preparatory studies for research on the eastern German *Lebensraum*' and Lück's book as 'a calm, strictly scholarly investigation' which, nonetheless, was 'a cry of warning to the mother nation'.[157] The author's acknowledgements somewhat shortened the financial wires involved in the production of his book by thanking Rauschning in Danzig for publication subventions. This was shortly to be a matter for embarrassment.[158] He also explained that because of the vast range of sources, which had 'forced him to his knees', the book represented a mere *Sondierungsversuch* which because of the author's mental exhaustion had to appear in first draft form.[159]

The provisional product confirms Lück's verdict on his own work. The book is compiled from extracts lifted from the work of Polish scholars, ill-digested source material, statistical tables and maps in great abundance. If one were to subtract the word German or its cognates, there would not be much of a text left. This would presumably also reflect what would remain of Polish civilization if the German contribution were to be removed. For given the existence of a West–East 'cultural gradient', there were not many areas of Polish cultural life that did not owe their existence to the Germans:

Many Polish national stories are of German origin. For example, the motif of the *Mäuseturm* [a 13th-century tower on the Rhine at Bingen where an avaricious bishop Hatto II of Mainz was supposed to have been devoured by mice] wandered from the Rhine to Lake Goplo. Even the rogue Till Eulenspiegel was taken over into the stock of Polish comic tales where he lived on, enhanced by many Polish characteristics as Sowizdrzał.[160]

... It is not being claimed that the German colonisation brought skilled crafts, as such, to Poland. They existed in a primitive indigenous form for certain branches of trade already. The Germans brought the division of labour, the organisation of gilds [Polish *cech* from the German *Zeche*], and the higher types of craft production. The best proof of this is the uncommonly high number of German loan-words in Polish craft terminology.[161]

... The Polish academic A. Brückner has already stressed that the university could only function in a well-organised town like German Krakau then was. The regular grants, one of the means of support for poor, i.e. for the most part Polish students, enjoyed the lasting support of the German bourgeoisie.[162]

... After all that has been said, it was not presumptuous of the Germans in those days to speak of 'our university'. With the departure of the German element, which partly resulted from the anti-German pressure of the Poles, with the progressive de-Germanisation of the university town, the university sank from its high level. It was never a transmission point for Polish intellectual culture. The fundamental strength of its being was due to the Germans.[163]

... A predecessor of Copernicus wandered from the demonstrably German-settled and still German-inhabited Silesian village of Köppernig, near Neisse, to German Krakau, from whence the astronomer's father 'Niklas' moved on to Thorn, which was then still nine-tenths German. There he married the patrician's daughter, Barbara Watzelrode, and became, for nineteen years, a juror of the Altstadt, an office that only a German could occupy then. His son, Nicolaus, our astronomer, enrolled as a student in Bologna as part of the German nation – and not as a member of the Polish nation which also existed there – which stipulated German as the mother tongue for admissions.[164]

Remorselessly, Lück went through the centuries in search of 'Germans as the creators of the paper industry',[165] 'German printers as the "technical levers of intellectual development"',[166] 'German bookdealers as the first purveyors of printed books in Poland',[167] 'German physicians, medical orderlies and apothecaries',[168] 'Germans in the building trade', 'Germans as bearers of Humanism',[169] 'German merchants. Their rapid rise'[170] and so on. Aided by such informed eighteenth-century commentators as David Hume, Lück contrasted the 'promised land of limited state power and the land with no restraint upon the nobles' with France, Prussia and Russia, and decided that because of international approbation from Herder, Voltaire and *der Weise von Weimar* the First Partitions must have been justified.[171] He was not so emphatic about the events of 1793, for if Prussia could claim an 'inner right' to the acquisitions of 1772, it was difficult to see what was German – to use his criteria – about the areas incorporated as 'South Prussia'. The mysteries of modern science came to his assistance:

> It is well known that the large town of Posen had once again become, in the course of the 18th century, an overwhelmingly German town, in which the Frenchman Parendier walked around for four days in 1784 – in other words before it became part of Prussia – without hearing Polish spoken. Here, as elsewhere, there were far more German Catholics than one has believed hitherto. Moreover, the other large towns were overwhelmingly German or Jewish. Certainly the very strong medieval Germandom in Great Poland had, for the most part, been lost in *Polentum* – most Poles in the region have no idea how much German blood is hidden in them, only their strong nordic characteristics, along with the many German family names, supplies the racial evidence of this – but the steady migration of the modern period again flooded the area with a new wave, saturating it with new German settlements, which were economically and culturally superior to those of the Poles.[172]

By the criteria of the eighteenth-century *Volkstumsstaat*, Poland was not really Polish at all. Only a third of the inhabitants of this pre-1772 'multi-coloured dual state' were Poles and, among the 52 per cent Roman Catholics after 1791 were substantial numbers of Lithuanians, White Russians and Germans of that confession. This *argen Mischmasch* had no more of a right to exist than the pre-1918 Habsburg monarchy.[173]

With Poland disposed of in this cursory, unreflective manner, Lück returned to the matter of filling the shelves of his cultural pantheon with the great Germans in Poland in the nineteenth century. These included captains of industry like Karl Scheibler in Łódź or the entrepreneur Peter Steinkeller, as well as the painters, printers and more ornamental gardeners. He was generous, to a fault, with the criteria for appropriation. The historian Lelewel was taken over on the grounds that his grandparents were Germans, the work of Polish poets like Kraszewski – whose work became 'nobler, the content livelier, the accounts more passionate and gripping' through contact with the work of E. T. A. Hoffmann and Richter – were stripped of their creative originality.[174] While Chopin and Paderewski had, perforce, to stay resolutely Polish, Lück managed to diminish their talents by stressing that they had 'derived their beginnings, like rivers from the source' from the German Joseph Elsner (1769–1854).[175] Conscious of the many who had escaped his trawl, Lück concluded with the observation 'we have merely been able to exhibit only a fraction of the felicitous influences of these bearers of civilisation, but to a certain extent that may already make an impression'.[176] The effects of this one-way transmission of culture led him to some final, broader, reflections on the nature of the two peoples. The 'German man of will' was characterized by 'pedantic diligence and a sense of order' and 'tenacity'; the Poles were 'a sentimental people', who lacked the capacity 'for abstract thought'. This apparently explained the success of the Counter Reformation in Poland. He ended with the ringing, boldly printed, declaration,

> The Germans have earned a right to live in their homeland through honourable work, apart from the fact that the Polish privileges they received most solemnly promised them just treatment.[177]

While there was nothing methodologically remarkable about *Deutsche Aufbaukräfte*, Lück's venture into comparative anthropology – *Der Mythos vom Deutschen* – demonstrates why his patrons were so enthusiastic about his work. Despite its primitive technique and obvious prejudices, *Der Mythos* was a pioneering example of what nowadays would be called the history of *mentalités*. The intellectual influences were Emil Lehmann's studies of German–Czech border conflict, and a spate of works, in most European languages, dealing with national stereotypes, engendered by the nationalist hysteria of the First World War; Max Scheler's 'The origin of hatred of the Germans' (1917) or Stanislaw Kot's 'The Polish Republic in the political literature of the West' (1919).[178] In *Der Mythos*, Lück combined oral evidence with studies of recurrent themes in popular literature and image-making; it was a history 'from below', a contribution to a future 'psychology of European ethnic frontiers'.[179] About fifty years later, these subjects are debated at learned conferences of international experts. Lück used proverbs, folk tales, jokes and popular literature to explore national stereotypes that had arisen out of centuries of close contact between the two peoples, and tried to discover why stereotypes endured long after the circumstances that had created them no longer applied. The conceptual framework he employed to explain the genesis and transmission of stereotypes was inevitably flawed. 'Eternal conflict' between Poles and Germans was the result of 'passive' Polish resentment against their 'active' German 'teachers'. Not all Poles, however, were the same. A small group comprised 'Poles 1' (those capable of rationally appreciating German cultural achievements); 'Poles 2' encompassed the mass of the population who subjectively and emotionally rejected anything German.[180] Polish practice was determined by the former: Polish custom by the latter. These reactions could be tabulated:

Polish reaction to the introduction of potatoes	
Example 2	
Cultural gradient	German colonists introduce potatoes to Poland.
Emotional reaction of Poles 2	Poles 2 are revolted by this new crop. They call the Germans 'potato gobblers' with 'potato bellies' and 'potato brains' and make up insulting verses. It takes 150 years before the new crop becomes the most important staple diet in the whole country.
Rational reaction of Poles 1	Poles 1 quickly recognize the importance of the new crop and promote its cultivation through the founding of exemplary German villages.
Influence on custom	Today the Polish people no longer knows that Germans brought the potato. According to statistics today a Pole eats eight times as many potatoes as a German. Despite this, the latter is still the 'potato gobbler' in both literature and popular tradition.[181]

In the main body of the book, Lück systematically rehearsed stereotypes which had arisen from conflicting confessions, languages, dress, food and 'national character'. Authentic popular stories were set in a pseudo-academic anthropological context. For example, in his discussion of why other peoples are said to smell differently Lück wrote:

Naturally different races perspire in characteristic ways, and the odour is unpleasant to others. The body odours of the Black are unbearable to the White, and those of the European to the Japanese . . . All over Germany, since time out of mind, the Semite has been considered to be a stinker, Jewish stinker, Stinking Jew. Naturally, as soon as he became Christian he ceased to stink.[182]

Passing through the learned exegesis of the etymology of the word smerd (stink), Lück interpolated a tale that could be heard along the 'entire eastern ethnic front'.

One day a German, a Pole and a Ukrainian passed by a shed containing a billy-goat from which a terrible stench wafted forth. They decided to make a bet as to which of them could stay the longest in the shed. The German went in first, but after a few moments he came out again. The Pole stayed inside for a quarter of an hour. The Ukrainian surpassed them both. They waited for half an hour but he still did not come out. Suddenly the door flew open – and the billy-goat leaped out in a wild jump. He could not stand it anymore.[183]

Similar tales and proverbs were used to objectify concepts like *polnische Wirtschaft* – one said to the sick *Du siehst ja so vergänglich aus wie ein polnischer Gutshof* – or to characterize 'Slav' and 'German' work rhythms.

A German wanted to show a Russian how well his servant worked. He called him and commanded him 'Johann, go and fetch me tobacco.' Then he took out his watch and said 'Now he's there, now he's there in the shop, now he's there, now he must be outside the door. Johann have you got the tobacco?' *Jawohl Herr* called the servant from behind the door, and came in.

The Russian said, 'My Ivan can do that too. Ivan, run to the shop and fetch me tobacco.' He took out his watch and said, 'Now he's there, now he's there, in the shop, now he's there, now he must be behind the door. Ivan have you got the tobacco?' *Ach, nein, Herr* muttered Ivan behind the door, 'I haven't found my cap yet.'[184]

And so the book went on, with sadistic Prussian schoolmasters who beat little girls unconscious who did not say their prayers in German, German Gradgrinds in German 'Lodsch' and, at the start, archetypically, the satanic Danveld and Siegfried de Löwe in Sienkiewicz's *Krzyzacy*.[185] The 1943 second edition made the purpose of this massive catalogue of human uncomprehension and ill-will perfectly clear. The Polish literature was a 'school of hatred' which blinded Germany's eastern neighbour.

And so it came to September 1939 in which the Poles gave vent to their hatred of the Germans through the murder of thousands of innocent people, but in which the fate of Poland was also finally sealed. As so often, 'myth' was dethroned by harsh reality. Have the Poles become more mature through experience? We do not believe so. Poland was always the promised land of germanophobic intrigue, myths and legends. That will not change in the future. In the interests of its own security the Great German Reich must draw the necessary conclusions.[186]

This was where the amusing anecdotes and (intrinsically) innocuous proverbs and tales led. Taken out of context, and catalogued in their thousands, they lent the present conflict an air of immutable inevitability. Lück's own role in depicting the 'September Massacres' in the most lurid terms and his involvement in the interests of security will be discussed in the following chapter.

Not all of the NODFG funds for work on Poland were dispensed from the pools of patronage around Lattermann and Kauder and not all of the recipients were permanently operational in Poland. In 1937 Theodor Oberländer, the chairman of the BDO and head of the *Institut für ostdeutsche Wirtschaft* in Königsberg, sent the NODFG a list of grant applications for the coming year. The list included a request for 200 RMs a month for Kurt Ballerstedt for work on agrarian reform in Poland.[187] Honestly, but unwisely, Ballerstedt mentioned in the application form that he had belonged to the SPD from 1 October 1930 to 31 December 1932. The PuSte assumed that this matter had been settled before Ballerstedt joined the IoW staff but wrote to Oberländer for immediate clarification.[188] This request caught up with Oberländer who was touring the East Pomeranian frontier. It gave him 'a little fright'.

> Certainly I knew that Ballerstedt did not belong to the NSDAP but otherwise I have not researched his political background. Ballerstedt should have told me about this, especially since I intervened personally on his behalf . . . First of all might I suggest you contact the responsible NSDAP office, in this case probably Rostock, for a judgement on Ballerstedt. If that is all right, everything is in order, if it isn't, then naturally we have a free hand.[189]

Two weeks later Ballerstedt wrote to the PuSte to explain this reddish mark in his political copybook.

> During my membership of the SPD I was always on the right wing of the Party. I always rejected the political Marxism of the left wing with its internationalist outlook and regarded it as the most important task facing the Party to make the workers into the co-bearers of the German idea of the state and to lead them to an understanding of the vital questions confronting the German people, in particular the Eastern problem and the importance of our peasant farmers.
>
> The motives for my joining the Party were not a desire to advance my professional career. That can be seen from the date upon which I joined (October 1930) . . . One can see that every form of Marxist

internationalist opinion was alien to me from the fact that after the
conclusion of my education I turned to the practice of rural settlement
upon which I had already decided during my preparatory service as a
lawyer.

Heil Hitler![190]

He appended the names of an NSDAP *Kreisleiter* and an SA-*Obergrup-penführer* who would testify on his behalf. With positive references
from them, the PuSte informed Oberländer on 29 October 1937 that
they had no objections to giving Ballerstedt a grant.[191]

Another young historian recommended by Oberländer occasioned
no such political difficulties. Peter-Heinz Seraphim was born in Riga in
1902. He came from a scholarly Baltic family and had been wounded
fighting the Soviets. He was also an NSDAP and SA member. At the
time of his grant application he was the IoW Referent concerned with
Poland. Oberländer stressed the importance of Seraphim's work in a
letter to Brackmann dated 16 January 1936:

> It has to do with the Jewish problem in the eastern European region.
> The [research project] seems to me to be particularly important because
> this very important and fateful question for all of the eastern Euro-
> pean states has never been scientifically dealt with from an impartial
> viewpoint. The investigations of the social situation and economic
> significance of Jewry seems to me to be of particular significance.[192]

Seraphim sent Brackmann a detailed submission on the work he
wished to do under the title *Das Judentum im osteuropäischen Raum*.
There were three sub-headings: (1) the distribution of Jews in the East,
(2) their social situation and economic significance, and (3) the Jews
within the 'social community'. The first part of Seraphim's work was
to consist of a 'demographic, political, statistical reckoning' of the
Jewish population of eastern Europe with particular emphasis upon
the 'urban demographic agglomerations'.[193] He then planned to study
the role of the Jews in the economies of eastern Europe:

> Certainly we speak of a Polish, Lithuanian, or Russian economy – but
> the notion is almost totally absent that in significant and decisive
> sectors of the economy we are dealing with a Jewish economy in
> Poland, Lithuania, Russia etc. Evidence of to what extent the entire
> distributive apparatus, credit system and so on is in the hands of Jews
> is much more important than their simple statistical role and propor-
> tionate significance within the countries of eastern Europe.[194]

This led to a consideration of the role of Jews as a separate element in social life, which was to include study of Zionism, assimilation and 'the undoubted significance of Jews as leaders of the proletarian–socialist line of thought'. He also wanted to study anti-Semitic movements and 'to try to establish critically whether and which possibilities exist for the solution of the eastern European Jewish problem'.[195] He included a long account of the significance of what he planned to write. 'Practically everything', he insisted, that has been written on the subject 'stems from Jewish pens.' Only through such a study of the importance of the Jews to the economies of the eastern European states 'would we become conscious of the economic danger that lies in the existence of these Jewish population groups for these peoples and states'. It would also clarify why eastern European Jewry 'which is simply a reservoir for Jewry as a whole, represents a standing danger for Central Europe and in particular for Germany'. He wanted 900 RMs for a long study trip from Königsberg to Kaunas, Riga, Wilna, Warsaw, Łódź, L'vov and Bucharest to ascertain how many newspapers had Jewish editors, how much 'Jewish' capital was involved in banks and the attitudes of Jews towards the 'host' states.[196] Any reservations about the project, of which there were none, would have been cleared up by a second report incorporated into a more forceful recommendation from Oberländer, which conveyed the intelligence that Seraphim was learning Yiddish and that his father, the historian Ernst Seraphim, was helping with the Russian material.[197] In July 1936 the PuSte informed Seraphim that they would give him a two-month travel grant of 800 RMs and would subsidise the publication of his book with a further 2,000 RMs.[198] The fruits of his efforts, as will be discussed below, subsequently adorned the pages of the NODFG journal *Jomsburg*.

iv. 'The times are gone when everyone can do what he likes': the NODFG, ethnic minorities and censorship

While strenuous and deliberate efforts were made to heighten the ethnic consciousness of German minorities abroad, the opposite policy was pursued towards ethnic minorities in Germany. The Lusatian Sorbs occupy an area some 90 kms long and 45 kms wide, that straddles the Spree south-east of Berlin and runs towards the Czechoslovak border. Although the Sorbs (the German term *Wende* has pejorative associations) are a protected minority within the DDR and live hard by their Slav neighbours, before the Second World War they formed a Slavic island some way behind the further shores of a German sea. Overwhelmingly rural, and speaking a form of West Slavonic that has a closer affinity to Polish than to Czech, the beginnings of their consciousness of ethnicity have been traced back to the influence of Panslavic ideology and the impact of the 1848 revolution. This manifested itself in the creation of the *Maćica Serbska* in 1847, a cultural association based, from 1904, in the *Serbski Dom*, which was designed to promote consciousness of Sorbian national identity.[199]

Attempts to achieve autonomous representation at Paris in 1919, and the fact that only the KPD group in the Saxon *Landtag* was active in pressing for the implementation of Sorbian rights under Article 113 of the Weimar Constitution, meant that the Sorbs were viewed with considerable suspicion by the authorities.[200] In 1920 a 'Wendish Department' was set up in Bautzen, the aims of which included 'strengthening work on Germandom in Wendish districts', 'promoting broader enlightenment on the treasonable character of all manifestations of Wendish nationalism', 'exposure of Wendish national consciousness as inimical to the Reich' and 'promotion of the merging of the Wends into Germandom'.[201] Nazi policy towards the Sorbs was essentially the same but confused in its execution. If they began by banning Sorbian newspapers, raiding the homes of prominent Sorbs, and deporting Sorbian teachers from Lusatia, the negative reverberations for the German minorities in Poland and Czechoslovakia, and international outcry, recommended the more subtle approach of building NSDAP support in the region.[202] Given the importance of scholarship, learned societies and libraries in the development of Sorbian national consciousness, it was inevitable that the German authorities, and Nazi organizations like the BDO, should be particularly concerned to obstruct the study of Sorbian civilization both within Lusatia, and among Slavists in Germany as a whole. BDO policy towards the Sorbs, which included the 'gift' of German Kindergarten to Sorbian villages, was encapsulated in the statement 'intermediary nationalities as exist in a few eastern regions, are survivals from an age of unconsolidated national consciousness', and the directive that, 'for reasons of state it is especially desired that the concepts "Wend", "Wendish", "Wendish nationality" disappear from all types of publication, brochures, journals etc.'[203] The task of vetting scholarly work on the Sorbs and other ethnic minorities, which involved massive interference by historians in disciplines about which they knew practically nothing, ultimately devolved upon the PuSte and NODFG.

All levels of intellectual enquiry – and especially history – on the Sorbs were touched by the deadening hand of the *Ostforscher*. For as the Leipzig historian Prof. R. Kötzschke put it in 1920 'precisely the lack of history of the Sorbs is a guarantee for the acceleration of their desired disappearance into Germandom'. In June 1938 an octogenarian clergyman called Tilka sent his memoirs to the chairman of the Lower Lusatian Society, Dr Lehmann, to sound out the possibility of publication. He had never written a book and wanted advice on how to go about publishing one.[204] The table of contents included 'Boys' games and all kinds of nonsense'; 'Mushrooms'; 'The weekly market in Cottbus'; 'How I came to Neubrandenburg'; 'money found in the vicarage garden'; 'non-believers (sectarians, Sabbatarians and Social Democrats in Kolkwitz)'; 'East Prussian refugees in Lippehne and the marriage of my daughter in Berlin'; *Das otium cum dignitate*; 'how many languages are there on our planet and attempts to unify them all'; 'the death of my dear wife'; and 'Kolberg, a first class spa town'.[205] This was history bounded by the garden fence, with the odd glance up at the cosmos or at the larger concerns of mankind that flitted through the parish. Tilka's manuscript and letters were forwarded by the *Oberpräsident* of the province of Brandenburg to the RMdI in June 1938.[206] Essen in the RMdI asked the PuSte to report on the old man's ramblings. The *Oberpräsident* had written 'this long-winded work is the product of an eighty-year-old, who himself can be considered politically harmless. Despite that, publication should be prevented; that might not come into question as no publisher will be found for such a diffuse manuscript'.[207] In November the *Oberpräsident* reported that he had instructed Lehmann to return the manuscript to Tilka with instructions to re-work it, and 'had drawn the attention of the Gestapo office in Köslin to Tilka and the projected publication of his work'.[208] Tilka's last, hopeful, letter to Lehmann asking whether he could expect the work of a decade to be published shows why the wanderings of an old man should have excited such high-level attention. He said that in order to escape boredom he had sought to 'set up a monument to Sorbianism, from which I come and which is now on its deathbed'. His rider that he had preached for twenty-five years in places where 'today and a thousand years ago Sorbs and Slavs lived' did not improve his chances of finding a publisher. Plaintively he added 'what one has written with the blood of one's heart, one does not like to throw into the wastepaper basket'.[209]

In their report, the PuSte staff insisted that Tilka's Section 3, Part 3 should be deleted.[210] This section was concerned with the history and language of the Sorbs. He was not alone, however, in experiencing difficulties with this subject.

On 10 August 1937 the *Deutsche Forschungsgemeinschaft* asked the PuSte for a report on a grant application made by Dr Paul Wirth (his Sorbian name was Pawoł Wirt)[211] for a 'linguistic–geographical study of the terminology used by Sorbian craftsmen' including fishermen, weavers, beekeepers, potters and rope-makers.[212] This was in accordance with a prior agreement whereby the NODFG would check all questions concerning works on the Sorbs. Wirth's earlier work – a Sorbian linguistic atlas – had been supported – by the Slavonic committee of the Prussian Academy which included not only Max Vasmer but Brackmann himself.[213] Kohte sent a confidential report on Wirth's project dated 21 August 1937:

> To our regret it is not possible for us to recommend the application by Dr Paul Wirth for a research grant for linguistic study of the terminology used by Sorbian craftsmen. It is generally undesirable that works on the Sorbian language should be published from the German side. The Sorbian language should remain as unnoticed as possible and its decline not be impeded by increased academic study . . .
>
> On these grounds [his earlier work] the projected study must also be described as dubious. The justification that we must rescue the disappearing Sorbian linguistic legacy for scholarship at the last moment because with it many German borrowings will be lost does not seem convincing. We see no reason why, on account of a few borrowings . . . Sorbian should be conserved in any way. In the last analysis – and despite the good intentions of the student – the work will give an unwarranted stimulus to the Poles and Czechs or at all events to the strengthening of Sorbian ethnicity. It was precisely earlier German study of Sorbian customs that led to their revival. On the basis of this experience we have no interest in promoting linguistic–geographical studies of the sort that the applicant has carried out hitherto and wishes to carry out in future. We ask you to treat our statement of reference highly confidentially and not to inform the applicant of its contents because through his family and his work he has relations with Sorbian circles and we should avoid disconcerting the latter.[214]

On 25 August 1937 Wirth was informed by the *Deutsche Forschungsgemeinschaft* that a grant was 'not possible at the moment'.[215]

If Tilka or Wirth were powerless to react to interference in their

work, it was otherwise with Professor Reinhold Trautmann. Trautmann (1883–1951) was, from 1926, Director of the Slavonic Institute
at the University of Leipzig, which was one of Germany's greatest
centres of Slavonic studies. Although Trautmann was a very distinguished scholar, known for his publications rather than his dexterity
on committees, student interest in Slavonic studies fell sharply in the
1930s. At one point he described lecturing as like being 'an actor
without an audience'.[216] After a number of publications on old Prussian, medieval Czech literature, and the novels of Turgenev, Trautmann turned in the late 1920s to the study of the Sorbian language. In
1928 he edited the *Wolfenbüttel Lower Sorbian Psalter*. His familiarity
with Sorbian then coalesced with an earlier interest in place-names and
in particular the problem of Slavic placenames in Germany.[217]

Trautmann's troubles began with a letter to the NODFG in March
1938 requesting information on whether an edict existed banning
publication of studies on early Sorbian settlements in Germany. He
had attended a meeting at the RMdI on 26 April 1937 on the Sorbian
question, but was unsure whether a ban had ensued or whether this
encompassed historical studies.[218] The conference had been called by
the NODFG to achieve 'a unified approach' among scholars working
on Sorbian questions. However, in letters to officials in Saxony, Breslau
and Brandenburg before the conference was held, the RMdI gave the
meeting a more narrow purpose. The conference was designed to
hinder the publication of undesirable academic studies on the Sorbs.[219]
The professional Slavists regarded the conference as an unwholesome
attempt by non-specialists in the PuSte to regulate Slavonic studies.
During the meeting Trautmann warned of the dangers of complete
cessation of Slavonic studies.[220] His Berlin colleague, Max Vasmer,
expressed his regret that 'people like Papritz have tried to play a role
in Slavonic studies at the expense of trained professionals, which is
forcing the coming generation of Slavists to seek other jobs'. Defending
what Vasmer called 'Papritz and Co.', Brackmann observed that
Slavonic studies were merely 'an auxiliary discipline'.[221]

Attended by representatives of the Foreign, Propaganda and Education ministries, BDO, NODFG and several scholars from Leipzig,
including Otto Reche, Trautmann and Kötzschke, the meeting in Unter
den Linden issued a series of 'Theses on the Sorbian question':[222]

1. There are no 'Sorbs' and no 'Lusatians in the German Reich, but
   merely Wends or Wendish-speaking Germans.

2. The Wends do not constitute a separate nationality but are a people who, in part, speak a Slavonic language within the context of the German people and state.

3. There is no *Wendei* and no self-contained Wendish area of settlement. The expression Wendish linguistic region is to be avoided. In case of need one should employ regional terms like Upper or Lower Lusatia or Spreewald.

4. The incidence of Wendish-speaking, Wendish costume and other manifestations of Wendish custom is no indication of a non-German nationality. The cultivation of Wendish customs within given limits is totally permissible. The Wendish language is declining through natural processes.

5. A small group in Saxony is trying to split the Wends from the German nation as a separate 'Sorbian people', a foreign national group. These efforts are supported from Czechoslovakia, Poland, South Slavia and France. Therefore it is recommended that the Wendish Question should not be dealt with in public in the Reich either publicistically or in a scholarly way.

6. Such questions which have to be dealt with for general scholarly reasons, should not be published or, if they are, only for internal use.

7. Treatment of the Wendish Question cannot be avoided in the context of academic studies of Eastern Germany, Saxony, Brandenburg and Silesia. In these studies the connection with the history and customs of the German people is to be emphasized strongly.

8. If, for whatever reason, for example because of hostile studies from home or abroad, it is still found to be necessary to refute the latter or to study the subject, it is strongly recommended that the manuscripts should be sent to the NODFG before publication, who in turn, for their part, will get in touch with the competent authorities.

On 22 March 1938 Brackmann informed Trautmann that there were no objections to studies of the early Sorbian settlements in Germany, 'however I would regard it as useful if in such cases the political authorities were asked for their permission'. He added that it could come to pass that the RMdI would 'intervene' if political consequences could be drawn from historical studies.[223] There had been some 'intervention' already. In January 1936 the PuSte had informed the local administration in Bautzen about two Sorbian students from Saxony who had been spotted in Poland assisting the archaeologist Kostrzewski in his investigations of *Urslav* Lusatian civilization.[224] The administration in Bautzen instructed the Gestapo to 'monitor' the two students when they returned home.[225] In March 1937 the Propaganda Ministry took exception to an article by Dagmer Ohlsen entitled 'Girls in the Wendei' published in the March issue of *Deutsche Jugendburg*, on the grounds that 'in reality the so-called Wends have been a pure German people for a long time and do not possess their own nationality'. A picture caption 'Wendish peasant children from the parish of Schleife' was to be excised.[226] In May 1937 the same ministry tackled the editor of NS-*Frauenwarte* about a piece entitled 'Easter in Bautzen' which maintained that there were 24,000 Catholic Sorbs in what the author designated Budyšin (Bautzen).

> I draw your attention to the fact that it is extremely undesirable and absolutely does not lie in the interests of the nationality policy of the Reich when old Wendish names are used in the German press, and again and again references to the Wendish 'nation' appear.[227]

Trautmann tried to reassure Brackmann that his work, which he wanted to publish in the *Jahrbuch des Vereins für mecklenburgische Geschichte*, was designed to refute the Russian historian Egorov, and to highlight the German cultural achievement by contrasting it with Sorbian civilization. Without the valleys, there are no peaks. He added, 'I have not only served the truth but have also worked throughout as a German Slavist.'[228] Brackmann told Trautmann that he should hold up publication of his work, for although there was no blanket ban, 'each case has to be checked to see if the political effect of the work could result in damage to German interests'.[229] At that point in time 'as little discussion as possible about the Wendish settlers' was desired by the authorities.[230] In May 1938 the educational department of the Ministry of State in Schwerin sought an opinion from the RMdI on Trautmann's work on placenames in Mecklenburg which they in turn had received from the *Jahrbuch der Vereins für mecklenburgische Geschichte*.[231] Apparently the local NSDAP Gauleitung had not responded. In June the PuSte informed Trautmann that they had been checking his work although 'our task, to do justice to the demands of scholarship as well as the irrefutable demands of politics is not easy'.[232] Trautmann, tired of delays, then complicated matters by withdrawing his manuscript from the *Jahrbuch* which he then sent, with its academic content endorsed by Professor Scheel in Kiel, to the History Society in Kiel.[233] Brackmann was soon in hot pursuit, although he managed to contact the referee rather than the editor of the journal concerned.[234]

Scheel assured Brackmann that a paper on Slavic placenames in East Holstein would be harmless as 'they possess no political actuality'.[235] This did not reassure Brackmann who dispatched the PuSte's North Germany expert, Koppe, to Kiel. He met Scheel in the Hotel Excelsior on 21 March 1939 and 'drew Scheel's attention to the indivisibility of the whole former Slavic-settled German territory and found his agreement'.[236]

Not surprisingly, Trautmann was furious about this interference in his work. It was not, however, a matter of manning the barricades on behalf of the Sorbs, for he was actually stressing separate Sorbian identity in order to diminish the territorial scope of Poland. Fifteen years before, he insisted, he had not been handled with such mistrust when he had demonstrated that the Memel area had been settled from Prussia rather than Lithuania. It would not do, merely to refute Polish work through 'trivial boyish pieces' like a recent review in the NODFG organ *Jomsburg*, but rather 'German scholarship is forced to wheel out the heavy artillery, I don't believe that in the case of warlike conflict our army high command would counter Polish machine-gun fire with rounds of shot.' A 'head in the sand policy' (*Vogelstrausspolitik*) in the face of the Poles did not correspond with 'our' character.[237] Brackmann tried to make Trautmann see reason by drawing his attention to recent Polish work that had extended historic *Slawentum* to the proximity of Hamburg, and asked him to send his work to the PuSte for comradely censorship.[238] Scheel agreed with Brackmann.

> It is not a matter of interference in the freedom of a German researcher or university teacher, but simply to establish whether or not publication of particular details is politically tolerable at the moment. That is an absolutely legitimate demand of the political leadership of the German people and it stands entirely beyond the question of freedom to research.[239]

Meanwhile, the editor of the journal involved, Pauls, sought formal clarification on government policy. Informed that *this did not exist*, to prevent it falling into the wrong (Polish) hands, Pauls observed that he found this 'very remarkable'. Papritz noted on the letter, 'it seems to me that good-will is lacking'.[240] In August 1938 the PuSte reported to the RMdI on Trautmann's work. It had little negative to say about his scholarly accomplishments. However Trautmann had mentioned the Slav origin of placenames like Bandelstorf, Dalldorf, Dambeck etc. and worse, had noted instances where Slav villages had received

German names. He had also said that 'Since we do not have a critical and above all German account of the history of the Elbe and Baltic Wends and do not anticipate one (although the academic forces for this patriotic task are available)' which could only imply to a (malevolent) Polish reader that the regime was censoring Slavonic studies. His chances were not improved by approving references to 'particularly good [Polish] theoretical work'. The PuSte report concluded 'for all of these reasons we regard the appearance of this book as impossible at the moment on political grounds'.[241] Trautmann received a copy of the report through an error on the part of the History Society in Kiel.[242] He informed Brackmann that 'if this involved a review of my work after its publication, I would regard it as beneath my dignity to reply even with one word to that sort of concoction'.[243] At no point had it been made clear to him at the RMdI conference on the Sorbs that the measures adopted applied to historical studies.[244] His threat to circulate a refutation of the report throughout the academic community was relayed to the RMdI.[245] Undaunted, Trautmann managed to set in motion the publication of his book in Schleswig-Holstein despite the machinations of the PuSte and NODFG. Brackmann enlisted Aubin to put pressure on Trautmann through a former student who, as Professor Frings, was one of Trautmann's Leipzig colleagues.[246] This approach failed. Trautmann's Leipzig friends banded together to demand a limited edition of his work which was at that time being printed. The decision to ban the book was taken by Goebbels.

> The above named book is added to the list of dangerous and undesirable publications and will be confiscated by the Gestapo.[247]

Gestapo agents in Kiel raided the printers but could only find three finished copies and a mass of unbound proofs.[248] Vollert in the RMdI ordered the Gestapo to hand over 50 sets of proofs to the PuSte.[249] With the issue thus disposed of, the PuSte file on Trautmann closed with the idea of producing a limited confidential edition from the proofs. But, in view of the 'happy quiet that has descended on the matter' and with the agreement of Goebbels who had found the time to dip into the book, the idea was dropped.[250] The case of Trautmann was quite felicitously summed up by the *Landeshauptmann* in Schleswig-Holstein. In January 1940 he wrote, 'I am convinced we are dealing here with one of the less pleasant accompaniments of academic life.'[251]

Racial studies of Slav minorities were also not friction free. The principal arbiter in this area was Professor Otto Reche of Leipzig university, the NODFG's expert on racial matters. Born in Glatz (Silesia) in 1879, Reche had moved from museum work to a lectureship at Hamburg university. In 1924 he became professor of anthropology and ethnology at Vienna, moving to Leipzig in 1927.[252] An attempt made in 1940 to backdate his NSDAP membership – the five million plus Party card was a source of embarrassment among his colleagues – tells us something about his earlier political activities. Apparently, in 1918 he had co-founded in Hamburg a *völkischsoziale Partei* with the motto 'Germany for the Germans'. It was safer, in 1940, to add that this effort to combat 'Jewdom, Freemasonry, Marxism and Ultramontanism', had failed because of the lack of an 'outstanding leading personality'. In Vienna, Reche's 'Institut zur Pflege deutschen Wissens' had become the rallying point for National Socialist students. The NSDAP itself had suggested that, for tactical reasons, he would be more effective outside the Party.[253]

Reche's academic work, for which he received grants from the *Reichsforschungsrat* and the NODFG, concerned twins, the families of criminals, and the Sorbs. During the 1930s the opinion of this pioneer was increasingly sought on a range of racial matters. For example, he was the obvious man to consult when the Reich's committee on public health services wrote to the RMdI about an article by a Dr Gangele entitled 'The dislocated hip-joint – an hereditary illness?' that had appeared in the *Zentralblatt für Chirurgie*.[254] In his essay Gangele had observed that the frequent occurrence of broad pelvises among the Saxons could be attributed to their Slav origins. The RMdI wanted a corrective of this aberrant physiology. The NODFG subcontracted the task to Reche.[255] In due course he produced a piece bearing the title 'On the territoriality of the Germans east of the Elbe' for the journal *Der öffentliche Gesundheitsdienst*.[256] In this he explained that the whole area had been permeated with German blood, to the point where the Slavs 'were not racially ascertainable with any certainty any more'.[257] A few years later, as we will see, this inveterate Slavophobe would question whether the Slavs had actually ever existed.

Reche was also involved in attempts to extend the silence upon the Sorbs to the racial anthropology of Silesia. In December 1937 the NSDAP *Gauleitung* in Silesia contacted the Education Ministry (and the NODFG/PuSte), concerning how Silesia was treated in academic studies. The local Party leadership complained that although studies of Silesia had demonstrated that the 'racial structure was overwhelmingly nordic', academics insisted on stressing the prevalence of *ostisches und ostbaltisches Menschentum* which was giving the Germans in Silesia 'an inferiority complex'.[258] As a Silesian, and a purist in these matters, Reche was less certain than the NSDAP leaders in Silesia. He could not shrug off the feeling that the authors of earlier studies had approached the subject 'with a certain predetermined optimism . . . about the share of the nordic race in the population'. Certainly the 'nordic inheritance' was in the ascendant, and asserted areas were 'overwhelmingly nordic', but there was undeniable proof of the strong presence of *ostische, sudetische, ostbaltische und dinarische* characteristics. He concluded: 'Anthropology is politically a really difficult subject! It would be better perhaps if nothing was said or written about it in public.' His rather indeterminate conclusions were relayed to the Education Ministry by Papritz who endorsed the suggested ban on public discussion.[259]

Many of those scholars affected by the censorship of the NODFG and PuSte could not be classed as members of any putative academic 'resistance'. In the case of Hans Mortensen (1894–1966), who from 1935 to 1945 and 1948 to 1962 occupied the chair of geography at Göttingen, the 'victim' described himself in 1934 as 'a convinced National Socialist for over a decade'.[260] The Mortensens – they were a husband and wife team – were producing a history of the colonization of East Prussia from the Middle Ages up to the early modern period, for Brackmann's series *Deutschland und der Osten*. As the series editor, Brackmann had the delicate task of relaying the instructions of the RMdI to his contributors. At the NODFG conference in Stolpmünde in May 1937, Brackmann announced that the RMdI had advised the non-employment of the word 'colonisation' because 'the Poles could reach certain conclusions from this that might not be very politically satisfactory for us', and its replacement with 'resettlement' in discussions of the German presence in the East.[261] In a letter to Aubin dated 25 May 1937 Brackmann mentioned that the advice was now a matter of 'firm instruction' and that a conference would shortly be held in the RMdI to lay down guidelines.[262] By June Brackmann was advising both the editor of the *Deutsches Archiv für Landes- und Volksförschung* to substitute 'settlement history' or 'settlement research' for 'history of the colonisation' and 'research on the colonisation' in an essay that Aubin was contributing to the next number. The RMdI had insisted that the word was 'to be avoided at all costs'.[263] Faced with the same demand, the Mortensens argued that the word 'colonisation' conveyed the necessary distinction between the superior

German presence and the 'primitive settlements without inner order or organisation' of the Lithuanians.[264]

If they bowed to Brackmann's more informed judgement on this issue, the next phase of ministerial interference was harder to accept. The Mortensens 'had often discussed during our work how nice it was that we only needed to maintain the truth in order to establish something politically favourable for Germany'. Faced with undeniable, Lithuanian numerical predominance in East Prussia, both in the past and present, the Mortensens had tried to deflate Lithuanian irredentism by establishing that the Lithuanians had been invited by the German Order to settle in a wilderness that clearly belonged to the territories of the Order. This dispensed with the notion of a Lithuanian *Urheimat*. The Lithuanians had no more rights there than German migrants to Brazil or Chile. Hans Mortensen added, 'I, for my part, would never publish or make known anything that would damage Germany or the German people, even if it was the scholarly truth.'[265]

As a prospective speaker at the next International Geographical Conference in Amsterdam, he did not wish to appear as 'a traitor to my country' and therefore requested Brackmann 'as the person in charge of all scholarly work on the East', to find out what ministerial policy was. Brackmann contacted Essen in the RMdI with whom Mortensen was also in communication by telephone.[266] There were meetings at the RMdI and in Essen's home where both the host and Papritz became more and more convinced of the political importunity of the Mortensens' work.[267] As the ground shifted to the question of why they broke their work off in 1618 – before the (superior) German colonization had begun – the Mortensens, already incensed by the continued use of the word 'colonisation' in other books, threatened to scrap the whole project.[268] Brackmann drafted the RMdI's appeal to their better nature. It would be politically consequential if 'the leading expert' on the subject inadvertently supplied proof of overwhelming Lithuanian settlement; disastrous if they suddenly stopped working for political reasons. Matters could only be set to rights if they could extend the work to cover the onset of German settlement and admin-istration, which would show 'the powerful German cultural achieve-ment which the enemy would have to recognise too'. This might involve more work, but one day they could look back 'with inner satisfaction' and 'would be able to say that you have done everything which promotes the well-being of your fatherland'.[269] The crux of the matter was that the RMdI wanted to scrutinize what had been written so far while the Mortensens wanted clear guidelines *before* they went any further.[270] Mortensen irately informed the RMdI that in view of the series in which the book was to be published, 'there is hardly any danger that my wife and I will publish anything whose contents are anti-German or undesirable'.[271] They saw no sense in extending their studies into areas which were the preserve of Kurt Forstreuter. 'Conscious of my national duty', Hans Mortensen had dispatched his wife to Königsberg to double check the question of who had filled the gaps left by plague in seventeenth-century Lithuania. The results were not encouraging. If there had been cultural and linguistic germanization in the nineteenth century, there 'was not any kind of considerable German settlement that broke the preponderant Lithuanian settlement' beforehand. Extending the scope of the book would not make any difference.[272]

Brackmann's role in this minor tussle is worth noting. On the one hand the Mortensens were grateful to him for his 'manly intervention' on behalf of oppressed *Ostforscher* during a conversation with Essen at the last NODFG conference.[273] However, Brackmann was simultaneously advising the RMdI not to answer Mortensen's last letter until he sent his manuscript to the RMdI for vetting. He assured Mortensen that he did not know why the RMdI wanted to see the work and that he could not understand their reluctance to hand it over.[274] Mortensen tried to reassure him that the book would help the political situation by supporting German claims to the Memelland and added 'the reservations stem from our present day racial and ethnic viewpoint with which the historically established settlement of the Memelland is not entirely in harmony'.[275] Throughout, Brackmann's role was to relay ministerial anxiety that the 'enemy could operate politically' in the wider world with the Mortensens' work.[276] This role continued long after Brackmann's staff were rummaging through the abandoned papers of Polish scholars in libraries stretching from Paris to Warsaw.[277]

v. The German–Polish Conferences on School History Books, 1937–8

As we have seen, the Hitler–Piłsudski Pact amounted to little more than 'linguistic regulation' for the *Ostforscher* gathered in the NODFG. There was one area, however, in which serious attempts were made to scrape away the encrusted prejudices that had weighed

down German–Polish relations for so long: the German–Polish Conferences on School History Books.[278] Both countries sent delegates to
meetings which were held alternately in Warsaw (28–9 August 1937)
and Berlin (27–9 June 1938). The Polish delegation consisted of
Professors Dabrowski, Nawroczynski and Kowalski; the German contingent of Aubin, *Oberschulrat* Fitzek and a translator called Arnulf
Schröder. The object of the negotiations, which seem to have been
quite amicable, with common ground in anticommunism and probably
anti-Semitism too, was

> To eradicate from teaching and reading books all expressions and
> usages which would insult or deprecate the treaty partners or which
> are intended to injure the national sensibilities of the other nation.[279]

According to *Der Angriff*, 'History Books for Peace' was to be
extended to include other subjects.[280] Both sides came armed with lists
of the issues they regarded as most crucial, and citations from books
that they thought tendentious. The German list at Warsaw in August
1937 consisted of:

1. treatment of the Teutons and German national character
2. accounts of the knightly orders and the colonization of the East
3. the Age of Frederick William I and Frederick the Great
4. Bismarck and his times
5. the world war and the post-war period.

The Polish list consisted of:

1. 'negative' accounts of Poland's role in German school history books:
   a) in the struggle with the Tatars
   b) in the liberation of Vienna
   c) with reference to the Partitions of Poland
2. the demands for a 'positive' treatment in German school history
   books:
   a) the rise and christianization of the Polish kingdom
   b) the role of Poland in eastern Europe
   c) the honouring of the historical significance of the battle of
      Warsaw (1920) in the liberation from Bolshevik onslaughts.[281]

The discussions began with Polish objections to the notion of a
'primeval ethnic German territory' in the East, which they regarded as
a pretext for revisionist claims in the present. The Germans argued
that they were not claiming to be the autochthonous inhabitants of the
region, that their textbooks acknowledged the existence of a Lusatian

civilization, and that the textbooks made no revisionist claims upon the basis of what had happened a thousand years before. Other issues were settled without much ado. The Poles did not care for a sentence in a description of the battle of Liegnitz (1241) which said 'a bloody battle flared up around the brave German warriors ... but the Germans gained the upper hand'. The Germans similarly took exception to the sentence 'at Liegnitz the Poles stood up against the Tatars ... they protected western Europe with their heroic breasts'. Both parties acknowledged the need to make the defending forces more internationally representative.[282] Concord reigned too on the need to emphasize that there was peace between Poles and Germans between 1466 and the First Partitions. The German delegation immediately introduced the jarring question of how Polish schoolbooks failed to give due credit to the German cultural contribution to Poland. The Poles said that German accounts were too narrowly germanocentric and neglected the role of other influences upon Polish cultural life.[283] It is doubtful whether they were reassured by the German statement that 'in particular, the present National Socialist perception of the autonomy of every ethnic culture recognizes, without limitation and most emphatically, the cultural independence of those peoples who have relations with Germany'.[284] No agreement could be reached on the nationality of Copernicus.

More topically, the Polish delegates detected a lack of appreciation for the significance of Poland's victory over 'Bolshevik Russia' in 1920, and the role of Piłsudski. The Germans assured them that:

At the time when the books used today in Germany were written, the authors did not yet have the necessary distance towards the newly created Polish state, the battle of Warsaw or the statesman-like achievements of Marshal Piłsudski. In view of the combative stance of the Third Reich towards Bolshevism, in future the German schoolbooks will not pass over the epoch-making significance of the battle of Warsaw. It is also well-known with what high regard Nazi Germany views the Marshal's great person and his inspired achievements as a statesman and commander in chief. This view will also be reflected in future German school history books.[285]

The Germans had their own armoury of offensive passages in textbooks. In a discussion of how war-guilt was described, they drew attention to passages like: 'The German government united imperialism and exaggerated nationalism and propagated among the German people the conviction of the superiority of the German race and their duty to rule the world or, 'Kaiser Franz Josef was not inclined to immediate military action but gave in to the pressure from the side of Kaiser Wilhelm.'[286]

The Poles were prepared to adjust these passages on the grounds that with the creation of a Polish state 'the Poles had no reason to look around for a guilty party'. Their historians would have to pay more attention to the role of Russia whom modern researchers were increasingly blaming for the outbreak of war.[287] The Poles were also accommodating on the matter of the sinking by German submarines of hospital and merchant shipping. Future accounts would have to stress the existence of maritime exclusion zones. Sensing almost limitless goodwill, the German delegates pointed to a passage which described the present German regime as 'A government supported by the preponderance of one Party and the recognition of the superiority of one race over the others has, in reality, destroyed the democratic basis of the equality and freedom of the citizen in Germany.' The Poles offered to remove the offending passage.[288] They also offered to 'retouch' a book designed for the fourth class which included the sentence: 'Danzig remained to one side of the most important economic movements which developed in Germany in the second half of the nineteenth century and finally sank from the fourth position it had occupied among the towns of Prussia at the beginning of the nineteenth century to that of nineteenth', so that it read, 'Although Danzig progressed considerably, like the rest of the towns in the East, it could not keep pace with the tempo of development in the West.' They were also ready to de-brutalize the *Król-sierzant* by stressing his cultural accomplishments, and by attributing to him merely the intention of partitioning Poland, at a time when the Russians wanted to annex the lot. They were not prepared to go any further on this 'matter of national feeling' which was as sensitive for them as the Treaty of Versailles for the Germans.[289]

As the negotiations moved backwards over time, the Germans sought to introduce some historical relativism. It was meaningless to condemn the German Knights for 'murder and arson' because 'the entire conduct of warfare in those times was brutal on all sides'. Finally, they cleared up misunderstanding resulting from the sentence in a Polish book that 'Poland was irritated by the fact that it had to justify itself before the League of Nations on account of unjustified charges which resulted from the misunderstanding or even ill-will of the plaintiffs' by assuring the Germans that the sentence was 'aimed in the first instance at Lithuanians, Jews and Ruthenians who caused particular difficulties'.

In addition to Aubin, representing the NODFG, the PuSte was involved in monitoring Polish press responses to the conferences – the *Kurjer Poznanski* took the opportunity to criticize the numbers of Jews who wrote textbooks[290] – and in keeping the delegates supplied with extracts from controversial books. In July 1938, for example, Fitzek asked the PuSte for more material; he had not combed through primary-school textbooks, to counter Polish objections to recent German publications. He also requested materials on atlases, geography, and teacher-training manuals.[291] The PuSte counselled against drawing in geography books, as this would occasion yet more Polish complaints against German books.[292] They also sent the delegates lists of extracts, and reports on particular books, for use at the negotiating table. They culled sentences like 'The thieving Vandals . . . pillaged Rome without pity' or 'It resulted in an inundation . . . by the Teutonic hordes' from J. Dabrowski's *Historja* (1930–3); ironic references to Heinrich V 'bringing the corpses of his soldiers back from Poland as tribute'; or representations of Frederick Wilhelm I as 'brutal, without cultural interests', 'the sergeant-king'. In Jakóbiec's *Deutschland und die Deutschen* (1919), a German book for the sixth class, they isolated passages like: 'The colonists who went to the hostile East, to the joyless young German settlement of Berlin, were either practically or entirely disinherited. They were energetic, booty-hungry and freedom-seeking people, disinherited sons, the oppressed, propertyless and the like who did not have a very good reputation at home', as well as the author's use of French loan-words (*Spirituosen*, *Gendarm* etc.), and the Polish form of Warsaw, which they felt were inappropriate in a German-language reader.[293]

In addition to these conferences, the PuSte also dealt with error in school books much closer to home. In May 1938 the archives in Elbing contacted Brackmann about W. Eggers's *Harms Grossen Schulatlas* (Leipzig 1938), in which a map had been published which maintained that in 1466 West Prussia became an integral part of Poland. Since this could be used by Polish propagandists, the archivists wanted 'forcible measures' and 'definite guidelines' which would 'force publishers not to bring anything out that offended against these formulations'.[294] The PuSte's cartographic expert Franz Doubek assured them that the shortcomings in the atlas 'would disappear', for 'it is a special responsibility of our office not only to isolate such flaws but to take care that they are eradicated'.[295] On the same day he wrote to the RuPMdI, Foreign Office, VOMI and education ministry to get the offending map removed.[296] The authorities ordered the publishers, List and Bressendorf, to revise the map.[297] Doubek's request that the archives in Elbing keep him abreast of similar errors resulted in a stream of offending extracts. Karl Kasiske had not drawn attention to an error in F. Mager's *Geschichte der Landeskultur Westpreussens und des Netzebezirks bis zum Ausgang der polnischen Zeit* in his review. The last three words of the title made certain assumptions that Kasiske should have challenged.[298] Inevitably, at no point in either the German–Polish Conferences, or the monitoring activities of the PuSte, were the larger presumptions that history was a developing 'national story', or an extended hike from one kingly peak to the next, subjected to any form of criticism. For that would have challenged the function of the subject as a means of reinforcing prejudice in depth while obliterating any wider, critical, perspectives, designed to broaden rather than contract the mind.

vi. *Jomsburg*: journal of the north and east

The NODFG leadership structure was reorganized in 1937.[299] Hitherto it had consisted of a committee of five: Brackmann and Papritz from the PuSte, Aubin from the *Osteuropa-Institut*, Oberländer from Königsberg and Walter Recke representing Danzig. In 1937 this was replaced by a smaller panel consisting of Brackmann and Aubin and two administrators, Papritz and Kohte, with two regional and subject advisory councils. In 1938 these included:

Regional Council[300]

Baethgen (Königsberg) *East Prussia*	Spohr (Dorpat) *Estonia*
Recke (Danzig) *Danzig*	Wittram (Riga) *Latvia*
Diestelkamp (Stettin) *Pomerania*	Lattermann (Poznań) *Poland*
Schmitz (Schneidemühl) *Grenzmark*	Lück (Poznań) *Poland*
Aubin (Breslau) *Silesia*	Kauder (Katowice) *Poland*
Kötzschke (Leipzig) *Saxony*	Weizsäcker (Prague) *Czechoslovakia*
Holst (Kiel) *Schleswig-Holstein*	Obersdorffer (Brüx) *Czechoslovakia*
Rörig (Berlin) *Baltic*	Gierach (Munich) *Czechoslovakia*

Subject Council[301]

Economics: Oberländer (Greifswald), Seraphim (Leipzig)
Volkskunde: Helbok (Leipzig), Kuhn (Breslau), Schier (Leipzig)

Geography: Krebs (Breslau), Creutzburg (Dresden), Mortensen (Göttingen)
Art history: Frey (Breslau), Heimpel (Dresden), Kestner (Greifswald)
Demography: Ipsen (Königsberg)
History: Pleyer (Königsberg)
Ecclesiastical history: Koch (Breslau)

By the end of the same year the regional council had risen to 28 while there were 26 subject advisers. Brackmann decided who was to be asked to join.[302] Those invited included Professor Otto Reche who became the NODFG expert adviser on *Rassenkunde* in September 1939.[303]

The NODFG conferences, whose costs were covered by the RMdI and Foreign Office,[304] were the occasions upon which the *Ostforscher* met and upon which they heard the government line on particular issues. The theme discussed was usually appropriate to the location of the conference, although it is important to remember that excursions to local sights, and informal contacts, were as important as anything set down in the formal minutes of the meetings. In late March–early April 1935 the *Ostforscher* descended upon the VDA 'Erzgebirgsheim' at Schellerhau about 30 kms from Dresden and 3 kms from the Czechoslovak border. The area was heavily wooded and isolated and although the hundred-bed establishment was *kein Luxushotel* it served as a suitably out of the way meeting-place for Sudeten Germans.[305] Any equivocation over the politicization of scholarship along the lines of the debate at Kahlberg was resolved by Brackmann's opening words that:

> the times are gone in which anyone can do what he liked. Our scholarly research will be involved wherever it is necessary to support and promote the interests of Germandom. We must all rationalise our academic efforts and let them be determined by one great thought: how can my work be of use to my fatherland? In other words political aims but scholarly methods. We will allow ourselves to be advised by the political authorities but we remain researchers with our own responsibilities.[306]

Erich Maschke thought that they should 'certainly' follow general political aims and directives but should avoid 'artificial politicisation' through work carried out at the behest of the state. However they should not miss the opportunity – and few of his audience or he himself did – to participate in the political educational activities of the various organizations concerned with the East.[307] Although busy with his new chair in Jena, Maschke's time was mostly taken up with educational–political work on behalf of the NSDAP and SA.[308]

In early September 1935 the NODFG reconvened at Landsberg in the Neumark. The accent here was as much on tourism as upon scholarship. Thirty-seven *Ostforscher* attended as well as *Regierungspräsident* Budding, and Essen from the RMdI. They were given a tour of Zantoch by Unversagt, and lectures on the archaeological dig by Unversagt and Lüpke, and wandered through the *Schloss* Filehne with the Graf von der Schulenbühl who treated them all to breakfast. They visited Schneidemühl to applaud Papritz's archival outpost and, after a tour of the *Landesmuseum*, settled down to a long lecture by Brackmann on 'Pomerania and Poland in the earliest times'. On Friday 6 September they went north to visit a forge at Kramski, and on to Flatow for more lectures. The *Oberpräsident* of the province Brandenburg Frick warned that conflicts in the Grenzmark should not upset the larger brushmarks of the Führer's policies:

> Everyone, right down to the last peasant and agricultural labourer must carry the idea of the mission which is to be performed on the frontier for the German nation. It is necessary that suitable people come East; the Grenzmark needs personalities! It is absolutely necessary to improve the standard of living in the province so that people are not only drawn here, but stay here.[309]

The same theme of enduring commitment to life on the frontier was picked up by *Regeirungspräsident* Kohte. Following a lecture by Papritz on ways to stimulate *Heimatforschung*, the party visited 'an ethnic-politically endangered village', the ruins of a castle and a BDO agricultural-labour unit before boarding the night express back to Berlin.[310]

In May 1937 the NODFG conference was held at Stolpmünde in East Pomerania. There were 64 participants, including Poralla from the Foreign Office, Sieg from the BDO and the ubiquitous Essen from the RMdI. Following Brackmann's customary attack on the rival Polish institutes in Toruń and Katowice, the conference settled down to gloomy accounts of local depopulation and economic backwardness, and a series of lectures designed to strip the Kashubians of their Polish nationality. Holmeister from Greifswald insisted on his conviction 'that there was no Kashubian nationality, the Kashubians are . . . Pomeranians and the name only designates their tribe'.[311] Simoleit from Lauenburg wanted more attention paid to the early history of

Pomerania and, in particular, to the 'bitter defensive struggle by the Pomeranians against the Poles' and the former's 'rapid, pacific, germanisation'. Werner Fast from the PuSte introduced a scientific note by stressing the affinities between Kashubian and the (dead) 'Polabian' tongue.[312] After excursions to a work camp in Bütow, folk-dancing in a school courtyard, and an evening meal in the hotel *Preussenhof*, the party assembled for a lecture by Kaiser on 'Problems of Ethnicity in the *Kashubei*'. Gluttons for punishment, the *Ostforscher* heard that very few Slav settlements in Pomerania were in fact of Slav origin, and that 'in the light of modern research the curve of Slavic phenomena in the whole of Pomerania has sunken to zero'.[313]

The journal *Jomsburg. Völker und Staaten im Norden und Osten Europas* made its first appearance in 1937. It was edited by Papritz and Koppe[314] with an editorial committee consisting of Brackmann, Aubin, Oberländer, Recke, Rörig, Scheel and Uebersberger. Each number cost about 3,000 RMs to produce – with a shop price of 5 RMs per annum – and the PuSte's publishers, Hirzel in Leipzig, were responsible for publishing it.[315] Production costs were covered by the RMdI.[316] The professed object of *Jomsburg* was to make scholarship available to a wider audience in an unpedantic format. To this end, 'essays which show the broader developments, surveys of the present state of research, and general accounts will be preferred above academic minutae'.[317] Among those particularly keen on popularizing the fruits of *Ostforschung* – which suffered from considerable tedium – was Vollert of the RMdI.[318] Having toyed with the rather flat *Nord- und Osteuropäische Rundschau* the editors decided to adopt the more resounding title as a

> way of expressing the historical juxtaposition of Teutons and Slavs in eastern Europe. Jomsburg was one of the first examples of these encounters. It stood at the beginning of a development in the history of relations between Teutons and Slavs in which the Germans were the fertilising element both politically and culturally for the Slavs ... In the entire north and among historically educated circles in the East, Jomsburg is a live concept.

Apart from the fact that it conjured up longships slinking out of Baltic ports, there were other, subtle reasons for the name.

> It is one of the first examples of the characteristically east European incongruity of state and nation, which is the precondition, and at the same time end result of the Teutonic–Germanic political and cultural

mission. The Sound and Carpathians, Elbe and Western frontier of Russia encompass an area which natural features hardly delineate and in which for centuries races of different types in their multi-formed, intermingled and colourful confusion have made the formation of national state boundaries difficult up to our own times.[319]

So much for the public profile of the journal. In fact it was to be the organ of the scholars involved in the NODFG – although this was never admitted publicly – and the German equivalent of the Baltic Institute's *Baltic Countries*, with a similar emphasis upon recruiting foreign scholars to lend partisanship an air of international complicity.[320] Although the PuSte–NODFG–government connection was never mentioned, they were all closely bound up with the journal.[321] In the course of suggesting to Hirzel that the latter might avail themselves of the *Reichsstelle zur Förderung des deutschen Schriftums*'s advertising facilities (they had those of the VDA and BDO), Papritz emphasized that 'one cannot make it public knowledge that the periodical serves the interests of German propaganda in eastern and western countries'.[322] A too obliging testimonial for *Jomsburg* by the *Reichsstelle* had to be drastically altered lest 'our propaganda aims are uncovered by interested circles abroad whereby we would not only destroy all the possibilities of involvement by well-known foreign scholars but also hand over to hostile foreigners (especially the Poles) the desired material to discredit German scholarship as a whole'.[323] Consequently a passage in the testimonial that read 'It serves, through rigorous academic research, German propaganda in Eastern and Northern European countries and will be an effective barrier to well-known Polish publications' became 'It has the task of dealing with historical and political questions in East and Northern European countries through rigorous academic research'.[324] The aims of the journal were expressed more explicitly in a letter from Papritz to Professor Ipsen in Königsberg dated 15 January 1934:

It involves critically observing the academically important literature of the Baltic peoples and Poles beyond our own frontiers; bringing to light hostile tendencies; giving recognition to those authors who are ideologically near to us, paving the way for good relations with academics in neutral countries who are still sceptical towards us, especially in the nordic states and Estonia; and to combat the intellectual hegemony of liberals, Marxists, Jewish and Jewish-connected academics in the North who today determine public opinion in those countries. Every academic of any political significance for the Baltic region will have his say.[325]

News of the journal was brought to the anticipated readership – teachers and the young in general[326] – through prospectuses circulated through the VDA and BDO apparatuses, or through academics with contacts in the Nazi press.[327] Thus Professor Habicht in Hannover offered to write a piece about *Jomsburg* in 'the leading National Socialist organ' of Lower Saxony, the *Tageszeitung*, and to spread the word among the *Gau* leadership and at the university.[328] Habicht also volunteered the information that the editors of *Jomsburg* should be careful if they were thinking of commissioning anything from Professor J. Roosvel in Stockholm 'who is certainly Swedish but a pupil of the Jew A. Goldschmidt and is hardly a friend of Germany today'.[329] But sometimes the enthusiasm of the friends of Germany had to be curtailed. In June 1938 Koppe communicated with Brackmann about copy for the latest number. Most of the essays were 'avowedly political' but they were going to include a neutral piece 'in order to underline the "objectivity" and pure scholarliness of the journal'. He had read a long essay entitled 'The Nordic States in Europe' by the Norwegian Aal but,

> his views are so pro-German and so anti the liberal-democratic West European great powers, and above all England; the League of Nations; and the USSR, that similar opinions from a German author would be immediately rejected abroad as tendentious. However since his work does not lack quotations and because he is a representative of the otherwise anglophile Norwegian people, his account may excite the greatest interest inside and beyond Germany. In any event, my expectations of Aal have been fulfilled.[330]

The ground rules for soliciting the work of foreigners were set down by Brackmann in a letter to Professor Friedrich Metz dated 15 June 1937:

> It is naturally not right that we ask foreigners to contribute to the *Deutsche Archiv* or *Jomsburg* and then afterwards send their essays back because they used other ethnic concepts than our own. Naturally we will send back attacks on modern Germany but foreigners must be given the chance to put their views openly otherwise the collaboration is pointless.[331]

The editors left their contributors in no doubt as to the themes to be stressed. Professor W. Boek was asked to 'mention each time the Germandom of the artists you mention' in an art-historical piece; Werner Conze, commissioned to write an article on ethnic minorities, was asked to emphasize 'how the territories concerned became a part of the Polish state and what was the fate of the populations under Polish rule', while Aubin was keen that *Jomsburg* should include treatments of 'ethnic biology or racial studies or something similar'.[332]

The Polish response to the journal was unfavourable. Admitting the correspondence with *Baltic Countries*, one commentator noted that *Jomsburg* was a symbol of 'germanic expansionism onto primeval Slav soil'. The presence of Aubin, Brackmann, Oberländer and Recke on the editorial board and the noticeably few foreign collaborators, called for a certain scepticism.[333] By November 1938 *Jomsburg* was banned in Poland.[334] In September 1937 Koppe was also prevented from distributing 150 free copies of his 'objective, distinguished and genuinely scholarly journal' at a conference in Riga.[335]

The staff of the PuSte were among the most regular contributors to what was, after all, their house journal. This was one result of Papritz's circularized injunction to contribute, complete with areas of interest marked against their names.[336] Areas of responsibility included Schaeder (political history 1772–1815); Doubek (geography and minority cartography, statistics); Loessner (military and naval); Conze (north-east Poland); Kossmann (geography and Poland) and Seraphim (Jews).[337] The shorter notes kept a watchful eye upon rival Polish institutes and journals. For example in 1937 it was noted that *Baltic Countries* defined its territory by claiming that Norway, Germany and Russia were not predominantly 'Baltic' in their geographical orientation.[338] An article by Loessner also chronicled the genesis of the *Liga Morska*, giving details of its membership, journals, leadership and income.[339] There were also reports on Hitler's ban on further acceptance of the Nobel Prize following the episode of the 'traitor' Ossietzsky, and information, culled from the reports of the Polish Central Statistical Office, on the decline of Poland's Jewish population.[340]

One of the first scholars to get in on the ground floor, so to speak, was Peter-Heinz Seraphim whose research project on the Jews of Eastern Europe we considered in an earlier section. In September 1937 he offered to write an article on the 'economic disharmony of Poland' whose object was to correlate regional economic performance with nationality.[341] A month later he suggested further articles, on either the industries in Poland that might prove vital to its wartime economy, or an article on the eastern European Jewish ghetto and its influence upon eastern European towns.[342] This idea appealed to Papritz who thought that Seraphim might like to include sketch maps showing where the ghettos were situated in the towns concerned.[343] In December and in the New Year, Seraphim sent maps of the ghetto in Wilna, charts giving the percentages of Jews in the Polish urban population, and photographs from his collection of shots of Jewish street-life.[344]

The article 'Das Ostjüdische Ghetto' dealt with the progressive urbanization of the Jewish population of eastern Europe in the late nineteenth century. It was copiously illustrated with simple maps and tables and a large number of photographs of ghetto life. The butchers, rabbis and coach-drivers occasionally smile quizzically at the photographer, but for the most part seem absorbed in their conversations or labours. It is as well to realize that for the most part they would soon be dead. Seraphim ascribed the process of urbanization and emigration not to any local difficulties in the acquisition of land but to 'the immanent compulsion to wander' of a race 'that felt foreign everywhere and which could therefore easily abandon their homes because unlike the indigenous population, they were not bound by ties of tradition, blood or relations with their surroundings'.[345] Medieval Jewish ghettos, he emphasized, were formed voluntarily both to 'protect' their Jewish inhabitants from pogroms, and so that the Jews themselves might maintain their own religion through a lessening of the possibilities of assimilation. Such population concentrations 'brought certain health disadvantages for the Jewish population'.[346] However, these ghettos were 'the great source of strength of Jewry' for, unlike other peoples, upon whom urbanization had a 'biologically destructive' effect, the Jews had accustomed themselves during two thousand years to urban life.[347] The ghettos were usually centrally situated in the older parts of towns where the Jews had taken over plots vacated by their German predecessors. This 'pattern' could be observed in the modern textile town of Łódź:

Today ⅖ths of the population of the *Altstadt* is Jewish, entire streets are totally occupied by Jews. An ever stronger movement of Jews from this Jewish core-ghetto runs from the north to the south following the north-south business and residential streets of Łódź along the Petrikauerstrasse. The shops here are for the most part in Jewish hands and, as we shall see, so are the residential houses.[348]

If the ghetto was a 'protective wall' to maintain Jewry, it was also a basis for expansion 'because in the ghetto lay a concentrated economic force that strived for the Judaization of the whole of urban economic life'.[349] This 'force' manifested itself in domination of the urban property market which was 'planned' with the 'connivance' of the rabbis. But this accumulation of property did not result in any improvement in living standards among urban Jews. On the contrary, the houses were desperately overcrowded, with 24 per cent of the inhabitants in a Jewish quarter of Warsaw living seven to a room and only a third of the houses in Warsaw and a fifth of those in Łódź possessing lavatory facilities. The 'social-hygienic condition' in the ghettos was 'extremely unfavourable'.[350] Remarking that 'although it sounds contradictory', Seraphim maintained that the overcrowded, barracks-like, dwellings harboured not only property speculators and religious zealots, but 'the most radical communists' and children who, 'through above average achievement', would eventually dominate politics, academe and the liberal professions. The implications for the states concerned 'needed only to be hinted at'.[351] Despite their predominance in the towns, the Jews had little influence upon architectural forms. He ascribed this creative 'sterility' to the sinister fact that the Jews sought to push into the towns without being noticed. *Therefore* they frequently hid their specifically Jewish communal buildings, like prayer rooms, schools etc. in out of the way corners and backyards in the Jewish ghettos. Nonetheless, the Jews managed to introduce an 'oriental note' into urban life with their 'strange' feasts, Hebrew shop signs, kosher butchers, hairstyles and dress, as well as 'the specific oriental smell' emanating from within their dwellings. The overall effect, he wrote, was 'non-European'. Fear of the foreign merged with fear of the poor. In a few years, Seraphim, expert economist, would be working on the 'rationalisation' of the Polish economy. Tidying up the economy entailed 'resettling' the Jews: the price of olfactory offence was high.

Many of the *Ostforscher* connected with the PuSte and NODFG were also authors of educational pamphlets for the BDO. Links with the latter were particularly close after 19 October 1934 when the director of the IoW, Theodor Oberländer, became the leader of the BDO.[352] Until October 1937, when he was replaced by SS-*Oberführer* Hermann Behrends and SS-*Brigadeführer* Hoffmeyer, the *Ostforscher* were dealing with one of their own.[353] Although the Hitler–Piłsudski Pact imposed restraints on the public activities of the BDO, so that from 1934 to 1938 it operated more or less in the shadows, Oberländer adopted a Clausewitzian view of relations between government foreign policy and the BDO's 'unofficial' propagation of German ethnic consciousness:

> The struggle for ethnicity is nothing other than the continuation of war by other means under the cover of peace. Not a fight with gas, grenades, and machine-guns, but a fight about homes, farms, schools, and the souls of children, a struggle whose end, unlike in war, is not foreseeable as long as the insane principle of the nationalism of the state dominates the Eastern region, a struggle which goes on for generations with one aim: extermination![354]

Oberländer's political philosophy, before he became a minister in Adenauer's regime, can be seen in a *tour d'horizon* he delivered in June 1937 under the title *Der Kampf um das Vorfeld*. The lecture began with the duality of state and nation which enabled him to establish a two-tier policy, consisting of the foreign policy of the state – the Ten Year Pact – and the struggle between ethnic groups. The object of the latter should be to draw the inhabitants of the central eastern European region towards Germany. This entailed stressing everything that was 'deleterious to the Communist drive forwards'. However, there were economic, political and structural faults in the central European states. They had 'gone over to the principle of authoritarianism', but 'had not consciously parted company with liberalism'. Poland, for example, was *ein weltanschauliches Chaos* and *Etatismus* the precursor of communism. The standard-bearers of communism in the region were the Jewish urban proletariat, rural proletariat and 'academic proletariat'.

> The east European Jews are, in so far as they are not orthodox but assimilated Jews, the most active carriers of communist ideas. Since Poland alone has 3.5 million Jews, of which over 1.5 million can be regarded as assimilated Jews, and since the Jews live in scarcely credible adverse social conditions in the urban ghettos, so that they are proletarians in the truest sense, they have little to lose but much to gain. They are the ones who are peddling the most militant and successful propaganda for communism in the countryside.[355]

The positive features of the scene included an 'army' of 8 million ethnic Germans and the anti-Semitism of the non-Jewish rural population of eastern Europe.

> The East European peasant . . . is a pronounced anti-Semite. Conversation with various peasants has always shown that respect for a Germany that has taken on the struggle with Jewry is uncommonly high, and through that sympathy with us, but only among the peasants.[356]

However, there were negative factors at work. In line with what he would later observe in the occupied eastern regions, Oberländer drew attention to the bad impression created by German arrogance towards other peoples and the 'unhappy' image of Germany created by a football crowd that had recently descended upon Warsaw. The German minorities should try to exhibit *ein kleines Drittes Reich in sich*, which would check the expansion of communism. The German minorities were to receive ideological encouragement but not assistance in subverting the host states with the exception of their 'liberal ideological properties'. Mastery of this 'apron' area was not to be underestimated as a form of 'preparation' for 'a power-political conflict'.[357]

Preparatory work included monitoring the activities of the 1,200,000 Poles living in Germany, including a card index of 'frontier-political untrustworthy' Poles and Germans; a campaign to 'germanise' Polish place, street and family names in the eastern regions and, as we have seen, efforts to foster German national consciousness at the expense of Sorbian ethnicity in Lusatia.[358]

If the BDO leaders attended the NODFG conferences, the PuSte staff and *Ostforscher* in general supplied the BDO with lecturers and authors of pamphlets. The PuSte was consulted about a speaker on matters Czech in March 1937; Aubin, Kuhn and Rörig lectured at the BDO meeting in Passau in December 1937, and Kohte spoke on 'The Political Scholarship of our Slav neighbours' at a meeting of the Greater Berlin BDO group.[359] When the BDO wanted to rework its educational material, it turned to the PuSte for translations of works that 'make it easy to recognise the mentality of the ethnic-political enemy and his fighting stance against Germandom'.[360] The PuSte obliged with extracts from *inter alia* Anton Plutyński's *Silesia and Pomerelia*, which was designed for Polish troops 'so that they should know what the struggle with Germany is about'.[361] Many of those we have encountered were responsible for the BDO educational pamphlets, each adorned with a swastika superimposed upon the German Order's shield: Werner Conze, *Die weissrussische Frage in Polen*;

Gerhard Sappok, *Das Deutschtum des Veit Stoss*; Peter-Heinz Sera-phim, *Das Judentum in Osteuropa*; Walter Kuhn, *Die deutsche Leis-tung in Ostmitteleuropa*; Friedrich Baethgen, *Die Anfänge des älteren polnischen Staates*; Erich Maschke, *Die treibenden Kräfte in der Entwicklung Polens*; Hermann Aubin, *Die deutsche Leitung in Ostmit-teleuropa*; H. Brückner, *Die gemischtsprachliche Bevölkerung der Lausitz*; Hans Mortensen, *Das Memelgebiet- Die Geschichte seiner Besiedlung* and the PuSte's own *Träger der polnischen Auslands-propaganda*.

vii. New enemies, new friends: Brackmann, Walter Frank and the SS

Late in September 1936 Brackmann received the following letter from Göring:

> Upon reaching the age limit you will be retiring on 1 October 1936. In 1929 you gave up many years of scholarly activity and took up, as General-Director of the State Archives, responsibility for the adminis-tration of the Prussian archives. It is due above all to your ceaseless efforts and creative energy that they have become the foundation for the future organisation of the archives of the Reich. I regard this result as the best form of recognition of your dutiful service to the province of Prussia, for which I, in the name of the Prussian State government, would like to express my especial gratitude.
>
> Heil Hitler!
> Göring[362]

A few days later *Staatssekretär* Körner presented Brackmann with a severance certificate in the Prussian Ministry of State.[363] As we have seen, Brackmann was anything but retired after 1936, although he did relinquish control of the administration of the archives to Zipfel, and had to vacate his villa in the Archivstrasse.[364] Since he was obvi-ously still in the best of health, to prise his grip from the archives by rigorously enforcing the retirement limit, rather than allowing him to soldier on until he was sixty-eight, was unusual. In the German academic profession as a whole, years of enforced asceticism meant that only those with nerves of steel got to the top. In 1907 the average age of a full professor at Berlin university was sixty and, after the rigours of the climb, those who reached the summit of their profession liked to stay there.[365] The conventional accounts of Brackmann's 'fall'

– which already evokes the world of Danton or Marat rather than that of a Prussian professor – is that 'he could not compromise either as a man or as a scholar with the new totalitarian course'.[366] The facts are more prosaic, involve no issues of principle, and largely concern the *homo novus* of National Socialist historical writing, Walter Frank. In the months when the latter's candidature for the directorship of the projected *Reichsinstitut für die Geschichte des neuen Deutschlands* was being mooted, Frank detected alarming signals that hostile forces in the Education Ministry were tending towards the appointment of 'a liberal *Geheimrat* of the old school', which in Frank's beleaguered world view, meant a member of the entrenched, 'liberal', academic mafia. This had serious implications for one whose mission in life was to rise to power and good fortune on the wave of committed scholarship and over the bodies of those against whom he launched his campaigns of destruction.

Although the precise circumstances remain unknown, for one could not dispose of Brackmann with the ease with which Frank had publicly character-assassinated Hermann Oncken, Frank claimed credit for toppling Brackmann, whom he over-generously described as 'this pillar of liberal and pro-Jewish academicism'.[367] His self-congratulation was a little premature, as in Brackmann he had an opponent endowed with as much low-cunning and vindictiveness as himself, tempered with years of experience of bureaucratic in-fighting. If Frank's description of Brackmann as being part of 'a grand coalition' to effect his downfall was characteristically overwrought, there is no doubt that Brackmann was on the lookout for any means, fair but preferably foul, to avenge himself on Frank. In 1937 Brackmann informed Himmler that there were materials in a repository of the Geheime Staatsarchiv which would 'yield important contributions to a characterization of Mr Walter Frank'.[368] Himmler deputed Heydrich to scour the sources.

No, Brackmann's 'fall' was more like the temporary jolt of switching points than injurious derailment. The contacts with the SS, a potent new ally, multiplied. After all, there was certain common ground – the Ottonians for instance – between the former General-Director and the modest polymath in the Prinz-Albrecht-Strasse. In November 1938 Brackmann wrote to the *Reichsführer* about SS archaeological excavations in the imperial palace at Quedlinburg. The SS archaeologists had unearthed the tombstone of Otto III's aunt, the abbess Matilda, whose inscription indicated that Otto had given her the title *patricia* of

Saxony while he was in Italy. The discovery evidently illuminated – in a sense that was unfavourable to Poland – the relationship between the German emperor and Boleslaw of Poland – his *patricius* – in 1000. This subject concerned Brackmann. He informed Himmler that:

> It does not merely lie in the interests of research but also in those of the scholarly underpinning of our German *Kulturpolitik* in the East, if a photographic reproduction or a reliable transcription could be made available.[369]

In May 1939 he sent the *Reichsführer* a copy of his article *Otto III und die staatliche Umgestaltung Polens und Ungarn*, drawing Himmler's attention to his use of the Quedlinburg inscription on pages 16–19.[370] An aide assured Brackmann that the piece would be set before the *Reichsführer* when he returned from an official journey.[371] Regular gifts of books to the enlightened amateur, in September 1939 Erich Keyser's *Geschichte des Weichsellandes*, ensued.[372]

Apart from these tokens of recognition, Brackmann entered into closer contact with the SS as an author for the SS *Ahnenerbe Verlag*. They paid well. On 26 September 1939 SS-*Untersturmführer* Dr Kaiser wrote to Brackmann setting out the terms under which he should produce 'a political-academic booklet' on the 'political history and destiny of Poland and Eastern Europe'. This venture into history and prophecy had to be ready in three weeks, and Brackmann would receive the royal sum of 500 RMs, and royalties of 10 per cent, on editions after the initial run of 5,000 copies. The booklet was to be a form of 'intellectual liquidation' of Poland, a reckoning before world history, for *Weltgeschichte=Weltgericht*. The Leitmotif of the work was that *Mitteleuropa* was the original *Lebensraum* of the German nation. German expansion westwards was the result of Roman Christian attempts to destroy German self-consciousness, by seducing the barbarians away from where their inner compulsion led them. A continuum of German purposiveness and dominance in the East stretched from Heinrich I, via Frederick the Great, Bismarck and, after a diversionary lapse under Weimar governments, to Hitler.[373]

There is a different account of the genesis of the booklet by Brackmann written in 1946. Referring to diary entries, Brackmann claimed that after an 'unsettling' visit from Dr Kaiser on 25 September, he had been assured by Papritz and Unversagt that the *Ahnenerbe Verlag* was only interested in purely scholarly publications. Having decided to set pen to paper on their behalf, he handed over the manuscript to Dr Kaiser on 20 October, and was told that it would be printed shortly. He scrutinized the proofs late on 27 October. In between the corrections and printed version, Brackmann claimed drastic alterations had been made. The title was no longer *The German role in the development of the East* but *Crisis and construction in Eastern Europe*. There were historical errors such as 'Heinrich I conquered France for Germany', and a number of quotations from *Mein Kampf* had been introduced without his knowledge. It was too late, he was told, for changes to be made. Apart from these alterations, and parts of the booklet do not read as though they are by the same author, in 1946 he declared himself satisfied with a booklet that was by then on an Allied index.[374]

Leaving aside the fact that Brackmann did not mind writing the booklet on the terms set out in Kaiser's letter, the *Ahnenerbe* records tell a rather different story. To begin with, Brackmann was fully in agreement with the new, short title – not that this matters much – when he wrote to Kaiser on 28 September 1939.[375] The *Ahnenerbe* staff only sent parts of the booklet to SS-*Standartenführer* Professor Dr Six of the SD-Hauptamt for his opinion about three weeks after it had been printed.[376] Moreover, acknowledging a Christmas present from the *Ahnenerbe Verlag*, their latest author made no mention of any objections to the content of the booklet, which was given a second run of 30,000 copies on New Year's Eve. The Wehrmacht bought 7,000 of them.[377] Brackmann hoped that the coming year would bring 'victory and well-being to the Fatherland'. Although some of his colleagues had commented on the booklet in 'a temperamental manner', he was more concerned about how the NSDAP Press had received it. His main concern, however, was not alleged sleights of hand performed on his booklet, but rather that Hans Frank had invited the PuSte to set up a sub-office in occupied Poland for 'cultural–political tasks'.[378]

Apart from the matter of ultimate responsibility for the copious quotations from *Mein Kampf* and appreciative references to the works of Kurt Lück, the booklet reflects what were probably Brackmann's enduring preoccupations expressed in a simplified form. He began with the axiom that 'the unmistakable lesson of history is that Europe only has peace and quiet as long as the hegemony of Germany in *Mitteleuropa* is secure'. This hegemony existed in the Bronze Age and was based upon a higher level of civilization than prevailed among the neighbouring Slavs.

The German people were the only bearers of civilisation in the East, and as the main power in Europe, defended Western civilisation and brought it to the uncivilised nations. For centuries Germany formed an eastern bulwark against lack of civilisation, and protected Europe against barbarism.[379]

The Slavs had merely filtered through into lands occupied by residual Germans, and worked as 'seasonal workers' for the German ruling class. It was as if they were the historic antecedents of the *Ostarbeiter* in the factories of the Ruhr, or on the estates of the East Elbian aristocracy.[380] Throughout the booklet, success and failure – or in other words whatever consolidated or diminished the power of Prussia/Germany – depended upon the personalities of those in power. Frederick Wilhelm III of Brandenburg-Prussia was a failure; he poured troops down the drain of the War of the Spanish Succession. Frederick Wilhelm I was a success, because he renounced territorial expansion in favour of the *Retablissement* in East Prussia. The latter's 'greatest monument' was his son Frederick the Great. He recognized the value of working subjects:

through him and Frederick Wilhelm I, the particular Prussian characteristic was created which knew nothing higher than the duty of incessant work. In this respect, the Prussia of Frederick the Great became the forerunner of modern Germany in which similarly only those people who fulfil their duty within the community of their nation have value.[381]

The booklet's extreme germanocentricity is evident in passages like his discussion of eighteenth-century Austrian settlement in the Banat. The noun German recurs with all the monotony of a hammer striking an anvil:

what the German miners achieved there in mining is demonstrated by the fact that today the Rumanian armaments industry is based upon these mines. Germans were in charge here, Germans provided the skilled labour, the mines of the Banat owe their present prosperity to the Germans.[382]

The subject of these settlements in the Banat served to set the scene for more ominous projects in the present.

Another method was tested in the context of these settlements which will be employed today, as was announced in the Führer's speech of 6 October 1939. Closed bands of Protestant peasants from the Austrian

Alpine region were sent to Transylvania, and this transmigration, which was carried out skilfully and cleverly, proved itself to be very worthwhile.[383]

The Polish Partitions were attributed to the failings of the Polish national character:

> The Poles have always complained about the great wrong that was done to them through the Partitions. But they forget to mention that they themselves bear the greatest responsibility for the decline of their state. History shows that the fundamental fault of the Polish people is their lack of awareness of the possibilities and limitations of their existence as a state.[384]

Oscillating indeterminately between the late eighteenth century and Poland after Piłsudski, Brackmann drew the stark conclusion:

> As in the age of the Jagiellonians and their successors from the house of Vasa [the Poles] were in the grip of an imperialistic drive to conquer, and the end result was the same: Poland ceased to exist.[385]

Brackmann's account of nineteenth-century Prussian and Austrian *Polenpolitik* condemns any halfway measures or concessions. He included in his litany of error, the creation of the Grand Duchy of Warsaw, the recall of Flottwell, 'weak concessions and emotive sympathy for the situation of the stateless Poles' after 1848, the regime of Goluchowski in Austrian Galicia and hesitant employment of the Expropriatory Laws of 1908.[386] By way of contrast, the Flottwell regime, Bismarck's Settlement Law of 1886, and the Expropriation Laws of 1908 received his approval. The section of the booklet that deals with Weimar *Polenpolitik* consistently, and insidiously, seeks to belabour 'democracy' with the charge that governments neglected provision for the German minorities in eastern Europe.

> As if overnight it was clear to the Germans that beyond the frontiers of the German Reich lived Germans with the same blood and same culture, who longed for closer relations with us so that they did not go under in a foreign environment. Political circles held back. Post-war Germany was a democracy like the others. Different criteria played the decisive role. But the souls of those who had been at the front, and who had hoped for a greater Germany after the war, started to burn when they compared the matter of their dreams with what reality had brought them.[387]

Having already employed early modern Muscovite expansionism to legitimize more recent territorial acquisitions by Soviet Russia, Brackmann – or whoever was responsible for this mishmash of puerile *Realpolitik* – concluded on a note of generosity to Nazi Germany's eastern ally:

> We know of Napoleon's expedition against Russia, about the burning of Moscow and the desolation of the crossing of the Beresina. We know too about the disaster that England brought upon Poland recently when it made its 'guarantees'. But we do not know of any cultural achievements of these countries which give them the right to speak about the future of the East.
>
> Only Germany, as the main power in Central Europe and as the only bearer of civilisation in the East for centuries, and Russia, as the strongest political force in the East next to us, have this right. The future of eastern Europe will depend upon the cooperation of these powers.[388]

Thanks to Frank, the SS and SD had conceived an animus against Brackmann as a 'type of wild man' which, on closer inspection, had no rational, political, justification. He had been handled not just 'wrongly' but 'despicably'.[389] Provided his erstwhile status was duly recognized, one could make of Brackmann what one would. That, at least, was the sense of a brief note concerning him which Kaiser wrote in January 1940:

> Professor Brackmann is a university professor in Berlin, before that in Göttingen, Marburg and elsewhere. Became prominent as the General Director of the Prussian Geheime Staatsarchive. Outstanding scholarly and political activity-position in the Prussian bureaucracy comparable with the rank of a general in the army.
>
> Political qualification: directly involved as an expert adviser in the drawing of frontiers in Czechoslovakia and Poland.[390]

Provided one pandered to his sense of self-importance, Brackmann had a utility to the regime far greater than the mere nuisance value of Walter Frank. We must turn to the wartime activities of this 'general' among scholars, and first to the matter of redrawing Germany's eastern frontiers.

4. WAR

i. Hour of the experts: frontiers and resettlement

The *Ostforscher* operated with a simple categorical equipment. Scholarship had to take account of political priorities; politicians were to be advised by academic experts; politicians should not determine the methods or goals of scholarship.[1] These ethical criteria swirled like detritus in a wind-swept square once war broke out. Several factors explain the Gadarene rush to serve the regime. Commitment to similar goals (which were as many as there were NSDAP, State or army agencies ready to implement them) ranging from territorial revisionism to a racialist reordering of Europe. The hubristic desire to be close to decision-making and the march of events. The need to make their work appear 'relevant' or, 'vital to the war effort' to secure government funds. In a few cases, fear that their controlled, revisionist goals would be outpaced by a younger generation bent upon realizing fantasies of 'boundless imperialism' built upon the figure of Otto the Great.[2]

After 1945 the racial experts disappeared like melting snow. The irrationality of their work assisted a process whereby they became an unaccountable and lunatic fringe somehow unconnected with the mainstream of academic life. Prior to that date it was otherwise. Although the voices of the racial experts soared in a shrill descant, increasingly 'respectable' academics were singing their tune. It was the 'respectable' who underwent a process of acculturation. The result was the steady permeation of their work with concepts, methods and practices derived from the developing miasma of racial science. Relations with the racial experts may sometimes have been uneasy, although instances of mutual cooperation are not difficult to find, but in the end capitulation to, and adoption by the 'respectable' of deeply irrational modes of thought is most striking. The racial experts were not some lunatic extra, but a force that exerted a magnetic pull on the rest, a force that derived strength from coincidence and identity with the ideological core of the regime. The tasks of the PuSte during and after the war were outlined in a paper by Papritz dated 30 November 1939. Rehearsing the obligatory Polish academic threat and the German institutional response, Papritz endeavoured to justify continued governmental funding. The PuSte would continue to refute Polish claims, although the latter would, perforce, emanate from Polish exiles in western Europe or the USA. It would also be necessary to carry out an 'intellectual re-conquest', parallel with the work of motorized divisions and bombers.

> The German cultural achievements of past centuries, which have set their seal on the cultural landscape of the occupied areas, the labour of German people in the towns and on the land which created the German 'Kulturboden', the immortal services of the Prussian administration which has left visible traces behind it, these and similar matters will need to be systematically and, since the sources are now at last available to us, finally studied. This research will be one of the principal means of strengthening the legitimacy of German action.[3]

The PuSte would have to liaise closely with the *Gauleiter* and Hans Frank in occupied Poland on the matter of reconstructing (German) research in the occupied territories. There had already been extensive cooperation with other agencies.

> The dissolution of the Czechoslovak state, and still more the Polish crisis, the campaign in Poland and the occupation of the German sphere of interest have had the strongest effects upon the work of the PuSte. The excellent aids produced by the PuSte (specialised library, map collection, index cards etc.), and the staff of qualified linguistic and subject experts were naturally comprehensively consulted by the political and military offices of the Reich (RMdI, Foreign Office, OKH, Ministry of Propaganda and many more) and by the NSDAP.[4]

Orders received for thousands of maps from the army, *Luftwaffe*, and administration were adequate proof of the indispensability of Papritz and his staff. The PuSte was also 'keenly concerned' to produce maps showing communal boundaries, German placenames or the extent of ethnic Germandom. These maps paid for themselves, since a list of Sudeten German placenames and maps of communal boundaries alone had generated 55,000 RMs of income. In addition to its cartographic tasks, the PuSte had also reorientated the Press translation service to cover exile newspapers, while keeping up a stream of propaganda publications which, Papritz claimed, had been used to good effect in the *Völkischer Beobachter* in the weeks immediately prior to the invasion of Poland.[5] Inevitably, war meant a certain distortion in the normal run of PuSte activities. Remarking that 'a large number of offices, especially the ministries in Berlin, have accustomed themselves to getting rapid, specialist, information on eastern questions from the PuSte', Papritz noted the PuSte's involvement in the redrawing of frontiers in the East, resettlement actions and, in the future, renaming places.

> Demographic questions, for whose treatment the PuSte is particularly and demonstrably qualified, will gain in importance. In particular, investigations of the migrations of Germandom and the influx of foreign peoples, and of the fundamental circumstances of earlier German public and private settlement and its success or failure.[6]

These efforts to demonstrate the relevance of the PuSte's brand of expertise were partly a reflection of the need to secure continued ministerial funding. In a letter to *Gauschulungsleiter* Loebsack in Danzig, Papritz drew attention to unspecified, misguided, individuals who thought that 'where the sword has spoken and resettlement is an accomplished fact' scholarship of this sort was 'no longer important'. He thought that the need to stimulate a 'healthy *Heimatgefühl*', in resettled areas, and to 'defend politically both within and without what had been gained' necessitated increased efforts and further resources.[7]

There was little that was immodest in Papritz's *tour d'horizon* of PuSte activities. Brackmann was of the same opinion. In a letter to Professor Friedrich Metz dated 23 September 1939 he observed:

> It gives us great satisfaction to see that the NODFG with its office in the PuSte, is now the central office for scholarly advice to the Foreign Office, RMdI, OKH and in part also the Ministry of Propaganda and a number of SS departments. We have reached the position whereby we will also be comprehensively consulted on the drawing of future frontiers.[8]

Papritz was a member of the Commission dealing with the Sudeten frontier that met in the Foreign Office in October 1938. Although it has been claimed that these measures were carried out with a scientific precision designed to separate conflicting ethnic groups – a view adhered to by some of those responsible – the sources suggest that more prosaic motives were at work.[9] The estates of the Prince Schwarzenberg at Prachatitz had to be kept intact; elsewhere, increased territory would also ensure the integrity (and German domination) of rail-lines or roads bringing access to sawmills; if Theresienstadt became part of Germany on account of its German majority, ethnic scruples about Raudwitz (with 4,050 Czechs and 1,352 Germans) were overcome 'because the rail and road connections to Trebnitz must be united in German hands'. The report concluded that sometimes 'simple ethnographic corrections' had proven impossible and that ethnic criteria had occasionally been abandoned in favour of a more drastic approach, based upon the concept of *Volksboden*. This meant that where the land was largely *owned* by Germans, it was possible to discount the 'mere' numerical predominance of landless Czech labourers.[10] These sophistic criteria were in turn abandoned, to the annoyance of the cartographic experts, when major figures and major interests were involved. Armed with a blue pencil, Göring decided to appropriate an arms factory and aerodrome at Brünn, overruling objections with the remark *Seien Sie ohne Sorge, Brünn holen wir uns*. With the aid of his dotted line (still visible on the maps) between 50,000 and 80,000 Czechs found themselves part of the Reich.[11]

The German–Soviet demarcation line of 28 September 1939 cut Poland into two almost equal parts. All of West, Central, and western South Poland or an area of 188,000 sq kms with some 20,200,000 inhabitants (17,300,000 Poles and 675,000 Germans) came under German domination. Since the Soviet-occupied areas included only 4,700,000 Poles in a population of 11,900,000, some three-quarters of the Polish population was in German hands. In accordance with instructions from Hitler, the occupied territories were to be further subdivided into an area to be incorporated and 'germanised', and another – the *Generalgouvernement* – of indeterminate status, where Poles and Jews were to be 'encapsulated', terrorized, and exploited in an ad hoc, constitutional and legal limbo.[12] The special status of the occupied East was further underlined by the fact that while the customs frontier extended up to the *Generalgouvernement*, the police or 'disease-policing' frontier corresponded with the frontiers of 1919. These dual lines meant that the 'incorporated' areas remained 'foreign', while restricting uncontrolled population movements, and acting as a screen for the major enormities taking place in the East.[13]

The location of the frontiers between the two regions rapidly became a subject of dispute between those in the Foreign Office or RMdI who were against exceeding the bounds of former Prussian territories, and those like Hitler or Göring who sought more 'generous' frontiers, encompassing valuable economic or strategic installations. The result of this unequal contest was the incorporation of the industrial region of Łódź, the extension of Upper Silesia to include Katowice, Königshütte and Austrian Silesia, and of East Prussia towards the south, with a colonial new territory of 12,000 sq kms acound Zichenau.[14] The irrelevance of ethnic niceties to these arrangements can be seen from the fact that of the 4,500,000 inhabitants of the *Warthegau*, 85 per cent were Polish, 8 per cent Jewish, and 7 per cent German. The details of these frontier adjustments were worked out by a commission under Vollert of the RMdI in October and November 1939. Papritz was a member of a sixteen-man commission whose task was to chart the boundaries of a future projected *Reichsgau Beskidenland* stretching from west of Cracow to the San in the east. His colleagues included Springorum from the RMdI, a *Wehrmacht* staff officer, and SS-*Hauptscharführer* Oskar Walther of *Einsatzkommando* I/i. Their report on the new Gau (of some 18,000 sq kms) began with a brief résumé of the demographic difficulties of the region. During the early modern period, the descendants of medieval German colonists had been submerged through catholicism into *Polentum*. However, despite the superficial, numerical predominance of the Poles, 'today German racial characteristics can still be traced in the countryside. The commission noticed the presence of predominantly nordic racial blond persons in the most different places.' This overcame the problem presented by a German element of 1,600 in a Polish, Ukrainian and Jewish population of 2,056,000. In the sections on the various ethnic groups they purported to discover in the region, the commissioners adopted similar racial criteria to cast doubt upon the homogeneity of the Polish population. The *Góralen* (Góra = mountain) mountain shepherds made 'an excellent racial impression although politically and confessionally they are not different from the rest of the Poles'.[15] They had other suggestions too. They counselled against the incorporation of loss-making oilfields, salt works, aircraft, and cellulose factories on the grounds that these had been established by the Poles to cure local unemployment in terms of a (now defunct) industrial plan. Using Oberländer's work on rural overpopulation in Galicia, they advised that in view of the minuscule size of 25–30 per cent of rural holdings, 'in an exchange of populations ten to twelve of the existing units must be merged to create an adequate base for one German settler'.[16] The actual frontier adjustments were made in order to maintain examples of Germandom or to secure German domination of rail junctions, strategic heights, and roads.

The new frontier adjustments in Upper Silesia resulted in the accession to Germany of the industrial area Katowice–Beuthen–Hindenburg–Königshütte, rural districts like Rybnik and Pless, former Austrian (Teschener) Silesia, and part of the districts of Zawiercie and Tschenstochau. Paradoxically, the *Oberpräsident* and *Gauleiter* Josef Wagner was dissatisfied with this increase of 10,000 sq kms and two and a half million inhabitants. On 2 February 1940 he proposed to the RMdI the retraction of the new frontiers. The PuSte's cartographic expert Doubek prepared a report on Wagner's proposals for a discussion held in the RMdI on 27 February. Essentially, Wagner thought that industry in the areas he wished to shed was obsolete, and that the incorporation of 400,000 'national Poles' would 'by their existence encumber the ethnic struggle in east Upper Silesia'. So many Poles would endanger the assimilation of the 'labile in-between class' of Silesian *Wasserpolen*. The loss of chemical, iron, fertilizer and locomotive factories was rationalized with an eye to labour conditions in the *Generalgouvernement*.

> The exploitation of these concerns during the war can carry on if these areas are ceded to the *Generalgouvernement*, perhaps better and certainly more cheaply, because then wages and prices do not need to be comparable.[17]

Although Hans Frank was interested in having the coal reserves of these areas, both he and Wagner were overruled by Hitler, who refused to pull the frontiers back on prestige grounds. The result was the division of Silesia into two *Gaue*.[18]

If Wagner wished to be unencumbered by uneconomic and ethnically dubious territories, his colleague *Gauleiter* Koch in East Prussia sought to extend his East Prussian fiefdom southwards to Płock. The dubiety of the ethnic criteria used to acquire 12,000 sq kms in the district of Zichenau was evident from the fact that 90 per cent of the inhabitants were Poles and 2 per cent Germans.[19] In his submission to the RMdI dated 15 December 1939, which was relayed to the PuSte for expert comment, Koch maintained that the ethnic German 'material' scattered throughout Zichenau was virtually indistinguishable from the surrounding Poles and, consequently, one had to conserve such concentrations of non-assimilated ethnic Germans as existed, even if this involved transferring Płock from the *Reichgau*

Posen (*Warthegau*). Careful where his red lines ran, Koch thought that Płock itself could do without its local town of Gostynin, which he described as 'a little Polish *Drecknest*'. The secret PuSte report conceded that Zichenau had the lowest percentage of Germans in the eastern territories and that hence an increase of 6,000 Germans would be significant. They concluded that the loss of Płock would have no adverse effects upon the *Reichsgau* Posen although the district of Gostynin would lose all coherence.[20]

The corollary of these new frontier arrangements was the forcible deportation of Poles and Jews to the *Generalgouvernement* and the resettlement of ethnic Germans from the Baltic and eastern Poland in the areas incorporated into the Reich. The PuSte and scholars connected with it through the NODFG were concerned in the planning and execution of resettlement actions, a further stage in the instrumentalization of scholarship. From early 1937 onwards there was a concerted drive on the part of the SS to control organizations concerned with ethnic German issues, and hence an area of German foreign policy. In January 1937 Himmler commissioned SS-*Obergruppenführer* Werner Lorenz, a former cavalry officer, estate owner and socialite, to organize an Ethnic German Liaison Office (*Volksdeutsche Mittelstelle*, or VOMI) which was to be the most aggressive attempt to co-ordinate the heterogeneous organizations working in this area.[21] Lorenz infiltrated his VOMI colleagues into positions of influence in organizations concerned with ethnic Germandom, and by 1938 had secured effective powers of veto over funds totalling 50–60 million RMs (equivalent to the entire budget of the Foreign Office for that year) available to these organizations. Both measures tied the ethnic German organizations closer to the changing foreign policy of the Third Reich. In October 1937 Lorenz's deputy SS-*Standartenführer* Dr Hermann Behrends, a jurist who had been instrumental in the founding of the SD, and SS-*Brigadeführer* E. Hoffmeyer pushed Oberländer from the leadership of the BDO, while in April 1937 Steinacher of the VDA was warned by Behrends that either he integrate the VDA into the Nazi movement or he would 'dig his own grave'. In November 1937 Steinacher was retired and replaced (for a short time) by SS-*Führer* Dr Wilhelm Luig.[22] Aptly described as a kind of iceberg, with refugee camps for ethnic Germans showing above the surface, VOMI established contact with the PuSte in April 1938.[23] On 7 April 1938 Papritz was invited by Behrends to discuss draft versions of a map of Germandom in the North East.[24] On 28 April Doubek represented the

NODFG at a conference including representatives of VOMI, the RMdI, DAI (Stuttgart), BDO and Ministry of Propaganda held to discuss small-scale maps of ethnic Germandom. The participants resolved to exclude Jews, assimilated or otherwise, on the grounds that they were not 'rooted in the soil' from cartographical displays, while including 'real nations' like the Germans, Poles and Hungarians.[25] These last concepts were to be subjected to considerable revision in the future. One of the participants suggested that they might proceed 'as if there are no Jews'.[26] On 5 May 1938 Doubek and Papritz again gathered in the offices of VOMI to discuss maps which divided the East into a German 'core area' and 'mixed' and 'scattered' areas.[27]

When Hitler commissioned Lorenz to take charge of resettlements from Latvia and Estonia in September 1939, Himmler outmanoeuvred his lightweight, but accomplished, subordinate by securing a decree dated 7 October 1939 from Hitler charging Himmler himself with the task of 'strengthening ethnic Germandom'. He assumed the portentous title *Reichskommissar für die Festigung deutschen Volkstums* (RKFDV).[28] Himmler proceeded to redistribute the administrative apparatus responsible for resettlements in a way that rendered Lorenz and VOMI one department among many. An RKFDV 'Controlling Office for Immigrants and Repatriates' was established at 142 Kurfürstendamm under the former factory manager SS-*Oberführer* Ulrich Greifelt. The latter was to be responsible for planning and the confiscation of Polish and Jewish property. VOMI would run transit camps and organize transport, and Otto Hoffmann of the RuSHA would assume responsibility for the racial evaluation of the repatriates.[29] Clashes with other powerful competitors in the field of expropriation (including Göring) and the ambitions of the leaders of these SS departments, were in turn minimized by keeping Greifelt's office small, and by farming out much of the technical work to outside experts and agencies.[30] Among those to benefit from this patronage were SS-*Oberführer* Professor Konrad Meyer, Director of the Institute for Agriculture and Agrarian Policy at the University of Berlin who established his own office in the professor's suburb of Dahlem, and the PuSte.[31] Doubek and the PuSte produced maps on the resettlement of the Volhynian Germans in the *Warthegau* from the summer of 1940. In June 1940 Dr von Dietel, of the statistical department of Greifelt's office, sent statistical materials on the Volhynian Germans for Doubek to convert into maps.[32] Pleased with the product, the SS approached Doubek in August 1940 to establish a cartographic section in the planning office at Podbielskiallee 25–27 with a salary of 700–800 RMs per month.[33] Although Doubek rejected the offer because 'most of the work carried out there does not accord with his personal views' and because he was working twelve hours a day in the PuSte's cartographic department, Greifelt persisted.[34] The latter assured the RMdI that he wanted Doubek to deputize for Dr Krause, as leader of the planning office, which would only involve Doubek in supervising academically trained personnel for a few hours a week.[35] With agreement from the RMdI, Doubek's time was divided between the PuSte and department VI/1 (resource and area investigations) of Meyer's group 'C' 'planning':

Monday, Wednesday, Friday	PuSte 8 a.m.–12.30 p.m.
Tuesday, Thursday	1 p.m.–4.30 p.m.
Monday, Wednesday Friday	RKFDV 1 p.m.–4.30 p.m.
Tuesday, Thursday, Saturday	RKFDV 8 a.m.–12.30 p.m.[36]

The maps that Doubek produced for the RKFDV in the calendar year 1941 included:

The settlement of Volhynian Germans in the Wartheland Part 1. 1: 1,000,000

Major classes of settlement corresponding to area plans in the incorporated eastern territories. 1: 1,000,000

The results of the Reich's estimation of resources in the incorporated eastern territories. 16 sheets. 1: 1,000,000

Investigations into former eastern Poland. 20 sheets. 1: 1,000,000

Distribution of the Kashubians 1: 300,000.[37]

The arrangement with the PuSte and Doubek also pleased Konrad Meyer who wished to visit his neighbours in Dahlem to inspect their work, and who thought that the two offices should work closely together in the future.[38] The PuSte also provided information for other agencies. On 23 October 1939 Däumling of the Gestapo telephoned with an urgent request for global statistics, extrapolated from the 1931 census, on the overall population, and proportion of Jews, in towns with 10,000 or more inhabitants in occupied Poland. The task was delegated to Klostermann with instructions to·use confessional rather than nationality or linguistic criteria.[39] A paper entitled 'Proportion of the Jewish population in the overall population of major and administrative Polish towns with over 10,000 inhabitants inside the German sphere of influence' dated 31 October 1939 was acknowledged by the RSHA in early November.[40]

The *Ostforscher* also had plans of their own. In a letter to Brackmann dated 18 September 1939 Aubin reflected with satisfaction on the fact that the 'highest authorities' had agreed with their proposals and hoped that Brackmann would act as a conduit to Vollert and the RMdI for memoranda on 'ethnic questions'.

> We must make use of our experience, which we have developed over many long years of effort. Scholarship cannot simply wait until it is called upon, but must make itself heard.[41]

On 28 September Aubin, Kuhn, Schieder, Birke and Petry gathered in Breslau to discuss the drafting of a memorandum on ethnic relations in the eastern territories. The Berlin group (the PuSte) was to investigate the extent of Polish expropriation of Germans before 1939; Kuhn was to establish the extent of Polish migration into former Prussian territories since 1918, while the Breslau group was to work on the historical pre-conditions for 'large scale settlement policy in the eastern territories'.[42] As part of these proposals, Kohte contacted the Reich's Office for Statistics for information on the estimated numbers of illegal Polish immigrants and *Wanderarbeiter* who had overstayed their welcome.[43] A PuSte memorandum dated 1 November 1939 sought to justify and outline the procedure for future resettlements. The paper rehearsed the demographic collapse of ethnic Germandom in inter-war western Poland, and the influx of Polish migrants, from Galicia and Congress Poland, into Poznania and West Prussia. This had resulted in the 'sinking of the standard of living in the towns and countryside of these areas'.[44] Since the numerical predominance of the Poles had been achieved 'only by force', appropriate 'adjustments of property' would have to occur to redistribute the ethnic balance. It was a matter of the *Wiedergutmachung* of an obvious 'political injustice'. The end goal was to be the 'clear separation of Polish and German ethnic groups which would avoid the dangers of ethnic and racial intermingling and infiltration'.[45] There were two lines to work from. The first was the frontier of 1914, which for centuries had been the borderline between 'two regions on different levels of civilisation', and another that encompassed German settlements strewn amidst a 'mixed population'. The second line had to be consolidated by population transfers. The preconditions for this were the registration of property in German hands in 1918 and the creation of powers to expropriate Poles *en masse*; the immediate expropriation of Poles known to be anti-German; the immediate deportation of Poles who had migrated to Poznania and West Prussia since 1919 and restrictions on the movement of Poles into the frontier areas of the old Reich.[46] Although the author of the paper saw the ideal solution in terms of Polish emigration overseas, he confronted the problems arising from overpopulation in the Polish *Reststaat*. The solution lay either in 'getting the Jews out of the Polish towns' or through intensified economic production in Poland to support an inflated population.

> The question of what will become of the Poles who are resettled is not a matter of indifference to the Reich: the removal of the Jews from *Restpolen* and the construction of a healthy ethnic order demands the employment of German resources and forces but brings the danger of the development of a new Polish ruling class from a new Polish bourgeoisie.[47]

With plans and administrative structures developing very rapidly, it was natural that those *Ostforscher* at a remove from Berlin should regard the PuSte as a source of information, and as a conduit for relaying their own ideas to the authorities. Otto Reche was one of the first to volunteer his services through the NODFG to the regime. On 19 September 1939 Reche sought an urgent meeting with Brackmann; reflecting upon thirty years of experience of 'racial and demographic–political questions', he insisted that 'we need *Raum* but no Polish lice in our fur'.

> I am absolutely of the opinion that the racial–scientific side is determinative in the solution of all of these questions since we do not want to build a German people in the East in the future that would only be a linguistically germanised, racial mishmash, with strong asiatic elements, and Polish in character. That would be no German *Volk*, nor a corner stone for a German future! . . . Since I also know the anthropological conditions in Poland and know what is racially and hereditarily useful in this people and what at all events is to be driven out of the German settlement area, I believe I have gathered together in the course of many years several ideas which should now be used for the general good and for our future.

It would be tantamount to a dereliction of duty (*Pflichtverletzung*) if he did not report for duty; but he needed to know who the appropriate authorities were.[48] Brackmann visited the RMdI on 21

September 1939 to inform the relevant official of Reche's views. He told Reche:

> I stressed how important exact knowledge of racial questions is for the future drawing of frontiers, and recommended to him that they draw upon you on these questions. He was enthusiastic about this suggestion.

Brackmann suggested that Reche send a position paper, formally through the NODFG, which would be more efficacious than the unsolicited musings of an individual. He added:

> Both the official and myself agreed completely with your fundamental view that 'we need *Raum* but no Polish lice in the fur', but there are people who think otherwise and so it is best if we are all on the spot.[49]

Reche spent the next Sunday afternoon in a frenzy at his typewriter. On 24 September he sent Brackmann a memorandum noting:

> Your suggestion that there are people who even want to include 'Polish lice' (in the figurative sense) has made me very apprehensive. It seems all the more necessary that racial and racial–hygienic considerations should be brought to the attention of the relevant and decisive officials as soon as possible and so I would be very grateful to you, if you – in the name of the NODFG – would take my memorandum as quickly as possible to the RMdI. It would certainly be particularly useful if it was to be set before the Führer himself.[50]

The object of their joint solicitations was entitled 'Basic Principles on the Demographic–Political Securing of the German East'.

Basic Principles

1) Acquisition of *Raum*

1. Only land won through settlement remains secure in possession of a people for a millennium.
2. The German people must secure in Europe – and certainly now after the crushing of Poland – a large, contained, settlement area adequate for a greater German nation (150,000,000) in the future. The German *Volk* will have to become so large since only really large peoples in a secure, state *Raum* will survive the struggles of the future.
3. The German people needs a new settlement area bordering its existing frontiers of at least 200,000 sq kms.
4. The entire German *Raum* must have strategically useful frontiers;

this point is to be taken into account in the detailed redrawing of frontiers.

2) Ethnic Settlement

1. The *Raum* to be won shall exclusively serve German people and the German future; German blood has been spilled for this goal only. The newly acquired land must be made empty of all foreign ethnic elements; all foreign races, foreign peoples are to be resettled.

2. The retention of foreign peoples and inhabitants of lesser racial value will inevitably result in a bastardisation of the German settlers, which must lead to a consequential weakening of the strength of the German *Volk* and their cultural capabilities. The German people in the East should not be merely a linguistically 'germanised', hybrid population, but true and pure German people. We do not need a bastard population there with Polish characteristics and Polish cultural incapability which is determined by blood! All the great peoples of pre-history have been brought to ruin by such racial hybridisation.

3. In order to settle the newly won and vacant areas not only interested persons, but as many peasants, craftsmen, skilled workers, businessmen from the Germans abroad are to be recruited. Every capable foreign German won for the homeland is a gain for the strength of the German *Volk*.

4. ... Settlement must take place with decisive regard to racial and racial–hygienic criteria and under the responsible control of a relevant expert since the German *Volk* has neither land, money or time for elements of a lesser genetic value. In *every* respect the new settlers should be outstanding sources of strength for the German future.

3) Further Remarks: I

1. The territories inside the eastern frontiers of the old Reich before 1914 come automatically to the Reich; similarly the territories within the former frontiers of the old Austrian monarchy, which Germany definitely requires for reasons of strategic security (about 50,000 sq kms).

2. In addition, as 'war reparations' and as atonement and compensation for the sacrifices of blood by the German army and for the mishandling, murder and economic harm of ethnic Germans in Poland a further area, in proximity to the former frontiers, of about 150,000 sq kms is to be incorporated into the Greater

German Reich, in so far as Germany needs it for strategic, settlement, or economic reasons.

3. The areas ceded under Point 2 will be cleared of their Polish and Jewish populations; these will be made available – from the point of view of a sort of 'population transfer' – to what remains of Poland or Russia.

4. In the areas ceded under Point 1 the following have to leave immediately: (a) all Jews and gypsies and their hybrids, (b) all Polish migrants since 1918, especially those who occupy former German landed estates.

5. All lands gained under Points 3 and 4 belong to the German Reich – firstly as state domain – also urban property.

Further remarks: II

1. The present inhabitants of the newly ceded areas are racially (and therefore in character, talents and capabilities too) for the most part totally useless. Above all the *c.* two million Jews and Jewish hybrids must be pushed out as soon as possible.

   The Polish population is for the most part a very unhappy melange of 'pre-Slavic' (related to Scandinavian Lapps), 'East Baltic' and '*ostisch*' races, with mongoloid characteristics very evident here and there. A mixing of this linguistically, but not racially 'Slavic' population with Germans is to be avoided at all costs; that can only be achieved through deportation of the Poles. Whether here and there parts of the Polish population are racially useful can only be decided by skilled racial experts; apparently strong nordic elements live by the lower reaches of the broad Vistula valley, perhaps linguistically slavicised, residual Germans.

   Anyone who knows the Polish rural population, knows how primitive, crude and often almost simpleminded the facial expressions of the people are and how crude their thought and behaviour is.

2. It may be suggested that as many as possible of the German peasant settlements in White Russia, the Polish and Russian Ukraine, on the Volga, in the Caucasus, Crimea, Bessarabia etc. should be included and that these settlers – in so far as they are racially and genetically useful – be exchanged with Poles, naturally so that compensation favours the new settlement areas so that exchange signifies a clear advantage for one group. Through such an exchange of population – in which it is only generally envisaged where the individual Polish emigrants are to go, which is not our problem – the emigration of the Poles will be facilitated.

3. This concerns the movement of many millions of people. However,

when one thinks that in the twentieth century the Poles have settled or resettled about four million people, that the Greeks succeeded, despite the weakness of their state (but with loans from England) in accommodating one and a half million Anatolian Greeks, one cannot doubt that powerful Germany with its excellent organisational gifts and its massive resources can resettle without difficulty 10 or still more millions in a few years, especially since the clearing of the land of Poles and Jews will occasion no appreciable costs since these will be covered by Poland or Russia.

4. The settlement of German peasants from abroad has the further advantage that most of them are very fertile; with them we can counterbalance the pressure of the Polish population on our frontiers.

5. The fact that the newly gained areas will be thinly populated for years after the immediate expulsion of the Jews and Poles – until the new settlements take effect – is no difficulty; by using machines and large fields on state farms it is intended to produce large harvests of grain, potatoes, and fodder as well as cattle on extensive pastures.

6. In the newly won industrial and mining areas it is self-evident that for the foreseeable future the present labour force is to stay – however without granting the Poles the great honour of German citizenship. But here one will always strive to slowly and surely drive out these foreign workers. The Poles did not do otherwise and drove out as many Germans as possible from the part of Upper Silesia that they stole . . .

7. The emigrant Poles can take their moveable goods – in so far as this does not contradict the interests of the German state – with them; one may proceed less charitably with the Jews.

8. . . .

9. German–Polish mixed marriages should be racial-politically examined to decide about whether they stay or emigrate; also, the views of the people and their past conduct must be considered.

10. Whichever Poles remain in the Reich – including Poles living there up to now in the old Reich – must fundamentally renounce their Polish nationality and naturally all corresponding political activity. Whoever continues to be active in the Polish cause will be immediately – except where they have first to be punished by the courts – deported without compensation together with their family. No right exists anywhere in Germany for any Polish schools or other establishments; naturally no Polish worship either. Anyone who does not like this has to leave Germany. There must be no 'Polish minority' in the Reich anymore. Naturally on no account must

anything Polish, either in writing, in the theatre, cinema or radio, be accorded recognition. No Polish officials!

Further remarks: III – The Question of a Polish State

As long as a Polish state, even as a protectorate, or any kind of self-contained Polish settlement area exists, the efforts of Polish politicians to restore a greater Poland will not cease, and above all the politicians of the 'democracies' and international Jewry will not rest in supporting such efforts with all the means available to them. This means allowing a standing source of crisis – to the detriment of Germandom – to exist. Therefore all traces of *Polentum* must disappear from the area of German settlement, whose presence supplies a pretext for Polish desires to conquer and which will fuel Polish irredentism which, as the experiences of centuries have shown, will be overcome with difficulty; even Tsarist Russia was not capable of denationalising *Polentum* . . .

Just how tenaciously a chauvinistically agitated Slavic people holds to its exaggerated claims is demonstrated by 'Czechdom' which will not abandon the secret hope of a 'rebirth' for decades. The reason for this is the lack of a sense of reality on the part of the Slavs. The few million Czechs will still give us many hard nuts to crack! How much greater is the danger from over 20 million Poles! In addition, the most extraordinarily refined agitation against the powers-that-be has become second nature to the Poles over many decades.

Prof. Dr O Reche
as adviser on racial questions to the NODFG[51]

Brackmann sent this memorandum – which reflects what was to be a Polish and Jewish reality – to Essen in the RMdI remarking, 'although one must put a question mark beside many points, by and large it still seems to me valuable to hear one of our leading racial researchers on these matters'.[52] Ever the skilful intermediary, Brackmann informed the author that he considered the paper 'very important, although perhaps on one or other points, I think otherwise'.[53] A regular correspondence on the matter of moving entire populations ensued. On 29 September Reche argued that the frontier fixed with the USSR provided a thinly settled area, and the chance 'to press together *Polentum* more and more over there'.[54] On 11 October he aired the dangerous thought whether *his* paper had inspired the recent Reichstag speech of the Führer on resettlement plans.

Modestly, Reche decided 'hardly probable, since the Führer has been planning something similar for a long time'. Having established the guidelines for mass deportations, Reche was keen to participate on the practical side. One had to be quick off the mark, for given the speed of decision making, the inexpert might make major errors.

> I do not like the role of a home-front soldier especially since I am a WW1 veteran. I am over 60 and they will not have me with the soldiers, naturally with reason, since on account of a war wound I am no longer up to real exertion and cannot do much . . . But I still feel that I have great energies within me, despite my sixty years.[55]

Brackmann informed his 'most esteemed colleague' that he had been in touch with the RMdI, but that the ministry was preoccupied with vital economic issues.[56] His rather literal correspondent deplored the fact that 'despite the removal of the Jews we still cannot get away from the Jewish mode of thought that "the economy is destiny"!' Fearing that malevolent spirits in the RMdI were sabotaging the progress of his paper, Reche thought that Brackmann might organize a man to man meeting with Frick while he tried Darré, whom he had known for decades: 'with allies one might perhaps make progress'. He also wanted to know who SS-*Obergruppenführer* Lorenz was, and how the latter had become responsible for resettling Germans from Estonia.[57] Brackmann relayed the intelligence that Lorenz was close to Hitler; was in charge of VOMI, and would ensure that the Poles would only remain 'shoved in between here and there'. There were plans to expel 'as many Poles as possible' to achieve a purely German frontier population. The only problem lay in where 'eight million' Poles were to go for '*Restpolen* is not in a position to receive them on account of overpopulation which you know about, and those areas in which they might find a place are in Russian hands.' He thought that similar ignorance prevailed in 'councils closest to the Führer' where *man nicht weiss, wohin man die Polen bringen soll.*[58] By late October Reche had abandoned Frick in favour of the apparently omnipotent Lorenz in his quest for action. He had the impression that the NODFG was acting behind the scenes in resettlements, and he had at last come to a solution of the question *wohin mit den Pollacken?* If the Ukrainians were to be moved eastwards, space would be found for the Poles.[59] In his reply, Brackmann underlined the fact that PuSte maps and statistical aids were used by Lorenz's VOMI office and that it had been recently said that 'without our staff the redrawing of frontiers would not have been possible'.[60] By this time Reche had discovered the elusive figure he had been seeking: with SS-*Gruppenführer* Günther Pancke of the RuSHA he could discuss the 'racial–political side' of the problem. The two had had a 'very fruitful' meeting. Inspired by Pancke, Reche urgently requested translations of Polish anthropological works – in triplicate with one copy of each for the SS – and maps of frontiers in the vicinity of Łódź. He was a seeker of absolutes.[61] Brackmann was pleased that Reche had at last discovered the right person and offered to support his work through the apparatus of the PuSte.[62] The newly established relationship between Pancke and Reche, with the PuSte as a sort of academic back-up service, can be pursued a little further. Through Pancke, Reche's ideas came to the attention of the *Reichsführer*-SS.

Reche had written to Pancke on 2 October 1939 in his capacity as the 'only specialist who knows about racial relations in the East'. He was particularly exercised about the 'tremendously important question of eastern Jews' and of how 'we can gain as much pure German settlement territory without being bothered by "Polish lice" whose presence also constitutes a considerable racial threat'.[63] A man to man discussion 'would produce total clarity in a very short time'. In his reply, Pancke explained that Lorenz's competence ended when repatriates entered German frontiers. He alone was responsible for 'racial hygienic' questions: the two should meet as soon as possible.[64] A meeting occurred on 13 November 1939. The specialist in anthropology and self-professed 'racial politician' could only 'welcome most warmly' the policies Pancke was pursuing. The two had agreed Reche's future competence. Reche was to act as a one-man 'court of appeal' in cases of doubtful racial ancestry. Three or four of his assistants were to be retrieved from the armed forces to carry out the racial categorization of persons moving through 'human sluicegates': Himmler should issue him with a general commission, 'say *Wissenschaftliche Kommission für Rassefragen der Ostsiedlung*', which would convince courts, the army, and other agencies of the vital nature of his activities. The two had also mooted more technical questions like the necessity of taking fingerprints from the left thumb and index finger to offset forgeries 'by Jews and other types of scoundrel'. Ever obliging, Reche appended a draft questionnaire for the racial–statistical encompassing of the Polish population.[65]

While the PuSte assisted Reche with translations from Polish anthropological works, Pancke brought Reche's suggestion to the attention of the *Reichsführer*-SS, for 'I certainly believe that [he] will agree with your recommendations and will very much welcome your ready collaboration'. It was *Selbstverständlich* that Reche would receive his commission.[66] By January 1940 Reche's attention had wandered to the matter of which Germans were fit for settlement in the annexed eastern territories. The prospect that 400,000 small farmers might be shifted from the South-west eastwards did not enthuse him. The population contained many 'non-Nordic' elements and was 'worn out' through earlier migration. The alternative – artisans from the industrialized centre – also consisted of 'material which is not exactly racially first class, at least on average'. His assistants were much in demand as racial inspectors in the 'Protektorat' and Łódź.[67] In the eyes of SS leaders he was 'fully on the right path'.[68] And indeed he was. In May 1940 he recommended the creation of a *Kriegeradel* ('in the original biological sense of the word "noble")' through the settlement of SS veterans in the East.[69] His cogitations on the concept of *Sippenschande* a year later were described as being 'a further important step forwards in the work of enlightenment'.[70] SS-*Brigadeführer* Hoffmann agreed that strict SS regulations on marriage – involving medical examinations and lengthy family trees – should be extended to the German population as a whole. What Reche said was heard in the highest quarters and it was heard with the respect accorded a long-time academic pioneer working in an 'experimental' field of knowledge. What he did was done in active partnership not only with senior SS figures, but also with sections of the German scholarly establishment. The categories were not hard and fast.

Like Reche, Walter Kuhn – from 1936 onwards Professor of German *Volkskunde* at Breslau – was immediately involved in resettlement actions in Poland. His own account of this period suggests that he was 'enlisted' in 1940, by whom is left in doubt, to 'make proposals' for the resettlement of the Galician Germans.[71] In fact, months before he returned to Galicia, Kuhn relayed a secret memorandum on 'ethnic political' issues to Theodor Schieder designed to correlate ethnic circumstances with the fluctuating arrangements that he picked up on the radio. On 29 September 1939 he sent Schieder a memorandum entitled 'German villages in Central Poland immediately beyond the former frontier of the Reich'.[72] The paper was an extended exposition of the theme of German *Volksboden*. Noting that the villages exhibited 'healthy colonial peasant strengths and a strong surplus of births', Kuhn argued that future frontiers should encompass areas that had been won for civilization through the efforts of German peasants.[73]

In the eventuality that in the course of the conflict with Poland, Poznania and West Prussia return to the Reich, it would be purposeless and would contradict the ethnic principles of the Third Reich if German ethnic territory directly beyond the new frontiers of the Reich were to be left in a foreign state.[74]

The methods Kuhn employed to establish the numbers of Germans and Poles in these villages are worthy of closer attention. Jews were counted as a separate category from 'Aryans' for reasons that 'require no justification'.[75] Elsewhere he observed:

> The ethnic exclave is divided elsewhere from Poznań by a narrow strip of old Polish villages in Prosnatale, with over 4,000 inhabitants, including 84 Germans. The entire area, which must be annexed to the Reich numbers 18,617 inhabitants with 9,500 or 51.3 per cent Germans. If the numerical majority of the Germans is only just adequate, the German *Volksboden* is more extensive than that of the Poles.[76]

His methods could also be elastic in a prospective rather than retrospective sense.

> The natural centre of the area dealt with (on the Vistula above Toruń) is the market town of Bobrowniki on the Vistula, in which certainly in 1921 there were only 119 Germans among 1,162 inhabitants, but which through natural influx *will* quickly be germanised.[77]
> . . . The villages (in an area around Wiżajny) number 1,400 or 71 per cent Germans in a population of 1,970 inhabitants, the market town of Wiżajny is the natural centre with 447 Germans, 617 Poles and 338 Jews. *Without* the Jews the entire area is 60.8 per cent German.[78]

Kuhn's conclusions aptly illustrate the way in which, armed with the appropriate conceptual presuppositions, it was possible to ignore reality by simply pretending that categories of person no longer existed.

> Together, the seven areas number 24,175 or 52.6 per cent Germans *in an Aryan population* of 45,881. They are almost all pure, healthy peasants, who inhabit a far greater *Volksboden* than the average for the same number of Germans in the Reich . . . Economically and in terms of settlement, the predominance of Germans in the areas dealt with is far greater than a bare numerical majority enables one to recognise.[79]

In the winter of 1939–40 Kuhn returned to the scene of his earlier enthusiasms to advise on the resettlement of the Volhynian Germans. In a report for the SD Immigration Centre (EWZ) in Łódź dated 22 January 1940, Kuhn endeavoured to tally the historical and present circumstances of the German repatriates, with soil and climatological conditions prevailing in the Reich.

> Resettlement could be made much easier if the Germans could be transferred to areas with whose climate and soil types etc. they are familiar and in which they would not have to extensively reorientate themselves economically.[80]

In this way, the Sudeten Germans from the East Carpathians were to be resettled in the Silesian Beskids, where the heights and woods would seem familiar; the north Germans from north Volhynia were destined for the area around Danzig or the *Warthegau*, and the *Holländer* from the Bug region, for the Vistula delta or Zichenau, where amidst the river flats they were to be mixed with Germans in order to learn the language of their new homeland.[81] Although the latter group had spoken Polish or Ukrainian since the eighteenth century, 'in race and consciousness they are thoroughly German and could be incorporated into the German national community without difficulty'. Their 'exceptional racial quality' had already been noticed by the 'sluicing-office' in Balut.[82]

During conversations with the peasants, Kuhn noticed their desire to be resettled as entire village communities. There were to be some exceptions. The villagers of Winsentówka, Klementówka and Rzeczyszcze and so on, exhibited characteristics 'associated' with incest. There was also the problem of the sectarian villages that the *Ostforscher* had discovered in 1926.

> Sectarianism in Volhynia is a form of spiritual sickness, due to exceptional suffering in WW1, the abduction of the entire German population to Russia, during which countless numbers died on the march, and the destruction of almost all of the German settlements during war-time hostilities.[83]

Villages 'infected' by sectarianism – Emelin, Slobodarke, Romanov I, Amelin and others – were to be 'broken up'. Further information on the sectarian villages could be had from the Lutheran pastor Kleindienst (with whom Kuhn and his friends had stayed in 1926 and whose research was also financed by the NODFG).[84] The spirit of sectarianism 'would soon blow over [*verrauchen*] in the more sober spiritual atmosphere of Germany'. Villages in a state of feud with one another would also have to be scattered.[85] Kuhn's report was read by SS-candidate Dr Werner Gradmann who agreed with the findings of 'the ultimate expert'. Gradmann, himself a cog in the process of screening repatriates, was particularly exercised by the effects of *Inzucht*:

> The effects [of in-breeding] are so shocking because a great percentage of the children are idiots. With reference to the destruction of the sectarian villages it is to be noted that these sects also constitute a danger in a health–policing sense.[86]

The corollary of these resettlement actions was the forcible evacuation of about three-quarters of a million Poles during the war years to the *Generalgouvernement*, which was neither able, nor willing, to make adequate provision for them.[87] In the organized deportations the victims were allowed a suitcase each and food for fourteen days, to minimize the loss of moveable goods awaiting the German repatriates, and were packed onto rail transports where they were often left freezing and hungry, while the authorities in the *Generalgouvernement* made up their minds where to deposit them. Deportations and resettlement actions took place in winter so as to minimize disruption of the harvests. The start of the searing trauma experienced by the Polish deportees was described by one of the VOMI experts in 1940:

> One evening a Polish village was surrounded by a group of SA men who had been entrusted with the action. A few ethnic Germans had been forcibly drafted into the unit. The village was encircled, and shortly before midnight the inhabitants were driven from their beds. Then came the order to be ready to travel in half or three quarters of an hour with 30 kgs of luggage. The most dreadful havoc resulted. Icons and crucifixes were smashed and thrown on the rubbish heaps. The Poles had to drive in their own vehicles to the local town and were put behind barbed wire. There were ethnic Germans waiting there already, who had been brought from elsewhere. These ethnic Germans were loaded onto the same trucks in which the Polish families had arrived. Naturally these ethnic Germans were very disturbed by the terrible things that they witnessed there.[88]

While not subjected to the same degree of terror or loss as the Polish deportees, the German repatriates were corralled in VOMI camps (abandoned factories, churches or Jewish sanatoria), subjected to a screening and quarantine process of up to two months' duration and, in many cases, condemned to an indeterminate, makeshift existence in the camps. By June 1941 some 275,000 had not been settled, as more refined screening processes, the need to conserve transport for the attack on the USSR, faltering purposiveness on the part of SS administrators, and the reluctance of the Führer's eastern satraps to lose skilled Polish labour or to assimilate deportees, conspired to slow down the entire operation.[89] The screening process, described by Werner Gradmann, occupied a considerable time. The repatriates filed through the EWZ or before 'flying squadrons' of experts sent to the camps. They were deloused, clothed, fed, and medically examined, X-rayed and photographed, and subjected to a 'racial estimate', while their papers were checked by officials in black, brown and grey uniforms. A large card contained information built up on each person. It was marked with a racial estimate ranging from 1aM/1 ('very valuable') to 1V 3c (a 'reject'); a Security Police recommendation on naturalization or delayed action; and the letters A, O, or S, designating future settlement in the old Reich, the East, or 'a special case' (Sonderfall). The 'special cases' were turned over to the Gestapo.[90]

Kurt Lück, by then an SS-Hauptsturmführer, was consulted by Gradmann about the relocation of the Volhynian Germans. He was also involved in presenting the official version of what was taking place. In Deutsche Volksgruppen aus dem Osten kehren helm ins Vaterland (1941), a pamphlet (in an edition of 945,000) for the backpacks of the Wehrmacht, Lück chronicled the return of hundreds of thousands of ethnic Germans to 'primordial germanic territory'. The object of these operations, in accordance with Hitler's Reichstag speech of 6 October 1939, was to 'achieve clear ethnographic relations by a separation of nationalities through resettlement'.[91] Using arguments that those involved still repeat, Lück maintained that the property and level of economic well-being left behind by the repatriates justified the expropriation and deportation of the Poles: 'in the great task of resettlement, no one-sided sacrifices will be imposed upon anyone'.[92] This meant that the German repatriates acquired the results of economie polonaise while the Poles took over neat, orderly, and business-like German villages in the East. Any discomfiture experienced by the Poles, and Lück was instrumental in mythologizing what happened, was rationalized by the treatment of ethnic Germans in Polish 'concentration camps' in September 1939.[93]

Lück dwelt on the administrative structures responsible for resettlements and upon the logistic and operational problems confronting those involved. His fetish for facts and figures was on a par with that of the Reichsführer-SS himself.

The Baltic Germans were brought back to the Reich on 41 ships, which made 126 trips and thereby traversed 121,000 nautical miles, i.e. five and a half times the circumference of the globe. Some 293,000 cubic metres of baggage had to be moved, which piled up to a height of 2.5 metres, would cover the 54.40 metres wide East–West axis in Berlin from the Brandenburg Gate to the middle of the Technische Hochschule for some 3.5 kilometres.[94]

He was sympathetic to the discomfort of the resettlement technicians under SS-*Standartenführer* Hoffmeyer in eastern Galicia.

The winter was bitterly cold, the roads were covered in snow. The resettlement commando, trusted colleagues from the VDA, BDO, SS, NSKK and ethnic Germans familiar with the eastern territories worked under the most difficult conditions, in inadequate offices, often for twenty hours a day. The orders of the Führer had to be carried out at all costs.[95]

In order to lend the operation a homely touch, Lück appended a number of short stories, verse and letters, designed to foster empathy between the settlers and the Reich in the minds of the soldiers. A Volhynian tale entitled 'Brother Germans' rather improbably related how a Volhynian German infantryman called Ivan Pawolowitsch Mathey, serving in the Tsarist army in the First World War, used to creep out of his trench at night in Pavlovian response to the Siren call of German harmonicas intoning *O Strassburg* in the opposing trenches. His children would one day wear the 'honourable field grey uniform of the German *Wehrmacht*'.[96] The verse was of the plangent sort:

> Ancient homeland behind the Pruth,
> land of sun on sea;
> rich through our sweat and bravery,
> sanctified through the blood of our fathers.
> Germany calls its sons homeward,
> farewells were taken,
> the Danube roars its ancient song.
> Fatherland we are coming! etc.[97]

Letters purportedly written by the repatriates lent the racial sieving of simple humanity an air of breathing immediacy. Sixty thousand Baltic Germans set off by steamer to the Reich. After much singing and dancing on the promenade deck, they reached 'Gotenhafen' on a winter night and were shipped by rail to the *Warthegau*:

The extraordinarily friendly reception and the exceptional helpfulness of our hosts was quite singular. Today we all feel that we have regained our homeland and thank the Führer for the care with which we were brought home, for his confidence in our strength as a people, and for his summons. As soon as I have found my ultimate destination in the *Warthegau* you will receive further news.

Heil Hitler!

Yours E.[98]

Lück and other ethnic German members of the SS were also responsible for a book chronicling the experiences of the German minority during the eighteen-day campaign in Poland. Despite warnings from the Foreign Office of the local consequences, some ethnic Germans may well have been used by German military intelligence as a fifth column.[99] The consequences for many innocent people were rough treatment, forced marches, internment and murder at the hands of panic-stricken and incensed Polish soldiers and civilians. Whether killed by German aircraft or lynched by their Polish captors, some 4,000–6,000 ethnic Germans died during the short war.[100] On 3 September 1939 retreating Polish troops claimed that they had been fired upon by ethnic Germans in Bromberg, and in a wave of retaliation many of the latter were murdered.[101] The German army high command ordered drastic measures to be taken against Polish troops involved, while on 5 September an advance party of thirty men from *Einsatzgruppe* IV moved into the town. Having shot a number of Poles en route, they stormed the town hall, which was being defended by members of a Polish youth organization called *Obrona Narodowa*. Later, about fifty of these young Poles were found to have been shot in the back of the head. The *Einsatzkommando* then executed the four town councillors who negotiated the surrender of the urban militia and, after some delay, began shooting hostages on the town square on 7 September. Between 200 and 400 persons were shot and a further 1,400 interned. They combed a quarter of the town called Schwedenhöhe with instructions to liquidate anyone with a weapon on his or her person. Shots fired at German soldiers during the night resulted in more hostages being executed the next morning. The arrival of Roland Freisler, an expert in judicial murder, on 9 September resulted in a further one hundred executions and massive jail sentences for forty-seven others.[102] Although these actions were separate from and post-date the 'rendering harmless' of the Polish intelligentsia, the 'September murders' served as an alibi for the intended decimation of the Poles.

On Hitler's orders the number of ethnic German victims was multiplied by ten, with an official figure of 58,000 killed or missing, agreed for the sake of consistent accounts from February 1940.[103]

Lück had spent the days of uncertainty hiding in the woods until German troops appeared. In 1940 he published a book called *Marsch der Deutschen in Polen* which contained accounts of ethnic German experiences by *inter alia* SS-*Oberführer* Dr Hans Kohnert, Alfred Lattermann (who joined the SS in November of that year), and SS-*Obersturmbannführer* Ludwig Wolff.[104] The book described in graphic terms the treatment meted out to the German minority in Poland during the short war. The preface spoke of 'the extermination of the German people openly proclaimed today by the Jewish plutocratic democracies' and of the need to make the Germans aware of the means being deployed to achieve their 'extermination'.[105] Lück set the events of September 1939, which he blamed on the Polish and Jewish Press in Poland, in a continuum of anti-German outbursts from riots in Cracow in 1312 to the 'Bloodbath in Thorn' in 1724.[106] Working with statistics of 'far beyond 50,000' Lück claimed that the Polish authorities had issued orders to shoot Germans involved in espionage, all those who fell by the wayside during the march to internment camps and, in the eventuality of further German advances, all internees.[107] The events in Bromberg were described as follows:

> English and Polish propaganda seeks in vain to shift the guilt for the largest bloodbath of all time onto the innocent victims. In Bromberg the Germans are supposed to have shot at Polish soldiers. But in reality, the German men had already been interned and taken away. Do the wretched liars maintain that the many children, women and elderly people who were numbered among the slain threatened the Polish army? Among the first 1,030 victims registered in the vicinity of Poznań were 70 women, 3 children under three years of age, and 47 elderly persons of between 61 and 86 years of age. That these people were abducted at all is already in itself a crime.[108]

Although the German accounts contain instances of appalling sadism by individual Polish soldiers and civilians, it is necessary to bear in mind that the experiences described in the book lasted for a number of hours or days, and that, as the accounts make clear, some of the fatalities resulted from German bombing, infirmity or suicide.[109] Spells in the converted sugar factory at Chodecz, or in the prison at Bereza Kartuska, which were described as 'concentration camps' may have been an ordeal, but were not comparable with the systematic destruction of persons that took place in vast industrialized installations run by the SS.[110] The accounts reflect a number of serious prejudices. In Bereza Kartuska 'Jewish spivs' received individual cells while 150 ethnic Germans were apparently crammed into a room with a capacity of forty.[111] The sensitivities of Heinrich Weiss were particularly exercised by having to eat his pearl-barley soup and potato from the same bowl as a Jew: 'did they know how one could best upset a racially conscious German?'[112] On the march through Kutno, a group of ethnic Germans were set upon by 'a crazed mob (mostly Jews) and badly beaten. The infamy of these beasts in human form can best be seen when one describes how they set about the seriously ill and half dead comrades lying on carts at the back of each column with clubs and iron bars.'[113]

Alfred Lattermann's experience was probably typical of most and may be taken as an exemplar of how a short sequence of events was worked up into a protracted nightmare. As a reserve officer he was arrested on 6 September and taken from Gosciniec to Sompolno, sleeping in woods and eating carrots along the way. In Sompolno he heard that three 'Hitler people' had been shot. Escaping his escort in Kutno, Lattermann and Richard Breyer established themselves in a cottage deserted by its Polish-peasant occupant. Discovered by Polish militiamen, the two were taken to a railway station where they had to stand facing a wall. After a spell in prison the two set off as part of an eighty-man column towards Gombin. An attempt to break out failed and, fearful of German gunfire, the two returned to Gombin where they encountered an advance party of German troops. This was on 17 September. On the way back to the Vistula their column was attacked by German aircraft. Lattermann's 'internment' had lasted eleven days, and not the 'three weeks' he mentioned, and the experience had been rendered potentially lethal largely by German forces. He concluded 'with gritted teeth we survivors recommence the work for *Volk* and *Heimat* as the most loyal followers of our Führer Adolf Hitler'.[114]

One of the more urgent questions facing the German authorities in the wake of resettlements and deportations was who was to be regarded as a German citizen. Although there was general agreement to exclude the Jews, a further step on their road to 'special status', there were serious differences about how one should categorize the rest. Traditionalists in the RMdI thought that after deporting those Poles not deemed to be assimilable, general German citizenship should be granted to whoever remained, with citizenship of the Reich as a sort of bonus for ethnic Germans to distinguish them from Germans being 'retrieved' from *Polentum*.[115] Among those interested in a more restricted definition of citizenship were ethnic Germans who stood to gain from the expropriation of doubtful cases, and the SS. Faced with a too generous bestowal of certificates confirming German ethnicity on about 40,000 persons in Poznań alone, the local specialist on ethnic questions. SS-*Obersturmführer* Dr Strickner, prompted by local ethnic German activists connected with the SD, created an 'Ethnic German List' (DVL) which was soon extended to the *Warthegau* as a whole.[116] The list divided ethnic Germans into categories A and B, denoting the degree of activism they had evinced before 1 September 1939. Between May 1940 and January 1941 as the intentions of the regime became clearer, categories C and D were added, denoting retrievable Germans lost in *Polentum* and 'salvageable' ethnic German 'renegades'. Inclusion in these four categories decided the matter of whether an individual remained in the East or was to be deported for accelerated germanization to the Reich and, in the case of 'asocial' or racially 'less valuable' members of Category D, translation to concentration camps.[117] These categories were re-worked in September–October 1940, so that 6,015,000 non-assimilable Poles came under Category D as 'protected members'. These criteria were not uniformly imposed throughout the incorporated territories. For example, *Gauleiter* Forster was loath to introduce these pedantic criteria once he had deported and expropriated the ethnically dubious or those whose property ethnic Germans coveted. In his drive to finish the germanization of his *Gau* as soon as possible, Forster set target percentages of Germans to be included in the DVL, regardless of whether the individuals concerned were Poles or acting in response to threats of force. This grotesque but relatively humane procedure drew upon Forster schoolmasterly communications from Himmler addressed to *Lieber Parteigenosse Forster* informing him that 'you yourself are a National Socialist of such long standing that you know that a droplet of the wrong blood which penetrates the veins of an individual can never be got out again'.[118]

The cards generated by the DVL and by earlier surveys were handed over to the PuSte in 1941. They received a copy of the DVL central register, the results of a RMdI survey of Poles living in the Reich extrapolated from the census of 17 May 1939, 250,000 cards from the Reich's Statistical Office on foreigners in the Reich, and 159,000 cards on foreigners in eastern areas of the Reich from the 'central index on foreigners' kept by the SD.[119] These cards were to be the basis of an 'Ethnic Card Index' whose purpose was:

> the removal of German citizenship from non-German ethnic elements in the Old Reich and their designation as 'protected dependants'; the clarification of the question of non-German ethnic elements with German family names, and many other questions relating to ethnicity (connection with mother-tongue, occupation property, religion, number of children, degermanisation, regermanisation etc.)[120]

The PuSte staff at Potsdamerstrasse 61 had to work through the cards sorting foreigners into national groups (Poles, Danes, Croatians etc.), creating a separate colour-coded index for four categories of Czech, and separating entirely 'Jews, gypsies, coloured persons, Asiatics' and 'other non-Europeans'. These were to be 'evaluated as a separate category'.[121] From 7 August 1941 the cards on gypsies were marked with five varieties of symbol ranging from 'Z' = gypsy, through 'ZN+' = gypsy hybrid with mostly gypsy blood, to 'ZM −' = gypsy hybrid with mainly German blood. The final goal was to build up four cards on each individual in the Reich of non-German nationality with index tabs running from 1 to 14, which would be deposited with the local authorities, and *Regierungspräsidenten*, while the PuSte retained two mastercards in turn catalogued alphabetically and according to regions.

The PuSte also received advanced notice of the plans for further resettlement actions in the form of *Kleine Umsiedlungsspiegel* issued half yearly by the SS. These gave the 'planning statistics', the name of the SS officer in charge of the operation and the 'type' of action envisaged. Thus SS-*Brigadeführer* Hoffmeyer was in charge of a 'normal resettlement' of Galician and Volhynian Germans between 11 December 1939 and 3 February 1940, while his colleague SS-*Hauptsturmführer* Lackmann was in charge of resettlements from Serbia whose type was described as 'asocial and refugees' and 'without means'. A further 720 'asocials' were to be resettled by Lackmann from Slovakia between 9 and 25 July 1942.[122]

ii. 'Divide et impera': the *Ostforscher* and the occupied East

The construction of a German civil administration in the *Generalgouvernement* following Hitler's edict of 26 October 1939, provided the PuSte with further opportunities to demonstrate its resourcefulness to the regime.[123] Hitler's insistence that there should not be 'too much' administration in the *Generalgouvernement* and that what there was had to be bluff, aloof and soldierly, threatened imminent administrative chaos.[124] Apart from a task force of 400 bureaucrats from the RMdI and the '*Sonderstab* Craushaar', which provided staff for the office of the *Generalgouverneur* in Cracow, Hans Frank and Seyss-Inquart had to manage with a motley array of lawyers from Munich, keen to shine in the sham-glitter of the Wawel, and surplus civil servants from Austria or on secondment from terms of imprisonment in the Reich.[125] The shortage of skilled administrators partly explains the size of the administrative districts formed after 1 January 1940: 6 Polish Voiwodships and 72 *Starosteien* were merged into four new districts (Warsaw, Radom, Lublin and Cracow), and 10 local captaincies.[126] The German officials were thinly spread; in January 1944 Frank estimated that excluding railway employees and policemen, there were 4,000–5,000 officials in the *Generalgouvernement*.[127] The scale of the problem may be deduced from telephone requests by the Foreign Office to the PuSte, for lists of ethnic Germans 'who might be suitable for administrative duties in the regime of occupation'.[128] Another cause for concern was that most of the imported officials had no knowledge of Polish and consequently were unable to use existing administrative aids.[129] Essen in the RMdI enlisted the help of the PuSte for the task of enlightening bureaucrats about the society they had to govern. He requested 'Poland in Figures', the catalogue of the publisher S. Hirzel, lists of PuSte translations, and regional studies.[130]

The publishing houses Hirzel in Leipzig and Oldenbourg in Munich saw a heaven-sent opportunity to unburden themselves of surplus stock. On 20 November 1939 Hirzel sent the PuSte 300 catalogues with a request for a list of 300 addresses in the 'liberated territories' while Oldenbourg drew attention to 2,576 unsold copies of Brackmann's *Deutschland und Polen*.[131]. The PuSte offered a range of titles suitable for officials from western or central Germany translated to the East. There was a discount of 25–30 per cent. The officials could study *Jomsburg*, Lück and Lattermann's 'Our *Heimat*' or the first volume of Brackmann's monumental *Festschrift*.[132] The list was forwarded by the RMdI to Greiser, Koch, Wagner and Frank whose local officials in turn ordered the books.[133]

Aubin in Breslau was well placed to establish the requirements of officials and soldiers in Poland. On 11 March 1940 he returned from lecturing to the troops and asked Hirzel to send catalogues to the army.[134] On 22 March he reported to Brackmann on the concrete results of his trip to Poland. The work of the *Ostforscher* during the last twenty years was not widely known, and only one lowly official was using Doubek's nationality maps. But almost half of the lectures to the troops were on historical–political subjects, and they needed material. Cases of books by members of 'our circle' and the products of the BDO could be circulated among the divisions, and pamphlets should be produced summarizing Lück's *Deutsche Aufbaukräfte*. The authors should be 'men of the pen' and not academics, although the latter – propriety had to be observed – should be in overall control. Officials had formed a large section of the audience at lectures he and Sappok had delivered in the Palais Brühl in Warsaw. Conscious of his 'duty as a publicist' Aubin sent copies of these proposals to *Obersleutnant* Dr Hesse of the OKH propaganda department and *Hauptmann* Dr Gerhardus on the staff of *Ober-Ost*.[135] In his reply Brackmann noted that a brochure by Aubin had been 'extremely well-received by the higher officers and also by their subordinates' but that Keyser's Vistula booklet was 'too dry'. He had enjoined Lück to do a propaganda version of his *Aufbaukräfte*. Academics were not well-suited to writing propaganda, but professional propagandists wrote 'colourlessly'. There were two types of historical talent, 'story-tellers' and 'the systematic', and the former were needed at that point.[136] In his address to the January 1940 NODFG conference in Berlin, Brackmann coyly suggested that he had the necessary skill:

> I myself was requested by various political offices to write the booklet 'Krisis und Aufbau in Osteuropa'. As I heard subsequently the army was behind the request. The high command has sent thousands of these booklets into the field and to all command posts. Several chiefs of staff have said to me that they urgency require booklets of a similar sort because it is vital that officers and the intelligent part of the ranks are given correct political education.[137]

As he well knew, the SS rather than the army had been behind the request.

Among the first casualties of the German invasion were chauvinistic Polish organizations and research institutes. The *Einsatzgruppen* I–VI (or about 2,700 men) who accompanied the five army groups as 'Operation Tannenberg' came armed with guidelines, prepared lists of suspects, and orders to liquidate sections of the Polish intelligentsia and upper class.[138] Among those systematically pursued were the members of the Western Marches Association and its subordinate organizations.[139] Among the *Ostforscher* there was a scramble for the resources of the Polish institutes, while local ethnic German scholars thought that their hour had come. Aubin was keen to discover whether the Silesian Institute in Katowice would be 'turned around in order to shoot at the Poles' while Viktor Kauder was insistent that the institute did not 'fall into the wrong hands'.[140] Having survived for five weeks without any means of subsistence, Kauder was appalled that a German from the Reich had been imported to run the public library in Katowice. He wrote to Papritz 'perhaps you can sympathize with us ethnic Germans who feel despondency creeping over us about this state of affairs'.

> Unfortunately I am still treated here as if my work to date counts for nothing. I am experiencing the greatest disappointment of my life and first have to learn to understand that the likes of us only come in question as hack writers for the gentlemen who rule here now. That is really bitter.[141]

The Baltic Institute, too, was immediately closed. When one of the visiting PuSte staff decided to inspect the contents of files on the PuSte he was ejected by the Gestapo, who informed him that 'what is going on here does not concern you'.[142]

The PuSte and NODFG members were quick to establish contact with those responsible for cultural policy in the *Generalgouvernement*. On 6 December 1939 the PuSte informed Hans Frank that:

> In the last few years scarcely any German academic work or periodical with significant contributions on German–Polish questions has appeared inside or outside the Reich that was not planned, promoted or supported by the PuSte and NODFG. The activity of the PuSte is completely confidential so that the involvement of the PuSte or NODFG is never mentioned in public. Before the war the PuSte was above all increasingly active in researching nationality relations in Poland and in turning the results into a series of clearly set out maps. In the course of that year an entire series of publications and maps on the history of Poland and of Germandom in this country have been produced which should afford reliable material for the overcoming of new problems.[143]

During late November and December 1939 the PuSte staff flocked to the occupied East. The NODFG conference was held in Katowice on 14 December which enabled Papritz and Aubin to visit Cracow.[144]

They were received for an hour by Frank. The 'lively' conversation on German-Polish problems was so animated that the two scholars hardly had time to admire the frescoes. Frank pronounced his 'solemn thanks' for the work of the PuSte and gave them to understand that 'his and our views were in complete accord'.[145] He assured the PuSte that:

> The academic and statistical works of the PuSte about which Professor Aubin and archive director Dr Papriz talked to me today are of considerable value for the administration of the *Generalgouvernement*. In order to ensure that the results of this work are quickly and reliably made available to the administration of the *Generalgouvernement* I think it would be advisable if a representative of the PuSte were to be ordered to Cracow in order to maintain the necessary link.[146]

On 18 December 1939 Frank commissioned Gerhard Sappok to open a sub-branch of the PuSte in Cracow. It opened on 1 January 1940.[147] He was to be on secondment to the *Generalgouvernement* for the duration of the war and the costs of the sub-branch were divided between the PuSte and the *Generalgouvernement*.[148] The tasks of the sub-branch included producing maps and statistics for the administration, and scholarly and publicistic work based upon local archival and library resources. The latter were to include a German guide to Cracow, research on relations between Poland and the Reich in the Middle Ages, studies of 'German culture and art in Polish history' and of the economic structure of the *Generalgouvernement*, and an edition of the *Beheim Codex* to bring to life the German character of medieval Cracow.[149]

Sappok was closely involved with plans for a future German university in Cracow. Like other members of the PuSte he was well aware of what had happened to the existing university. On 26 February 1940 he informed Brackmann that the Gestapo had asked him for information on the Polish historian Professor W. Semkowicz who was among those Polish scholars deported to Sachsenhausen after the arrest by the SS of the entire professoriate on 6 November 1939. Unlike most of the professors arrested excepting the fifteen who had already died – who were eventually released, Semkowicz was still in 'protective custody'.[150] The reason given for his continued detention, Sappok assumed, was 'the testimony of some gentlemen in Breslau, in my estimate pre-historians, who described him as particularly anti-German'.[151] Sappok made efforts to help Semkowicz by stressing in his report to the Gestapo that Semkowicz was not hostile to National Socialism, and had helped a number of German scholars gain access to Polish archives before the war.[152] Semkowicz returned from Sachsenhausen on 18 October 1940, although he had to report several times a week to the security Police, and his clandestine seminar was shut down in December.[153]

On 10 April 1940 Sappok visited the Wawel to discuss the role of the PuSte and plans for a projected German institute with *Staatssekretär SS-Standartenführer* Dr Mühlmann, the *Reichsführer* SS's special representative in the *Generalgouvernement*. Plans for the institute seemed to be emanating from the propaganda department in Cracow. Two days later Sappok was received by Frank. He presented Frank with copies of Brackmann's work on early Polish history, Kossmann's settlement studies, Lück's work on Cholm and Lublin and a few of his own offprints. Enthusing over these gifts Frank requested the PuSte's assistance in the creation of the projected institute.[154] The following morning Sappok toured the Jagiellonian Library of the University of Cracow in the company of Frank and 'a great entourage of thirty men' including a group of surveyors. They spent an hour in the building with Sappok relating the history of the university to Frank. The object of the visit was to see whether the building would be suitable for Frank's projected *Institut für deutsche Ostarbeit* (IdO). Sappok assured the PuSte that he would endeavour to secure their interest on the steering committee of the IdO, and the visit ended with Frank examining PuSte products in their 'work room' in the library.[155] Sappok informed Brackmann that the IdO was 'almost a certainty' and that Frank had described it as being 'the core cell of a future German university in Cracow'. He speculated about possible influences on the form the institute would ultimately take. The Ministry of Propaganda wished to use the institute to train administrators.[156]

Since Brackmann had to attend the NODFG conference in Berlin, Aubin attended the opening ceremony of the IdO alone. In a letter to Brackmann dated 24 April 1940 he reported on a long conversation with Seyss-Inquart. The steering committee of the IdO was to consist of five, with Aubin as a full member and Brackmann as an honorary member. Research and the training of officials were to be divided between two distinct institutes. Although he had not accepted the offer of leadership of the IdO, Aubin had made a number of suggestions about leaders of academic sections: Sappok was to be academic leader and head of history, and the names of Kuhn and Oberländer had been canvassed for other posts. The results of the discussion had been very satisfactory 'for our circle' but there was always the danger that the

ambitious and unscrupulous would bring their influence to bear.[157]
A few days later Aubin sent detailed proposals to Seyss-Inquart. He
recommended Sappok as the future 'General Secretary' of the IdO,
Professor Dagobert Frey (Breslau) for art history, Kuhn (Breslau) for
Volkskunde, Martin Jahn (Breslau) for prehistory, Willi Czaska (Breslau) for geography and Oberländer (Greifswald) for economics, while
Aubin himself was to assume responsibility for history until a regular
appointment was made. Since the emphasis was to be on 'comparatively
rapid production', it was necessary to hire younger scholars and wartime man-power shortages could be bridged by calling upon the services
of officials, judges and teachers. He offered to produce a detailed plan
for co-ordinated research on ethnic Germandom in Poland.[158] Brackmann had a number of reservations about these proposals. He thought
that Aubin's recommendations were 'very Silesian' and that the IdO
should not appear to be *ein Breslauer Filiale*. A number of academic
parties had expressed interest in appointments in Cracow including
Unversagt and the jurist Ernst Heymann. Since the PuSte was 'godfather'
to the IdO, Brackmann wanted his interest secured.[159] The question of
'godfather' to what will be discussed in Part III below.

Although the Brackmann circle was to be outmanoeuvred by those
in charge in Cracow, the extent of PuSte/NODFG involvement in the
early stages of the IdO can be seen from the timetable of the first
formal conference held in the IdO.

Thursday 20 June

9 a.m. Ceremonial Chamber:

1 Schubert *String Quartet in C Major*
2 Speech by Hans Frank
3 H. Aubin 'The Reich and the Peoples of the East'

3 p.m.

1 G. Sappok 'Cracow's German Past'
2 Barthel (Breslau) 'The artistic face of Cracow' (slides)
3 Tour of the city

Friday 21 June

9 a.m.

1 Professor Czaska 'Development and form of the lands of the
   Generalgouvernement'
2 E. O. Kossmann 'German Settlement of the Vistula region in the
   Middle Ages'
3 Walter Kuhn 'Modern Settlement of the Vistula region'

4 E. Randt 'The Archives of the *Generalgouvernement*'
5 Arlt 'Nature and Structure of the Population of the
   Generalgouvernement'
6 P.-H. Seraphim 'The Jews in Poland'

Saturday 22 June

9 a.m.
1 Dr Weh 'Law in the *Generalgouvernement*'
2 T. Oberländer 'Agrarian Problems in Eastern Europe'
3 D. Frey 'German Art in the Vistula Region'
4 Tour of the Wawel and cathedral

9 p.m. – Concert
Haydn: *Concerto for viola and orchestra in D-Major*
Wagner: *Siegfried Idyll*
Schubert: *Symphony No. 5 in B-Major*

Three-quarters of the lecturers were members of the NODFG.[160]

The work carried out by Sappok and the PuSte sub-branch for the occupying regime ranged from the symbolic and historical, to radical attempts to change the face of Poland. Whether symbolic or not, both types of work are symptomatic of the regime. They reveal a desire to forge continuities with the past in order to relativize the ahistorical aspects of the ideology informing action in the present, and show how by judicious selectivity, history could be made to conform with the dictates of that ideology.

On 18 May 1940 *Das Generalgouvernement*, the official organ of the regime, devoted a full page to the ceremony in Marienburg at which Frank solemnly handed over to *Gauleiter* Forster copies of eighteen banners captured by the Poles at Tannenberg in 1410, that had hitherto stood in a corner of Frank's office. In his speech to the assembled representatives of the armed forces, Frank observed:

> It is a proud feeling for us to be in the happy position, through the bravery of our army and their victory over the Poles, to return these symbols of such an unhappy hour in Germany's history, but now with the exhilarating feeling of the approaching National Socialist world empire of Adolf Hitler, to the home from which they were once carried out, and to return them to the proud castle of the East – Marienburg. The grandiose history of the German people has moved forward half a century. The Poland of Versailles no longer exists and will never re-arise again. Marienburg is German today, Cracow is German and both will remain German.[161]

Although they managed to get their history right on the day, a major error was only averted by Erich Keyser, the director of the local history museum in Danzig. In March 1940 he asked the PuSte whether they realized that the banners that Frank was about to present to Forster were not original.[162] The PuSte contained Sappok who assured his colleagues that the copies had been ordered by the Polish historian Długosz in 1448. He added 'They look old.'[163] Informed of Sappok's report, Keyser pointed out, correctly, that Długosz had been referring to copies of the banners made in a manuscript, the *Banderia Prutenorum*, and that the items Frank was about to hand over to Forster had been manufactured in the 1930s.[164] The curator of the museum in the Wawel, Professor Syszko-Bohusz, informed Sappok that the banners had been produced in 1938, but had been made to appear tattered by time.[165] It was a near run thing, for the correct chronology was only inserted into a telegraph reporting the impending ceremony which was wired to the *Berliner Morgenaüsgabe* on 26 April 1940.[166]

As well as attempts to forge continuities between the remote past and the present, the PuSte was engaged in systematically germanizing the countenance of Polish towns and villages in line with their version of history, their conceptions of the German role as 'bearers of civilisation', and their anti-Semitism. On 22 August 1940 Sappok issued a memorandum on the germanizing of urban streetnames that illustrates all three processes:

Guidelines on the renaming of streetnames in the towns of the *Generalgouvernement*
22 August 1940

With the renaming of main squares in the towns of the *Generalgouvernement* as 'Adolf Hitler Square' it will be necessary

1. to check the names of existing streets and public squares for the presence of places named after anti-German personalities, events, Jews, and how these are to be obliterated and replaced by other names.
2. in renaming [streetnames] one should try to choose names which are closely bound up with the history of Germandom or German cultural achievements.
3. If one opts for translations, it is to be borne in mind that these translations should be as complete and grammatically accurate as possible.

On Point 1:

All names, e.g. which are connected with the struggle of the Poles against the German Knights are to be renamed: e.g. *ulica Grund-waldzka* (the battle of Tannenberg of 1410 is normally called the battle of Grunwald by the Poles) or streets and squares which have been named after the writer H. Sienkiewicz (the author of the notorious agitatorial novel *Krsyzacy*). Furthermore, all names of anti-German politicians, like for example, the name of the former Polish Minister of the Interior B. Pieracki, who was notorious because of his measures against the Ukrainian and German ethnic groups in Poland, or places named after Marshal Foch (*Aleja Focha*), J. Paderewski [the notorious anti-German leader of the Polish National Democrats and opponent of Piłsudski] are to be obliterated. Places named after Jews e.g. after General Berek Jozelewicz, the rabbi Meisel, the Jew Warschauer are widespread and common. The designation *Aleja zg Listopada* (Avenue of the 29 November) refers to the beginning of the Polish–Russian war on 29 November 1830 so there is no immediate need for the German administration to change this name. The same applies to the name *Aleja 3 Maja* (Avenue of the 3 May) which commemorates the consti-tution of 3 May.

On Point 2:

The history of Polish towns is rich in German men who were the bearers of German civilisation and the German will to create. The new placenames must recall these names. For Cracow, for example, it is possible to find the names of innumerable worthy Germans who could supply living proof of the German past of the city. By way of example one could name:

Artists: Veit Stoss, Hans Dürer, Pankraz, Labewolf, N. Koeber (Court painter to King John Sobieski), Zipsen (Gothic architect), Heinrich Finch (the greatest late Gothic composer was chief choral director in Cracow), Valentin Greff (famous 16th-century German lutanist), Jörg Huber (assistant to Veit Stoss from Passau), Köcher (famous instrument maker who was court supplier to four Polish kings), J. Laitner (Baroque architect, builder of the extension to the Jagiellonian Library, Annagasse 12), M. Lindentold (Builder of the Cloth Hall in Cracow), J. Münz (Builder of the Baroque Church on the Skalka), Parler (relative of a Prague family of artists, demonstrable in Cracow), Peter von Rennen (Danzig goldsmith, creator of Stanislaw sarcophagus), Hans Süs von Kulmbach (painter). The German patri-cian families: Boner, Schilling, Bethmann (all from Alsace), Thurzo, Wirsing, Kreidler, Georg Schwarz, Johann Heydeke.

German printers: Johann Haller, the brothers Scharffenberg, Sebald

Veyl (the first to print in Cyrillic type), Florian Ungler, Kasper Hochfeder, Hans Krüger etc.

One should remember that in 1791 Goethe stayed in Cracow.

On Point 3:
In translating streetnames one should first of all check which names the streets had in the Middle Ages. In literal translations one should take care that the grammar has been grasped correctly. If one translated the *plac Kossaka*, the translation must read *Kossak-Platz*, and not *Kossaka-Platz* because the original name is *Kossak* [famous Polish painter of animals]. The translation of the term *Rynek Kleparski* must not be *Ring Kleparski* but *Klöpperer Ring* because the term stems from the former suburb Klöpper or Kloppard.

The IdO history section Cracow Annagasse 12 is ready to help with working out these new streetnames, or with checking new names for the towns of the Generalgouvernement.

Sappok.[167]

The renaming of places was one of the tasks undertaken by the PuSte during the war. The procedure for changing the names in a given area was for a commission to be formed consisting of *Ostforscher*, local government officials and the local German bourgeoisie who would make suggestions, whose appropriateness was then examined by the PuSte. The sixteen-man commission in Upper Silesia was chaired by Wagner and included Sappok, Maydell, Kauder, Kuhn, Lück, Sczodrok and a textile factory owner.[168] The rationale behind transforming Olkusch into Ilkenau was explained as follows:

> The retention of the name Olkusch, as well as variations like Ilkusch or Elkusch, *as was used in Germany in the Middle Ages*, cannot be considered in the view of the commission, *because of the undoubted Slavonic ring of the name*. Use of the other form common in the Middle Ages – Ilkenau – will bring agreement on all sides, especially from the rural council.[169]

In the *Warthegau*, where 4,000–6,000 names had to be invented, 'politically insupportable names, e.g. *Jesuitenbruch* and the like will naturally have to be eradicated'. The new names had to be as imaginative as those they replaced for an endless series of 'Neudorf's', or 'Altdorf's' would result in the ruination of the entire *Gau*.[170] By the end of 1941 Kohte and Fast had processed about 7,450 names from West Prussia and the *Warthegau* but still had 10,200 to deal with.[171]

Sappok and Weidhaas also produced a guide to Cracow for the PuSte series 'German Guides to the towns in the East'. The introduction explained the significance of Cracow as a 'German cultural centre that once exercised a strong and lasting influence on the entire *Ostraum*', and emphasized 'the influences emanating from the German homeland' upon the history and artistic development of the town.[172]

Sappok contributed a lengthy essay on the historical development of 'this monument to German creative forces' on the Upper Vistula.[173] Although the guidebook is leaden and monotonous, the facility with which Sappok telescoped time in order to make his point, or slipped into a casual anti-Semitism, is worth stressing in what might otherwise be dismissed as a piece of Nazi ephemera. Creative 'Germans' were at work in the region from the late Stone Age. After an Illyrian period from 2,000 to 1,200 BC whose connection with the Slavs was dismissed, east germanic tribes settled on the banks of the Vistula in about 200 BC.

> All of these germanic tribes have left us an impression of their high level of culture through the things they left behind: beautiful black-glazed urns, artistic gold fibulae and other splendid burial gifts still remind us today of those who paved the way for civilised life in early pre-history on the banks of the Upper Vistula who were there before a single Slav set foot in the area.[174]

While credit for the founding of the first Polish state was bestowed upon the Vikings, the tenth- and eleventh-century origins of Cracow as a Slav princely residence, trading, and ecclesiastical centre were quietly passed over in favour of an account of the refounding of Cracow as a town under German law.[175] Since Poles were not allowed to migrate to the town from the countryside (in order to preserve the labour force on seigneurial estates rather than because of any nationalistic prejudice on the part of the medieval citizenry) 'it is clear that the founding of the town of Cracow, in accordance with the will of its founder, was a purely German undertaking and that it owes its rise to German creative strength'.[176] With the ethnic credentials of Cracow thus appearing to endorse medieval subscription to the notion of *polnische Wirtschaft*, Sappok blithely proceeded to attribute *every* manifestation of artistic, publishing, business or academic excellence to Germans residing in Cracow. This was quite simple as Germans had formed a large proportion of the citizens of the town. Absurd continuities were made between the university where Copernicus had studied

in 1491, and the present occupants of the Annagasse who had recently
stepped into the shoes of Polish professors sent to concentration camps.

> In the buildings of the earlier university, in whose courtyard a monu-
> ment to Copernicus commemorates a great son of the university, a
> German scholarly institute was established in 1940 (the IdO) forging
> a link with the great and honourable tradition of renowned German
> research work which issued forth from this place hundreds of years
> ago.[177]

The sections of his essay became deliberately shorter as time progressed. The beneficiaries of German creativity were the Jews. Despite
periodic anti-Jewish riots the latter had succeeded in gaining influence
in urban affairs through domination of credit. Quite how this differed
from the massive political influence of the German financier Hans
Boner during the reign of Sigismund I was not discussed. He described
how, in 1538, the Polish parliament had ordered that Jews should
wear distinguishing clothing, and how despite these measures Cracow
had become a 'playground for Jewry' (*einem Tummelplatz des Judentums*).[178] National decline in the form of a powerful nobility and
foreign rulers had ensued. A brief rebirth of the town under Austrian
rule after 1795 had unfortunately also resulted in German university
teachers and German writers providing the Poles with 'the intellectual
weapons' which they were to employ against the Germans.[179] The
suggestion that education for the Poles would be counterproductive
for the present German regime lay not very far beneath the surface.
Although Sappok had a few good words to say about Piłsudski and
the missed opportunity afforded by the Polish Legion, the inter-war
Polish state was never directly mentioned. The Stone Age warranted
closer attention than modern Poland. With no sense of irony Sappok
concluded:

> The most recent evidence of the German achievement in the town are
> also at the same time the most moving. These are the simple wooden
> crosses on the graves of our German soldiers who through heroes'
> deaths have prepared the way for our people for new and great German
> creative tasks in the East.[180]

The NODFG also continued to subsidize the ever burgeoning
output of Kurt Lück. In March 1939 Lück had informed the PuSte
that he wished to produce a book of biographical portraits of German
'path-finders and pioneers' in Poland.[181] With a publication subsidy of
2,200 RMs Lück produced *Deutsche Gestalter und Ordner im Osten*

(1940).[182] This series of essays on thirty-five German 'creative pioneers' contrasted

> The Poles [who] have always had a tendency to be ruled by disorder and erraticism and who rejoice in doing nothing and indulgence ... [with] The Germans [who] were organisers, creators and bearers of progress. When will a great museum of German cultural achievement in the East be built in the frontier areas?[183]

Leaving aside the fact that the designer of the Lazienski Park in Warsaw (Johann Schuch); 'the first organiser of Polish scholarship' the librarian Georg Bandtke; and Ludwig Bosanus, the first Professor of Veterinary Science in Wilna, do not come readily to mind as being particularly significant in the cultural history of Poland, as well as its absolute germanocentricity, the book makes a number of concessions to current ideological preoccupations.[184] In his essay on the Cracowian merchant Wirsing, Erich Maschke dwelt upon the influence of blood, which had become a regular casual agency in his work:

> Like Wirsing many members of the German bourgeoisie in Poland were received into the Polish nobility. Polish nobles were often keen to contract marriages with the daughters of rich German merchants. In this way a stream of German blood went through the women into the Polish nobility ... These hereditary factors benefited the Polish upper class and became the foundation of their achievements.[185]

There were not many achievements, for implicitly or explicitly, the essays stressed the political and cultural incapability of the Poles, and spoke of 'the Hydra of Polish noble indiscipline and self-centredness' or 'a thin Polish ruling class' in Volhynia which 'was never able to complete political, military or cultural tasks with their own resources and so over the centuries they again and again summoned German assistance to the East', until 'piece after piece of the rotting body of the multi-ethnic republic broke off until in 1795 it disappeared from the map entirely'.[186]

In the same year Lück also published *Der Lebenskampf im deutschpolnischen Grenzraum* for the central press of the NSDAP. The series in which the book appeared was designed for the political education of new NSDAP members, and to disseminate a view from the ethnic frontier among those living in the German heartlands.[187] Unlike *Deutsche Gestalter*, this book was not a recycling of Lück's earlier work on second-rate composers and obscure botanists, but an official version of German–Polish history culminating in a series of guidelines on how those who would rule or settle in the East should conduct themselves towards the subject population. National Socialism represented the culmination of German history and was the most developed form of the 'world view' of the frontier fighter; in the future every German would be a frontier fighter and hence a National Socialist.[188]

Commencing in deep time, Lück established the permanence, and hence axiomatic irreconcilability, of 'German give' and 'Polish take' in the 'total struggle' fought along the line of a West–East 'cultural gradient'.[189] Running beneath his ellision of the various prejudices of a century was a subtle, coded message to the effect that when the Poles allied with the Germans they gained empire in the East, but if they confronted the Germans nemesis ensued. It was 'no accident' that the signatory of the Treaty of Kalisch in 1334 had received the epithet 'the great'.[190]

The state of the German Order in Prussia was 'an eastern bastion', 'German bulwark' or an 'outpost' protecting ethnic Germandom against 'polonisation' (*Verpolung*).[191] Eighteenth-century Poland, 'the promised land of limited power of the state, of lack of restraint ['freedom'!] on the part of the nobility' was contrasted with Berlin where 'well-trained soldiers . . . unity, readiness to make sacrifices and love of country' prevailed. In Warsaw 'drunken, chattering nobles kicked up a row against the King and State, the priests preached the most laughable stupidities to the people, and all was lost in feuding, immaturity and characterlessness'.[192] Nationality conflict was permanent, remorseless and timeless and there were no instances of cooperation between the two peoples. In the fifteenth century the Poles had launched 'a war of extermination against Germandom' and maps captured in 1939 showed that the 'machinery of repression that called itself the Polish state' wished to 'exterminate the whole of Germandom in the East' and to extend the Polish frontier to a line running from Rostock to Leipzig or even to the gates of Berlin.[193] With the conflict eternalized in this manner, Lück suggested that the resettlements (and deportations) of the present were the logical outcome.

The desire to separate the nationalities is deeply anchored in the consciousness of both peoples, especially after recent experiences. National Socialism, which today under the leadership of Adolf Hitler is in touch with the healthy instincts of the people, wishes to create a clear and final dividing line through settlement measures [bringing back the German ethnic exclaves] and has inaugurated a new epoch in the history of German settlement and a meaningful solution to the question of frontier areas in a part of the world where nationalities are intermingled.[194]

The permanence of nationality conflict suggested that it was rooted in the 'life of the soul' and had its own 'techniques, psyche and tactics ranging from healthy competition to the death blow'.[195]

The Germans worshipped at 'the cult of work', were 'superior', and faced the Poles 'calmly and with self-control'. The Poles were given over to 'enjoying life, negligence and carelessness' in their 'paradise of carelessness'.[196] Unfortunately the inevitability of the conflict had not been clearly understood by the rich who had often betrayed the *Volk*. The Prussian Estates had rebelled against the German Knights and Prussian *Polenpolitik* had pursued a 'zig-zag course' from 1815 to 1871.[197] Even Bismarck was not 'a supporter of a total struggle against *Polentum*'.[198] His successors had 'only' availed themselves four times of the Expropriatory Laws of 1908 and (Lück implicitly argued for the educational retardation of the Poles in the present), German teachers had turned a population that was '90 per cent illiterate' into an 'equally well educated opponent', through 'a detour via German schools the Polish illiterate was given the chance to decode Polish books and newspapers'.[199]

All pretence at objectivity deserted Lück as he raved against the Poland of the *Versailler Schanddiktat*. Scholarship and the siege mentality finally succumbed to hysteria. The German minority had been exposed to 'a satanically organised system to cut them down'. Ministers in a country with 'the lowest consumption of soap in Europe' had closed down German schools or dairies on hygienic grounds, and official chicanery was designed 'to wear down and exterminate the Germans'. Teachers had been transferred to 'the Jewish nests in the East'.[200] Lück's earlier studies of ethnic stereotypes in literature and proverbs degenerated into lists of Polish character faults 'fantasising, feeling, indulgence'; 'lack of restraint (regarded by them as 'freedom'), lack of discipline and perseverance, superficiality, inclined to parliamentarism' which he contrasted with German 'subordination of the individual to the good of the community', 'tenacity', 'thoroughness' and 'recognition of the leadership principle'.[201] The 'taciturn' and 'credulous' German was easily deceived by the Pole. Beneath the frivolity was a murderous hatred that was expressed in proverbs like,

'What's new?' 'Nothing much! They saw someone today who looked like a German and hanged him'.[202]

Lück concluded this litany of hate with a number of suggestions on how those settled or working in the East should behave towards the subject population. Only those who practised a 'soldierly, Prussian, mode of life, workers and thinkers' were needed. Although they would have to exercise 'tact' to promote the assimilation of 'racially and morally acceptable persons' from 'intermediary ethnic groups', moderation had resulted in 'fiasco' in the past.[203] Events like the 'bloodbath of September 1939' would have to be punished: 'bachelorhood and birth control' were 'sins' against the interests of the *Volk* and those who married 'nationally-conscious Polish partners' were to be treated as 'traitors'.[204] All Polish influences had to be 'cleaned out' of the repatriates and they would have to learn German habits like punctuality. It was a permanent, ongoing struggle for survival in which 'the frontier German remains the guard of honour of Greater Germany'.[205]

The PuSte itself kept government and NSDAP departments supplied with bi-monthly *Polenberichte*. These short hectographed reports were designed to keep interested politicians and administrators abreast of claims made by Polish propaganda, while providing them with the evidence of German achievements in Poland in the past. Thus Number 4 (12 June 1939), 'Polish Midsummer Night Dreams', attributed a postcard, produced by the Association of Popular Reading-Rooms in Poznań, depicting Polish claims to territory stretching up to Berlin to the recent spate of warm weather.[206] Number 5 took as its text a memorandum entitled 'Questions relatives aux territoires polonais sous la domination prussienne', which had been presented by Polish academics at Versailles. The professors had claimed that Danzig had been a Polish city since 997 and that East Prussia had to be isolated as 'a centre of Prussian militarism'. Despite the efforts of Lloyd George and General J. Smuts, an American professor called Lord had managed to convince Wilson of the Polish view of things.[207] Lloyd George himself was deemed worthy of an entire report. Number 22 quoted extensive extracts from his 'The Truth about the Peace Treaties' (1938) and, in particular, corrosive remarks he had made after a meeting with Paderewski who had laid claim to Galicia and Upper Silesia. The Welshman did not think that millions of Allied soldiers had laid down their lives in order to support Polish imperialism.[208] The PuSte's Wolfgang Kohte also endeavoured to undermine British–Polish amity by a report on the comments of an ambassador to Poland written in

1598. William Bruce's 'objective report' on the Noble Commonwealth no doubt brought a warm glow of fellow-feeling to Kohte's heart. The Scot had lambasted Polish 'mulishness', 'wrong-headedness', 'incapacity', 'factionalism', 'barbaric cruelty' and 'slovenliness' in language that would not have embarrassed Eduard Flottwell. Bruce had contrasted German cities like Thorn with the surrounding Polish disorder, while his remarks about antipathies between Poles, Germans and Hungarians underwent a sea change here to fit descriptions of modern Poland as 'a state of nationalities' as opposed to 'a nation state'.[209]

The theme of *polnische Wirtschaft* was stressed in many of the reports. Number 26 was entitled *Anarchie, Verwirrung und Unordnung* (!), and referred to comments made by Frederick the Great about West Prussia prior to 1772. The report used comments made by eighteenth-century Prussian commissioners – not known for their objectivity on conditions in Poland – to describe untilled fields surrendered to the thorny clutches of wild nature; desolate farm buildings; soil erosion caused by heedless asserting, and economic conditions in which peasants regarded bread as a delicacy. It was a classic statement of *economie polonaise*:

> The existence of the peasants who were severely oppressed by the taxes imposed by the Polish regime was more like that of beasts than human beings. The Oberpräsident von Domhardt reported to Frederick the Great on 24 February 1773 concerning the Starosteien Mirchau, Putzig, Schöneck, Berent and Parchau: Most of the peasants exist throughout the year without bread and live off roots and rotten vegetables while selling their meagre stocks of grain which they cultivate only in order to pay the burdens laid upon them.[210]

As well as uncritically purveying the prejudice of over a century, the PuSte reports painted a picture of Poland in which all cultural and economic achievement resulted from German endeavour. The woodcarvings of Veit Stoss, Frederickian colonization in West Prussia; German influences upon the Polish language, and the industrialization of Łódź were all grist to their mill.[211] German entrepreneurs like Scheibler, Biedermann or Peters had built industrial Łódź; the workforce consisted of Polish peasants. The only beneficiaries of Polish attempts to expel the Germans were the Jews:

> The only beneficiary of WW1 and the post-war years here was the Jew who now got his hands on most of the industrial capital and the textile factories which almost exclusively had been set up by Germans. Even

the tactics used by the Poles to push out the Germans only benefited the Jews. Łódźer Germandom defended its economic position with its characteristic tenacity as best as it could until the united mass of 300,000 Poles and 250,000 Jews broke over the heads of the 60–70,000 German souls in the town in the Summer of 1939. They appeared to have reconciled themselves to decline until they were saved from it by the victorious entry of our troops.[212]

Five reports later, the banners of the German Order were fluttering in the breeze at Marienburg.[213]

So far the activities of the *Ostforscher* have been seen to consist of involvement in resettlement actions and the production of a leaden stream of propaganda literature justifying German hegemony in the occupied East. The work of Sappok or Lück has been examined but there were many others – responsible for similar works. Further analysis would not promote understanding. There was a third area in which the *Ostforscher* were uniquely equipped to serve the regime. Policy towards the subject population pivoted on the existence of many intermediary ethnic groups. The German regime was not dealing with 'the Poles', but rather with several peoples who had been artificially subordinated to a series of imperialistic Polish states culminating in the 'Versailles state'. Their existence was to be stressed, and the *Ostforscher* had done precisely that, for as long as they were a convenient means of emphasizing the transient, superstructural, and artificial nature of the Polish state. Once that state had ceased to exist, and the intermediary groups had in some cases become part of the German Reich, they would in turn have to cease to exist. The example of the Lusatian Sorbs, who had provided an encapsulated and controllable experimental 'case' since the late 1930s, was probably paradigmatic for what ensued.

How the Masurians, Kashubians, Upper Silesians, and Teschener 'Schlonsaks', were treated in scholarly writing and in the Press depended largely upon changing propaganda priorities. On 8 September 1939 the Ethnic Liaison Office (VOMI) sent the RMdI a corrected version of a series of guidelines on the propagandistic treatment of these ethnic groups.

Guidelines on the Treatment of Masurians, Schlonsaks, Upper Silesians and Kashubians.

Current propaganda demands that the following four ethnic groups receive increased and careful notice:

The Masurians in the district of Allenstein,
the Schlonsaks in the Teschener area,
the 'Upper Silesians' and the Kashubians in northern Pomerelia.

The varying ethnic-political relations of these peoples makes it impossible to formulate generally valid principles for these four population groups. One can only say that none of them are to be described as Polish and that it would be equally unintelligent to describe their customs or the dialects that separate them from the surrounding population as Slavic, or to associate them in general in public with the concept 'Slavic'. It also seems undesirable to describe these demographic groups as 'mixed' races or their languages as 'mixed' tongues, because that could result in an individual having a feeling of inferiority, which could set an insurmountable obstacle on their path to German self-consciousness.

The following points should be observed for each group:

The *Masurians* (predominantly Protestant) are not to be described as Poles; and the dialect spoken at home by older people, or the bilingual, is Masurian and not Polish. Since this linguistic overlapping is the only example of what distinguishes the Masurians from the rest of the population of East Prussia – one thinks of their vote for the Reich of almost 100 per cent in the referendum after WW1 – it is generally not desirable that accounts of the historical development of their germanisation should refer to any sort of particularities.

The *Schlonsaks* were described up to now as a particular demographic group in the Teschener area, so that one spoke of four ethnic groups in the Teschener area: Germans, Schlonsaks, Czechs and Poles. Under the latter one understood migrant industrial workers from Galicia and Congress Poland, by Schlonsaks one understood the native peasantry (the Schlonsaks are mostly Protestant).

After the occupation of the Teschener area the words 'Schlonsak' and 'Schlonsakdom' must disappear from the German vocabulary. The word Schlonsak must only remain as the Polish translation of the word 'Silesian' in the form 'Slazak'. German linguistic usage can only recognise Germans, Czechs and Poles. The German population in the Teschener area consists of German inhabitants of the towns, i.e. Germans pure and simple, and the German Silesian rural population, in which concept Schlonsakdom can be subsumed.

The population of parts of Upper Silesia hitherto called 'Wasserpollaken' are in future to be described as *Upper Silesians*. Today one understands by 'Upper Silesian' the German speaking inhabitants of Upper Silesia as well as that part that still speaks a particular dialect. The term Upper Silesian is not entirely clear. With respect to the ethnic political situation it is not desirable to coin a new term. It is particularly important to stress that the latter are not Poles. It is important to stress the origins of the Upper Silesians and their transitional development to German consciousness . . . The Upper Silesians are not in general to be described as anything in particular. With respect to their Roman Catholic confessionality it is unintelligent to speak of a conflict between Polish–Catholic and German–Protestant in Upper Silesia.

The *Kashubians* are not Poles. One can trace the remnants of the ancient Pomeranians in them. In treatments of the Kashubians, opposition towards *Polentum*, of which there are many instances, is to be emphasised. In the long view however, such treatments of the Kashubians must take care not to force them into the role of a particular – even Slavic – ethnic group which might hinder their transition to Germandom of which there are many indications both in the past and at the present time. In the case of the Kashubians the temptation is always there to use the concept Slavic. Under all circumstances that must be avoided. On account of their adherence to the Roman Catholic church the conflict of Polish–Catholic and German–Protestant is also inappropriate.

Cartographic displays of the Masurians, Schlonsaks and Upper Silesians are not to distinguish them in any particular way, and they are always to be counted as part of the German ethnic or linguistic area. Under certain circumstances the Kashubians can be described as such.

The above guidelines recommend themselves for newspapers, periodicals and brochures etc. Since these guidelines stem from ethnic-political necessity, in the case of academic works, one must check whether with respect to these guidelines publication is permitted.[214]

The PuSte report on these VOMI guidelines specified that 'what is decisive is whether the areas inhabited by these groups belong to the Reich or not'. If the areas *did* then 'the principles tested in the Sorbian Question must be applicable'. This meant that the group concerned would not be mentioned in the Press and scholarly work would cease. If the ethnic groups lay *outside* the frontiers of the Reich then 'it is in the German interest to mention them as often as possible in public in order to divide them from the Poles'.[215] What this meant in practice can be seen from reports concerning the Kashubians and Masurians that passed through the PuSte office in the course of the war and from the treatment of the Sorbs, who amounted to an 'experimental case' for Nazi policy towards Slav ethnic minorities in general. In November 1939 the RMdI forwarded the PuSte a report on the Kashubians by a

Dr Petzsch, the chief medical officer in the West Prussian provincial labour office. Petzsch noted that the Kashubians around Stolp, Lauenburg and Bütow used German words with Polish endings while continuing to count in German. The rural proletariat was miserably poor, while the better off worked for the railways. Petzsch observed that 'the Kashubian is vigorous and thrifty, but has no initiative of his own, and needs someone standing behind him all of the time'. In an almost imperceptible slide from 'conventional' prejudice into thoroughgoing 'scientific' racism Petzsch suggested that members of the Kashubian upper class who had belonged to organizations like the Western Marches Association, intellectuals, and officials would have to be 'deported'; that the railway workers could be 'salvaged' if German Catholic priests were imported to undo the harm caused by the Polish clergy, and that 'less valuable elements' could be ultimately eliminated through 'sterilisation'.[216] The PuSte commentary on this report, sent to the RMdI on 20 December 1939, observed that 'we can only recommend the carrying out of the suggestions raised in the special report for the future handling of the Kashubian Question'.[217] That presumably extended to *all* of Petzsch's suggestions.

They also agreed with the contents of a report forwarded by the RMdI from the *Gauleitung* of East Prussia on the Masurian question. This deplored the fact that Masurians in western areas in the Reich were being discriminated against as foreigners. Some 98 per cent of the Masurians had voted for Germany in the referendum of 1920, and most had also voted for the NSDAP in 1932. All that they had in common with the Poles was their language, but that was so different from Polish that a Masurian speaker could hardly understand 'high Polish'. The Masurians were also Protestant. The report suggested that in future the term 'Masurian' was to 'disappear' in order to diminish the chances of 'members of our ethnic group' being treated as foreigners. All those Masurians who tried to 'conserve' their 'foreignness' were to be deported.[218]

Prompted by Benninghausen of the BDO, Vollert in the RMdI extended the blanket of silence that had been drawn over the Sorbs to these other ethnic groups.[219] Papritz thought that the ban was correct since 'final policy towards the Kashubians has not been determined' while Brackmann raised the unhappy affair of Reinhold Trautmann and the Sorbs as an unfortunate example of how scholarship could interfere with 'largely unclarified' ethnic–political relations.[220]

How these questions were going to be 'clarified' is already evident from Dr Petzsch's report and from Nazi policy towards the Sorbs. Nazi persecution of the Sorbs, which it is argued was paradigmatic for what was in store for other Slav minorities, included the closure of Sorbian cultural associations and newspapers between June and August 1937, the punitive transfer of Sorbian schoolteachers and clergymen out of Lusatia, a ban on the use of Sorbian as a medium of instruction in schools in 1938, the construction of a network of spies and informants, and the arrest and imprisonment in concentration camps of politically active or prominent Sorbs.[221]

The success of these measures can be gauged from an SD report dated 30 May 1940 on the Sorbs. A census carried out in Lower Lusatia in the previous year had revealed only 3,484 Sorbian speakers although the SD was certain that at least 20,000 existed. They attributed the discrepancy to the reluctance of the Sorbs to acknowledge their ethnicity for political reasons.[222] Since only costume and language appeared to distinguish the Sorbs, 'experts' advised that Sorbian festive gatherings and folk dancing should be banned and the participants drafted into the armed forces. The following measures were to be observed to accelerate germanization:

1. Any emphasis and promotion of Sorbian ethnicity must cease, although forcible measures or political denigration should be avoided.
2. The Sorbian ethnic splinter should be absorbed through peaceful cultural penetration. The most beneficial factors are German kindergarten, German schools, use of female labour, service in the army or NS formations.
3. The influence of the extraordinarily thin Sorbian intellectual class must be cut out. This can be achieved, since only teachers and clergy come into question here, mostly through transfers, without needing to occasion any disquiet in the population as a whole.[223]

In future, 'ethnic–political criteria' would determine the choice of teachers since the 'existence' of twenty Sorbian teachers in Lower Lusatia was contributing to the survival of the language. Transfers could be effected under cover of the war.

The German annexation of Czechoslovakia provided the regime with an opportunity to strike at Sorb sympathizers there, which in turn was a calculated stage in the isolation of the Sorbs in Lusatia. There was nothing pacific about the measures adopted, rather they were an advanced and violent stage of a process of negating Sorbian nationality pursued by a variety of agencies, whose earlier stages had seemed to consist of interfering with the publications of Tilka, Wirth or Trautmann. In June 1939, following the occupation of Czechoslovakia, the RMdI asked the *Reichsprotektor* in Bohemia and Moravia to prevent the Czech professors Josef Páta and Kretzschmer from lecturing at the university 'and if necessary to remove them from their chairs'. Páta was a leading member of the Society of Friends of Lusatia and, according to a BDO report, 'had always stirred up the Sorbs against Germany'. He had extensive connections in Lusatia with 'malevolent Panslavic agitators and anti-Germans', presented the Sorbian case for parity of treatment with the German minority in Czechoslovakia, and had helped Sorbian students with grants to enable them to attend the university of Prague.[224] This meant that Páta was a marked man. It did not avail him that most of his students were Czechs, since 'for as long as Sorbian is still taught, the desired result with regard to the Sorbian question cannot be attained'.[225] The RMdI was behind the times on Páta. On 3 May 1939 Dr Werner Best of the Gestapo reported to the authorities in Bautzen that the *Einsatzkommando* in Prague had raided the offices and homes of members of the Society of Friends of Lusatia, and had confiscated the libraries of Páta, Adolf Černý and Kretzschmer. The haul included the first printed Sorbian Bible.[226] Although the records of the Society had been destroyed before they arrived, the *Einsatzkommando* had arrested its administrator Dr Vladimir Zmeškal, 'who obdurately refused even to name a single German citizen' who had supplied the Society with material from Lusatia. The Gestapo were investigating Páta's 'misuse' of his professorship, asked the RMdI whether his chair could be abolished, and added that they had taken his passport to prevent his flight to Bulgaria or Yugoslavia.[227] Páta was imprisoned in Theresienstadt. He was sentenced to death on 23 June 1942 and executed the following day.[228]

The PuSte was a direct beneficiary of the eradication of Sorbian scholars and scholarly organizations. In February 1941 Essen in the RMdI asked the Security Police and SD to hand over to the PuSte the Sorbian Macica library in Cottbus.[229] The SD agreed, although they indicated that Professor Prinzhorn in Leipzig also had his eye on the books.[230] Cosack pleaded the PuSte claim on the grounds that 'the administration, and in particular the RMdI, will also in future have things to do with the Sorbs and the so-called Sorbian question'.[231] In December 1941 the Gestapo informed the PuSte that they would receive the looted books.[232] Cosack and Engel travelled via Dresden to

Bautzen. From their temporary abode in the Hotel Gude the two reported to Brackmann and Papritz about their tour of the confiscated libraries in the company of SS-*Oberführer* Klein. In Bautzen they found 8,000 religious books (25 per cent in Sorbian), and the Gestapo loaned them some prisoners – 'prisoners cost us nothing' – to help pack them.[233] On 18 February they went to Cottbus where the Gestapo officers from Frankfurt on the Oder helped orientate them. In a church tower at Selow, and in a barn at Döbrick, they found more school and language books. Cosack remarked, 'I took them with us because they will soon be a rarity.' On 19 February Cosack and Engel, aided by five prisoners, loaded 3,840 kg of books onto two furniture vans. The prisoners were cheap since 'one may not even give them cigarettes'.[234] In July 1942 the authorities in Bautzen had unearthed a further ten Sorbian book depositories.[235]

Armed with this material the PuSte could, and did, claim to be a repository of scholarly expertise on the Sorbian 'question' which was increasingly being given a racial solution. Work on the Sorbs was still subject to a ban regardless from which ideological quarter it issued. In July 1941 Essen in the RMdI sent the PuSte a copy of an essay by Heinrich Gottong entitled 'Are there still Sorbs?' Essen had instructed the Ministry of Propaganda to hinder similar publications, because 'the author believes one can decide ethnic or tribal relations with the methods of racial studies'.[236] Gottong had contrasted historical and archaeological evidence which suggested that the Sorbs had once been 'dark-haired' because of inter-breeding with extra-European races with the results of his own racial investigations in the present. Changes in field forms, dress and dwellings at the time of the German settlement of the East suggested that the Sorbs had ceased to exist some time ago. Only their language, which the Church had used to make Christianity *schmackhafter*, appeared to connect them with earlier Slav settlements. They had disappeared in a social-darwinian struggle with the Germans.

> Sorbiandom was not destroyed by war or exterminated, but slowly died out. It went under in a competition with people of germanic origin because it did not have such an unshakeable will to exist or so great a strength for life as the people who set out to create *Lebensraum* and a homeland for themselves and their children in the East.[237]

The RMdI asked the PuSte to report on Gottong's dissertation on the population in the Hoyerswerda area.[238] His work had been supported by the Institute for Racial Studies, Ethnic Biology and Rural

Sociology under H. K. F. 'Rassengünther' Günther. Essentially Gottong had tried to prove the greater affinity between Sorbian skulls and those found in germanic graves than appeared to exist between the former and skulls found on the Upper Dnieper. The PuSte commentators thought that even accounts like Gottong's which were entirely in accordance with the German view should not be published since an ethnic group 'in the process of germanisation' should not be brought into any connection with Slavs further afield and because 'the Sorbian question can only continue its artificial existence with the help of publications on the Sorbs'.[239] The same view was echoed in a second report on Gottong's work by Sappok.[240]

Clearly no longer so disturbed by academic work – of a precise racial type – on the Sorbs, the RMdI requested the names of academics capable of producing an anthropological study of the Sorbs.[241] In his letter asking Otto Reche whether he could do the work, Brackmann insisted that the RMdI wished to have a study of the 'racial composition of the present day Sorbs in Upper and Lower Lusatia, of the changes that took place in historical times and of whether the socio-biological settlement processes that could have influenced these changes could be clarified'. The object of the work was to settle the question of relative German, Polish and Czech influence upon the Sorbs. Reche had been investigating the Sorbs around Bautzen for 'eight years' already, but was too busy to do the work himself. For no longer a desk-bound warrior,

> I am overburdened with work to the limits of my strength, by teaching and administration, as a member and adviser to a considerable number of State and NSDAP offices, *and as an adviser on references on people's racial origins for various civil and military agencies and the courts.*[242]

He would need two of his assistants to be released from military service.[243] Although this work was indefinitely postponed in December 1942 (because plans to resettle the Sorbs in the mining regions of Lorraine or the Crimea, whose opening moves had already occurred in the form of deporting teachers and clergy, were shelved), what was in store for them at the hands of racial experts like Reche can indirectly be seen from an example of methodological infighting that broke out among the racial experts over Silesia. In August 1941 the PuSte called upon Reche to comment upon the series 'Race, Nation and Heredity in Silesia' edited by Arlt and Eichstedt.[244] A number of personal animosities were barely kept below the surface. Reche thought that the series was *ein regelrechtes Ungluck* and that despite *his* warnings (*invidia collegialis*), Eichstedt had pressed on in search of 'new', and 'sensationalist' findings. 'In many respects' Eichstedt was 'a journalist' who had dared to impugn 'blood-group refereeing' (*Blutgruppengutacherei*). Eichstedt and Arlt had purported to discover a 'Silesian *Gau* type', as well as six different racial categories in Silesia. These categories could be expressed numerically, so that a '6/6' meant 100 per cent nordic, or by letters, so that 'n.o.d.' expressed the presence of nordic, '*ostisch*' and dinaric characteristics in the proportion 2:2:2. A purist on these matters, Reche thought that Eichstedt and Arlt had omitted 'Lappoid' and 'Mongoloid' elements.[245] Worried by the uncomradely and *unsachlich* tone of Reche's report, the PuSte consulted Professor Lenz of the Institute for Racial Hygiene at the university of Berlin who suggested that, by Eichstedt and Arlt's criteria, only a third of the inhabitants of Silesia were nordic and that their maps of racial boundaries bore an unfortunate correspondence with boundaries depicted in pre-war Polish propaganda. Both of these discoveries were open to serious misuse by the enemies of the Reich.[246]

The racial experts whom the PuSte consulted and assisted were not armchair activists. Fritz Rudolf Arlt was born in 1912, joined the NSDAP in November 1932, and the SS in 1937.[247] He studied theology, anthropology and sociology at Leipzig, gaining his doctorate in 1936 for a 'racial–psychological contribution' to the study of women in Icelandic sagas.[248] Parallel with his thesis (and activities as the spokesman of the theology students of Leipzig), Arlt carried out an 'ethnic–biological investigation' of the population of Leipzig in his capacity as local representative of the Racial-Political Office of the NSDAP. This involved analysing the places of birth, addresses, distribution in the city, numbers of children, occupations and so forth of Leipzig's Jewish population. The result was to have the whole Jewish population of Leipzig, with details concerning whether they were 'full, three quarter, half or a quarter Jewish', on index cards.[249] Arlt's cards became the model for the card index on Jews being built up at that time by department II 112 of the SD. This department, where the career of SS-*Hauptscharführer* Adolf Eichmann had its modest beginnings, made contact with Arlt in July 1936.[250] Arlt's researches had a pioneering, paradigmatic value.

Working entirely on his own initiative, Arlt moved to Silesia to construct similar card indexes on a larger scale. He also published a number of articles on Jewish questions in NSDAP journals like *Der Schulungsbrief* or *Der Weltkampf*. In 1938 he published a piece entitled *Der Endkampf gegen das Judentum* in which he explained the nature of the 'new hostility towards the Jews' based upon 'blood'. All bridges of assimilation were cut off:

> The Jew can stress ideas, confession, membership of a nation as much as he likes. As long as his parents were Jews, he remains a Jew, and therefore different in spirit, belief, character and behaviour. There is no bridge for him to the community of non-Jews. Consequently, hostility to Jews on a racial basis represents a final struggle in the history of the struggle against the Jews as a whole.[251]

In July 1937 Arlt, leader of the Racial-Political Office of the NSDAP in Silesia since January, made contact with SS-*Gruppenführer* von dem Bach-Zelewski. The SS, he wrote, needed his expertise on 'migratory movements, demographic developments, racial reconstruction, and Jews in Silesia'. His office could provide a *Gesamtorientierung* in the region *and* information about foreign peoples in the *neighbouring* states.[252] He was taken into the SS shortly afterwards.[253] From 2 November 1939 until September 1940 Arlt was in charge of the department for demographic questions and welfare policy in the *Generalgouvernement*. A referee subsequently reported that he had devoted himself successfully to the question of how to handle the various 'elements' in the population and had organized a resettlement office which, under 'the most difficult circumstances', had 'resettled hundreds of thousands of people'.[254] Elsewhere Arlt suggested ways of solving Polish 'overpopulation' through seasonal migration, permanent resettlement, or the physical extermination of groups like the very young, the old and the sick through the removal of welfare provision. The resettlement of 1,500,000 Jews would also reduce the population density from 126 per square kilometre to 110, and create industrial or commercial jobs for the Polish rural proletariat.[255] Mass murder was coming into dangerous proximity with economic 'rationalisation'.

Wherever he worked, Arlt pleased. From September 1940 until May 1943 he was a *Stabsführer* with *Gauleiter* Bracht in Upper Silesia. There he carried out the resettlement of 35,000 persons and the 'inventorisation and seizure of property in the hands of foreign races etc. . . . in an irreproachable and most clean way'.[256] This last activity included determining whether the property left behind by Jews sent to concentration camps was allocated to German settlers or appropriated by the state.²⁵⁷ Despite his administrative labours, Dr Arlt still found time to be among scholars. In May 1942 he had a 'scholarly discussion' with a Professor Clauberg of the women's clinic in Königshütte. Clauberg wanted to extend his experiments on 'positive and negative' fertility from rabbits to 'five to ten women' in Auschwitz. This meant sterilizing them by injecting a caustic substance into the cervix to obstruct the fallopian tubes. Arlt had remarked that 'those in Germany with a particular interest in such things and who could help' included the *Reichsführer* SS. Hence Clauberg wrote that 'an annexe to your camp in Upper Silesia would provide the best preconditions' for his research.²⁵⁸ The annexe was the infamous 'Block 10'.

Arlt's contacts with the PuSte began in November 1940 when he asked the RMdI for information on the Teschener Schlonsaks. The PuSte sent him material by Aubin, Walter Kuhn (written under the pseudonym Georg Kursus), and Viktor Kauder, with the suggestion that he make contact with Karl Sczodrok in Opole.²⁵⁹ The SS requested further material on Schlonsaks, Górals, Masurians and Kashubians in February 1941 and received books in German, Polish and English.²⁶⁰ Himmler's own thoughts on these intermediary ethnic groups were contained in a secret memorandum which he set before Hitler on 25 May 1940. Entitled 'Some Thoughts on the Treatment of Foreign Peoples in the East' the paper was not merely a 'classical document of National Socialist hubris'.²⁶¹ Although it reflects Himmler's tendency to merge sweeping plans with seemingly absurd details, the paper was an accurate statement of what was being planned (and done) to both the ethnic groups discussed here and the Slavs in general. The quirky details merely camouflage the earnest intentions of the whole. Intentions which were essentially similar to those in Reche's memorandum of September 1939.

Himmler thought that it was in the German interest to discover as many ethnic groups as possible, including Ukrainians, White Russians, Górals, Lemkes, and Kashubians because this would facilitate dividing the population of the East 'into as many parts and fragments as possible'.²⁶² Ethnic consciousness among the small fragments would in turn be dissolved by using members of these groups as policemen and officials to watch over the rest. By dissolving the 'ethnic mush' (*Völkerbrei*) in the *Generalgouvernement* it would be possible to 'fish out' of the sieve 'racially valuable' elements who would be taken to Germany to promote their assimilation.²⁶³ Having used these groups to fragment the homogeneity of Poland, 'in four or five years time the concept of Kashubians, for example, must be unknown'. With the Jews dispatched to 'Africa', the 'concepts' of Ukrainian, Góral, or Lemke, as well as the Poles, were 'to disappear'. The subject population was to be reduced to helotry by restricting education to the ability to write their name, count up to 500, and learning that being obedient to the Germans was 'a command from God'. Learning to read was 'not desirable'. Although individual cases might be 'tragic', these policies seemed more humane than 'the Bolshevik method of physically exterminating a people' which was 'ungermanic and impossible'.[264] With racially valuable elements removed to the Reich, the population of the *Generalgouvernement* would consist of a residue of individuals of 'lesser value', those deported from the Reich, and peoples 'of the same racial and human type' like elements of the Sorbs.[265] This human reservoir was to be a source of manual labour for the major engineering works of the Reich. Neither the grotesque sanctimoniousness about the Soviet regime, nor the incongruous finer details (not to speak of the plan to send the Jews to Africa), should distract from what was an accurate description of what was being done to the 'intermediary' ethnic minorities at the time. The fate of the Sorbs was to befall the rest. Their consciousness of ethnicity would be first negated and then broken down by arresting, deporting or killing the leaders, and appropriating the tools of their culture; they would be sieved by racial experts like Reche or Eichstedt; and the results of that sieving would be the assimilation of the 'valuable' and the condemnation to, at best, a life of abject exploitation and, at worst, extinction through sterilization of the rest.

The invasion of the USSR considerably extended the scope of PuSte activities. Although the DDR historian Rudi Goguel was incorrect in arguing that from November 1941 the PuSte's *Polenberichte* were renamed *Nordostberichte*, for this had occurred in July 1940, there was undoubtedly a sudden increase in interest in the USSR from August 1941.[266] The titles of the PuSte reports produced in 1941 are indicative of this change of emphasis.

No. 50 (May) – The distribution of the Germans in Lithuania.
No. 51 (June) – Prague in German history.
No. 52 (June) – German academic life in Posen.
No. 53 (July) – Franconian art in Cracow.
No. 54 (July) – The *Ostpolitik* of the *Grosse Kurfürst*.
No. 55 (August) – Albert Brackmann and *German Ostforschung*.

No. 56 *(August)* – The formation of states by germanic peoples in
  the East.

No. 57 *(September)* – The Bolshevisation of schools in Latvia.

No. 58 *(September)* – The peasants of Estonia under Bolshevism.

No. 59 *(October)* – The Finns in NW Russia.

No. 60 *(October)* – The impoverishment of Estonia during a year of
  Bolshevik rule.

No. 61 *(November)* – 'The expropriation of the propertied classes'
  in Estonia by the Soviet Russians.[267]

The shift in emphasis was also stressed by Papritz in his contribution to a conference held in the Foreign Office from 29 September to
1 October 1941 on 'ethnic-political questions'. According to the
minutes of his speech, Papritz included among the objects of research
'the ethnic German past as well as biological investigations and
Rassenkunde, and the ethnic German achievement in the construction
and culture of foreign states'.[268] Present work carried out by the
NODFG and PuSte included the translation of books on the national
and racial characteristics of the Ukrainians, and the production of
maps of western Russia, the Kola peninsula, Karelia, 'Ingermanenland'
or the area around Leningrad, the Baltic states and the Ukraine. They
were also producing nationality maps that were ominously reminiscent
of earlier work on Górals, Kashubians and Lemkes. The list was
now extended to include 'Karelians, Finns, Ingrier' (both Protestant
and Orthodox), '*Wepsen*', Estonians, '*Sekuteren*', Latvians, Poles and
Jews.[269] This shift of emphasis towards the USSR was reflected in the
work of the cartographic department. A list of maps produced between
1 January 1942 and 31 December 1942 was dominated by maps of
the USSR. Six maps on the distribution of Russians, Finno-Ugrians,
Latvians, White Ruthenians, Poles and Jews on the scale 1: 2,500,000;
population density in European Russia in 1941; maps of new administrative boundaries and ethnographic maps of Karelia, Murmansk,
Leningrad, Pskov, Novgorod and maps of the strategically important
Kola peninsula.[270]

One of the smallest ethnic groups to exercise the *Ostforscher* was a
tribe of six or seven hundred Karaite Jews in Nowi Troki west of
Kaunas in Lithuania. Although the numbers involved pale into insig-
nificance beside the Jewish population systematically wiped out in
Poland and Russia, the fate of these people illustrates how questions
of survival or extermination quite literally hung on the decisions of
racial 'experts'. In August 1941 the General Kommissar in the Ukraine,

Essen – the PuSte's former RMdI controller – and two others visited Nowi Troki to decide whether the Karaites were Jews. The Karaites had been settled in the area as captives taken from the Tatars since the late fourteenth century and had acted as royal bodyguards for both Lithuanian and Polish rulers. They were part of a fundamentalist sect with adherents in Turkey, Egypt, and the Crimea; spoke an old form of Turkish or Russian 'devoid of [Yiddish] jargon', and practised a religion containing elements of Judaism, Islam and Christianity. The report on the Karaites reveals the extreme subjectivity of supposedly 'scientific' racial criteria:

> Judging by their appearance, the Karaites make an overwhelmingly Tatar–Near Asiatic impression; dark, with wide brown eyes, prominent cheekbones, and partly 'armenoid' extended skulls, and smooth Near Asian noses. Neither their gestures nor their overall appearance makes a Jewish impression.[271]

Leibbrandt in Rosenberg's Eastern Ministry eventually decided that since the Karaites farmed and were not engaged in Jewish 'parasitic' activities, they were not to be handled as Jews. This meant that 'all unnecessary hardness' was to be avoided lest this had unfortunate political consequences in the Orient.[272]

Through administrative or military service in the occupied East, some of the *Ostforscher* directly witnessed what 'necessary hardness' involved. 'Necessary hardness' was a euphemism for shooting as many Jews as the security police could get their hands on. Professor Peter-Heinz Seraphim, whose studies of Jewish ghettos were discussed in the previous chapter, was an expert on logistics in the Ukraine. On 2 December 1941 an armaments inspector forwarded a report by Seraphim to General Thomas which discussed the *economic* (!) consequences of scenes Seraphim had witnessed in the Ukraine. The report condemns the 'manner' of execution and invited the reader to sympathize with the psychological problems of the executioners. The sufferings of 'between 150,000 and 200,000' people were thoroughly incidental for him because in his myopic universe people were so many units of 'surplus mouths'.

c) *Jewish Question*

The resolution of the Jewish Question in the Ukraine was already a difficult problem because the Jews constitute a large part of the urban population. Therefore one is dealing with a demographic-political mass problem as in the *Generalgouvernement*. Many of the towns have a

Jewish population of over 50 per cent. Only the rich Jews fled from the German troops. Most of the Jews have been left to the German administration ... Getting rid of the Jews must have far-reaching economic and even direct military–economic consequences (production for the needs of the troops).

From the start the attitude of the Jewish population was fearful. They sought to avoid everything that would antagonise the German administration. That within they hate the German administration and army is understandable and one should not be surprised. But it is not proven that the Jews as a group have taken part in acts of sabotage to any extent. Certainly there have been a few terrorists or saboteurs among them, as among the Ukrainians. But one cannot maintain that the Jews as such represent any sort of danger to the German army. The troops and German administration are satisfied with the work of the Jews, which is naturally motivated by no other consideration than fear.

At first the Jewish population remained unscathed by direct military engagements. Weeks, and in part months later, the Security Police carried out the systematic shooting of the Jews. These actions moved from East to West. They took place in the open, with the help of Ukrainian militiamen, but often, unfortunately with the voluntary participation of members of the army. The manner of execution, which included men, the elderly, women and children was appalling. The order of numbers executed was so huge that it was unlike any similar measures hitherto carried out in the USSR. All together between 150,000 and 200,000 Jews in the parts of the Ukraine belonging to the *Reichskommissariat* have been executed, up to now without any regard to economic priorities.

Overall one could say that the solution of the Jewish Question carried out in the Ukraine obviously in terms of ideological perspectives has had the following effects:

a) getting rid of part of the surplus mouths [*überflüssiger Esser*] in the towns.

b) getting rid of part of the population which doubtless hates us.

c) getting rid of urgently needed craftsmen who were also indispensable to the needs of the army.

d) Foreign policy and propagandistic consequences which are obvious.

e) Ill-effects upon those troops who came into direct contact with the executions.

f) A brutalising effect upon the units (Security Police) who carried out the executions.

The creaming-off of agricultural surpluses from the Ukraine as food supplies for the Reich is only conceivable if trade in the Ukraine is pushed down to a minimum. Efforts to achieve this will be made by:

1. Eradicating surplus mouths (Jews and the population of the large Ukrainian cities) which, like Kiev, will receive no quota of supplies.
2. By radical reduction of the rations made available to the Ukrainians in the other towns.
3. By lowering the consumption of the peasant population.

One must be clear that in the Ukraine only the Ukrainians will produce anything of any economic value. If we shoot the Jews, let prisoners of war die, and deliver a large part of the population of the major towns to death by starvation, and in the coming years lose a part of the rural population through hunger, the question that will remain unanswered is 'Who will actually produce anything of economic value here?'

. . . [Summary]

A considerable part of the Jews in the towns of the RK, constituting more than half the population in some places, have been executed. This has removed a large part of the craftsmen and that has affected the needs of the army (troop needs, billets).

Billeting, care, clothing and state of health of prisoners of war is bad, mortality very high. One must reckon on the demise of many tens or hundreds of thousands this winter. Among them there are elements which could have been used with profit in the economy of the Ukraine as skilled workers and craftsmen.[273]

Seraphim's colleague Theodor Oberländer was also active in the Ukraine, as an expert on 'ethnic psychology', and as an officer with units of Ukrainians formed from the remnants of the Polish army. He operated with a unit called the 'Nightingale Battalion' – they sang – in the Ukraine, and then with the 'Bergmann Battalion' in the Caucasus.[274] In January 1942 Oberländer sent Brackmann a detailed report on conditions in the Ukraine. At first, only 10 per cent of the population consisting of 'Jews, Communist Party people left behind, and a small section of the young' had opposed the invaders.[275] The old and the farmers anticipated the end of collectivization. Success in the Ukraine lay in 'winning over the masses and pitilessly exterminating partisans as deleterious to the people'. Conditions in the Ukraine had sharply deteriorated since October 1941: German conduct was alienating the populace and driving them into the hands of the partisans.

It can be established that we frequently confuse Jews and Ukrainians and that the treatment applied to the Jews is frequently extended to the Ukrainians which leads to serious grievances among them.

Certainly there have been cases where German soldiers have been too trusting; but how much more frequent are the cases in which we have behaved unpsychologically, and through casually made errors, have lost every vestige of sympathy among the population. The shooting of prisoners who could go no further, in the middle of villages and larger places, and the leaving about of their bodies are facts that the population cannot understand, and which confirm the worst distortions of enemy horror propaganda.[276]

By starving the population of Kiev and looting villages along their lines of march, the Germans had played the Ukrainian population into the hands of the partisans. In a few weeks they had lost all support. Partisans backed by, and recruited from, the local population and led by 'Bolshevik agents', would never be defeated. The results were attacks on bridges, trains, and agricultural machinery. The idea that the Ukrainians would embrace the Germans because of their hatred of the Poles and Russians was 'self-delusive'. Propaganda would have to enlighten the Ukrainians about life in Germany to counter enemy propaganda that described the Nazi race laws; capital would have to be found to stimulate private enterprise in the Ukraine; and skilled workers would have to be sent to Germany whence they could avail themselves of generous postal facilities to explain to their families and friends how good life in the Reich was. An auxiliary force of police and a network of centres to assist informers would help deal with the partisans.[277] Leaving aside the complex question of whether Oberländer's 'Nightingales' were responsible for shooting several hundred Jews in Lemberg (L'vov) in early July 1941 – and the Poles cleared Oberländer of war crimes charges in 1975 – the question comes to mind of how anyone who advocated 'pitilessly exterminating' partisans, or who led the BDO, managed to have a political career at all after 1945, let alone one culminating in a ministerial portfolio in Adenauer's government.[278]

The problems presented by the USSR dominated a conference of interested academics and officials that was held under the patronage of Rosenberg's Ministry for the Occupied Eastern Territories between 24 and 27 March 1942. Speaker after speaker unfurled their portmanteau notions of Soviet society and how the USSR could best be digested. The Soviet 'madness of world domination' was rooted in the Orthodox religion, Tsarism, and Pan-Slavism. Russia had 'never existed' and parts of continental European Russia would have to be 'orientated' away from Asia.[279] The Germans would have to set out on a path once taken by the Goths who had been diverted elsewhere by the Hunnic hordes. On account of the high proportion of Germans who had served the Tsars as officers and officials, and because of the achievements of the latter, Germany had an absolute right to the 'region'.[280] Lines of thought already familiar from the Polish experience recurred:

> The racial, psychological and culture-promoting strength of the individual peoples of the USSR, who appear in the statistics as about 150,000,000 people, of which perhaps only 12,000,000 are significant for a political and economic new order in Europe, must be investigated.[281]

or,

> In the new area of ethnic research the racial question has to be solved, which is very difficult since the USSR is a conglomerate of races. Up to now, neither the Russians nor the Germans have produced work on this. The first preparatory works are now being undertaken with Soviet prisoners.[282]

or,

> We are beginning to make appropriate measurements in prison camps. It is astonishing how many West European types one finds. A much higher percentage of nordic racial elements in the Greater Russian as well as the Finno-Ugrian races is to be found than one earlier assumed.[283]

Other speakers discussed whether or not any more Russian physicians should be trained; the need for 'step by step reprivatisation' of state owned property; the desirability of large-scale industrial plant to rival the USA; the desirability of teaching the children of foreign peoples 'respect for Germany as the creator of Europe' and of the closure of Jewish-dominated Soviet universities; of how the Germans should appear as a self-confident 'master race' or, of the ways in which Soviet Communism had appropriated Dostoievskian messianism.[284]

Rosenberg summed up the proceedings. The Russian plain was an open door for invaders from Europe and Asia. Centrifugal forces, in Finland, the Baltic, Ukraine, Caucasus and Turkestan, would have to be exploited to accelerate the demise of the overall Soviet superstructure.[285] When the Germans overcame their class differences and when the nations of Europe were united, a new internationalized *Ostlandritt* could resume.[286] One of the few concrete results of these three days of academic and bureaucratic grand strategy was the formation of an international steering committee under Seraphim at the *Osteuropa-Institut* Breslau, designed to develop contacts between German scholars and their colleagues in Croatia, Bulgaria, Turkey, the Ukraine and Hungary.[287]

Otto Reche was also keen to destroy the USSR through the agency of centrifugal ethnic forces. It is worth stressing that only the tone and unscientific erraticism of his various suggestions, and not the substantive content meant that his plans were not taken up. If his ideas sometimes soared shrilly above those of the regime, for much of the time the two were in harmony. The points where agreement prevailed are as worthy of notice as where it did not. In March 1942 he sent Kohte an article on the future of the Soviet Union. Kohte forwarded it to Rosenberg's Ministry for the Occupied Eastern Territories at the end of the month. In his covering letter, Reche explained:

> It can hardly be a coincidence that the words 'Russia' and 'Russian' have disappeared for some time from the vocabulary of newspapers and radio announcers; hopefully not just to underline the difference between 'Russian' and 'Bolshevism'!
>
> In my opinion the concept 'Russian' is in itself very suspect, and must be eradicated in the future, so that it does not become a crystallisation point for a new, and for us, politically dangerous structure, or even for renewed Pan-Slavism, whose reemergence must be hindered for all time.
>
> The eastern European *Raum* must not only be heavily subdivided into single countries, but also the individual peoples must keep *or receive* their ancient names and the name Russia must be replaced by older names. Rivalries between the races are to be encouraged. The smaller the individual area, the easier they will be to command; even White Ruthenia, and in particular the Ukraine (in its present extent) seem to me to be dangerously large ... The more we encourage self-consciousness in the individual peoples, the fewer political difficulties we will have in future, and so less the danger that racial mixing with the Germans who rule or settle there will take place: the ethnic distance must be as great as it can possibly be, and no one should arrive at the biologically destructive thought that these peoples of foreign race should be 'germanised'! The territories that we need for the settlement of German peasants must be totally cleared of the natives![288]

The Ministry thought that Reche's stress on the plurality of ethnic groups in the USSR was correct 'in itself', but that his plans to revive obscure groups like the *Wiatitschen* or *Sewerjanen* would not greatly assist the struggle against the claims to hegemony of *Russentum*.[289] Undeterred, Reche sought to elaborate his two main ideas of '*das "divide et impera"*' and the eradication of the term Russia.[290] In a further letter to Kohte he explained that:

> As an eastern German – a Silesian – I have been involved in the ethnic struggle against Slavism since my schooldays. For example, even as a schoolboy I gave a lecture to the class on *Polentum* and the inevitability of conflict between Germans and Slavism. Over the years I have always been struck by the strong suggestive power that the word Russia exercises on all of the other Slav peoples: 'little old mother Russia' has understood how to carry out a long and well-financed propaganda campaign as the great protectress of all of the Slavs; without Russia it would never have come to the far more menacing Pan-Slavism. Russia gave birth to it, naturally to pave the way for a large-scale imperialistic policy. Even in Tsarist times they wanted to expand their sphere of influence with the aid of Pan-Slavic ideas, beyond Constantinople to the whole of the Balkans up to Adria, and at least as far as the Oder!
>   . . . In my opinion it would be a mistake if we allowed the concept 'Russian' to remain. It would be a further error if we did not split up 'Greater Russiandom'; however the parts must receive names, and there it seems to me that the ancient historical names – although they no longer endure in popular consciousness (*in the area of ethnicity much has already been successfully brought back to life!*) – would perhaps be better than any sort of new inventions. Perhaps it would be possible to use terms connected with the main towns in each area?[291]

Just how closely these ideas corresponded to reality can be illustrated by a series of 'Provisional Semantic Regulatory Guidelines on the Concepts of the East' issued by the RMdI on 14 March 1942. The term 'Russia' was permissible for the 'Petersburg empire and for its "democratic" latecomers from Peter the Great to the October Revolution of 1917'. The period from about 1300 to Peter the Great was to be referred to as the time of the 'Muscovite state'.

> Fundamentally only those ethnic and geographical terms are to be used which reflect ethnic relations and thereby correspond with German conceptions. The terms which the bureaucracy of the [Petersburg] empire and the Soviets used and sought to make credible, mostly had definite aims and are suited to supporting Greater Russian propaganda.[292]

Concepts like:

White Russia (instead of White Ruthenia)

Little Russia (for the Ukraine)
Russian Sea (for the Black Sea)
Russian Asia (for Siberia)

are to be absolutely avoided since they belong to the terminology of Muscovite imperialism (Russification measures).

Acounts and expressions which refer to the linguistic or racial community between Finns and Estonians (Finno-Ugric peoples) are to be avoided. The *Ingermanländer* are to be described as a people who are closer to the Estonians than the Finns.[293]

Tatars: The concept is a Russian (Muscovite) pejorative collective term for the Volga, Crimean and Aserbeidschan Turks and is to be avoided and replaced by the concepts 'Idel-(Volga)-Uraler', 'Crimean Turks' and 'Aserbeidschaner'.

Separatists: The term 'Separatists' as applied to members of the peoples of the former USSR who strive for national independence is a discovery of the Muscovite bureaucracy. Therefore it is to be eradicated. A 'Separatist' is one who seeks to treasonably separate himself from *his people*. Precisely that does not apply to the peoples of the former USSR who seek to break away from Moscow.[294]

Terms like 'Bolshevism' or 'Communistic' could be used to describe the Soviet system, as in 'bolshevistic chaos' or 'communistic elements', but one could not speak of a 'Communist Empire'.[295] The tone of the report was drier and less intemperate than the work of Reche, but in essentials it said precisely the same things. Uncharted distances, and peoples known only as terms on maps, were to be made manageable in a continuous cycle of rebirth and destruction according to racial criteria, and in terms of the maxim *divide et impera*.

iii. From the Quay d'Orleans to Kharkov: the Einsatzstab Rosenberg and SS-Sonderkommando Grüppe-Künsberg

The triumph of German arms provided German academics with the opportunity to appropriate libraries and archives from the occupied territories. The first libraries to be looted were close to home: those of the Sorbian cultural associations and of the Polish minority in Germany. The PuSte scooped up a wide range of libraries and collections of books built up by the Poles in Germany. In January 1940 the RMdI sent the PuSte a catalogue of books confiscated on their orders by the Gestapo from a number of Polish libraries. The list included

240 books from the Polish school association 'Bremenja' in Bremen; 500 books from the Gymnasium in Marienwerder; 1,000 patriotic novels taken in Gleiwitz; 2,500 books from Bochum, 670 from Münster, 430 from Gelsenkirchen, 90 volumes belonging to the Association of Polish Women in Oberhausen and so on.[296] The PuSte was interested in the historical novels and in 2,000–3,000 titles taken from libraries in Beuthen and Darmstadt.[297]

The RMdI instructed the SS to hand over the items requested by the PuSte, and to turn the 'literary and politically neutral' pulp fiction over to Hans Frank in Cracow where 'it is envisaged that these books will be used as a basis for a newly created state lending library for the Polish inhabitants of the *Generalgouvernement*, in order to minimize the politically harmful influences of the many existing private lending libraries'.[298] In October 1940 the PuSte staff met Essen and Böhmer from department IV B.4 b. of the RSHA to distribute the spoils.[299] Subsequently, the PuSte sent Böhmer a book by Viktor Kauder and Sappok's guide to occupied Cracow as tokens of gratitude 'for worthwhile collaboration over many years'.[300]

There were far greater libraries on offer than 8,000 Sorbian books or the libraries of Polish schools and cultural associations. In October 1940 Brackmann informed Aubin that:

> With respect to our relations with the *Amt Rosenberg* I can only tell you – with a request for the utmost discretion – that the Amt is inclined to hand over to us one of the Polish libraries in return for collaboration over certain questions. We immediately informed the RMdI of the proposal and learned from there that the ministry is in agreement. We want to wait to see how matters develop and for this reason it seems expedient if we postpone negotiations for a while. Incidentally, Papritz has returned very satisfied from Prague. We will receive a number of books from there which we lack at present and thereby will be in a position to increase our Czech collection.[301]

In a letter to the RMdI dated 15 July 1940 Wolfgang Kohte argued that the incorporation of Poles and Czechs into the Reich made accurate study of their way of life, and of propaganda emanating from Czech or Polish exiles abroad, a pressing task. He continued:

> The present circumstances offer the chance to considerably expand our library which, in view of the tasks for the future outlined in the introduction, should not, in my opinion remain unexploited. First of all we can definitely anticipate, on the basis of negotiations with the

Foreign Office archives and its representatives in Prague, the handing over of certain collections of Czech or foreign language books concerning Czechoslovakia. It can also be assumed that *Staatsarchivdirektor* Dr Papritz will succeed in securing a large number of double copies from Baltic German libraries for the PuSte.

Concerning Poland, a short while ago a large library in Warsaw was offered to us. It is not possible at the moment to say whether its removal to Berlin is feasible. We are trying to clarify the question. In principle *Ministerialdirektor* Dr Vollert has agreed some time ago to the PuSte's acceptance of the library of about 100,000 books.

It seems most urgent to take steps concerning the Polish and Czech libraries in Paris. We have already drawn attention in our report of 20 May to the importance of the Polish and Czech establishments in Paris and to the foreign–political necessity of their transfer to the Reich. Considerable difficulties will arise today over the acquisition of these libraries. Precisely these collections will correspond particularly well to the needs of the PuSte, as by the same token, the PuSte has the first claim to these libraries on account of its activities to date.[302]

The object of their attentions in Paris had been inspected by Sappok during a visit to Paris in the spring of 1939. In a memorandum dated 7 October 1940 Sappok rehearsed the history of the *Bibliotheka Polska* from its founding by Prince Adam Czartoryski in 1838, the number and names of staff employed in its building on the Quay d'Orleans, and the scope of its holdings. The latter included about 130,000 volumes, 7,000 medals and coins dating from the fourteenth to the nineteenth centuries, a photographic archive, 1,000 manuscripts, 2,560 maps and atlases and 9,000 objets d'art.[303] Since several parties were interested in 'securing' the library – the RSHA had already quietly moved off with the equivalent Czech library – speed was imperative.[304]

A Polish library employee managed to relay a report on the fate of the library to the London-based exile paper *Dziennik Polski i Dziennik Zolnierza*. At first *Wehrmacht* officers had searched the building for secret documents. They were replaced by forty-five men from the *Einsatzstab Rosenberg* some of whom spoke Polish. The latter tore down the Jagiellonian eagle adorning the building and began cataloguing and packing the books. The Polish librarian went in vain to protest to the army high command and the Gestapo in the Avenue Foch. Threatened by the latter, he decided to smuggle books to his home on the Rue St Louis by cart. Eventually he had to move his furniture out in order to accommodate the books.[305] Others managed to rescue Chopin scores.[306]

On 19 September 1940 the Foreign Office informed the PuSte that the *Amt Rosenberg* had inherited the library from the soldiery.[307] On the afternoon of 11 October a meeting was held in the RMdI between Vollert, Essen, the director of the Berlin Staatsbibliothek, Papritz, Sappok and Krüss the General Commissioner for Libraries in the occupied West. The meeting resulted in the decision that the books, maps and copperplate engravings should go to the PuSte and duplicates to the Staatsbibliothek. A pencilled list marked the 'score' as 'us 120,000'/'Staatsbibliothek duplicates 20,000'.[308]

Although Rosenberg made much of a commission from Hitler empowering him to use books confiscated in the western zone of operations as the basis for the library of a future Nazi university, he came to an agreement with Frick whereby:

1. The Paris Polish library is the property of the university and stands under the sole disposition of *Reichsleiter* Rosenberg.
2. The library will be put at the unrestricted disposal of the RMdI.
3. The RMdI commissions the PuSte, which is subordinate to him, with the administration of the library whose leader thereby assumes responsibility for leadership of the library.
4. In so far as for purposes of looking after the library it is necessary to employ persons over and above the personnel of the PuSte, these appointments will be made after prior agreement with *Reichsleiter* Rosenberg.
5. Tasks will be allotted to the leadership of the library by mutual agreement between the *Reichsleiter* and RMdI.[309]

With the question of ownership resolved in this provisional way, the PuSte staff pressed on with the technicalities of transporting over 100,000 books. In December 1940 they asked the SS whether the latter had the services of middle-ranking librarians 'available in your orbit' who could read Polish, Russian and French or an academic from Bessarabia able to read Ukrainian.[310] Aided by three assistants, Kohte spent six months up to September 1941 packing 2,050 metres of books.[311] In the winter of 1941 the wagons rolled towards Berlin with a total of 766 cases including the *Encyclopedia Britannica*, 66 volumes of Voltaire, a portrait of Piłsudski and busts of Miekiewicz.[312]

The books were stored in magazine VI of the Geheime Staatsarchiv while the contents of the Miekiewicz Museum went to the second floor of Potsdamerstrasse 61 which was made available by the RMdI.[313] The books remained in the Geheime Staatsarchiv until February 1943 when they joined books looted from the Maćica Serbska in the Potsdamerstrasse.[314]

The PuSte library also benefited from looting operations undertaken by the *Einsatzstab Rosenberg* in the occupied East. In October 1942 Cosack and Kohte paid a visit to the *Buchsammelstelle* at Alt-Moabit 130 to inspect a catalogue of duplicates newly acquired in Riga.[315] They asked for a copy of the catalogue and to be kept informed when the books arrived in Berlin. With no sense of irony, Rosenberg's staff indicated that the books were only to be considered as on loan to the PuSte since the matter of ultimate ownership would be determined after the war. They also objected to the term *Buchsammelstelle*, preferring the less forthright 'library in the process of construction'.[316] Trips made to the East by PuSte staff also enabled them to put their markers down at an early stage in the looting process. In April 1944 Hermann Weidhaas made a trip to Kowno, Wilna, Minsk and Bialystok. Armed with a pass bearing the RF-SS seal, Weidhaas was well-received by various SS and SD officers like SS-*Untersturmführer* Schlemm in Wilna or SS-*Sturmbannführer* Sepp in Minsk. In Wilna he was allowed to use the SD canteen. In Minsk he negotiated the surrender to the PuSte of 20,000 books on White Ruthenia with SS-*Standartenführer* Langkopf and Dr Richel from the *Einsatzstab Rosenberg*.[317]

The SS was also active in the book trade in the USSR. According to the testimony of SS-*Obersturmführer* Dr Förster, who was captured by the Red Army at Mozdok, in August 1941 he had been invited by a friend from university days who worked in the Foreign Office to join a special *Waffen*-SS battalion of about 303 men under SS-*Sturmbannführer* Eberhard Freiherr von Künsberg. The unit consisted of four companies which were attached to each army group to plunder diplomatic archives, museums, libraries, and art treasures. Förster's company operated alongside Army Group 'South' and looted the Ukrainian Academy of Sciences and medical laboratories in Kiev.[318] These SS units were accompanied by expert civilians. In Kharkov they looted the Korolen Library including a few thousand valuable editions.[319]

The civilian experts probably came from the circle of the NODFG. In July 1942 the SS-*Sonderkommando* 'Gruppe-Künsberg' wrote to the NODFG seeking assistance.

The SS-*Sonderkommando* 'Gruppe-Künsberg' is again in action in the *Ostraum*. Our tasks have been increased considerably through the taking over of the entire field of Geography into the categories of materials to be secured by the commando. The commando can only do justice to these increased tasks through increased employment of suitable co-workers. Since your office has already received considerable material from the work of the commando in past years, and is interested in the supply of further material, we ask you to name from your circle suitable forces to strengthen the commando in the field of Geography and who would come in question for participation in actions in the East.[320]

The object of this odd collaboration between a battalion of the *Waffen-SS* and a library in Dahlem were cases of books plundered from libraries in the Soviet Union. In May 1942 three cases of books on Russian intellectual history consisting of 253 volumes, were delivered to the PuSte;[321] in October 1942 17 cases;[322] and in November further cases were ready for collection from the SS store in the Hardenbergstrasse.[323] The trade in looted books continued in early 1943.

At the same time we dispatch 7 cases of books for the NODFG. You are requested to unpack the cases and to send them back as soon as possible and to unpack cases nos. 49 and 134 whose contents are destined for the SODFG in Vienna and to store them since at present no transport facilities exist.[324]

The principal Polish state archives consisted of five archives in Warsaw and others in Cracow, Poznań, Lublin, Bydgoszcz, Kielce, Piotrkow, Płock and Radom.[325] There were also ministerial archives in Warsaw for military, foreign and judicial records; some 200 municipal archives; several capitular, consistorial and monastic archives and a number of private archives like the Zamoyski or Radziwill collections. The Zamoyski archive alone contained some 30,000 items from the sixteenth to the twentieth century.[326] During the short war, some archives were subjected to outright vandalism – as when documents were thrown out of the Wawel to make room for Hans Frank – and others in Warsaw were destroyed by bombing and shelling. The archive of Public Education lost about 40,000 units; the Treasury Archives some 130,000 units.[327]

According to a report by Zipfel, the Director of the Prussian State Archives, dated 7 December 1939, the RMdI had charged the Prussian archival administration with responsibility for 'securing' Polish archives. Following the 'lightning victory of our army', in the first half of September teams of Prussian archivists descended upon the Polish archives: Weise (Berlin), Buttkus (Magdeburg) and Eilers (Dresden) to the central archives in Warsaw; Randt and Goetting (Breslau) to Łódź, Katowice, Cracow, Radom, Toruń and Gnesen; Gollub and Forstreuter (Königsberg) to Poznań. The scenes they discovered were not encouraging. In the Warsaw ministries they found charred records covered in soot and broken glass and evidence that a Colonel Waldenfels of the Herresarchiv in Potsdam was making off, *manu militari*, with thousands of metres of military records.[328] Elsewhere they experienced difficulties in getting access to ecclesiastical archives 'since many leading clergy have been arrested'.[329]

Before leaving Berlin for Poland, Randt received instructions:

1. To secure and take care of all archival material to be found in State or non-State archives and in other places and to make them accessible to officials and German research workers.
2. To define the documents of German origin and prepare them to be returned to Germany.
3. To support German research requirements, particularly those which served to maintain German claims to Poland and to shed light on the history of the German nation and German cultural influences in Poland.[330]

During October and November Randt – he was appointed as chief of the archives on 12 October 1939 – established an archival administration in the *Generalgouvernement* with a central directorate in Cracow and four *Archivämter* in Warsaw, Lublin, Radom and L'vov.[331] The archives in North and West Poland were incorporated into the network of Prussian archives and subordinated to the Central Directorate of the Prussian archives in Berlin. This dual division of the archives mirrored the political division of Poland into an incorporated area to be germanized and an indeterminate residual state. Divide and rule was to be extended to the historical record.[332]

The first documents to be removed from Poland were those records which had been returned to Poland under international agreements from any of the German states. These were shortly followed by records issued by the partitioning powers between 1772–1806. In this way some 22,000 bound volumes of Prussian central records concerning South, New East and West Prussia were loaded onto three railway wagons and shipped to the Geheime Staatsarchiv.[333] Three more wagonloads of records concerning Austrian Galicia – which had not been unpacked since being returned to Poland under a treaty with Austria in 1932 – were sent to Vienna.[334] Some seventy-four charters from the Polish Royal Archive which had been handed over to the King by the German Knights in 1525 were removed to Königsberg.[335]

Following a meeting between Zipfel and the archival administrators in the *Generalgouvernement* in late May 1940 it was decided to further reduce the homogeneity of the Polish archives by returning records to their place of origin in the incorporated territories.[336] Since the duchies of Auschwitz and Zator were now part of Silesia, in May 1940 four large lorries moved court and land records from Cracow to Katowice.[337] These were followed by three wagonloads of records from the Central Archives of Earlier Records in Warsaw destined for Poznań and several thousand volumes of records and maps to Königsberg and Katowice.[338] Individual German researchers also demanded the shipment of groups of records pertinent to their investigations: in 1943 168 documents dating from 1215–1456 from the Livonian department of the Crown Archives were dispatched to Berlin.[339] For the tasks of the Prussian archives had altered since the Brackmann era. If in the 1930s it was a matter of 'weakening Polish claims to Reich's territory with proof of ancient German settlement', by 1940 the object was 'to bring forth evidence that all higher life in the eastern *Raum* is of German or Nordic origin and that the Slavic peoples themselves, need the disciplining hand of the Germans in order to achieve peace and prosperity'.[340] This meant producing studies of the achievements of 'Germandom' in the East, including the 'German' system of towns and studies of the Jews through the employment of records systematically looted from Polish archives.[341] Reviewing the work of his subordinates, Zipfel concluded:

> All German archivists have fully and entirely fulfilled their duty, as is self-evident to them, as National Socialist officials, for Führer, Nation and Fatherland. In the future too, they will labour tenaciously and indefatigably, with cool heads but with fire in their hearts, in keeping with the maxim: *Mehr sein als scheinen.*[342]

This 'famous page in the history of the Prussian archival administration' was repeated following the attack on the Soviet Union.[343] Polish territories vacated by Soviet forces yielded a rich haul of records which the Poles (or the Russians) had moved eastwards. In Ossolini in July 1941 Randt discovered the Pless archives and records from the plebiscite in Upper Silesia, in a Bernardine monastery, and personnel records from the administration in Katowice in the cellars of the Soviet archives. Seeberg-Elverfeldt operating in Volhynia unearthed the records of the Ministry of Justice in Dubno and of the Ministry of Posts in Zdolbúnow. Since the Soviets were also in the business of 'securing' archives, Buttkus discovered the Radziwill papers, two-thirds of the records of the Grand Duchy of Lithuania and 50,000 registry records in Minsk, while Kurt Forstreuter discovered the Lithuanian central state archives in a nunnery at Pažaislis.[344]

The most serious losses suffered by the Polish archives were not the work of Randt and Zipfel. During the course of the Warsaw Rising in August 1944, German aircraft dropped incendiary bombs which destroyed 400,000 bound volumes in the Archive of Earlier Records in the Old Town. Artillery fire resulted in the loss through fire of a further 30,000 bound volumes in the Treasury Archives.[345] On 2 September 1944 German troops set fire to the Archive of Earlier Records, which meant the loss of over 1,600,000 records dating from the sixteenth to the nineteenth centuries.[346] A month after the Poles had formally surrendered, SS 'clearance-commandos' destroyed a further 1,200,000 records in the Archive of Recent Records and 400,000 items in the Municipal Archives. The combined losses of the archives of Warsaw alone have been estimated at 92.8 per cent.[347]

iv. 'Your firm, our firm': disintegration and reconstruction

The war took a savage toll of the ranks of those scholars working in the PuSte or under the aegis of the NODFG. The archivist and SA-*Sturmführer*, Dr Fritz Morré, fell outside Leningrad on 21 November 1941.[348] Brackmann fondly recalled Morré's debut at his graduate seminar ten years earlier 'in a Brown shirt'.[349] The medievalist, Dr Karl Kasiske, died on a reconnaissance mission near Leningrad on 25 November 1941.[350] Brackmann observed that matters were 'now almost as bad as in WW1'.[351] A month later SS-*Hauptsturmführer* Dr Kurt Lück was killed fighting partisans in the USSR.[352] In July 1944 the PuSte's SS-*Untersturmführer* Dr Gerhard Masing, a veteran of the 1st Battalion SS-Panzer grenadiers 'Totenkopf I' who had been stationed in Warsaw, was killed fighting partisans at Mitau.[353] Two months later Gerhard Sappok disappeared after an encounter with the Maquis in Autun.[354] By January 1943 eight of the PuSte's academic staff of 16 were in the field; Ost with the *U-Booten* in the Arctic Circle; SS-*Oberscharführer* Dollinger in Italy, shortly to be joined by SS-*Untersturmführer* Dr Jürgen von Hehn, in charge of an *Einsatzkommando* at Minsk.[355]

Like the rest of the Berlin population, the PuSte staff were subject to worsening air raids. An English night raid, on 1–2 March 1943, caused superficial damage to Brackmann's house, but his daughter's apartment block in Lichterfeld was destroyed.[356] In July 1944 Carl Wagener of the photographic department was killed by a bomb in Spandau.[357] Constant bombing resulted in strained nerves and fractious disputes in a profession not notable for its comradely solidarity. In July 1944 Wolfgang Kohte was sacked after having accused Papritz of cowardice in the face of bombing.[358] Both men had been badly shaken by the raids – in November 1943 Papritz had lost everything – and Kohte thought he could use Papritz's nervous state as a way of getting rid of him. On one occasion Kohte seized Papritz's pulse to prove incapability; on another he diagnosed syphilis on the evidence of a nervous tick.[359] Maydell supported Kohte and made accusations of such severity against Papritz that the latter considered a suit for slander or demanding 'personal satisfaction'.[360] As the plots thickened, Papritz spoke darkly of 'torpedoes' and 'boomerangs' and of how 'in Berlin one can daily experience how otherwise entirely calm people completely lose their senses under the slightest pressure'.[361]

Inevitably some of the PuSte employees were subjected to the repressive attentions of the security apparatus. On 12 September 1943 Dr Hildegard Schaeder was arrested by the security police. Papritz attributed her arrest to her 'exaggerated Christianity', which had manifested itself hitherto in an insistence on retaining crosses (as opposed to runic symbols) in *Jomsburg* obituaries for those colleagues who had met a heroic death on the eastern Front. According to SS-*Sturmbannführer* Hannerbruch, who had investigated her case, Schaeder belonged to the Niemöller circle. She had hidden Jewish children, and had helped Jews with false identity papers and money to reach Switzerland. Even more damagingly, she had declared that biblical commands outweighed all other forms of command. He concluded that Schaeder was liable to be sent to a concentration camp.[362] After months in a Gestapo cell, Schaeder was sent to Ravensbrück in March 1944 where she remained until 29 April 1945.[363] Papritz tried to use the PuSte's immediate SS superiors to secure her release by appealing to her sense of duty. She would 'render unto Caesar', he thought provided no binding declarations of loyalty were demanded.[364] Schaeder appears to have been the only individual connected with either the PuSte, NODFG or *Ostforschung* as a whole, who essayed anything that could be reasonably described as resistance, or opposition.

From the beginning of 1943 the depleted staff of the PuSte increasingly worked on intelligence projects. The Press extracts were taken from a wide range of exile newspapers provided by the Gestapo and the Press department of the Foreign Office.[365] They obtained the *Codzienny Niezalezny Kurier Polski w Argentynie* from Buenos Aires; *Wdrodze* from Jerusalem, the *Kurier Polski* from Baghdad, *Polak w Irancie* from Tehran, *Free Europe* from London, *Polak w Francji* (Paris), *Nowy Swiat* (New York) and *Dziennik Chicagoski* from Chicago.[366] In March 1941 these hectographed Press extracts were sent to 250 government agencies, including six Foreign Office departments; the *Reichskanzlei*; OKH; OKW; three Gestapo offices; the RSHA; three SD departments; VOMI; twelve NSDAP departments; Reche's Institute in Leipzig; and Hans Frank in Cracow.[367] Information gleaned from the exile Press was partly designed to stimulate anti-Soviet sentiment in the *Generalgouvernement*. In a letter dated 27 January 1943 Papritz suggested to Hans Frank that Polish exile warnings of 'the Soviet Russian danger' could be used to stimulate Polish dependence upon Nazi Germany. The Press service would stress Soviet territorial claims on eastern Poland and dwell upon the treatment of Poles abducted to the USSR. The words of prominent London Poles about the Soviet threat would carry more weight in Poland than anything German journalists might write.[368]

There was also one final flurry of activity in the area of resettlements. Neither the *Heim ins Reich* programme, nor attempts to interest the youth of Germany, were able to close the gap between plans to settle the East and the manpower available to do it with. The problem of a shortage of skilled labour became acute following the deportation of the Poles and mass extermination of the Jews. A solution, and one with the advantage of appearing to have historical precedents, was to move people from the Netherlands to the East. 'Hollanders' had played an important part in the draining of the Vistula delta and other low-lying areas in the Middle Ages, and Dutch Mennonites had strayed as far as Russia in the seventeenth century to escape religious persecution. The initiator of schemes to renew these migrations in the present was the RKFDV representative in Danzig SS-*Sturmbannführer* Dr Appel, who towards the end of 1940 began preparatory work in the form of exchange visits, lectures and exhibitions.[369] The Danzig museum director Erich Keyser took it upon himself to lend the endeavour historical credentials with an exhibition entitled 'The Netherlands and Danzig' which was held in Utrecht in March 1942.[370]

The subject was also discussed at NODFG conferences in October 1942 and February 1943 as well as at a meeting held in East Friesland by the WDFG in late 1942.[371] Although Brackmann and Papritz stressed the importance of work on ethnic groups and strategically important regions of the USSR, they also debated plans to resettle the Dutch. Keyser reported on the enthusiasm of Dutch collaborators in the local equivalent of the *Ahnenerbe* organization or 'Saxofrisia' (led by the Rektor of Groningen University) for plans to settle a Dutch colony in the Ukraine. However, archivists in the Netherlands were loath to lend exhibits 'which could be used against themselves'. Keyser indicated that the best way to lodge the idea in the consciousness of the Dutch would be by stressing their historical role as intermediaries in Baltic trade.[372] During the ensuing discussion the facade of German–Dutch historical community eventually fell away to reveal the naked economic purpose of these plans. Essen remarked that the Dutch could be used to settle and drain the Pripet swamps between the Black Sea and the Baltic and 'as a substitute for the Jews removed from the towns'.[373] Both Brackmann and Papritz stressed the need to avoid mentioning 'germanisation' in connection with the projected Dutch settlements although that was precisely the end in view.[374]

Virtually the entire circle of scholars connected with the PuSte and *Forschungsgemeinschaften* was marshalled for the second Brackmann *Festschrift*. The idea seems to have been raised by Aubin in March 1940 and he, Kohte, Papritz and Otto Brunner formed the editorial team.[375] The title was decided by Aubin and Kohte. *Deutsche Ostforschung, ibre Aufgaben, Methoden und Ergebnisse* was too imprecise; *Deutscher Osten und deutsche Wissenschaft* or *Wissenschaft im deutschen Osten* too academic; *Leistung und Erbe des deutschen Ostens* approximated what they had in mind, and *Deutschland und der Osten* had to be ruled out since it was the title of a PuSte series. In the end they settled for *Deutsche Ostforschung. Ergebnisse und Aufgaben seit dem ersten Weltkrieg*.[376] The editors also had to resolve issues like how to mention Jewish authors in the footnotes, and the substitution of the term *Ostsiedlung* for *Ostkolonisation* in line with NSDAP rulings since 1937.[377]

Deutsche Ostforschung, volumes 1 and 2, was like a review of the fleet, as opposed to an exercise in sycophantic self-indulgence. Ernst Vollert of the RMdI contributed a brief review of the honorand's achievements and in particular Brackmann's role in building 'a tested circle of German scholars and especially a staff of young researchers joyful in action' who were willing to satisfy the research needs of the state.[378] Both Lattermann and Keyser reviewed the achievements of a host of historical associations and societies in purveying the notion of the Germans as 'bearers of civilisation'; as a unifying force amidst the 'many peoples and fragments of peoples in the East' and in consolidating popular perception of the area between the Elbe, Gulf of Finland, Inn and Black Sea as 'a unified *Lebensraum* for the German people'. According to Keyser these tasks had now been supplanted by others that reflected the steady march of scientific racism.

> It will not be so much a question of showing German achievements in the East as of conveying the biological foundations of its existence. In future German *Ostforschung* will not be mainly concerned, as Aubin's celebration of the past decade showed, with cultural research, but must be almost exclusively [concerned with] ethnic research.[379]

As his own contribution makes abundantly clear, biological–racial criteria totally informed the content and purpose of Keyser's work. The most virile elements among the Goths had migrated westwards leaving the weaker specimens behind to deal with the Slavs. In this way Germanic blood had found its way into the veins of the Sorbs, Czechs and Poles. In his concern to prove both the primordial and continuous presence of *Restgermanen* in the East, Keyser made the claim that 'Weapons [finds] presuppose men who knew how to use them. Weapon use is racially determined and is therefore bound up with the race'.[380] Medieval colonization had in turn resulted in a classless 'ethnic community of blood' from which a second German race had appeared. He spoke of 'cell formation' and 'multiplication of reserves of blood'. The Treaty of Versailles had opened the sluice gates to the threatening 'Slavic flood'. By these criteria nothing changed, or could change.

> Just as the driving forces of peoples and the dangers which threaten their blood do not fundamentally change in themselves, so the experiences of the past can certainly be used as guidelines for future conduct.[381]

People responded to the sort of compulsions that result in migrations of birds and were part of a continuous biological struggle that took place beneath the superficial vicissitudes of events, or the conflict of classes, and beyond time.

By April 1944 Keyser was working with the Institute for Racial Studies of the Danzig medical academy, carrying out 'ethnic and racial investigations' on German repatriates from the Black Sea in camps near Danzig and was about to embark on studies of the Kashubians.[382]

Otto Reche's contribution on the nordic role among the West Slavs ventured somewhat further down the road of biological ahistoricity. Writing to Kohte in July 1940 Aubin had been particularly keen to include a treatment of 'racial problems' and had suggested Reche.[383] By the time the latter's contribution lay before him he was not so certain. He tried to excise some of the wilder 'fantasising' of the Leipzig expert, and would not accept descriptions of the migrant Slavs as 'slaves of the *Restgermanen*'. It would also be difficult to attribute the influx of Slavs to Varangian slavers if the Slavs had settled in the region long before the Vikings.[384] By page 3 point 7 Aubin was reduced to scribbling 'again pure fantasy'.

Reading Reche's essay one shudders to think of the original, uncorrected typescript. He made no attempt to conceal the contemporary 'relevance' of his research. Since the Greater Reich had taken 'West Slavdom' under its 'protection' (!) the question was 'what have we before us of racial value?'[385] How would it be possible to set the necessary 'biological boundaries against elements that are racially far apart from us?' Polish research on the subject was 'a confused mess' but at last the original materials of scholarship, as well as the present population, were now available to research. The subject had its internal difficulties:

The delineation [of races] in the eastern *Raum* is so difficult because races are so heavily intermingled, and in many respects they more or less resemble one another; one only has to think of the common tendency to shorter and broader shaped heads, of lower and broader facial formation, of prominent cheekbones, primitive nasal formation and of thick, taut hair.[386]

Aided by maps, statistics and the prevalence of Blood Group A, Reche was beginning to find correspondences between the numbers of 'nordic long heads' and the territory occupied by East and West Prussia, Posen and 'the Corridor'.[387] In fact they appeared to be coterminous with the eastern frontier of the *Warthegau*. Like a diviner of water, Reche then purported to have unearthed archaeological evidence which appeared to give prehistoric support to his scientific investigations in the present. Working amid the skulls in Germanic and *Urslav* graves, Reche detected a difference between the length and breadth of skulls, which suggested to him that the incoming Slavs had already inter-bred with 'east Baltic and *ostisch*' elements.[388] The object of these enquiries was to prove the enduring presence of residual Germans beyond the barbarian migrations. Like the Germans in East Africa whose children had learned Swahili (!), the *Restgermanen* ruling elite had disappeared into the Slavic flood by learning the language of their servants. It could not have been otherwise as the Slavs were racially incapable of conquering the Germans. This led him, ineluctably, to the thought that if leadership had always been in German hands, and if early Slav rulers were racial Germans in a Slav guise, perhaps there had never actually been a Slav period in history at all? History meant *Herrschaft*, and without *Herrschaft* there was no history.[389] It is as well to recall that the decisions of the individual responsible for this nonsense could decide whether Poles and Czechs had long or short heads, and therefore whether they were liable to be deported for assimilation or extermination.[390] Brackmann's response to an essay which already heralded the end of historical writing in any rational form, is symptomatic of how far the parameters of debate had shifted in Reche's direction. It would be 'an extraordinarily important foundation for all other works in the field of German ethnic research', 'I read the essay with the greatest interest, and am very grateful to you that it appeared in this context.' He hoped that the two would encounter each other *noch recht oft* in the field of German *Ostforschung*.[391] An essay by Peter-Heinz Seraphim on *Deutschtum und Judentum in Osteuropa* adorned the second volume. Although by 1943 a substantial proportion of the Jewish citizens of Poland and the USSR had already been murdered by the *Einsatzgruppen* or in the gas chambers of Auschwitz, Seraphim continued to rehearse the 'historical' predeterminatedness of German–Jewish antipathy and the ways in which the Jews had 'seeped' into positions of strength in the economies of eastern Europe. Acting in accordance with the maxim *Mit der Macht zu gehen*, and driven by 'their intrinsic drive to wander', the Jews had occupied key positions along East–West trade routes and eventually as the unproductive heirs of German cultural and economic achievement.[392] In the 1870s the Jews had 'similarly' latched onto the industrial achievements of German entrepreneurs, and through bribery, 'unobtrusiveness', and mobility of capital had managed to survive the worst exigencies of local economic measures designed to weaken the hold of minorities on the economy.[393] Since the author of the essay had first-hand knowledge of what was happening to the Jews in the Ukraine, his attempts to perpetuate and provide historical legitimization for an image of the Jews as 'outsiders' and 'parasites' whom it was in the nature of things to detest, must be regarded as particularly, and sinisterly, cynical.[394]

The Brackmann *Festschrift* represents a high-water mark in *Ostforschung*: a survey of the achievements of the past, and shoulder to shoulder, so to speak, the fusion in one work of nationalistic historical writing and biological ahistoricity. If one had to predict which way the future lay, then on the evidence of accommodation to racial terminology, sooner or later most of those concerned would have more or less consciously surrendered to the ahistorical, obsessional, and irrational view of existence purveyed by Otto Reche. History, as such, would probably have ceased to have been written.

By 1943 administrative changes affecting the PuSte had ensured that to all intents and purposes they stopped writing history. Himmler's appointment as Minister of the Interior in August 1943 meant the dissolution of Department VI, and the subordination of the PuSte and other research institutes to Department VIg of the RSHA under the Austrian *Ostforscher SS-Hauptsturmführer* Dr Wilfried Krallert. One of Krallert's sixteen-man team, SS-*Untersturmführer* Dr Jürgen von Hehn, was already on the staff of the PuSte, and Krallert himself was a member of the SODFG.[395] The PuSte became one of a number of 'sources of information on foreign countries' subordinated to an SS committee consisting of SS-*Standartenführer* Dr Ehlich (IIIB); Krallert (VIg); SS-*Standartenführer* Dr Luig (VOMI); SS-*Hauptsturmführer* Dr Mäding (Planning Department RKFDV); SS-*Hauptsturmführer* Dr Storz (IIIB) and Hehn (VIg/PuSte).[396] The presence of men representing Otto Ohlendorf's 'Inland SD' (offices III and VI) meant that the PuSte was regarded primarily as a means of evaluating intelligence material, and ethnic questions were relegated to second place.[397] Like the Wannsee Institute or the East Asia Institute, the PuSte was to supply the SD with its 'fundamental weapons'. In order not to prejudice this activity, department VIg was given the innocuous title 'Central Office for Regional and Ethnic Research of the RMdI'.[398]

In a policy paper dated 25 August 1944, Krallert insisted that either the research institutes conform to being 'instruments of the foreign information service' or they would be closed. They were to concentrate upon work of immediate military or political value, and the personnel was to be sieved for those who could be sent to the Front. Among those projects that Krallert regarded as important were the evaluation of enemy technical publications, the questioning of prisoners of war, and providing improved information on targets for the *Luftwaffe* in the USSR.[399] When the Foreign Office showed signs of wishing to reduce its contribution of 38,000 RMs per annum to the PuSte in May 1944, SS-*Standartenführer* Dr Ehlich ensured that the SS met the difference.[400] For allowing for communications' confusion and the conscription of PuSte personnel, Papritz's institute was performing what the SS regarded as important wartime work. This was the considered view of Ohlendorf and Schellenberg who informed *Gauleiter* Mutschmann of Saxony on 19 January 1944 – when the removal of the PuSte to Bautzen was imminent – that:

> The PuSte observes on behalf of the highest authorities in the Reich the cultural, academic, and political relations in the North and East of Europe. It is particularly concerned with geographical and ethnic questions and thereby supplies the highest authorities in the Reich with the basis for important decisions and measures.[401]

Brackmann and Papritz may have been prone to hubristic exaggeration of the importance of what they were doing; SS managers like Otto Ohlendorf were not.

Much of the work done by the PuSte for the SD was probably destroyed or thrown away after it had been used. From requests made by the SD it is possible to catch glimpses of what was being done. The SD required information on Polish exiles in the USA or a translation of an economic geography of the USSR;[402] evaluations of the publications of Czech exile organizations;[403] analysis of materials concerning Polish exiles found in Budapest;[404] a translation of a list of names and addresses of Poles in England found by the *Einsatzkommando* in Budapest;[405] information on the treatment of partisans in the First World War;[406] and lists of Czech exile organizations extending to Cadogan Square, Notting Hill Gate and Milton Road, Cambridge.[407] Books supplied by the Gestapo enabled them to flesh out the picture they were assembling on the composition and plans of exile organizations.

Since the SS increasingly demanded the services of Doubek and

Maydell, the PuSte was reliant upon the work of the wounded, women and refugees.[408] Ominously, the SD proffered the services of individuals whose collaboration with the German regime had led them to flee from advancing Russian forces. In October 1944 Hehn offered Papritz an Estonian SD operative from Reval; in November the *Auslandsamt* of the German Lecturers Association proffered the services of some Finnish academics from the University of Dorpat; there were other displaced persons – historians from Estonia and Latvia – digging trenches in Silesia.[409] As bombing made work in Berlin impossible, Krallert decided to move the PuSte to Bautzen. In the summer of 1943 twenty train wagons of equipment and materials moved south-eastwards and in November the personnel followed.[410] The continued advance of Soviet forces led Papritz to relocate the PuSte to Coburg in February 1945.[411] American soldiers occupied the town on 13 April and about a month later Papritz reported to the US military authorities.[412]

Although institutional reconstruction of *Ostforschung* after 1945 will be dealt with in chapter 6 below, a brief review of where those who have occupied our attention were situated in 1945 seems pertinent. Panic had set in among those most deeply compromised by their actions some time before the end. In a letter to Papritz dated 20 January 1945, Reche had expressed fears about an article by Eli Hecksher in *Dagens Nyheter* in which the author had called for 'a black list' of German academics culpably involved with 'Nazi crimes'. Reche wanted to contact the Foreign Office who would 'turn the spear point around' by drawing up a list of academics who had shown themselves to be 'anti-German'.[413] Unaware of the PuSte's SD involvement, Reche offered to use *his* SD contacts – he evaluated racial publications for the SD – on the PuSte's behalf. Retired to Gross-Hansdorf, from 1958 he was an honorary member of the German Anthropological Society.[414] His fellow adept on the Jewish Question, Seraphim, was captured by US troops. Writing to Papritz in July 1946 he observed that he had spent an agreeable year doing 'regional research' in the vicinity of Washington, and hoped that a place would be found for his professional skills now that he was back, none the worse for his year abroad, in Germany.[415] Wilfried Krallert was imprisoned in a POW camp in Austria. Through the offices of Papritz and Kossmann, ensconced in the US military intelligence base at Camp King, Krallert was brought back to Germany to work on strategic maps of the USSR.[416] Although by July 1948 his movements were still subject to restrictions, he was negotiating a role for himself with US intelligence and with 'a more northerly situated firm'.[417] The latter seemed to be interested in 'bringing the work back to life again as in the old days'.[418] He offered to find a role for Papritz with British intelligence but Papritz turned down the offer in view of Britain's insignificant economic position in relation to the USA.[419] By June 1949 Krallert was working as an adviser to the 'northerly firm' and had hired Hehn as his assistant.[420] Krallert's retirement from the intelligence community left Hehn unemployed. Although 'no great friend of refugee work, but today one cannot be choosy', Hehn decided to pin his hopes on the developing political career of Theodor Oberländer, for 'perhaps under his direction there will be entirely new perspectives'.[421]

Walter Kuhn was similarly indisposed by the sudden lack of demand for experts on *Volkskunde*. He had money troubles and was thinking of going to Chicago.[422] Through the good offices of Aubin some temporary teaching at the university of Hamburg was eventually translated into the chair of Settlement History and Ethnic Research.[423] Mortensen and Wittram were more rapidly 'rehabilitated' in Göttingen despite their recent markedly 'Brown' pasts.[424] Mortensen in Göttingen was one of those scholars whom Papritz approached in order to put indirect pressure upon the British Military Government for a revival of the PuSte in a university context.[425] Despite his 'denazification', which included ludicrous testimony from Brackmann to the effect that they had both been on the periphery of the July 1944 bomb plot against Hitler, Papritz and the PuSte were regarded with considerable suspicion by the Americans and British. One US officer remarked in January 1947 that Papritz was still 'flitting about' the remnants of an institute 'with which [he] has nothing more to do', while it was Cosack's opinion that many of the British 'feared to do anything that would harm the USSR'.[426] In the course of 1947 these attitudes were revised. Papritz spent a year, until August 1948, putting the PuSte library in order within the US intelligence base at Camp King. His former superior, Krallert, was imported from a POW camp in Austria on account of his cartographic expertise concerning eastern Europe. Sometime between July 1948 and June 1949 the PuSte library was shipped to Washington although Papritz turned down the offer of a job as an 'academic specialist' in the 'land of chewing-gum culture'.[427] Perfunctory Allied 'denazification' proceedings, in which individuals like Brackmann provided references for people like Papritz, were presumably not assisted by the decision to appoint a Lt Col. G. R. Gayre as SHAEF's Civil Affairs Officer responsible for educational and religious affairs in Germany and Austria. In his *Teuton and Slav on the Polish Frontier* (1944), Gayre not only referred to 'Professor Hans F. K. Günther's authoritative work on German racial science' but reproduced dozens of photographs of persons and skulls from the latter's *Rassenkunde Europas*.[428] Having abandoned an Oxford D.Phil. after two years of study, Gayre had been lecturing on anthropology at German universities up to 1939.

Brackmann was left ill and isolated in the Soviet Zone. The Americans had taken Blankenberg in the Harz, but had been superseded by the British in June 1945, and then by the Russians. Brackmann's villa in Berlin-Dahlem had been occupied by US officers. His pension had been stopped on 4 April and his bank account was frozen: the future was *nicht gerade rosig*.[429] By March 1946 his correspondence – including numerous 'denazification' testimonies for friends – had assumed dimensions requiring the services of a secretary.[430] Although almost eighty and confined to bed with a severe rash, Brackmann received a research commission from the University of Berlin and was told to concern himself with the future of the MGH. By August 1946 he was confirmed as an ordinary member of the Academy.[431] An indefatigable master of intrigue to the last, in September 1946 he tried to negotiate the removal of the PuSte to Berlin.[432] His erstwhile subordinate took an altogether more realistic view of the PuSte's 'rarity value' in the West and of likely 'denazification' proceedings in the East.[433] By the time he died on 17 March 1952 at the age of eighty-one, Brackmann had cause for cautious optimism concerning the reconstruction of his life's work. Shorn, perhaps, of its recent, racist, components, but skilfully accommodating to the developing rhetoric of the Cold War.

PART THREE

5. SCHOLARSHIP AS POWER: RESEARCH INSTITUTES
IN THE OCCUPIED EAST, 1940–45

Three days before the university year was due to commence early in November 1939, the Rektor of the University of Cracow, Tadeusz Lehr-Spławiński, was summoned to the Gestapo offices on Pomorska Street. SS-*Obersturmbannführer* Dr B. Müller explained that he would like to address the entire faculty on the relationship of the Third Reich to scholarship and higher education. Responding to Lehr-Spławiński's invitation, the scholars assembled on 6 November in lecture theatre 56 of the Collegium Novum, an austere room furnished with dark wooden desks. Shortly before midday, Müller strode to the podium and spoke for a few minutes. The university authorities had begun the year without the express permission of the occupying regime, which had recently changed because of the cessation of military administration. Since it was 'well known' that the lecturers were hostile to German scholarship, all those present were to be removed to concentration camps: 'Any discussion and any comment on this matter is forbidden. Whoever offers any resistance to my orders will be shot.'[1] The relationship of National Socialism to the Polish universities was brutally clear.

Some 183 academics were hustled with rifle butts onto canvas-covered trucks and, over the next few weeks, transported via Breslau and Berlin to Sachsenhausen. Their numbers included twenty teachers from the Mining Academy who had had to hold a meeting in the same building because their own had been occupied, and a couple of students who had gone to collect degree certificates. On 8 February 1940 those over forty were released – excepting the thirteen who had already died from malnutrition or misuse – while the younger scholars were transferred to Dachau. None of the Jewish scholars returned to Cracow.[2] The *Sonderaktion Krakau* was ordered by Seyss-Inquart on the prompting of Reich's Education Minister Rust. Hans Frank's opinion was that it would have been better to have dealt with the professors 'on the spot'. The release of those arrested was the result of international outcry. It should be noted that apart from Max Vasmer, the Africanist Westermann, Sinologist Haenisch, and physicists von Laue and Hahn, the German professoriate conspicuously failed to sign a letter objecting to the arrest of their Polish colleagues.[3]

The removal of Polish scholars left the many constituent institutes of the university of Cracow open to plunder. The total value of equipment that went missing was estimated at fifty million złoty: only ten of the 137 institutes survived the war completely intact.[4] The losses covered all subjects: Frank and Otto Wächter decided to adorn their official residences with rare plants from the Botanical Gardens and greenhouses. The plants perished in the wrong temperatures. The head of the University of Breslau, Professor Staemmler, sought to refurbish his university at minimal cost from the equipment of the Jagiellonian University. Ten thousand books from the Library of the League of Nations were removed to the *Osteuropa-Institut* Breslau. Professor Roland Brinkmann of Hamburg stripped the Geological Institute; the equipment of the physics and chemistry departments was removed to Germany; the pharmacological institute was subsumed by I. G. Farben.[5]

The creation of the *Institut für deutsche Ostarbeit* amidst the ruins of one of the most venerable universities in Europe cannot be fully understood without some consideration of the man responsible for its foundation: Hans Frank. Although the official photographs seek to convey bull-like strength, Frank was, to use Joachim Fest's apt phrase, 'an imitation man of violence'.[6] Pitifully subservient to a leader who equated education with weakness, and who once informed Frank 'Here I stand with my bayonets, there you stand with your law! We'll see which counts for more!', this middle-class lawyer found himself surrounded in Poland by professional murderers, like Krüger and Globocnik, who experienced no precious, metaphysical, qualms about killing. In this company Frank felt obliged to imitate their casual brutality, although the result was rhetorical posturing rather than the 'ice-cold' quality he was endeavouring to convey. In an interview with a correspondent of the *Völkischer Beobachter* on 6 February 1940, Frank was asked about the differences between the *Protektorat* and *Generalgouvernement*. 'I can give you a tangible difference. In Prague, for example, large red posters are put up on which one can read that today seven Czechs have been shot. I said to myself: if I had to put up a poster for every seven Poles who had been shot, the forests of Poland would not be enough to produce the paper for such posters.'[7] The educated bourgeois lawyer also contained an imitation Renaissance prince who readily succumbed to the manner of an oriental despot. The Italian war correspondent-cum-novelist Curzio Malaparte visited Frank's 'court' in January 1942. Most of the scenes that Malaparte recorded took place around the dinner table in the Wawel. They were all there: Frank, Keith, Wächter, Krüger and their wives – gathered in an orgy of collective pretentiousness, gluttony, and murderous insensitivity a few yards from the tombs of six centuries of Polish kings. The rooms were bedecked with tapestries and furniture purloined from the homes of Polish aristocrats; light glinted on the stolen Bohemian crystal and Meissen porcelain; and the sheen of sweat made their faces seem like 'masks of cellophane'. The conversation, larded with the odd phrase in French to convey 'culture', was of Schumann, Brahms, Donatello and Botticelli. 'My single ambition', Frank said, as he stretched his hands against the edge of the table and leant back deeply in his chair, 'my single ambition is to raise the Polish people to the level of European civilisation.'[8] The *grosser Künstler* would rule Poland from the piano as a sort of 'Polish Orpheus'. But the culture was superficial, and excess quickly surfaced: *Gouverneur* Fischer spooned a golden sauce over slices of venison to illustrate the manner of interment in the ghetto. 'A layer of corpses and a layer of quicklime . . . a slice of meat and a layer of sauce.' 'It is the most hygienic method,' explained Wächter. 'If we are speaking of hygiene,' Emil Gassner added, 'the living Jews are more contagious than the dead.' 'I think so too,' Frau Fischer cried emphatically. 'The dead do not bother me,' Frank said.[9] In this manner a class given over to mindlessness, consumption and destruction took refuge from its own awfulness.

Frank's thoughts on the *Generalgouvernement* were set out in a piece entitled *Deutsche Ordnung und polnische Wirtschaft* (1941). The Germans had given the 'Polish settlement region' form and value, but the Poles had responded with 'hate and the desire to exterminate Germandom'.[10] A country on a 'primitive level of development' was to be enmeshed in 'an iron net' of a 'German total administration' which 'without the least sentimentality' was to make available to the Reich the resources of labour, agriculture and industry. Productive labour was the watchword, and whoever obstructed this goal would be 'pitilessly wiped out'. In the next breath Frank mentioned the Jews who had been granted 'asylum' (!) in the ghettos of the *Generalgouvernement* to limit their 'harmful influence and their shady practices'.[11]

The NSDAP would have to create 'a model type of German eastern official', free from the 'modernising ideals of a rotten era' or 'bloated enjoyment' (!). In other words Poland was to be dragged into the twentieth century by an administration informed by what it perceived to be the values of the Middle Ages: engravings of 'Gothic Krakau' jostled uneasily with rigid, schematized charts of administrative structures. The obsession with structure bore no relation to the chaos of reality.

The opening session of the IdO was held on Hitler's birthday, 20 April 1940. In his speech in the Gothic ceremonial chamber of the university Frank paid fulsome tribute to the work of the institutes in Breslau, Danzig and Königsberg, the NODFG and those scholars 'at the furthest front' grouped around Lattermann and Kauder. Kurt Lück and Hermann Aubin were given special praise.[12] The IdO was designed to resolve 'immediate questions of the German people in the eastern areas' and to become 'the focal point of German intellectual work in the East'. The work was to be carried out 'in the German sense' and in opposition to 'slander and distortion which seeks to challenge the workings of the administration and military apparatus in this area'. It was to construct an 'intellectual bulwark for Germandom' and to forge 'intellectual weapons' for the Führer's fight against 'the enemies of Germany'. The more one stressed the historical inevitability of German dominance of the region, the quicker the Poles would reconcile themselves to 'German protective lordship'.[13]

The IdO was housed in Renaissance buildings off one of the streets running from Cracow's ring of trees called Planty to the central market square Rynek Głowny. Its formal structure was copied from both the Akademie für deutsches Recht and the Osteuropa-Institut Breslau.[14] The name was chosen by Frank so as to reflect areas of interest like agriculture or horticulture which would have seemed inexplicable in an Institut für Ostforschung.[15] According to its statutes, the IdO was subordinate to the Generalgouverneur who assumed its presidency. It was the equivalent of a government department and the personnel wore the grey and blue uniforms of German officials.[16] The President was to nominate a committee, the Director, administrator and academic leader.[17] Funds for the IdO came from the administration of the Generalgouvernement. In the first year of its existence, the IdO received a subsidy of one million złoty from an overall education budget of about ninety-four million złoty. Over the next four years the IdO received 2,664,150 złoty in 1941, 3,525,000 złoty in 1942,

3,002,800 złoty in 1943, and 354,200 złoty in 1944. It is worth noting that by 1944 the sums allocated to education and security had risen from respectively ninety-four and sixty-two million to 227,545,050 and 397,330,850 złoty.[18] Cracow became a progressively dangerous place.

The first appointments were reported by the BDO's organ *Ostland* on 1 May 1940. The institute was designed to train German officials, police and SS members active in the *Generalgouvernement*. Frank had appointed Seyss-Inquart as his permanent representative, Dr Copitz (*sic*) as Director, and Gerhard Sappok as provisional academic leader and head of history. The IdO was situated in the library of the university, and 'thereby obviously had taken over the tradition of an academic teaching institution which was founded in 1364 in German "Krakau", and which until the sixteenth century was attended over-whelmingly by German students, and achieved European significance through the teaching activities of mostly German professors'. The IdO was to 'intellectually secure the military victory and political leadership of the German people in this region'.[19] Wilhelm Coblitz was born in Munich in 1906. A graduate in law from Munich University, he was an NSDAP member and SA-*Hauptsturmführer*. By the time he came to Poland he had worked for Frank for seven years, first in the *Eher-Verlag* – the NSDAP publishing house – and then as a section leader in the NSDAP *Reichsrechtsamt*.[20] Faceless and tyrannical, Coblitz lived in some style in occupied Cracow, with Polish maids and chauffeurs, large cars, regular hunting trips, and comradely get-togethers with fellow *Burschenschaftler* like SS-*Obersturmbannführer* Dr Schumacher ('Germania'/Würzburg) or *Waffen*-SS *Generalmajor* Voss ('Germania'/Hannover). He listened to Verdi's *Otello* and read about Nero, emperor of Rome.[21]

Coblitz's own account of the first year of the IdO both changed the purpose of his institute, and overlooked the role of Sappok and the PuSte in its creation. The IdO was founded 'as a place of pure research in which the researchers active there can leave aside the business of teaching and concentrate exclusively upon research'.[22] The academic leader of the IdO 'from 1 September 1941' was Professor Werner Radig of Elbing who had replaced the lawyer Dr Siegmund Dannbeck, 'who played a leading role in the construction of the institute'.[23] In late August 1940 Coblitz reported to Frank on 'certain machinations of Dr Sappok'. The latter had described himself as 'commissary leader of the IdO' on visiting cards and had appeared to be spying on the IdO on behalf of the PuSte in Berlin.[24] Sappok was given twenty-four hours to leave the *Generalgouvernement*.[25] Although Frank had stressed the importance of cooperation with the PuSte and NODFG in his opening speech, Coblitz had other ideas and was in any case intolerant of anyone of greater ability than himself. In April 1941 he informed Hess that negotiations with Aubin had been broken off because of Aubin's political leanings towards the Centre Party. Aubin had also 'not freed himself' from his fundamental scholarly principles 'even though he is loyal and correct in his behaviour to the National Socialist state'.[26] Being connected in any way 'with the Brackmann circle' rapidly became a reason for non-employment in the IdO.[27]

Sappok's lengthy attempts at self-exculpation shed some light upon the first months of the IdO, when ideas were being turned into structures. He claimed that since the PuSte were paying his salary, they had a right to regular reports on his activities.[28] In a hand-written memorandum for Brackmann, he rehearsed the 'intrigues and actions' that had resulted in his dismissal. Coblitz was too young for the job, and had no experience in the ways of the East. He had hired academic staff without any checks on their quality, and after six months the IdO still did not have a budget. As the business of the IdO seemed to be running through Sappok's hands, Coblitz had launched *eine allgemeine Hetzjagd* against him. In this Coblitz was assisted by a legal historian called Ernst Niemann, Sappok's own secretary – who reported telephone conversations and mail to Coblitz – and Dr Heinrich Kurtz, 'one of the most dangerous slanderers in the East', who had been appointed chief of the section for demographic studies without Sappok's knowledge.[29] Sappok then produced an eighteen-page refutation of the charges made against him. His desk had been searched for the incriminating visiting cards and a copy of a letter sent to Brackmann, and inquiries had been made to the *Mitropa-Schlafwagengesellschaft* to discover whether he had falsified his travel expenses on a recent trip to Berlin.[30] Sappok argued that at no point had the competences of the Director and himself been defined. He had tried to recruit suitable personnel but this was difficult in wartime and in any case, Coblitz had not managed to find suitable quarters for the IdO by August 1940. If there were difficulties in the IdO, these lay at the top.[31] These attempts to shift responsibility onto Coblitz's shoulders were in vain, for the latter had taken the precaution of informing Frank that Sappok had remarked 'It is well known that Dr Frank has great experience in the founding of institutes but he stays silent about what becomes of them.'[32] That remark probably sealed Sappok's fate. This type of petty academic intrigue became a characteristic of the institute.

The IdO experienced considerable difficulty in recruiting personnel of the desired calibre. The staff eventually assembled to fill the eleven subject sections largely consisted of the young and mediocre. Initially Coblitz had thought in terms of staffing the IdO with members of government departments. A Nazi journalist called Zarske was to run *Ostpolitik*, the Freiherr Du Prel of the propaganda department was to be in charge of *Kulturpolitik* and *Ministerialrat* Dr Weh of Frank's *Staatssekretariat* was to take over the administration of the IdO.[33] Although by June 1940 the IdO had been in existence for two months, it was an institute without any personnel. A conference held in that month listed only one IdO speaker – Sappok – alongside the old hands of *Ostforschung* Kuhn, Seraphim and Oberländer.[34]

By January 1941 some eleven sections existed on paper, including prehistory, history, art history, racial and ethnic research, law, economics, linguistics (which never existed), geography, agriculture, horticulture, forestry and forest economy.[35] It proved difficult to entice anyone of stature to replace Sappok. The names of Kuhn, Aubin, Oberländer and Lück were repeatedly canvassed, but informed sources thought that such powerful personalities would quickly clash with Coblitz and hence follow Sappok into exile.[36] Coblitz endeavoured to make the terms of employment as attractive as possible. The sections corresponded to the faculties of a future university to be opened after the war. A section leader was on a par with an *Ordinarius*. He held out the prospect of exemption from military service, since service in the *Generalgouvernement* counted as *Osteinsatz*. The salaries were equivalent to those of a professor with a supplement of 420 RMs or 240 RMs per month, depending on marital status, to cover the higher costs of living in the *Generalgouvernement*.[37] He omitted to point out that he and his staff had to carry weapons lest they were assassinated by the Polish underground.[38] Both Ludat and Maschke turned down the offer of leadership of the history section, while Kuhn rejected the offer of leadership of the race and ethnic section.[39] Word of mouth was all among the *Ostforscher* with Rudolf Kötschke recommending Maschke to his nephew Radig, and Kuhn once again recommending Lück.[40] Ironically, Coblitz was reduced to attempts to poach PuSte employees. In April 1941 he tried to lure Kurt von Maydell to the history section in Cracow.[41]

While Coblitz undermined Sappok, his own control of appointments was in turn undermined by the enthusiasms of Hans Frank. The latter was personally responsible for the creation of the sub-section 'Jewish studies', for the projected 'biology faculty', and for studies of the Ukraine.[42] Frank's NSDAP cronies endeavoured to slip their protégés into the institute. The *Reichsdozentenführer* recommended Prof. Hermann Brüske to lead the section for Slavonic Philology, chiefly because Brüske had almost singlehandedly won the University of Greifswald for National Socialism.[43] One of the bigger catches made by Frank was Professor Maurer, the Director of the Institute for Horticulture at the University of Berlin.[44] Frank had appeared at the Christmas festivities of Maurer's unit and had invited the professor to a working breakfast to discuss the creation of a horticultural section. He offered him some 1,000 *Morgen* as an experimental station and assured him, in a way which typifies the IdO, that he need not actually come to Cracow, but could delegate the work to a younger assistant.[45] The eventual terms were not ungenerous: a salary of 800 RMs per month and some sixty days duty in the *Generalgouvernement* per annum.[46]

By January 1942 Maurer and two assistants had organized a section consisting of six sub-sections including the history of horticulture, statistics, 'the human being', production, markets, and landscaping. Although the section has been described as a curiosity, in fact it had more strategic significance than most. By the winter of 1941/2 Germany had to export grain to France and Spain while imports were frozen from Holland, Italy and the Balkans. Some 2,100,000 foreign workers and 4,000,000 Soviet prisoners had to be fed, and there was a need for the vitamins and salts in vegetables, as well as jams and substitutes for fats.[47] Inevitably, in this context, even the cultivation of shrubs was not value-free. Outlining the work of his section, Maurer explained that cultivation in the *Generalgouvernement* was 'on a primitive level' in terms of harvest techniques, seed production and soil care. But the main obstacle to progress was 'the living human being', or in other words, 'Polish dwarf-farmers' (*Zwergbauern*) whose minuscule holdings 'had to be got rid of'. The *Zwergbauern* had no 'feeling' for the soil and evinced 'hostility to trees' (*Baumfeindlichkeit*).[48] It would be necessary to resettle the land with German farmers, and especially horticulturalists, who tended to produce larger families than regular farmers. Again one notices how biological criteria marginalized more rational concerns. Horticulture was not about intensified production of fruit and vegetables but intensified production of people. The mode of life of the horticulturalists was 'the simplest', which in turn, kept 'the race healthy'. Advancing further into the light of universal biological clarification, Maurer claimed that the most significant Russian or Polish horticulturalists 'stemmed from the best horticultural blood in the Reich which had fallen victim to slavicisation in the third or fourth generation'.[49] His section was to research the extensive cultivation of berries – labour costs were low – as well as the possibilities for the late cultivation of vegetables to eradicate Egyptian competition, and the cloning of frost-resistant apple, cherry and plum trees.[50] He also casually essayed the idea of transforming the whole eastern European landscape to make the Germans feel more at ease. The 'wasted and monotonous eastern European plain' was to be transformed into the undulating greenery of a landscape 'over-arched by German trees'. This would involve pushing back the 'squat, treeless, Slav villages' into the Steppe and swamps of Russia.[51] A second memorandum explained how what had been pressed back was to be kept out for all time. Woods, he informed the commander-in-chief *Ost Generaloberst* Blaskowitz, had played a decisive defensive role since the battle of the Teutoburger Wald in AD 9. A belt of trees some 30 kms in depth would serve to conceal defensive installations, and a further belt some 50 kms deep, strewn with market gardeners and small towns, would make the frontier impenetrable.[52]

The section for Racial and Ethnic Research consisted of 32 staff working in three sub-sections: anthropology, ethnology and Jewish studies.[53] This was an academic growth area, spawning new 'disciplines' like 'ethnic – psychology'. The first leader of the section was Fritz Arlt who was then working in the demographic office of the *Generalgouvernement*.[54] Coblitz outlined the work of the section in a reference for its second leader Anton Plügel, an ex-radio scriptwriter. Plügel's tasks included 'the racia–biological investigation of particular ethnic groups'; 'racial–biological investigations of the Polish resistance movement' (!); racial evaluation of 'intermediate' groups like the Góralen and Ukrainians; the detection of 'hidden German blood' among the Poles; advising on the 'germanisation' of specific ethnic groups; and the investigation of persons who came into 'biological contact' with the Germans.[55] The first IdO annual amplified these points. The work was to supply the 'practical basis for the leadership of the state and administration'. Ethnology was understood to involve study of the racial, biological and 'ethnic psychological properties' of particular peoples, including their 'collective health' and the incidence of hereditary disease.[56] A series of questionnaires would cast a fine meshed net over the population of the entire *Generalgouvernement*. The anthropology sub-section was to work on the assumption that cultural achievement determined the *Lebensraum* allocated to each people. The object of research was to seek out German 'achievers' amidst the 'racial confusion' of the 'so-called Polish people'. Maps would plot the relative 'ethnic–biological significance' of each ethnic group.

These racial–biological investigations were carried out by IdO staff on Soviet prisoners of war, ethnic 'splinters' like the Göralen and, of course, Jews. On 12 March 1942 Plügel applied to the Army High Command via the Ministry of Education for access to Soviet prisoners of war to conduct 'racial, ethnic and linguistic surveys'. He argued that similar tests had been carried out during the First World War by Professor von Eichstedt and the *Institut für Osten und Orient* in Vienna.[57] The army had no objections. His subordinate, Dr Heinrich Gottong, a pupil of 'Rassengünther', was engaged in the quest for hidden German blood both in individuals and among entire village communities. The work was subsidized by the RKFDV, OKW and the Racial–Political Office of the NSDAP.[58] Gottong, Dr Elfriede Fliethmann, Dr Rudolf Stark and Dr Ingeborg Sydow carried out anthropometric measurements on the Göralen who lived in the valleys of the Tatra mountains near Zakopane. The entire Carpathian region, Plügel reported, constituted 'a racial–ethnic museum' with Herculen, Bojken, Ruthenen, Lemken and Góralen. In the latter Plügel thought he had detected 'a unique race with definite cultural characteristics and racial composition'.[59] This was due to pre-historic nordic influences and a wave of German migrants in the Middle Ages. The pastoral economy came from 'proto-Rumanian Walach shepherds; the Göralen scrupulously avoided interbreeding with their Jewish or gypsy neighbours'.[60] Efforts were made to stimulate Góral ethnic consciousness by a committee to preserve their customs, economic subventions and periodic get-togethers with Hans Frank.[61]

Racial investigations of the Jews were carried out by teams from the section in close association with a Dr Dora Maria Kahlich of the Anthropological Institute in Vienna and, more significantly, the local SD commanders. The latter provided local information, scholarly references, and protection when the Jews resisted.[62] The SS did the photography. Work had to be carried out with alacrity since 'we do not know what measures are being planned for the coming months for the resettlement of the Jewish population'. 'Valuable material' might elude them, and it could happen that 'our material will be torn from its natural family surroundings and customary context' so that the work would have to be conducted under 'very difficult circumstances'.[63] Kahlich, who was interested in tracing the sources of Jewish migration to Vienna, suggested that they do tests – blood-groupings, fingerprints, iris structure and so on – on a sample 100 families 'so that we can save at least some material if any particular measures should be taken'.[64] Studies of Jews in Tarnow and Galicia were undertaken in close cooperation with the local SD. An SS-*Hauptsturmführer* Schenk questioned a Jewish anthropologist on their behalf and sent references culled from the library in Lemberg concerning rural Jewish populations and their religious practices.[65] The IdO obliged the SD with ethnological maps to be used in the search for German blood in the Lublin area. Although the IdO researchers asked the SD to preserve certain communities intact until their arrival, the SS worked to their own schedule. In September 1942 Schenk informed them that because of 'special circumstances' he could no longer permit their visit. By way of compensation he suggested that the IdO might study 1,500 Karaite Jews in Halicz as this could be 'very important for practical policies'.[66] Elfriede Fliethmann reported to her colleagues in Vienna:

> I cannot investigate Jews in Galicia anymore. There are still 8,000 left from the Jews of Tarnow, but as [SS-*Obersturmführer*] Bernhardt told me, almost none of ours are left. Today our material already has a rarity value.[67]

By September 1942, when Fliethmann and Kahlich were frantically counting and sorting their index cards most of their 'material' was dead. The fate of the Jewish population of eastern Europe was hardly secret, since the files of the IdO contained reports circularized by other academics concerning the Ukraine. A report on a journey through the Ukraine by a Professor Hans von Grünberg and colleagues in August 1942 – and it bears no particular classification about secrecy – made the following observations about the Jewish population of the towns visited:

> *Stolbunow* – The liquidation of all the Jews was received with satisfaction by the population.
> *Winnizia* – 40,000 Jews have been liquidated in the area. There are merely still 300 skilled craftsmen in the clothing factory. They

are in barracks to the rear of the building. The removal of the Jews
was welcomed by the population.

Alexandrowka – From the 700 Jews in the area there are still 60 living
in Alexandrowka as craftsmen. The liquidation of the Jews occasioned great satisfaction among the population.

Kirowograd – There are merely 3 Jewish craftsmen available who are
still needed.

Alexandrija – There are no longer any Jews in the area.

Dnjepropetrowsk – 120,000 Jews fled before the entrance of German
troops into Dnj. after carrying out much destruction. Of the 11,000
Jews still there, 10,000 were liquidated, the remaining 1,000 work
in the town. A strict watch is kept over them.[68]

The tasks of the sub-section on the Jews, which was created on Frank's
orders, were to research the whole Jewish population of the *Generalgouvernement* in close connection with the Institute for Research on
the Jews of the NSDAP in Frankfurt, of which Coblitz was himself an
honorary member.[69] Since the section was led by an historian, the
approach adopted was largely historical. Work focused upon conflicts
between the Jews and their 'host peoples', and was designed to make a
scholarly contribution to the 'political solution of the Jewish problem
through National Socialism'.[70] Specific themes to be studied included
the socio-economic struggle between Germans and Jews in the East;
the development of anti-Semitic movements, and the role of the Jews
in pre-war Poland.[71] Since this was a new discipline, it was necessary
to collect Judaica and to train young scholars in modern Hebrew. To
this end the sub-section's expert on oriental languages endeavoured
to obtain access to the ghetto in Podgórze to study with a Jewish
instructor. The sub-section also employed two Ukrainians to comb
sources in Slavonic languages, and to carry out statistical work on the
Jews.[72]

The IdO's organ *Die Burg* contained numerous articles on the
Jewish Question both by IdO staff members and outside experts. Peter-
Heinz Seraphim recycled his earlier work on ghetto formation and
supplied statistics to demonstrate that despite extensive Jewish migration to the USA in the previous century, the 'rising' Jewish population
of the *Generalgouvernement* 'proved' that it was the *Engzuhtgebiet* for
Jewry in eastern Europe as a whole.[73]

Fresh Jewish population elements have streamed into the already
'Jew saturated' area of the *Generalgouvernement* who are, as will be
demonstrated elsewhere, almost entirely without the means of subsist-

ence and who represent a heavy burden in a socio-economic sense for
the *Generalgouvernement*.[74]

Like the question of rural overpopulation, the Jewish question
needed resolution. The Jews were 'blocking up' the towns and retard-
ing their 'healthy development'. The long-term aim would have to be
the 'ethnic cleaning up' of the region. The search for a solution was
discussed by Dr Sommerfeldt of the sub-section on the Jews and Dr
Kloss of the DAI Stuttgart on 28 or 29 March 1941. Contrary to the
view in the Reich, there appeared to be no clear view about *Juden-
politik* in the *Generalgouvernement*. Policy appeared to be limited to
'police measures', especially in the matter of housing, and a different
policy seemed to be pursued in each of the four administrative districts.
In the Warsaw district, Jews had been rounded up from the smaller
towns and congregated in the ghetto of the former capital. In Cracow
nearly 60,000 Jews were gradually expelled to the surrounding villages
or into the ghetto of Podgórze across the Vistula. The Jews of Cracow
could leave the ghetto to work: those of Warsaw could not. Sommerfeldt was keen that the Jews attend technical courses – with Yiddish as
the language of instruction to encourage their sense of being a separate
people – to prepare them for eventual deportation. Kloss concluded:

> Today there are the most wild and contradictory rumours among the
> police and administrative authorities about the future course, with one
> person claiming that all the Jews will shortly be shot, and another that
> they will all be sent to Alaska.[75]

Following countless discriminatory measures, Cracow's Jewish population was expelled from Kasimierz towards the end of 1941 and
'rehoused' in Podgórze. From there they were transported to Bełzec,
Majdanek, Auschwitz or, much nearer, Płazów where they were
murdered.

Sommerfeldt's own work involved giving anti-Semitism historical
and popular credentials. He combed Polish books and the work of
Lück in search of the 'underlying currents' of popular anti-Semitism.
This was designed to reveal the 'foundations of European anti-Semitism' and to invest the present 'war of liberation' against 'world Jewry'
with tradition and purpose.[76] To this end he assembled examples of
the use of the word '*Zyd*' to denote damp patches, mould on walls,
or blunt knives; stereotypes of Jews; and proverbs like *Wypchieszli
żtda drzwiami, on ci piecem wlezie* (If you throw a Jew out of the
door, he will creep back into the house through the stove), *Panskie*

jutro, a żydowskie zaraz (The nobles 'tomorrow' and the Jews
'immediately'), *Zdatny jak żyd do roli* (As useful as a Jew at farming),
or *Czysty jak żydowskie pomyje* (Clean as a Jew's bathwater). There
were some 350 examples in this vein.[77]

Sommerfeldt and Gottong's thoughts on the Jews were repeated
again and again in the newspapers of the *Generalgouvernement*. Both
of them graced the front page of *Aus Zeit und Geschichte* which was
produced by the propaganda department of the administration in
conjunction with the IdO. While Sommerfeldt described a noxious
Polish anti-Semitic tract from 1618, his colleague chronicled 'the
destiny of Polish Jewry'. This consisted of 'an endless chain of persecution, oppression, and deportation'. The article presupposed the
inevitability of periodic pogroms since there was no peaceful solution
to the Jewish problem. The Jews were an alien people with extra-
European racial characteristics. Remorselessly closing the avenues of
escape, Gottong argued that assimilation of the more prosperous Jews
was a mistake, since this merely unleashed a threat 'to the civilised
world' from the 'mass of Jewish proletarians' who would seek to
follow their more affluent co-religionists. Poverty too was condemned
since it resulted in large families and hence pressure to escape the
ghetto. The Jews would have to engage in productive labour 'outside
the circle of non Jewish demographic groups . . .'

> If the Jews do not succeed in doing this, then Jewry itself has pro-
> nounced sentence on itself, and destiny will take its course on a people
> who up to now has had a deleterious effect on the development of the
> peoples and which now no longer has a place and *no justification for
> existence.*'[78]

By December 1942 Sommerfeldt had developed a line of argument
to justify deportations by claiming that the Jews had 'exterminated'
the German townsmen of medieval eastern Europe. 'Wherever they
appear they show themselves to be the destroyers of the social, political
and spiritual unity of the peoples.'[79] Sommerfeldt's last published
thoughts on the Jewish Question were contained in an article in *Die
Burg* concerning projects for a Jewish state formulated by nineteenth-
century Polish publicistic writers. The common view was that the
Jews were destined to wander: a Jewish state would liberate the Jews
from their extra-territorial destiny and other peoples from the 'heavy
burden' of the Jews.[80] Wincenty Krasinski had argued that a 'surgical'
solution to the Jewish 'plague' might entail forming the Jews into 300

columns of 1,000 persons each, who would be marched along three parallel routes to the banks of the Dnieper. A Jewish *Miliz* would keep order, and the costs of deportations would be covered by the sale of Jewish assets.[81] The Polish 'Anonymous 1841' had argued in favour of deporting the Jews on the analogy of the amputation of a diseased limb.[82] They could be dispatched to a 'waste land'. Other authors advised resettlement in Nebraska or Kansas. When Sommerfeldt regurgitated the fantasies of forgotten authors in January 1944 most of the Jewish population of Poland had already been annihilated in the gas chambers of Auschwitz. These lay about fifty miles away from where he was writing. One of the architects of the camp, SS-*Sturmbannführer* Dr von Troschke, had been invited to an IdO conference in 1941.[83] About 15,000 Cracowian Jews were killed in the concentration camp of Płaszów which lay near the ghetto in a suburb of the city. It was within easy walking distance from the IdO.

The sections pre-history, history and art history were similarly closely involved with the propaganda apparatus of the regime. The pre-history section was led by Professor Werner Radig (1903–), a member nowadays of the Academy of Sciences in East Berlin.[84] He was recommended to Coblitz by a member of Hans Reinerth's office for pre-history in the *Amt Rosenberg*.[85] Radig had attended the humanistic Gymnasium in Wurzen and the universities of Tübingen, Munich, Lausanne and Leipzig. A member of the SA from 1933 and the NSDAP since 1937, Radig also belonged to the NS-*Lehrerbund* and *Dozentenbund*.[86] He came to the IdO from the directorship of a teacher-training institute in Elbing and from 1941 represented the *Amt Rosenberg* in the *Generalgouvernement*.[87] The subject Radig studied had considerable value for the Nazis. No one knew very much about it, and the subject itself was largely speculation. The reconstruction and interpretation of bones and pots could be used at will to confirm Nazi racial dogma. It was possible to invest a drawing of a Bronze Age man or woman with whatever physical or racial features one liked. Radig's patron Reinerth had a career that in some ways resembled that of Walter Frank. He made the anti-classical tendencies in the work of Gustav Kossinna (1858–1931) his own, and used them to assail the dominant figures in the archaeological establishment.[88] Kossinna's work was a reflection of both the uneven distribution of Romano-German finds, as one moved from West to East Germany, and of exaggerated nationalism before the First World War. His teachings on how the incidence of finds enabled archaeologists to determine the dominant ethnic group also had obvious political application in regions of nationality conflict.[89] Like Frank, Reinerth was not averse to the public character assassination of his professional rivals, or to the use of *Stammbaumschnuffelei* to discredit those of them who were Jews. Reinerth nominated the members of Radig's section.[90]

The work of the IdO's pre-history section was in line with the dogmas of the Reinerth group. It had to prove pre-historic germanic settlement of the region and to contribute to 'the new view of history of Greater Germany'.[91] The section was responsible for the care of monuments and the organization of exhibitions. The exhibitions afforded Frank opportunities to affirm the role of his regime in public. The exhibition *Germanenerbe im Weichselraum* was opened by Frank on 12 September 1941. In a thoroughly typical confusion of cultures, Beethoven's Allegro con brio from the String Quartet Opus 18 No. 1 set the mood for an audience surrounded by maps of prehistoric Europe, model log houses and rows of ceramic urns.[92] Coblitz stressed that the exhibition 'proved' primeval German settlement of the Vistula region. Frank endeavoured to make the most of the inscrutable pots of a vanished civilization by turning their opacity to good account. He reflected gravely on 'this planet full of secrets that carries us through the cosmos':

> This exhibition is a religious celebration of our germanic mission in the world ... How small, how unrecognisably small are systems like that of the United States of North America. Mr Roosevelt, compared with this pot – impossible! How risible, how small, how jumped-up, how shabbily imitative, how low and empty are the arguments of the representatives of the world against Adolf Hitler!

Demonstrating his familiarity with one of the main preoccupations of the Reinerth group, he continued:

> The criticism of Germandom that it exhibited symptoms of decline and degeneration must be rejected right from the start. We were never barbarians, never! The Germans were never bearers of the mundane or of decline, the Germans never brutally trampled underfoot the sublime.

And so to the function of the exhibition,

> The work of the *Generalgouvernement* arises too from this solemn mission, and so this exhibition is a symbol of the profound spiritual and historically, deeply-rooted mission of the Germans in the *Generalgouvernement*.[93]

The selfless anonymity of the men who made the urns was to characterize their lineal successors several thousand years later.

In Radig's hands a subject that was long on speculation but short on evidence was given teleological dynamism and a racial–biological accent, oddly at variance with the simple artifacts of forgotten and impenetrable cultures. A grave near Breslau containing a corpse from 4000 BC 'who without doubt belonged to the west European long-headed race'; 'in the early Stone Age ethnic waves of nordic expansion broke into the *Ostraum*'; 'in the late Stone Age waves of nordicisation broke more stormily and frequently across ancient Europe and thereby over the *Ostraum* too'. Complex and discrete phenomena were invested with a purposiveness, continuity and dynamism that they did not possess.

> The nordic ethnic waves show an extraordinary dynamism whose power must have had strong roots in the homeland of the North and in the character of its carriers. Their domestic buildings, burial grounds and large-scale settlement of new lands, suggests a unified, organised, will which could only have been the product of clear, purposive, political behaviour ... These triumphal movements would have been unthinkable if they were not based upon racial superiority and cultural properties which were innate to the primeval Germans and in particular to the Indogermanen.[94]

The history and art history sections similarly served to manufacture propaganda affirming the regime. The leader of the history section was Dr Erwin Hoff, a member of the SS since 1936.[95] He had been dismissed from the University of Breslau for cheating in the oral part of his doctoral examination.[96] The task of his section was to produce sources which demonstrated German creative forces in the development of a Polish state, and to justify the German claim to political and cultural leadership.[97] It was as if the work of Kurt Lück had been institutionalized. An article by Hoff entitled 'Why German leadership in the *Generalgouvernement*?' typifies the way in which *Ostforschung* had set rigid as the dogmatic repetition of a few canons. Open frontier relations in the East were juxtaposed with the existence of a 'cultural gradient' running West to East. Medieval settlement was a matter of 'regaining ancient Germanic settlement areas'. The Germans brought education, progressive economy, culture and order.[98] The Polish disaster of 1939 was attributed to character failings – as described by Philippe Desportes in 1574! The sources for Hoff's view of history were Aubin, Brackmann and Kötzschke: indeed his conclusion repeats parts of Brackmann's *Ahnenerbe* booklet verbatim.[99]

The IdO's art history section was designed to rediscover the totality of German artistic achievement in the East and to reappropriate artists like Veit Stoss whom the Poles had claimed as their own.[100] The leader of the section, Dr Ewald Behrens, explicitly rejected classical or Renaissance canons of artistic excellence in favour of the individual evaluation of each work of art.[101] Behrens's pre-war research in Poland had been subsidized by the PuSte.'[102] Like the pre-history section, the art history section served the regime through exhibitions. In May 1941 Behrens and Weidhaas from the PuSte organized an exhibition devoted to the work of Veit Stoss: in July 1942 another entitled 'Early German art from Krakau and the Carpathian region'. Frank put the purpose of the former exhibition quite succinctly: 'Veit Stoss was a German. He lived and worked as a German and he died a German.'[103] The second exhibition was the pretext for a homily on how German officials could study the quiet self-assurance in the faces of anonymous Madonnas carved in the Middle Ages.[104] In this fashion works of art and the lives of wood-carvers were bastardized as a form of exemplification for a host of minor government functionaries.

The quatercentenary of the death of Copernicus presented the regime with a further opportunity to appropriate the great by way of self-celebration. In 1941 Frank introduced a Copernicus Prize and requested the production of monographs on the astronomer. He also invited Planck, Heisenberg and Sauerbruch to lecture at the IdO and founded an observatory.[105] Plans for the celebrations were drawn up by Coblitz in conjunction with the propaganda department and included concerts, films on Copernicus and Paracelsus, a special issue of *Die Burg* and commemorative editions of stamps and postcards.[106] The prize was instituted by Frank on 20 April 1941 and consisted of 50,000 złoty. Frank, Coblitz and the relevant subject experts were to be the judges.[107] The IdO was also responsible for supplying Frank with materials to use in his speech at the awards ceremony.[108] The ceremony itself was held in the *Staatstheater* in Cracow on 24 May 1943. Following some music, dedicated to Frank, and a few words from Coblitz, the *Generalgouverneur* proceeded to give the amateur view of the cosmos. Dispensing with 'Polish pseudo-science' that had claimed Copernicus as a Pole, Frank made off with the astronomer into the symbolic realm. Copernicus was 'the proudest legitimisation' of 'German leadership in this region'. It was a 'meaningful coincidence' that his work had been entitled *De revolutionibus* for this 'revolution-ary' genius had challenged the encrusted scholarship of his own time. He was a 'spiritual symbol' for the 'gigantic struggle for freedom of the European mind against bolshevik tyranny'. As the speech continued in this banal manner, Frank permitted himself a few reflections on man's lonely travels through the dark cosmos: Copernicus had rescued the human race from hopelessness in the face of infinity. Returning to the task in hand, Frank awarded the prize to five astronomers and physicists from Berlin and Potsdam.[109] In the following year the prize was to be awarded to an historian working in the field of German–Polish relations. Laubert, Randt and Albert Brackmann were the judges.[110]

While the arts subjects functioned as a means of legitimizing and affirming the policies of the regime, the technical and applied sciences were involved in the location and exploitation of the human and natural resources of the *Generalgouvernement* in close cooperation with departments in the administration. The leader of the economics section, Dr Emmerich, was president of the department for eco-nomic affairs in the government, and Professor Christiansen-Weniger, leader of the agricultural section, was in charge of the government research station at Pulawy. This consisted of some 2,792 ha and included institutes for bacteriology, soil science and stockbreeding.[111] The forestry section under Prof. Dr Kurt Mantel and Prof. Dr Ing. Anton Kriesche, also worked closely with the forestry department in the administration. The tasks of the section were to develop laws to prevent reckless asserting, and consequent soil erosion, but on the other hand to transform the *Generalgouvernement* into a timber-based economy.[112] The section was also concerned with the problem of *Wald und Mensch*, which involved studying the damage done to forests and woods by small peasant farmers and large private estates. These studies were to be the basis of new forestry laws and were therefore instrumen-tal in the creation of a 'coercive economy'.[113] Conservation plans were at variance with wartime demands for timber; in April 1942 the forest administration of Galicia alone was ordered to supply some 800,000 metres of timber.[114] The studies of *Wald und Mensch* were for Himm-ler who wished to 'retrieve' German forest dwellers for Germandom.[115] The agriculture section, which incorporated Maurer's horticultural section in September 1942, was intended to contribute to the rational-ization of agricultural production. It was closely involved in the planning of food production, as well as in studies demonstrating why agriculture in pre-war Poland was in a parlous condition.[116] Like the forestry section, the work also involved studies designed to eliminate the parcelling of rural holdings which were preparatory to the drafting of legal measures.[117]

Close relations between the economics section and the regime were personified by the section's leader Emmerich, who was also president of the department of economics in Frank's administration.[118] Theory was subordinated to the applied solution of economic problems in the *Generalgouvernement*.[119] Economic studies carried out in close consultation with government departments were designed to 'liberate' the labour resources of an 'overpopulated', 'undercapitalised', and 'backward' rural economy for employment in industry. This necessarily involved a reordering of the whole economy.[120] How closely 'objective' descriptive analyses dovetailed with economic planning can be demonstrated by examining Peter-Heinz Seraphim's 1941 survey of the economy of the *Generalgouvernement*. The book began with a description of the German administration and of the 'cultural landscape'. Among the noteworthy 'environmental influences' were the Germans who had created the towns: Jewish traders and craftsmen had introduced 'a strange, oriental life'.[121] In keeping with the dominant dogma, Seraphim argued that the Germans were the original inhabitants of the region and that the more 'primitive' West Slavs had 'seeped in' in the ninth century. Repression of the German element and the development of 'a selfish, faction-ridden noble oligarchy' were coterminous with the rise of 'the adaptable Jew'.[122] The statistical, occupational, and geographical isolation of the latter formed a sort of Leitmotiv throughout the book. Surveying the rural economy, Seraphim argued that it was structurally imbalanced in favour of small farms. Partible inheritance resulted in proletarianization and atomization which in turn meant rural overpopulation. Oberländer's studies of overpopulation suggested comparisons with Japan and China.[123] Given rural overpopulation of about 50 per cent, there was a considerable reservoir of surplus labour. Comprehensive agrarian reform should endeavour to create a middling peasantry by removing the 'rural proletariat' from their lands.[124] Productivity was to be further rationalized by cutting the meat rations in the towns to lower demand, and by increasing the production of cereals and sugar beet. The object of these measures occasionally surfaced: the transformation of the *Generalgouvernement* into an area producing agricultural surpluses for the Reich achieved by enmeshing reduced numbers of peasants in a coercive economy.[125]

Since 'resettlement' of the Jews would not create adequate employment for the surplus, rural, proletarians, Seraphim envisaged significant industrialization.[126] New industries were to be created in proximity to the heavy industry of Silesia. Craft production and domestic industry were to be severely rationalized by 'eradicating' Jewish distributors.[127] This sector, which had a significant black economy, was to be severely regulated. The Jews were similarly to be excluded from commerce, an area in which they had 'deeply nested themselves'. Regulations like those in the Reich could not be introduced as this would paralyse Poland's trade, but Jewish businesses could be forced into liquidation through zealous enforcement of price and sanitary regulations.[128] The organization of communal credit for the Poles would further reduce the power of Jewish middlemen. Seraphim's book was not a survey of existing economic conditions but a blueprint for the future. It was not just a matter of selectively loading the evidence so that those who read the book were faced with a pre-selected range of options; but also an example of how an obsession pushed aside any other relevant concerns. The implicit message of the book was that the economic ills of the *Generalgouvernement* could be rectified by removing the Jews.

The economics section was also responsible for studies recommending extensive reprivatization in the Ukraine, and ways of solving the 'problem' of rural overpopulation.[129] Labour reserves, underemployed in a subsistence economy, were to be 'set free', through a 'rationalised' rural economy, either as migrant forced labour, as factory workers in occupied Poland or in the interests of further colonization eastwards.[130] That this involved, necessarily, tearing peasants from their lands, dividing families, and brutally imposing an alien economic order appeared to be incidental. It would be 'painful' for those affected. One 'painful' project essayed by Meinhold was to solve overpopulation by further settlement eastwards. Since it was necessary to avoid offending the ethnic sensibilities of Ukrainians and White Russians, whose collaboration was deemed essential for the 'construction of the European East', he entertained the idea of using the Poles and Jews in order to reclaim the Pripet swamps, or as settlers in thinly populated areas rich in raw materials in the Voiwodships of Lemberg and Tarnopol. Carefully discounting any personal responsibility for the various options *he* had adumbrated, Meinhold allowed that ultimately these were matters for politicians to decide.[131]

The terms 'propaganda' or 'applied science' do not adequately encompass the sort of work carried out in the IdO sections. Both were certainly in evidence, but they are too neutral as descriptive terms to capture that comprehensive scholarship-as-power, in which scholars doubled as functionaries, and scholarship *in itself* became instrumental in the exercise of power. This can be demonstrated by examining a programmatic statement by Dr Hans Graul of the geographical section. The work of his section was 'only a part of the programme of German work in the East in general'.[132] If scholarship in the Reich as a whole had long ceased to be pursued 'by a small circle as an end in itself', in the *Generalgouvernement* scholarship was particularly 'at the centre of the life of the people'. The methods were to be strictly scholarly: the ends 'ethnic-political'. Scholarship was to be the 'bearer of development' and scholars, not merely experts, but 'responsible for the long-term academic underpinning of political actions' that would extend over generations. They would solve the 'most burning questions of the future' as opposed to adumbrating 'grey theories'.[133] To this end, the section had been entrusted with *Raumforschung* by the office for *Raumordnung* in the *Staatssekretariat* of the *Generalgouvernement*.[134] The fundamental task of the section consisted of social engineering. To extend the German *Volksboden* and strengthen an independent peasantry or, in other words, to transform the East over the next generations, in terms of the 'German colonisation of the East of the 20th century'.[135] The direction, thrust and success of this colonization was determined by the interaction of race, climate, and soil types. The end goal was to establish 'optimal Lebensraum' for the German people in the East, and to make the problem of 'limitless' space manageable through regional analysis. This had a direct political application since the section would be engaged in establishing a 'final division of the eastern region into a net of carefully chosen centres of power and economy'.[136] Part of the search for the 'Lebensraum of the ethnic community of the will' involved studying the 'slavicisation' of the landscape – 'a devastated landscape, woods plundered, wild water economy, decayed seed and animal breeding, and in wide areas the proletarianisation of the entire country' – so that the new German reformation of the landscape could begin again from fundamentals.[137] The products of this 'research' were to be made instantly available to the regime in the form of typescript manuscripts to offset the delay inherent in publications.

The development of the IdO as a source of 'scholarship as power' was inevitably interrupted by the course of the war. That does not mean that the activities carried out in Cracow were either harmless or ephemeral. By February 1943 the arts sections, pre-history, history, and art history, were merged to form an 'Historical Section' under Radig.[138] Many of the male staff had been conscripted, and Coblitz was obliged to seek academics wounded in the war as replacements.[139] By October 1943 the arts subjects had been dropped altogether.[140] Allied bombing of the western areas of the Reich resulted in the relocation of defence research to the East, and the creation of a 'General Military Sciences' section. For security reasons this was never mentioned in public.[141]

By early 1945, when what remained of the IdO was relocated to Bavaria, there were five defence sections including inorganic chemistry, physical chemistry and electro-chemistry, general physics, astronomical calculation and geography. Their work was described in a secret memorandum on the occasion of their translation to two castles Zandt and Miltach in Bavaria and the Upper Palatinate. The chemistry section was working on defence contracts for the navy (corrosion of metals); for the Reichsforschungsrat (securing of pectin); the Luftwaffe (magnesium and aluminium for aircraft fuselages, and coolants for rock-drilling equipment). The physics section was engaged in research for the navy on directional antennae for aircraft, or to enable submarines to locate large surface ships; jamming devices to disorientate aircraft; radios that could operate without quartz for Zeiss, and research on the harnessing of wind power to armaments factories.[142] It is worth noting that, in contrast to the remorseless propaganda about the incapability of the Slavs, virtually all of these projects were led by Russian scientists using knowledge developed in Soviet aircraft factories.[143] The section for mathematical calculation under Prof. Dr Walther was engaged in research for the Luftfahrtforschungsanstalt Hermann Göring on statistical tables for the flight paths of aircraft and 'new weapons'.[144] This section was relocated to Mecklenburg in September 1944 where the section leader availed himself of skilled workers hired from Ravensbrück concentration camp.[145] The chemistry section similarly used prisoners from Flossenbürg under arrangements with the SS-WVHA.[146] Of the original eleven sections, only one remained in Poland. Graul's geography section was concerned with the study of foreign publications and aerial photographs, in order to produce maps for tank crews operating on the eastern front. To that end his section stayed in Cracow until the bitter end to maintain contact with army commanders in the East.[147]

*

Any evaluation of the work of the IdO would be incomplete without some mention of its contemporary critics. As we have seen, Dr Kloss of the DAI attended an IdO conference in March 1941. He was not impressed. The conference was 'fantastically badly organised' and most of the other guests were members of Frank's administration. The only areas that seemed to function well were those working on concrete questions on behalf of the regime. Two of the best minds, Szabok (*sic*) and Kurtz, had left, and the influence of Coblitz – 'purely an administrative lawyer' with no knowledge of research – was disastrous. The IdO had some worthwhile staff and a good periodical, 'but in view of the unsuitable personality of the leader, it may well not pursue any clear course for a long time and the question of collaboration with the DAI is out of the question at the moment'.[148] The director of the Cracow *Staatsbibliothek*, Abb, was similarly unenthusiastic. In March 1942 Coblitz reported some of Abb's remarks about the IdO to the education department, claiming that Abb had tried to 'sabotage' his institute.[149] Abb evidently thought that the IdO was a sort of over-financed Potemkin village on the academic scene. It had no qualified staff, produced nothing original, and merely compiled the work of others. In the IdO one was dealing with *Ignorantentum*.[150] Papritz was similarly of the opinion that the IdO had reaped the *Ostforscher* of the *zweite Garnitur* although that may reflect the fact that the influence of the PuSte had been excluded at an early stage in the IdO's development.[151] Possibly the most accurate verdict on the IdO was pronounced by the Polish historian Władysław Semkowicz in the course of the Bühler trial in February 1946. The product of the sections was 'a worthless pile of insolent bragging and total nonsense'; but nonsense that had 'propagated anti-Polish sentiment and legitimised a policy of extermination'.[152] It might be added that the IdO represented the complete perversion of scholarship as an active arm of the power of the state.

The IdO also brought Poles and Germans together in a working context. During its brief period of full activity, in 1941–3, the IdO employed some 195 people of whom 125 were non-Germans.[153] The documents occasionally shed some light on what it was like to work in the IdO. The balance between collaboration and resistance was fine and hence dangerous for those involved. For the Poles, the IdO afforded some possibilities for continuing academic work in a culture being remorselessly reduced to the lowest denominator. Mieczysław Małecki, the leader of the underground university of Cracow, was employed in the institute to work on a dictionary of German loan words in Polish. His Polish students were able to use his work as a cover for their own studies.[154] Since the German staff were largely ignorant of Polish, there were opportunities for academic sabotage and for playing one German authority off against another. Poles in the institute were able to draw the attention of the library director Abb to books stolen by German institute employees.[155]

While the Polish resistance regarded work in the IdO as 'particularly ominous on political grounds', all employees were under observation by an agent of the SD – Rudert – who had come to the institute after working as a translator in Radom.[156] He recruited at least one Polish informant while certain institute sections employed someone specifically to watch the Poles.[157] A passive and underpaid workforce, which could be terrorized with threats of the concentration camps, seems to have been separately exploited by Coblitz and Rudert for private ends.[158] The experience of working in the IdO or its branches cannot be detached from the permanent terror of living in a state with unlimited police power. In July 1944 Antek Maryański resigned after two years' work in the Warsaw filial of the IdO. In his letter of resignation to its leader, Professor Heinrich Wolfrum, he explained the reasons for his sudden departure

You already know that I was once put in prison because of an unhappy misunderstanding and without the least cause on my part, and that only because of a happy accident could I see the sun again. On Friday I accidentally overheard part of a conversation between the police and Frl. Wolfrum. At the time I was in the next room, and understood that these present representatives of law and order wanted to arrest me. I still do not know why or what for, perhaps only for interrogation. But I know these situations and also that many people who are sent for interrogation have ended their lives in concentration camps. I also know that I want nothing to do with these people, because I genuinely know nothing about Tabęcki. My brother-in-law was arrested by the Gestapo in April and was released after two days. After a week at home he went out of the house and until now has not returned. His family have heard nothing from him. We do not know where he is or whether he is still alive. His mother reported this to the Gestapo. Now you will understand that I know as much as the police and cannot supply any information about Tabęcki, moreover I cannot be held responsible for the activities of my brother-in-law.[159]

Apart from the real danger of just simply disappearing into the subuniverse of the camps, there was the atomization from family and friends, mistrust of colleagues, insomnia and illnesses resulting from strained nerves.

Below the level of exclusively male section chiefs were a considerable number of female white-collar workers including women like Fliethmann or Sydow. Although it is difficult to determine their reasons for being there, personal files shed some light on the question. For some it was a matter of voluntary idealism, like the typist who thought that the German conquest of the East required people of 'character'[160] or the secretary who had deepened her knowledge in the 'ideological–political field' through lectures at the Berlin *Hochschule für Politik*.[161] Others either had a background of employment in pre-war Poland or husbands in the administration of the East.[162] For the female racial scientists, Fliethmann and Kahlich – who took a dim view of the competence of their male superiors – conscription provided a chance 'to show that women can also do things'. Most of the Russian employees were skilled engineers and technologists who either had relatives serving in the German armed forces or who had been compromised by their collaboration with the Germans in the Soviet Union.[163] One Russian biochemist had deliberately surrendered to German troops.[164] The Gothic buildings around the 'Copernicus courtyard' housed a sort of aggregate of human tragedy. Ada Schmidt-Kowtanjuk in the geography section, an ethnic German educated in Tomsk and Leningrad, had lost her father and first husband in Stalin's purges. From August 1942 to January 1943 she had worked as a translator in a Wehrmacht hospital. Having followed the retreating troops, she hoped to train as a teacher in order to work in a school in a German colony.[165] There were many people who had similarly drifted into the institute on the tide of war.

The shabby reality of the IdO was oddly at variance with Frank's plans for it to become the basis for a future 'Copernicus University' of Cracow. Frank aired this idea both during discussions with Sappok in 1940 and on a number of subsequent occasions in the following year.[166] According to his diaries, Frank discussed these plans with Hitler in early May 1941. The object was to move one of the smaller German universities like Giessen, Marburg or Greifswald to Cracow. The plans seem to have peaked in May, as Frank ordered Watzke to find suitable buildings, insisted on the need for a faculty of biology, and charged Coblitz with the founding of the Veit-Stoss-Prize.[167] By

July Frank insisted that the founding of a new university could not be considered at that juncture. Nevertheless, planning went ahead to turn the IdO into an 'Academy of Sciences' with certain sections to be hived-off into the new university.[168] In September Frank, Coblitz, and Watzke decided to postpone plans for a university until after the war: there were not enough students and lecturers available for the projected foundation.[169] This was not quite the end of the matter as in November Frank ordered that planning should continue, along with the transformation of existing institutions into a form suitable for a future university. Public discussion of the project, however, was to cease.[170] The form the university was to take was outlined by Watzke in an article in the *Schlesische Volkszeitung* on 26 June 1941. The 'second oldest university on German soil' (!) was to be the basis for 'the first real National Socialist university'. 'Tradition', 'questions of prestige', 'the chains of bureaucracy' and 'obsolete perspectives' had hindered the penetration by National Socialism of the existing universities in the Reich. The projected university would sweep away all of these obstacles and, through the medium of new faculties, would set to work on the 'direct problems of the East'. The corner stone of the new university was to be that queen of the National Socialist sciences – biology. There were to be three sub-sections concerned with the biology of plants, animals, and men, which in turn would be closely linked with all other subjects. The university already existed in embryo since the arts subjects would grow from the sections of the IdO, while the mathematical–technical faculties would issue forth from the *Generalgouverneur*'s great observatory. The *Staatsbibliothek* would form the basis of the university library.[171] In the event, the IdO followed the path of integration into the regime rather than towards the relative autonomy of an 'Academy of Sciences'. In February 1943 an ordinance ended the legal autonomy of the IdO which henceforth became an integral part of the administration of the *Generalgouvernement*.[172] To the dispassionate observer that is what the IdO had been since its creation.

Although the IdO was the most thorough-going example of scholarship as power, it was not unique. Both the importance which leading Nazis attached to *Ostforschung*, and the 'anarchy of competences', that characterized the regime, ensured that rival institutions appeared on the scene. Expenditure on research institutes in the middle of a global war is testimony of a kind to the importance of the subject to those in power.

During a speech delivered in Litzmannstadt (Łódź) in March 1941,

Gauleiter Greiser announced the foundation of a *Reichsstiftung für deutsche Ostforschung* (RSfdO) to be based in Posen.[173] Since the *Reichsstiftung* was very closely involved with Greiser's *Reichsuniversität Posen* it will be necessary to briefly describe the earlier foundation. The choice of Posen for a new German university was determined by the prior existence of a Polish university of Poznań, and by the tradition of the Prussian 'Royal Academy of Sciences of Posen' (1903–19).[174] The impetus behind the founding of a Nazi university came from Hitler and the Ministry of Education which, in October 1939, sent SS-*Sturmbannführer* Dr Hans Streit to Poznań, to assess the resources of the (closed) Polish university, and to make plans for a German foundation. Armed with a commission from Hitler, and with the express support of the *Reichsführer*-SS, who was keen to promote studies in agriculture – there were to be 21 chairs in this field alone – forestry and veterinary science, Streit approached Greiser on 17 November 1939.[175] Greiser designated Streit 'university and academic representative of the *Reichsstatthalter*' (Greiser), and 'registrar' of the future university. Since Streit was already 'eastern representative of the *Reichsdozentenführer* and *Reichsstudentenführer*, he could dispose of a considerable range of academic contacts essential to his task.[176] The facilities of the existing university were incorporated into the new foundation. A number of, by now, familiar names, cropped up in Posen. The university library was entrusted to SS-*Oberführer* Dr Alfred Lattermann, while Dr Jürgen von Hehn was charged with running a book collection depot, which 'acquired' 150,000 volumes from the Society of Friends of Scholarship, 200,000 from the archiepiscopal archives and libraries, and 80,000 volumes from the cathedral chapters of Posen, Gnesen and Włocławek.[177] By 1941 Hehn had collected some 1,300,000 volumes of which 400,000 were handed over to the university library. The rest were pulped on the grounds that their contents were undesirable. In addition to staff recruited from the Leipzig *Stiftung für Volks- und Kulturbodenforschung*, Breslau, and the *Institut für ostdeutsche Wirtschaft* in Königsberg, Streit availed himself of about 40 of the 119 Baltic German academics under Professor R. Wittram, who had surfaced in the *Warthegau*, to fill the six faculties. Those recruited included the historian Leonid Arbusov, and the historian of ideas Kurt Stavenhagen.[178] The presence of Wittram, the NODFG representative in Latvia, provided a further window of opportunity for Brackmann to influence the matter of appointments. In October 1942 he was to be found recommending names to Wittram for the vacant chair in Agrarian and Settlement History. Since Karl Kasiske was no more, he recommended Kossmann, Ost, Theodor Penners and Detlef Krannhals, adding 'you see, the choice is not great'.[179] Since there was a considerable delay between the conception and the creation, a number of voices made themselves heard about the form the university was to assume. This included specific plans for particular subjects. Thus Dr Rudolf Hippius from Estonia sent a memorandum on 'demographic planning in the *Warthegau*' dated 5 December 1939. This spoke of 'inspecting and analysing the human building material' in terms of 'ability to live, capacity to work, social behaviour, character structure and particular characteristics' and the analysis of groups in terms of 'origin, race and circumstances'. The studies proposed would be the 'raw material' for population planning in terms of 'the principles of the National Socialist ordering of life'. This in turn – for one had to struggle through the words – would contribute to 'the maximal usage of human building material in structurally legitimate ways' and the stage by stage 'total exclusion' of the Poles from the *Warthegau*.[180]

The opening ceremony of the university was held on 27/28 April 1941 in the presence of Rust, Greiser, the *Reichsdozentenführer* SS-*Brigadeführer* Schultze, the President of the *Reichsakademie* of German Science SS-*Oberführer* Vahlen, the heads of the German universities and *Generalfeldmarschall* von Bock.[181] The head of the new university, a veterinary geneticist, SS-*Standartenführer* Dr Peter Johannes Carstens, had been an SS member since 1933 and, from 1940, a member of the *Waffen*-SS *Leibstandarte* Adolf Hitler. Carstens outlined the tasks of the university, namely to solve the 'practical questions' that had arisen from the resettlement of ethnic Germans in the *Warthegau*. These 'practical questions' included studies of the division of holdings, businesses and factories; the 'clarification' of ethnic relations in an 'ethnically mixed zone', and studies of the 'history, characteristics and racial composition' of the Poles. Thus, the agricultural faculty would liaise closely with the legal and economics faculties, in the service of 'the complete re-ordering of property relations in the East'. The tasks of the new university were not restricted to local concerns.

As a university of the East there are no frontiers for us as scholars towards the East. The tasks of our university do not end either at the frontiers of the *Warthegau* or on the Bug, rather, in our teaching and research we must encompass the furthest reaches of the Soviet Union.[182]

There were to be chairs in 'Ethnic and Geographical Studies of the USSR', 'The History and Language of Jewry', 'Racial-Politics', '*Volks-kunde*' and 'Volkslehre'. Like the new head of the Posen institute for 'agrarian politics and settlement systems', the ubiquitous SS-*Obergrup-penführer* Professor Konrad Meyer, Carstens had considerable practical experience in the area of resettlement. Since 1933 he had worked as a deputy section leader in the RuSHA and, from 1937, in the office concerned with agrarian questions attached to SS-*Oberabschnitt* South West, and then directly in resettlement actions.[183]

One of the essential functions of the *Reichsuniversität* was to act as a 'leadership school of the German East'.[184] Prospective students had to complete lengthy forms concerning their political background, and were then subjected to political vetting. Whoever had *not* belonged to a Nazi youth formation before 1939, or had Polish relatives or, in the case of Baltic Germans, had not responded promptly to the call homeward before 15 December 1939, was debarred. By way of contrast, membership of one of the nationalist and conservative student corporations in Latvia and Estonia was considered to be an asset.[185] Student and staff numbers actually increased throughout the war. In 1941 there were 49 staff, 85 in 1942 and 118 in the winter of 1943/4. The corresponding figures for the student body were 191, 482 and 868, reaching a high point of 1,228 in the summer of 1944.[186] By this last date, some 45 per cent of the students consisted of invalided soldiers.[187] Together with their teachers, the students were to be formed into 'a new type of academic' who would 'demonstrate the significance to Germany and Europe of the entire East, and [who] will make the East productive'.[188] Emphasis was placed upon 'character formation', physical training and practical involvement in the actions of the regime. Comradely evenings and practical trips to resettlement camps, joined lectures by Aubin and Maschke on history, or seminars on punitive legal measures directed at the Poles.[189] The accent was on inculcating 'hardness', by battering down sensitivities through constant activity, or lectures of mind-stunning tedium, to penetrate the inner self in order to obliterate normal ethical values. The lecture theatre and the academic 'practical' were used to ease the young into the habit of deciding matters of life and death. An SS professor of criminal pathology confronted his students with a fifteen-year-old boy who had been sentenced to death for stealing from military mail. The sentence could be carried out, if it could be demonstrated that the boy exhibited the mental characteristics of a sixteen-year-old. Collectively the students decided that their 'subject' was old enough to die. The sentence was carried out.[190]

While the young were eased into the circle of murderous culpability, their teachers became part of the apparatus of murder. The cellar of the medical faculty building in Friedrich-Nietzsche-Strasse 6 contained facilities for the cremation of anatomical remains. The Gestapo, aided by the professor of criminal pathology, availed themselves of this facility to dispose of their victims. In July 1941 the director of the Anatomical Institute, Professor Voss, reached an agreement with the Gestapo whereby some of the corpses would be retained for autopsy. This deal enabled Voss to develop a lucrative business with colleagues in Hamburg, Leipzig, Vienna and Königsberg.[191] Some 4,916 Poles disappeared in a manner described in Voss's diaries.

Saturday 24 May 1941: Here in the cellar of the institute building there is a crematorium for burning corpses. It is now exclusively at the service of the Gestapo. The Poles shot by them are delivered by night and burned. If only one could reduce the whole of Polish society to ash. The Polish people must be exterminated, otherwise there will be no peace in the East.

Sunday 15 June 1941: Yesterday I visited the 'corpse cellar' and the ovens which are in the cellar. These ovens were supposed to be for getting rid of anatomical parts used in anatomy classes. Now they are used to transform the Poles who have been executed into ash. Almost daily a grey van arrives with men in grey uniforms, i.e. SS men from the Gestapo, bringing material for the oven. Since it was not in action yesterday, we could look inside. The remains of four Poles were in there. How little remains of a person when all organic matter has been burned! A glimpse inside the ovens is very thought-provoking. How did Marshal Ney put it before his execution: *ou (sic) bientôt un peu de poudre*. At the moment the Poles are very uppity, and consequently our oven has a lot to do. How nice it would be if one could chase the whole society into such ovens. Then there would finally be peace in the East for the German people.

Tuesday 17 June 1941: Today there is once again a notice from the special court on the poster column, that 5 Poles from Posen, who were sentenced to death on account of murder, have been executed. Why aren't 100 Poles, or more as far as I am concerned, got rid of for every German murdered?

Tuesday 19 May 1942: Herr von Hirschheydt said to me on Sunday that on Saturday he had picked up a few lice from a louse-ridden Jewish corpse. He is making plaster-casts of Jewish heads for the anthropological museum in Vienna. That was a lovely piece of news because the Jewish corpses delivered here often died of typhoid fever.[192]

Hirschheydt died of typhoid fever on 4 June.

Greiser's *Reichsstiftung* grew out of this 'university'. It enjoyed the protection of Göring and was designed to co-ordinate research carried out in, though not exclusively restricted to, the *Warthegau*.[193] Significantly, the *Reichsstiftung*'s original title was to have been *Reichsstiftung Ost für praktische Forschung*.[194] This new foundation was opposed by Frick who argued that 'his' PuSte staff had general competence for research in the East, whose fruits they made available to all authorities in the Reich: 'in my opinion there is no necessity in the ethnic–political area for a new general office for *Ostforschung*'.[195] The close connections between the regime, university, and *Reichsstiftung* can be seen in the latter's statutes. Greiser assumed the presidency, Carstens became academic leader, and Streit was designated the *Reichsstiftung*'s administrator. A committee, consisting of Göring, Ribbentrop, Rust, Goebbels, Ley and Frick, was to watch over its affairs.[196] The resources of the new organization consisted of 24,000 ha of land confiscated from the Polish National Foundation Kornik, and estates and castles, both confiscated and bequeathed, by the Prince Michael Radziwill. These estates yielded considerable sums of money. In 1942 the *Reichsstiftung*'s forests yielded a profit of 250,000 RMs, in 1942 400,000 RMs, while in January 1943 the foundation had some 500,000 RMs in the bank.[197]

Organizationally, the *Reichsstiftung* consisted of about ten study groups and institutes, all of which were led by members of the university staff. The orientation was completely practical: 'Settlement of the East' (Carstens/Zoch); 'Ethnic-politically useful deployment of Polish rural labour' (Blohm); 'Draft settlement structure'; 'New methods of field reorganisation in specific rural areas'; 'Methods for securing clay and other building materials'; 'East European economy' (Brenner); 'Reforestation of the East' (Sommermeyer); 'Legal research in the East', and so forth.[198] Like his colleague in Cracow, Greiser instituted a number of prizes for academic research. There was a

'Clausewitz Prize' for work on 'ethnic political forces' vital to the East, and a *Preis des Grossen Königs* for work on the potentialities of the German peasantry for the East.[199] The Clausewitz Prize was awarded to the poet Erhard Winter and an SS-*Sturmmann* in 1941, to the historian Manfred Laubert in 1942, and (posthumously) to Kurt Lück in 1943.[200]

From the description of the various study groups, it is obvious that the *Reichsstiftung* was designed to cater for the research requirements of the regime. In the case of the study group *Ostsiedlung* this took the form of organizing exhibitions on 'Planning and Construction in the East', studies to correlate labour resources with individual rural holdings, or to 'secure unmarried labour from within the villages'. There was nothing theoretical about these projects. On 21 October 1943 members of the group met to discuss the response of officials from the RKFDV to their various proposals. These had *already* resulted in the removal from German villages of all 'not absolutely essential Polish labour in accordance with the directives produced'.[201] The study group under the geographer W. Geisler, concerned with 'settlement structure', helped to determine the precise status of the Poles in the new rural order while planning major alterations in the economy as a whole, away from labour-intensive agriculture. The study group emphasized that:

> The German is the lord of the land, and the Pole is subordinate to him. It is inconceivable that a Pole should occupy any form of leading position ... Through the employment of Polish labour, the labour potential of German national comrades will be released for higher tasks. In his attitude to the Poles, every national comrade must bear in mind that the Pole is our enemy ... There is nothing further to do here, except to pull everything down and build anew![202]

This new entrant into the field of *Ostforschung* was closely watched by Brackmann. In a letter to Aubin dated 10 March 1941, Brackmann surveyed the new foundation. He thought that the patronage of Göring was significant since the *Reichsstiftung* was 'obviously a countermove against the founding of the IdO in Cracow'. Since lesser networks of power were involved below the rivalry of Frank and Greiser, Brackmann noted with some satisfaction that the existence of the new foundation had forced Coblitz to adopt a more accommodating attitude towards the PuSte.[203] Relations between the *Reichsstiftung* and

IdO were cool, consisting only of an agreement to exchange historical documents.[204]

The intense politicization of these institutes inevitably rendered them particularly sensitive to sudden changes in the geopolitical terrain. Surveying the *Reichsstiftung* in December 1942, Zipfel noted that since the onset of the war in the USSR, the significance of the *Reichsstiftung* as a 'bulwark against the East' had been considerably diminished. The university would also sink into provinciality, since Dorpat was likely to become the new university of the East.[205] Coblitz in Cracow was shortly to be menaced in a more immediate fashion by the *Reichsführer*-SS. On 3 February 1943 he informed Frank that Himmler was planning to open a research institute of his own in Cracow. This would lead to 'endless trouble' since it would automatically result in the exclusion of the IdO from 'all ethnic academic work'. Frank was equally apprehensive about this further extension of SS power: he hoped that Coblitz would succeed in 'removing the danger'.[206]

The SS had entered the business of founding institutes for *Ostforschung* a year before with the 'Reinhard-Heydrich-*Stiftung*' in Prague. According to a report delivered to Brackmann and Papritz on 29 June 1943, the Heydrich-*Stiftung* consisted of a number of separate institutes which dealt with particular problems. These included law, history and economics, geography and settlement studies, ethnic research, social biology and anthropology, linguistics, ancient history and settlement research. Cryptically, the report added that 'their pretensions extend beyond the *Sudetenraum*'.[207] Although next to nothing is known about the Heydrich-*Stiftung*, one of its ascertainable functions was to supply educational materials to students serving in the *Waffen*-SS on the eastern front. The materials supplied included essays on 'ethnic-biology and ethnic leadership', Erich Keyser's 'People and Population' and essays by Günther Franz, himself an SD figure, on 'The historical demographic consequences of the Thirty Years War'.[208] In 1942 the Heydrich-*Stiftung* and the *Reichsstiftung* in Posen concluded a form of demarcation agreement whereby the former would be chiefly concerned with Bohemia and Moravia and the south east, while the latter worked on the 'central eastern areas'.[209]

The final entrant into this scramble to establish institutes for *Ostforschung* was Alfred Rosenberg. In 1943 he created a *Reichszentrale für Ostforschung*. He announced this new foundation during a speech in Dresden in October 1943. The object of the *Reichszentrale* was to relay to the German people knowledge about their 'region of destiny', and to work up a 'new version of the history of the East'. Surveying the existing institutes, Rosenberg praised their individual efforts, while cunningly emphasizing the absence of overall coordination. This deficiency was to be corrected by the *Reichszentrale* which, operating from within Rosenberg's ministry, and in close connection with the *Reichsforschungsrat*, would take over the financing of research projects in *Ostforschung*. The *Reichszentrale* was to consist of a committee of representatives of the NSDAP and state, an administrative office, study groups, and some 400 academic institutes in the occupied East. This meant that Rosenberg's experts would commission and finance research carried out in institutions like the agricultural academy in Mitau or the technical university of Reval.[210] The director of the *Reichszentrale*, Dr Coulon, explained to Papritz that henceforth it would be the only institute allowed to deal with the *Reichskommissariat* Ostland. It is worth noting that in this case all pretence at scholarly autonomy had been abandoned, since the institute was actually housed within a ministry in Berlin, and was largely staffed by Rosenberg's experts like Reinerth.[211]

The total subordination of *Ostforschung* to the state was further in evidence during a conference held in the Heydrich-*Stiftung* in February 1944. The conference was attended by Brackmann, Papritz, Meynen, Steinacher, Metz, Beyer, von Loesch, and Seraphim who reported to their SS masters on the work carried out by their various institutes. SS-*Standartenführer* Ehlich outlined the future direction the subject was to take. The SS would set the political 'direction and goals' for academic work. The work was clearly of some importance, since Ehlich mentioned that he was about to give Himmler a list of names to relay to Keitel, in order to release *Ostforscher* from service in the armed forces. For their scholarship was 'of tremendous significance for future arrangements and planning'. The 'direction and goals' of scholarship were now set by the *Reichsführer*-SS. This meant studies designed to 'maintain and strengthen Germandom', 'to regain submerged Germandom' and to educate those of German brood 'combed out' of foreign peoples. He hoped that in future 'an even closer working community would develop in which each member will work freely but in terms of political goals which we need at the moment'.[212] Having set the terms of inquiry, Ehlich could afford to pander to the professional scruples of his audience, which by then had a sort of curiosity value from a time that had passed. The scholarship of the *Ostforscher* had been totally harnessed to the practical exercise of power. The subject *itself* had become an instrument for ruling conquered populations or, more insidiously, for effecting the inner transformation of those set in positions of power over those peoples. How those responsible for these developments managed to negotiate the total military defeat of Germany, and succeeded in reconstructing the subject in the altered circumstances after 1945, will occupy the following chapter.

6. THE 'BAND OF THE UNBROKEN' AND THEIR CRITICS:

ASPECTS OF *OSTFORSCHUNG* AFTER 1945

A critical perspective on the relationship between *Ostforschung* and the Nazi regime has been slow to develop in the post-war period. Following Germany's military defeat, the *Ostforscher* were more concerned with establishing a new institutional base in altered political circumstances than with clarifying their role in the previous decade. Ironically enough when, in the mid-1950s, criticism did ensue, the source of the criticism enabled the *Ostforscher* to postpone self-reflection. Their critics across the inner-German divide were enemies of Western freedom and servants of the state–political interests of the DDR or Poland. The substance of the criticisms went unanswered. Recently, a more complex situation has arisen. Certainly the *Ostforscher* successfully carved out an institutional niche in the Federal Republic. But as they themselves are increasingly marooned in memory, and as more about their past activities becomes known, they have become a source of apologetic embarrassment for their ever-younger successors. The academic futures of the younger generations depend upon institutions funded by governments concerned with trade and coexistence – if not understanding – with the crystallized states of eastern Europe. The position reached at the moment would seem to be as follows. The *Ostforscher* discussed here are increasingly the stuff of obituaries, commemorative addresses and *Festschriften*: genre notorious for an absence of critical detachment from their subject. Their critics in the DDR have switched their attention to new priorities such as the selective reevaluation of Prussian history. The immediate beneficiaries of the post-war institutional foundations have no incentive to rake over awkward areas in the history of their own discipline or to examine the careers of figures of whom they were very often pupils. Funds are tight nowadays. The political colours of *Bund* and *Länder* do not necessarily overlap and so a discreet silence ensues. Consequently, what critical literature there is stems largely from outside the narrow confines of the subject. A *tour d'horizon* would have to include the work of historians of ideology, of contemporary eastern Europe, and social scientists interested in personal and theoretical continuities between those who served the Third Reich and those who serve the Federal Republic.[1] The separate schools of *Osteuropaforscher* have also tried to look at the past and present of their respective disciplines although it seems that much of this discussion – with the notable exception of Friedrich Kuebart – remains trapped in the semantic and methodological spheres. This is not to suggest, facilely, that nothing has changed. While 1945 (unlike 1933) may not represent a decisive break in the careers of individuals, the political context in which they work has changed. To labour along the same groove despite these changes is to become irrelevant. The main contours of these developments will be essayed here, but all conclusions must be regarded as highly provisional.

From the middle of the 1950s the *Ostforscher* were refracted through two mutually antagonistic literatures. Their own was compounded of nostalgia, and old animosities refashioned for a global, Cold War, setting. The DDR critics sought to place the *Ostforscher* as 'ideological precursors' to a demonic succession running from Wilhelmine imperialism, via the Nazis, to the 'military–clerical' dictators in Bonn'.[2] In addition to their inner German political function, both literatures reflect a concern to manufacture a community of opinion with their respective political and military allies. These literatures contain a number of serious flaws even in terms of their own theoretical dynamics. The one that purports to be Marxist-Leninist is too personalized, and over-responsive to the fluctuating political interests of the DDR. It also manages to reify concepts like *Drang nach Osten* that are part of the unscientific armoury of the *Ostforscher* themselves and, paradoxically, of the DDR's larger eastern neighbours.[3] The literature produced by the *Ostforscher* totally fails to engage with the Nazi past, transforms symbolic gesture and metaphor into 'resistance', and sometimes contains more or less explicit declarations of political intent which, if extrapolated from the wider political context, confirm the worst fears of their DDR and Polish critics. The literature becomes an extended hall of mirrors for, paradoxically, both interlock at certain points, in an odd dialectic where criticism results in evasion, and evasion stimulates increased criticism. This process, and the wider question of continuities across 1945 can best be approached by considering the senior survivor of post-war *Ostforschung* Hermann Aubin (1885–1969).

A series of speeches delivered in Bonn on 23 March 1970 reflected the official view of some of the German historical establishment on the life and work of their erstwhile colleague. Rehearsing the stages of an academic life, the interludes in Bonn and Giessen at the start, and at Hamburg at the end, figured more prominently than the fifteen years in Breslau from 1929 to 1945. There, apparently, Aubin had applied his work on 'cultural streams' to the 'zone of destiny'.[4] There were difficulties with the Nazi regime – experienced by the Jew Richard Koebner and Aubin's brother Gustav the *Rektor* of Halle – but 'the optimum of what was achievable' was to stay in his post.[5] Having rationalized why he remained, it was necessary to explain his position thereafter. Aubin had become 'Janus-faced', and steered a scholarly course through the Scylla of Polish tendentiousness and the Charybdis of Nazi 'interference' with history.[6] 'Consequently' Breslau escaped the worst effects of Nazi *Gleichschaltung*. Aubin emerged, unsullied, and armed with an essay in a book designed to retrieve Charlemagne from those who traduced him as the 'slayer of the Saxons', and three semesters of lectures devoted to the Merovingians – the '*Götterdammerungsära* of germanic history' – to demonstrate his prescient opposition to the regime.[7] Resistance was in metaphor. There was the matter of lectures to the troops in Rostov-on-the-Don (lectures to Hans Frank or at the 'university' in Posen were too difficult to rationalize), but all must have been well in the world of learning if, in 1942, a chapter (commissioned in 1934), had adorned the pages of the *Cambridge Economic History*. This had a symbolic significance on a par with mayhem at the court of Clovis.[8] By the winter of 1945/6 Aubin was lecturing at Göttingen; a chair at Hamburg followed the year after. Honour and recognition ensued for the distinguished, international, professor. In 1950 he created the *J. G. Herder Forschungsrat* and three years later he became chairman of the *Verband der Historiker Deutschlands* and a member of the *Comité International des Sciences Historiques*.[9]

Across the inner-German border there was a different Aubin, the creation of Rudolf Graf. This was the malignant shade of the benign figure conjured up in Bonn. Graf's title 'Hermann Aubin in the service of the fascist policy of occupation in Poland and clerical-militaristic anti-bolshevism' contained the essential elements of the local exegesis. Aubin was 'an old apologist for German imperialism and militarism' who had ideologically 'prepared' the Second World War.[10] He had propagated notions like 'master race' and Lebensraum, organized 'fifth columnists' in Poland and Czechoslovakia, and had served the 'fascist racial theory' in the occupied East. His more recent enthusiasm for a 'western community of interest' was the latest example of 'diversionary' tactics, designed to disaffect the citizens of the 'people's democracies' in order to achieve a better 'point of departure for the assault upon the Soviet Union'.[11]

Although Graf's view of the relationship between historians and government probably tells us more about working arrangements in the DDR than in the Federal Republic, his article *does* raise a number of disquieting questions about elements of continuity in the work of *Ostforscher* to justify a closer examination of what they were writing before and after 1945. The work of Aubin has been chosen, not for reasons of personal denunciation, but because his writings span the 1930s and 1950s, and continue to enjoy some sort of academic reputation.

In 1965 Aubin republished, in an unaltered form, articles entitled 'Zur Erforschung der deutschen Ostbewegung', which had first appeared in 1937. The essays were a celebration of how 'before our eyes', academic research had become part of actual national consciousness. Acknowledging a considerable debt to the work of geographers in the 1920s, Aubin advocated a 'total' approach to phenomena that had hitherto been regarded as being separate in time and character. 'Dynastic-territorial historiography' had narrowed the view to regional episodes in the 'movement east', but the 'tearing asunder' of German 'Lebensraum' after 1918 had forced historians to construct a unified, wider, picture which in turn had 'contributed a great deal to awaken the Germans from a territorial, state-focused, to a wider, overall-German, *völkisch* view of history'. The language of contemporary political polemic, of a 'unified destiny of the lands of the East', had given an 'intellectual stimulus' to academic research. *Ostforschung* itself had been responsible for lowering the obstructive frontiers 'in the consciousness of the German people', for terms like *Volksboden* or *Kulturboden* dispensed with political frontiers.[12] What he regarded as a continuous movement eastwards from the Middle Ages to the early modern period was to be studied as a chronological and spatial totality. Although, in narrow historiographical terms, this approach contained some progressive elements, it was also, profoundly, politically reactionary.[13] The retreat from the specificities of time and place

– *l'histoire evenementielle* if you will – into the vaguaries of *Raum*, served to underline the contingency of political arrangements that Aubin, and most of the German professoriate, wished to do away with. By investing his 'movement' with the force of timeless, natural, inevitability, he was, in effect, trivializing the political status quo. The metaphors he chose further helped to establish causality outside time and human agency. Throughout his extensive *oeuvre* he spoke of 'streams',[14] 'waves',[15] 'floods',[16] and 'rivers'[17] to describe a process whereby the Germans were strewn like 'seed' across eastern Europe.[18] In a further conceptual development, the cliches of bourgeois historical writing – the 'pioneer spirit'[19] – were replaced by biological explanations. A 'migration of selection' by 'the strongest and most valuable parts of the population';[20] German blood 'that flowed through the channels of the Austrian state system';[21] 'national–psychological preconditions',[22] and last, but not least, 'drives' compelling the Germans eastwards, rendered current political arrangements contingent and by implication 'unnatural'. The greater the retreat into historical–geographical *Ganzheitsforschung* – with a biological edge – the lesser the need to countenance frontiers, social organization, class relations, institutions, diplomacy and politics – the human substance of history – in the present.[23] Despite all of the pseudo-scientific convolutions, one only has to compare this work with that of some of Aubin's French contemporaries like Marc Bloch – who, of course, was familiar with research done in several countries – to realize that one is dealing with a provincial literature of a rather ponderous, germanocentric sort.

With considerable monotony, Aubin repeated the same metaphors and notions of cultural superiority and made the same resort to 'Blood' as a causal agent, in numerous publications on the history of Silesia – the 'exit gate for German being to the East'.[24] By 1940 he was lecturing on these themes to Hans Frank in occupied Cracow, when it was common knowledge that the Polish professoriate had been abducted to concentration camps. As in his earlier essays, Aubin made light of any firm, national frontiers, opting instead for the deliberate vagaries of 'the German ethnic frontier', the 'massive Lebensraum' of 'greater Russiandom', the 'zone of peoples and ethnic splinters', the 'in-between zone', 'between Europe', 'ethnic mosaics', and 'the limited value' of hard inter-state frontiers.[25] The Slavs, he argued, were only indigenous to 'the smallest part of their present area'. The 'primitiveness' of their cultural situation and their 'constitutional incapability' meant that they had to defer to the dominant Germans. From the time of Charlemagne, the Germans had given 'blood from [their] blood to the neighbouring peoples'. Speaking in Reichenberg in October 1940, he described the treaty of Versailles as 'an unnatural state of affairs' and of the 'hearts filled with gratitude' towards the liberator of German minorities, Adolf Hitler, who had been 'given in gift' to the German people.[26]

By the early 1950s the *Ostforscher* were congratulating themselves upon having survived the difficult times. In 1952 Aubin and 'the band of the unbroken' issued a new journal entitled the *Zeitschrift für Ostforschung*.[27] The language, metaphors, and images, were curiously familiar, but worked into a global, Cold War, context.

> The troops of the Soviet Republics stand on the Elbe, in the heartland of central Europe. To the east the unified influence of Bolshevism prevails. The frontiers of two distinct spheres of civilisation run straight through Europe. World views and forms of existence collide against one another whose differences threaten to tear the world apart into two irreconcilable camps.[28]

What had resulted in this state of affairs was ignored; instead he dwelt upon the 'expulsion', 'abduction' and 'extermination' (in industrialized death camps?) of 'over twelve million Germans' for there was safety in the approximation of large numbers. Surveying his own time, Aubin remarked that the Nazi regime had 'posed the question of a lasting order in eastern central Europe' and had begun by recognizing the nationality principle 'for all peoples'. The 'serious application' of this principle could have united the forces of the West 'in common defence'. Only Hitler's imperialism had sabotaged the construction of 'a frontier wall of the West against bolshevik Russia'. The result was that 'a form of existence alien to the West' was established across the slim divide of the Elbe. Hitler's subscription to the idea of national self-determination was genuine: at some point in time there had been a wrong turning.[29]

Having assumed the role of a Cold War warrior, Aubin rode forth in defence of freedom. In late September 1958 he used his position as chairman of the *Verband der Historiker Deutschlands* to assail the twenty-three delegates from the DDR attending a conference in Trier. In a statement which was published in the *Historische Zeitschrift*, Aubin queried the representationality of the delegation from the recently founded *Deutsche Historiker Gesellschaft*; dwelt upon the obstacles facing non-Marxists in the 'Soviet Occupied Zone', and added that 'a scholarly dialogue with discussion partners who avowedly subject scholarship to political aims is pointless'. To refuse the right to speak to Professors Ernst Engelberg, Max Steinmetz and Leo Stern, was a matter of obeying the 'dictates of self-respect' on the part of the members of the VHD.[30] Whatever the specific rights and wrongs of the events in Trier – which revolve around the point that the invitations were sent to individuals but a delegation appeared – Hermann Aubin was not the best person to deliver speeches on the subordination of scholarship to politics.

Offering so many hostages to fortune, it was inevitable that Aubin should have become the specific target of assault from East German scholars like Graf. In fact, the decision to focus attention upon West German *Ostforschung* had been taken some years before Aubin's ill-chosen words in Trier. In July 1955 the Central Committee of the SED resolved to intensify the struggle against 'the ideologists of anti-Communism and revanchism in West Germany'.[31] The accent was placed upon the study of imperialist *Ostforschung* by the Leipzig historian F.-H. Gentzen, in an article in the theoretical journal *Einheit* later that year. Gentzen traced continuities between the propagandists of the Eastern Marches Association and the *Ostforscher* who had manufactured the 'intellectual armoury' of German fascism.[32] They were currently responsible for propagating revanchism, revisionism and chauvinism under the mantle of an ideology of the West. The aim was a war of aggression against the Soviet Union and its allies.[33] The activities of the *Ostforscher* had found a new institutional base in the Federal Republic in the form of the Göttinger Arbeitskreis, Herder Institute and Deutsche Gesellschaft für Osteuropakunde in Stuttgart. The perceived threat from these institutes was discussed at a meeting held in December 1958 between a number of DDR historians and the educational department of the Central Committee, in the presence of Ulbricht, and the chairman of the Politburo.[34] University institutes were encouraged to study West German *Ostforschung*. Initially studies were coordinated from the Leipzig Institut für Geschichte der europäischen Volksdemokratien, where a study group 'Struggle against West German *Ostforschung*' was formed in May 1959, under the direction of Gentzen and the former professor of journalism Basil Spiru.[35] Gentzen was one of the four contributors to a major East German article on '*Ostforschung* – shock troops of German imperialism' that appeared in 1958. This was a form of counter-attack following the 'scandalous incidents in Trier', from a scholarly camp dedicated to the 'securing of peace' and 'the construction of socialism'. As the 'ideologists of German imperialism', the West German *Ostforscher* were active 'in the aggressive policies, the Cold War, and psychological warfare of the ruling circles of West Germany against the socialist countries'.[36] Moving from the general to the specific, the four DDR authors accused the *Ostforscher* of training administrative specialists for '*Tag X*';[37] creating an institutional apparatus for the resumption of 'imperialist plans for expansion eastwards';[38] revanchism as a means of 'liquidating the order of people's democracies' and of transforming the states of eastern Europe into colonies of West German monopoly capitalism;[39] the subversion of the state and social foundations of the DDR and encouragement of counter-revolutionary elements elsewhere;[40] 'research' on behalf of United States and West German intelligence agencies;[41] the whitewashing of Nazi terror in occupied eastern Europe, and the creation of a martyrological literature concerning post-war expulsions.[42] This line of argument was stated more crudely, in a popular form, in Gentzen and Eberhard Wolfgramm's 1960 book on *Ostforschung*. They drew attention to the fact that 'the murderers of yesterday occupy ministerial positions in the Bonn state', and that the 'intellectual fathers of Nazi crimes' were again teaching at West German universities.

> The *Ostforscher* in West Germany are like poisonous spiders who spin their fine web in all directions in an attempt to influence the widest sections of the West German population. From the elderly 'expellee', to the ten-year-old child, from the East Prussian landowner, to small farmers brought back from Bessarabia under the 'Home to the Reich' programme of the Nazis, from the Baltic clergyman, to the Sudeten German Social Democrat.[43]

Case studies of particular individuals like Aubin and Oberländer accompanied attempts to discredit specific research institutes as 'centres of diversion and espionage'.[44] Inevitably, in this rather simple discussion, there was no effort to isolate specific relationships between academic research and government, or to discriminate between scholarship, legitimate information gathering, and criminal activity carried out in another state.

This Leipzig literature doubtless benefited from the fact that Eberhard Wolfgramm was himself a former *Ostforscher*. In 1959 he published an autobiographical account of his odyssey from *Ostforscher* to academic at the Karl Marx University of Leipzig. Born in Bohemia in 1908, Wolfgramm's interest in authoritarian models of the state was aroused by the *Wandervogel* and the ideas of Othmar Spann and Stefan George.[45] He passed from the *Kameradschaftsbund* into the Sudeten German Party, producing a number of articles purveying the notion of a German 'cultural mission' and a brochure entitled *Germans and Czechs in History*. As a member of staff of the NSDAP *Gauleitung* in the Sudetenland, Wolfgramm worked on maps and statistical tables designed to isolate 'ethnic–political danger zones' and hence areas subsequently subjected to 'germanisation'.[46] In an attempt to escape complicity in activities he increasingly regarded as criminal, Wolfgramm joined the army. After the war, he worked for the 'German Office for Peace Questions' in Bonn and was encouraged, he wrote, to make contact with Peter-Heinz Seraphim, who, ensconced beside the Starnberger See, had forsaken anti-Semitism for intelligence gathering and the production of memoranda on eastern European problems.[47] With a glancing blow at the trinity of ministries in Bonn, expellee organizations, and Standard Oil, Wolfgramm returned to his own career as a lecturer in Slavonic languages in Stuttgart. Membership of the 'German–Soviet Friendship Society' proved incompatible with stipulations of the Adenauer regime concerning 'enemies of democracy', and since Wolfgramm refused to sign a declaration renouncing his political contacts, he lost the right to teach in Baden-Württemberg. Fearing the resurgence of fascism, he fled to East Germany in March 1956. There he was well-placed – like the academic exiles going the other way – to provide up-to-date information on his erstwhile colleagues, with all the unselfconsciousness of the recently converted.

In June 1960 a further department 'for the history of imperialistic *Ostforschung*' was established at the Humboldt University in East Berlin under the direction of the KPD veteran Rudolf Goguel (1908–76). The department evaluated publications in search of tendencies within the discipline, and made the results available to corresponding institutes in other states like the Institut Zachodni in Poznań. A further study group devoted to 'the philosophical and historiographical clarification of the "European" and "Western" theories of German imperialism' – for the ways of imperialism were circuitous – was founded in November 1961 at Halle-Wittenberg. These various groups, whose activities were coordinated, organized exhibitions and conferences between historians and Slavists from east European states, and supplied expert testimony for legal proceedings conducted in the highest court of the DDR against Theodor Oberländer.[48] According to a programmatic statement, the study groups regarded *Ostforschung* as representing the interests of the ruling classes 'independently of the dominant political system of the time', or, in other words, from the *Kaiserreich* to the *Bundesrepublik*. The *Ostforscher* researched whatever target of imperialism came next.[49] By studying this subject, the East German historians hoped to clarify the 'historical roots of contemporary West German *Ostpolitik*' and to discover 'valuable analogies' between past and present.[50]

Goguel's route to an academic post in East Berlin was as circuitous as that of Wolfgramm, although in Goguel's case it was a career deeply embedded in the KPD. His education had come to a halt in the early 1930s because of the financial necessity of his parents.[51] As the leader of a Communist trade union for white-collar workers in Düsseldorf, Goguel was subject to arrest, imprisonment, and conditional release by the Gestapo in their effort to penetrate and destroy the KPD cells. In late September 1934 he was again arrested and confronted with the battered face of another KPD functionary, Erich Krause, from the Lower Rhine District. Since both men were going to be tortured into mutual recognition, Krause hanged himself the same evening; Goguel threw himself from a fourth-floor window.[52] Having survived this attempt at suicide, in February 1935 he was sentenced to ten years' imprisonment for conspiracy to commit high treason. After serving the sentence in Lüttringhausen and Hameln, Goguel was put in 'protective custody' in Sachsenhausen and then Neuengamme concentration camps. Having survived the efforts of the SS to drown the surviving inmates on the ship *Cap Arkona*, Goguel worked as an editor on various Communist newspapers until, in 1953, he moved East.[53] From 1953 he worked as an editor in the German Institute for Contemporary History, and then in the department within the Humboldt university.

Goguel's work in Berlin included a number of published articles and a doctoral dissertation which, in its austere way, is the most significant work on the role of *Ostforschung* during the Second World War.[54] It was produced without the cooperation of senior West German *Ostforscher* who, with the exceptions of Conze and Wittram, refused to assist him, despite the fact that their own enquiries to the Ministry of Overall-German Affairs had revealed that Goguel was out of sorts with the SED, had probably helped three persons to leave, and was an *anständiger Charakter*.[55] As the *Ostforscher* closed upon Goguel, he tried to explore the trends in post-war West German *Ostforschung*. In 1960 he produced a study of institutions concerned with *Ostforschung* in the Federal Republic and posed the question why there was no global *Westforschung* devoted to Britain and France, or *Sudforschung* covering Italy, Spain and Portugal.[56] The emphasis in this research was not merely anti-Communist, but actively revanchist. A speech by Max Hildegard Böhm to the 'Ostdeutsche Kulturrat' in 1954 spoke of the day when 'the bolshevised areas would be regained for Europe', of a Western 'mission' more onerous than that of the Middle Ages, and of the urgency of training legal and economic specialists conversant with 'the zone' for *Tag X*.[57]

By 1964 attention in the DDR had shifted from *Ostforschung* to the more modish and americanized discipline of 'Sovietology'. Assuming rather than proving the influence of academic research upon the foreign policy of the Federal Republic, Goguel detected 'hard' and 'soft' approaches among scholars towards *Ostpolitik*. The objective of the 'soft' group was to prise Poland from the state socialist camp, by dismantling the 'anti-Polish complex', recognizing the Oder-Neisse frontier, and isolating the DDR.[58] The vocal revanchist camp threatened to upset a policy of seducing the peoples of eastern Europe into a false sense of security. It was unfortunate that the work of these departments was so immensely responsive to the political interests of the DDR, for this served to prevent any coming to terms with the substantive criticisms made by DDR historians. This responsiveness also meant that these departments were subject to immediate dissolution should the interests of the state require it. For reasons that remain obscure, by the late 1960s the Berlin and Leipzig departments ceased to function.[59]

The overt political objectives of the DDR critics – of which the DDR historians make no secret – should not obscure the striking personal and institutional continuities between pre- and post-war *Ostforschung*. If the scene surveyed by Klaus Mehnert in 1951 was depressing, by 1958, when Jens Hacker listed the main umbrella organizations and institutes there were grounds for optimism.[60] He began with the Göttinger Arbeitskreis, which was founded in 1946 by refugee scholars, in order to produce memoranda on the importance of East Prussia for the Moscow conference of Foreign Ministers in that year.[61] Although the Western occupying authorities were not initially well-disposed to the work of the Arbeitskreis – banning Professor Götz von Selle's 'Deutsches Geistesleben in Ostpreussen' – this does not seem to have obstructed the work of this self-proclaimed community of the like-minded.[62] By the late 1940s the Arbeitskreis was producing publications designed to tell the young about German achievements in the East, which was described as an integral part of Europe, and various information sheets which serviced the Press and interested individuals in mainly north and south America. Interest in the latter sub-continent was particularly strong, since a separate Buenos Aires edition of the *Pressedienst der Heimatvertriebenen* was produced for sympathizers residing in Chile and Argentina.[63] Hans Mortensen, Theodor Oberländer and Ernst Vollert were on the steering committee.

From the early 1950s there was a marked proliferation of research institutes in the Federal Republic: the Johann Gottfried Herder Institute (Marburg 1950–); the Osteuropa-Institut (Munich 1952–); the Norddeutschen Akademie (Lüneburg 1951–); the Südost-Institut (Munich 1952); and umbrella organizations like the Deutsche Gesellschaft für Osteuropakunde (Stuttgart 1948–); Südosteuropa-Gesellschaft (Munich 1953–); and the Ostkolleg der Bundeszentrale für Heimatdienst (Cologne 1957–). There were also six chairs for east European history, two chairs in Kiel for *Ostkunde* and six specialist institutes attached to the universities of Tübingen, Mainz, Wilhelmshaven, Munich, Münster and Giessen as well as the Osteuropa-Institut at the Freie Universität, Berlin (1951–).[64] In 1953 the Bundestag resolved to promote the study of East and South-East European subjects at all levels of the West German educational system. A year later a committee consisting of representatives from the cultural department of the Interior Ministry, the ministers of culture of the *Länder* and the Rektors of the universities was formed to suggest ways of allocating funds.[65] As in the past, the funds came from the Foreign and Interior ministries, with the former assuming responsibility for the cost of the Deutsche Gesellschaft für Osteuropakunde, and the latter covering the institutes in Berlin and Munich. Hacker, at least, made no secret of one aspect of this considerable financial input.

> Is it not one of the overall German tasks of our universities to include the [Soviet Occupied] Zone in their curricula? However the restitution of the unity of the German state, in our sense, will one day occur, there must be people before and on *Tag X* who are particularly conversant with the legal and economic development of the Zone.[66]

Statements like this, not to speak of the prominent positions occupied by Oberländer (Minister of Overall German Affairs), or Seraphim (Director of the Administrative Academy in Bochum), suggest that the fears of the DDR critics of West German *Ostforschung* may not have been entirely groundless.[67]

The motor behind the creation of the *J. G. Herder Forschungsrat* in

April 1950 was Hermann Aubin. The currency reform, and the imminent creation of federal authorities, provided a window of opportunity for the institutional revival of *Ostforschung*. The route to the money was via Dr Schreiber, the President of the Office for Expellees, who in turn presented Aubin's proposals to the incipient finance administration. Since Brackmann was old, infirm and a pensioner of the DDR, leadership devolved upon Aubin. The structures adopted were explicitly modelled upon those of the past. Conferences of interested scholars (the NODFG), a central institutional apparatus (the PuSte), and a journal (*Jomsburg*).[68] Papritz, Erich Keyser and Aubin were prominent in the Forschungsrat which met biannually to coordinate research.

The objectives of the 'new German *Ostforschung*' were outlined by Keyser in 1952. 'Necessity' and 'a sense of duty' had compelled them all to begin anew. The German people were duty-bound to study some seven hundred years of their history in the East. The decisions of Yalta and Potsdam reflected an 'unknowing' of German history. Narrow chauvinism was to be replaced by a sense of a European community to which the peoples of the East belonged. In practice this meant that the Germans had brought Christianity, cultural improvement, political order and economic development to the East in collaboration with other European nations.[69] This internationalizing of traditional German chauvinism barely concealed the legacy from the past.

A Western community of interest, juxtaposed against an undefined 'East', was apparent in much of the historical work produced by the *Ostforscher* in the late 1950s. To anyone familiar with what the same men had produced shortly before, these efforts to revise the past in terms of transnational community of interest are jarring and unconvincing. A few examples of this genre will suffice. In a monograph on the right of resistance in later medieval Prussia (1955), Erich Weise suggested that the Knights were the finest example of the interweaving of the destinies of Germany with those of Europe as a whole.[70] The Order represented 'the concentrated energy of European culture'. It was a 'bulwark' against 'threats from the East'.[71] Foreign visiting crusaders like John of Bohemia or Henry of Derby went to Prussia in the fourteenth century, not for the festivities or 'thrills' (*Nervenkitzel*) but for 'political reasons' like inspecting the 'level of culture' of the pagan Lithuanians. In the end, the efforts of these armoured anthropologists were in vain, for at Tannenberg 'not only the power of the Order, but the solidarity of Europe was badly affected'.[72] The history of the Order was given a similar Cold War accent by Walter Kuhn, in an article entitled 'Military Religious Orders as Frontier Guards of the West against eastern Heathenism', which appeared in 1959. The various military–religious orders had failed in their plan to create a series of frontier states, acting as a 'bar' between Poland and Hungary and 'the Greek-Orthodox world'.[73]

As in the 1930s, the *Ostforscher* tried to make their work more internationally accessible through translations and books specifically aimed at an international, Anglo-Saxon audience. A number of familiar names were involved in the production of *The German East* which arose from an exhibition devoted to 'Germany's Eastern Homeland', organized by the Berlin city council and the Ministry for Overall German Affairs in November 1950. A number of revealing claims were made in the book:

> The subjects chosen cover all those spheres of life which can be formed by human effort. And in every field the truth is revealed, that this is German land, since the German peasant's plough turned it into arable land, since the word of God spread in the German tongue in monasteries and churches, since German law guided the life of its inhabitants, since western civilisation and morality came to prevail and reached their full flower. This all came to pass on ground which was undeveloped, almost without a history; certainly not everywhere without injury to the rights of others, and at the cost of opposition from other forces, as is inherent in the course of historical events; but still with more justification than the naked violence in use against the Germans today. The world knows that the present solution is not a solution that can last.[74]

The 'present solution', the Minister for Overall German Affairs stated, was 'not a German, not a Polish, not even a Russian solution', but 'a Bolshevik solution'. The essays endeavoured to show that German expansion eastwards was carried out 'on behalf of the nascent West'. This was given a highly aggressive accent, which again demonstrates that the almost hysterical reaction in the DDR to this type of literature had some basis in fact, when the editor remarked that the Germans were the 'shieldbearers' on the eastern 'flank' of Europe '*and are today and will be tomorrow*'.[75] The Stuttgart Charter of the Expellees was appended to the end of the book.

The form and content of the essays resembled that of Brackmann's *Germany and Poland* of the early 1930s. Wolfgang La Baume was still shadow-boxing with the 'Slav' Lusatian civilization, and endeavouring to demonstrate the continuity of 'Germanic culture' in the north-east. The Slavs had 'infiltrated' into these areas, absorbing the Germanic remnants into 'Slavdom'. Elsewhere, the Polish kingdom was described as 'a political power-complex of feeble coherence', while the Germans had brought 'inspiration and order' to the 'German-Slav frontier belt'. The 'decades-long migratory movement' was invested with a European character:

> It was a task on behalf of the West, carried out in the new Germany. It was not accidental that the imperial charter instructing and empowering the Knights of the Teutonic Order to overthrow the persistently pagan Prussians was issued in Rimini, Arminium of the Romans, a city of the Adriatic Sea, in the classical heart of the western empire. And it was not accidental that the commission was given to an Order which had emerged in the east in the struggle against the menacing power of the Orient and had withstood its ordeal of fire on the Transylvanian border, on the frontier of the West.[76]

A curious intermingling of *völkisch* historiography and an ideology of the West is particularly apparent in Erich Keyser's chapter. The author was unaware of any problems concerning the categories, concepts, and language he was using, which, even to the most obtuse English reader, must have appeared to have come from the stockroom of intellectually damaged goods.

> The most striking achievement of the Germans was the productive reform of the land. The Germans were the first to convert Prussia into 'Lebensraum' and to wrest the harvest from its soil to nourish a constantly increasing population. For long after the arrival of the Germans the Prussians and Pomerani earned a meagre existence, scratching superficially at the soil with the primitive swing plough or fishing and hunting ... All towns and most of the villages were built by the Germans.[77]

While the impact of works like this upon an English reading public can safely be described as minimal, one can only speculate about the influence of former *Ostforscher* upon sections of the West German public. In an article in *Der Stahlhelm*, the organ of former *Frontsoldaten*, in 1962, the retired Theodor Oberländer rehearsed the nature of 'the revolutionary war'. The 'dictatorship in the East' was conducting an 'offensive revolution' against the West. It was a 'war' that had no definite beginning, involved no sudden movement of troops, but began with 'publicism', 'infiltration', and 'espionage'.

> There is no coexistence between the free and the unfree world. Khrush-
> chev described it himself as international class-struggle. Some in the
> West, and in particular part of the rootless intelligentsia, believed in
> the possibility of leftist coexistence.
>
> It is one of the most dangerous utopian ideas of our time that the
> East–West conflict can be solved by an approximation and later a
> merging of both blocs and systems.[78]

The West talked of defence, but 'gives up one position after another'.
Those who traded in essential goods with the USSR were digging their
own graves. To appease 'the enemy' was to further world revolution.[79]
The fact that the 'unfree' might not have wished to be 'liberated' by
Theodor Oberländer or the *Bund der Frontsoldaten* – who themselves
had passed that way twenty years before – eluded him.

Further repetition of examples of this Cold War literature would
not promote understanding and deserves a fuller treatment in the
context of contemporary East–West relations than can be given here.
A critical West German literature on *Ostforschung* developed in the
mid-1970s. Criticism from the DDR and Poland, which could be easily
brushed off through reference to its political purposes, was gradually
accompanied by a growing domestic interest in the culpable involvement of bourgeois, educated groups – physicians, lawyers and academics – with the Nazi regime.[80] Younger scholars discovered that beneath
the smooth mask of academic respectability, with its subscription to
professional values and humanistic culture, lay the more sophisticated
colleagues of the witless sadists whose actions have become all too
horribly familiar. In a lesser key, the advent of detente seems to have
triggered an internal crisis of confidence within the discipline, as the
assumptions that had guaranteed *Ostforschung* generous funding in
the decade after the war were brought into question.

A conference held in Bad Hönnigen in 1974 debated the nature and
future of the discipline, and the question of whether the term *Ostforschung* should be dropped in favour of 'Osteuropaforschung', 'Sovietology'? 'Ostwissenschaft' or 'Osteuropakunde'.[81] Behind this rather
self-conscious semantic exercise lay concern about diminishing recruitment and budgetary stagnation.[82] The founder generation – the Aubins
and Papritzs – had retired. Their forty-five- to sixty-year-old successors,
who had benefited from expansion from the late 1950s, were securely
– some would say too securely – in place. Those whose training, and
expectations, had been formed in the years of expansion had fewer
opportunities when contraction ensued. These problems were further

compounded by the fact that whereas many of the middle generation had been born outside the Federal Republic, their younger pupils had no immediate personal link with the countries to be studied. It was not just a matter of what sort of torch was to be handed on but whether there would be anyone with an interest in taking hold of it.

The conference also discussed the relationship between academic expertise, politics and the mass media in a way that suggests that a new realism had developed. The disciplines subsumed under the term *Ostforschung* had to become more 'consumer' orientated. Politicians had no time to digest abstruse academic research – which, the *Ostforscher* acknowledged, often went unread even in the most distilled form – and were primarily interested in functional information about, for example, the political weight of their opposite numbers in Warsaw or Bucharest.[83] The journalists and television networks had their own specialists and, more importantly, their own professional notions of the relationship between background analysis and 'news'. If the scholars had a greater awareness of their role, so too did the politicians and bureaucrats. While the scholars wished to be 'in the proximity but not in the tow of politics', the politicians wanted accurate information on developments within the various Communist states of eastern Europe and the USSR. That was why the subject received generous Federal funding.[84] These contacts between research and the bureaucracy have been formalized. In 1953 the Ministry of the Interior established a committee for research on eastern Europe consisting eventually of the heads of the eleven major research institutes, and representatives from the Interior, Foreign and Inner-German Relations ministries.[85] In 1974 an Inter-Ministerial Study Group for Osteuropaforschung, with a permanent secretariat, was formed to coordinate the interests of government departments and the work of the research institutes.[86] The secretariat informs the directors of institutes about the general areas of research that most interest the bureaucrats, while the institutes forward some 250 information sheets a year to the secretariat which in turn sends the information to 'discussion partners' in the ministries. These more formalized relationships have resulted in some discussion of the different tempo of political and academic work, the differences between 'academic' and 'political' truth (!), and the information gap between diplomats and scholars.[87] Although it is difficult to establish whether this is so or not, the work is said to consist of 'basic political work' (background information) which is distilled by middle echelon bureaucrats at some remove from where decisions are taken.[88] In other words the easy access and personal–social contacts of a Schiemann, Hoetzsch or Brackmann have been replaced by more formalized relationships. This might be described as a positive development.

As the generation directly involved in giving the subject its extreme germanocentric emphasis passes away, their successors have had the difficult task of adapting to new international and domestic political realities, while not casting overboard the entire legacy from the past. Personal loyalties and the ties of academic patronage have not assisted the process of confronting the recent history of the discipline. Cosmetic changes – like altering the title of a journal – resolve nothing. However changes will probably accelerate – unless the subject is to become irrelevant – as the wider scholarly landscape becomes more internationalized. In some areas of medieval history, for example, there have been genuine attempts to treat once sensitive issues in a broad, thematic and comparative way, by informal teams of scholars from east and west Europe. Some of the most interesting work on 'towns', 'nobilities', 'estates' or 'colonisation' has resulted from international conferences organized by the *Konstanzer Arbeitskreis*, while Polish, West German and Scandinavian medievalists meet regularly in Toruń for the comparative study of military religious orders.[89] If the trend in medieval studies is away from the uniqueness of national historical experience, a reverse tendency, away from mechanistic theorizing and global models of systems, is perceptible in more contemporary work. There are also successful examples of international scholarly debate, reflecting an awareness of the variegated influences of many cultures and political systems, in the specialized field of *Südosteuropaforschung*.[90] Collectively, these developments represent a *Verwissenschaftlichung* of, and increased specialization within, the various disciplines and regions hitherto subsumed under the term *Ostforschung*. Although there are still those who continue to plough the old germanocentric furrow, this represents again one school among many. Since the intellectually interesting developments occur elsewhere, stagnation ensues.[91]

NOTES

INTRODUCTION

1. On German liberal *Polenfreundschaft* see Eberhard Kolb, 'Polenbild und Polenfreundschaft der deutschen Frühliberalen. Zu Motivation und Funktion aussenpolitischer Parteinahme im Vormärz', *Saeculum* (1975), 26, especially pp. 124–7 for the change in attitudes between 1846 and 1848; Hans-Adolf Jacobsen, 'Vom Wandel des Polenbildes in Deutschland (1772–1972)', *Aus Politik and Zeitgeschichte* (1973), 21/73, especially pp. 6–7; Wolfgang Wippermann, 'Die Ostsiedlung in der deutschen Historiographie und Publizistik. Probleme, Methoden und Grundlinien der Entwicklung bis zum Ersten Weltkrieg' in Wolfgang Fritze, ed., *Germania Slavica* (Berlin 1980), 1, especially pp. 57–60, and his 'Die deutsche und polnische Frage in der deutschen Historiographie', *Aus Politik und Zeitgeschichte* (1987), 14/87, pp. 29–31; Martin Broszat, *Zweihundert Jahre deutsche Polenpolitik* (Frankfurt am Main 1972₂), especially pp. 113ff. On 1848 as a turning point in German perceptions of the Slavs see Gerard Labuda, 'The Slavs in Nineteenth Century German Historiography', *Polish Western Affairs* (1969), 10, pp. 194–6.

2. On *'polnische Wirtschaft'* see Wolfgang Wippermann, *Der Ordensstaat als Ideologie. Das Bild des Deutschen Ordens in der deutschen Geschichtsschreibung und Publizistik. Einzelveröffentlichungen der Historischen Kommission zu Berlin*, 24 (West Berlin 1979), pp. 128–30; 'Die Ostsiedlung in der deutschen Historiographie' p. 54; Bernhard Stasiewski, 'Polnische Wirtschaft und Johann Georg Forster, eine wortgeschichtliche Studie', *Deutsche Wissenschaftliche Zeitschrift im Wartheland* (1941), pp. 207–16; on antagonisms between forms of state and society see for example Broszat, *Zweihundert Jahre deutsche Polenpolitik* pp. 33ff., and William W. Hagen, *Germans, Poles, and Jews. The Nationality Conflict in the Prussian East, 1772–1914* (Chicago 1980), especially pp. 31–7; Günther Stökl, *Osteuropa und die Deutschen* (Stuttgart 1982₃), pp. 33–51. Stökl's book is, deservedly, the standard introduction to these problems.

3. Hagen, *Germans, Poles, and Jews* pp. 36–7; see also Michael Burleigh, 'The Knights, Nationalists and the Historians: Images of Medieval Prussia from the Enlightenment to 1945', *European History Quarterly* (1987), 17, p. 38.

4. Josef Körner, 'Die Slaven im Urteil der deutschen Frühromantik', *Historische Vierteljahreszeitschrift* (1936–7), 31, pp. 569–71; Wolfgang Wippermann, 'Das Slawenbild der Deutschen im 19. und 20. Jahrhundert', *Slawen und Deutsche zwischen Elbe und Oder. Vor 1000 Jahren: Der Slawenaufstand von 983* (Berlin 1983), p. 69.

5. Johann Gottfried Herder, *Ideen zur Philosophie der Geschichte der Menschheit. Vierter Theil, Sechzehntes Buch*, in B. Suphan, ed., *Herders Sämmtliche Werke* (Berlin 1909), 14, pp. 472–3. On Herder and the Slavs see Konrad Bittner, *Herders Geschichtsphilosophie und die Slawen. Veröffentlichungen der Slavistischen Arbeitsgemeinschaft an der Deutschen Universität in Prag*, eds. F. Spina and G. Gesemann (Reichenberg 1929), 6, especially pp. 97ff.; and on Herder in general, K. Stavenhagen, 'Herders Geschichtsphilosophie und seine Geschichts prophetie', *Zeitschrift für Ostforschung* (1952), 1, pp. 16–43, and Isaiah Berlin, *Vico and Herder: Two Studies in the History of Ideas* (London 1980). For the reappraisal of the Order by *inter alia* Reitemeier and Johannes Voigt, see Wippermann, *Der Ordensstaat als Ideologie*, pp. 120–35, and his *Der 'Deutsche Drang nach Osten': Ideologie und Wirklichkeit eines politischen Schlagwortes* (Darmstadt 1981), pp. 24–9, and Burleigh, 'The Knights, Nationalists and the Historians', pp. 37–9.

6. Wippermann, *Der 'Deutsche Drang nach Osten'* pp. 34ff.; and for Marx and Engels his 'Das Bild der mittelalterlichen deutschen Ostsiedlung bei Marx und Engels', Wolfgang Fritze, ed., *Germania Slavica*, I, pp. 71–97.

7. Gustav Freytag, *Soll und Haben* (Berlin 1855), p. 551; on Freytag's historical novels see Wippermann, 'Gen Ostland wollen wir reiten!' Ordensstaat und Ostsiedlung in der historischen Belletristik Deutschlands', Wolfgang Fritze, ed. *Germania Slavica* (West Berlin 1981), 2, pp. 207–9; see also Rolf-Dieter Kluge, 'Darstellung und Bewertung des Deutschen Ordens in der deutschen und polnischen Literatur', *Zeitschrift für Ostforschung* (1969), 18, pp. 15–53, and on Freytag in general, Walter Bussmann, 'Gustav Freytag. Massstäbe seiner Zeitkritik', *Archiv für Kulturgeschichte* (1952), 34, pp. 261–7.

8. Heinrich von Treitschke, 'Das Deutsche Ordensland Preussen', *Preussischer Jahrbücher* (1862), 10, p. 95; on this essay see Walter Bussmann, *Treitschke. Sein Welt- und Geschichtsbild* in H. Goetting *et al.*, eds., *Göttinger Bausteine zur Geschichtswissenschaft* (Göttingen 1981₂) 3/4, pp. 85–91; Wippermann, *Der Ordensstaat als Ideologie*, pp. 155–67; *Der 'Deutsche Drang nach Osten'*, pp. 92–3; Werner Magdefrau, 'Zur

Beurteilung der mittelalterlich-deutschen Ostexpansion in der bürgerlichen Geschichtsschreibung von Herder bis Treitschke', *Jahrbuch für Geschichte der UdSSR und der volksdemokratischen Länder Europas* (1966), 9, especially pp. 284–5; Burleigh, 'The Knights, Nationalists and the Historians', pp. 40–3; on Treitschke in general see Andreas Dorpalen, *Heinrich von Treitschke* (New Haven/London 1957) and his 'Heinrich von Treitschke', in *Historians in Politics* eds. W. Laqueur and G. Mosse (London 1974), pp. 21–36.

9. Treitschke, 'Das Deutsche Ordensland Preussen', p. 110.

10. Wippermann, *Der 'Deutsche Drang nach Osten'*, pp. 38–44.

11. Gerard Labuda, 'A Historiographic Analysis of the German *Drang nach Osten*', *Polish Western Affairs* (1964), 5, pp. 239–40; on the concept see also Henry Cord Meyer, 'Der "Drang nach Osten" in den Jahren 1860–1914', *Die Welt als Geschichte* (1957), 17, pp. 1–8; Hans Lemberg, 'Der "Drang nach Osten". Schlagwort and Wirklichkeit', in F. Krause and R. Stasiewski, eds., *Deutsche im europäischen Osten. Verständnis und Missverständnis* (Cologne/Vienna 1977), pp. 1–17; Benedykt Zientara 'Zum Problem des geschichtlichen Terminus "Drang nach Osten"', in Lothar Dralle, ed., *Preussen. Deutschland. Polen im Urteil polnischer Historiker. Eine Anthologie*. Band 1, *Millenium germanopolonicum (Einzelveröffentlichungen der Historischen Kommission zu Berlin 37)* (Berlin 1983), pp. 171–81; and above all Wippermann, *Der 'Deutsche Drang nach Osten'*, pp. 12–13, 38–46, 85–104.

12. Adalbert Forstreuter, *Der endlose Zug. Die Deutsche Kolonisation in ihrem geschichtlichen Ablauf. Kampfschriften der Obersten SA Führung* (Munich 1939), 14, p. 12.

13. Käthe Schirmacher, *Unsere Ostmark, Deutsche Michel, wach auf! Eine Reihe nationaler Schriften*, ed. Oberst a. D. Immanuel (Leipzig 1923), 11, pp. 38ff. On Schirmacher see Wippermann, *Der Ordensstaat als Ideologie*, pp. 220–1, and Adam Galos, F.-H. Gentzen and Witold Jakóbczyk, *Die Hakatisten. Der deutschen Ostmarkenverein 1894–1934. Ein Beitrag zur Geschichte der Ostpolitik des deutschen Imperialismus* (Berlin East 1966), pp. 177 and 187.

14. Wilhelm Kotzde, *Der Deutsche Orden im Werden und Vergehen* (Jena 1928), pp. 72–5. For a good discussion of the psychopathology of these metaphors see R. Chickering, *We Men Who Feel Most German: A Cultural Study of the Pan-German League 1886–1914* (London 1984), especially pp. 82ff. and pp. 122–30.

15. Wippermann, *Der 'Deutsche Drang nach Osten'*, pp. 104–8.

16. See, for example, Erich Maschke, 'Quellen und Darstellungen in der Geschichtsschreibung des Preussenlandes', ed. by order of the Landeshauptmann der Provinz Ostpreussen *Deutsche Staatenbildung und deutscher Kultur im Preussenlande* (Königsberg 1931), p. 39.

17. Adolf Hitler, *Mein Kampf*, trans. R. Manheim (London 1974ff.), pp. 128–9; Wippermann, *Der Ordensstaat als Ideologie*, pp. 253–8.

18. Hitler, *Mein Kampf*, p. 598.

19. *Ibid.*, p. 598; on Hitler's 'creative synthesis' of anti-Semitism, expansion eastwards and anti-Communism see Eberhard Jäckel, *Hitler's World View. A Blueprint for Power* (Cambridge, Mass. 1981), especially pp. 106–7.

20. Josef Ackermann, *Heinrich Himmler als Ideologe* (Göttingen 1970), p. 205; for SS manipulation of historical models see also B. Wegner, *Hitlers politische Soldaten: Die Waffen SS 1932–45* (Paderborn 1982) pp. 39ff. and Wippermann, *Der Ordensstaat als Ideologie* pp. 258–65.

21. 'Rede des Reichsführer-SS am 16. September 1942 in der Feldkommandostelle vor den Teilnehmern an der SS- und Polizeiführer-Tagung, einberufen von SS-Obergruppenführer Prützmann, Höherer SS- und Polizeiführer Russland-Süd', in H.-A. Jacobsen and W. Jochmann, eds., *Ausgewählte Dokumente zur Geschichte des Nationalsozialismus 1933–1945* (Bielefeld 1961), IV, pp. 4–5.

22. BDC, *Aubin* Reichswaltung des NS-Lehrerbundes. Begutachtungsstelle für des pädagogische Schrifftum, reference on Aubin 30.7.37.

23. BA R153/291 Aubin to Albert Brackmann 18.9.39.

24. Much can be learned about these subjects from Götz Aly and Karl Heinz Roth, *Die restlose Erfassung. Volkszählen, Identifizieren, Aussondern im Nationalsozialismus* (Berlin 1984)

25. Recently two exceptionally good collections of essays have appeared: Peter Lundgreen, ed., *Wissenschaft im Dritten Reich* (Frankfurt am Main 1985), and Jörg Tröger, ed., *Hochschule und Wissenschaft im Dritten Reich* (Frankfurt am Main/New York 1986). More specialized monographs include Helmut Heiber's fascinating *Walter Frank und sein Reichsinstitut für Geschichte des neuen Deutschlands* (Stuttgart 1966); Alan D. Beyerchen, *Scientists under Hitler. Politics and the Physics Community in the Third Reich* (New Haven/London 1977); and Otthein Rammstedt, *Deutsche Soziologie 1933–1945* (Frankfurt am Main 1986). There are also recent English-language studies of theologians and psychologists to which no reference is made here. Heiber's monograph remains the best guide to the historical profession under the Nazi regime, although there are a number of interesting studies, not least by Henryk Olszewski and Wolfgang Wippermann of the historical components of Nazi ideology. Reference to these works can be found in the bibliography of secondary literature.

1. THE RISE OF A PROFESSION: CLASSICAL *OSTEUROPAFORSCHUNG* 1902–33

1. Manfred Hellmann, 'Zur Lage der historischen Erforschung des östlichen Europa in der Bundesrepublik Deutschland', *Jahrbuch der historischen Forschung*, ed. Fritz Wagner *Berichtsjahr* 1979 (Stuttgart 1980), pp. 14–16; Friedrich Kuebart, 'Zur Entwicklung der Osteuropaforschung in Deutschland bis 1945', *Osteuropa* (1980), 30, pp. 658–9; Klaus Zernack, *Osteuropa. Eine Einführung in seine Geschichte* (Munich 1977), pp. 14–15; C. Klessmann, 'Osteuropaforschung und Lebensraumpolitik im Dritten Reich', *Wissenschaft im Dritten Reich*, ed. Peter Lundgreen (Frankfurt am Main 1985), pp. 354–5.
2. Klaus Meyer, *Theodor Schiemann als politischer Publizist. Nord- und osteuropäische Geschichtsstudien*, ed. Paul Johansen (Frankfurt am Main 1956), 1, pp. 29ff.; Andreas Dorpalen, *Heinrich von Treitschke* (New Haven 1957), p. 292 for Schiemann as Treitschke's spiritual successor.
3. Horst Giertz, 'Das Berliner Seminar für osteuropäische Geschichte und Landeskunde (bis 1920)', *Jahrbuch für Geschichte der UdSSR und der volksdemokratischen Länder Europas* (1967), 10, pp. 184–5. Both Giertz and Gerd Voigt have made very significant contributions to our technical knowledge of the early organization of *Osteuropaforschung*. Nothing of comparable quality has been produced in the Federal Republic.
4. Meyer, *Theodor Schiemann als politischer Publizist*, pp. 32–3.
5. Hellmann, 'Zur Lage der historischen Erforschung', pp. 14–16; Giertz, 'Das Berliner Seminar', pp. 187–8.
6. Giertz, 'Das Berliner Seminar', pp. 185–6.
7. *Ibid.*, pp. 190–1.
8. Meyer, *Theodor Schiemann als politischer Publizist*, p. 46; Giertz, 'Das Berliner Seminar', p. 192; Kuebart, 'Zur Entwicklung der Osteuropaforschung', p. 659.
9. Giertz, 'Das Berliner Seminar', p. 196; Klessmann, 'Osteuropaforschung und Lebensraumpolitik', pp. 354–5.
10. Giertz, 'Das Berliner Seminar', p. 202; Kuebart, 'Zur Entwicklung der Osteuropaforschung', p. 659.
11. Meyer, *Theodor Schiemann als politischer Publizist*, p. 47.
12. Gerd Voigt, *Otto Hoetzsch, 1876–1946 Wissenschaft und Politik im Leben eines deutschen Historikers. Quellen und Studien zur Geschichte Osteuropas*, eds. Eduard Winter, Heinz Lemke *et al.* (East Berlin 1978), 21, *Anhang*, p. 305, Document 2, p. 305 'Denkschrift von Hoetzsch zwecks Gründung einer Deutschen Gesellschaft zum Studium Russlands', February 1913, for a clear exposition of the necessity for multidisciplinary studies of eastern Europe.

13. Hellmann, 'Zur Lage der historischen Erforschung', p. 16; Giertz, 'Das Berliner Seminar', pp. 208–9.

14. Giertz, 'Das Berliner Seminar', pp. 210–11.

15. Voigt, *Otto Hoetzsch, 1876–1946*, p. 19; Friedrich Kuebart, 'Otto Hoetzsch – Historiker, Publizist, Politiker. Eine kritische biographische Studie', *Osteuropa* (1975), 25, p. 605.

16. Voigt, *Otto Hoetzsch, 1876–1946*, pp. 33–6; Kuebart, 'Otto Hoetzsch – Historiker, Publizist, Politiker', pp. 607–10.

17. Voigt, *Otto Hoetzsch, 1876–1946*, pp. 34–5.

18. *Ibid.*, pp. 41–3.

19. Fritz Fischer, *War to Illusions: German Policies from 1911 to 1914* (London 1975), p. 39.

20. Klaus Meyer, *Theodor Schiemann als politischer Publizist*, p. 90; Fritz T. Epstein, 'Friedrich Meinecke in seinem Verhältnis zum europäischen Osten', *Jahrbuch für die Geschichte Mittel- und Ostdeutschlands* (1954), 3, p. 135.

21. Meyer, *Theodor Schiemann als politischer Publizist*, pp. 90ff. for a discussion of Schiemann's *Russlandbild*.

22. *Ibid.*, pp. 93–103; see also Walter Laqueur, *Russia and Germany. A Century of Conflict* (London 1965), p. 37 for a description of Schiemann.

23. Fischer, *War of Illusions*, p. 39.

24. Voigt, *Otto Hoetzsch, 1876–1946*, pp. 84–100; see also Fritz T. Epstein, 'Otto Hoetzsch als aussenpolitischer Kommentator während des Ersten Weltkrieges', *Gedenkschrift für Otto Hoetzsch. Schriftenreihe Osteuropa*, no. 3. (Stuttgart 1957), pp. 10 and 15–17 for a skilful analysis of Hoetzsch's war-time journalism; Kuebart, 'Otto Hoetzsch – Historiker, Publizist, Politiker', pp. 607, 613–16.

25. Voigt, *Otto Hoetzsch, 1876–1946*, p. 49 for his travels and pp. 59–60 for his thoughts on Russian literature. See Meyer, *Theodor Schiemann als politischer Publizist*, pp. 105ff. for Schiemann's views on Russian literature. The professor thought that Tolstoy (the '*russische aller Russen*') and Gorky were '*Symptome der Krankheit*'. In the case of Tolstoy this was because '*Der Kern seiner Lehre ist doch die Negierung des Staatsgedankens*'.

26. Voigt, *Otto Hoetzsch, 1876–1946*, p. 59.

27. *Ibid.*, p. 61.

28. Meyer, *Theodor Schiemann als politischer Publizist*, pp. 202ff., and Fritz T. Epstein, 'Der Komplex "Die russische Gefahr" und sein Einfluss auf die deutsch-russischen Beziehungen im 19. Jahrhundert', in *Deutschland in der Weltpolitik des 19. und 20. Jahrhunderts. Fritz Fischer zur 65. Geburtstag*, eds. Imanuel Geiss and Bernd Jurgen Wendt (Düsseldorf 1973), especially pp. 144–5.

29. Meyer, *Theodor Schiemann als politischer Publizist*, p. 199; Kuebart, 'Otto Hoetzsch – Historiker, Publizist, Politiker', pp. 612–13.

30. Voigt, *Otto Hoetzsch, 1876–1946*, pp. 66ff.; Werner Markert, *Fünfzig Jahre Osteuropa-Studien* (Stuttgart-Obertürkheim 1963), p. 5. The later parts of this essay – those concerning Markert himself – seem selective and unreliable. I am grateful to Dr Hugo Weczerka for this reference and for a memorable discussion on the beginnings of *Ostforschung*.

31. Voigt, *Otto Hoetzsch, 1876–1946*, pp. 303–11, 'Denkschrift von Hoetzsch zwecks Gründung einer Deutschen Gesellschaft zum Studium Russlands', February 1913.

32. *Ibid.*, p. 67.

33. *Ibid.*, p. 68.

34. Giertz, 'Das Berliner Seminar', p. 213 for the sordid details.

35. Meyer, *Theodor Schiemann als politischer Publizist*, p. 204.

36. *Ibid.*, pp. 226–7.

37. On Hoetzsch's relationship with Westarp at this time see Kuebart, 'Otto Hoetzsch – Historiker, Publizist, Politiker', p. 613; more generally see Fritz J. Epstein, 'Otto Hoetzsch als aussenspolitischer Kommentator', pp. 9–13.

38. Epstein, 'Otto Hoetzsch als aussenpolitischer Kommentator', p. 10 and Klaus Schwabe, *Wissenschaft und Kriegsmoral. Die deutschen Hochschullehrer und die politischen Grundfragen des Ersten Weltkrieges* (Göttingen 1963), p. 106 for Hoetzsch's views in the much wider context of academic discussion of war aims.

39. Otto Hoetzsch, *Russland als Gegner Deutschlands. Zwischen Krieg und Frieden* (Leipzig 1914), no. 6, p. 6.

40. *Ibid.*, pp. 13–14.

41. *Ibid.*, p. 15.

42. Epstein, 'Otto Hoetzsch als aussenpolitischer Kommentator', p. 12, citing Hoetzsch's 25.10.16 article in the *Kreuzzeitung*, 'Die Verfassungsform eines anderen Staates geht uns nichts an, kann jedenfalls nicht Preis eines Weltkampfes für uns sein'; Kuebart, 'Otto Hoetzsch – Historiker, Publizist, Politiker', p. 615; Schwabe, *Wissenschaft und Kriegsmoral*, pp. 57ff. for *Kannegiesserei*. Hans Peter Bleuel, *Deutschlands Bekenner. Professoren zwischen Kaiserreich und Diktatur* (Bern n.d.) pp. 88–93 for the wilder flights of the professorial imagination.

43. Hoetzsch, *Russland als Gegner Deutschlands*, p. 56: 'Es kann nur schärfster widerspruch erhoben werden gegen eine Teilung da Felles des Bären, bevor er erlegt ist, wenn dieses abgenutzte Schlagwort gebraucht werden darf. Und es war kein Zeichen von politischer Reife, wenn sich daren schon in den ersten Tagen auch sehr hochstehende Männer unseres Geisteslebens beteiligten und das russische Reich auflösten, wie man Blätter einer Artichocke abpflückt, wie es auch eine geradezu kindliche

Unterschätzung und Unkenntnis des Gegners verriet, wenn man hoffte, es würden sich gleich bein Einreiten der ersten preussischen Ulanen alle Grenzvölker und die Massen zugunsten der Befreiung bringenden Deutschen und Osterreicher erheben'.

44. Meyer, *Theodor Schiemann als politischer Publizist*, p. 210.

45. Hoetzsch, *Russland als Gegner Deutschlands*, p. 36; Voigt, *Otto Hoetzsch, 1876–1946*, p. 64.

46. Epstein, 'Otto Hoetzsch als aussenpolitischer Kommentator', p. 21.

47. On the 'Intellektuelleneingabe' see Schwabe, *Wissenschaft und Kriegsmoral*, pp. 70ff. and Imanuel Geiss, *Der polnische Grenzstreifen 1914–1918. Ein Beitrag zur deutschen Kriegszielpolitik im Ersten Weltkrieg. Historische Studien* (Lübeck/Hamburg 1960), Heft, 378. pp. 52–3; Voigt, *Otto Hoetzsch, 1876–1946*, pp. 105–6.

48. Geiss, *Der polnische Grenzstreifen*, p. 25.

49. *Ibid.*, p. 44. This aspect of Hoetzsch's attitude to Poland is not dealt with by Epstein, 'Otto Hoetzsch als aussenpolitischer Kommentator', pp. 19–22 and hence Hoetzsch emerges as a rather more 'progressive' figure than he probably was. On the constitutional implications of § 13 of the Ansiedlungsgesetz (March 1908) see Hans-Ulrich Wehler, 'Von den „Reichsfeinden" zur „Reichskristallnacht": Polenpolitik im Deutschen Kaiserreich 1871–1916', in Wehler, ed., *Krisenherde des Kaiserreichs, 1871–1916. Studien zur deutsche Sozial und Verfassungsgeschichte* (Göttingen 1970), especially pp. 190–2.

50. Geiss, *Der polnische Grenzstreifen*, p. 44.

51. *Ibid.*, p. 50 and pp. 76–7.

52. On Schwerin see Geiss, *Der polnische Grenzstreifen*, pp. 78–84, and Martin Broszat, *Zweihundert Jahre deutsche Polenpolitik* (Frankfurt am Main 1972₂), pp. 183–4.

53. Geiss, *Der polnische Grenzstreifen*, p. 76.

54. *Ibid.*, pp. 148–50; Broszat, *Zweihundert Jahre deutsche Polenpolitik*, p. 184.

55. Voigt, *Otto Hoetzsch, 1876–1946*, pp. 105–6; Geiss, *Der polnische Grenzstreifen*, p. 46.

56. Geiss, *Der polnische Grenzstreifen*, p. 49.

57. Voigt, *Otto Hoetzsch, 1876–1946*, p. 106.

58. *Ibid.*, pp. 80–1; Schwabe, *Wissenschaft und Kriegsmoral*, pp. 97–9; and on Hoetzsch's rationality see Epstein, 'Otto Hoetzsch als aussenpolitischer Kommentator', p. 10 and Schwabe, *Wissenschaft und Kriegsmoral*, pp. 183ff.

59. Voigt, *Otto Hoetzsch, 1876–1946*, p. 101; Kuebart, 'Otto Hoetzsch – Historiker, Publizist, Politiker', p. 615; Manfred Hellmann, 'Der Disput aus heutiger Sicht', *Osteuropa* (1975), 25, pp. A 442–8.

60. Schwabe, *Wissenschaft und Kriegsmoral*, p. 36.

61. Voigt, *Otto Hoetzsch, 1875–1946*, p. 101 n 41.

62. Klaus Schreiner, 'Führertum, Rasse, Reich. Wissenschaft vom der Geschichte nach der nationalsozialstischen Machtergriefung', in Lundgreen, ed., *Wissenschaft im Dritten Reich*, pp. 231–2, 'Die Nacht, die uns umgab, ist einer neuen Morgenröte gewichen. Schneller, als das kühnste Hoffen es zu denken gewagt hätte, ist die Sonne über Deutschland aufgegangen, und ihre ersten Strahlen verheissen einen neuen lichten Tag, der das Erlittene vergessen lasse'. He left out the next line 'Kommen wird der Tag, wo einst zugrunde geht die heilige Ilios'.

63. Fritz T. Epstein, 'Hamburg und Osteuropa. Zur Gedächtnis von Professor Richard Salomon (1884–1966)', *Jahrbücher für Geschichte Osteuropas* (1967), 15, p. 65.

64. F. K. Mann, 'Ostdeutsche Wirtschaftsforschung', *Schriften des Instituts für ostdeutsche Wirtschaft an der Universität Königsberg* (Jena 1926), 15, pp. 11–12.

65. *Ibid.*, pp. 12–14; see also F. K. Mann, 'Die neuen Aufgaben des Instituts für ostdeutsche Wirtschaft', *Ein Vortrag*, 24.6.22 p. 3, and on the IoW in general see Gerd Voigt, 'Aufgaben und Funktion der Osteuropa-Studien in der Weimarer Republik' in *Studien über die deutsche Geschichtwissenschaft. Die bürgerliche deutsche Geschichtsschreibung von der Reichseinigung von oben bis zum Befreiung Deutschlands vom Faschismus*, ed. J. Streisand (East Berlin 1965), 2, pp. 374–6.

66. *Das Institut für ostdeutsche Wirtschaft an der Albertus-Universität in Königsberg Pr. Ein Führer für Studierende* (Königsberg n.d.), pp. 7–8.

67. *Ibid.*, pp. 8–10.

68. *Ibid.*, 'Grundsatzung des Instituts für ostdeutsche Wirtschaft', § 2, p. 26.

69. *Ibid.*, pp. 24–5.

70. Mann, 'Ostdeutsche Wirtschaftsforschung', p. 13.

71. *Ibid.*, pp. 13–14; 'Das Institut für ostdeutsche Wirtschaft. Ein Führer für Studierende', p. 15.

72. Mann, 'Ostdeutsche Wirtschaftsforschung', p. 40.

73. *Ibid.*, p. 42.

74. P. Diehls, 'Das Osteuropainstitut in Breslau', *Zeitschrift des oberschlesischen Berg- und Hüttenmännischen Verein* (1920), 59, pp. 149ff.; on the Osteuropa-Institut see also Voigt, 'Aufgaben und Funktion der Osteuropa-Studien', pp. 376–7.

75. Diehls, 'Das Osteuropainstitut in Breslau', pp. 149–50.

76. Voigt, 'Aufgaben und Funktion', p. 376.

77. Diehls, 'Das Osteuropainstitut in Breslau', p. 150.

78. *Ibid.*, pp. 151–2.

79. For this important shift in emphasis see Klessmann, 'Osteuropaforschung und Lebensraumpolitik', p. 363; see also Hellmann, 'Zur Lage

der historischen Erforschung', pp. 19–20; Kuebart, 'Zur Entwicklung der Osteuropaforschung', especially pp. 666–8.

80. On the Leipzig Stiftung see Voigt, 'Aufgaben and Funktion', p. 378; *Volk unter Völkern. Bücher des Deutschtums*, 1, ed. for the *Deutsche Schutzbund*, K. C. von Loesch (Breslau 1925).

81. Albrecht Penck, 'Deutscher Volks- und Kulturboden', *Volk unter Völkern*, p. 62; on Penck see Mechthild Rössler, 'Die Geographie an der Universität Freiburg 1933–1945. Ein Beitrag zur Wissenschaftsgeschichte des Faches im Dritten Reich', *Zulassungsarbeit* (Freiburg 1983), pp. 47–8. I am grateful to Mechthild Rössler for a copy of her work and for a number of discussions on the role of geographers in *Ostforschung*.

82. Penck, 'Deutscher Volks- und Kulturboden', p. 63; on Penck see Voigt, 'Aufgaben und Funktion', pp. 388–9.

83. *Ibid.*, p. 64.

84. *Ibid.*, p. 65.

85. *Ibid.*, pp. 67–9.

86. *Ibid.*, p. 70.

87. *Ibid.*, p. 70.

88. *Ibid.*, p. 69.

89. *Ibid.*, p. 62.

90. *Ibid.*, p. 72.

91. *Ibid.*, 'Karte des deutschen Volks- und Kulturbodens', between p. 72 and p. 73.

92. Fritz Jaeger, 'Die Siebenbürger Sachsen, geographisch betrachtet', *Volk unter Völkern* p. 168.

93. *Ibid.*, p. 171, 'Die kulturelle überlegenheit machte sie in gewissem Sinne zum Herren-volk'.

94. *Ibid.*, pp. 171–4.

95. *Ibid.*, pp. 179–83.

96. Wilhelm Volz, ed., *Der ostdeutsche Volksboden. Aufsätze zu den Fragen des Ostens* (Breslau 1926), pp. 5–6; see also Klessmann, 'Osteuropaforschung und Lebensraumpolitik', p. 356; Voigt, 'Aufgaben und Funktion', pp. 389–90; and K. Fiedor, J. Sobczak and N. Wrzesiński, 'The image of the Poles in Germany and of Germans in Poland in Inter-War Years and its Role in Shaping the Relations between the Two States', *Polish Western Affairs* (1978), 19, pp. 204–5.

97. The importance of *Der ostdeutsche Volksboden* was noticed by Gerhard Heitz, 'Rudolf Kötzschke (1867–1949). Ein Beitrag zur Pflege der Siedlungs- und Wirtschaftsgeschichte in Leipzig', *Karl-Marx-Universität Leipzig 1409–1959. Beiträge zur Universitätsgeschichte* (Leipzig 1959), 2, p. 269. Heitz seems to have overlooked Kötzschke's dubious behaviour towards the Sorbs in the 1920s.

98. Hans Witte, 'Slawische Reste in Mecklenburg und an der Niederelbe', *Der ostdeutsche Volksboden*, p. 194.

99. Rudolf Kötzschke, 'Die deutsche Wiederbesiedelung der ostelbischen Lande', *Der ostdeutsche Volksboden*, p. 154.

100. Rudolf Kötzschke, 'Über den Ursprung und die Geschichtliche Bedeutung der ostdeutschen Siedlung', *Der ostdeutsche Volksboden*, p. 26.

101. Wolfgang La Baume, 'Das Land an der unteren Weichsel in vor- und frühgeschichtlicher Zeit', *Der ostdeutsche Volksboden*, pp. 90–1.

102. *Ibid.*, p. 95.

103. *Ibid.*, p. 100.

104. Max Vasmer, 'Die Urheimat der Slawen', *Der ostdeutsche Volksboden*, p. 140; on Vasmer see Hans Holm Bielfeldt, 'Die Geschichte des Lehrstuhls für Slawistik an der Berliner Universität', *Beiträge zur Geschichte der Slawistik*, in eds. H. H. Bielfeldt and K. Horálek *Veröffentlichungen des Instituts für Slawistik* (East Berlin 1964), no. 30, pp. 275–6.

105. Hans Witte, 'Slawische Reste in Mecklenburg', *Der ostdeutche Volksboden*, p. 205.

106. Hermann Aubin, 'Zur Erforschung der deutschen Ostbewegung', reprinted in his *Grundlagen und Perspektiven geschichtlicher Kulturraumforschung und Kulturmorphologie*, ed. Franz Petri (Bonn 1965), p. 569 n 1. This essay was first printed in the *Deutsches Archiv für Landes und Volksforschung* (1937) 1, pp. 37–70, 309–31, 563–602. Aubin was referring to R. Kötzsche and W. Ebert, *Geschichte der ostdeutschen Kolonisation* (Leipzig 1937).

107. Kötzsche, 'Die deutsche Wiederbesiedelung der ostelbischen Lande', *Der ostdeutsche Volksboden*, p. 153.

108. *Ibid.*, pp. 165–74.

109. *Ibid.*, p. 169.

110. H. Gollub, 'Die Masuren', *Der ostdeutsche Volksboden*, p. 295. On the history of Masuria see Max Töppen, *Geschichte Masurens. Ein Beitrag zur preussischen Landes- und Kulturgeschichte* (Danzig, 1870).

111. *Ibid.*, p. 297.

112. *Ibid.*, p. 305.

113. Friedrich Lorentz, 'Die Kaschuben', *Der ostdeutsche Volksboden*, pp. 245ff. On the status of the Kashubian dialect see G. Stone, 'The Language of Cassubian Literature and the Question of a Literary Standard', *The Slavonic and East European Review* (1972), 50 pp. 521–9. I am grateful to Dr Stone for offprints of his articles on Kashubians and Sorbs.

114. Lorentz, 'Die Kaschuben', *Der ostdeutsche Volksboden*, p. 264. On Lorentz see Friedhelm Hinze, 'Zum Leben und Werk von Friedrich Lorentz (1870–1937)', Beiträge zur Geschichte der Slawistik, pp. 71ff.

115. Erich Maschke, for example, published work on Piłsudski in *Osteuropa* and Hoetzsch contributed to Brackmann's *Deutschland und Polen* (Munich/Berlin 1933); 'Brandenburg- Preussen und Polen von 1640–1815', pp. 185–206.

116. Voigt, *Otto Hoetzsch, 1876–1946*, pp. 164–5; Epstein, 'Otto Hoetzsch als aussenpolitischer Kommentator', p. 26.

117. Voigt, *Otto Hoetzsch, 1876–1946*, pp. 136–8; Kuebart 'Otto Hoetzsch – Historiker, Publizist, Politiker', pp. 616–18.

118. Kuebart, 'Otto Hoetzsch – Historiker, Publizist, Politiker', p. 618.

119. Voigt, *Otto Hoetzsch, 1876–1946*, p. 166; Jutta Unser, '"Osteuropa" Biographie einer Zeitschrift', *Osteuropa* (1975), 25, pp. 557–8.

120. Voigt, *Otto Hoetzsch, 1876–1946*, p. 175.

121. *Ibid.*, p. 176.

122. *Ibid.*, pp. 180–1

123. O. Hoetzsch, 'Deutschland und Russland', *Osteuropa* (1925/6), 1, p. 7. Jutta Unser, '"Osteuropa" Biographie einer Zeitschrift', p. 557. See also Fritz T. Epstein, 'Otto Hoetzsch und sein „Osteuropa" 1925–1930', *Osteuropa* (1975), 25, pp. 541ff.

124. In addition to the titles cited in note 123 above, see Voigt, *Otto Hoetzsch, 1876–1946*, pp. 164ff.

125. Unser, '"Osteuropa" Biographie einer Zeitschrift', p. 565, for the percentage of Hoetzsch's contributions, and pp. 562–3 for a biographical sketch of Auhagen.

126. *Ibid.*, p. 564; Epstein, 'Otto Hoetzsch und sein „Osteuropa"', pp. 551–2.

127. Unser, '"Osteuropa" Biographie einer Zeitschrift', p. 583.

128. 'Das Russische Wissenschaftliche Institut in Berlin', *Osteuropa* (1925/6), 1, p. 125.

129. Unser, '"Osteuropa" Biographie einer Zeitschrift', p. 569.

130. Oskar Vogt, 'Die Russische Forscherwoche in Berlin' (19–25.6.27), *Osteuropa* (1926/7), 2, pp. 459–61; Otto Hoetzsch, 'Eröffnungsreden', *Osteuropa* (1927/8), 3, pp. 745–51; 'Deutsche Technische Woche in Moskau', *Osteuropa* (1928/9), 4, pp. 440–2; Werner Markert, *Fünfzig Jahre Osteuropa-Studien*, pp. 11–15; Epstein, 'Otto Hoetzsch und sein „Osteuropa"', p. 546.

131. Voigt, *Otto Hoetzsch, 1876–1946*, pp. 212ff.

132. *Ibid.*, pp. 213–16.

133. *Ibid.*, pp. 218–19 and ch. 1, sec. ii below.

134. Unser, '"Osteuropa" Biographie einer Zeitschrift', p. 585.

135. Otto Hoetzsch, 'Die Lage in Polen und den Randstaaten', *Osteuropa* (1933/4), 9, p. 70; Unser, '"Osteuropa" Biographie einer Zeitschrift', p. 583.

136. Unser, '"Osteuropa" Biographie einer Zeitschrift', p. 583.

137. *Ibid.*, p. 584.

138. Voigt, *Otto Hoetzsch, 1876–1946*, p. 259; Unser, ' "Osteuropa" Biographie einer Zeitschrift', p. 585.

139. Werner Markert, 'Das Studium Osteuropas als wissenschaftliche und politische Aufgabe', *Osteuropa* (1933/4), 9, p. 396.

140. *Ibid.*, p. 400; on Markert see Unser, ' "Osteuropa" Biographie einer Zeitschrift', pp. 586ff.

141. Unser, ' "Osteuropa" Biographie einer Zeitschrift', p. 590; Voigt, *Otto Hoetzsch, 1876–1946*, p. 263. Voigt manages to overlook the racial aspect of Hoetzsch's dismissal in his otherwise remarkable intellectual biography. On this see Walter Laqueur, *Russia and Germany. A Century of Conflict* (London 1965), pp. 179–80.

142. BDC, *Uebersberger*, Hans Uebersberger to the Reichministerium für Wissenschaft, Erziehung und Volksbildung 17.3.36, pp. 7–9.

143. Peter-Heinz Seraphim, 'Antisemitismus in Osteuropa', *Osteuropa* (1936/9), pp. 341ff.; Unser, ' "Osteuropa" Biographie einer Zeitschrift', pp. 597–6.

144. Epstein, 'Hamburg und Osteuropa', pp. 89–90.

145. Voigt, *Otto Hoetzsch, 1876–1946*, pp. 189–90. Until 1964 Loewenson was librarian in the School of Slavonic and East European Studies, University of London. On Epstein see Fritz T. Epstein, *Germany and the East*, ed. R. F. Byrnes (Bloomington 1973), pp. xii–xiv.

146. Manfred Unger, 'Georg Sacke- Ein Kämpfer gegen den Faschismus', *Karl-Marx-Universität Leipzig, 1409–1959. Beiträge zur Universitätsgeschichte* (Leipzig 1959), 2, p. 309.

147. Voigt, *Otto Hoetzsch, 1876–1946*, p. 190; for a sensitive appreciation of Sacke's work see Dietrich Geyer, in 'Georg Sacke', *Deutsche Historiker*, ed. H.-U. Wehler (Göttingen 1973), pp. 603–13.

148. Unger, 'Georg Sacke- Ein Kämpfer gegen den Faschismus', pp. 307–8; Geyer, 'Georg Sacke', p. 603.

149. Unger, 'Georg Sacke- Ein Kämpfer gegen den Faschismus', p. 320.

150. *Ibid.*, p. 327; Geyer, 'Georg Sacke', p. 604; see also Klessmann, 'Osteuropaforschung und Lebensraumpolitik', p. 362.

2. ENTER THE GENERAL

1. 'Im Kampf um den deutschen Ostraum', *Kurier Tageblatt* 13.7.41, no. 192, p. 5. See also BA 153/ no. 1674, Wolfgang Kohte, 'Albert Brackmann und der deutsche Ostforschung', *Nordostberichte* of the PuSte 16.6.41, no. 55 and BA R1531/no. 1039 for further biographical material including Brackmann's autobiographical sketch 'Die wissenschaftliche Entwicklung' (1941), and, hagiographically W. Kohte,

'Albert Brackmann, der deutsche Ostforscher', *Königsberger Allgemeine Zeitung*, 24.6.41, Ernst Vollert, 'Albert Brackmann und die ostdeutsche Volks- und Landesforschung', in *Deutsche Ostforschung. Ergebnisse und Aufgaben seit dem ersten Weltkrieg*, eds. H. Aubin, D. Brunner, W. Kohte and J. Papritz (Leipzig 1942), 1, pp. 1–12, 'Albert Brackmann', *Ostland* (1941) pp. 252–3, Hans Goetting, 'Albert Brackmann', *Neue Deutsche Biographie* (Berlin 1955), 2, pp. 504–5. On Brackmann's role in *Ostforschung* in general see M. Burleigh, 'Albert Brackmann, Ostforscher (1871–1952): the Years of Retirement', *JCH* (1988), 23, pp. 573–88.

2. BA R153/ no. 1674, *Glückwunsch-Depeschen*, 24.6.41 for a list of telegrams received.

3. BA R153/ no. 1050, Brackmann to the Führer and Reichskanzler 27.6.41.

4. BA R153 no. 1050, Brackmann to Frick 28.6.41.

5. BA R1531 no. 1050, SS-*Obersturmführer*, Worninghoff to J. Papritz 26.1.43, and RF-SS, *Persönlichen Stab* (*Feld-Kommandostelle*) to Papritz 30.1.43.

6. BA R153 no. 1039 Brackmann, 'Die Wissenschaftliche Entwicklung', p. 1; see also Hermann Meinert, 'Albert Brackmann und das deutsche Archivwesen', *Archivalische Zeitschrift* (1954), 49, pp. 127ff.

7. F.-H. Gentzen, J. Kalisch, G. Voigt and E. Wolfgramm, 'Die „Ostforschung" – ein Stosstrupp des deutschen Imperialismus', *ZfG* (1958), 6, pp. 1193.

8. A. Brackmann, *Ostpreussens Kriegsschicksale. Ein geschichtlicher Rückblick in ernster Zeit* (Königsberg, *c.* 1917), pp. 3–7. See also his *Ostpreussische Kriegshefte auf Grund amtlicher und privater Berichte*, eds. A. Brackmann, E. Joachim, D. Krauske and A. Seraphim (Berlin 1916), parts 1–4; see also Gerd Voigt, *Otto Hoetzsch, 1876–1946 Quellen und Studien zur Geschichte Osteuropas*, ed. E. Winter and H. Lemke, vol. 21 (East Berlin 1978), p. 70.

9. *Geheimes Staatsarchiv*, eds. E. Henning and C. Lowenthal-Hensel (Berlin 1974), pp. 8–9.

10. BA R153/ 1039, Brackmann, 'Die wissenschaftliche Entwicklung', p. 1, and H. Heiber, *Walter Frank und sein Reichsinstitut für Geschichte des neuen Deutschlands* (Stuttgart 1966), pp. 851–2.

11. *Ibid.*, p. 852; GStA Rep. 92 *Nachlass Brackmann* no. 61 Reichswehr-Gruppen-Kommando 3 to Brackmann 22.10.19; no. 47 OMV Chairman to Brackmann 27.8.26; and no. 57 NSDAP *Ortsgruppe* Dahlem to Brackmann 2.3.33.

12. Klaus Schreiner, 'Führertum, Rasse, Reich. Wissenschaft von der Geschichte nach der nationalsozialistischen Machtergreifung', in Peter Lundgreen, ed., *Wissenschaft im Dritten Reich* (Frankfurt am Main

1985), p. 224. The remark was made by Friedrich Rödinger, a deputy to the Frankfurt parliament.

13. GStA Rep. 92 *Nachlass Brackmann* no. 2 Brackmann to Professor Otto Becker 12.9.31.

14. BDC, *Brackmann* undated report; Heiber, *Walter Frank*, p. 852.

15. E. Posner, 'Der Neubau des Geheimen Staatsarchivs in Berlin-Dahlem', *Archivalische Zeitschrift* (1925), 35, pp. 24ff.

16. *Ibid.*, pp. 32ff.

17. W. Leesch, 'Das Institut für Archivwissenschaft und geschichtswissenschaftliche Fortbildung (IfA) in Berlin-Dahlem (1930–1945)', *Brandenburgische Jahrhunderte. Festgabe für Johannes Schultze zum 90. Geburtstag*, eds. G. Heinrich and W. Vogel, *Veröffentlichungen des Vereins für Geschichte der Mark Brandenburg* (Berlin 1971), 35, pp. 224–5. See also Hermann Meinert, 'Albert Brackmann und das deutsche Archivwesen', pp. 135–6.

18. Leesch, 'Das Institut für Archivwissenschaft', p. 226.

19. *Ibid.*, p. 234 and Meinert, 'Albert Brackmann und das deutsche Archivwesen', p. 136.

20. *Hessisches Staatsarchiv Marburg* (hereafter HStA) *Nachlass* Papritz 340, C12 '*Entnazifizierung*' '*Wissenschaftlicher Lebenslauf*' (1948) p. 2. See also Henning and Lowenthal-Hensel, *Geheimes Staatsarchiv*, p. 13; on the formation of the new Province from the remnants of the territories taken by the Poles see J. Wąsicki, 'Origins of „Grenzmark Posen-Westpreussen" Province', *Polish Western Affairs* (1965), 6, pp. 150ff. The Grenzmark was designed to keep German claims to the detached territories 'green'.

21. HStA *Nachlass* Papritz 340, C12c, 12 Papritz memo 24.4.29.

22. Die Pflege des Heimatgedankens', *Der Gesellige* (Schneidemühl), 1.2.30 no. 27 for an account of a lecture delivered by Papritz to the *Grenzmärkischen Gesellschaft zur Erforschung und Pflege der Heimat* and the Press brief of a lecture given in Wiesbaden on 3.9.34 which contains material on the evolution of Department I and the *Zweigstelle* in Schneidemühl under a Dr Salewsky.

23. R. Franz and R. Gross, 'Wissenschaftliche Beziehungen zwischen sowjetischen und deutschen Archiven in den Jahren 1917–1933', in *Archivmitteilungen. Zeitschrift für Theorie und Praxis des Archivwesens*, ed. Der Staatlichen Archivverwaltung der Deutschen Demokratischen Republik (1966), 16, pp. 85–6 for the texts of these agreements.

24. BA R153/ no. 1310, Brackmann to RuPMdI 20.1.37 enclosing a copy of his lecture 'Polens Grenzmarkforschung und die deutsche Wissenschaft' delivered on 12.1.37, p. 9 for the abrogation of the treaties. See also BA R153/ 882, Brackmann's lecture, 'Bericht über die Tätigkeit der Nord- und Ostdeutschen Forschungsgemeinschaft erstattet in der Sitzung

der Beiräte am 4. Januar 1939' pp. 3–4 where he described the conse-
quences of the treaties as being 'dass wir im Arbeitssaal des Geheimen
Staatsarchivs und in anderen Staatsarchiven einen sowjet-russischen
Kommunisten neben dem anderen sitzen hatten'.

25. H. U. Wehler, 'Radikaldemokratische Geschichtswissenschaft: Eckart
    Kehr', *Krisenherde des Kaiserreichs, 1871–1918* (Göttingen 1970),
    p. 273.

26. BA R153/ 1, 'Protokoll über die Konferenz im grossen Sitzungssaal des
    Preussischen Staatsministeriums' 15.7.31, p. 1.

27. 'Protokoll', p. 2; for the account of the Polish institutes I have relied
    upon the PuSte's translation of Baltic Institute materials e.g. GStA
    Rep. 92 *Nachlass* Brackmann no. 81 'Bericht der Direktion des Bal-
    tischen Instituts' II (Toruń 1933) and III (Toruń 1935) which contain
    detailed information on the Baltic Institute's membership, structure and
    constitution. For Brackmann's views on the Polish institutes see also
    BA R153/ 1310, for his lecture 'Polens Grenzmarkforschung und die
    deutsche Wissenschaft' (1937), especially pp. 1–8.

28. BA R153/ 1701, Papritz to Brackmann 9.1.31 for the report and HStA
    Nachlass Papritz 340 C12c/13 'Beschwerde deutscher Benutzer über
    die Behandlung deutscher Forscher in polnischer Archiven' (1931) for
    the Papritz report based on enquiries to Maschke, Schmauch and the
    Osteuropa-Institut Breslau throughout April 1931.

29. BA R153/ 1, 'Protokoll' p. 4; the official grounds for restricted access to
    documents are mentioned in BA R154/44 in a memorandum for Brack-
    mann dated 6.6.35.

30. BAR153/ 1, 'Protokoll pp. 6–7.

31. *Ibid.*, p. 11.

32. *Ibid.*, p. 19; on D. N. Egorov see W. Wippermann, *Der 'Deutsche Drang
    nach Osten': Ideologie und Wirklichkeit eines politischen Schlagwortes*
    (Darmstadt 1981), pp. 60–1.

33. BA R43I/ 1811, Prussian Ministerpräsident to RMdI 19.9.31.

34. BA R43I/ 1812, 'Vermerk über die kommissarische Beratung am 11
    Dezember 1931 betreffend wissenschaftliche Ostmarkenforschung',
    RMdI to Staatssekretär in der Reichskanzlei incorporating Brackmann's
    suggestions, pp. 48–55.

35. For the lobbying, see BA R43I/ 1811, Prof. Dr Seppelt (Domkapitular
    Breslau) to the Reichskanzler 21.11.31, p. 134; BA 54I/ 1912, 'Vermerk
    über die kommissarische Beratung', p. 4.

36. BA R43I/ 1812, 'Vermerk über die kommissarische Beratung', p. 4.

37. On this see in particular Norbert Krekeler, *Revisionsanspruch und
    geheime Ostpolitik der Weimarer Republik. Die Subventionierung der
    deutschen Minderheit in Polen 1919–1933* (Stuttgart 1973), especially
    pp. 29ff., and his 'Der deutsche Minderheit in Polen und die Revisi-

onspolitik des Deutschen Reiches 1919–1933', in W. Benz, ed., *Die Vertreibung der Deutschen aus dem Osten* (Frankfurt am Main 1985), especially pp. 20–2.

38. BA R43I/ 1812, 'Protokoll über die Besprechung im grossen Sitzungssaal des Preussischen Staatsministeriums in Sachen der Ostmarkenforschung am 24.2.32', p. 215.

39. BA R153/ 1 memorandum/circular from Papritz 31.3.33, '*Laut Anordnung vom Herrn Generaldirektor der Staatsarchive heisst unsere Firma in Zukunft ... Publikationsstelle*'. For reasons of convenience, the callmark 'Pu-Fo' was retained for new book accessions.

40. BA R153/ 1, 'Aufgaben des Publikationsfonds' (1932), p. 16.

41. BA R153/ 1, 'Aufgaben des Publikationsfonds', p. 5.

42. BA R153/ 1, 'Aufgaben des Publikationsfonds', pp. 10–11.

43. *Deutsche Staatenbildung und deutsch Kultur im Preussenlande* ed. *Landeshauptmann der Provinz Ostpreussen* (Königsberg 1931).

44. BA R153/ 1, 'Aufgaben des Publikationsfonds', p. 16.

45. BA R153/ 1573, 'Rechnungslegungen der PuSte für die Rechnungsjahre 1931–1944', 1 (1931), pp. 1ff.

46. BA R153/ 882, 'Ausgaben des Publikationsfonds bis 10.10.32, section III', Polnische Bücherei.

47 BA R153/ 47, Gestapo to PuSte 20.10.33 and PuSte to Gestapo 26.10.33.

48. BA R153/ 1, 'Übersicht über die Arbeiten der PuSte des Preussischen Geheimen Staatsarchivs', 12.7.33, p. 1.

49. Leesch, 'Das Institut für Archivwissenschaft', p. 242 for Kohte. He studied in IfA between 1.5.30 and 12.9.31; and BA R153/ 1573, 'Rechnungslegungen' (1932) for payments to Maschke and Forstreuter.

50. BA R153/ 1573, 'Rechnungslegungen' (1932) for grants to Lüpke, and BA R153/ 1233, for the text of Lüpke's oath to the PuSte on 1.10.32 and for a brief description of his duties.

51. BA R153/ 1233, Helmut Lüpke to Brackmann 'Jahresbericht über meine im Auftrage der Publikationsstelle des Preuss. Geheimen Staatsarchivs unternommenen Arbeiten 1932/33', p. 4.

52. BA R153/ 1233, Lüpke to Brackmann, 'Jahresbericht', pp. 5–6.

53. BA R153/ 1, 'Übersicht', p. 3, section C, sub-section 3.

54. BA R153/ 1233, Lüpke, 'Jahresbericht', p. 7.

55. BA R153/ 1573, 'Rechnungslegungen' (1932); BA R153/ 1113, Forstreuter to Papritz 1.8.32 responding to Papritz to Forstreuter 25.7.32 offering him a grant.

56. BA R153/ 1113, Forstreuter to Brackmann 5.5.32 outline of his work.

57. For an autobiographical sketch see Erich Maschke, 'Begegnungen mit Geschichte', *Städte und Menschen. Beiträge zur Geschichte der Stadt, der Wirtschaft und Gesellschaft 1959–1977. Vierteljahrschrift für Sozial- und Wirtschaftsgeschichte* Beihefte no. 68 (Wiesbaden 1980), pp. vii–xi

and, largely derivatively, Eckart Schremmer, 'Erich Maschke (2. März 1900–11 February 1982)', *HZ* (1982), 235, pp. 251–5.

58. Erich Maschke, 'Quellen und Darstellungen in der Geschichtsschreibung der Preussenlandes', *Deutsche Staatenbildung*, pp. 37–9.

59. BA R153/ 1220, Maschke to Brackmann 7.10.31, and PuSte *Aktennotiz* 11.10.33 for information on Maschke's financial affairs.

60. BA R153/ 1200, PuSte to Maschke 12.5.32. See also HStA *Nachlass* Papritz 340, C12c/13, Maschke to Papritz, n.d., report on archives in Poland in late 1928.

61. BA R153/ 1220, Maschke to Brackmann 4.3.34.

62. BA R153/ 1220, Brackmann to Maschke 7.3.34 and Maschke to Brackmann 28.3.34.

63. BA R153/ 1220, Maschke to Brackmann 20.6.34.

64. Hermann Reincke-Bloch, 'Der Sechste Internationale Historikerkongress zu Oslo 14–18/8/1928', *HZ* (1929), 139, pp. 313–33 for the decision to hold the next meeting in Warsaw, and Karl Brandi, 'Der Siebente Internationale Historikerkongress zu Warschau und Krakau, 21–29 August 1933', *HZ* (1934), 149, p. 214.

65. *Ibid.*, p. 214.

66. BA R153/ 65, 'Vademecum für die deutschen Teilnehmer mit Information über die beiderseitigen Argumente in der deutsch-polnischen historisch-politischen Auseinandersetzung' (1933), pp. 2–4.

67. BA R153/65, 'Vademecum', pp. 6ff. On whether Kashubian is a language or dialect see Gerald Stone, 'The Language of Cassubian Literature and the Question of Literary Standard', *The Slavonic and East European Review* (1972), 50, pp. 521ff. See also Peter Brock, 'Florjan Cenôva and the Kashub Question', *East European Quarterly* (1968), 2, p. 261. I am grateful to Dr Stone for this and other papers on West Slavonic languages and for a number of discussions about minorities in Central Europe.

68. BA R153/ 65, 'Vademecum', p. 33.

69. BA R153/ 216, Brackmann circular to potential contributors 26.11.32; on Krahmer-Möllenberg see Norbert Krekeler, *Revisionsanspruch und geheime Ostpolitik*, p. 16.

70. BA R153/ 216, Brackmann to Prof. Eduard Wechssler 22.12.32; Foreign Office to Brackmann 22.12.32; Brackmann to Dr Dammann (RMdI) 28.12.32; and Verlag Oldenbourg to Brackmann 10.1.33 agreeing to a first run of 5,000 copies.

71. BA R153/ 216, 'Protokoll der Besprechung in Sachen des Sammelwerkes *Deutschland und Polen*' (Prussian Ministry of State), 8.2.33.

72. BA R153/ 216, Verlag Oldenbourg to Brackmann 22.2.33.

73. BA R153/ 216, Gerhard Ritter to Brackmann 1.1.33.

74. BA R153/ 216, Brackmann to Ritter 11.2.33.

75. BA R153/ 216, Max Hein to Brackmann 26.1.33.
76. BA R153/ 216, A. O. Meyer to Brackmann 4.4.33.
77. BA R153/ 217, Brackmann to Drost 9.5.33. See also Brackmann to Drost 19.5.33 'in this national effort, the interests of the individual should bow to the whole'.
78. BA R153/ 217, Brackmann to Aubin 17.6.33.
79. BA R153/ 217, Brackmann to Hans Rothfels 10.7.33.
80. BA R153/ 217, Brackmann to Rothfels 10.7.33.
81. BA R153/ 216, A. O. Meyer to Brackmann 7.4.33.
82. BA R153/217, Brackmann to RM für Volksaufklärung und Propaganda (Dr Krieg) 8.6.33 and Preuss. Min. für Wissenschaft, Kunst und Volksbildung (Dr Gerullis), to Brackmann 24.7.33.
83. BA R153/ 217, Brackmann to Karl Brandi 26.7.33.
84. BA R153/ 217, undated list of addresses for review copies; BA R153/ 219, Brackmann to Reichspräsident von Hindenburg 1.9.33.
85. BA R43II/ 1480a, Brackmann to Hitler 11.8.33.
86. BA R43II/ 1480a, Der Persönliche Referent des Reichskanzlers Dr Meerwald to Brackmann 12.8.33.
87. Volkmar Kellermann, *Schwarzer Adler-Weisser Adler. Die Polenpolitik der Weimarer Republik* (Cologne 1970), p. 160.
88. *Ibid.*, p. 164; see also Martin Broszat, *Zweihundert Jahre deutsche Polenpolitik* (Frankfurt am Main 1972, second edition 1978), pp. 239–40.
89. Kellermann, *Schwarzer Adler-Weisser Adler*, pp. 164–5.
90. Broszat, *Zweihundert Jahre deutsche Polenpolitik*, p. 241.
91. *Deutschland and Polen. Beitrage zu ihren geschichtlichen Beziehungen*, ed. A. Brackmann (Munich and Berlin 1933), p. iv.
92. W, Unversagt, 'Zur Vorgeschichte des ostdeutschen Raumes', *Deutschland und Polen*, pp. 3–5.
93. *Ibid.*, p. 6.
94. *Ibid.*, pp. 11–12.
95. Hermann Aubin, 'Die historisch-geographischen Grundlagen der deutsch-polnischen Beziehungen', *Deutschland und Polen*, p. 14.
96. Albert Brackmann, 'Die politische Entwicklung Osteuropas vom 10–15. Jahrhundert', *Deutschland und Polen*, p. 30.
97. Max Hein, 'Ostpreussen', *Deutschland und Polen*, p. 126.
98. Walther Recke, 'Westpreussen', *Deutschland und Polen*, p. 145.
99. Hein, 'Ostpreussen', p. 132; Hermann Oncken, 'Preussen und Polen im 19. Jahrhundert', *Deutschland und Polen*, p. 224.
100. Aubin, 'Die historisch-geographischen Grundlagen', p. 22.
101. Walther Vogel, 'Polen als Seemacht und Seehandelsstaat', *Deutschland und Polen*, p. 113.
102. Recke, 'Westpreussen', p. 136.

103. Aubin, 'Die historisch-geographischen Grundlagen', pp. 14 and 23.

104. Brackmann, 'Die politische Entwicklung', p. 39.

105. BA R153/ 1701, Brandi to Brackmann 23.2.33; BA R153/ 1573, 'Rechnungslegungen' (1933) for travel grants totalling 6000 RMs from the Foreign Office.

106. For these and other details of the Warsaw Congress see K. Brandi, 'Der Siebente Internationale Historikerkongress', pp. 216–17.

107. Wolfgang Kohte, 'Der VII Internationale Historikertag in Warschau', *Volk und Reich* (1933) 10, pp. 897–900.

108. BA R153/ 218, O. Halecki to Dölger (and a copy from Dölger to Brackmann) 21.12.33.

109. *Gazeta Warszawska* 28.10.33.

110. D. Krzemicka, *Wiedza i Zycie* (1934), 4. See also reviews in *Prawda Katolika* (1934) 5, and Stanisław Kot, 'Deutschland und Polen, Czy rewizja historji stosunków polskoniemieckich?', *Wiadomości Literackich*, 24.12.33.

111. BA R153/ 219, Brackmann to Handelsman 9.4.34 enclosing Deutsche Rundschau in Polen (Bromberg) list of banned books 31.1.34.

112. BA R153/ 1220, Maschke to Brackmann 20.6.34 and BA R153/219 Papritz memo to Brackmann 23.1.36.

113. BA R153/ 1573, 'Rechnungslegungen' (1933); for a detailed account see BA R153/ 219, '*Verwendungsnachweis für Deutschland und Polen*', 10.10.34.

114. BA R153/ 218, Papritz memo 9.10.33.

115. BA R153/ 1076, Drögereit to Brackmann 21.2.35. Drögereit attended IfA between 24.4.33 and 4.7.34 see Leesch, 'Das Institut für Archivwissenschaft', p. 243.

116. BA R153/ 1076, Drögereit to Brackmann 24.2.35, and Brackmann to Drögereit 27.2.35 see also R153/ 219, PuSte to Verlag Oldenbourg asking for four copies of the book to be dispatched to Drögereit.

117. BA R153/ 1076, Brackmann to Drögereit 27.2.35.

118. Krekeler, *Revisionsanspruch und geheime Ostpolitik*, p. 29ff.

119. Ernst Ritter, *Das Deutsche Ausland-Institut in Stuttgart: 1917–1945. Ein Beispiel deutscher Volkstumsarbeit zwischen den Weltkriegen*, Frankfurter Historische Abhandlungen, eds. W. Gembruch, P. Herde, P. Kluke, W. Lammers, K. Schwabe and K. Zernack, 14 (Wiesbaden 1976), p. 14.

120. *Ibid*., p. 26; see also Gerd Voigt, 'Aufgaben und Funktion des Osteuropa-Studien in der Weimarer Republik', *Studien über die deutsche Geschichtswissenschaft*, ed. Joachim Streisand, I, *Die bürgerliche deutsche Geschichtsschreibung von der Reichseinigung von oben bis zur Befreiung Deutschlands vom Faschismus* (Berlin 1965), pp. 380–1.

121. Ritter, *Das Deutsche Ausland-Institut*, p. 26; for an account of the

relationship between the Leipzig *Stiftung* and the *Forschungsgemeinschaften* see Brackmann's lecture in BA R153/ 882, 'Bericht über die Tätigkeit der Nord- und Ostdeutschen Forschungsgemeinschaften' etc., pp. 3ff.

122. Rudi Goguel, 'Über die Mitwirkung deutscher Wissenschaftler am Okkupationsregime in Polen im 2. Weltkrieg, untersucht an 3 Institutionen der deutschen Ostforschung', *Phil. Diss.* (East Berlin 1964), pp. 56ff.; and 'Die Nord- und Ostdeutsche Forschungsgemeinschaft im Dienste der faschistischen Aggressionspolitik gegen Polen 1933–1945', *Archivmitteilungen. Zeitschrift für Theorie und Praxis der Archivwesens* (1967), 17, pp. 82–9; and on the VDA and Steinacher see R. M. Smelser, *The Sudeten Problem 1933–1938. Volkstumspolitik and the Formulation of Nazi Foreign Policy* (Folkestone 1975), pp. 16–24.

123. BA R153/ 1269, 'Bericht über die Gründungstagung der Nordostdeutsche Forschungsgemeinschaft im ehemaligen Herrenhaus zu Berlin', 19–20.12.33, p. 4.

124. *Ibid*, pp. 10–12.

125. *Ibid*, p. 14; for the text of Kuhn's address see BA R153/ 1309, 'Stand und Aufgaben der Deutschtumsforschung in Polen', 20.12.33.

126. BA R153/ 233, Protokoll of a meeting held on 1.11.33 between the BDO leaders and various *Ostforscher* to discuss the BDO's exhibition 'Der Osten – das deutsche Schicksalsland' to be held between 1.12.33 and 10.1.34; on the BDO in general see Manfred Weissbacker, 'Bund Deutscher Osten 1933–1934', Dieter Fricke, ed., *Lexikon zur Parteiengeschichte* (Leipzig 1983), 1, pp. 308–9, and Maria Rothbarth, 'Der Bund Deutscher Osten- Instrument des aggressiven faschistischen deutschen Imperialismus', *Wissenschaftliche Zeitschrift der Universität Rostock* (1972), 21, pp. 213–15.

127. *Ibid.*, pp. 156–7.

128. BA R153/ 72, PuSte report on the BDO 5.7.33.

129. BA R153/ 1701, Brackmann to Fritz Rörig 14.7.33.

130. BA R153/ 233, Protokoll of the BDO leaders meeting with Brackmann *et al.*, 1.11.33, and Brackmann, 'Kampfland – von deutschen Blute besiedelt', *Berliner Illustrierte Nachtausgabe*, 4.12.33.

131. For the preparations for Kahlberg see BA R153/ 1277, Brackmann to Budding 28.7.34, in which he mentioned that the Foreign Office had stressed the need for great secrecy.

132. BA R153/ 1269, 'Vertraulicher Bericht über die Tagung der NODFG Kahlberg', p. 36.

133. *Ibid.*, p. 37 for Papritz's contribution.

134. *Ibid.*, p. 38; see also Broszat, *Zweihundert Jahre deutsche Polenpolitik*, p. 245 for the wider ramifications of these remarks.

135. BA R153/ 1269, 'Vertraulicher Bericht', pp. 40–2 for Oberländer's

paper and the resulting discussion; p. 50 for Reche and p. 51 for the itinerary after the conference was formally over. On Oberländer and the BDO see M. Rothbarth, 'Bund Deutscher Osten', pp. 215–17.

3. WATCH IN THE EAST

1. BA R153/ 1549, NODFG *Jahresbericht* 1938/9 (*Entwurf*) p. 6.
2. BA R153/ 2, *Organisatorische und räumliche Trennung der PuSte vom GstA Berlin-Dahlem*, draft by Brackmann 20.8.36 pp. 1–2.
3. BA R153/ 2, 'PuSte Berlin-Dahlem', *Raumbedarf* 21.9.36 p. 1.
4. BA R153/ 2. PuSte to RuPMdI 19.2.37, and PuSte Berlin-Dahlem *Raumbedarf* 21.9.36, p. 2.
5. BA R153/ 2, PuSte Berlin-Dahlem *Raumbedarf* 21.9.37 pp. 3–4; HStA *Nachlass Papritz* 340, C12 *Wissenschaftlicher und politischer Lebenslauf* (1948–53), p. 7. Papritz was formally relieved of his duties in the GStA in 1938. Interview with Dr Papritz 2.8.86.
6. BA R153/ 2, Papritz to the Prussian Finance Minister 10.8.37 enclosing an *Übersicht über die zum Ausbau des PuSte erforderlichen Mittel*.
7. BA R153/ 2, *Mietvertrag* 23.9.38, which gives the rent, and BA R153/ 1573, *Rechnungslegungen der PuSte* (1938) for the removal costs of 19.994 RMs. See BA R153/ 1571, comparative budgets 1936–7, for the salaries.
8. Interview with Dr Papritz in Marburg 11.8.86.
9. HStA *Nachlass Papritz* 340, C12 *Wissenschaftlicher Lebenslauf* (1948), pp. 1–9.
10. HStA *Nachlass Papritz* 340, C12 *Politischer Lebenslauf* (pre-1945), pp. 16ff. and interviews with Dr Papritz on 26.7.86; 28.7.86; 2.8.86; 11.8.86; 14.8.86; 16.8.86 in Marburg.
11. On this see Fritz K. Ringer, *The Decline of the German Mandarins. The German Academic Community, 1890–1933* (Cambridge, Mass. 1969), p. 80; C. E. McClelland, *State, Society and University in Germany 1700–1914* (Cambridge 1980), pp. 314ff.; Georg G. Iggers, *New Directions in European Historiography* (London 1984), pp. 83f.; Reinhard Kuhnl, 'Reichsdeutsche Geschichtswissenschaft', in Jörg Tröger, ed., *Hochschule und Wissenschaft im Dritten Reich* (Frankfurt am Main 1986), pp. 94–7, and Bruno Reimann, 'Die -Selbst Gleichschaltung- der Universitäten 1933', pp. 38ff.; and for how this affected the ways in which history was purveyed by the professoriate see Klaus Schreiner, 'Führertum, Rasse, Reich. Wissenschaft von der Geschichte nach der nationalsozialistischen Machtergriefung', Peter Lundgreen, ed., *Wissenschaft im Dritten Reich* (Frankfurt am Main 1985), especially pp. 222ff.

12. BA R153/ 1134, Sergei Jakobson, *Lebenslauf*, 3.10.31.

13. BA R153/ 1134, Jakobson to Brackmann 8.10.31.

14. BA R153/ 1134, PuSte reference for Jakobson 9.8.1933.

15. BA R153/ 1, *Übersicht über die Arbeiten der PuSte* 12.7.33, p. 3, C i.

16. BA R153/ 1134, Jakobson, *Lebenslauf*, 3.10.31 and *Einbürgerungsakten* 6.3.30.

17. BA R153/ 1134, Brackmann to Jakobson, '*Im Sinne des § 3 des Gesetzes betreffend Wiederherstellung der Berufsbeamtentums sehen wir uns genötigt das Ihnen gewährte Forschungsstipendium mit dem 30 September 1933 einzustellen*'; Jakobson to GStA 17.10.33 for the address 2 Asmus Hill, Hampstead Way NW11; and *Bericht über die Gründe, die zur Erteilung eines Forschungsauftrages an Dr S. Jakobson im Jahre 1931 geführt haben* 20.5.1936, pp. 1–3 for the PuSte's apologia.

18. BA R153/ 1134, *Bericht über die Gründe* p. 3.

19. BA R153/ 1212, Brackmann to Schwarz 21.9.31.

20. BA R153/ 1212, Schwarz, *Lebenslauf*, 20.10.31.

21. BA R153/ 1212, *Notgemeinschaft* to Brackmann 24.10.32.

22. BA R153/ 1212, Brackmann to Schmidt-Ott 8.4.33.

23. BA R1531/ 1212, *Durchsuchungs-Bericht* 5.4.33.

24. BA R153/ 1212, *Interrogation Protocol* 5.4.33, pp. 3–9 for Schwarz and pp. 1–4 for Bing-Nan Wang.

25. BA R153/ 1212, Papritz memo for Brackmann 13.4.33

26. BA R153/ 1212, Brackmann to Schmidt-Ott 8.4.33.

27. BA R153/ 1212, GStA memo 13.4.33 banning Schwarz; *Notgemeinschaft* to Schwarz 12.5.33 ending her grant; GStA/PuSte to *Polizeipräsidium* informing them of the above measures.

28. BA R153/ 1212, Schwarz to Papritz 13.11.34.

29. On Cosack see *Osteuropa in der historischen Forschung der DDR*, ed. M. Hellmann, vol. 2 *Bibliographie und biographische Notizen* (Düsseldorf 1972), p. 362. For a good biographical study see Ingetraud Spill, 'Prof. Harald Cosack vom "Ostforscher" zum akademischen Lehrer an der Universität Rostock', *Staatsexamensarbeit* (Humboldt-Universität, Berlin 1965), pp. 3–16.

30. GStA Rep. 92 *Nachlass Brackmann* Nr. 82, Cosack to the *Geschaftsführenden Senator der 5 Abteilung des Senats der Freien Stadt Danzig* 5.8.37, enclosing an extensive c.v., pp. 262–4. Spill, 'Prof. Harald Cosack' pp. 15–16 for Cosack's time in Breslau.

31. HStA *Nachlass Papritz* 340 C12a/5 *Entnazifizierung*, Cosack's testimony for Papritz 12.11.45. Spill, 'Prof. Harald Cosack' pp. 20–1 on his employment by the PuSte.

32. BA R153/ 1142, *Verhandlung am 18/12/1934 in GStA* p. 1.

33. *Ibid.*, p. 2.

34. *Ibid.*, p. 2. On the compulsory use of the 'German Greeting' for public

employees see Ian Kershaw, *The 'Hitler Myth'. Image and Reality in the Third Reich* (Oxford 1987), p. 60.

35. *Ibid.*, p. 5.
36. *Ibid.*, pp. 23–7.
37. *Ibid.*, p. 56.
38. *Ibid.*, p. 65 for Cosack's defence and BA R153/ 1142 *Preussische Staatsbibliothek* to Papritz 5.1.35 answering his request of 19.12.34.
39. K. H. Augustin and P. Nasarski, 'Ein Leben für die Forschung', in E. O. Kossmann, *Deutsche mitten in Polen. Unsere Vorfahren am Webstuhl der Geschichte* (Berlin 1985), p. 8. I am grateful to Dr Kossmann for a copy of his book.
40. HStA *Nachlass Papritz* 340, C12g 'K' for an undated c.v. by Kossmann.
41. Otto Heike, *Das Deutsche Schulwesen in Mittelpolen. Ein Kapitel mühsamer Abwehr staatlichen Unrechts. Veröffentlichungen der Ostdeutschen Forschungsstelle im Lande Nordrhein-Westfalen*, Reihe A, no. 6 (Dortmund 1963), pp. 87–90.
42. K. H. Augustin and P. Nasarski, 'Ein Leben', p. 9.
43. HStA *Nachlass Papritz* 340, C12 d 31 Brackmann to Krahmer-Möllenberg 4.1.35.
44. HStA *Nachlass Papritz* 340, C12 d 31, Verlag Justus Perthes to Prof. E. Meynen (VDA) 7.11.34 and Meynen to Brackmann 20.12.34.
45. HStA *Nachlass Papritz* 340, C12 d 31, Krahmer-Möllenberg to Brackmann 20.2.35.
46. HStA *Nachlass Papritz* 340, C12 d 31, Brackmann to Kurt Lück 25.2.35.
47. BA R153/ 1140, oath of allegiance August 1936; grant 1.8.36.
48. GStA Rep. 92 *Nachlass Brackmann* no. 82 PuSte *Personalbestand* 2.11.36, with language abilities and regional responsibilities.
49. BA R153/ 1140, PuSte to *Arbeitsamt* 21.1.39.
50. Interviews with Dr E. O. Kossmann in Marburg 28.7.86 and 8.8.86.
51. HStA *Nachlass Papritz* 340, C12 d 31, Brackmann to Krahmer-Möllenberg 4.1.35; BA R153/ 1143, Franz Doubek, *Personalfragebogen* 25.10.41, for Doubek's political affiliations. See also BDC *Doubek* SS service street. He joined the SA on 1.8.32 and the SS on 25.2.39.
52. BA R153/ 1125, Lattermann to Brackmann 30.3.32; Lattermann to Brackmann 12.3.33 seeking a grant for Doubek on the grounds that, like Kuhn and Lück, Doubek was *schon einmal mit den Nerven zusammengeklappt*; and Brackmann to Dr Stieve (Foreign Office) 29.3.33 mentioning Doubek's *kümmerliche Gehalt von złoty 250*.
53. BA R153/ 1125, *Express Wilenski* 3.12.32, and Doubek to Lattermann with his version of the story 14.5.33.
54. BA R153/ 1125, Brackmann to Lattermann 15.6.33; Brackmann to

Gerullis (Prussian Education Ministry) 14.7.33 and 1.8.33 seeking a grant for Doubek.

55. BA R153/ 1125, Papritz to Doubek 28.11.33 asking him to report to Brackmann's villa on 5.12.33; BA R153/ 1143, Papritz to Doubek 15.10.34; Doubek to Brackmann 29.10.34 thanking him for his help; and Brackmann to Foreign Office 30.1.35 mentioning the job in Danzig. Doubek worked in Danzig from 1.4.34–31.3.35 and then for the VDA from '1.4.35–15.10.36 and for the PuSte from 16.10.36–31.3.43, see PuSte to RMdI 20.3.43.

56. BA R153/ 1239, Ost *Lebenslauf* 6.6.37.

57. BA R163/ 1239, Ost *Lebenslauf* 6.6.37.

58. BA R153/ 1239, Brackmann to Foreign Office 20.11.37.

59. GStA Rep. 92 *Nachlass Brackmann* Nr. 82, *Geschäftsverteilung bei der PuSte* 16.1.39.

60. BA R153/ 1228, PuSte reference for Maydell 24.10.39.

61. BA R153/ 1228, Maydell to Brackmann 22.10.37.

62. BA R153/ 1228, Kohte memo 8.11.38 and PuSte memo 2.11.39.

63. This table has been produced by merging several sets of data on the staff of the PuSte. The information in columns 1 and 2 comes from GStA Rep. 92 *Nachlass Brackmann* no. 81 '*Personalbestand* 2/11/1936'; column 3 is based upon HStA *Nachlass Papritz* 340 C 12d 30 *PuSte Personalia, Referatseineilung* 1/6/1937; column 4 on BA R153/ 1590 *Jomsburg* Papritz to PuSte staff *Aufforderung zur Mitarbeit* 22.12.36; column 5 on BA R153 1570 personal data on PuSte staff collected after a circular dated 10.2.38; and column 6 upon BA R153/ 1571, comparative budgets for 1936–7 and wage lists for clerical staff (undated) 1931–44. Since rates and terms of pay fluctuated e.g. when a grant became a salary, these figures should be treated with caution.

64. BA R153 1571, *Örtliche Prüfung der Verwendung der Reichsosthilfemittel, die der PuSte usw. im Rechnungsjahr 1934 und früher zur Verfugung gestellt worden sind* RuPMdI 30.7.36 p. 4.

65. Norbert Krekeler, *Revisionsanspruch und geheime Ostpolitik der Weimarer Republik. Die Subventionierung der deutschen Minderheit in Polen 1919–1933* (Stuttgart 1973), pp. 46–7.

66. BA R153/ 1573, *Rechnungslegungen der PuSte für die Rechnungsjahre 1931–1944*. These figures do not include interest on money in the PuSte/ NODFG accounts or, with one exception, funds carried over from previous years. Hence actual income should be reckoned to have been slightly higher than the figures in this table. There are no figures for 1939.

67. BA R153/ 1571, *Örtliche Prüfung* comparative budgets for 1936–7.

68. BA R153/ 1571, *Haushaltsvoranschlag für die Rechnungsjahr 1937*. These figures roughly tally with the total grant for 1937.

69. Krekeler, *Revisionsanspruch und geheime Ostpolitik*, pp. 88–9. See also section 3 below.

70. GStA Rep. 92 *Nachlass Brackmann* Nr. 81 *Karteien der PuSte* 1.11.36

71. BA R153/ 1085, Papritz to Swientek (*Entwurf*) April 1933.

72. BA R153/ 49, Polish Historians D–G 1931–1939, PuSte report to General-Director of the *Staatsarchive* 24.5.33.

73. BA R153/ 49, PuSte memo on Górski (no date). I am grateful to Professor Górski for correspondence on the background to these events (5.11.86).

74. BA R153/ 49, PuSte *Polnische Presseauszüge* no. 164 24.4.35 *Kurjer Poznanski* 18.4.35 report on April issue of *Przeglad Powszechny*. General-Director of the *Staatsarchive* to *Staatsarchive der Freien Stadt Danzig* 1.12.38.

75. BA R153/ 49, Kohte to Brackmann report on Górski 23.1.35.

76. BA R153/ 49, Staatsarchiv Königsberg, report by Forstreuter 29.11.38 signed by Max Hein.

77. BA R153/ 43, PuSte memo 25.3.36.

78. BA R153/ 44, Uebersberger to PuSte 7.4.36.

79. BA R153/ 44, PuSte to Uebersberger 27.5.36 with the (marked) list.

80. BA R153/ 43, Schieder to PuSte 20.2.1938 and PuSte to Schieder 24.2.38.

81. BA R153/ 44, Uebersberger to PuSte 11.2.39.

82. BA R153/ 44, PuSte to Uebersberger 18.2.39.

83. BA R153/ 1372, Brackmann to Foreign Office/RMdI 15.9.37.

84. BA R153/ 43, Krahmer-Möllenberg to Brackmann, Foreign Office, RMdI and War Ministry 22.4.37.

85. BA R153/ 43, *General-Director der Staatsarchive* to PuSte 17.8.39 and PuSte to above with list of names required.

86. BA R153/ 1305, PuSte memo 21.3.35. The Upper Silesian Geographical Institute received 3,000 RMs from respectively the Foreign Office, RMdI, local sources and the Oberpräsident in Silesia.

87. BA R153/ 1302, NODFG to Aubin 11.9.35; Sczodrok to Brackmann 12.9.35 and 15.12.36.

88. BA R153/ 1302, Sczodrok to Brackmann 17.9.35.

89. BA R153/ 1302, Sczodrok to Brackmann 22.10.35 and Sczodrok to NODFG 18.8.36.

90. BA R153/ 1302, Sczodrok to NODFG 18.8.36.

91. BA R153/ 1302, Sczodrok to Brackmann 15.10.35.

92. BA R153/ 1302, Sczodrok to NODFG 2.12.36.

93. BA R153/ 1302, Sczodrok to NODFG 15.12.36.

94. BA R153/ 1305, Sczodrok to PuSte 3.6.35 recommending translation of a Polish work and Sczodrok to PuSte 28.10.36 on Eichstedt.

95. BA R153/ 1305, Aubin to Brackmann 10.12.35.

96. BA R153/ 1305, PuSte memo 24.11.36.

97. BA R153/ 1305, Brackmann to Eichstedt 16.2.37. Eichstedt was the editor of *Zeitschrift für Rassenkunde*.

98. GStA Rep. 92 *Nachlass Brackmann* no. 81, list of translations produced up to 1.11.36.

99. BA R153/ 1571, Brackmann to Dr Roedinger, Foreign Office 18.10.35.

100. BA R153/ 1245, Vollert (RMdI) to Papritz 12.8.37.

101. GStA Rep. 92 *Nachlass Brackmann* no. 81, p. 123, *Die Übersetzungen der PuSte* 1.11.36.

102. BA R153/ 505, *Preussische Geheime Staatspolizei* (Dr Best) to PuSte 20.3.36 and PuSte to Gestapo 24.2.36.

103. BA *Findbuch* 153 pp. 84–119 for lists of the translations including dates of publication and translation, and Ingetraud Spill, 'Prof. Harald Cosack', pp. 24ff. for a good discussion of the contents of some of the books translated.

104. Krekeler, *Revisionsanspruch und geheime Ostpolitik*, p. 11; 'Der deutsche Minderheit in Polen', pp. 15–16; Gotthold Rhode, 'Das Deutschtum in Posen and Pommerellen in der Zeit der Weimarer Republik', *Studien zum Deutschtum im Osten* ed. E. Hökle *et al.*, 3, *Die Deutschen Ostgebiete zur Zeit der Weimarer Republik* (Cologne/Graz 1966), p. 94.

105. Broszat, *Zweihundert Jahre deutsche Polenpolitik*, pp. 226–7; Rhode, 'Das Deutschtum in Posen und Pommerellen', pp. 102–9. On the nineteenth-century background see H. U. Wehler, 'Von dem "Reichsfeinden" zur "Reichkristallnacht": Polenpolitik im Deutschen Kaiserreich 1871–1918', *Krisenherde des Kaiserreichs*, pp. 186ff., and W. H. Hagen, *Germans, Poles and Jews. The Nationality Conflict in the Prussian East 1772–1914* (Chicago 1980).

106. Kellermann, *Schwarzer Adler – Weisser Adler*, p. 52.

107. F. H. Gentzen, 'Die Rolle der deutschen Regierung beim Aufbau deutscher Minderheitsorganisationen in den an Polen abgetretenen Gebieten (1919–1922)', *Jahrbuch für Geschichte der UdSSR and der volksdemokratischen Länder Europas* (1967), 10, p. 166.

108. Krekeler, *Revisionsanspruch und geheime Ostpolitik*, pp. 64ff.; Rhode 'Das Deutschtum in Posen und Pommerellen', pp. 100–1; Broszat, *Zweihundert Jahre deutsche Polenpolitik*, p. 212.

109. Krekeler, *Revisionsanspruch und geheime Ostpolitik*, p. 53.

110. *Ibid.*, pp. 16–22, pp. 79–87; Gentzen, 'Die Rolle der deutschen Regierung', pp. 173ff., and his 'Zur Geschichte des deutschen Revanchismus in der Periode der Weimarer Republik', *Jahrbuch für Geschichte der UdSSR und der volksdemokratischen Länder Europas* (1960), 4, pp. 48–53.

111. Krekeler, *Revisionsanspruch und geheime Ostpolitik*, pp. 87–8.

112. Gentzen, 'Die Rolle der deutschen Regierung', pp. 168–9, and Krekeler, *Revisionsanspruch und geheime Ostpolitik*, pp. 22–4.

113. BA R153/ 1571, RuPMdI, *Ortliche Prüfung der Verwendung der Reichsosthilfemittel, die der Publikationsstelle im Rechnungsjahr 1934 und früher zur Verfügung gestellt worden sind 30.7.36*, p. 4.

114. These figures are from BA R153/ 1573, *Rechnungslegungen der Publikationsstelle für die Rechnungsjahre 1931–1944*.

115. *Ibid.*

116. BA R153/ 1542, *Forschungsgemeinschaft Jahresbericht 1933–1934*, p. 3.

117. BA R153/ 1388, PuSte to Foreign Office 9.11.38.

118. BA R153/ 1388, NODFG to *Oberfinanzpräsidenten Devisenstelle Berlin* 22.8.38; *Oberfinanzpräsident Schlesien Devisenstelle* to NODFG 30.9.38; Deutsche Bank Berlin to NODFG 5.10.38; BA R153/ 1388, NODFG to Deutsche Bank 13.10.38; PuSte to Foreign Office (*Kulturpolitische Abteilung*) 9.11.38; Foreign Office to NODFG 29.11.38. 5932 RMs were then transferred from the Prussian *Staatsbank* (*Seehandlung*) to the Deutsche Bank and then on to the consulates in Kattowitz and Posen, see BA R153/ 1388, NODFG to Deutsche Bank 9.12.38. The consulates were informed of the true purpose of the funds sent to them.

119. BA R153 1442, Kohte report on his arrest 12.7.37, pp. 1–10.

120. Rhode, 'Das Deutschtum in Posen und Pommerellen', p. 129; A. Lattermann, 'Deutsche Forschung im ehemaligen Polen 1919–1939', *Deutsche Ostforschung. Ergebnisse und Aufgaben seit dem ersten Weltkrieg*, eds. H. Aubin, O. Brunner, W. Kohte and J. Papritz (Leipzig 1943), 2, pp. 465–7; G. Rhode, 'Die Historisch-Landeskundliche Kommission für Posen and das Deutschtum in Polen', *ZfO* (1955), 4, pp. 559–60 for the journals edited by Lattermann and Kauder.

121. On Lattermann, see his c.v. in GStA Rep. 92 *Nachlass* Brackmann no. 84 p. 172 (no date), BA R153/ 1233, Lattermann to Papritz 17.1.40 and BDC *Lattermann*. SS service sheet/c.v., and the obituary by H. M. Meyer, 'Alfred Lattermann', *ZfO* (1952), 1, pp. 423–5; on Kauder see principally W. Kuhn, 'Das Lebenswerk Viktor Kauder', *Der Kulturwart* (1969), 17, pp. 1–10.

122. For examples see BA R153/ 1387, *Verband Deutscher Volksbüchereien* (Kauder) to Papritz 15.11.37 *Aufstellung unserer Vorschläge für 1938*; R153/ 1388, *Haushaltsvorschläge für die deutsche Forschung in Polen 1937*; R153/ 1385, Lattermann to Papritz on requirements for 1938 19.1.38; R153/ 1309, *Vorschläge über Beihilfen zur wissenschaftlichen Arbeit der Deutschen in Polen für 1934* and *Beihilfen und Stipendien der NODFG im Haushaltsjahr 1935/1936* (no date) with the proposals, sums agreed and dates of transfer of funds to Poland. These proposals consisted of blocks of grant applications which the NODFG forwarded

to the ministries; see for example BA R153/ 1549, 'Jahresbericht der NODFG 1938/39', p. 14.

123. BA R153/ 1309, 'Vorschläge über Beihilfen', pp. 5–6.

124. BA R153/ 1309, W. Kuhn, *Stand und Aufgaben der Deutschtumsforschung in Polen* 20.12.33; R153/ 1269, *Bericht über die Gründstagung der NODFG 19–20.12.33*, p. 25.

125. On Lück see W. Kuhn, 'Kurt Lück 1900–1942', *ZfO* (1952), 1, pp. 425–6 and the sad exchange between Kuhn and Lück's son Walter Lück, 'Mit Dr Kurt Lück . . . etc.' and W. Kuhn, 'Zum Gedenken an Kurt Lück' *Posener Stimmen. Heimatblatt des Hilfskomittees der Glieder der Posener Evgl. Kirche* (1967) 14, pp. 5–7; the exchange was reprinted as 'Die zornigen jungen Männer', *Der Kulturwart* (1969), 17, pp. 13–18.

126. Kurt Lück, 'Die Bauern im polnischen Roman des 19. Jahrhunderts', *Schrift zur Erlangung der philosophischen Doktorwürde bei der Philosophischen Fakultät der Schlesischen Friedrich Wilhelms-Universität zu Breslau* (Poznań 1926). The copy I have read came from the former GStA Grenzmark section.

127. BA R153/ 1233, Lattermann to Brackmann 22.9.31.

128. BA R153/ 1233, Brackmann to Lattermann 4.3.32 and 24.3.32.

129. BA R153/ 1233, Brackmann to Lattermann 22.4.33 and 7.5.33; R153/ 1309, Brackmann to Hassinger (SODFG) 16.1.34 and NODFG to Kauder 25.1.34 and R153/ 1573, NODFG budget 1933 including 500 RMs for Lück in 1933 etc. According to BA R153/ 1309, Papritz to Kauder 25.7.34 payments to Lück went via the consulate in Katowice.

130. BA R153/ 1233, Lattermann to Papritz 22.9.31.

131. BA R153/ 1233, Lattermann to Brackmann 7.5.33.

132. BA R153/ 1309, Brackmann to Lück 18.6.34.

133. BA R153/ 1385, PuSte to Lück 28.12.39 referring to payments sent on 22.12.38 and 600 RMs for 1939.

134. BA R153/ 1309, Lattermann to Brackmann 17.12.33.

135. BA R153/ 1309, Hassinger to Brackmann 12.1.34; Brackmann to Hassinger 16.1.34 and NODFG to Kauder 25.1.34; Kuhn, 'Stand und Aufgaben' 20.12.33, p. 5. See also W. Kuhn, 'Ein Jugend für die Sprachinselforschung', *Jahrbuch der Schlesische Friedrich-Wilhelms-Universität zu Breslau* (1982), 23, p. 243. I am grateful to Dr Hugo Weczerka for this and other references to Kuhn.

136. BA R153/ 1309, Kuhn to Brackmann 19.9.34 complaining about the nature of the grant and '*Beihilfen und Stipendien der NODFG 1935/ 1936*', p. 2.

137. Kuhn, 'Ein Jugend für die Sprachinselforschung', p. 226.

138. *Ibid.*, p. 227.

139. *Ibid.*, pp. 227–8.

140. *Ibid.*, pp. 232–3; see also G. Rhode and H. Weczerka, 'Zum Tode von Walter Kuhn (1903–1983)', *ZfO* (1983), 32, pp. 161ff.

141. 'Ein Jugend für die Sprachinselforschung', p. 255. Alphons Dopsch made the oral part of the examination easier by asking him questions on the medieval German colonization of the East.

142. BA 153/ 1309, 'Beihilfen and Stipendien', p. 2.

143. Walter Kuhn, 'Meine Forschungsarbeiten in Wolhynien' (no place of publication *c.* 1977), pp. 2–4.

144. Hans Frhr. von Rosen, *Wolhynienfahrt 1926*. Schriften der J. G. Herder-Bibliothek Siegerland e.V. (Siegen 1982), 10, pp. 2–3.

145. *Ibid.*, p. 10.

146. *Ibid.*, pp. 16–24.

147. *Ibid.*, pp. 36–7 for a reproduction of one of the forms.

148. *Ibid.*, p. 30 and the photographs between p. 40 and p. 41, especially no. 3 showing Kuhn with the peasant Jakob Bäuerle, and Kuhn, 'Meine Forschungsarbeiten in Wolhynien', pp. 8–11.

149. Rosen, *Wolhynienfahrt 1926*, p. 43 citing Kuhn, 'Wege und Ziele ostlanddeutscher Heimatforschung', *Deutsche Blätter in Polen* (1926), p. 379.

150. Kuhn, 'Ein Jugend für die Sprachinselforschung', p. 234.

151. Rosen, *Wolhynienfahrt 1926*, p. 46.

152. *Ibid.*, p. 50.

153. *Ibid.*, p. 58.

154. *Ibid.*, p. 59.

155. *Ibid.*, p. 64.

156. *Ibid.*, p. 73.

157. Kurt Lück, *Deutsche Aufbaukräfte in der Entwicklung Polens. Forschungen zur Deutschpolnischen Nachbarschaft im ostmitteleuropäischen Raum*, ed. Viktor Kauder (Plauen i. Vogtland 1934) 1, p. ix.

158. *Ibid.*, p. xii.

159. *Ibid.*, p. 4.

160. *Ibid.*, p. 127.

161. *Ibid.*, p. 133.

162. *Ibid.*, p. 155.

163. *Ibid.*, p. 156.

164. *Ibid.*, p. 161.

165. *Ibid.*, pp. 189ff.

166. *Ibid.*, pp. 191ff.

167. *Ibid.*, pp. 197ff.

168. *Ibid.*, pp. 207ff.

169. *Ibid.*, pp. 224ff.

170. *Ibid.*, pp. 215ff.

171. *Ibid.*, pp. 293–321.

172. *Ibid.*, p. 322.

173. *Ibid.*, p. 323.

174. *Ibid.*, p. 381 for Lelewel and p. 400 for Kraszewski.

175. *Ibid.*, the section on Elsner was inserted, unpaginated between pp. 412–13.

176. *Ibid.*, p. 450.

177. *Ibid.*, p. 452.

178. 'Kurt Lück, *Der Mythos vom Deutschen in der polnischen Volksüberlieferung und Literatur. Forschungen zur deutsch-polnischen Nachbarschaft im ostmitteleuropäischen Raum*, vol. 2, *Ostdeutsche Forschungen*, ed. Viktor Kauder (Leipzig 1943 and enlarged edition), 7, pp. 10 and 293ff.

179. *Ibid.*, pp. 22–3.

180. *Ibid.*, p. 20.

181. *Ibid.*, pp. 18–20.

182. *Ibid.*, p. 168.

183. *Ibid.*, pp. 770–1.

184. *Ibid.*, p. 218.

185. *Ibid.*, pp. 421ff.; 306ff.; 388–402.

186. *Ibid.*, p. 484.

187. BA R153/ 98, PuSte to Oberländer 10.7.37 and Ballerstedt to PuSte 18.1.38.

188. BA R153/ 98, PuSte to Oberländer 10.7.37.

189. BA R153/ 98, Oberländer to Papritz 20.7.37.

190. BA R153/ 98, Ballerstedt to the PuSte 27.7.37.

191. BA R153/ 98, PuSte to all referees 14.7.37 and W. Gebert to NODFG 3.9.37 and PuSte to Oberländer 29.10.37.

192. BA R153/ 98, Oberländer to Brackmann 16.1.36 and Seraphim to NODFG 21.7.36 enclosing a c.v. and questionnaire in which he gave his political affiliations.

193. BA R153/ 98, Peter-Heinz Seraphim, 'Bericht über den Entwurf einer Arbeit "Das Judentum im osteuropäischen Raum"' 9.1. 36, p. 2.

194. *Ibid.*, p. 3.

195. *Ibid.*, p. 4.

196. *Ibid.*, pp. 8–9.

197. BA R153/ 98, Oberländer to Brackmann 29.1.36. Brackmann had earlier expressed reservations about the length of the project and that it might stray on to areas worked on by Frank's *Reichsinstitut*; see Brackmann to Oberländer 20.1.36.

198. BA R153/ 98, PuSte to Seraphim and NODFG to Seraphim 29.7.36, and PuSte to Seraphim 1.7.39 for a publication subsidy of 2,000 RMs.

199. Gerald Stone, *The Smallest Slavonic Nation. The Sorbs of Lusatia* (London 1972), pp. 21–9.

200. *Ibid.*, pp. 32–3 and Jan Šołta, K. Schiller, M. Kasper and Frido Mětšk, *Geschichte der Sorben*, 4 vols., vol. 3, *Von 1917 bis 1945* (Bautzen 1976), pp. 82–3.

201. *Geschichte der Sorben* p. 132; see also Frido Mětšk, *Bestandsverzeichnis der Sorbischen Kulturarchivs in Bautzen*, Teil III, *Das Depositum Wendenabteilung. Němska akademija wědomosćow w Berlinje Spisy Instituta za serbski ludospyt w Budyšinje* (Budyšin/Bautzen 1967), pp. 11ff., and F. Mětšk, 'Das Sorbenbild in der westdeutschen „Ostforschung"', *Zeitschrift für Geschichtswissenschaft* (1965), 13, p. 1178.

202. *Ibid.*, p. 44.

203. *Ibid.*, pp. 155–6; see also Manfred Weissbecker, 'Bund Deutscher Osten (BDO) 1933–1937', Dieter Fricke, ed., *Lexikon zur Parteiengeschichte* (Leipzig 1983) 1, pp. 312–13. I am grateful to Wolfgang Wippermann for this reference, and Frido Mětšk, *Bestandsverzeichnis des Sorbischen Kulturachivs*, pp. 19–20.

204. Frido Mětšk, *Bestandsverzeichnis*, p. 43 for the citation from Kötzschke. BA R153/ 1461 Tilka to *Niederlausitzer Gesellschaft* (Lehmann) 21.5.38.

205. BA R153/ 1461, Tilka to *Niederlausitzer Gesellschaft* 21.5.38 enclosing list of contents of his manuscript.

206. BA R153/ 1461, Oberpräsident der Provinz Brandenburg to RMdI 17.6.38.

207. BA R153/ 1461, RMdI (Essen) to PuSte 1.7.38 and Oberpräsident der Provinz Brandenburg to RMdI 5.11.38.

208. BA R153/ 1461, Oberpräsident der Provinz Brandenburg to RMdI 5.11.38.

209. BA R153/ 1461, Tilka to Lehmann 28.10.38.

210. BA R153/ 1461, PuSte to RMdI 17.9.38.

211. *Geschichte der Sorben* 3, p. 162 for Wirt's name.

212. BA R153/ 1263, *Deutsche Forschungsgemeinschaft* to NODFG 10.8.37.

213. BA R153/ 1455, Vasmer to Brackmann 1.6.33. On Vasmer see H. H. Bielfeldt, 'Die Geschichte des Lehrstuhls für Slavistik an der Berliner Universität', H. H. Bielfeldt, K. Horálek, *Beiträge zur Geschichte der Slawistik. Veröffentlichungen des Instituts für Slawistik* (Berlin 1964), no. 30, pp. 275–6. The SD had 'certain reservations' about the polonophile content of lectures at Vasmer's Institute. See *Meldungen aus dem Reich. Die geheimen Lageberichte des Sicherheitsdienstes der SS 1931–1945*, ed. Heinz Boberach (Herrsching 1984), 2, p. 257.

214. BA R153/1263, NODFG (Kohte) to *Deutsche Forschungsgemeinschaft* 21.8.37.

215. BA R153/ 1263, *Deutsche Forschungsgemeinschaft* to Wirth 25.8.37.

216. Rudoff Fischer, 'Reinhold Trautmann in der deutschen Slawistik', *Beiträge zur Geschichte der Slawistik*, p. 175.

217. *Ibid.*, pp. 176f.

218. BA R153/ 1258, Trautmann to Brackmann 20.3.38.

219. BA R153/ 1455, NODFG to BDO 9.11.36 and Professor R. Kötzschke to NODFG 19.11.36 and RMdI to officials in Saxony, Breslau and Brandenburg 9.4.37.

220. BA R153/ 1455, 'Notizen über Wendenbesprechungen im RMdI' 26.4.37 for Trautmann's cryptic interjection.

221. GStA Rep. 92 *Nachlass Brackmann* no. 82 Vasmer to Brackmann 11.5.37 and Brackmann to Vasmer 19.5.37 defending his staff.

222. BA R153/ 1455, RMdI to NODFG, Foreign Office, enclosing results of conference on 26.4.37 'Thesen zur Wendenfrage'. On Prof. R. Kötzschke see F. Mětšk, *Bestandsverzeichnis* p. 43. Kötzschke saw it as the task of academic research 'die Meinungsbildung von der Primitivität der Wenden und Slaven wissenschaftlich zu untermauern und die Gesetzmässigkeit des Sieges der überlegenen deutschen Kultur zu erweisen' and to hinder 'der Gefahr der Herausbildung eines eigenen Geschichtsbewusstseins unter den Wenden' and 'alle Ansätze dazu energisch zu bekämpfen and als Auswüchse einiger Fanatiker aufzuzeigen'.

223. BA R153/ 1259, Brackmann to Trautmann 22.3.38.

224. BA R153/ 1455, Kohte to Amtshauptmann zu Bautzen 23.12.35.

225. BA R153/ 1455, Amtshauptmann zu Bautzen to Brackmann 8.1.36.

226. BA R153/ 1455, RM für Volksaufklärung und Propaganda to Hauptschriftleiter *Hilf Mit!* and *Deutsche Jugendburg* 30.3.37.

227. BA R153/ 1455, RM für Volksaufklärung und Propaganda to '*NS-Frauenwarte*' 3.5.37.

228. BA R153/ 1258, Trautmann to Brackmann 23.3.38.

229. BA R153/ 1258, Brackmann to Trautmann 23.4.38.

230. BA R153/ 1258, Brackmann to Trautmann 27.4.38.

231. BA R153/ 1258, Mecklenburgisches Staatsministerium to RMdI 17.5.38 and W. Strecker (Jahrbuch) to Mecklenburgisches Staatsministerium 21.12.37.

232. BA R153/ 1258, PuSte to Trautmann 14.6.38.

233. BA R153/ 1258, Der Landeshauptmann der Provinz Schleswig-Holstein als Vorsitzender der Gesellschaft für Schleswig-Holsteinische Geschichte to RMdI 20.1.40 recounting the route taken by Trautmann's manuscript.

234. BA R153/ 1258, Brackmann to Scheel 15.3.39.

235. BA R153/ 1258, Scheel to Brackmann 17.3.39.

236. BA R153/ 1258, Koppe, PuSte memo 21.2.39.

237. BA R153/ 1258, Trautmann to Brackmann 13.4.39.

238. BA R153/ 1258, Brackmann to Trautmann 25.4.39.

239. BA R153/ 1259, Scheel to Brackmann 27.4.39.

240. BA R153/ 1258, Pauls to the PuSte 26.6.39.

241. BA R153/ 1258, PuSte to RMdI enclosing a report on Trautmann's work dated 25.8.39.

242. BA R153/ 1258, Der Landeshauptmann der Provinz Schleswig-Holstein to RMdI 20.1.40 on this oversight.

243. BA R153/ 1258, Trautmann to Brackmann 18.10.39.

244. BA R153/ 1258, Trautmann to Brackmann 3.12.39.

245. BA R153/ 1258, PuSte to RMdI 9.12.39 relaying Trautmann's threat.

246. BA R153/ 1258, Brackmann to Aubin 1.2.40 and 8.2.40 and Brackmann to Essen (RMdI)

247. BA R153/ 1258, RM für Volksaufklärung und Propaganda to RMdI 3.5.40.

248. BA R153/ 1258, Der Chef der Sicherheitspolizei und des SD to PuSte 7.8.40.

249. BA R153/ 1258, RMdI toPuSte 11.5.40; PuSte to Gestapo 10.8.40 and Gestapo (local office Kiel) to PuSte 16.9.40 sending 5 copies of Trautmann's book.

250. BA R153/ 1258, PuSte memo on the Trautmann case 16.9.40.

251. BA R153/ 1258, Landeshauptmann der Provinz Schleswig-Holstein to RMdI 20.1.40.

252. *Reichthandbuch der Deutschen Gesellschaft. Das Handbuch der Persönlichkeiten in Wort und Bild* (Berlin 1931), 2, pp. 1484–5 for Reche's career and major publications.

253. BDC, *Reche* Justizrat W. von Zezschwitz to Reichsschatzmeister Schwarz 19.9.40 supporting Reche's efforts to alter his membership card.

254. BA R153/ 396, Reichsausschuss für Volksgesundheitsdienst beim Reichs- und Preussischen Ministerium des Innern to Essen (RMdI) 19.7.37. For grants to Reche see BDC *Reichsforschungsrat* cards.

255. BA R153/ 396, NODFG to Reche 2.6.37.

256. Otto Reche, 'Über die Bodenständigkeit des Deutschtums östlich der Elbe', *Der Öffentliche Gesundheitsdienst* (1937), 3, pp. 625–8.

257. *Ibid.*, p. 628.

258. BA R153/ 1361, NSDAP Gauleitung Schlesien to RuPM für Wissenschaft, Erziehung und Volksbildung 31.12.37; RMdI to NODFG 7.3.38; NODFG to Reche 2.9.38.

259. BA R153/ 1361, PuSte to RuPM für Wissenschaft, Erziehung und Volksbildung 22.4.39.

260. Mechthild Rössler, 'Die Geographie an der Universität Freiburg 1933–1945. Ein Beitrag zur Wissenschaftsgeschichte des Faches im Dritten Reich', *Zulassungsarbeit* (Freiburg 1983), p. 24 citing Hans Mortensen, 'Inwiefern kann die Hochschulgeographie den Bedürfnissen der Schulgeographie und der allgemeine Volksbildung gerecht werden?', *Geographischer Anzeiger* 23/24 (1934), p. 539. I am grateful

to Mechthild Rössler for this reference and for a number of memorable discussions on *Ostforschung* in Koblenz.

261. BA R153/ 1281, NODFG Tagung in Ostpommern 6–8.5.37, p. 7.

262. GStA Rep. 92 *Nachlass Brackmann* no. 82 Brackmann to Aubin 25.5.37.

263. GStA Rep. 92 *Nachlass Brackmann* no. 82 Brackmann to Klante 21.6.37 and Brackmann to Aubin 21.6.37.

264. BA R153/ 627, Mortensen to Brackmann 18.5.37.

265. BA R153/ 627, Mortensen to Brackmann 15.1.38.

266. BA R153/ 627, Brackmann to Essen (RMdI) 19.1.38.

267. BA R153/ 627, RMdI memo 10.2.38.

268. BA R153/ 627, Mortensen to Brackmann 29.12.38.

269. GStA Rep. 92 *Nachlass Brackmann* no. 83 Brackmann to Essen 25.8.38 and RMdI to Mortensen August 1938 and BA R153/ 627, Vollert (RMdI) to Mortensen 31.8.38.

270. BA R153/ 627, RMdI to Mortensen 10.8.38 and Mortensen to RMdI 19.8.38.

271. BA R153/ 627, Mortensen to RMdI 19.8.38.

272. GStA Rep. 92. *Nachlass Brackmann* no. 83 Mortensen to RMdI 8.9.38.

273. BA R153/ 627, Brackmann to Mortensen 9.1.39 and Mortensen to Brackmann 13.1.39.

274. BA R153/ 627, Brackmann to RMdI 9.3.39.

275. BA R153/ 627, Mortensen to Brackmann 5.4.39.

276. BA R153/ 627, Brackmann to Mortensen 22.5.39.

277. BA R153/ 627, Brackmann to Mortensen 19.4.41.

278. There is a brief reference to these conferences in Enno Meyer, 'Probleme einer Deutschpolnischen Diskussion über den Inhalt der Geschichtstlehrbücher' *GWU* (1958), i, pp. 13–14. See also H. Aubin, 'Ergänzung zu Enno Meyer, Probleme einer deutsch-polnischen Diskussion über den Inhalt der Geschichts-Lehrbücher' *GWU* (1958), 9, pp. 429–30.

279. BA R153/ 1371, 'Deutsche Aufzeichnung über die Verhandlungen zur Frage der Angleichung der Schulbücher mit Polen im Kultusministerium zu Warschau am 28. und 29. August 1937', p. 2.

280. BA R153/ 1371, 'Geschichtsbücher für den Frieden', *Der Angriff* 4.7.38.

281. BA R153/ 1371, 'Deutsche Aufzeichnung', pp. 2–3.

282. BA R153/ 1371, 'Deutsche Aufzeichnung', p. 6.

283. BA R153/ 1371, 'Deutsche Aufzeichnung', p. 7.

284. BA R153/ 1371, 'Deutsche Aufzeichnung', pp. 7–8.

285. BA R153/ 1371, 'Deutsche Aufzeichnung', p. 9.

286. BA R153/ 1371' 'Deutsche Aufzeichnung', p. 11.

287. BA R153/ 1371, 'Deutsche Aufzeichnung', pp. 12–13.

288. BA R153/ 1371, 'Deutsche Aufzeichnung', p. 13.

289. BA R153/ 1371, 'Deutsche Aufzeichnung', p. 17.

290. BA R153/ 1371, PuSte Polish Press extract no. 283 29.6.38 from Kurjer Poznanski no. 280 23.6.38.

291. BA R153/ 1371, Fitzek to the PuSte 27.7.38.

292. BA R153/ 1371, PuSte to Fitzek 4.8.38.

293. BA R153/ 1371, PuSte *Gutachten* on W. Mosczenska, H. Mrozowska, *Podrecznik do nauki historji II* (1934), pp. 1–4; Tadeusz Bornholtz, *Historja dla Klasy ii*, pp. 1–8 and 'Polnische Geschichtsbücher' including Dabrowski, *Wiadomosci z dziejow Polski* (1928–9).

294. BA R153/ 379, Stadtarchiv Elbing to Brackmann 21.5.38.

295. BA R153/ 379, Doubek to Stadtarchiv Elbing 1.6.38.

296. BA R153 379, Doubek to RuPMdI, Foreign Office, Vomi etc. 1.6.38.

297. BA R153/ 379, RMdI to List and Bressendorf 13.10.38 and PuSte to Stadtarchiv Elbing 13.10.38 reporting this action.

298. BA R153/ 379, Stadtarchiv Elbing to PuSte 20.6.38. See also Professor Carstenn to the PuSte 1.7.38 and Stadtarchiv Elbing to the PuSte 28.3.39 and 8.5.39.

299. GStA Rep. 92. *Nachlass Brackmann* no. 81 Brackmann to Aubin 17.7.37.

300. BA R153/ 1550, NODFG Jahresbericht 1937–1938 1.4.37–31.3.38.

301. GStA Rep. 92 *Nachlass Brackmann* no. 82 list of subject advisors 18.2.38, p. 138.

302. GStA Rep. 92 *Nachlass Brackmann* no. 81 Brackmann to Aubin 17.7.37 suggesting the inclusion of Kleo Pleyer; BA R153/ 1220 Brackmann to Erich Maschke asking him to join.

303. BA R153/ 288, Reche to Brackmann 19.9.39.

304. BA R153/ 1571, 'Übersicht über den Haushalt der NODFG und PuSte 1934/1935' for the costs of the meeting in Neisse and Kahlberg to which the RMdI contributed 7,000 RMs and the Foreign Office 3,000 RMs.

305. BA R153/ 1278, VDA (Landesverband Sachsen) to NODFG 27.2.35.

306. BA R153/ 1269, 'NODFG Tagungen: Erzgebirgsheim bei Waldbärenburg-Schellerhau 30/3/1935–1/4/1935', p. 5.

307. BA R153/ 1269, 'NODFG Tagungen: Schellerhau', Erich Maschke, 'Wissenschaft und politische Praxis', p. 6.

308. BA R153/ 1220, Brackmann to Maschke 26.11.35 congratulating him on the call to Jena and Maschke to Papritz 10.1.39 reporting on work financed by the NODFG in which he remarked that he had been held up by his political–educational work for the *Reichsleitung* of the NSDAP and for his Ortsgruppe of the SA. See also BDC, *Erich Maschke* for details of his NSDAP/SA affiliations.

309. BA R153/ 882, 'Vertraulicher Bericht über die Tagung der NODFG in der Neumark und Grenzmark vom 4 bis 6 September 1935', p. 22.

310. BA R153/ 822, 'Vertraulicher Bericht über die Tagung der NODFG in der Neumark', pp. 5–26.

311. BA R153/ 1281, 'NODFG Tagung im Ostpommern' 6–8.5.37, p. 2.

312. BA R153/ 1281, 'NODFG Tagung im Ostpommern', p. 9.

313. BA R153/ 1281, 'NODFG Tagung im Ostpommern', Kaiser, 'Volkskundliche Probleme in der Kaschubei', pp. 14ff.

314. BA R153/ 1138, for the file on W. Koppe.

315. BA R153/ 1779, for the contract between the PuSte and the *Verlagsbuchhandlung* S. Hirzel Leipzig 11.1.37 and Hirzel to Papritz on the production costs.

316. BA R153/ 1573, for annual grants for *Jomsburg* from the RMdI of between 5,000 and 6,000 RMs from 1935 onwards.

317. GStA Rep. 92 *Nachlass Brackmann* no. 81 Papritz and Koppe prospectus for *Jomsburg* (no date).

318. GStA Rep. 92 *Nachlass Brackmann* no. 82 Brackmann to Aubin 18.11.37 'Es traf unmittelbar nach einer längeren Unterredung mit Ministerialdirektor Vollert bei mir ein, der wiederum, wie schon so oft, auf Popularisierung unserer wissenschaftlichen Ergebnisse drang.'

319. GStA Rep. 92 *Nachlass Brackmann* no. 81 Papritz and Koppe prospectus for *Jomsburg* (no date).

320. GStA Rep. 92 *Nachlass Brackmann* no. 81 Brackmann to Professor W. Vogel 21.12.36. See also BA R153/ 1783 Papritz and Koppe to Professor Ipsen 15.1.37 and BA R153/ 1590 Papritz to Dr Goeken (Foreign Office) 8.12.41 on the aims of the journal.

321. BA R153 1783, Brackmann to Professor J. Hansen 16.1.37 mentioning that both the RMdI and Foreign Office were subsidizing the journal. See also BA R153/ 1589 Kohte to Dr Gerner-Waldmann, Leitung der 'Bücherkunde' des Organs der Reichsstelle zur Förderung des deutschen Schrifttums 3.3.37 in which he remarked 'Wir bereiten diese Zeitschrift in engster Zusammenarbeit mit den für die Deutschtumspolitik zuständigen Stellen vor . . .'

322. BA R153/ 1589, Papritz to Verlagsbüchhändler Hirzel 5.10.37.

323. BA R153/ 1589, Papritz to Reichsstelle zur Förderung des Deutschen Schrifftums 7.10.37.

324. BA R153 1589, Papritz to Reichsstelle zur Förderung des Deutschen Schrifftums 7.10.37 enclosing the original and amended versions of the reference dated 14.9.37 and 12.10.37.

325. BA R153/ 1783, Papritz to Professor Ipsen 15.1.37.

326. BA R153/ 1783, PuSte to Werner Gieve 26.5.37 asking him to promote *Jomsburg* at the next meeting of the NSLB.

327. BA R153/ 1779, RM für Volksaufklärung und Propaganda to editors of *Jomsburg* 22.12.37.

328. BA R153/ 1587, Habicht to Koppe 16.5.37 and PuSte to Habicht 14.5.37.

329. BA R153/ 1587, Habicht to Koppe 16.5.37.

330. GStA Rep. 92 *Nachlass Brackmann* no. 82 W. Koppe to Brackmann 21.6.38.

331. GStA Rep. 92 *Nachlass Brackmann* no. 82 Brackmann to Professor Friedrich Metz 15.6.37.

332. BA R153/ 1587, PuSte to Dr W. Boek 26.10.37; Papritz to Werner Conze 8.7.37 and R153/1779 Aubin to Papritz 27.2.37.

333. *Dziennik Poranny* no. 195 24.8.37.

334. BA R153/ 1590 W. Koppe, to Aubin 28.11.38.

335. BA R153/ 1538, 'Bericht des Herrn Dr Koppe über seine Reise nach Riga 5/9/1937'.

336. BA R153/ 1590, Papritz to all PuSte staff 'Aufforderung zur Mitarbeit' 22.12.36.

337. Hildegard Schaeder, 'Die Ursachen des Untergangs des alten polnischen Staats im Urteil der heutigen polnischen Öffentlichkeit', *Jomsburg* (1937), 1, pp. 31–7; 'Die historischen Ostgrenzen Polens im Verhältnis zur heutigen polnischen Volkstumsmehrheit', *Jomsburg* (1938), 2, pp. 28–34; 'Die neuen polnischen Wojewodschaftsgrenzen', *Jomsburg* (1938), 2, pp. 197ff.; Franz Doubek, 'Die litauisch-polnische Volkstumsgrenze', *Jomsburg* (1938), 2, pp. 168ff.; 'Die zahlmässige Verbreitung des Deutschtums in Mittelpolen', *Jomsburg* (1938), 3, pp. 380ff.; Anton Loessner, 'Die polnische See- und Kolonialliga', *Jomsburg* (1937), 1, pp. 229ff.; 'Der polnische Offizier im Dienste der Wissenschaft', *Jomsburg* (1937), 2, pp. 315–29; 'Hinter der litauischen Mauer', *Jomsburg* (1938), 2, pp. 192ff., E. O. Kossmann, 'Stammesspiegel deutscher Dörfer in Mittelpolen', *Jomsburg* (1937), 3, pp. 329–42 etc.

338. 'Nachrichten', *Jomsburg* (1937), 1, p. 124.

339. Loessner, 'Die polnische See- und Kolonialliga', pp. 229f.

340. 'Der Bevölkerung der Juden in Polen nimmt ab', *Jomsburg* (1937), 1, p. 401.

341. BA R153/ 1589, Seraphim to Papritz 24.9.37.

342. BA R153/ 1589, Papritz to Seraphim 28.10.37.

343. BA R153/ 1589, Papritz to Seraphim 24.11.37.

344. BA R153/ 1589, Seraphim to Papritz 18.12.37; 15.12.37; 4.1.38 and 7.1.38.

345. Peter-Heinz Seraphim, 'Das ostjüdische Ghetto', *Jomsburg* (1937), 1, pp. 439–65, p. 442.

346. *Ibid.*, pp. 446–7.

347. *Ibid.*, p. 449.

348. *Ibid.*, p. 452.

349. *Ibid.*, p. 457.

350. *Ibid.*, p. 460.

351. *Ibid.*, p. 462.

352. BA R153/ 1218, Oberländer to Papritz 13.1.38. Oberländer was Director of the IoW until 1.1.38 and thereafter Professor of History at Greifswald from 1.4.38.

353. Manfred Weissbecker, 'Bund Deutscher Osten', pp. 308–11.

354. *Ibid.*, p. 311 citing T. Oberländer, *Der neue Weg* (Königsberg 1936) p. 3. On Oberländer see 'Drittes Reich im Kleinen', *Der Spiegel* 2.12.59, pp. 29–42, and, perhaps, more scurrilously, *Die Wahrheit über Oberländer. Braunbuch über die verbrecherische faschistische Vergangenheit des Bonner Ministers.* Ed. by the Ausschuss für Deutsche Einheit (no place or date of publication).

355. BA R153/ 1202, T. Oberländer, 'Der Kampf um das Vorfeld', 7.6.37, p. 4.

356. 'Der Kampf um das Vorfeld', pp. 6–7.

357. 'Der Kampf um das Vorfeld', pp. 8–10.

358. Manfred Weissbecker, 'Bund Deutscher Osten', p. 312.

359. BA R153/ 1202, BDO (Benninghaus) to PuSte 8.3.37 and PuSte to Schieche 12.3.37; BDO invitation to the conference in Passau 4–5.12.37 including list of lectures to be delivered and BDO Landesgruppe Gross-Berlin to the PuSte 9.12.37.

360. BA R153/ 1202, BDO (Benninghaus) to Papritz 26.3.38.

361. BA R153/ 1202, PuSte to BDO 25.4.38.

362. BA R153/ 2, Göring to Brackmann 30.9.36.

363. BA R153/ 2, PuSte memo 3.11.36.

364. BA R153/ 2, PuSte memo 13.5.38.

365. Ringer, *Decline of the German Mandarins*, p. 54.

366. Hermann Meinert, 'Albert Brackmann und das deutsche Archivwesen', *Archivalische Zeitschrift* (1954), 49, p. 137.

367. Helmut Heiber, *Walter Frank und sein Reichsinstitut für Geschichte des neuen Deutschlands* (Stuttgart 1966), p. 855.

368. BDC, *Brackmann SS-Hauptsturmführer* Prof. Eckhardt to SS-*Gruppenführer* Wolff 7.7.37; Heiber, *Walter Frank*, p. 856.

369. GStA Rep. 92 *Nachlass Brackmann* no. 61 Brackmann to Himmler 2.11.38. For Himmler and the Ottonians see *Das Schwarze Korps* (8 July 1937) 'Herr Heinrich hat nun seine Ruhe' and also Bernd Wegner, *Hitlers Politische Soldaten: Die Waffen-SS 1933–1945* (Paderborn 1982), pp. 61–2.

370. GStA Rep. 92 *Nachlass Brackmann* no. 61 Brackmann to SS-*Hauptsturmführer* R. Brandt (Der RF-SS Persönlicher Stab) 26.5.39.

371. GStA Rep. 92 *Nachlass Brackmann* no. 61 SS-*Hauptsturmführer* Brandt to Brackmann 21.6.39.

372. BA R153/ 1393, Der RF-SS Persönlicher Stab to the PuSte 15.9.39.

373. GStA Rep. 92 *Nachlass Brackmann* no. 44 SS-*Untersturmführer* Kaiser to Brackmann 26.9.39; see M. H. Kater, *Das 'Ahnenerbe' der SS 1935–1945. Ein Beitrag zur Kulturpolitik des Dritten Reiches* (Stuttgart 1974), pp. 199 for brief discussion of Brackmann's booklet.

374. HStA *Nachlass Papritz* 340, C12 g, Brackmann to Papritz 5.4.46.

375. BA NS 21/444 Brackmann to the *Ahnenerbe-Stiftungs Verlag* 28.9.39.

376. BA NS 21/444 *Ahnenerbe-Stiftung* to SS-Standartenführer Prof. Dr Six (SD-Hauptamt) 21.11.39; on Six see Gerd Voigt, 'Methoden der „Ost-forschung"', *Zeitschrift für Geschichtswissenschaft* (1959), 7, p. 1790 and note 51. Six was gaoled by a West German court in 1948 for twenty years for murdering Soviet POWs in Smolensk.

377. BA NS 21/444, *Ahnenerbe Verlag* memo 7.5.1940 on the sales figures.

378. GStA Rep. 92 *Nachlass Brackmann* no. 44 *Ahnenerbe Stiftung-Verlag* to Brackmann 20.12.39 for his present and Brackmann to SS-*Untersturmführer* Kaiser 6.1.40.

379. Albert Brackmann, *Krisis und Aufbau in Osteuropa. Ein weltgeschicht-liches Bild* (*Ahnenerbe-Stiftung Verlag* Berlin 1939), p. 11.

380. *Ibid.*, p. 13.

381. *Ibid.*, p. 44.

382. *Ibid.*, p. 46.

383. *Ibid.*, p. 46.

384. *Ibid.*, p. 53.

385. *Ibid.*, p. 54.

386. *Ibid.*, pp. 58–61.

387. *Ibid.*, p. 64.

388. *Ibid.*, p. 68.

389. BDC, *Brackmann*, Memorandum on a telephone conversation between SS-*Untersturmführer* Kaiser and SS-*Hauptsturmführer* Prof. Dr Harmjanz 30.9.39 concerning Brackmann: 'B. hängt nach seiner Her-kunft noch mit einem gewissen Kreis mehr oder weniger reaktionären Leuten zusammen, dass man deshalb mit Erfolg versucht hat, ihn herauszubugsieren, war aber unrecht. B. ist ein sehr williger Mann. Er ist ein wenig machthungrig. Aus den verschiedensten Gründen ist er im Laufe der Zeit für SS und SD eine Art wilder Mann geworden, das stimmt aber nicht B. ist völlig falsch, ja sogar niederträchtig behandelt worden. Man hat ihn, der ein Beamter in sehr hoher Dienststellung war, offensichtlich falsch behandelt. Und wenn B. heute hier und da sich quergelegt hat, so geschah das nicht aus politischen, sondern persönlich-menschlichen Gründen.'

390. BDC, *Brackmann*, SS-*Untersturmführer* Kaiser, 'Notiz für Herrn Hart-wich', 20.1.40.

4. WAR

1. GStA Rep. 92 *Nachlass Brackmann*, no. 3, Aubin to Brackmann 25.1.39.

2. GStA Rep. 92 *Nachlass Brackmann*, no. 83, Aubin to Brackmann 25.1.39. Wohin neuestens ein Teil der deutschen Wissenschaft und namentlich der Jugend segelt, darüber haben Sie, wie ich sehe, ebenso wenig einen Zweifel wie ich. Diese Leute können es gar nicht abwarten, sich in einen hemmungslosen Imperialismus hineinzustürzen. Geben Sie acht, wie bald Otto I und Friedrich I obenauf sein werden, weil sie das Beispiel gegeben haben, wie man eine 'deutsche Ordnung' aufzurichten hat. Diese Männer werden die deutsche Wissenschaft um ihren letzten Kredit bringen.

3. BA R153/ 6, 'Einsatz der PuSte in und nach dem Kriege' 30.11.39, pp. 3–4.

4. BA R153/ 6, 'Einsatz der PuSte', p. 5.

5. BA R153/ 6, 'Einsatz der PuSte', p. 6.

6. BA R153/ 6, 'Einsatz der PuSte', p. 7.

7. BA R153/ 6, Papritz to *Gauschulungsleiter* Loebsack 7.12.39.

8. GStA Rep. 92 *Nachlass Brackmann* no. 83, Brackmann to Prof. F. Metz 23.9.39.

9. Interview with Dr Papritz in Marburg 11.8.86 in the company of Professor R. Schmidt of the Herder Institute, Marburg.

10. HStA *Nachlass Papritz* 340, C12dI, Foreign Office 'Ressort- Besprechung des Grenzausschusses' 26.10.38, p. 16, and 'Bericht über die Tätigkeit des (deutschen) Ausschusses für die endgültige deutsch-tschechoslovakische Grenzziehung' no date, p. 4.

11. HStA *Nachlass Papritz* 340, C12dI, RMdI memorandum 9.10.38, on a conversation between Göring and Dr W. Branzcik, and map bearing Göring's alterations.

12. M. Broszat, *Nationalsozialistische Polenpolitik 1939–1945* (Frankfurt am Main 1965$_2$), pp. 31–2, and C. Klessmann, *Die Selbstbehauptung einer Nation. NS-Kulturpolitik und polnische Widerstandsbewegung. Studien zur modernen Geschichte*, eds. F. Fischer, K.-D. Grothusen and G. Moltmann (Düsseldorf 1971), pp. 29–31.

13. Broszat, *Nationalsozialistische Polenpolitik*, p. 37.

14. *Ibid.*, pp. 34–7.

15. HStA *Nachlass Papritz* 340, C12d2, 'Grenzkommission für Grenzstrecke von westlich Krakau bis San', 'Reichsgau Beskidenland', no date, pp. 4–5 on ethnic minorities.

16. *Ibid.*, pp. 6–7. See also 'Bemerkungen zum Verlauf der Grenze des geplanten Reichsgaues Beskidenland im Norden', points 1–6, for the elasticity of the ethnic criteria employed.

17. Broszat, *Nationalsozialistische Polenpolitik*, pp. 36–7 for Wagner and these attempts to retract the frontiers of Silesia, and BA R153/ 774, PuSte (Frank Doubek) report on Wagner's proposals 23.2.40, p. 3.

18. Broszat, *Nationalsozialistische Polenpolitik*, p. 37.

19. *Ibid.*, pp. 35–6.

20. BA R153/ 774, RMdI to the PuSte 23.12.39, enclosing report by the *Oberpräsident* in Königsberg (Koch) dated 15.12.39, with a request for comment. PuSte report (marked 'Secret') 5.1.40 on Roch's proposals.

21. For the best account of the evolution of the Ethnic Liaison Office see Hans-Adolf Jacobsen, *Nationalsozialistische Aussenpolitik 1933–1938* (Frankfurt am Main 1968), pp. 234ff. There is also a succinct account in Heinz Höhne, *The Order of the Death's Head. The Story of Hitler's SS*, translated by R. Barry (London 1972), pp. 254–5; see also R. Koehl's *RKFDV: German Resettlement and Population Policy 1939–1945. A History of the Reich Commission for the Strengthening of Germandom* (Cambridge, Mass. 1957), pp. 28–39.

22. Jakobsen, *Nationalsozialistische Aussenpolitik*, pp. 245–6 on the VOMI powers of veto and sums involved and pp. 246ff. for the removal of Steinacher and Oberländer. On Oberländer's fall see also M. Weiss-becker, 'Bund Deutscher Osten', *Lexikon zur Parteigeschichte* (Leipzig 1983), 1, pp. 313, and M. Rothbarth, 'Bund Deutscher Osten – Instrument des aggressiven faschistischen deutschen Imperialismus', *Wissenschaftliche Zeitschrift der Universität Rostock* (1972), 32, p. 217.

23. Koehl, *RKFDV: German Resettlement and Population Policy*, p. 37.

24. BA R153/ 110, (VOMI) Dr Wilhelm Luig to Papritz 7.4.38.

25. BA R153/ 110, (VOMI) 'Besprechung am 22.4.38 über ein Kleinmassstäbliches Kartenbild des deutschen Volkstums' 22.4.38.

26. BA R153/ 110, Dr K. C. von Loesch, 'Bemerkungen zu den Ergebnissen der Besprechung über grossmassstäbige Volkstumskarten mit Flächenkolorit am 22/4/38' 17.5.38, p. 2.

27. BA R153/ 110, minutes of a meeting in the VOMI offices to discuss 'Darstellung der deutschen Volksgrenze im Osten' 30.5.38, pp. 1–4.

28. Broszat, *Nationalsozialistische Polenpolitik*, pp. 19–20; Höhne, *The Order of the Death's Head*, pp. 284–5; for the decree dated 7 October 1939, Koehl, *RKFDV: German Resettlement and Population Policy*, pp. 247–9, and, for a discussion of the administrative structure of the RKFDV, see Hans Buchheim, 'Die SS – das Herrschaftsinstrunent', in H. Buchheim, M. Broszat, H.-A. Jakobsen and H. Krausnick, *Anatomie des SS – Staates* (Munich 1979), 1, pp. 182ff.

29. Koehl, *RKFDV: German Resettlement and Population Policy*, pp. 64–8, and Buchheim, 'Die SS – das Herrschaftsinstrument', pp. 187–95 for the different competences of Lorenz's and Greifelt's offices. The latter was created in June 1939 in order to resettle the South Tyrolean Germans.

Its title was changed in mid-October 1939 from 'Leitstelle für Ein- und Rückwanderung' to 'Dienststelle des RKFDV', with six departments, and in June 1941 to the 'Stabshauptamt' (StHA/RKF), with three subgroups of offices (A, B, C), each containing three departments. In June 1941 VOMI also became one of the SS *Hauptämter* with eleven departments. The RuSHA had a sort of mobile competence throughout the RKFDV sphere of activities, with outlying offices in Prague and Łódź and responsibility for racial investigations.

30. Koehl, *RKFDV: German Resettlement and Population Policy*, pp. 56–61.

31. *Ibid.*, pp. 70–3; on Meyer, see also Helmut Heiber, 'Der Generalplan Ost', *VfZG* (1958), 6, pp. 289–92, and Wolfgang Benz, 'Der Generalplan Ost. Zur Germanisierungspolitik des NS-Regimes in den besetzten Ostgebieten 1939–1945', in *Die Vertreibung der Deutschen aus dem Osten*, ed. Wolfgang Benz (Frankfurt am Main 1985), pp. 43–4.

32. BA R153/ 2105, Dr von Dietel (RFSS/RKDFV) to the PuSte 29.6.40; SS-*Brigadeführer* Greifelt to the PuSte 1.7.40; and W. Kohte to SS-*Brigadeführer* Greifelt 9.7.40. PuSte maps produced between 1.4.40 and 1.4.41 for the RKFDV included maps on the resettlement of the Volhynian Germans in the *Warthegau* and on the Kashubians; see BA R153/ 1143, 'Zusammenstellung der vom 1/4/1940 bis 141940 bei uns hergestellten wichtigsten Karten', Section C.

33. BA R153/ 1143, PuSte memorandum (W. Kohte) 15.8.40 on the offer to Doubek. For the structure of Meyer's department see BDC, RF-SS 32, RKFDV, 'Organisation und Geschäftsverteilungsplan des Stabshauptamtes 1/8/1942, p. 34 Amt Planung (VI) 1. Bestandsaufnahme and Raumuntersuchung (Doubek)'.

34. BA R153/ 1143, Papritz to RMdI 22.10.41.

35. BA R153/ 1143, SS-*Gruppenführer* Greifelt to RMdI 6.10.41 and RMdl to SS-*Gruppenführer* Greifelt 8.11.41.

36. BA R153/ 1143, PuSte 'Allgemeiner Umlauf' timetable for Doubek 16.1.42 signed by Papritz.

37. BA R153/ 1143, 'Zusammenstellung der vom 1/4/1940 bis 1/4/1940 bei uns hergestellten wichtigsten Karten' Section C 10 and 11. See also BA R153/ 1517, 'Jahresbericht 1941/1942 der NODFG and der PuSte', pp. 7–8 for list of maps produced for the RF-SS, and BA R153/ 1521, PuSte, 'Jahresbericht 1941/42', p. 10 for list of maps produced for the SS and Doubek, 'Bericht über meine dienstliche and wissenschaftliche Tätigheit im Kalenderjahr 1941', p. 2 nos. 18–22.

38. BA R153/ 1143, Prof. Konrad Meyer RKFDV IIa to PuSte 2.12.41 and Meyer to Papritz 3.2.42 Wie sehr ich mich freue, wenn unsere Dienststellen künftig eng zusammenarbeiten; BA R153/ 1521, PuSte 'Jahresbericht 1941/42', p. 10 on Doubek's office with the RKFDV.

39. BA R153/ 286, PuSte memorandum on conversation with Dr Däumling 27.10.39.

40. BA R153/ 286, RSHA to PuSte 2.11.39 acknowledging 'Anteil der jüdischen Bevölkerung an der Gesamtbevölkerung der polnischen Haupt- und Kreisstädte und sonstigen Städten über 10,000 Einwohner innerhalb des deutschen Interessengebietes', 31.10.39.

41. BA R153/ 291, Aubin to Brackmann 18.9.39.

42. BA R153/ 291, 'Arbeitsplan für die Denkschrift über die ostdeutsche Reichs- und Volkstumsgrenze'. Protocol of a meeting in Breslau 28.9.39.

43. BA R153/ 291, W. Kohte (PuSte) to the *Präsident* of the Reich's Statistic Office 3.10.39 and GStA to the PuSte with references on Polish seasonal workers 11.10.39.

44. BA R153/ 291, PuSte paper, 'Bevölkerungstragen im Polen' 1.11.39, p. 1.

45. *Ibid.*, p. 2.

46. *Ibid.*, p. 4.

47. *Ibid.*, p. 7.

48. BA R153/ 288, Professor Otto Reche to Brackmann 19.9.39.

49. BA R153/ 288, Brackmann to Otto Reche 22.9.39. See also GStA Rep. 92 *Nachlass Brackmann*, no. 83, Brackmann to Prof. F. Metz, 'Man will hier aus wirtschaftlichen Gründen soviel Gebiete in das Reich mit hineinbeziehen dass wir gegen 4× 100, 000 waschechte Polen bekommen würden, eine ungeheuere Gefahr für das deutsche Volkstum'.

50. BA R153/ 288, Otto Reche to Brackmann 24.9.39.

51. BA R153/ 288, Otto Reche, 'Leitsätze zur bevölkerungspolitischen Sicherung des deutschen Ostens' 24.9.1939, pp. 1–6.

52. BA R153/ 288, Brackmann to Essen (RMdI) 28.9.39.

53. BA R153/ 288, Brackmann to Reche 28.9.39.

54. BA R153/ 288, Reche to Brackmann 29.9.39.

55. BA R153/ 288, Reche to Brackmann 11.10.39.

56. BA R153/ 288, Brackmann to Reche 13.10.39.

57. BA R153/ 288, Reche to Brackmann 19.10.39.

58. BA R153/ 288, Brackmann to Reche 20.10.39.

59. BA R153/ 288, Reche to Brackmann 26.10.39.

60. BA R153/ 288, Brackmann to Reche 1.11.39.

61. BA R153/ 288, Reche to Brackmann, 14.11.39.

62. BA R153/ 288, Brackmann to Reche, 22.11.39.

63. BDC *Reche*, Otto Reche to SS-*Gruppenführer* Günther Pancke 2.10.39. Pancke rapidly became a one-man clearing house for the projected involvement of academic racial experts. See for example BDC *Friedrich Lenz*. Lenz was a professor at the *Institut für Rassenhygiene* at Berlin University. On 5.1.40 he sent Pancke some comments ('Bemerkungen zur Umsiedlung unter dem Gesichtspunkt der Rassenpflege'). Pancke to Lenz 13.1.40, 'Der Reichsführer-SS and damit wir als seiner Durchführ-

ungsorgane stehen auf genau demselben Standpunkt wie Sie. Es wäre daher eine enge Zusammenarbeit auch uns sehr erwünscht'. On Pancke see BDC *Pancke*, SS service sheet.

64. BDC *Reche* Pancke to Reche 8.11.39 explaining Lorenz's limited competence and requesting a meeting on Monday 13 November 1939.

65. BDC *Reche* Reche to Pancke 14.11.39 and Reche to Pancke 18.11.39 with 'Entwurf für einen bevölkerungsstadstischen Fragebogen'.

66. BDC *Reche* Pancke to Reche 22.11.39.

67. BDC *Reche* Reche to Pancke 10.1.40. Pancke's reply on 13.1.40 was heavy with unintended irony: 'Bezüglich der Gefahr, dass rassisch nicht einwand freie Menschen in die neuen Ostprovinzen hereinkommen, brauchen Sie nicht zu beunruhigen, da vom Reichsführer-SS Vorkehrungen getroffen und noch beabsichtigt sind, die dass ausschliessen.'

68. BDC *Reche* SS-*Brigadeführer* Otto Hoffmann to SS-*Oberführer* Prof. Dr Saure (Prague) 19.12.40, 'Reche ist mit seinen Ausführungen völlig auf dem richtigen Wege, wenn er davon spricht, dass es ausserordentlich wichtig ist, festzustellen, inwieweit im Protektorat noch Germanen leben und welchen Umfang die Slawisierung angenommen hat. Es ist ausserordentlich wichtig, dass baldmöglichst in einer geeigneten Form – ich denke, in Zusammenarbeit mit dem Gesundheitswesen – an die Erhebung des Volkstums im Protektorat herangegangen und gemeinschaftlich mit dem Chef der Ordnungspolizei eine Tätigkeit durchgeführt werden könnte.'

69. BDC *Reche* Reche to Pancke 15.5.40 enclosing a copy of Reche to Rudolf Hess 15.5.40.

70. BDC *Reche* SS-*Brigadeführer* Otto Hoffmann to Reche 2.12.41.

71. Walter Kuhn, 'Eine Jugend für die Sprachinselforschung', *Jahrbuch der Schlesischen Friedrich-Wilhelms-Universität zu Breslau* (1982), 23, p. 269.

72. BA R153/ 289, Walter Kuhn to Theodor Schieder 29.9.39 enclosing the memorandum.

73. W. Kuhn, 'Deutsche Dörfer in Mittelpolen, unmittelbar jenseits der alten Reichsgrenze' (Geheim!), dated 5.9.39.

74. *Ibid.*, p. 2.

75. *Ibid.*, p. 3.

76. *Ibid.*, p. 5.

77. *Ibid.*, pp. 6–7.

78. *Ibid.*, p. 8.

79. *Ibid.*, pp. 8–9.

80. On the activities of the EWZ in Łódź see Koehl, *RKFDV: German Resettlement and Population Policy*, pp. 104–10; and BA R57 DAI/1386 Prof. Dr W. Kuhn (Breslau) to the Chef der Sicherheitspolizei and des SD-Einwandererzentrale Nord-Ost 'Lodsch' 22.1.40, 'Stammesgruppen,

Bodenverhältnisse, Anbaufrüchte usw. in Galizien und Wolhynien und die sich daraus für die Umsiedlung ergebenden Gesichtspunkte', p. 4.

81. Kuhn, 'Stammesgruppen usw.', p. 6.
82. *Ibid.*, p. 3.
83. *Ibid.*, p. 13.
84. Hans Frhr. von Rosen, *Wolhynienfahrt 1926. Schriften der J. G. Herder Bibliothek* (Siegen 1982), 10, pp. 28–9.
85. Kuhn, 'Stammesgruppen, Bodenverhältnisse', Anbaufrüchte usw.', p. 14.
86. *Ibid.*, 'Stellungnahme', W. Gradmann, p. 15.
87. Broszat, *Nationalsozialistische Polenpolitik*, p. 102.
88. *Ibid.*, p. 97, citing a report by Karl Schoepke, who was part of a VOMI team.
89. For a good discussion of repatriation procedures see Koehl, *RKFDV: German Resettlement and Population Policy*, pp. 104–10; the material is largely based upon Werner Gradmann, 'Die Erfassung der Umsiedler', *Zeitschrift für Politik* (1942), 32, pp. 346–51.
90. *Ibid.*, p. 110.
91. SS-*Hauptsturmführer* Dr K. Lück, 'Deutsche Volksgruppen aus dem Osten kehren helm ins Vaterland', *Tornisterschrift des Oberkommandos der Wehrmacht* (1941), Heft 19, p. 1. Lück's pamphlet was given a print run of 945,000 copies; see BA R153/ 1385, Lück to Papritz 4.3.41. Lück joined the SS on 5 May 1940. By November 1940, at the latest, he was involved in ethnic studies of repatriates in the Warthegau. See BDC, *Lück*, SS-*Sturmbannführer* Dr Brandt to RF-SS 28.11.40 and Lück's SS service sheet.
92. *Ibid.*, p. 4.
93. *Ibid.*, p. 9.
94. *Ibid.*, p. 5.
95. *Ibid.*, p. 7.
96. *Ibid.*, 'Bilder aus dem deutschen Leben im Nordosten', pp. 16–18.
97. Ibid., p. 23.
98. *Ibid.*, p. 30. Members of the PuSte also served up accounts of resettlements; see W. Kohte, 'Arbeit im Osten – Heimat im Osten', *Wille und Macht* (1941), 16, pp. 9–14.
99. Helmut Krausnick, *Hitlers Einsatzgruppen. Die Truppen des Weltanschauungskrieges 1938–1942* (Frankfurt am Main 1985), p. 45.
100. Martin Broszat, *Zweihundert Jahre deutsche Polenpolitik*, pp. 281–2.
101. Krausnick, *Hitlers Einsatzgruppen*, p. 46.
102. *Ibid.*, pp. 48–50.
103. Broszat, *Nationalsozialistische Polenpolitik*, p. 48; *Zweihundert Jahre deutsche Polenpolitik*, p. 282; Tomasz Szarota, 'Poland and Poles in German Eyes during World War II', *Polish Western Affairs* (1978), 19, p. 233.

104. GStA Rep. 92 *Nachlass Brackmann* no. 83 Brackmann to Prof. F. Metz describing Lück's whereabouts 23.9.39. BDC, *Lattermann*, SS service sheet. Lattermann joined the SS on 9 November 1940, becoming an SS-*Obersturmführer* a year later.

105. For Lattermann's membership of the SS see R153/ 1233, RMdI to the PuSte enclosing Lattermann's c.v., and *Marsch der Deutschen in Polen. Deutsche Volksgenossen im ehemaligen Polen berichten über Erlebisse in den Septembertagen 1939.* Zusammengestellt und bearbeitet von Dr Kurt Lück (Berlin 1940), p. 7.

106. *Ibid.*, p. 9.

107. *Ibid.*, p. 10. There was of course no basis for this claim.

108. *Ibid.*, p. 16.

109. *Ibid.*, p. 23.

110. *Ibid.*, pp. 25–6 and 113–14 for the very short periods of detention.

111. *Ibid.*, p. 35.

112. *Ibid.*, p. 38.

113. *Ibid.*, p. 27.

114. *Ibid.*, pp. 63–7.

115. Broszat, *Nationalsozialistische Polenpolitik*, p. 119; Koehl, *RKFDV: German Resettlement and Population Policy*, p. 81.

116. Broszat, *Nationalsozialistische Polenpolitik*, pp. 121–2.

117. *Ibid.*, pp. 122–5 and p. 113 n 3 for removal to concentration camps of the 'asocial' and erbiologisch minderwertig.

118. *Ibid.*, p. 130 n 3, citing BA R43II/ 1332, Himmler to Forster 26.11.41.

119. BA R153/ 1517, 'Jahresbericht 1941/1942 der NODFG and der PuSte' p. 3, and R153/810, RMdI to the PuSte 12.3.41 on the collection of cards from the *Sicherheitspolizei* and *Statistischen Reichsamts*.

120. BA R153/ 810, RMdI 'Vermerk betr. Volkstumskartei' June 1941, p. 1.

121. BA R153/ 810, RMdI 'Vermerk betr. Volkstumskartei' June 1941, p. 5; Götz Aly and Karl Heinz Roth, *Die restlose Erfassung: Volkszählen, Identifizieren, Aussondern im Nationalsozialismus*, pp. 49–50. The importance of 'sorting the population' as a precondition for 'evacuating the lesser races' was recognized by Heydrich in the 'Protektorat'. These measures were camouflaged as an 'ethnic census'. I am grateful to Wolfgang Wippermann for this reference.

122. HStA *Nachlass* Papritz 340, C12d 64 a, b, c, d, *Kleine Umsiedlungsspiegel* July 1942, February 1943, July 1943 and d, Bericht über den Stand der Um- und Ansiedlung am 1.10.42, 1.12.40 and October 1944, pp. 11–13.

123. C. Klessmann, *Die Selbsbehauptung einer Nation*, pp. 39ff.

124. Broszat, *Nationalsozialistische Polenpolitik*, pp. 71–2.

125. *Ibid.* pp. 52 and 72; Frank was the NSDAP's *Starjurist* as founder of the NS-*Juristenbund* (*NS-Rechtswahrer-Bund*), and from 1933 President

of the *Akademie für Deutsches Recht*. Many of his *Akademie* colleagues, including Lasch, Bühler, Weh and Coblitz, the Director of the IdO, surfaced later in senior positions in the *Generalgouvernement*. On this see C. Klessmann, 'Der Generalgouverneur Hans Frank', *VjZG* (1971), 19, pp. 249–50. For an unflattering account of Frank's court see Curzio Malaparte, *Kaput* (Frankfurt am Main 1982), Part Two, pp. 87ff.

126. Broszat, *Nationalsozialistische Polenpolitik*, p. 72, and *Zweihundert Jahre deutsche Polenpolitik*, pp. 294–5.

127. Broszat, *Nationalsozialistische Polenpolitik*, p. 73 n 1.

128. BA R153/ 284, PuSte memorandum on conversation with Dr Triebe (Foreign Office) 8.9.39 and PuSte to Dr Essen (RMdI) 12.9.39 with a list of nine ethnic German lawyers and economists.

129. BA R153/ 284, Kossmann to the RMdI 14.11.39.

130. BA R153/ 284, PuSte memorandum 12.9.39 and Kossmann to Essen 23.12.39.

131. BA R153/ 284 Verlag S. Hirzel to Papritz 20.11.39 and 27.11.39 and Verlag Oldenbourg to PuSte 18.9.39.

132. BA R153/ 284 PuSte to Dr Essen (RMdI) 5.4.40.

133. BA R153/ 284 RMdI to Reichsstatthalter in Danzig and Posen, Oberpräsidenten in Königsberg and Breslau 5.4.1940, and Der Landrat des Rreises Rippin to the PuSte 3.4.40 ordering books.

134. BA R153 284, Aubin to Verlag Hirzel 11.3.40.

135. GStA Rep. 92 *Nachlass Brackmann* no. 84, Aubin to Brackmann 22.3.40.

136. GStA Rep. 92 *Nachlass Brackmann* no. 84, Brackmann to Aubin 27.3.40.

137. GStA Rep. 92 *Nachlass Brackmann* no. 84, 'Eröffnungsansprache in der Sitzung der Nord- und Ostdeutschen Forschungsgemeinschaft am 23 Januar 1940', p. 5 (p. 229).

138. Krausnick, *Hitlers Einsatzgruppen*, pp. 27f., and Broszat, *Zweihundert Jahre deutsche Polenpolitik*, p. 280.

139. Krausnick, *Hitlers Einsatzgruppen*, p. 36; Broszat, *Nationalsozialistische Polenpolitik*, p.44.

140. BA R153/ 291, Aubin to Brackmann 18.9.39 and BA R153/ 1387, Kauder to Papritz, 16.9.39.

141. BA R153/ 1387, Kauder to Papritz 11.10.39 and 24.10.39. Kauder shortly became Director of the Upper Silesian *Landesbibliothek* in Beuthen-Kattowitz and in 1942 director of the municipal library in Kattowitz; see W. Kuhn, 'Das Lebenswerk Viktor Kauders', *Der Kulturwart* (1969), 17, p. 9. Younger ethnic German scholars like Richard Breyer were given grants to study at the Osteuropa-Institut by W. Kuhn; see BA R153/ 1385, Alfred Lattermann to W. Kohte 27.8.40.

142. Interview with Dr Kossmann in Marburg 8.8.86.

143. BA R153/ 304, PuSte to H. Frank 6.12.39.

144. BA R153/ 1545, Report of the NODFG conference held in Katowice on 14.12.39. Only 20 *Ostforscher* attended and the conference was a short one. On 23.11.39 Kohte applied for travel passes for Aubin, Brackmann, Papritz, Kohte, Doubek, Kossmann, Sappok and Weidhaas to visit the *Generalgouvernement*; see BA R153/ 304, Kohte memo 23.11.39; for the minutes of the conference see GStA Rep. 92 *Nachlass* Brackmann no. 85, pp. 397ff.

145. GStA Rep. 92 *Nachlass Brackmann* no. 83, Aubin to Brackmann 16.12.39.

146. GStA Rep. 92 *Nachlass Brackmann* no. 83, Hans Frank to the PuSte 15.12.39.

147. BA R153 304, PuSte to Generalgouvernement Abt. Innere Verwaltung 29.1.40 referring to an agreement between Frank, Papritz and Aubin on 15.12.39 to establish the sub-branch, and PuSte memorandum 11.1.40 on Frank's choice of Sappok on 19.12.39 to run the sub-branch and the date on which it opened.

148. BA R153/ 304, budget proposals for the sub-branch 19.2.40, and BA R153/ 784, PuSte 'Etatsentwurf für die geplanten Nebenstelle der PuSte des RMdI' 19.2.40.

149. BA R153/ 304, G. Sappok, 'Ziele und Aufgaben der Nebenstelle Krakau der PuSte Berlin' 19.2.40, pp. 2–4, and BA R153/ 784 'Übersicht über die von der Nebenstelle Krakau der PuSte in Arbeit genommenen oder geplanten wissenschaftlichen Forschungsarbeiten und Publikationen' 8.4.40.

150. BA R153/ 304, Sappok to Brackmann 26.2.40. On Semkowicz see Stanislaw Gawęda, *Die Jagiellonische Universität in der Zeit der faschistischen Okkupation 1939–1945. Veröffentlichung der Friedrich-Schiller-Universität Jena* (Jena 1981), p. 53 and pp. 15–27, and Henryk Batowski, 'Nazi Germany and Jagiellonian University', *Polish Western Affairs* (1978), 19, pp. 113–20 for the *Sonderaktion Krakau* of 6 November 1939; see also C. Klessmann, *Die Selbstbehauptung einer Nation*, pp. 54–6, and his 'Osteuropaforschung und Lebensraumpolitik im Dritten Reich', in *Wissenschaft im Dritten Reich*, ed. P. Lundgreen (Frankfurt am Main 1985), p. 364.

151. BA R153/ 304, Sappok to Brackmann 26.2.40.

152. BA R153/ 304, Sappok to Herr Pappke (Gestapo Krakau) 26.2.40.

153. Gawęda, *Die Jagiellonische Universität*, p. 53.

154. BA R153/ 304, Sappok to the PuSte H.4.40; R 52 II/ 176, Hans Frank, *Tagebuch*, 1940, vol. 2/i (April 1940), 10.4.40, p. 286.

155. BA R153/ 1197, Sappok to the PuSte 12.4.40. On the IdO see G. Voigt, 'Das "Institut für deutsche Ostarbeit" in Krakau', in *September 1939*,

ed. Basil Spiru (Berlin 1939), pp. 109ff.; C. Klessmann, *Die Selbstbe-hauptung einer Nation*, pp. 61ff.; Rudi Goguel, 'Über die Mitwirkung deutsche Wissenschaftler', pp. 132ff. See also Part III, ch. 5 below.

156. BA R153 H97, Sappok to Brackmann 18.4.40.

157. BA R153/ 1197 Aubin to Brackmann 24.4.40 and 27.4.40 with a list of proposed appointments. Aubin had a ten-minute audience with Frank on 21.4.40; see BA R 52 II/176, Hans Frank, *Tagebuch*, 1940, vol. 2/i (April 1940), 21.4.40, p. 335.

158. BA R153/ 1197 Aubin to Seyss-Inquart 27.4.40, pp. 1–6.

159. BAS R153/ 1197, Brackmann to Aubin 30.4.40.

160. BA R153/ 1197, 'Arbeitstagung da IdO 20–22/6/1940' programme.

161. 'Generalgouverneur Frank übergibt Ordensfahnen an Gauleiter Forster', *Das Generalgouvernement* (18.5.40), no. 116, p. 1. On the ceremony see Sven Ekdahl, *Die Schlacht bei Tannenberg 1410. Quellenkritische Untersuchung* (West Berlin 1982), 1, pp. 25 and 65–6, and Wipper-mann, *Der Ordensstaat als Ideologie*, p. 360.

162. BA R153/ 525, Erich Keyser to the PuSte 20.3.40.

163. BA R153/ 525, Sappok to the PuSte 23.3.40.

164. BA R153/ 525, PuSte to Keyser 1.4.40 and Keyser to the PuSte 4.4.40.

165. BA R153/ 525 Sappok to the PuSte 7.5.40.

166. 'Alte Ordensfahnen kehren zurück', *Berliner Morgenaüsgabe* 26.4.40. See also Herder Institut, Marburg, 32, XV, JZ2 PuSte, *Nordostberichte* no. 35, 'Die Deutschordensfahnen in der Marienburg', 29.5.40, pp. 1–3, and 'Vom Wawel zur Marienburg', *Ostland* (1940), 11, pp. 262–5.

167. BA R153/ 951, G. Sappok, 'Richtlinien für die Umbenennung von Strassennamen in den Städten des Generalgouvernements' 22.8.40.

168. BA R153/ 1035, PuSte to the Oberpräsident der Provinz Schlesien 31.1.40 naming Sappok as their representative on the commission, and 'Protokoll über die Besprechung der Kommission über die Ortsnamen-änderungen in den eingegliederten Ostgebieten der Provinz Schlesien' 19.3.40 for lists of names and *modus operandi*.

169. BA R153/ 1035, Der Graf von Matuschka to the RMdI 12.11.40.

170. BA R153/ 790, Reichsstatthalter im Reichsgau Wartheland to the RMdI 2.11.40.

171. BA R153/ 1131, W. Kohte, 'Bericht über meine Tätigkeit im Kalender-jahr 1941', p. 2.

172. *Krakau. Hauptstadt des deutschen Generalgouvernements Polen. Deutsche Städte-Führer im Osten*, eds. J. Papritz and G. Sappok (Leipzig 1940), pp. v–vi.

173. *Ibid.*, p. 8.

174. *Ibid.*, p 11

175. *Ibid.*, pp. 12–15.

176. *Ibid.*, p. 16.

177. *Ibid.*, p. 27.

178. *Ibid.*, p. 31.

179. *Ibid.*, p. 33.

180. *Ibid.*, p. 33.

181. BA R153/ 1385, Kohte PuSte memorandum 9.3.39.

182. BA R153/ 1385, PuSte to Alfred Lattermann 12.8.40 mentioning two subsidies for Lück of 300 RMs for an index for a new edition of *Deutsche Aufbaukräfte* and 2,200 RMs for *Deutsche Gestalter*.

183. Kurt Lück, *Deutsche Gestalter und Ordner im Osten. Forschungen zur deutsch-polnischen Nachbarschaft im ostmitteleuropäischen Raum* (Posen 1940), 3, p. xi. This was reissued with a conspicuously shorter title as *Deutsch-polnische Nachbarschaft. Lebensbilder deutscher Hefer in Polen*, ed. V. Kauder (Würzburg 1957), Göttinger Arbeitskreis, Veröffentlichung no. 178; see C. Klessmann, 'Osteuropaforschung und Lebensraumpolitik', p. 381 n 66.

184. Lück, *Deutsche Gestalter*, pp. 184ff., 208ff., 233ff., etc.

185. Erich Maschke, 'Krakauer Bürger als Geldgeber und Gastgeber von Königen. Nikolaus Wirsing und seine Familie', *Deutsche Gestalter*, p. 13. For similar use of blood as a causal agent in his work see E. Maschke, 'Hanse und Ritterorden im Zug nach Osten', *Der Schulungsbrief* (1936), 3, 4 Folge, p. 132. See W. Wippermann, *Der Ordensstaat als Ideologie Einzelveröffentlichungen der Historischen Kommission zu Berlin* (Berlin 1979), 24, pp. 275ff.

186. Lück, *Deutsche Gestalter*, pp. 138, 293, 197 etc.

187. Kurt Lück, *Der Lebenskampf im deutsch-polnischen Grenzraum. Der Osten Europas*. Schriftenreibe der NSDAP Gruppe VII, Band 4 (Zentralverlag der NSDAP, Berlin 1940), p. 7.

188. *Ibid.*, p. 68.

189. *Ibid.*, p. 9.

190. *Ibid.*, pp. 10–13.

191. *Ibid.*, pp. 13–14.

192. *Ibid.*, p. 17.

193. *Ibid.*, pp.20–1.

194. *Ibid.*, pp. 30–1.

195. *Ibid.*, pp. 26, 32.

196. *Ibid.*, pp. 31.

197. *Ibid.*, pp. 38, 44.

198. *Ibid.*, pp.40–1.

199. *Ibid.*, p. 43.

200. *Ibid.*, p. 46.

201. *Ibid.*, p. 48.

202. *Ibid.*, p. 51.

203. *Ibid.*, p. 70.

204. *Ibid.*, p. 72.

205. *Ibid.*, pp 74–7.

206. Herder Institute, Marburg, 32, XV, JZ2 *Publikationsstelle* 'Polenberichte', no. 64 (12.6.36), 'Sommerliche polnische Wunschträume', pp. 1–2.

207. Herder Institute, Marburg, 32, XV, JZ2 PuSte 'Polenberichte', no. 5 (20.6.39) 'Danzig auf der Versailler Konferenz', p. 2.

208. Herder Institute, Marburg, 32, XV, JZ2 PuSte 'Polenberichte' no. 22 (no date), 'Wem verdankt Polen seine Entstehung? Lloyd George über polnische Masslosigkeit und Undankbarbeit – Was Lloyd George zu sagen vergass', p. 3.

209. Herder Institute, Marburg, 32, XV, JZ2 PuSte 'Polenberichte' no. 25 (9.11.39), '. . . anno 1958' (*sic*) Ein Engländer über Polens Weg ins Chaos', pp. 2–3.

210. Herder Institute, Marburg, 32, XV, JZ2 PuSte 'Polenberichte' no. 26 (no date), '. . . Anarchie Verwirrung and Unordnung . . .', p. 4. The same points were made in no. 8, 'Friderizianische Kulturleistungen in Westpreussen' (28.7.39).

211. Herder Institute, Marburg, 32, XV, JZ2 PuSte 'Polenberichte' no. 1 (30.5.39), 'Deutsche Kunsteinflüsse in Polen'; no. 8, 'Friderizianische Kulturleistungen in Westpreussen' (28.7.39); no. 21, 'Deutsche Kultureinflüsse in Polen im Spiegel der polnischen Sprache'; no. 27, 'Textilzentrum Lodz – das Werk deutscher Industriepionere'. See also no. 9, 'Das Städtewesen in Polen – eine deutsche Schöpfung' (4.7.39); no. 14, 'Alles war demnach deutsch . . . Westpreussische Zeugnisse über den deutschen Charakter Westpreussens'; no. 31, 'Gebaute Zeugen deutscher Kultur in Westpreussen'.

212. Herder Institute, Marburg, 32, XV, JZ2 PuSte 'Polenberichte' no. 27, 'Textilzentrum Lodz', pp. 2–3.

213. Herder Institute, Marburg, 32, XV, JZ2 PuSte 'Nordostberichte' no. 35 (29.5.40), 'Die Deutschordensfahnen in der Marienburg' etc.

214. BA R153/ 280, Volksdeutsche Mittelstelle to RMdI 8.9.39 'Richtlinien zur Behandlung der Masuren-, Schlonsaken-, Oberschlesier- und Kaschuben', pp. 1–3.

215. BA R153/ 280, PuSu to RMdI 4.10.39.

216. BA R153/ 280, Dr Martineck (Reichsarbeitsminister) to RMdI 11.11.39 and RMdI to the PuSte enclosing Dr Petzsch's report, 'Sonderbericht zur Kaschubenfrage' 15.10.39, p. 4, 'Es wird nötig werden, durch Massnahmen der Rassenpflege die minderwertigen Elemente allmählich auszuschalten (Sterilisation) und die brauchbare durch behebung ihrer Lebensführung (Erschliessung des Absatzgebietes, Wohnungsfürsorge etc.) zu verdeutschen'.

217. BA R153/ 280, PuSte to RMdI 20.12.39. On the need for 'clarification'

of the 'Kaschuben problem' see *Meldungen aus dem Reich*, ed. H. Boberach (Herrsching 1984), 3, p. 566.

218. BA R153/ 547, Response of *Gauleitung* East Prussia to 'Volkspolitische Lagebericht' no. 1 of the RMdI enclosed with RMdI to the PuSte 3.9.41 and PuSte to RMdI 17.10.41.

219. BA R153/ 537 Benninghausen (BDO) to RMdI and RM für Volksaufklärung und Propaganda 11.12.40 and Vollert (RMdI) to Dr Krieg RM für Volksausklärung und Propaganda 13.1.41.

220. BA R153/ 280, RMdI to NODFG 15.8.423 with hand comments by Papritz, p. 3, and Brackmann to RMdI 14.9.42.

221. *Geschichte der Sorben* 3, pp. 174ff.

222. *Meldungen aus dem Reich. Die geheimen Lageberichte des Sicherheitsdienstes der SS 1938–1945*, ed. Heinz Boberach (Herrsching 1984), 4, pp. 1195. I am grateful to Prof. Wolfgang Wippermann for this reference.

223. *Ibid.*, p. 1196.

224. BA R153/ 1458, RMdI to Reichsprotektor Böhmen and Mähren 7.6.39 enclosing BDO Bundesleitung to RMdI 15.5.39. On Páta see *Geschichte der Sorben*, 3, pp. 174–9 and 191.

225. BA R153/ 1459 RMdI to Reichsprotektor Böhmen und Mähren 7.6.39.

226. BA R153/ 1458, Dr Werner Best to the Landrat Bautzen 3.5.39.

227. BA R153/ 1458, Gestapo to the PuSte 10.5.39.

228. *Geschichte der Sorben*, 3, p. 191.

229. BA R153/ 1452, Essen (RMdI) to the Chef der Sicherheitspolizei und des SD 4.2.41 enclosing Landrat zu Bautzen to the RMdI 5.12.40 with details of the library.

230. BA R153/ 1452 RMdI to the PuSte 12.5.41 and 14.10.41 enclosing Chef der Sicherheitspolizei und des SD to RMdI 4.10.41 with details of Prinzborn's interest.

231. BA R153 1452, Cosack (PuSte) to RMdI 30.10.41; for a brief reference to PuSte involvement see Frido Mětšk, *Bestandsverzeichnis des Sorbischen Kulturarchivs in Bautzen*, Teil III, *Das Depositum Wendenabteilung. Němska akademij wědomosćow w Berlinje. Spisy Instituta za serbski Lvdospyt w Budysinje* (Budyšin/Bautzen 1967), pp. 22–3.

232. BA R153/ 1452, Chef der Sicherheitspolizei und des SD to RMdI 18.12.41 and Gestapo Dresden to the PuSte 22.1.42 and PuSte to Gestapo Dresden 17.1.42.

233. BA R153/ 1452, Cosack to Papritz 14.2.42.

234. BA R153/ 1452, Cosack to Papritz 18.2.42 and PuSte to RSHA (Schutzhaftreferent) 26.2.42 on supply of prisoners and PuSte memorandum 27.2.42 containing instructions from the SS on how to treat the prisoners.

235. BA R153/ 1452, Landrat zu Bautzen to the PuSte 8.7.42.

236. BA R153/ 1456, RMdI (Essen) to the PuSte 3.7.41 and to the Ministry of Propaganda, and Ministry of Propaganda to the RMdI 5.8.41 agreeing on banning publication.

237. Heinrich Gottong, 'Gibt es noch Wenden?', *Neues Volk. Blätter des Rassenpolitischen Amtes der NSDAP* (1941), 6, p. 3.

238. BA R153/ 1456, RMdI to the PuSte 27.2.42.

239. BA R153/ 1456, PuSte (W. Kohte and G. Sappok) to the RMdI 21.4.42. Günther, known as *Rassengünther*, was one of those responsible for advising on the 'Gesetzes zur Verhütung erbkranken Nachwuchses' (14.7.33) which legalized the sterilization of the 'hereditarily' insane, schizophrenic, blind, deaf and alcoholic. It has been estimated that between 350,000 and 400,000 people were sterilized in Germany before 1939 under these laws. See Peter Weingart, 'Eugenik- Eine angewandte Wissenschaft. Utopien der Menschen-züchtung zwischen Wissenschaftsentwicklung und Politik', *Wissenschaft im Dritten Reich*, pp. 332–3. Many of these victims of Nazi laws have never been compensated for their very private suffering.

240. BA R153/ 1456, Sappok to the RMdI 12.8.42.

241. BA R153/ 1456, RMdI to the PuSte 20.8.42. See PuSte to RMdI 21.9.42 recommending Fischer in Breslau, Eichstedt in Breslau and Reche in Leipzig. Eugen Fischer's 'Kaiser-Wilhelm-Institut' at Berlin University was responsible for training SS physicians in genetics and anthropology. See Weingart, 'Eugenik-Eine angewandte Wissenschaft', p. 334.

242. BA R153/ 1456, Brackmann to Prof. Otto Reche 14.10.42 and Reche to Brackmann 19.10.42. The approximation of the language used by both men is worth careful attention, as is, of course, Reche's role as an advisor to the courts.

243. BA R153/ 1456, Otto Reche to Brackmann 18.11.42.

244. BA R153/ 1456, PuSte to Otto Reche 24.12.42 and *Geschichte der Sorben*, 3, pp. 186–7 on the postponement of plans to resettle the Sorbs: BA R153/ 1356, RMdI to the PuSte 16.6.41; PuSte to Otto Reche 2.8.41 and Reche to Papritz 5.8.41. For plans to resettle the Sorbs in Lorraine see Frido Mĕtšk, *Bestandsverzeichnis*, p. 22.

245. BA R153/ 1356, Reche to Papritz 25.10.41.

246. BA R153/ 1356, Wolfgang Kohte (PuSte) to Prof. Friedrich Lenz. On Lenz see Weingart, 'Eugenik – Eine angewandte Wissenschaft', pp. 328ff.

247. BDC *Arlt*, SS service sheet and personal file including 'Tätigkeit in der Partei, ihren Gliederungen und angeschlossen Verbänden nach der Machtergreifung', no date.

248. Götz Aly and Karl Heinz Roth, *Die restlose Erfassung*, p. 73.

249. *Ibid.*, pp. 73–4.

250. *Ibid.*, pp. 72–4.

251. Fritz Arlt, 'Der Endkampf gegen das Judentum', *Der Weltkampf* (1938), 15, p. 128.

252. BDC *Arlt*, 'Tätigkeit in der Partei', for these dates and Arlt to SS-*Gruppenführer* von dem Bach-Zelewski 11.5.37.

253. BDC *Arlt*, SS Oberabschnitt Südost (Breslau) to Chef des SS-HA (SS-Personalamt Berlin) 19.5.37.

254. BDC *Arlt*, Ministerialrat Dr Siebert (Abtl. Innere Verwaltung) reference for Arlt 1.9.40 in his personal file.

255. Götz Aly and Karl Heinz Roth, *Die restlose Erfassung*, pp. 84–5.

256. BDC *Arlt*, Gauleiter Bracht (Upper Silesia) reference for Arlt 26.5.43.

257. BDC *Arlt*, Arlt to RKFDV Hauptabtl. Wirtschaft 26.6.42 with reference to 'Verwertung des Mobilarrücklasses der Evakuierten'. From the document appended it is clear that Arlt was involved in sifting the property of Jews sent to concentration camps.

258. BDC *Arlt*, Prof. Dr med. C. Clauberg to the *Reichsführer*-SS 30.5.42 with references to having discussed his research project with Arlt. On Clauberg's experiments in Block 10 of Auschwitz see Robert Jay Lifton, *Nazi Doctors. A Study in the Pychology of Evil* (London 1986), pp. 271–8.

259. BA R153/ B49, SS-*Sturmbannführer* Arlt to RMdI 9.11.40 and Essen (RMdI) to Arlt 25.11.40 and 14.2.41. The PuSte sent Arlt material on Silesia by Aubin, Kuhn and Mak; see PuSte to Arlt 19.12.40.

260. BA R153 280, RF-SS (RKFDV) to the PuSte 22.2.41 requesting material and 5.3.41 returning the books borrowed.

261. Helmut Heiber, 'Denkschrift Himmlers über die Behandlung der Fremd-völkischen im Osten', *VjZG* (1957), 2, p. 194.

262. *Ibid.*, p. 196.

263. *Ibid.*, p. 197.

264. *Ibid.*, p. 197, see also Gerald Fleming, *Hitler and the Final Solution* (Oxford 1986), p. 44.

265. *Ibid.*, p. 198. For Himmler's wider thoughts on the East see Josef Ackermann, *Heinrich Himmler als Ideologe* (Göttingen 1970), pp. 195ff.

266. Rudi Goguel, 'Über die Mitwirkung deutsche Wissenschaftler', p. 77.

267. Herder Institute, Marburg, 32, XV, JZ2 *Publikationsstelle* 'Polenber-ichte' no. 50–61, May–November 1941.

268. BA R153/ 58, Foreign Office to NODFG 31.12.41 Minutes of Volkspol-itische Tagung im A.A. 31.12.41, p. 30. During the meeting Papritz was invited to lunch with SS-*Obergruppenführer* Werner Lorenz of VOMI, VOMI to Papritz 26.9.41.

269. BA R153/ 58, Foreign Office to NODFG 31.12.41 minutes p. 31.

270. BA R153/ 1521, Franz Doubek, 'Bericht über meine dienstliche und

wissenschaftliche Tätigkeit im Kalenderjahr 1941', pp. 1–3; Doubek and Maydell also produced in 1942 a map entitled 'Die Verbreitung der Juden im nordwestlichen Europäischen Russland. Auf Grund der Nationalität-enzahlungen USSR 1926, Estland 1934, Lettland 1935, Litauen 1923, Polen 1931 dargestellt auf der Verwaltungskarte des nordwestlichen Europäischen Russland innerhalb der Grenzen der Sowjetunion von 1941 1: 1,500,000', Herder Institute, Marburg K41iii Fi a/b. Places with Jewish populations ranging from 10 to 100,000 and over were marked with dots and ever-larger Stars of David. Unfortunately the cartographic expert was not available to elucidate the uses of this document.

271. BA R153/ 1669, 'Karaimenfrage in Litauen: Nichteinordnung als Juden', General Kommissar (Kauen) to Ostministerium 1.9.41. See also *Encyclopaedia Judaica* (Jerusalem 1971), 10, pp. 771–6. The Karaites were subsequently favourably treated.

272. BA R153/ 1669, Leibbrandt (Reichsministerium für die besetzten Ostgebiete) to RSHA, NSDAP, RMdI, OKW, PuSte etc. 12.6.43. On Leibbrandt see BDC, George *Leibbrandt*, personal file.

273. 'Report from an Armament Inspector in the Ukraine to General Thomas personally, 2 December 1941: Description of Mass Execution of Jews in the Ukraine and Reduction of the Population by Starvation; unfavourable consequences for Germany of these measures' (Exhibit USA-290), *IMT*, 32, pp. 71–5 (this extract from pp. 73–5).

274. These details of Oberländer's military career are taken from 'Oberländer. Drittes Reich im Kleinen', *Der Spiegel* (2.12.59), pp. 37–9.

275. BA R153/ 1048, Oberländer to Brackmann 13.1.42, p. 2.

276. BA R153/ 1048, Oberländer to Brackmann 13.1.42, pp. 3–4.

277. *Ibid.*, pp. 8–9. See Alexander Dallin, *German Rule in Russia, 1941–1945: A Study in Occupation Policies* (London 1981₂), pp. 513–14 for a discussion of Oberländer's various memoranda.

278. This charge is raised implicitly in 'Oberländer. Drittes Reich im Kleinen', p. 39, citing the evidence of diaries kept by SS-*Oberscharführer* Landau who had come upon hundreds of corpses in Lemberg in early July 1941 shortly after Oberländer's 'Nightingales' had passed through. According to Peter Steinbach, *Nationalsozialistische Gewaltverbrechen. Die Diskussion in der deutschen Öffentlichkeit nach 1945* (Berlin 1981₂), pp. 103–4, Oberländer was cleared by a Polish commission in 1975 of war crimes. I am grateful to Wolfgang Wippermann for this reference.

279. R57/DAI 937 'Die Osttagung deutscher Wissenschaftler vom 24–27 März in Berlin, speech by Hauptabteilungsleiter Leibbrandt, p. 2.

280. *Ibid.*, p. 2.

281. *Ibid.*, p. 3.

282. *Ibid.*, Prof. Dr von Mende, 'Volkstumsfragen im Osten', p. 11.

283. *Ibid.*, Prof. Lenz, 'Bevölkerungsbiologische Lage im Osten', p. 19.
284. *Ibid.*, Oberstabsarzt Dr Waegener, 'Aufgaben der Gesundheitsführung im Osten', pp. 6–7; Generalkonsul Dr Bräutigam, 'Eigentumsfragen in den besetzten Ostgebieten', p. 8, Dr Graue, 'Forschungsaufgaben der Chemie und Physik im Osten', p. 10; Oberführer Scheidt, 'Aufgaben der Kulturpolitik im Osten', p. 12; Hasselblatt, 'Völkerordnung und Völkerzuordnung im Ostraum', p. 15; Frl. Dr Woltner, 'Russlandsdeutschtum', p. 25.
285. *Ibid.*, closing speech by A. Rosenberg, p. 26.
286. *Ibid.*, p. 27.
287. *Breslauer N.N.* 20.6.42.
288. BA R153/ 1250, Otto Reche to the PuSte (W. Kohte) 18.3.42.
289. BA R153/ 1250, *RM Für die besetzten Ostgebieten* to the PuSte 25.4.42.
290. BA R153/ 1250, Reche to Kohte (PuSte) 24.5.42.
291. BA R153/ 1250, Reche to Kohte 24.5.42.
292. BA R153/ 584, RMdI to the PuSte 'Vorläufige Sprachregelung über Begriffe des Ostens' 14.3.42, p. 5.
293. BA R153/ 584, 'Vorläufige Sprachregelung', p. 6.
294. BA R153/ 584. 'Vorläufige Sprachregelung', p. 7.
295. BA R153/ 584, 'Vorläufige Sprachregelung', p. 6.
296. BAR153/ 613, RMdI to the PuSte 15.1.40; on Nazi policy towards the Polish minority see Mirosław Cygański, 'Nazi Persecution of Polish National Minorities in the Rhineland-Westphalia Provinces in the Years 1933–1945', *Polish Western Affairs* (1976), 17, pp. 130 and 137 for confiscations of libraries in 1937 and Sepember 1939.
297. BA R153/ 613, PuSte to RMdI 4.4.40 and 'Charakteristik der polizeilich geschlossenen Büchereien der polnischen Volksgruppe im Reich'.
298. BA R153/ 613, RMdI to RSHA 5.8.40.
299. BA R153/ 613, RMdI to the PuSte 8.10.40.
300. BA R153/ 613, PuSte to Amtsrat Hermann Böhmer (Gestapo Abt. IV B 4a) 4.1.41.
301. GStA Rep. 92 *Nachlass Brackmann* no. 83 Brackmann to Aubin 23.10.40.
302. BA R153/ 6, Kohte to RMdI 15.6.40 and R153/ 1650, Brackmann to Ministerialrat Dr Conrad RMdI 15.7.40 forwarding the PuSte report on the Bibliotheka Polska and the PuSte's requirements.
303. BA R153/ 1650, Sappok memorandum 7.10.40.
304. BA R153/ 1650, Wolfgang Kohte memorandum 24.8.40.
305. *Dziennik Polski i Dziennik Zolnierza* (London), no. 247 18.10.44.
306. BA R153/ 1650, Leibbrandt (Rosenberg staff) to Essen (RmdI) 19.11.40.
307. BA R153/ 1650 Foreign Office to RMdI 19.9.40.
308. BA R153 1650, Sappok memorandum on the meeting in the RMdI 11.10.40.

309. BA R153/ 1650, 'Entwurf zu einem Ubereinkommen zwischen Reichs-
     leiter Rosenberg und dem Herrn RMdI betr. die polnische Bibliothek
     aus Paris', 27.11.40. On the *Amt Rosenberg* in general see R.
     Bollmus, *Das Amt Rosenberg und seine Gegner: Studien zur Machtkampf im
     Nationalsozialistischen Herrschaftssystem* (Stuttgart 1970), pp. 145ff.

310. BA R153/ 1650, PuSte (Kohte) to RF-SS (RKFDV) Dr Bethge 3.12.40.

311. BA R153/ 1131, Wolfgang Kohte, 'Bericht über meine Tätigkeit im
     Kalenderjahr 1941', p. 3.

312. BA R153/ 1569, Catalogue of the Bibliotheka Polska, contents of cases
     MI-MVII 9.3.42.

313. BA R153/ 1516, 'Jahresbericht 1940/1941 der NODFG and der PuSte',
     p. 10; BA R153/ 1650, PuSte to the RMdI 1.11.40 on the shelf-space
     needed to accommodate the books (3 kilometres); and Kohte to the RMdI
     3.3.42 on the whereabouts of the books in the Geheime Staatsarchiv.

314. BA R153/ 1522, 'Bericht des Bibliotheksleiters für das Jahr 1942'
     30.1.43, and R153/ 1523, 'Bericht des Bibliotheksleiters für das Jahr
     1943' 27.6.44.

315. BA R153/ 1161, Kohte to *Stab Rosenberg Bücherei* 2.10.42.

316. BA R153/ 1161, *Einsatzstab Rosenberg* to the PuSte 7.10.42.

317. BA R153/ 1008, 'Vertrauliche Bericht des wissenschaftlichen Referenten
     der PuSte Dr Hermann Weidhaas über seine Erfahrungen and Tätigkeit
     während der nach Weissruthenien unternommenen Reise im April
     1944'; and GStA Rep. 92 *Nachlass Brackmann* no. 86/14, Papritz to
     Brackmann 10.4.66 on Weidhaas's efforts to 'secure libraries in Minsk
     for the PuSte'.

318. *IMT Prozess gegen die Hauptkriegsverbrecher* 8, 29.2.46–7.3.46,
     pp. 69ff. For the Freiherr Eberhard von Künsberg's SS career from June
     1929 onwards see BDC, Künsberg, including a breakdown of the
     composition of his unit.

319. *Ibid.*, p. 71. See also David Thomas, 'Foreign Armies East and German
     Military Intelligence in Russia, 1941–1945', *JCH* (1987), 22, p. 265.

320. BA R153/ 1209, SS-Sonderkommando 'Gruppe-Künsberg' to the
     NODFG 29.7.42. The PuSte's future SS controller W. Krallert was a
     member of the Künsberg unit. See GStA Rep. 92 *Nachlass Brackmann*
     no. 85 Foreign Office to Brackmann 17.11.42. On Krallert see sec. iv
     below.

321. BA R153/ 1209, PuSte to SS-Sonderkommando 'Gruppe-Künsberg'
     29.5.42.

322. BA R153/ 1209, PuSte memorandum 1.10.42.

323. BA R153/ 1209, PuSte memorandum 23.11.42.

324. BA R153/ 1209 SS-*Untersturmführer* Scheibert (Batallion der Waffen-
     SS) to library of the NODFG 18.2.43.

325. Adam Stebelski, *The Fate of Polish Archives during World War II*, The

Central Directorate of State Archives (Warsaw 1964), pp. 5–7. I am indebted to the Polish Library in London for this booklet.

326. *Ibid.*, p. 10.
327. *Ibid.*, pp. 14–15.
328. BA R153/ 5, Zipfel to the NODFG 14.12.39 enclosing 'Archivmassnahmen in den befreiten and besetzten Gebieten des Ostens' 7.12.39, pp. 2–4 for the itineraries of his subordinates, BA R153/ 161, Zipfel, 'Kriegsmassnahmen deutscher Archivare' (1941?), pp. 5–6, and Stebelski, *The Fate of Polish Archives*, pp. 22–3 for Waldenfels.
329. BA R153/ 1545, Zipfel speaking at the NODFG conference in Katowice 14.12.39, p. 5.
330. Stebelski, *The Fate of Polish Archives*, p. 24.
331. *Ibid.*, pp. 17–18. There is a good discussion of Randt's archival administration in the *Generalgouvernment* in Klessmann, *Die Selbstbehauptung einer Nation*, pp. 75–8.
332. Stebelski, *The Fate of Polish Archives*, pp. 32ff.; Klessmann, *Die Selbstbehauptung einer Nation*, pp. 76–7.
333. Stebelski, *The Fate of Polish Archives*, pp. 33ff.
334. *Ibid.*, p. 35.
335. Klessmann, *Die Selbstbehauptung einer Nation*, p. 77.
336. BA R153/ 161, Zipfel, 'Kriegsmassnahmen deutscher Archivare', p. 8; Stebelski, *The Fate of Polish Archives*, pp. 35–7.
337. BA R153/ 161, Zipfel to Papritz 23.2.41 enclosing 'Kriegsmassnahmen deutscher Archivare', p. 9.
338. For comprehensive lists of records looted see Stebelski, *The Fate of Polish Archives*, pp. 38–41.
339. *Ibid.*, p. 42; according to Klessmann, *Die Selbsbehauptung einer Nation*, Kurt Forstreuter also acquired 70 volumes of Polish court records from Ostrołęka of the period 1455–1802 to assist his researches; p. 77.
340. BA R153/ 161, Zipfel, 'Kriegsmassnahmen deutscher Archivare', p. 12.
341. BA R153/ 5, Zipfel to the PuSte 16.1.40, pp. 2–4.
342. BA R153/ 161, Zipfel, 'Kriegsmassnahmen deutscher Archivare', p. 15.
343. BA R153/ 161, Zipfel to Papritz 26.8.40.
344. BA R153/ 161, Zipfel, 'Archivmassnahmen in besetzten sowjetrussischen Gebiet' 26.9.41, pp. 1–2.
345. Stebelski, *The Fate of Polish Archives*, pp. 50ff.
346. *Ibid.*, pp. 50–1.
347. *Ibid.*, p. 51. Losses in Warsaw were: Archives of the Age of Enlightenment, Treasury and Municipal Archives 100 per cent; Archive of Recent Records 97 per cent; Central Archives of Earlier Records 90 per cent; Archives of Earlier Records 80 per cent. In January 1945 German troops also destroyed over 320,000 bound volumes and about 5,000 maps in the State Archives in Poznań.

348. W. Kohte, 'Fritz Morre', *Jomsburg* (1941), 5, pp. 424–5.

349. GStA Rep. 92, *Nachlass Brackmann*, no. 84, Brackmann to Dr Diestelkamp 5.2.42.

350. Max Hein, 'Karl Kasiske', *Jomsburg* (1941), 5, pp. 426–7.

351. GStA Rep. 92, *Nachlass Brackmann*, no. 85, Brackmann to Diestelkamp and F. Metz to Brackmann 22.2.43; Brackmann to Lattermann 6.5.42 and Brackmann to F. Metz 4.4.42.

352. GStA Rep. 92, *Nachlass Brackmann*, no. 85, Lattermann to Brackmann 12.3.42; see the obituaries in the *Ostdeutscher Beobachter* 24.10.43 BA R52 IV/131, p. 25, and by Walter Kuhn, 'Kurt Lück 1900–1942', *ZfO* (1952), 1, pp. 425–6. See also BA R52 IV/ 114, p. 51, Dr W. Coblitz to Alfred Lattermann 20.3.42 on Hans Frank's plans to commemorate the death of one of the 'grössen Vorkämpfer der deutschen Wissenschaft im Osten'. BDC, *Lück*, SS service record. Lück joined the SS in May 1940.

353. GStA Rep. 92, *Nachlass Brackmann*, no. 86/13, Papritz to Brackmann 20.10.44, and BA R153/ 1222, Masing to the PuSte 21.3.43 on his address in Warsaw, and BA R153/ 1217 'Feldpostbriefwechsel mit eingezogenen Arbeitskameraden' for Masing's regimental affiliations, 3.6.43. BDC, *Gerhard Masing*, SS service record.

354. GStA Rep. 92, *Nachlass Brackmann*, no. 86/11, Papritz to Brackmann 9.1.45 on Sappok's disappearance in Autun.

355. GStA Rep. 92, *Nachlass Brackmann*, no. 85, Brackmann to Ministerialdirektor a.D. Dr Fischer 13.1.43. See also Brackmann to Ost 15.12.42; BA R153/ 1217, 'Feldpostbriefwechsel' 3.6.43 for Dollinger; and BA R58/ 101 RSHA To II C 2v in house 13.1.44, p. 15 and To VI F 3 13.1.44 requesting winter kit, machine-pistols, magazines and ammunition for an expedition led by Hehn to Minsk.

356. GStA Rep. 92, *Nachlass Brackmann*, no. 85, Brackmann to Aubin 6.3.43, and Brackmann to A. Feuerereisen 10.3.43.

357. GStA Rep. 92, *Nachlass Brackmann*, no. 86/13, Papritz to Brackmann 20.10.44; on 11 October 1944 Brackmann's son-in-law was killed at Libau; see Brackmann to Kohte 1.12.44.

358. GStA Rep. 92, *Nachlass Brackmann*, no. 86/12, Brackmann to Zipfel 17.7.44.

359. GStA Rep. 92, *Nachlass Brackmann*, no. 86/81 Kohte to Papritz 3.2.44 and Papritz to Brackmann 21.2.44; no. 86/11, Papritz to Brackmann 21.10.44.

360. HStA *Nachlass Papritz*, 340, C12d 40 Maydell to the PuSte 3.2.44, and Papritz to Dr Wilfried Krallert 3.2.44.

361. HStA *Nachlass Papritz*, 340, C12d 40 Papritz to Brackmann 21.2.44, p. 3.

362. BA R58/ 125 (RSHA) Hehn III/IV 22.12.43 Ref. Dr H. Schaeder investigation by SS-*Sturmbannführer* Hannerbruch RSHA IV B.2., p. 206.

363. HStA *Nachlass Papritz*, 340, C12d 31 Krallert to the PuSte 9.8.44, and Papritz questionnaire on Schaeder 13.1.58.

364. HStA *Nachlass Papritz*, 340, C12d 31 Papritz to Prof. Dr H.-H. Schaeder February 1944; Papritz to Krallert February 1944; Krallert to the PuSte B.7.44; Papritz to Krallert 14.8.44; and Hildegard Schaeder to Papritz 20.11.53 giving the date of her release.

365. BA R153/ 665, PuSte to the Gestapo 12.10.39 and memorandum by Kohte 24.1.40 on Foreign Office sources of newspapers.

366. BA R153/ 665, PuSte to the Gestapo 12.10.39; Kossmann to RSHA Oberinspektor Schönfelder 7.5.42.

367. BA R153/ 665, RMdI to the PuSte 22.7.42 with list of recipients of the Press translation service.

368. BA R153/ 665, Papritz to *Generalgouverneur* Hans Frank 27.1.43.

369. Goguel, 'Über die Mitwirkung deutscher Wissenschaftler' Document 12 Wendland to Zipfel 19.2.43, pp. 35ff.

370. Goguel, 'Über die Mitwirkung deutscher Wissenschaftler', p. 80.

371. For these conferences see Goguel, 'Über die Mitwirkung deutscher Wissenschaftler', p. 80. In a circular letter dated 7.12.42 Brackmann stressed the need for studies of the Dutch role in settlements in the East by way of preparation for the Dutch search for *Lebensraum* in the present; see R153/ 1057, Brackmann to Lattermann, Hein, Aubin, Metz and Kötzschke 7.12.42.

372. Goguel, 'Über die Mitwirkung deutscher Wissenschaftler', p. 36, 'Bericht Keyser's auf der Tagung der NODFG in Posen 25–27/2/1943'. The minutes of the conference in Posen seem to be missing from the otherwise complete sets of minutes of NODFG conferences in the *Bundesarchiv*.

373. Goguel, 'Über die Mitwirkung deutscher Wissenschaftler'(Anhang), pp. 37–8.

374. *Ibid.*, p. 38. These notes were taken by Zipfel.

375. BA R153/ 1049, Papritz to Aubin 30.3.40 replying to Aubin to Papritz 24.3.40 about Aubin's idea for a second Brackmann *Festschrift*; Kohte to Otto Brunner 9.10.40 offering him co-editorship.

376. BA R153/ 1049, Kohte to Aubin 26.2.41 on suggested titles and Kohte to Verlag Hirzel 12.5.41 with the agreed version. For the costs of the book see Verlag Hirzel to Kohte 13.4.40, and 19.10.40; Verlag Hirzel to the NODFG 8.1.42 on the need for a publication subsidy and Papritz to the Parteiamtliche Prüfungskommission zum Schutz des NS-Schrifttums 10.3.42 on support from the Foreign Office and RMdI.

377. BA R153/ 1049, Kohte to Aubin 7.3.41 and Aubin to Kohte 10.3.41 and BA R153/ 1050, Foreign Office to NODFG 7.5.42.

378. E. Vollert, 'Albert Brackmann und die ostdeutsche Volks- und Landes-forschung', *Deutsche Ostforschung. Ergebnisse und Aufgaben seit dem ersten Weltkrieg*, eds. H. Aubin, O. Brunner, W. Kohte and J. Papritz (Leipzig 1942), 1, p. 11.

379. Erich Keyser, 'Die Erforschung der Bevölkerungsgeschichte des deutschen Ostens', *Deutsche Ostforschung*, 1, p. 93; W. Wippermann, *Der 'deutsche Drang nach Osten'. Ideologie und Wirklichkeit eines politischen Schlagwortes* (Darmstadt 1981), p. 113 contains a substantial analysis of Keyser's essay.

380. Keyser, 'Die Erforschung der Bevölkerungsgeschichte', p. 95.

381. *Ibid.*, p. 103.

382. GStA Rep. 92 *Nachlass Brackmann*, no. 84/14, Brackmann to Papritz 27.4.44.

383. BA R153/ 1049, Aubin to Kohte 16.7.40.

384. BA R153/ 1049, Aubin to Papritz 12.11.41 with notes on Reche's essay.

385. Otto Reche, 'Stärke und Herkunft des Anteils nordischer Rasse bei den Westslawen', *Deutsche Ostforschung*, 1, p. 58; Wippermann, *Der 'deutsche Drang nach Osten'*, pp. 113–14 on Reche's essay.

386. Reche, 'Stärke und Herkunft', p. 64.

387. *Ibid.*, p. 67.

388. *Ibid.*, p. 75.

389. *Ibid.*, p. 88.

390. Wippermann, *Der 'deutsche Drang nach Osten'*, p. 115.

391. BA R153/ 1050, Brackmann to Otto Reche 10.7.42.

392. Peter-Heinz Seraphim, 'Deutschtum und Judentum in Osteuropa', *Deutsche Ostforschung* (Leipzig 1943), 2, p. 429.

393. *Ibid.*, pp. 439–46.

394. *Ibid.*, p. 430, 'Rein instinktiv wurde der Jude abgelehnt, die Berührung, insbesondere auch die Eheschliessung mit einem Juden vermieden. Man kann sagen, dass, obwohl bis 1933 ein fundierter Rassenantisemitismus bei den deutschen Volksgruppen in Osteuropa eigentlich nicht vorhanden war, praktisch die Ablehnung der Juden von allen deutschen Volksgrup-pen dieses Raumes durchgeführt wurde'; p. 431, 'Die Rückstrahlung dieser Gedanken in die deutschen Volksgruppen Osteuropas weckte und vertiefte, zumal in der jüngeren Generation, den Gedanken der scharfen Trennung und Ablehnung des Judentums'; p. 433, 'So bedeutet die Handelsstellung in Polen-Litauen für die Juden den Erwerb der Schlüs-selposition für einen bedeutenden Teil des damaligen Welthandels'; p. 434, 'Man sollte zutreffender statt von einer Einwanderung der Juden nach Osteuropa vom Vorgang ihres Einsickerns sprechen' etc.

395. For Krallert see BDC, *Krallert*. Krallert had worked for the SD in the SE

since March 1939. Goguel, 'Über die Mitwirkung deutscher Wissenschaftler' (Anhang), p. 24 Document 7, 'Unterstellung unter das RSHA', Brackmann to Zipfel 4.11.43: 'Nur eins ist sicher, dass wir dem RSHA seit dem 1.X. unterstellt sind'.

396. BA R58/ 101, 'Erlass des Chef des Sicherheitspolizei und SD' 3.5.44, p. 52. BDC, SS records of Ehlich, Luig.

397. On these SD departments see Heinz Boberach, ed., *Meldungen aus dem Reich. Die geheimen Lageberichte des Sicherheitsdienstes der SS 1938–1945* (Herrsching 1984), 1, p. 15. Section IIIB was concerned with 'Volkstum' and was divided into a further five sections: Volkstumsarbeit, Minderheiten, Rasse- und Volksgesundheit, Staatsangehörigkeit und Einbürgerung, Besetzte Gebiete or sections IIIB 1–5; on Schellenberg see Heinz Höhne, *The Order of the Death's Head*, pp. 450ff. He took over the *Ausland SD* in 1942 with the intention of achieving a monopoly of external espionage and intelligence activities.

398. BA R58/ 101, 'Decknamen für VIg' 3.5.44, p. 43.

399. BA R58/ 101, 'Gesichtspunkte über die Fortsetzung der Arbeit von VIg angesichts des totalen Krieges', Krallert 25.8.44, pp. 134–5.

400. BA R58/ 101, Dr von Hehn memorandum 22.5.44, p. 337 on the PuSte budget.

401. BA R58/ 125, *Obergruppenführer* III/VI Ohlendorf and Schellenberg to *Gauleiter Mutschmann* 19.1.44, p. 20.

402. BA R58/ 125, Krallert to the PuSte 22.5.44, p. 73.

403. BA R58/ 125, VIg to IVDI 22.5.44, p. 74.

404. BA R58/ 125, Krallert to the PuSte 22.8.44, p. 76.

405. BA R58/ 125, VIg to the PuSte 1.6.44, p. 78.

406. BA R58/ 125, Hehn to SS-*Obersturmführer* Dr Teich VIc/Z 30.6.44, p. 97.

407. BA R58 125, VIg to IIIB/VIe 11.8.44, pp. 118–20 with list of addresses supplied by the PuSte.

408. BA R153/ 1088, Papritz to Lattermann 22.2.44 and Papritz to Erich Keyser 23.3.44; Papritz to W. Recke 25.2.44 and Papritz to R. Wittram 25.2.44 trying to find staff.

409. BA R153/ 1088, Hahn to Papritz 19.10.44; Auslandsamt der Dozentenschaft der Deutschen Universitäten und Hochschulen to the PuSte 7.11.44; Professor E. Birke to Papritz 4.12.44.

410. BA R58/ 125, *Obergruppenführer* III/VI to Gauleiter Mutschmann (Saxony) 19.1.44, p. 20.

411. HStA *Nachlass Papritz* 340, C12d/41 'Die PuSte in den Jahren 1945–1947'; 'Wissenschaftlicher Lebenslauf' (1948), p. 8; interviews with Dr J. Papritz in Marburg 2.8.86 and 11.8.86.

412. HStA *Nachlass Papritz*, 340, C12d 41, Papritz official memo 26.2.46. He was interrogated by a Captain Stuart.

413. BA R153/ 1675, Otto Reche to Papritz 20.1.45.

414. BA R153/ 1675, Otto Reche to Papritz 20.1.45; for Reche's post-war years see Karl Saller, *Die Rassenlehre des Nationalsozialismus im Wissenschaft und Propaganda* (Darmstadt 1961), p. 48.

415. HStA *Nachlass Papritz*, 340, C12g 32 Seraphim to Papritz 21.11.46. For Seraphim's career as director of the Academy of Public Administration and Economy at Bochum see 'Reactionary Professors', *Wiener Library Bulletin* (1958), 12, p. 7.

416. Interviews with Dr J. Papritz and Dr E. O. Kossmann in Marburg 11.8.86; 16.8.86 and 8.8.86.

417. HStA *Nachlass Papritz*, 340, C12g, Krallert to Papritz 30.7.48.

418. HStA *Nachlass Papritz*, 340, C12g, Krallert to Papritz 31.1.49.

419. HStA *Nachlass Papritz*, 340, C12g, Papritz to Krallert 23.2.49.

420. HStA *Nachlass Papritz*, 340, C12g, Krallert to Papritz 4.6.49 and Krallert to Papritz 21.5.51 on his 'retirement'.

421. HStA *Nachlass Papritz*, 340, C12g, Hehn to Papritz 20.10.53.

422. HStA *Nachlass Papritz*, 340, C12g, Walter Kuhn to Papritz 16.10.48.

423. Walter Kuhn, 'Eine Jugend für die Sprachinselforschaung', p. 277 for Aubin's assistance.

424. HStA *Nachlass Papritz*, 340, C12g, Papritz to Ernst Vollert 14.5.47.

425. BA R153/ 963, Papritz to Hans Mortensen 1.11.45.

426. BA R153/ 963, Aktennotiz H. Cosack 13.1.47 and Aktennotiz H. Cosack 12.10.46.

427. HStA *Nachlass Papritz*, 340, C12, 'Wissenschaftlicher Lebenslauf', p. 13 and C12g, Papritz to von Brandt 26.1.49 and Brandt to Papritz 29.1.49.

428. G. R. Gayre, *Teuton and Slav on the Polish Frontier. A Diagnosis of the Racial Basis of the Germano-Polish Borderlands with Suggestions for the Settlement of German and Slav Claims* (London 1944), p. 40. The *New Stateman*'s 'London Diary' (5.8.44) summed up this appointment accurately when the diarist remarked, 'I cannot believe that this appointment can really be made.' I am grateful to Dr Robert Evans for these references.

429. HStA *Nachlass Papritz*, 340, C12g, Brackmann to Papritz 11.1.46.

430. HStA *Nachlass Papritz*, 340, C12g, Brackmann to Papritz 2.3.46, and Brackmann to Papritz 2.2.46.

431. HStA *Nachlass Papritz*, 340, C12g, Brackmann to Papritz 2.4.46 and 9.8.46.

432. HStA *Nachlass Papritz*, 340, C12g, telegram Brackmann to Papritz 30.9.46, and 19.10.46 on the possibility of moving the PuSte to the Soviet Zone.

433. HStA *Nachlass Papritz*, 340, C12g, Papritz to Brackmann 23.8.46 and 1.12.46.

5. SCHOLARSHIP AS POWER: RESEARCH INSTITUTES IN THE OCCUPIED EAST, 1940–45

1. Gawęda, *Die Jagiellonische Universität in der Zeit der faschistischen Okkupation 1939–1945* (Jena 1981), pp. 17–18; Klessmann, *Die Selbstbehauptung einer Nation*, pp. 54–5.
2. Henryk Batowski, 'Nazi Germany and Jagiellonian University', *Polish Western Affairs* (1978), 19, pp. 113–19. I am grateful to Professor Henryk Batowski for a memorable discussion about the 'Sonderaktion Krakau'.
3. Klessmann, *Die Selbstbehauptung einer Nation*, p. 56.
4. Gawęda, *Die Jagiellonische Universität*, pp. 35ff.
5. *Ibid.*, pp. 31–6. On Brinkmann see BA /A11. Proz. 21/90 *Prozesse gegen Deutsche im europaische Ausland*, p. 6, 'Lebenslauf', and pp. 13ff., 'Meine Tätigkeit im Generalgouvernement Polen in den Jahren 1940/ 1944'.
6. Joachim Fest, *The Face of the Third Reich* (London 1979), p. 317.
7. 'C. Klessmann, 'Der Generalgouverneur Hans Frank', *VjhZg* (1971), 19, p. 252.
8. Curzio Malaparte, *Kaputt* (Frankfurt am Main 1979), pp. 92–5; Klessmann, 'Der Generalgouverneur Hans Frank', p. 253.
9. Malaparte, *Kaputt*, p. 131.
10. Hans Frank, 'Deutsche Ordnung und polnische Wirtschaft', *Der Schulungsbrief* (1941), 8, pp. 88–90. This special 'eastern' issue was commissioned by Frank; see BA R52 II/ 179, Hans Frank, *Tagebuch* 1940, p. 1000, 24.10.40.
11. 'Frank, 'Deutsche Ordnung', p. 89.
12. G. Voigt, 'Das Institut für deutsche Ostarbeit in Krakau', in B. Spiru, ed., *September 1939* (East Berlin 1959), pp. 110–11.
13. *Institut für deutsche Ostarbeit Krakau. Jahrbuch 1941* (Krakau 1941), pp. 7–8.
14. Klessmann, *Die Selbstbehauptung einer Nation*, p. 62; Voigt, 'Das Institut für deutsche Ostarbeit', p. 112 for the Osteuropa-Institut as a model.
15. BA R52 II/ 181, Hans Frank, *Tagebuch* 1941, p. 152, 23–24.3.41.
16. *Verordnungsblatt des Generalgouvernements für die besetzten polnischen Gebiete* (Krakau 1939ff.), Teil 1, no. 30, 20.4.40, pp. 149–50 § 1–4; on the uniforms see BA R52 IV/ 99, p. 102, Coblitz to Regierung des Generalgouvernements Abtl. Innere Verwaltung 2.9.40.
17. *Verordnungsblatt des Generalgouvernements Teil* 1, no. 30, 20.4.40 § 1–4, pp. 149–50.
18. *Haushaltsplan des Generalgouvernements für das Rechnungsjahr 1940* (Krakau 1940ff.), vols. 1–5, 1, p. xi; 1948, 2, p. 294; 1942, 3, p. 376; 1943, 4, p. 275; 1944, 5, p. 344 for these figures.

19. *Ostland* (1.5.40), 9, pp. 217–18.
20. Coblitz's personal IdO file is suspiciously thin. This information has been compiled from BA R52 IV/ 100, p. 18, Coblitz to Hauptabtl. Propaganda (Press department) 11.7.41 and BA R52 IV/ 22, p. 2 (undated) military service record. See also K. Klssmann, 'Der Generalgouverneur Hans Frank', p. 250 n 21, for Coblitz's earlier connections with Frank.
21. BA R52 IV/ 13d; list of names for a Burschenschaftler-Abend 8.7.43; and Coblitz to Forstmeister Dr Baumgarten 15.12.43; Coblitz to Waffen-Habemeyer 18.2.43 and to Richard Hake 20.12.44 and p. 187, *Staatsbibliothek* to Coblitz 26.11.43 for a list of overdue books.
22. *Institut für deutsche Ostarbeit Krakau. Jahrbuch 1941*, p. 11.
23. *Ibid.*, p. 14.
24. BA R52 II/ 178, Hans Frank *Tagebuch* 1940 1.9.40, p. 787.
25. BA R52 IV/ 101, p. 171, Coblitz to Watzke 24.7.41 and BA R153/943, Coblitz to the PuSte 12.9.40 announcing Sappok's dismissal.
26. BA R52 IV/ 102, p. 108, Coblitz to the Stellvertreter des Führers 3.4.41.
27. BA R52 IV/ 86, p. 75, Werner Radig to Coblitz 5.12.40.
28. GStA Rep. 92 *Nachlass Brackmann* no. 84, pp. 49–50, Sappok to an unspecified *Staatssekretär* 23.10.40.
29. GStA Rep. 92 *Nachlass Brackmann*, no. 84, pp. 66–7, Sappok memo for Brackmann 1.10.40.
30. BA R153/943, Sappok to the PuSte, no date, pp. 1, 3–4, 7.
31. *Ibid.*, p. 17
32. BA R153/ 943 Coblitz to the RMdI 7.8.41.
33. Klessmann, *Die Selbstbehauptung einer Nation*, p. 66; Goguel, 'Über die Mitwirkung deutscher Wissenschaftler', p. 136.
34. BA R153/ 1197, 'Arbeitstagung des IdO 20–22/6/1940' programme.
35. Voigt, 'Das Institut für deutsche Ostarbeit', p. 112; and Klessmann, *Die Selbstbehauptung einer Nation*, pp. 63–5 for brief characterizations of the sections of the IdO.
36. Goguel, 'Über die Mitwirkung deutscher Wissenschaftler', p. 139, and *Anhang*, p. 103, Streitmüller (Leipzig) to Wissenschaftsministerium 12.11.40, and p. 102, Klumbert (Königsberg) to Wissenschaftsministerium 29.10.40.
37. BA R52 IV/ 6, Coblitz to Herbert Ludat 21.3.41, p. 147.
38. BA R52 IV/ 99, p. 15, Coblitz to Regierung des Generalgouvernement 11.10.43 requesting arms permits for two of his staff who had to visit fuel dumps and factories.
39. BA R52 IV/ 138, p. 80, Werner Radig to Erich Maschke 31.1.41 and R52 IV/ 6, p. 108, Dr S. Bannbeck to Staatssekretariat and Personalamt 19.6.42 and Coblitz to Ludat 22.4.42, p. 123. On Kuhn see BA R52/IV/

113, p. 101, Kuhn to Coblitz 18.12.40 and p. 102, Coblitz to Kuhn 28.11.40 offering him leadership of the section. The names Lück, Kuhn and Oberländer were recommended to Coblitz by *Oberregierungsrat* Scurla; see BA R52 IV/ 121, Scurla to Coblitz 21.11.40, p. 7.

40. BA R52 IV/ 86, p. 75, Radig to Coblitz 5.12.40, and p. 86, Radig to Coblitz 31.10.40 recommending Maschke and BA R52 IV/ 113, Kuhn to Coblitz recommending Lück 18.12.40, p. 101.

41. BA R153/ 1228, G. Sappok to Kurt von Maydell 28.6.40 and BA R52 IV/ 116, p.60, Coblitz to Maydell 29.4.41, and p. 59, Maydell to Coblitz 11.5.41.

42. BA R52 IV/ 62, p. 121, Coblitz to Inspektor des Sonderdienstes in Hauptabteilung Innere Verwaltung 10.7.42; BA R52 II/ 182, Hans Frank, *Tagebuch*, p. 442, 9.5.41; BA R52 II/ 184, p. 664, 21.7.41.

43. BA R52 IV/ 62, Brüske to Frank 10.10.40, p. 311; Brüske to Abtl. Finanzen 23.9.40, p. 316, for his c.v.; p. 338, Reichsdozentenführer to Frank 9.5.40; SA to NSDAP reference for Brüske 3.11.37, p. 341, and Brüske to Coblitz 14.6.40, p. 334.

44. BA R52 II/ 147, p. 129, Protocol of a meeting between Maurer and Coblitz 21.1.41.

45. BA R521 IV/ 147, p. 143, Maurer to Coblitz 28.12.40 and BS R52 II/ 179, Hans Frank, *Tagebuch*, p. 1169, 20.12.40.

46. BA R52 IV/ 147, p. 122, Coblitz to Maurer 3.2.41, and p. 79, Maurer to Abtl. Finanzen in der Regierung des Generalgouvernement, no date.

47. BA R52 IV/ 147, p. 82, Maurer report to Coblitz 5.1.42, and pp. 52–3, Maurer memo on the importance of horticulture 5.8.42.

48. BA R52 IV/ 147, Maurer Denkschrift: 'Der Landbau im Generalgouvernement. Forschung im Rahmen des IdO im besonderen; Planung and Aufbau der Forschung auf dem gesamtgebiete der Gartenkultur', no date, p. 5.

49. *Ibid.*, p. 10.

50. *Ibid.*, pp. 23–5.

51. *Ibid.*, p. 33.

52. BA R52 IV/ 147, Maurer, 'Der Ostwall: Ein Besiedlungsplan zum Schutze des Grossdeutschen Reiches nach Osten', Maurer to Oberbefehlshaber Ost, Generaloberst Blaskowitz via General von Höberth (Stadtkommandant Krakau), no date, pp. 35ff.

53. *Institut für deutsche Ostarbeit Krakau. Jahrbuch 1941*, p. 36.

54. UJA IDO 1, 'Das IdO' (typescript, no date), p. 19.

55. BA R52 IV/ 85, pp. 35ff. Coblitz letter of support for Anton Plügel in order to exempt him from military service, no date.

56. *Institut für deutsche Ostarbeit Krakau. Jahrbuch 1941*. pp. 34–5.

57. UJA IDO/ 70, Anton Plügel to OKW Abteilung Kriegsgefangene 2.3.42. From Dora Kahlich to Elfriede Fliethmann 4.5.42; in the same file it is

apparent that tests were also being carried out on English prisoners in
Wolfsberg in Kärnten.

58. BA R52 IV/ 78, p. 40, application to exempt Gottong from military
service 19.5.42.

59. For the backgrounds of these researches see BA R52 IV/ 67, pp. 19ff.,
Fliethmann's c.v.; BA R52 IV/ 76, pp. 55ff. Stark's c.v.; BA R52 IV/ 74,
pp. 113, a reference for Sydow 20.4.43. For Plügel's views on the
Góralen see his 'Die Podhalanischen Góralen im südlichsten Teil des
Kreises Neumarkt', *Die Burg* (1941), 2, p. 59.

60. *Ibid.*, p. 64.

61. Lothar Weirauch, 'Die Volksgruppen im Generalgouvernement', *Europ.
Revue* (1942), 18, p. 255 as well as photographs of receptions in the
Wawel that occur in the regime's press.

62. UJA IDO/ 70, E. Fliethmann to Dora Kahlich, no date, with references
to 'Der Widerstand bei der Bevölkerung war wiederum einmal ganz
stark, sodass wir nur mit Grenzschutz und Polizei arbeiten konnten.'

63. UJA IDO/ 70, Anton Plügel to Dora Maria Kahlich 22.10.41.

64. UJA IDO/ 70, Anton Plügel to Dora Kahlich 13.3.42 and Kahlich to
Plügel 3.11.41 on the nature of the tests.

65. UJA IDO/ 70, SS-*Hauptsturmführer* Schenk to IdO Sektion Rassen- und
Volkstumsforschung 22.5.42.

66. UJA IDO/ 70, IdO Sektion Rassen- und Volkstumsforschung to SS-
Hauptsturmführer Schenk 23.4.42, and Schenk to Dr E. Fliethmann
16.9.42.

67. UJA IDO/ 70, E. Fliethmann to Dora Kahlich, no date but before
October 1942, as she refers to a projected trip on 10.10.42 in the letter.

68. UJA IDO/ 61, 'Bereisung des Reichskommissariats' description of a
journey by Prof. Hans von Grünberg and five others in August 1942.
The references are to pp. 2, 8, 14, 16, 20, 24. See also Götz Aly
and Susanne Heim, *Ein Berater der Macht* (Hamburg/Berlin 1986),
pp. 48–9. The report is contained in a file with material for maps on
the USSR.

69. BA R52 IV/ 62, p. 104 reference for Magister Richard Böhm 27.9.43;
BA R52 IV/ 101, p. 115, Coblitz to Hauptabtl. Wissenschaft and
Unterricht 31.7.42 on his membership of the Frankfurt Institute. See
also J. Sommerfeldt, 'Aufgaben des Referats Judenforschung', *DFO*
(1941), 1, pp. 29–35.

70. *Institut für deutsche Ostarbeit Krakau. Jahrbuch 1941*, pp. 38–40.
Sommerfeldt was in charge of the sub-section for research on the Jews
from 1 October 1940 until 15 July 1944, when he became chief of the
(defunct) history section, see BA R52 IV/ 52, p. 22, Coblitz reference
for Josef Sommerfeldt 19.4.44. Sommerfeldt was an SA-Scharführer
from 26 May 1933 and an NSDAP member since May 1937; see BA

R52 IV/ 52, Sommerfeldt c.v., pp. 1–3, no date. Gottong joined the NSDAP in May 1937 and was an administrator with the International Congress on Racial Hygiene; see BA R52 IV/ 78, p. 3, c.v., no date. His work on the search for 'hidden German blood' was subsidized by the Racial–Political Office of the NSDAP, the OKW and the RKFDV, p. 40, application for Gottong to be released from the army 19.5.42. In March 1941 the section hired Dr Erhard Riemann, an NSDAP member since May 1933 with a background in museums and local-history societies in Königsberg; see BA R52 IV/ 87, p. 2 for Riemann's c.v., no date.

71. *Institut für deutsche Ostarbeit Krakau. Jahrbuch* 1941, p. 40.

72. BA R52 IV/ 62, pp. 126 application to Sonderdienstes in Hauptabtl. Innere Verwaltung 14.8.41, and p. 118 for Böhm's c.v. See also UJA IDO/ 11, Sommerfeldt to Coblitz 4.9.41 for the two Ukrainians.

73. Peter-Heinz Seraphim, 'Die Judenfrage im Generalgouvernement als Bevölkerungsproblem', *Die Burg* (1940), 1, pp. 57–62.

74. *Ibid.*, p. 63.

75. BA R57. DAI/ 344, Reisebericht Dr Kloss 30.3–1.4.41, p. xvii, 'Die Judenfrage im Generalgouvernement'.

76. Josef Sommerfeldt, 'Die Juden in den polnischen Sprichwörten und Sprichwörtlichen Redensarten', *Die Burg* (1942), 3, p. 314.

77. *Ibid.*, pp. 332–6; see also his 'Die Entwicklung der Geschichtsschreibung über die Juden in Polen', *Die Burg* (1940), 1, pp. 64ff.

78. Heinrich Gottong, 'Schicksale des polnischen Judentums', *Aus Zeit und Geschichte*, 13–14 October 1940, p. 1.

79. Josef Sommerfeldt, 'Die Aussiedlung der Juden als letzte Rettung', *Krakauer Zeitung*, 23. 12.42.

80. Josef Sommerfeldt, 'Judenstaatsprojekte in der polnischen Publizistik des 19. Jahrhunderts', *Die Burg* (1944), 5, p. 14.

81. *Ibid*, pp. 17–18.

82. *Ibid.*, p. 18.

83. BA R52 IV/ 138, Dr Radig to SS-*Sturmbannführer* Dr von Troschke, Gauleitung des KL Auschwitz/Upper Silesia, 15.3.41, p. 44.

84. C. Klessmann, 'Osteuropaforschung und Lebensraumpolitik im Dritten Reich', *Wissenschaft im Dritten Reich*, ed. P. Lundgreen (Frankfurt am Main 1985), p. 365.

85. BA R52 IV/ 86, p. 87, Dr Hülle (Amt Rosenberg) to Dr Coblitz 31.8.40, and Coblitz to Werner Radig 29.8.40, and Radig to Coblitz 7.9.40 accepting Coblitz's offer of a post.

86. BA R52IV/86, Coblitz to Radig 29.8.40, and p. 3 for Radig's c.v.

87. BA R52IV/ 86, Radig c.v., pp. 2–3.

88. R. Bollmus, *Das Amt Rosenberg and seine Gegner. Studien zur Macht-kampf in nationalsozialistischen Herrschaftssystem* (Stuttgart 1970),

pp. 155–7; for the comparison with Frank see Klaus Schreiner, 'Führertum, Rasse, Reich. Wissenschaft von der Geschichte nach der national-sozialistichen Machtergreifung', *Wissenschaft im Dritten Reich*, pp. 218–21.

89. On Kossinna, see Hans Jürgen Eggers, *Einführung in die Vorgeschichte* (Munich 1986₃), pp. 199ff., and Gustav Kossinna, *Altgermanische Kulturhöhe. Eine Einführung in die deutsche Vor- und Frühgeschichte* (Leipzig 1934₄); The Amt Rosenberg's *Der Schulungsbriefe* were saturated with work on prehistory. See in particular Rudolf Ströbel, 'Der Kampf um die deutsche Vorgeschichte', *Der Schulungsbrief* (1935), 2, pp. 48ff. for the official view of Kossinna and 'Gustav Kossinna' (1936), 3, etc.

90. Bollmus, *Das Amt Rosenberg*, p. 159; Schreier, 'Führertum, Rasse, Reich', p. 219.

91. *Institut für deutsche Ostarbeit Krakau Jahrbuch* 1941, pp. 26–7.

92. *Ibid.*, pp. 19–20; 'Germanischer Führungsanspruch im Weichselraum', *Krakauer Zeitung* no. 215, 13.9.41, and 'Ausstellung „Germanenerbe im Weichselraum" verlängert', *Krakauer Zeitung* no. 234, 5.10.41 for a photograph of the exhibition.

93. BA R52 II/ 185, Hans Frank, *Tagebuch* 1941, pp. 51–5, 12.9.41.

94. W. Radig, 'Die Vorgeschichte des Ostdeutschen Lebensraumes', *Die Burg* (1941), 1, pp. 12–13. See also Radig's 'Indogermanen und Germanen im Weichselraum', *Institut für deutsche Ostarbeit Krakau Jahrbuch*, 1941, pp. 169ff.

95. BA R52 IV/ 67, p. 58, Hoff's c.v., no date.

96. BA R52 IV/ 67, p. 82, Dean of the Philosophical Faculty Breslau to the IdO 8.2.43.

97. Klessmann, *Die Selbstbehauptung einer Nation*, p. 63.

98. Erwin Hoff, 'Warum deutsche Führung im Generalgouvernement?', *Europ. Revue* (1942), 18, pp. 258–9.

99. *Ibid.*, p. 263. For Hoff's propaganda work see his 'Polen und die Politik der Nachbarn', *Krakauer Zeitung* 6.9.42; 'Das Generalgouvernement als verpflichtende geschichtliche Aufgabe', *Krakauer Zeitung* (date unknown); 'Recht und Sprache im alten Polen', *Krakauer Zeitung*, 16.8.42.

100. *Institut für deutsche Ostarbeit Krakau Jahrbuch* 1941, pp. 32–3. See also BAR52 IV/ 141, p. 78, Behrens to Coblitz 2.5.41 with plans for his section.

101. BA R52 IV/ 5, pp. 82ff., Behrens, 'Kunstgeschichte im Dienste der Volksforschung', no date. On Behrens see BA R52 IV/ 103, p. 95, c.v. 4.3.41, and BA R52 IV/ 15, pp. 2–6, c.v., no date, and p. 72, c.v. 12.11.40.

102. BA R52 IV/ 15, p. 72, c.v. 12.11.40.

103. 'Veit Stoss-Zeuge deutscher Berufung im Osten', *Krakauer Zeitung* no. 105, 9.5.41.

104. BA R52 IV/ 141, p. 41, 14.7.42 for Frank's opening speech for 'Altdeutsches Kunst aus Krakau und dem Karpathenland'.

105. BA R52 II/ 181, Hans Frank, *Tagebuch* 1941, pp. 150–2, 26.3.41.

106. BA T52 IV/ 95, p. 8, plans for celebration of Copernicus's death 1543–1943, no date, and p. 46, meeting on 31.3.43 to plan the celebrations; 'Nikolaus Kopernikus zum 400. Todestag am 24 Mai 1943', *Die Burg* (May 1943), 4.

107. BA R52 IV/ 95, p. 87, Erlass des Generalgouverneurs 20.4.41. See also *Institut für deutsche Ostarbeit Krakau Jahrbuch* 1941, pp. 22–5, for the terms of the Copernicus and Veit Stoss Prizes.

108. BA R52 IV/ 95, p. 62, Coblitz to Staatsanwalt Dr Meidinger 12.5.43.

109. Hans Frank, 'Ansprache anlässlich der Verteilung des Kopernikuspreises des Instituts für Deutsche Ostarbeit am 24 Mai 1943 in Krakau', *DFO* (1943), 3, pp. 109–10, and 'Wie es zu dem „polnischen" Kopernikus kam. Verwechseltes Grab und weitere Irrtümer-Vortrag von Professor Wolfrum', *Krakauer Zeitung*, 1.6.43. 'Das Werk des Kopernikus Symbolik deutschen Ringens', *Das Generalgouvernement* 23.5.43, p. 1. See also Erwin Hoff, 'Nikolaus Kopernicus', *Pressedienst des Generalgouvernements*, ed., *Der Pressechef der Regierung des Generalgouvernements* no. 70, 20.5.43, and BA R52 IV/ 113, Fritz Kubach (Kommission für die Kopernikus-Gesamtausgabe) 6.5.42 'Zur Schreibweise des Namens "Kopernikus"' for the matter of how to spell the astronomer's name. The PuSte was also involved in the general celebrations in 1943; see J. Papriz and Hans Schmauch, eds., *Kopernikus-Forschungen* (Leipzig 1943). For the totally insignificant battle over the nationality of Copernicus see Klessmann, *Die Selbstbehauptung einer Nation*, p. 51, and from a large range of earlier works, Adolf Warschauer, *Die Geschichte des Streites um die Nationalität des Kopernikus* (Berlin 1925). For the background to Copernicus monuments in nineteenth-century Prussia see *Nicolaus Copernicus. Dokumente seines Lebens. Archivalienausstellung des Staatlichen Archivlagers in Göttingen aus den Beständen der Stiftung Preussischer Kulturbesitz* (Göttingen 1973), p. 36.

110. BA R52 IV/ 96, p. 2. NODFG Albert Brackmann to Coblitz 17.7.44 agreeing to join the panel, and p. 5 Coblitz to Brackmann setting out the terms of the prize and the names of the other judges.

111. BA R52 II/ 178, Hans Frank, *Tagebuch* 1940, p. 708. Frank toured the research station at Pulawy. UJD IDO/ 83, 'Bericht über die Studienfahrt des Instituts für deutsche Ostarbeit, Krakau nach Pulawy vom 27–29/ 7.1942' (E. Hoff), pp. 1–8.

112. BA R52 IV/ 148, p. 22, memo by Dr Dannbeck on the work of the section 10.10.40.

113. *Institut für deutsche Ostarbeit Krakau. Jahrbuch* 1941, pp. 54–5.

114. Goguel, 'Über die Mitwirkung deutscher Wissenschaftler', p. 156.

115. BA R52 IV/ 68, p. 308, Dr Heinrich Kurtz to Coblitz 18.11.40.

116. *Institut für deutsche Ostarbeit Krakau. Jahrbuch* 1941, pp. 50–1.

117. *Ibid.*, p. 52 and Fritz Christiansen-Weniger, 'Die Landwirtschaft des Weichselraumes, ihr Zustand vor dem Kriege und ihre Entwicklungsmöglichkeiten', pp. 247ff.

118. Klessmann, *Die Selbstbehauptung einer Nation*, p. 64.

119. *Institut für deutsche Ostarbeit Krakau. Jahrbuch* 1941, pp. 44–5.

120. *Ibid.*, p. 45.

121. BA R52 IV/ 144b, Peter-Heinz Seraphim, *Die Wirtschaftsstruktur des Generalgouvernements* (Krakau 1941), p. 19.

122. *Ibid.*, p. 21.

123. *Ibid.*, p. 33. For a good discussion of how 'overpopulation' was measured see Susanne Heim and Götz Aly, *Ein Berater der Macht*, pp. 30–1.

124. Seraphim, *Die Wirtschaftsstruktur*, pp. 34–5.

125. *Ibid.*, pp. 44–5.

126. *Ibid.*, pp. 63–4.

127. *Ibid.*, pp. 68–9.

128. *Ibid.*, p. 87.

129. Goguel, 'Über die Mitwirkung deutscher Wissenschaftler', pp. 152ff.

130. On Meinhold, see BA R52 IV/ 68, pp. 188ff., p. 192 18.5.44, c.v.; BA R52 R52 IV/ 144a, H. Meinhold, 'Die Erweiterung des Generalgouvernements nach Osten (July 1941), pp. 1–2 and p. 10. For what follows, Susanne Heim and Götz Aly, *Ein Berater der Macht*, pp. 33ff. is both fundamental and comprehensive.

131. *Ibid.*, pp. 1 and 11. Susanne Heim and Götz Aly, *Ein Berater der Macht*, pp. 47–8.

132. H. Graul, Aufgaben und Bedeutung der Sektion Landeskunde', *Deutsche Forschungen im Osten* (1941), 1, p. 21.

133. *Ibid.*, p. 21.

134. *Institut für deutsche Ostarbeit Krakau. Jahrbuch* 1941, pp. 47–8

135. Graul, 'Aufgaben und Bedeutung der Sektion Landeskunde', p. 22.

136. *Ibid.*, p. 26.

137. *Ibid.*, p. 25.

138. BA R52 IV/ 2, p. 116, Anordnung 18.2.43.

139. BA R52 IV/ 118, p. 29, Coblitz to *Reichskriegsopferführer* Oberlinder 30.6.44.

140. BA R52 IV/ 5, pp. 122, Coblitz to Holrat Prof. Dr Kallbrunner 5.10.43.

141. BA R52 IV 101, Regierung deg Generalgouvernements to Coblitz', p. 57 2.9.43.

142. BA R52 II/ 173, 'Bericht über Aufbau des IdO in Zandt' 3.2.45, pp. 14–24 for the individual research projects.

143. Some 250 Russian and Ukrainian academics were working in the Generalgouvernement, see BA R52 II/ 208, Hans Frank, *Tagebuch* 1943, p. 1044, 19.10.43. This was at variance with Coblitz's desire to deny any scientific achievements of the Slavs. See BA R52 IV 101, p. 70, Hauptabtl. Wissenschaft und Unterricht to Coblitz 25.8.43, giving him permission to remove a plaque from the walls of the IdO building commemorating two Poles responsible for discovering the liquefaction of air.

144. BA R52 II/ 173, 'Bericht über Aufbau des IdO in Zandt' p. 22, and BA R52 IV/ 13c, p. 4, Coblitz to Frank 11.10.44.

145. BA R52 IV/ 133, p. 180, Professor Walther to the IdO 2.1.45 and account for small debts incurred (the prisoners' wage bill), p. 178 November 1944, and p. 172 Walther to the IdO's accountant 1.2.45.

146. UJA IDO/ 92, Dr Hans-Paul Müller to Dr Pietsch 4.10.44 and 5.10.44 referring to telephone conversations and a meeting with SS-*Obergruppenführer* O. Pohl (SS-WVHA) and a visit by Müller to Flossenbürg planned for 5 October. See also BDC SS-HO 'Häftlinge im wissenschaftlichen Einsatz' (Geheim!) 6.1.45 for a detailed account of negotiations between the IdO and the SS concerning the employment of 100 prisoners from KZ Plaszow and Flossenbürg.

147. BA R52 II/ 173, 'Bericht über Aufbau des IdO in Zandt', p. 23.

148. BA R75 DAI/ 344, 'Reisebericht Dr Kloss', p. xvi.

149. BA R52 IV/ 101, p. 137, Coblitz to Hauptabteilung Wissenschaft und Unterricht der Regierung des Generalgouvernement 12.3.42.

150. *Ibid.*, p. 137.

151. Goguel, 'Über die Mitwirkung deutscher Wissenschaftler', p. 120, *Anhang* Document 8(b), *Aktennotiz* Zipfel on conversation with Papritz 1.12.41.

152. *Ibid.*, p. 138 Document no. 13, Semkowicz testimony during the Bühler-Prozess 27.2.46.

153. Klessmann, *Die Selbstbehauptung einer Nation*, p. 140.

154. *Ibid.*, p. 140; Gawęda, *Die Jagiellonische Universität*, pp. 48ff. for Małecki.

155. Goguel, 'Über die Mitwirkung deutscher Wissenschaftler', *Anhang* Document no. 12, p. 134, Testimony of Władysław Semkowicz, Bühler-Prozess 27.2.46 and Document (b), p. 135, Testimony of Prof. M. Małecki 22.1.46.

156. On Rudert's background see BA R52 IV/ 88, p. 7, 'Studiengang und bisherige berufliche Tätigkeit' 17.3.44.

157. BA R52 IV/ 61, p. 56, Werner Radig reference for a Pole in the geography section, 5.9.41, and BA R52 IV/ 88, pp. 39–40, Rudert to Coblitz 10.10.42 on his successful recruitment of an informer among the non-German staff.

158. BA R52 IV/ 13g, p. 7, Testimony of SS-*Sturmführer* Albrecht, 'Angaben des Herrn. Dr Rudert über die von ihm beabsichtigte Meldung an den SD' 13.2.44 and pp. 8ff. Coblitz to Frank 13.2.44 with counter-accusations.

159. UJD IDO/ 40, Antek Maryański to Professor Heinrich Wolfrum 2.7.44.

160. BA R52 IV/ 66, p. 60, Charlotte Gorn to Arbeitsamt 13.2.42.

161. BA R52 IV/ 65, p. 52, c.v. Gretchen Foyer, no date.

162. BA R52 IV/ 69, pp. 117–18, Erna Löwenberg job application 17.8.40, and p. 21, Erika Löptien c.v., no date, and BA R52 IV/ 75, pp. 64f., Ursula Schmidt c.v., no date.

163. BA R52 IV/ 64, p. 49, Julia Dsinkas c.v., no date, and pp. 49–58 work record and c.v. 9.6.43, and pp. 65ff. Prof. A. Schatsky c.v., no date.

164. BA R52 IV/ 90, p. 71 c.v. Alexis Zwetikow, no date.

165. BA R52 IV/ 75, p. 39f., Ada Schmidt-Kowtanjuk c.v., no date, pp. 46–7 for the disappearance of her husband and father in Siberia. See also UJA IDO/39, personal file including her c.v. 10.5.43.

166. BA R52 II/ 182, Hans Frank, *Tagebuch* 1941, p. 335 23.4.41. See ch. 4, sec. ii above on the role of Sappok.

167. BA R52 II/ 182, Hans Frank, *Tagebuch* 1941, pp. 440–2 9.5.41.

168. BA R52 II/ 184, Hans Frank, *Tagebuch* 1941, p. 629 17.7.41.

169. BA R52 II/ 185, Hans Frank, *Tagebuch* 1941, p. 785 4.9.41.

170. BA R52 II/ 187, Hans Frank, *Tagebuch* 1941, p. 1086 21.11.41.

171. Klessmann, *Die Selbstbehauptung einer Nation*, Anhang, pp. 247–8, Adolf Warzke, 'Die Kopernikus-Universität in Krakau', *Schlesische Volkszeitung*, 26.6.41. See also 'Neuartige Struktur der künftigen Coppernicus-Universität', *Krakauer Zeitung*, 11.6.41.

172. *Verordnungsblatt für das Generalgouvernement*, ed. *Amt für Gesetzgebung in der Regierung des Generalgouvernements* (Krakau 1942), 7, p. 49, 5.2.43 Artikel II, clause 2.

173. 'Gauleiter Greiser verkündet die Reichsstiftung für deutsche Ostforschung', *Ostdeutscher Beobachter* 10.3.41.

174. Goguel, 'Über die Mitwirkung deutscher Wissenschaftler' p. 91, and Herder Institut Marburg, 32, XV, JZ2 PuSte Nordostberichte no. 52, 8.4.41 'Deutsches akademisches Leben in Posen' pp. 3d. and 'Jüngste Reichsuniversität in der Gauhauptstadt', *Litzmannstadter Zeitung* 9.3.41.

175. J. Kalisch and G. Voigt, 'Reichsuniversität Posen', *Juni* 1941, ed. A. Anderle (East Berlin 1961), pp. 190–1, and Goguel, 'Über die Mitwirkung deutscher Wissenschaftler', p. 96, and *Anhang*, p. 40 for Himmler's interest. On the *Reichsuniversität*, see also F. Paprocki and K. M. Pospieszalski, 'Reichsuniversität Posen', *Przegląd Zachodni* (1956), 12, pp. 275ff., and Klessmann, 'Osteuropaforschung und Lebensraumpoli-

tik', pp. 367ff. For Hitler's role see Hans Streit, 'Der Ostauftrag der Reichsuniversität Posen', *Völkischer Beobachter*, 2.3.41.

176. J. Kalisch and G. Voigt, 'Reichsuniversität Posen', p. 191.

177. *Ibid.*, pp. 191–2.

178. *Ibid.*, p. 192.

179. GStA Rep. 92 *Nachlass Brackmann* no. 85, Brackmann to Wittram 7.10.42.

180. Goguel, 'Über die Mitwirkung deutscher Wissenschaftler', *Anhang* Document (b) Hippius 'Entwurf über die Aufgaben and Wege einer Bevölkerungsplanung im Warthegau' 5.12.39.

181. Kalisch and Voigt, 'Reichsuniversität Posen', p. 188.

182. Goguel, 'Über die Mitwirkung deutscher Wissenschaftler', *Anhang*, pp. 51–2, 'Die Aufgabenstellung der Reichsuniversität', Carstens speech 27.4.41. Streit, 'Der Ostauftrag der Reichsuniversität Posen', *Völkischer Beobachter*, 2.3.41.

183. *Ibid.*, p. 53, SS-*Sturmbannführer* Carstens 'Angaben über meine politische Tätigkeit', no date.

184. Kalisch and Voigt, 'Reichsuniversität Posen', p. 189.

185. *Ibid.*, p. 193, and Goguel, 'Über die Mitwirkung deutscher Wissenschaftler', pp. 112–13.

186. Kalisch and Voigt, 'Reichsuniversität Posen', p. 195.

187. Goguel, 'Über die Mitwirkung deutscher Wissenschaftler', p. 113.

188. Klessmann, 'Osteuropaforschung und Lebensraumpolitik', p. 367, Kalisch and Voigt, 'Reichsuniversität Posen', p. 189, and Streit, 'Der Ostauftrag der Reichsuniversität Posen', *Völkischer Beobachter*, 2.3.41.

189. Kalisch and Voigt, 'Reichsuniversität Posen', p. 194.

190. F. Paprocki and K. M. Pospieszalski, 'Reichsuniversität Posen', p. 286. Citing H. Kłab 'Wspomnienia z wykładu medycyny sadowej', *Archiwum Historii i Filozofii Medycyny*, 18, pp. 295–8.

191. Goguel, 'Über die Mitwirkung deutscher Wissenschaftler', pp. 124–5.

192. K. M. Pospieszalski, 'Z pamietwika professora 'Reichsuniversität Posen', *Przegląd Zachodni* (1955), 1/2, pp. 288, 290, 294. For extracts from Voss's diaries see now *Biedermann und Schreibtischtäter. Materialien zur deutschen Täter-Biographie*, eds. Götz Aly, Peter Chroust, H. D. Heilmann, H. Langbein, *Beiträge zur nationalsozialistischen Gesundheits- und Sozialpolitik* (Berlin 1987), 4, pp. 15ff.

193. 'Gauleiter Greiser verkündet die Reichsstiftung für deutsche Ostforschung', *Ostdeutscher Beobachter*, 10.3.41.

194. Kalisch and Voigt, 'Reichsuniversität Posen', p. 198 n. 57.

195. *Ibid.*, p. 201 n 73.

196. Goguel, 'Über die Mitwirkung deutscher Wissenschaftler', *Anhang*, p. 66 Satzung der Reichsstiftung für deutsche Ostforschung 3.3.41, § 3–4.

197. *Ibid.*, § 4, ii and Kalisch and Voigt, 'Reichsuniversität Posen', p. 199 on the profits derived from these properties.

198. Goguel, 'Über die Mitwirkung deutscher Wissenschaftler', *Anhang*, pp. 68–9, 'Liste der Leiter der Arbeitsgemeinschaften, Arbeitskreise und Institute der Reichsstiftung' in August 1943.

199. *Thorner Freiheit* 19.3.41.

200. *Stuttgart NS-Kurier* 28.10.41.

201. Goguel, 'Über die Mitwirkung deutscher Wissenschaftler', p. 70.

202. Kalisch and Voigt, 'Reichsuniversität Posen', p. 202.

203. GStA Rep. 92 *Nachlass Brackmann* no. 83, Brackmann to Aubin 10.3.41.

204. 'Wissenschaft im Osten', *Frankfurter Zeitung* 12.3.41. In April 1941 a journalist in 'Krakau' was sacked for suggesting that relations between the IdO and Reichsstiftung were cool. See BA R52 II/ 181, Hans Frank *Tagebuch*, 1941, pp. 262–3 8.4.41.

205. Goguel, 'Über die Mitwirkung deutscher Wissenschaftler', *Anhang*, p. 69, Zipfel memo 1.12.42.

206. BA R52 II/ 200 Hans Frank, *Tagebuch* 1943, p. 53 3.2.43.

207. BA R153/ 1152 PuSte memo on the Heydrich-*Stiftung* 29.6.43.

208. BA R153/ 1206, Reinhard Heydrich *Stiftung* to Papritz 22.4.44 and 18.5.44. On Franz see Helmut Heiber, *Walter Frank und sein Reichsinstitut für Geschichte des neuen Deutschlands* (Stuttgart 1974), pp. 106 and 186, and SS-*Leithefte* (1938), 'Der deutsche Bauernkrieg' no. 3, ix, pp. 85–90 and (1938), 4, i 'Deutschlands Weg durch den Dreissigjährigen Krieg', pp. 59–69. For Franz's thoughts on National Socialism and History see 'Das Geschichtsbild des Nationalsozialismus und die deutsche geschichtswissenschaft', *Geschichte und Geschichtsbewusstsein*, ed. O. Hauser (Göttingen 1981), pp. 91ff.

209. Kalisch and Voigt, 'Reichsuniversität Posen', pp. 200–1.

210. 'Waffenschmiede des Geistes. Tagung der Zentrale für Ostforschung', *Berliner Börsen Zeitung*, 30.10.43.

211. BA R153/ 1165, Papritz memo on a conversation with Dr Coulon 7.6.43.

212. BA R153/ 1283, RF-SS (RKFDV) to the PuSte 30.3.44 'Vermerk' on *Arbeitstagung* in Prague, pp. 4–12.

6. THE 'BAND OF THE UNBROKEN' AND THEIR CRITICS ASPECTS OF *OSTFORSCHUNG* AFTER 1945

1. 'Wolfgang Wippermann, *Der Ordensstaat als Ideologie* (Berlin 1979); *Der 'Deutsche Drang nach Osten': Ideologie und Wirklichkeit eines politischen Schlagwortes* (Darmstadt 1931); 'Die Ostsiedlung in der deutschen Historiographie und Publizistik. Probleme, Methoden und Grundlinien der Entwicklung bis zum Ersten Weltkrieg', in W. Fritze,

ed., *Germania Slavica* (Berlin 1980), 1, pp. 41–70; C. Klessmann, 'Osteuropaforschung und Lebensraumpolitik im Dritten Reich', in P. Lundgreen, ed., *Wissenschaft im Dritten Reich* (Frankfurt am Main 1985), pp. 350ff., reprinted in shorter form in *Aus Politik und Zeitgeschichte* B 7/84 (1984), pp. 33–45; and, from the *Osteuropaforscher*, Manfred Hellmann, 'Zur Lage der historischen Erforschung des östlischen Europa in der Bundesrepublik Deutschland', *Jahrbuch der historischen Forschung*, ed. Christoph Frhr. von Maltzahn, *Berichtsjahr*, 1979 (Stuttgart 1980), pp. 13ff.; Helmut König, 'Ostforschung- Bilanz und Ausblick', *Osteuropa* (1975), 25, pp. 786ff.; Friedrich Kuebart, 'Zur Entwicklung der Osteuropaforschung in Deutschland bis 1945', *Osteuropa* (1980), 30, pp. 657ff.; Oskar Anweiler, '25 Jahre Osteuropaforschung – Wissenschaft und Zeitgeschichte', *Osteuropa* (1977), 27, pp. 183ff.; and for research on south-eastern Europe see Klaus-Detlef Grothusen, 'Südosteuropa und Südosteuropa-Forschung in der Bundesrepublik Deutschland', in H. Lemberg, P. Nitschke and E. Oberländer, eds., *Osteuropa in Geschichte und Gegenwart. Festschrift für Günther Stökl zum 60. Geburtstag* (Cologne/Vienna 1977), pp. 408ff.; Franz Ronneberger, 'Zwischenbilanz der Südosteuropa-Forschung: Leistungsstand, Schwierigkeiten, Zukunftsprognosen', *Südosteuropa-Mitteilungen* (1980), 20, pp. 3–17. Most recently see Hans Lemberg, 'Lage und Perspektiven der Zeitgeschichtsforschung über Ostmitteleuropa in der Bundesrepublik Deutschland', *ZfO* (1986), 35, pp. 191ff. These last three titles are mainly concerned with methodological questions arising from the study of contemporary central and south-eastern Europe and not with the history of their respective disciplines in the Nazi period. For a more radical approach see Susanne Heim and Götz Aly, *Ein Berater der Macht. Helmut Meinhold oder der Zusammenhang, zwischen Sozialpolitik und Judenvernichtung* (Hamburg/Berlin 1986).

2. Rudolf Graf, 'Hermann Aubin im Dienste der faschistischen Okkupationspolitik gegenüber Polen und des klerikal-militarischen Antibolshewismus', *Beiträge zur Geschichte der Arbeiterbewegung* (1960), 2, p. 188 for an example of this genre. In addition to the DDR works discussed below see W. Stzeczinowski, 'Die Organisation der Ostforschung', *ZfG* (1954), 2, pp. 288–309; and Gerd Voigt, 'Methoden der Ostforschung', *ZfG* (1959), 7, p. 1793ff.

3. Wippermann, *Der 'Deutsche Drang nach Osten'*, pp. 117–20 and his *Der Ordensstaat als Ideologie*, pp. 304ff.

4. Ludwig Petry, 'Hermann Aubin in Giessen und Breslau', *Hermann Aubin 1885–1969. Werk und Leben. Reden gehalten am 23. März 1970 bei der Trauefeier des Instituts für geschichtliche Landeskunde an der Rheinischen Friedrich-Wilhelms Universität Bonn* (Bonn 1970), p. 27; from a large range of obituaries see G. Rhode and Walther Kuhn, 'Hermann

Aubin und die Geschichte des deutschen und europäischen Ostens', *ZfO* (1969), 18, pp. 601–21.

5. Petry, 'Hermann Aubin in Giessen', p. 28.

6. *Ibid.*, p. 28.

7. *Ibid.*, pp. 31–2.

8. *Ibid.*, pp. 32–3.

9. *Ibid.*, Otto Brunner, 'Hermann Aubin in Hamburg', p. 36; Hans Rothfels, 'Zur Gedenken an der Vorzitzenden des Verbandes der Historiker Deutschlands', pp. 70–1.

10. Graf, 'Hermann Aubin im Dienste', p. 187.

11. *Ibid.*, pp. 209–10.

12. Hermann Aubin, 'Zur Erforschung der deutschen Ostbewegung', in *Grundlagen und Perspektiven geschichtlicher Kulturraumforschung und Kulturmorphologie*, ed. Franz Petri (Bonn 1965), p. 548; see also W. Wippermann, *Der 'Deutsche Drang nach Osten'*, pp. 108–9; Klessmann, 'Osteuropaforschung und Lebensraumpolitik', pp. 372–3.

13. On this see Klessmann, 'Osteuropaforschung und Lebensraumpolitik', pp. 353 and 375 n 10 for similar observations about the work of Otto Brunner. Present-day admirers of Aubin's work might deepen their acquaintance with the work of the earlier *Annaliste* historians in France.

14. Aubin, 'Zur Erforschung der deutschen Ostbewegung', pp. 553, 556, 578, 581, 593, 613.

15. *Ibid.*, pp. 551, 554, 559, 562, 564, 569, 577, 604, 606, 610, 625.

16. *Ibid.*, pp. 555, 593, 580.

17. *Ibid.*, pp. 578, 593, 615, 625.

18. *Ibid.*, pp. 563, 567, 609, 611.

19. *Ibid.*, p. 556.

20. *Ibid.*, pp. 556, 557, 562, 604, 615.

21. *Ibid.*, p. 564.

22. *Ibid.*, pp. 565, 567 for these and pp. 558, 575, 613ff. for 'drives'.

23. For a good discussion of the primacy of politics from a radical perspective see Tony Judt 'A Clown in Regal Purple: Social History and the Historians', *History Workshop* (1979), 7, pp. 56–94.

24. See for example Hermann Aubin, *Schlesien als Aufallstor deutscher Kultur nach dem Osten im Mittelalter* (Breslau 1937), pp. 8, 11, 13, 21 (higher civilization); 9, 11, 17, 19, 39 (waves/streams etc.); 19 (blood).

25. Hermann Aubin, 'Das Deutsche Reich und die Völker des Ostens', *Die Burg* (1940), 1, pp. 7–8.

26. *Ibid.*, p. 13. See also Hermann Aubin, *Die geschichtlichen Kräfte für den Neuaufbau im mittelalterlichen Osten. Festvortrag aus Anlass der Eröffnung der sudetendeutschen Anstalt für Landes- und Volksforschung im Reichenberg am 13. Oktober 1940* (Berlin 1940), p. 7 for Versailles and p. 37 for 'die Macht des deutschen Volkes unter dem Führer, der ihm

geschenkt wurde, neu erwacht war ... etc.' Although in this lecture Aubin *defers* an approach based upon scientific racism (see p. 20), on pp. 19 and 35 he resorts to biology and blood as causal agencies. The distance between the 'respectable' academic norm and the full-blown racial scientists does not seem to have been that great in their respective resorts to the irrational.

27. The phrase 'band of the unbroken' comes from the foreword to the *ZfO* (1952), 1.

28. Hermann Aubin, 'An einem neuen Anfang der Ostforschung', *ZfO* (1952), 1, p. 3; on this see Wippermann, *Der 'Deutsche Drang nach Osten'*, pp. 126–7.

29. *Ibid.*, p. 10.

30. For the statements in the journals see W. Kienast and T. Schieder, 'Der Historikertag in Trier', *HZ* (1958), 185, pp. 728–31, and E. Engelberg, L. Stern, M. Steinmetz etc. 'Zu den Vorfällen auf der 24. Versammlung des westdeutschen Historiker-Verbandes in Trier', *ZfG* (1958), 6, pp. 1134ff. For the details of the DDR case see *Trier- und wie Weiter? Materielen, Betrachtungen und Schlussfolgerungen über die Ereignisse auf dem Trierer Historikertag am 25 September 1958*, eds. E. Engelberg, W. Berthold and R. Rudolph (Berlin 1959), pp. 7–24. See also H. Elsner, 'Die Geschichte des östlichen Europa in Forschung und Lehre im Rahmen der Wissenschafts- und Hochschulpolitik der DDR', in M. Hellmann, ed., *Osteuropa in der historischen Forschung der DDR* (Düsseldorf 1972), 1, p. 46, and Klessmann, 'Osteuropaforschung und Lebensraumpolitik', p. 372.

31. Elsner, 'Abteilung für Geschichte der imperialistischen Ostforschung', *Osteuropa in der historischen forschung der DDR* 1, p. 123.

32. F.-H. Gentzen, 'Die "Ostforschung" westdeutscher historiker – eine Hetze gegen die Sowjetunion und Volkspolen', *Einheit. Zeitschrift für Theorie und Praxis des wissenschaftlichen Sozialismus* (1955), 11, p. 1215. This appeared in Polish as '"Ostforschung" zachodnio-nie-mieckich historykow', *Przeglád Zachodni* (1956), 12, pp. 291–300. On Gentzen see Hellmann, ed., *Osteuropa in der historischen*, Forschung der DDR, 2, p. 365. These two volumes contain much useful biblio-graphical and biographical material.

33. Gentzen, 'Die "Ostforschung" ', pp. 1214, 1216, 1218.

34. Elsner, 'Abteilung für Geschichte der imperialistischen Ostforschung', p. 124.

35. Claus Remer, 'Über die Tätigkeit der Arbeitsgemeinschaft zur Bekämp-fung der westdeutschen Ostforschung', *Jahrbuch für die Geschichte der UdSSR und der volksdemokratischen Länder Europas* (1963), 7, pp. 451–3; Elsner, 'Abteilung für Geschichte', pp. 124–5.

36. F.-H. Gentzen, J. Kalisch, G. Voigt and E. Wolfgramm, 'Die "Ostfor-

schung" – ein Stosstrupp des deutschen Imperialismus', *ZfG* (1958), 6, p. 1184.

37. *Ibid*, p. 1200
38. *Ibid.*, p. 1202
39. *Ibid.*, p. 1204.
40. *Ibid.*, pp. 1208, 1216–17.
41. *Ibid.*, pp. 1214–15.
42. *Ibid.*, pp. 1214–15.
43. F.-H. Gentzen and Eberhard Wolfgramm, „Ostforscher" – „Ostforschung" Taschenbuch Geschichte 8 (East Berlin 1960), p. 16.
44. *Ibid.*, p. 88.
45. Eberhard Wolfgramm, 'Kämpft für den Frieden, arbeitet für die Zukunft des deutschen Volkes. Abrechnung mit der Vergangenheit, von einer ehemaligen „Ostforscher"', *Deutsche Aussenpolitik* (1959), 4, p. 992.
46. *Ibid.*, p. 995.
47. *Ibid.*, p. 996.
48. On the Berlin and Halle groups see Elsner, 'Abteilung für Geschichte', p. 125, and Remer, 'Über die Tätigkeit der Arbeitsgemeinschaft', pp. 452ff. For an example of the work of the Berlin group see *Information* (Vertraulich) *Abteilung für Geschichte der imperialistischen Ostforschung an der Humboldt-Universität* (East Berlin 1962), 2, pp. 1–81. I am grateful to a friend for this publication. For conferences see 'Wissenschaftliche Arbeitstagung zur Kritik der westdeutschen "Ostforschung"', *ZfG* (1964), 12, pp. 1224–6.
49. Remer, 'Über die Tätigkeit der Arbeitsgemeinschaft', p. 454.
50. Elsner, 'Abteilung für Geschichte', p. 129.
51. Goguel, 'Über die Mitwirkung deutscher Wissenschaftler am Okkupationsregime in Polen im 2. Weltkrieg, untersucht an 3 Institutionen der deutschen Ostforschung', Phil. Diss. (East Berlin 1964), in *Lebenslauf*, p. 181.
52. *Rudi Goguel, Es war ein langer Weg. Ein Roman unserer Zeit* (Düsseldorf 1947), pp. 18–22. I am grateful to Rolf Huhn for a copy of Goguel's autobiographical novel. See also Karl Schabrod, *Widerstand gegen Flick und Florian. Düsseldorfer Antifachisten über ihren Widerstand 1933–1945* (Frankfurt am Main 1978), pp. 113–22 and 199; Allan Merson, *Communist Resistance in Nazi Germany* (London 1965), pp. 137–9. I am very grateful to Dr Merson for the loan of books on the KPD resistance and for a letter about Rudi Goguel.
53. Goguel, *Es war ein langer Weg*, pp. 149ff. *Der rote Grossvater erzählt. Berichte und Erzählungen von Veteranen der Arbeiterbewegung aus der Zeit von 1914 bis 1945*, ed. by the Werkstatt Düsseldorf des Werkkreises Literatur der Arbeitswelt (Frankfurt am Main 1974), pp. 148ff., for Goguel as the composer of the *Moorsoldatenlied*.

54. Rudi Goguel, 'Über die Mitwirkung deutscher Wissenschaftler'.
55. HStA *Nachlass Papritz* 340, C12c 108, 12 'Goguel. Ostzonale Geschichte der PuSte 1963– ', Rudi Goguel to Papritz 12.12.63 'Für die Beurteilung des historischen Ablaufs scheinen mir auch die subjektiven Faktoren- z.B. persönliche Motive der handelnden Persönlichkeiten, des allgemeine politische Klima und dergl. -von nicht unterschätzender Bedeutung zu sein'; Papritz to H. Weiss (Director of the Herder Institute) 17.12.63 requesting that Goguel's name be put on the next agenda of the Forschungsrat; Papritz memo 4.2.64 noting that Werner Conze and R. Wittram had agreed to cooperate with Goguel 'Weil Goguel die Posener Universitätsakten in Händen haben dürfte'; Papritz to Goguel 6.2.64 rejecting his request for an interview; Papritz to Aubin 9.3.64 enclosing all correspondence on Goguel; Papritz to Ministerialdirigent Dr Freiherr von Zahn (Ministry for Overall German Affairs) 12.3.64 'Es wird Sie vielleicht interessieren zu erfahren, dass mit einem massiven ostzonalen Versuch zu rechnen ist, die Beziehungen der deutschen Ostforscher zu ostmitteleuropäischen Fachgenossen zu stören. Dazu soll eine Darstellung der Geschichte der deutschen Ostforschung vor dem zweiten Weltkrieg dienen'. Hostility to *Ostforschung* seems also to have been *communis opinio* across the Atlantic. This letter continues, 'übrigens bemüht sich auch Herr Epstein USA, um die Geschichte der deutschen Ostforschung; Es ist ein zweibändiges Werk im Entstehen, und man darf auch hier eine unfreundliche Darstellung erwarten. "Ostforscher" ist, auf einem Deutschen bezogen, heut wie schon vor 30 Jahren ein Schimpfwort'. Goguel to Papritz 17.2.64, arguing that refusal to cooperate with him implied continuing identification with past activities; Zahn (Ministry of Overall German Affairs) to Papritz 27.4.64, 'Ich hätte gern Herrn Wittram gefragt, was ihn veranlasst, an einer marxistischen Historiographie mitzuwirken'; Papritz to Zahn 29.4.64 stressing the need for a history of German *Ostforschung* and for information on Goguel; Zahn to Papritz 25.5.64, 'Er (Goguel) soll wegen seiner kritischen Einstellung bei der Partei wenig beliebt gewesen sein'. Ironically, by the time this correspondence took place, the work of the departments in the DDR had almost come to an end.
56. Rudi Goguel, 'Über Ziele und Methoden der Ostforschung', *„Ostforschung" und Slawistik. Kritische Auseinandersetzungen. Vorgetragen auf der Arbeitstagung am 3. Juli 1959 am Institut für Slawistik der Deutschen Akademie der Wissenschaften zu Berlin* (East Berlin 1960), ed. Gerhard Ziegengeist, pp. 14–15.
57. *Ibid.*, p. 17.
58. Rudi Goguel, 'Ostpolitik und Ostforschung', *ZfG* (1964), 12, pp. 1352–3. This article was particularly 'responsive' to shifts in West

German opinion and policy. It also endeavours to lump together the most miscellaneous historians under the rubric of *Ostforschung*.

59. Elsner, 'Abteilung für Geschichte der imperialistischen Ostforschung', pp. 130–1 sees 1966 as a turning point.

60. Klaus Mehnert, 'Abriss der slawischen und Osteuropa-Forschung in Deutschland seit 1945', *Johann Gottfried Herder-Institut Wissenschaftliche Beiträge zur Geschichte und Landeskunde Ostmitteleuropa* (Marburg 1951), 1, pp. 2ff. Jens Hacker, 'Die Entwicklung der Ostforschung seit 1945. Ein Blick auf die bestehenden Institute und ihre Arbeitsweise', ed. Landeskuratorium UNTEILBARES DEUTSCHLAND Schleswig-Holstein (Kiel 1958), pp. 6ff. I am grateful to Mechtild Rössler for all these references.

61. Hacker, 'Die Entwicklung der Ostforschung', pp. 6, 10.

62. Joachim Freiherr von Braun, 'Fünf Jahre Arbeit für den deutschen Osten. Der Göttinger Arbeitskreis. Tätigkeitsbericht zu seinen funfjährigen Bestehen', *Jahrbuch der Albertus Universität zu Königsberg/Pr.* (1952), 2, pp. 210–12.

63. *Ibid.*, pp. 229–30.

64. Hacker, 'Die Entwicklung der Ostforschung', pp. 6–11 for brief surveys of each institute.

65. *Ibid.*, p. 18.

66. *Ibid.*, p. 19.

67. Apart from the large DDR literature on Oberländer, e.g. *Die Wahrheit über Oberländer. Braunbuch über die verbrecherische faschistische Vergangenheit des Bonner Ministers*, ed. Ausschuss für Deutsche Einheit (n.d., n.p.), which consists of indiscriminate personal denunciation, see 'All Honourable Men', *Wiener Library Bulletin* (1952), 7, pp. 43–51 for Seraphim, 'Reactionary Professors', *Wiener Library Bulletin* (1958), 12, p. 7 (Seraphim); and 'Stirrings of Nationalism', *Wiener Library Bulletin* (1955), 9, p. 6 (Oberländer), for the post-war careers of former *Ostforscher*.

68. HStA *Nachlass* Papritz 340, C12g, Aubin to Papritz 2.6.49.

69. Erich Keyser, 'Der Johann Gottfried Herder-Forschungsrat und des Johann Gottfried Herder-Institut', *ZfO* (1952), 1, p. 102.

70. Erich Weise, *Das Widerstandsrecht im Ordensland Preussen und das mittelalterliche Europa* (Göttingen 1955), p. 10.

71. *Ibid.*; on this tendency see Wippermann, *Der Ordensstaat als Ideologie*, pp. 328–9.

72. Weise, *Das Widerstandsrecht*, p. 45 for visiting aristocrats and European solidarity in the fourteenth century.

73. L. Kuhn, 'Ritterorden als Grenzhüter des Abendlandes gegen das östliche Heidentum', *Ostdeutsche Wissenschaft. Jahrbuch des Ostdeutschen Kulturrates*, ed. Max H. Boehm, F. Valjavec and W. Weizsäcker (1959), 6,

pp. 68–9; see also Wippermann, *Der Ordensstaat als Ideologie*, pp. 329–30 n. 55.

74. *The German East*, ed. Karl Pagel (Berlin 1954), p. 7. I am grateful to Dietz von Beulwitz for giving me this curious publication.

75. *Ibid.*, p. 8 (Introduction).

76. Karl Pagel, 'The West and German Expansion', in *ibid.*, pp. 31–2.

77. Erich Keyser, 'German Achievement in Prussia', in *ibid.*, pp. 39–40.

78. Theodor Oberländer, 'Der revolutionäre Krieg', *Der Stahlhelm. Organ des Stalhelm/Bund der Frontsoldaten* (1962), 29, no. 2, front page.

79. *Ibid.*, p. 2.

80. From a growing literature see most recently *Wissenschaft im Dritten Reich*, ed. Peter Lundgreen (Frankfurt am Main 1985), and *Hochschule und Wissenschaft im Dritten Reich*, ed. Jörg Tröger (Frankfurt am Main 1986), and Hochschule und Wissenschaft im Faschismus', *Forum Wissenschaft* (1985), no. 2, pp. 3–50, as well as monographs on particular disciplines, e.g. Ottheim Rammstedt, *Deutsche Soziologie 1933–1945 Die Normalität einer Anpassung* (Frankfurt am Main 1986), or Alan D. Beyerchen, *Scientists under Hitler. Politics and the Physics Community in the Third Reich* (Yale 1977). Although Heiber's monumental study of Walter Frank remains, to my mind, the single most important work on academics under the Nazi regime, one should mention K. F. Werner's *Das NS-Geschichtsbild und die Geschichtswissenschaft* (Stuttgart 1967), although this makes no use of archival sources and takes an unnecessarily optimistic view of the ability of historians to 'resist' the 'incursions' of Nazi ideology into their work. Here it has been argued that the differences between what passed for normality and what the Nazis themselves thought were not mutually exclusive or unconnected.

81. Helmut König, 'Ostforschung – Bilanz und Ausblick. Bericht und Gedanken zu einer erweiterten Redaktionskonferenz', *Osteuropa* (1975), 25, p. 787.

82. *Ibid.*, pp. 794–9. See also Hans Lemberg, 'Lage und Perspektiven der Zeitgeschichtsforschung über Ostmitteleuropa in der Bundesrepublik Deutschland', *ZfO* (1986), 35, pp. 214–15 for what follows on the different problems of three generations of *Ostforscher*. I am grateful to Albrecht Kannegiesser for this reference.

83. König, 'Ostforschung – Bilanz und Ausblick', pp. 799–801 for a good discussion of the advisory function of academics.

84. This point was made by Arnold Buchholz in 'Koordination und Ressortbezug in der bundesgeförderten Osteuropaforschung', *Osteuropa* (1980), 30, p. 689. For the phrase in 'the proximity but not in the tow of politics', see O. Anweiler, '25 Jahre Osteuropaforschung – Wissenschaft und Zeitgeschichte', *Osteuropa* (1977), 27, p. 190, and his

'Aspekte und Probleme der Osteuropaforschung seit 1945', *Osteuropa* (1980), 30, pp. 683ff.

85. *Ibid.*, pp.691–2.

86. *Ibid.*, p. 695.

87. *Ibid.*, p. 700.

88. *Ibid.*, p. 704.

89. For a good discussion of these developments see Manfred Hellmann, 'Zur Lage der historischen Erforschung des östlichen Europa in der Bundesrepublik Deutschland', *Jahrbuch der historischen Forschung*, ed. Fritz Wagner (Stuttgart 1980), *Berichtsjahr*, 1979, p. 32.

90. Klaus-Detlef Grothusen, 'Südosteuropa und Südosteuropa- Forschung in der Bundesrepublik Deutschland', in H. Lemberg, P. Nitschke and E. Oberländer, eds., *Osteuropa in Geschichte und Gegenwart. Festschrift für Günther Stökl* (Cologne/Vienna 1977), p. 413.

91. Reinhard Olt, 'Kalter Krieg mit anderen Mitteln', *FAZ* (1987), no. 23 28.1.87. I am grateful to Albrecht Kannegiesser for this reference.

BIBLIOGRAPHY

UNPUBLISHED SOURCES

Berlin Document Center (BDC)

Personal files and other material on:

Fritz Arlt	Wolfgang Kohte	Klaus Mehnert
Hermann Aubin	Wilfried Krallert	Helmut Meinhold
Max Hildegard Boehm	Walter Kuhn	Konrad Meyer
Albert Brackmann	Eberhard von Künsberg	Theodor Oberländer
Wilhelm Coblitz	Alfred Lattermann	Günther Pancke
Franz Doubek	Georg Leibbrandt	Johannes Papritz
Hans Ehlich	Friedrich Lenz	Anton Plügel
Werner Essen	Werner Lorenz	Werner Radig
Hans Frank	Kurt Lück	Otto Reche
Wilhelm Gradmann	Wilhelm Luig	Robert Ritter
Ulrich Greifelt	Werner Markert	Peter-Heinz Seraphim
Jürgen von Hehn	Erich Maschke	Hans Uebersberger
Erich Keyser	Gerhard Masing	Reinhard Wittram

Bundesarchiv, Koblenz (BA)

R 153 (*Publikationsstelle Berlin-Dahlem*) – Numbers: 1, 2, 5, 6, 12, 43, 44, 45, 46, 47, 48, 49, 53, 55, 57, 58, 59, 72, 98, 106 110, 111, 146, 151, 161, 216, 217, 218, 219, 220, 233, 240, 280, 284, 286, 288, 289 290, 291, 304, 379, 388, 396, 441, 505, 515, 525, 526, 532, 537, 542, 547, 551, 580 583, 584, 591, 594, 608, 613, 618, 627, 628, 630, 632, 665, 666, 669, 710, 733, 758, 769, 774, 783, 784, 790, 791, 795, 810, 876, 882, 937, 943, 948, 950, 951, 952, 962, 963, 1008, 1035, 1039, 1040, 1042, 1044, 1048, 1049, 1050, 1057, 1070, 1076, 1085, 1088, 1112, 1113, 1121, 1125, 1131, 1134, 1138, 1140, 1142, 1143, 1147, 1152, 1161, 1165, 1173, 1174, 1197, 1202, 1206, 1209, 1212, 1216, 1217, 1218, 1220, 1222, 1228, 1233, 1239, 1245, 1250, 1258, 1262, 1263, 1271, 1278, 1280, 1281, 1283, 1293, 1202, 1305, 1309, 1310, 1333,

1348, 1349, 1352, 1356, 1361, 1371, 1372, 1375, 1385, 1387, 1388, 1393, 1442, 1452, 1453, 1455, 1456, 1458, 1461, 1465, 1512, 1516, 1517, 1521, 1522, 1523, 1538, 1541, 1542, 1544, 1545, 1549, 1550, 1566, 1569, 1570, 1571, 1572, 1573, 1587, 1588, 1589, 1590, 1646, 1650, 1666, 1669, 1674, 1675, 1677, 1701, 1704, 1708, 1779, 1784, 2105

R521V (*Institut für deutsche Ostarbeit*) – Numbers: 2, 5, 6, 7, 8, 9, 13a, b, c, d, g, 15, 22, 39, 44, 51, 52, 59, 60, 61, 62, 64, 65, 66, 67, 68, 69, 70, 74, 75, 76, 77, 78, 85, 86, 87, 88, 90, 92, 93, 95, 96, 98, 99, 100, 101, 102, 103, 104, 105, 106, 107, 108, 109, 110, 111, 112, 113, 114, 115, 116, 117, 118, 120, 121, 122, 123, 124, 129, 130, 131, 132, 133, 138, 139, 140, 141, 142, 144a, b, 145, 147, 148, 152

R58 (*Reichssicherheitshauptamt*) – Numbers: 101, 125, 126

R57/DAI (*Deutscher Auslands-Institut, Stuttgart*) – Numbers: 344, 889, 890, 891, 910, 937, 1386

NS 21 (*SS-Ahnenerbe*) – Number: 444

R431/II (*Reichskanzlei*) – Numbers: 1480a, 1800, 1811, 1812, 1815

R52 II (*Akten der Regierung des Generalgouvernements*) – Numbers: 143, 173, 174–246 = Hans Frank *Tagebuch* (here TB) consisting of about 11,000 typed sides of speeches, meetings, conferences, timetable of visits/ visitors etc.; 250

All. Proz. 21 – Numbers: 92–7 case against Prof. Roland Brinckmann

Geheimes Staatsarchiv, Berlin-Dahlem (GStA)

(Rep. 92 *Nachlass* Brackmann) – Numbers: 1, 2, 7, 8, 16, 17, 20, 22, 25, 29, 44, 47, 50, 51, 53, 57, 61, 62, 65, 81, 82, 83, 84, 85, 86, 104

J. G. Herder Institut, Marburg

32 xv JZ2 Publikationsstelle *Polenberichte*
Publikationsstelle maps catalogued under Doubek, F. and Maydell, K. von

Hessische Staatsarchiv, Marburg (HStA)

(*Nachlass* Papritz Number 340) – C 12, C 12d 32, C 12d 40, C 12d/10, C 12a/5, C 12d/31, C 12d 106/12, C 12g 32; general correspondence A–Z, C 12d/41, C 12d/30, C 12d 64–5, C 12 dI, C 12 d2, C 12 a31, C 12c 12, C 12d 104/627, C 12 d104/e27, C 12 d79–80, C 12h 2, 4

Uniwersytet Jagielloński Archimum, Cracow (UJA)

Institut für deutsche Ostarbeit (IdO) – Numbers: 1, 2, 3, 5, 6, 10, 11, 19, 20, 34, 35, 36, 37, 38, 39, 40, 41, 42, 47, 48, 57, 59, 61, 70, 71, 77, 79, 80, 81, 83, 84, 85, 86, 91, 92, 96, 97, 98, 100, 107, 108, 111, 112, 113, 114, 115, 116, 117, 118

Wiener Library, London (WL)

P.C 105g, 177/G10f 1, and films of books and periodicals

PUBLISHED SOURCES

Arlt, Fritz. 'Der jüdische Einbruch in den deutschen Arbeitsraum', *Der Schulungsbrief* (1938), 5, pp. 185–9

—— 'Die Unterjochung der Nichtjuden', *Der Weltkampf* (1938), 15, pp. 199–202

—— 'Der Endkampf gegen das Judentum', *Der Weltkampf* (1938), 15, pp. 125–8

—— 'Hardenbergs Briefwechsel mit dem Ältesten und Vorstehern der Judengemeinde zu Breslau', *Der Weltkampf* (1939), 16, pp. 163–70

—— *Siedlung und Landwirtschaft in den eingegliederten Gebieten Oberschlesiens. Die Wirtschaftlichen Entwicklungsmöglichkeiten in den eingegliederten Ostgebieten des Deutschen Reiches. Im Auftrage der Haupttreuhandstelle Ost and des Reichskommissars für die Festigung Deutschen Volkstums, Stabshauptamt,* ed. Walther Geisler (Berlin 1942), vol. 10

Arlt, Fritz, ed. *Die Ukrainische Volksgruppe im Generalgouvernement. Volkspolitischer Informationsdienst der Regierung des Generalgouvernements. Innere Verwaltung* (Krakau 1940), Heft 1

Aubin, Hermann. 'Die historische-geographischen Grundlagen der deutschpolnischen Beziehungen', *Deutschland und Polen. Beiträge zur ihren geschichtlichen Beziehungen,* ed. Albert Brackmann (Munich/Berlin 1933), pp. 13–25

—— *Schlesien. Ausfallstor deutscher Kultur nach dem Osten,* ed. by the Landesstelle für Heimatpflege in Niederschlesien und der niederschlesischen Landesgruppe der Deutschen Akademie (Breslau-Deutsch Lissa 1937)

—— 'Zur Erforschung der deutschen Ostbewegung', *Deutsches Archiv für Landes- und Volksforschung* (1937), 1, pp. 37–70, 309–31, 563–602, reprinted in *Grundlagen und Perspektiven geschichtlicher Kulturraumforschung und Kulturmorphologie,* ed. Franz Petri (Bonn 1965), pp. 537–626

—— 'Das Deutsche Reich and die Völker des Ostens', *Die Burg* (1940), 1, pp. 7–20

—— 'Deutschlands Leistung und Aufgabe für Ostschlesien', *Schlesien. Zeitschrift für den gesamtschlesischen Raum* (1940), 2, pp. 17–19

—— *Die geschichtlichen Krafte für den Neuaufbau im mittelalterlichen Osten.* Festvortrag aus Anlass der Eröffnung der sudetendeutschen Anstalt für Landes- und Volksforschung im Reichenberg am 13. Oktober 1940 (Berlin 1940)

—— *Die volkspolitische Bedeutung von Gewerbe und Industrie in Ostdeutschland* (Breslau 1941)

—— 'The Lands East of the Elbe and German Colonization Eastwards', *The Cambridge Economic History of Europe*, vol. 1, *The Agrarian Life of the Middle Ages*, eds. J. H. Clapham, E. Power (Cambridge 1941), pp. 449–86

—— 'Das Gesamtbild der mittelalterlichen deutschen Ostsiedlung', *Deutsche Ostforschung. Ergebnisse und Aufgaben seit dem ersten Weltkrieg*, eds. H. Aubin, O. Brunner, W. Kohte and J. Papritz (Leipzig 1942), vol. 1, pp. 331–61

—— 'An einem neuen Anfang der Ostforschung', *ZfO* (1952), 1, pp. 3–16

—— 'Die Deutschen in der Geschichte des Ostens', *GWU* (1956), 7, pp. 512–45

—— 'Ergänzung zu Enno Meyer, Probleme einer deutsch-polnischen Diskussion über den Inhalt der Geschichts-Lehrbücher', *GWU* (1958), 9, pp. 429–30

—— *Hermann Aubin 1885–1969. Werk und Leben.* Reden gehalten am 23 März 1970 bei der Trauerfeier des Instituts für geschichtliche Landeskunde an der Rheinischen Friedrich-Wilhelms-Universität Bonn. *Alma Mater. Beiträge zur Geschichte der Universität* (Bonn 1970), no. 32

Augustin, K. H. and P. Nasarski. 'Ein Leben für die Forschung', in E. O. Kossmann, ed., *Deutsche mitten in Polen. Unsere Vorfahren am Webstuhl der Geschichte* (Berlin 1985), pp. 7–12

Baedeker, Karl. *Das Generalgouvernement. Reisehandbuch* (Leipzig 1943)

Boberach, Hans. *Meldungen aus dem Reich. Die geheimen Lageberichte des Sicherheitsdienstes der SS 1938–1945* (Herrsching 1984), vols. 1–17

Brackmann, Albert, E. Joachim, O. Krauske and A. Seraphim, eds. *Ost-Preussische Kriegshefte auf Grund amtlicher und privater Berichte* (Berlin 1916)

—— *Ostpreussens Kriegsschicksale. Ein geschichtlicher Rückblick in ernster Zeit* (Königsberg 1917)

—— 'Die politische Entwicklung Osteuropas vom 10–15 Jahrhundert', in *Deutschland und Polen. Beiträge zu ihren geschichtlichen Beziehungen*, eds. Albert Brackmann and Karl Brandi (Munich/Berlin 1933), pp. 28–39

—— 'Germany and Eastern Europe', *Research and Progress* (1937), 3, pp. 175–8

— 'Deutschlands Bedeutung für den osteuropäischen Raum', *Raumforschung und Raumordnung. Monatsschrift der Reichsarbeitsgemeinschaft für Raumforschung* (1939), 3, pp. 497–501

— *Krisis and Aufbau in Osteuropa. Ein weltgeschichtliches Bild* (Ahnenerbe-Stiftung Verlag, Berlin 1939)

Brackmann, Albert, ed. *Deutschland und Polen. Beiträge zu ihren geschichtlichen Beziehungen* (Munich/Berlin 1933)

— ed., with H. Aubin, M. Hein, J. Papritz, E. Randt, W. Recke and H. Uebersberger. *Deutschland und der Osten. Quellen and Forschungen zur Geschichte ihre Beziehungen* (Leipzig 1936ff.), vols. 1–14.

Brandi, Karl. 'Der Siebente Internationale Historikerkongress zu Warschau und Krakau, 21–29 August 1933', *HZ* (1934), 149, pp. 213–20

Braun, Joachim Freiherr von. 'Fünf Jahre Arbeit für den deutschen Osten. Der Göttinger Arbeitskreis. Tätigkeitsbericht zu seinem fünfjährigen Bestehen', *Jahrbuch der Albertus-Universität zu Königsberg Pr.* (1952), 2, pp. 208–51

Bühler, Josef, ed. *Das Generalgouvernement. Seine Verwaltung und seine Wirtschaft* (Krakau 1943)

Coblitz, Wilhelm. 'Das Institut für deutsche Ostarbeit', *Institut für deutsche Ostarbeit Jahrbuch 1941* (Krakau 1942), pp. 7–57

Conze, Werner. 'Die weissrussische Frage in Polen', *Bund Deutscher Osten. Schulungsbrief* (Berlin n.d.), no. 6

Diehls, P. 'Das Osteuropainstitut in Breslau', *Zeitschrift des oberschlesischen Bergund Hüttenmännischen Verein* (1920), 59, pp. 149–53

Doubek, Franz. 'Die Ostgrenze der polnischen Volkstumsmehrheit', *Jomsburg* (1936), 2; 'Die litauisch-polnisch Volkstumsgrenze,' *Jomsburg* (1938), 2, pp. 168–91

— 'Die zahlmässige Verbreitung des Deutschtums in Mittelpolen', *Jomsburg* (1938), 2, pp. 380–1

Du Prel, Max Freiherr, ed. *Das Generalgouvernement* (Würzburg 1942)

Europas Schicksalskampf im Osten. Exhibition catalogue (Berlin 1938)

Forstreuter, Adalbert. *Der endlose Zug. Die Deutsche Kolonisation in ihrem geschichtlichen Ablauf. Kampfschriften der Obersten SA Führung* (Munich 1939), no. 14

Frank, Hans. 'Deutsche Ordnung und polnische Wirtschaft', *Der Schulungsbrief* (1941), 8, pp. 88–90

Geisler, Walter. *Deutscher! Der Osten Ruft dich! Die Wirtschaftlichen Entwicklungsmöglichkeiten in den eingegliederten Ostgebieten des Deutschen Reiches*, vol. 1 (Berlin 1941)

Gottong, Heinrich. 'Das biologische Bild einer deutschen Gemeinde in Polen Jablonna, Kreis Warschau-Land', *DFO* (1941), H. 1–2

— 'Stand der anthropologischen Forschung im früheren Polen', *DFO* (1941), H. 4

—— 'Eine polnische Bevölkerungsgruppe in Generalgouvernement', *DFO* (1941), H. 5

—— 'Bedeutung and Aufgaben der Sektion Rassen- und Volkstumsforschung', *DFO* (1941), H. 1

Graul, Hans. 'Das Weichselgebiet, eine mitteleuropäische Landschaft', *Institut für deutsche Ostarbeit. Jahrbuch 1941* (Krakau 1941), pp. 216–35

Hacker, Jens. 'Die Entwicklung der Ostforschung seit 1945. Ein Blick auf die bestehenden Institute und ihre Arbeitsweise', ed. *Landeskuratorium UNTEILBARES DEUTSCHLAND Schleswig-Holstein* (Kiel 1958)

Hagemeyer, Hans and Georg Leibbrandt, eds. *Europa und der Osten* (Munich 1939, 1943$_2$)

Haushaltsplan des Generalgouvernement. Vols. 1–4 (Krakau 1941–4)

Hein, Max. 'Ostpreussen', *Deutschland und Polen. Beiträge zu ihren geschichtlichen Beziehungen*, eds. A. Brackmann and K. Brandi (Munich/Berlin 1933), pp. 123–34

Herrschaft, Hans. *Das Banat. Ein deutsches Siedlungsgebiet in Südosteuropa* (Berlin 1942$_2$)

Himmler, Heinrich. *Die Schutzstaffel als antibolschewistische Kampforganisation* (Munich 1936)

—— 'Künder ewiger Grösse. Deutsche Burgen im Osten', *Der Schulungsbrief* (1941), 8, pp. 42–3 (reprinted as 'Deutsche Burgen im Osten', SS-*Leitheft* (1941) 6, pp. 12ff.

—— 'Denkschrift Himmlers über die Behandlung der Fremdvölkischen im Osten', ed. H. Krausnick, *VjHSZG* (1957), 5, pp. 194–8

Hitler, Adolf. *Mein Kampf*, trans Ralph Manheim (London 1974)

Hoetzsch, Otto. 'Russland als Gegner Deutschlands', *Zwischen Krieg und Frieden* (Leipzig 1914), no. 6

—— *Russland. Eine Einführung auf Grund seiner Geschichte vom 1912 bis 1914* (Berlin 1915$_2$)

—— 'Brandenburg-Preussen and Polen 1640–1815', *Deutschland und Polen. Beiträge zu ihren geschichtlichen Beziehungen*, eds. A. Brackmann and K. Brandi (Munich/Berlin 1933), pp. 185–206

'Das Institut für ostdeutsche Wirtschaft an der Albertus-Universität in Königsberg Pr.', *Ein Führer für Studierende* (Königsberg, n.d.)

Jaeger, Fritz. 'Die Siebenbürger Sachsen, geographisch betrachtet', in *Volk unter Völkern*, ed. K. C. von Loesch (Breslau 1925), pp. 168–83

Kasiske, Karl. 'Neuere Forschungen zur Geschichte des Deutschen Ordens', in *Deutsche Ostforschung. Ergebnisse und Aufgaben seit dem ersten Weltkrieg*, eds. H. Aubin, O. Brunner, W. Kohte and J. Papritz (Leipzig 1941), 1, pp. 446ff.

Kasiske, Karl and E. Maschke, *Der Deutsche Ritterorden. Seine politische und kulturelle Leistung im Deutschen Osten* (Berlin 1942)

Keyser, Erich. *Danzigs Geschichte* (Danzig 1921), pp. 101–6

—— 'Das Ordensland und die Deutsche Hanse', in *Deutsche Staatenbildung und deutsche Kultur im Preussenlande*, ed. *Landeshauptmann der Provinz Ostpreussen* (Königsberg 1931), pp. 89–103

—— *Geschichte des deutschen Weichsellandes* (Leipzig 1940)

—— 'Die Erforschung der Bevölkerungsgeschichte des deutschen Ostens', in *Deutsche Ostforschung. Ergebnisse und Aufgaben seit dem ersten Weltkrieg*, eds. H. Aubin, O. Brunner, W. Kohte and J. Papritz (Leipzig 1942), 1, pp. 90–104

—— 'Der Johann Gottfried Herder-Forschungsrat and das Johann Gottfried Herder-Institut', *ZfO* (1952), 1

Koch, Erich. 'Aufbau im neuen Ostpreussen', *Der Schulungsbrief* (1941), 8, pp. 39–41

Kohte, Wolfgang. 'Der VII Internationale Historikertag in Warschau', *Volk und Reich* (1933), 10, pp. 897–900

—— Deutsch-polnisches Schicksal an den Weichsel', *Wille und Macht* (1939), H. 20, pp. 12–19

—— 'Deutsche Ostforschung – Überlieferung und Aufgabe', *Der Student der Ostmark. Kampfblatt der Deutschen Studenten im Osten* (1940), F. 9, pp. 284–92

—— 'Arbeit im Osten – Heimat im Osten', *Wille und Macht* (1941), 16, pp. 9–14

—— 'Wirtschaftsentwicklung und Volkstumskampf der neueren Zeit im deutschwestslawischen Grenzraum', in *Deutsche Ostforschung. Ergebnisse und Aufgaben seit dem ersten Weltkrieg*, eds. H. Aubin, O. Brunner, W. Kohte and J. Papritz (Leipzig 1943), 2, pp. 357–98

Kossmann, Eugen Oskar. 'Die preussischen Landesaufnahmen in Polen', *Jomsburg* (1937), 1, pp. 19–31

—— 'Stammesspiegel deutscher Dörfer in Mittelpolen', *Jomsburg* (1937), 1, pp. 329–42

—— 'Urlandschaft und deutschrechtliche Siedlung in Mittelpolen', *Jomsburg* (1939), 3, pp. 139–42

—— 'Voraussetzungen der deutschen Ostsiedlung seit dem Mittelalter', *Jomsburg* (1939), 3, pp. 276–93

—— *Die Anfänge des Deutschtums im Litzmannstädter Raum. Hauländer und Schwabensiedlung im östlichen Wartheland* (Leipzig 1942)

—— 'Historisch-geographische Kräfte in der deutschen Ostbewegung des Mittelalters', *Deutsche Ostforschung. Ergebnisse und Aufgaben seit dem ersten Weltkrieg*, eds. H. Aubin, O. Brunner, W. Kohte and J. Papritz (Leipzig 1942), 1, pp. 31–57

—— *Deutsche mitten in Polen. Unsere Vorfahren am Webstuhl der Geschichte* (Berlin/Bonn 1985)

Kötzschke, Rudolf. 'Über der Ursprung und die geschichtliche Bedeutung der ostdeutschen Siedlung', *Der ostdeutsche Volksboden. Aufsätze zu den Fragen des Ostens*, ed. Wilhelm Volz (Breslau 1926$_2$), pp. 7–26

—— 'Die deutsche Wiederbesiedelung der ostelbischen Lande', *ibid.*, pp. 152–79

Kötzschke, Rudolf and Wolfgang Ebert. *Geschichte der ostedeutschen Kolonisation* (Leipzig 1937)

Kuhn, Walter. 'Die deutsche Leistung in Ostmitteleuropa. Die Lebensformen der ostdeutschen Volksinseln', *Bund Deutscher Osten. Schulungsbrief* (Berlin 1938)

—— 'Die Erforschung der neuzeitlichen deutschen Ostsiedlung', *Deutsche Ostforschung. Ergebnisse und Aufgaben seit dem Ersten Weltkrieg*, eds. H. Aubin, O. Brunner, W. Kohte, J. Papritz (Leipzig 1943), 2, pp. 155–235

—— 'Kurt Lück 1900–1942', *ZfO* (1952), 1, pp. 425–6

—— 'Ritterorden als Grenzhüter des Abendlandes gegen das östliche Heidentum', *Ostdeutsche Wissenschaft* (1959), 6, pp. 7–70

—— 'Das Lebenswerk Viktor Kauders', *Der Kulturwart* (1969), 17, pp. 1–10

—— 'Meine Forschungsarbeiten in Wolhynien', ed. *Historischer Verein Wolhynien e. V.* (Schwabach *c.* 1977)

—— 'Eine Jugend für die Sprachinselforschung. Erinnerungen', *Jahrbuch der schlesischen Friedrich-Wilhelms-Universität zu Breslau* (1982), 23, pp. 224–78

La Baume, Wolfgang. 'Das Land an der unteren Weichsel in vor- und frühgeschichtlicher Zeit', in *Der ostdeutsche Volksboden. Aufsätze zu den Fragen des Ostens*, ed. W. Volz (Breslau 1926₂), pp. 87–100

—— 'Das Land an der unteren Weichsel in vorgeschichtlicher Zeit', in *Deutsche Staatenbildung und deutsche Kultur im Preussenlande*, ed. Landeshauptmann der Provinz Ostpreussen (Königsberg 1931), pp. 1–7

Lattermann, Alfred. 'Frühere deutsche Kulturarbeit im Wartheland', *NS-Monatshefte* (1941), F. 130, pp. 1–7.

—— 'Deutsche Forschung im ehemaligen Polen 1919–1939', in *Deutsche Ostforschung. Ergebnisse und Aufgaben seit dem ersten Weltkrieg*, eds. H. Aubin, O. Brunner, W. Kohte and J. Papritz (Leipzig 1943), 3, pp. 461–87

Leibbrandt, Georg and Hans Hagemeyer, eds. *Europa und der Osten* (Munich 1939, 1943₂)

Loesch, K. C. von, ed. *Volk unter Völkern. Bücher des Deutschtums* (Breslau 1925), vol. 1

Loessner, Anton. 'Der polnische Offizier im Dienste der Wissenschaft', *Jomsburg* (1937), 1, pp. 315–29

—— 'Die polnische See- und Kolonialliga', *Jomsburg* (1937), 1, pp. 229–33

—— 'Hinter der litauischen Mauer', *Jomsburg* (1938), 2, pp. 192–6

Lorentz, Friedrich. 'Die Kaschuben', in *Der ostdeutsche Volksboden. Aufsätze zu den Fragen des Ostens*, ed. W. Volz (Breslau 1926₂), pp. 244–64

Lorentz, Friedrich, Adam Fischer and Tadeusz Lehr-Spławinski. *The Cassubian Civilisation* (London 1935)

Lück, Kurt. 'Die Bauern im polnischen Roman des 19. Jahrhunderts', *Schrift zur Erlangung der philosophischen Doktorwürde bei der Philosophischen Fakultät der Schlesischen Friedrich-Wilhelms-Universität zu Breslau* (Poznań 1926)

—— *Deutsche Aufbaukräfte in der Entwicklung Polens. Forschungen zur Deutschpolnischen Nachbarschaft im ostmitteleuropäischen Raum*, ed. Viktor Kauder (Plauen i. Vogtland 1934), 1

—— *Marsch der Deutschen in Polen. Deutsche Volksgenossen im ehemaligen Polen berichten über Erlebnisse in den Septembertagen* 1939 (Berlin 1940)

—— *Der Lebenskampf im deutsch-polnischen Grenzraum. Der Osten Europas*, vol. 4 (Berlin 1940)

—— *Deutsche Gestalter und Ordner im Osten. Forschungen zur deutschpolnischen Nachbarschaft im ostmitteleuropäischen Raum*, ed. Viktor Kauder, vol. 3 (Posen 1940)

—— 'Deutsche Volksgruppen aus dem Osten kehren heim ins Vaterland', *Tornisterschrift des Oberkommandos der Wehrmacht Abt. Inland* (1941), Heft 19

—— *Der Mythos vom Deutschen in der polnischen Volksüberlieferung und Literatur. Forschungen zur deutsch-polnischen Nachbarschaft im ostmitteleuropäischen Raum*, vol. 2, ed. Viktor Kauder (Leipzig 1943$_2$)

Lück, Walter. 'Mit Dr. Kurt Lück . . .', *Posener Stimmen. Heimatblatt des Hilfskomitees der Glieder der Posener Evgl. Kirche* (1967), 14, no. 3, pp. 6–7

Malaparte, Curzio. *Kaputt* (Frankfurt am Main 1979)

Mann, Fritz Karl. 'Die neuen Aufgaben des Instituts für ostdeutsche Wirtschaft', *Ein Vortrag* (Königsberg 1922)

—— 'Ostdeutsche Wirtschaftsforschung', *Schriften des Instituts für ostdeutsche Wirtschaft an der Universität Königsberg* (Jena 1926), H. 15 (2 Reihe, Heft 4)

Maschke, Erich. 'Quellen und Darstellungen in der Geschichtsschreibung des Preussenlandes', in *Deutsche Staatenbildung und deutsche Kultur im Preussenlande*, ed. Landeshauptmann der Provinz Ostpreussen (Königsberg 1931), pp. 17–39

—— *Der Deutsche Ordensstaat. Gestalten seiner grosser Meister* (Hamburg 1936$_2$)

—— 'Das deutsche Gemeinschaftsleben im Mittelalter', *Der Schulungsbrief* (1936), 3, pp. 90–105

—— 'Hanse und Ritterorden im Zug nach Osten', *Der Schulungsbrief* (1936), 4, pp. 130–46

—— 'Das mittelalterliche Deutschtum in Polen', in *Deutsche Ostforschung. Ergebnisse und Aufgaben seit dem ersten Weltkrieg*, eds. H. Aubin, O. Brunner, W. Kohte and J. Papritz (Leipzig 1942), 1, pp. 486–515

—— 'Begegnungen mit Geschichte', in *Städte und Menschen. Beiträge zur*

Geschichte der Stadt, der Wirtschaft und Gesellschaft 1959–1977. Viertel-jahrschrift für Sozial und Wirtschaftsgeschichte. Beihefte no. 68, ed. W. Conze, H. Kellenbenz, E. Maschke, H. Pohl and W. Zorn (Wiesbaden 1980), pp. vii–xix

Maschke, Erich and Karl Kasiske. *Der Deutsche Ritterorden. Seine politische und kulturelle Leistung im Deutschen Osten* (Berlin 1942)

Meinhold, Helmut. 'Die verkehrspolitische Bedeutung der Weichsel', *Jahrbuch des Instituts für deutsche Ostarbeit 1941* (Krakau 1942), pp. 194–215

—— 'Das Generalgouvernement als Transitland. Ein Beitrag zur Kenntnis der Standortslage des Generalgouvernements', *Die Burg* (1941), 2, pp. 24–44

—— 'Die Arbeiterreserven des Generalgouvernements', *Die Burg* (1942), 3, pp. 273–91

—— 'Der Aufgabenbereich der Sektion Wirtschaft. Grundlagen der Wirt-schaftsforschung im Generalgouvernement', *DFO* (1941), H. 4, pp. 39–43

—— 'Die Erweiterung des Generalgouvernements nach Osten' (IdO Krakau July 1941 typed manuscript)

Mortensen, Hans. 'Des Memelgebiet – Die Geschichte seiner Besiedlung', *Bund Deutscher Osten Schulungsbrief* (Berlin, n.d.), no. 34

Mortensen, Hans and Gertrud. *Die Besiedlung des nordöstlichen Ostpreussen bis zum Beginn des 17. Jahrhunderts.* Part 1: *Die preussisch-deutsche Siedlung am Westrand der Grossen Wildnis um 1400.* Part 2: *Die Wildnis im östlichen Preussen, ihr Zustand um 1400 and ihre frühe Besiedlung. Deutschland und der Osten. Quellen und Forschungen zur Geschichte ihrer Beziehungen*, eds. H. Aubin, A. Brackmann, M. Hein, J. Papritz, E. Randt, W. Recke and H. Uebersberger, vols. 7–8 (Leipzig 1937–8)

Oberländer, Theodor. 'Die Bevölkerungsdichte im Generalgouvernement', *Das Generalgouvernement* (1940), 1, pp. 47–52

—— 'Grundgedanken zu einer völkischen Sozialpolitik', *Neues Bauerntum* (1941), 33, pp. 145–7

—— 'Die agrarische Überbevölkerung Ostmitteleuropas', in *Deutsche Ost-forschung. Ergebnisse und Aufgaben seit dem ersten Weltkrieg*, eds. H. Aubin, O. Brunner, W. Kohte and J. Papritz (Leipzig 1943), 2, pp. 416–28

Oncken, Hermann. 'Preussen und Polen im 19. Jahrhundert', in *Deutschland und Polen. Beiträge zu ihren geschichtlichen Beziehungen*, eds. A. Brack-mann and K. Brandi (Munich/Berlin 1933), pp. 220–37

Pagel, Karl, ed. *The German East* (Berlin 1954)

Papritz, Johannes and Gerhard Sappok, eds. *Krakau. Hauptstadt des deutschen Generalgouvernements Polen. Deutsche Städte-Führer im Osten*, vol. I (Leipzig 1940)

Papritz, Johannes, H. Aubin, O. Brunner and W. Kohte, eds. *Deutsche*

Ostforschung Ergebnisse und Aufgaben seit dem ersten Weltkrieg (Leipzig 1942–43), 1–2

Penck, Albrecht. 'Deutscher Volks- und Kulturboden', in *Volk unter Völkern. Bücher des Deutschtums*, vol. 1, ed. K. C. von Loesch (Breslau 1926), pp. 62–73

Plügel, Anton and Heinrich Gottong. 'Bedeutung and Aufgaben der Sektion Rassen- und Volkstumsforschung', *DFO* (1941), 1, pp. 28ff.

— 'Rassen- und Volkstümer im Generalgouvernement', *Zeitschrift für Erkunde* (1942), 10, pp. 351–60

— 'Die Podhalnischen Góralen im südlichsten Teil des Kreises Neumarkt', *Die Burg* (1941), 2, pp. 54–86

Radig, Werner. 'Die Vorgeschichte des ostdeutschen Lebensraumes', *Die Burg* (1941), 2, pp. 5–24

— 'Indogermanen und Germanen im Weichselraum', *Jahrbuch des Institut für deutsche Ostarbeit* (Krakau 1941), pp. 169–93

Reche, Otto. Über die Bodenständigkeit des Deutschtums östlich der Elbe', *Der Öffentliche Gesundheitsdienst* (1937), 3, pp. 625–8

— 'Der Wert des erbbiologischen Abstammungsnachweises. Eine amtliche Stellungnahme', *Informationsdienst Rassenpolitisches Amt der NSDAP. Reichsleitung* (1939), no. 93

— 'Stärke und Herkunft des Anteils nordischer Rasse bei des Westslawen', in *Deutsche Ostforschung. Ergebnisse und Aufgaben seit dem ersten Weltkrieg*, eds. H. Aubin, O. Brunner, W. Kohte and J. Papritz (Leipzig 1942), 1, pp. 58–89

Reimers, Erich. *Der Kampf um den deutschen Osten* (Leipzig 1939)

Rhode, Gotthold. 'Das Bild des Deutschen im polnischen Roman des 19. und beginnenden 20. Jahrhunderts and das polnische Nationalgefühl', *Ostdeutsche Wissenschaft* (1961), 8, pp. 327–66

— 'Wolfgang Kohte (1907–1984), *ZfO* (1984), 33, pp. 407–10

Rhode, Gotthold and Walter Kuhn. 'Hermann Aubin and die Geschichte des deutschen and europäischen Ostens', *ZfO* (1969), 18, pp. 601–21

Rosen, Hans Freiherr von. *Wolhynienfahrt 1926. Schriften der J. G. Herder-Bibliothek, Siegerland e.V.* (Siegen 1982), vol. 10

Rosenberg, Alfred. 'Der deutsche Ordensstaat', *Der Schulungsbrief* (1934), 1, pp. 10–16

Schaeder, Hildegard. 'Die Ursachen des Untergangs des alten polnischen Staats im Urteil der heutigen polnischen Öffentlichkeit', *Jomsburg* (1937), 1, pp. 31–7

— *Geschichte der Pläne zur Teilung des alten polnischen Staates seit 1386. Part 1: Der Teilungsplan von 1392. Deutschland und der Osten. Quellen und Forschungen zur Geschichte ihrer Beziehungen*, eds. H. Aubin, A. Brackmann *et al.* (Leipzig 1937), vol. 5

—— 'Die historischen Ostgrenze Polens im Verhältnis zur heutigen polnischen Volkstumsmehrheit', *Jomsburg* (1938), 2, pp. 28–34

—— 'Die neuen polnischen Wojewodschaftsgrenzen', *Jomsburg* (1938), 2, pp. 197–9

—— 'Epochen der Reichspolitik im Nordosten von den Luxemburgern bis zur Heiligen Allianz', *Deutsche Ostforschung. Ergebnisse und Aufgaben seit dem ersten Weltkrieg*, eds. H. Aubin, O. Brunner, W. Kohte and J. Papritz (Leipzig 1943), 2, pp. 1–42

Schiemann, Theodor. *Geschichte Russlands unter Kaiser Nikolaus I* (Berlin 1904–8), vols. 1–2

Schirmacher, Käthe. *Unsere Ostmark. Deutsche Michel, wach auf! Eine Reihe nationaler Schriften*, ed. Oberst a.D. Immanuel (Leipzig 1923)

Schlenger, Herbert. 'Hans Mortensen', *ZfO* (1966), 15, pp. 401–3

Schmitt-Ott, Friedrich. *Erlebtes und Erstrebtes* (Wiesbaden 1952)

Seraphim, Peter-Heinz. 'Das Judentum in Osteuropa', *Bund Deutscher Osten Schulungsbrief* (Berlin n.d.), no. 28

—— 'Das ostjüdische Ghetto', *Jomsburg* (1937), 1, pp. 439–65

—— *Das Judentum im osteuropäischen Raum* (Essen 1938)

—— 'Die Judenfrage im Generalgouvernement als Bevölkerungsproblem', *Die Burg* (1940), 1, pp. 56–63

—— 'Bevölkerungs- und wirtschaftspolitische Probleme einer europäischen Gesamtlösung der Judenfrage', *Weltkampf* (1941), 18, pp. 46–51

—— *Die Wirtschaftsstruktur des Generalgouvernements* (IdO Krakau 1941)

—— 'Deutschtum und Judentum in Osteuropa', in *Deutsche Ostforschung. Ergebnisse und Aufgaben seit dem ersten Weltkrieg*, eds. H. Aubin, O. Brunner, W. Kohte and J. Papritz (Leipzig 1943), 2, pp. 428–46

Sommerfeldt, Josef. 'Die Entwicklung der Geschichtsschreibung über die Juden in Polen', *Die Burg* (1940), 1, pp. 64–79

—— 'Die Juden in den polnischen Sprichwörtern und Sprichwörtlichen Redensarten', *Die Burg* (1942), 3

—— 'Die Ostjudenfrage als Problem der preussischen Verwaltung im 18. und 19. Jahrhundert', *Jahrbuch des Institut für deutsche Ostarbeit* (Krakau 1942), pp. 136–68

—— 'Judenstaatsprojekte in der polnischen Publizistik des 19. Jahrhunderts', *Die Burg* (1944), 5, pp. 14–26

'Träger der polnischen Auslandspropaganda', *Bund Deutscher Osten. Schulungsbrief* (Berlin 1937)

Uebersberger, Hans. 'Österreich', *Deutschland und Polen. Beiträge zu ihren geschichtlichen Beziehungen*, eds. A. Brackmann, K. Brandi (Munich/ Berlin 1933), pp. 172–83

Vasmer, Max. 'Die Urheimat der Slawen', *Der ostdeutsche Volksboden. Aufsätze zu den Fragen des Ostens*, ed. Wilhelm Volz (Breslau 1926₂), pp. 118–43

—— 'Der deutsche Einfluss in der polnischen Literatur', in *Deutschland und Polen. Beiträge zu ihren geschichtlichen Beziehungen*, eds. A. Brackmann and K. Brandi (Munich/Berlin 1933), pp. 41–50

Verordnungsblatt des Generalgouvernements fur die besetzten polnischen Gebiete (Krakau 1939ff.)

Vollert, Ernst. 'Albert Brackmann und die ostdeutsche Volks- und Landesforschung', in *Deutsche Ostforschung. Ergebnisse und Aufgaben seit dem ersten Weltkrieg*, eds. H. Aubin, O. Brunner, W. Kohte and J. Papritz (Leipzig 1942), 1, pp. 3–11

Volz, Wilhelm, ed. *Der ostdeutsche Volksboden. Aufsätze zu den Fragen des Ostens* (Breslau 1926₂)

SECONDARY LITERATURE

Abendroth, Wolfgang. 'Universität im Faschismus', Hochschule und Wissenschaft im Faschismus, *Forum Wissenschaft* (1985), 2, pp. 3–7

—— 'Die deutschen Professoren und die Weimarer Republik', in *Hochschule und Wissenschaft im Dritten Reich*, ed. Jörg Tröger (Frankfurt am Main 1986), pp. 11–25

Ackermann, Josef. *Heinrich Himmler als Ideologe* (Göttingen 1970)

Aly, Götz and Karl Heinz Roth. *Die restlose Erfassung. Volkszahlen, Identifizieren, Aussondern im Nationalsozialismus* (West Berlin, 1984)

Aly, Götz and Susanne Heim. *Ein Berater der Macht. Helmut Meinhold oder der Zusammenhang zwischen Sozialpolitik und Judenvernichtung* (Hamburg/Berlin 1986)

Anweiler, Oskar. '25 Jahre Osteuropaforschung- Wissenschaft und Zeitgeschichte', *Osteuropa* (1977), 27, pp. 183–90

—— 'Aspekte and Probleme der Osteuropaforschung seit 1945', *Osteuropa* (1980), 30, pp. 673–87

Bartov, Omer. *The Eastern Front 1941–45, German Troops and the Barbarisation of Warfare* (London 1985)

Batowski, Henryk, 'Nazi Germany and Jagiellonian University', *Polish Western Affairs* (1978), 19, pp. 113–20

Benz, Wolfgang. 'Der Generalplan Ost. Zur Germanisierungspolitik des NS-Regimes in den besetzten Ostgebieten 1939–1945', *Die Vertreibung der Deutschen aus dem Osten. Ursachen, Ereignisse, Folgen*, ed. Wolfgang Benz (Frankfurt am Main 1985), pp. 39–48

Berlin, Isaiah. *Vico and Herder. Two Studies in the History of Ideas* (London 1976)

Berthold, Werner. 'Die Wandlung des Historikers Otto Hoetzsch. Sein Beitrag zur Entwicklung eines fortschrittlichen Geschichtsbewussteins 1946', *ZfG* (1966), 14, pp. 732–44

Beyerchen, Alan D. *Scientists under Hitler. Politics and the Physics Community in the Third Reich* (New Haven/London 1977)

Bielfeldt, Hans Holm. 'Die Geschichte der Lehrstuhls für Slawistik an der Berliner Universität', in *Beiträge zur Geschichte der Slawistik*, eds. H. M. Bielfeldt and K. Horálek, *Veröffentlichungen des Instituts für Slawistik*, ed. H. H. Bielfeldt (East Berlin 1964), no. 30, pp. 267–80

Bittner, Konrad. *Herders Geschichtsphilosophie und die Slawen. Veröffentlichungen der Slavistischen Arbeitsgemeinschaft an der Deutschen Universität in Prag*, eds. Franz Spina and Gerhard Gesemann (Reichenberg 1929), *Heft* 6

Bleuel, Hans Peter. *Deutschlands Bekenner. Professoren zwischen Kaiserreich und Diktatur* (Bonn, Munich, Vienna n.d.)

Bollmus, Reinhard. *Das Amt Rosenberg und seine Gegner. Studien zum Machtkampf im nationalsozialistischen Herrschaftssystem* (Stuttgart 1970)

Broszat, Martin. *Nationalsozialistische Polenpolitik 1939–1945* (Frankfurt am Main 1965₂)

—— *Zweihundert Jahre deutsche Polenpolitik* (Frankfurt am Main 1972₂)

—— *The Hitler State*, trans. John Hiden (London 1981)

—— *Die Machtergriefung. Der Aufstieg der NSDAP und die Zerstörung der Weimarer Republik. Deutsche Geschichte der neuesten Zeit vom 19. Jahrhundert bis zur Gegenwart*, eds. M. Broszat, W. Benz and H. Graml (Munich 1984)

Buchholz, Arnold. 'Koordination und Ressortbezug in der bundesgeförderten Osteuropaforschung', *Osteuropa* (1980), 30, pp. 688–704

Burleigh, Michael. 'The Knights, Nationalists and the Historians: Images of Medieval Prussia from the Enlightenment to 1945', *European History Quarterly* (1987), 17, pp. 35–55

—— 'Albert Brackmann, *Ostforscher* (1871–1952): the Years of Retirement', *Journal of Contemporary History* (1988), 23, pp. 573–88

Bussmann, Walter. 'Gustav Freytag. Massstäbe seiner Zeitkritik', *Archiv für Kulturgeschichte* (1952), 34, pp. 261–87

—— 'Treitschke als Politiker', *HZ* (1954), 177, pp. 249–69

—— *Treitschke. Sein Welt- und Geschichtsbild. Göttinger Bausteine zur Geschichtswissenschaft*, ed. H. Goetting, H. Grebing *et al.* (Göttingen 1981₂), vol. 3/4

Chickering, Roger. *We Men Who Feel Most German. A Cultural Study of the Pan-German League 1886–1914* (London 1984)

Chodera, Jan. *Die deutsche Polenliteratur 1918–1939. Stoff- und Motivgeschichte* (Poznań 1966)

—— '"Deutsche Mission im Osten" und Germanisierung der polnischen Bevölkerung in der deutschen Literatur des 20. Jh.', in *Studia Historica Slavo-Germanica*, eds. A. Czubinski, H. Orlowski, B. Piotrowski and J. Strzelczyk (Poznań 1973), 1, pp. 195–213

Cygański, Mirosław. 'Nazi Persecutions of Polish National Minorities in the

Rhineland-Westphalia Provinces in the Years 1933–1945', *Polish Western Affairs* (1976), 17, pp. 115–38

Dallin, Alexander. *German Rule in Russia 1941–1945. A Study of Occupation Policies* (London 1981₂) .

Dorpalen, Andreas. *Heinrich von Treitschke* (New Haven/London 1957)

—— 'Heinrich von Treitschke', in *Historians in Politics*, eds. W. Laqueur and G. Mosse (London 1974), pp. 21–35

—— 'Die Geschichtswissenschaft in der DDR', in *Geschichtswissenschaft in Deutschland. Traditionelle Positionen und gegenwärtige Aufgaben*, ed. Bernd Faulenbach (Munich 1974), pp. 121–86

—— *German History in Marxist Perspective. The East German Approach* (London 1985)

Elsner, Helmut. 'Abteilung für Geschichte der imperialistischen Ostforschung', in *Osteuropa in der historischen Forschung der DDR*, ed. M. Hellmann (Düsseldorf 1972), 1, pp. 123–31

Engelberg, E., L. Stern, M. Steinmetz *et al.* 'Zu den Vorfällen auf der 24. Versammlung des westdeutschen Historiker-Verbandes in Trier', *ZfG* (1958), 6, pp. 1134–6

Engelberg, E., ed. *Trier – und wie weiter? Materialen, Betrachtungen, und schlussfolgerungen über die Ereignisse auf dem Trierer Historikertag am 25.9.1958* (Berlin 1959)

Epstein, Fritz T. 'Friedrich Meinecke in seinem Verhältnis zum europäischen Osten', *Jahrbuch für die Geschichte Mittel- und Ostdeutschlands* (1954), 3, pp. 119–44

—— 'Otto Hoetzsch als aussenpolitischer Kommentator während des Ersten Weltkrieges', *Gedenkschrift für Otto Hoetzsch. Schriftenreihe Osteuropa* (Stuttgart 1957), no. 3, pp. 9–28

—— 'Hamburg und Osteuropa. Zum Gedächtnis von Professor Richard Salomon (1884–1966)', *Jahrbücher für Geschichte Osteuropas* (1967), pp. 59–98

—— 'Otto Hoetzsch', *Neue Deutsche Biographie* (West Berlin 1972), 9, pp. 371–2

—— 'Der Komplex "Die russische Gefahr" and sein Einfluss auf die deutsch-russischen Beziehungen im 19. Jahrhundert', *Deutschland in der Weltpolitik des 19. und 20. Jahrhunderts. Fritz Fischer zum 65. Geburtstag*, eds. I. Geiss and B. J. Wendt (Düsseldorf 1973), pp. 143–59

—— *Germany and the East. Selected Essays*, ed. Robert F. Byrnes (Bloomington/London 1973)

—— 'Otto Hoetzsch und sein "*Osteuropa*" 1925–1930', *Osteuropa* (1975), 25, pp. 541–54

—— *Russland-Deutschland-Amerika. Festschrift für Fritz T. Epstein zum 80 Geburtstag*, eds. A. Fischer, G. Moltmann and K. Schwabe (Wiesbaden 1978)

Faulenbach, Bernd. 'Deutsche Geschichtswissenschaft zwischen Kaiserreich und NS-Diktatur', *Geschichtswissenschaft in Deutschland. Traditionelle Positionen und Gegenwärtige Aufgaben*, ed. B. Faulenbach (Munich 1974), pp. 66–85

Fest, Joachim. *The Face of the Third Reich* (London 1970)

Fiedor, Karol, Janusz Sobczak and Wojciech Janusz. 'The Image of the Poles in Germany and of the German in Poland in inter-war years and its role in shaping the relations between the two States', *Polish Western Affairs* (1978), 19, pp. 202–28

Fischer, Fritz. *War of Illusions: German Policies from 1911 to 1914* (London 1975)

—— 'Zum Problem der Kontinuität in der deutschen Geschichte von Bismarck zu Hider', *Nationalsozialistische Diktatur 1933–1945, Eine Bilanz*, eds. K. D. Bracher, Manfred Funke and H.-A. Jacobsen, *Schriftenreihe der Bundeszentrale für politische Bildung*, vol. 192 (Bonn 1983), pp. 770–82

Fischer, Rudolf. 'Reinhold Trautmann in der deutschen Slawistik', *Beiträge zur Geschichte der Slawistik*, eds. H. H. Bielfeldt and K. Horálek, *Veröffentlichungen des Instituts für Slawistik*, ed. H. H. Bielfeldt, no. 30 (East Berlin 1964), pp. 171–82

Fleming, Gerald. *Hitler and the Final Solution* (Oxford 1986)

Franz, Günther. 'Das Geschichtsbild des Nationalsozialismus and die deutsche Geschichtswissenschaft', in *Geschichte und Geschichtswissenschaft*, ed. O. Hauser (Göttingen/Zurich 1981), pp. 91–111

Franz, R. and R. Gross. 'Wissenschaftliche Beziehungen zwischen sowjetischen und deutschen Archiven in den Jahren 1917–1933', *Archivmitteilungen. Zeitschrift für Theorie und Praxis des Archivwesens* (1966), 16, pp. 81–90

Galos, Adam, F.-H. Gentzen and W. Jakóbczyk. *Die Hakatisten. Der deutschen Ostmarkenverein 1894–1934. Ein Beitrag zur Geschichte der Ostpolitik des deutschen Imperialismus* (East Berlin 1966)

Gawęda, S. *Die Jagiellonische Universität in der Zeit der faschistischen Okkupation 1939–1945* Jena 1981)

—— 'The Image of a Pole in 19th Century Germany', *Polish Western Affairs* (1978), 19, pp. 175–96

Geiss, Imanuel. *Der polnische Grenzstreifen 1914–1918. Ein Beitrag zur deutschen Kriegszielpolitik im Ersten Weltkrieg. Historischen Studien. Heft 378* (Lübeck/Hamburg 1960)

Gentzen, Felix-Heinrich. 'Karl Marx über Polen', *ZfG* (1953), 1, pp. 310–44

—— 'Die „Ostforschung" westdeutscher Historiker – eine Hetze gegen die Sowjetunion und Volkspolen', *Einheit. Zeitschrift für Theorie und Praxis des wissenschaftlichen Sozialismus* (1955), 10, pp. 1214–22

—— 'Zur Geschichte des deutschen Revanchismus in der Periode der Weimarer Republik', *Jahrbuch für Geschichte der UdSSR und der volksdemokratischen Länder Europas* (1960), 4, pp. 40–78

—— 'Die Rolle der deutschen Regierung beim Aufbau deutscher Minderheits-organisationen in den an Polen abgetretenen Gebieten (1919–1922)', *Jahrbuch für Geschichte der UdSSR und der volksdemokratischen Länder Europas* (1967), 10, pp. 159–82

Gentzen, Felix-Heinrich, J. Kalisch, G. Voigt and E. Wolfgramm. 'Die „Ost-forschung" – ein Stosstrupp des deutschen Imperialismus', *ZfG* (1958), 6, pp. 1181–220

Gentzen, Felix-Heinrich and E. Wolfgramm. *„Ostforscher" – „Ostforschung". Taschenbuch Geschichte*, 8 (Berlin 1960)

Geyer, Dietrich. 'Georg Sacke', in *Deutsche Historiker*, ed. Hans-Ulrich Wehler (Göttingen 1973), pp. 603–15

Giertz, Horst. 'Das Berliner-Seminar für osteuropäische Geschichte und Landeskunde (bis 1920)', *Jahrbuch für Geschichte der UdSSR und der volksdemokratischen Länder Europas* (1967), 10, pp. 183–217

Goguel, Rudolf. *Es war ein langer Weg. Ein Roman unserer Zeit* (Düsseldorf 1947)

—— 'Über Ziele und Methoden der Ostforschung', *„Ostforschung" und Slawistik. Kritische Auseinandersetzungen. Vorgetragen auf der Arbeitstagung am 3 Juli 1959 am Institut für Slawistik der Deutschen Akademie der Wissenschaften zu Berlin*, ed. Gerhard Ziegengeist (Berlin 1960), pp. 12–39

—— 'Ostpolitik und Ostforschung', *ZfG* (1964), 12, pp. 1340–58

—— 'Über die Mitwirkung deutscher Wissenschaftler am Okkupationsregime in Polen im 2. Weltkrieg untersucht an 3 Institutionen der deutschen Ostforschung', *Phil. Diss.* (East Berlin 1964)

—— 'Die Nord- und Ostdeutsche Forschungsgemeinschaft im Dienste der faschistischen Aggressionspolitik gegen Polen 1933–1945', *Archivmitteilungen. Zeitschrift für Theorie und Praxis des Archivwesens* (1967), 17, pp. 82–9

Gollwitzer, Heinz. *Europabild und Europagedanke. Beiträge zur deutschen Geistesgeschichte des 18. und 19. Jahrhunderts* (Munich 1964)

Graf, Rudolf. 'Hermann Aubin im Dienste der faschistischen Okkupationspolitik gegenüber Polen und des klerikalmilitarischen Antibolshewismus', *Beiträge zur Geschichte der Arbeiterbewegung* (1960), 2, pp. 187–211

Graus, Frantisek. 'Geschichtsschreibung und Nationalsozialismus', *VjHZG* (1969), 17, pp. 87–95

Grothusen, Klaus-Detlev. 'Südosteuropa und Südosteuropaforschung. Zur Lage der Südosteuropa-Forschung in der Bundesrepublik Deutschland', in *Osteuropa in Geschichte und Gegenwart. Festschrift für Günther Stökl zum 60. Geburtstag*, eds. Hans Lemberg, Peter Nitsche and Erwin Oberländer (Cologne/Vienna 1977), pp. 408–26

Hagen, William W. *Germans, Poles, and Jews. The Nationality Conflict in the Prussian East 1772–1914* (Chicago 1980)

Hartwig, Edgard. 'Deutscher Ostmarkenverein' (DOV), *Lexikon zur Parteien-*

geschichte. Die bürgerlichen und kleinbürgerlichen Parteien und Verbände in Deutschland (1789–1945), vols. 1–4, eds. Dieter Fricke, Werner Fritsch, Herbert Gottwald, Siegfried Schmidt and Manfred Weissbecker (Leipzig 1983), 2, pp. 225–44

Heiber, Helmut. 'Der Generalplan Ost', VjHZG (1958), 6, pp. 281–325

—— Walter Frank und sein Reichsinstitut für Geschichte des neuen Deutschlands. Quellen und Darstellungen zur Zeitgeschichte (Stuttgart 1966), vol. 13

Heitz, Gerhard. 'Rudolf Kötzschke (1867–1949). Ein Beitrag zur Pflege der Siedlungs- und Wirtschaftsgeschichte in Leipzig', Karl-Marx-Universität Leipzig 1409–1959. Beiträge zur Universitätsgeschichte (Leipzig 1959), 2, pp. 262–74

Hellmann, Manfred, ed. Osteuropa in der historischen Forschung der DDR (Düsseldorf 1972), 1–2

—— 'Der Disput aus heutiger Sicht', Osteuropa (1975), 25, pp. 442–57

—— 'Zur Lage der historischen Erforschung des östlichen Europa in der Bundesrepublik Deutschland', in Jahrbuch der historischen Forschung im Auftrag der Arbeitsgemeinschaft ausseruniversitäter historischer Forschungseinrichtungen in der Bundesrepublik Deutschland, ed. F. Wagner et al. Berichtsjahr 1979 (Stuttgart 1980), pp. 13–38

Hiden, J. and J. Farquarson. Explaining Hitler's Germany. Historians and the Third Reich (London 1983)

Hinze, Friedhelm. 'Zum Leben und Werk von Friedrich Lorentz (1970–1937). Eine Würdigung anlässlich seines 25. Todestages', Beiträge zur Geschichte der Slawistik, eds. H. H. Bielfeldt and H. Horálek, Veröffentlichungen des Instituts für Slawistik, ed. H. H. Bielfeldt, no. 30 (East Berlin 1964), pp. 81–112

Hühne, Heinz. The Order of the Death's Head. The Story of Hitler's SS, trans. R. Barry (London 1972)

Iggers, Georg G. 'Heinrich von Treitschke', in Deutsche Historiker, ed. Hans-Ulrich Wehler (Göttingen 1971), 2, pp. 66–80

—— 'Die deutschen Historiker in der Emigration', in Geschichtswissenschaft in Deutschland. Traditionelle Positionen and gegenwärtige Aufgaben, ed. Bernd Faulenbach (Munich 1974), pp. 97–111

—— New Directions in European Historiography (London 1985, revised edn)

Jäckel, Eberhard. Hitler's World View. A Blueprint for Power, trans. H. Arnold (Cambridge, Mass. 1981)

Jacobsen, Hans-Adolf and Werner Jochmann, eds. Ausgewählte Dokumente zur Geschichte des Nationalsozialismus 1933–1945 (Bielefeld 1961)

—— Nationalsozialistische Aussenpolitik 1933–1938 (Frankfurt am Main 1968)

—— 'Vom Wandel des Polenbildes in Deutschland (1772–1972)', Aus Politik und Zeitgeschichte (1973), 21, pp. 3–21

—— '„Kampf um Lebensraum": Karl Haushofers „Geopolitik" and der Nationalsozialismus', *Aus Politik und Zeitgeschichte* (1979), 34/35, pp. 17–29

Kaczmarczyk, Zdzisław. 'German Colonisation in Medieval Poland in the Light of the Historiography of both Nations', *Polish Western Affairs* (1970), 11, pp. 3–40

Kalisch, Johannes and Gerd Voigt. ' "Reichsuniversität Posen". Zur Rolle der faschistischen deutschen Ostforschung im Zweiten Weltkrieg', *Juni 1941*, ed. A. Anderle (Berlin 1961), pp. 183–204

Kalisch, Johannes, F.-H. Gentzen, G. Voigt and E. Wolfgramm, 'Die „Ostforschung" – ein Stosstrupp des deutschen Imperialismus', *ZfG* (1958), 6, pp. 118–220

Kater, Michael. 'Die Artamanen- Völkische Jugend in der Weimarer Republik', *HZ* (1971), 213, pp. 577–638

—— *Das „Ahnenerbe" der SS 1935–1945. Ein Beitrag zur Kulturpolitik des Dritten Reiches* (Stuttgart 1974)

Kellermann, Volkmar. *Schwarzer Adler – Weisser Adler. Die Polenpolitik der Weimarer Republik* (Cologne 1970)

Kienast, W. and T. Schieder. 'Der Historikertag in Trier', *HZ* (1958), 186, pp. 728–31

Klessmann, Christoph. *Die Selbstbehauptung einer Nation. NS-Kulturpolitik und polnische Widerstandsbewegung. Studien zur modernen Geschichte*, eds. F. Fischer, K.-D. Grothusen and G. Moltmann (Düsseldorf 1971), vol. 5

—— 'Der Generalgouverneur Hans Frank', *VjHZG* (1971), 19, pp. 245–60

—— 'Polen in deutschen Geschichtsbüchern', *GWU* (1972), 23, pp. 731–53

—— 'Osteuropaforschung und Lebensraumpolitik im Dritten Reich', in *Wissenschaft im Dritten Reich*, ed. Peter Lundgreen (Frankfurt am Main 1986), pp. 350–82

Kluge, Rolf-Dieter, 'Darstellung und Bewertung des Deutschen Ordens in der deutschen and polnischen Literatur', *ZfO* (1969), 1, pp. 15–53

Koehl, Robert L. *RKFDV: German Resettlement and Population Policy 1939–1945. A History of the Reich Commission for the Strengthening of Germandom* (Cambridge, Mass. 1957)

Kolb, Eberhard. 'Polenbild und Polenfreundschaft der deutschen Frühliberalen. Zu Motivation und Funktion aussenpolitischer Parteinahme im Vormärz', *Saeculum* (1975), 26, pp. 111–27

Körner, Josef. 'Die Slaven im Urteil der deutschen Frühromantik', *Historische Vierteljahreszeitschrift* (1936/37), 31, pp. 565–76

Krausnick, Helmut, Hans Buchheim, Martin Broszat and Hans-Adolf Jacobsen. *Anatomie des SS-Staates* (Olten/Freiburg im Breisgau 1965, 1979₂), vols. 1–2

—— *Hitlers Einsatzgruppen. Die Truppen des Weltanschauungskrieges 1936–1942* (Frankfurt am Main 1985)

Krekeler, Norbert. *Revisionsanspruch und geheime Ostpolitik der Weimarer Republik. Die Subventionierung der deutschen Minderheit in Polen 1919–1933* (Stuttgart 1973)

—— 'Der deutsche Minderheit in Polen and die Revisionspolitik des Deutschen Reiches 1919–1933', in *Die Vertreibung der Deutschen aus dem Osten*, ed. W. Benz (Frankfurt am Main 1985), pp. 15–28

Kuebart, Friedrich. 'Otto Hoetzsch – Historiker, Publizist, Politiker. Eine kritische biographische Studie', *Osteuropa* (1975), 25, pp. 603–21

—— 'Zur Entwicklung der Osteuropaforschung in Deutschland bis 1945', *Osteuropa* (1980), 30, pp. 657–71

Kühnl, Reinhard. 'Weltbild und Nation: Ideologische Motive präfaschistischer Geschichtswissenschaft', *Hochschule und Wissenschaft im Faschismus. Forum Wissenschaft* (1985), 2, pp. 26–7

—— 'Reichsdeutsche Geschichtswissenschaft', in *Hochschule und Wissenschaft im Dritten Reich*, ed. Jörg Tröger (Frankfurt am Main 1986), pp. 92–104

Labuda, Gerard. 'Geschichte der deutschen Ostkolonisation in den neueren westdeutschen Forschungen', *Polish Western Affairs* (1961), 2, pp. 260–83

—— 'A Historiographic Analysis of the German „Drang nach Osten"', *Polish Western Affairs* (1964), 5, pp. 221–65

—— 'The Slavs in Nineteenth Century German Historiography', *Polish Western Affairs* (1969), 10, pp. 177–234

Laqueur, Walter. *Russia and Germany. A Century of Conflict* (London 1965)

Leesch, W. 'Das Institut für Archivwissenschaft und geschichtswissenschaftliche Fortbildung (IfA) in Berlin-Dahlem (1930–1945)', in *Brandenburgische Jahrhunderte. Festgabe für Johannes Schultze zum 90. Geburtstag*, eds. G. Heinrich and W. Vogel. *Veröffentlichungen des Vereins für Geschichte der Mark Brandenburg* (Berlin 1971), 35, pp. 219–54

Lemberg, Eugen. 'Ostmitteleuropa im deutschen Geschichtsbewusstsein', *Deutscher Osten und slawischer Westen. Tübinger Vorträge* (Tübingen 1955), pp. 111–27

Lemberg, Hans. 'Der „Drang nach Osten". Schlagwort und Wirklichkeit', in *Deutsche im europaischen Osten. Verständnis und Missverständnis*, eds. F. B. Kaiser, B. Stasiewski (Cologne/Vienna 1976), pp. 1–17

—— 'Lage und Perspektiven der Zeitgeschichtsforschung über Ostmitteleuropa in der Bundesrepublik Deutschland', *ZfO* (1986), 35, pp. 191ff.

Lifton, Robert Jay. *The Nazi Doctors. A Study in the Psychology of Evil* (London 1986)

Magdefrau, Werner. 'Heinrich von Treitschke and die imperialistische „Ostforschung", *ZfG* (1963), 11, pp. 1444–65

—— 'Zur Beurteilung der mittelalterlich-deutschen Ostexpansion in der bürgerlichen Geschichtsschreibung von Herder bis Treitschke', *Jahrbuch für*

Geschichte der UdSSR und der volksdemokratischen Länder Europas (1966), 9, pp. 277–85

McClelland, C. E. *The German Historians and England. A Study in Nineteenth-Century Views* (Cambridge, Mass. 1971)

—— 'Berlin Historians and German Politics', in *Historians and Politics*, eds. W. Laqueur and G. L. Mosse (London 1974), pp. 191–221

—— *State, Society and University in Germany 1700–1914* (Cambridge 1980)

Meinert, Hermann. 'Albert Brackmann und das deutsche Archivwesen', *Archivalische Zeitschrift* (1954), 49, pp. 127–38

Merson, Allan. *Communist Resistance in Nazi Germany* (London 1985)

Metsk, Frido. 'Das Sorbenbild in der westdeutschen „Ostforschung"', *ZfG* (1965), 13, pp. 1174–85

—— *Bestandsverzeichnis der Sorbischen Kulturarchivs in Bautzen* Teil III. *Das Depositum Wendenabteilung. Schriftenreihe des Instituts für sorbische Volksforschung in Bautzen* (Bautzen 1967)

Meyer, Henry Cord. 'Der „Drang nach Osten" in den Jahren 1860–1914', *Die Welt als Geschichte* (1957), 17, pp. 1–8

Meyer, Klaus. *Theodor Schiemann als politischer Publizist. Nord- und osteuropäische Geschichtsstudien*, ed. Paul Johansen (Frankfurt am Main 1956), 1

Mückenberger, Christiane. 'Zum Wesen and zur Entwicklung der „Ostforschung"', in *Beiträge zur Geschichte der Slawistik*, eds. H. H. Bielfeldt and K. Horálek. *Veröffentlichungen des Instituts für Slawistik* no. 30 (East Berlin 1966), pp. 281–93

Nolte, Ernst. 'Konservativismus und Nationalsozialismus', *Zeitschrift für Politik*, NF (1964), 11, pp. 5–20

—— 'Zur Typologie des Verhaltens der Hochschullehrer im Dritten Reich', *Aus Politik und Zeitgeschichte* (1965), 46, pp. 3–14

Nolte, Hans-Heinrich. *"Drang nach Osten". Sowjetische Geschichtsschreibung der deutschen Ostexpansion. Studien zur Gesellschaftstheorie*, eds. Norbert Altmann, Martin Baethge, Gerhard Brandt *et al.* (Cologne/Frankfurt am Main 1976)

Olszewski, Henryk. 'Das Geschichtsbild – ein Bestandteil der NS-Ideologie', in *Tradition und Neubeginn. Internationale Forschungen zur deutschen Geschichte im 20. Jahrhundert. Referate und Diskussionen eines Symposiums der Alexander von Humboldt-Stiftung*, eds. Joachim Hütter, Reinhard Meyers and Dietrich Papenfus (Cologne/Berlin/Bonn/Munich 1975), pp. 299–316

Orlow, Dietrich. 'Die Adolf-Hitler Schulen', *VjHZG* (1965), 13, pp. 272–84

Posner, Ernst. 'Der Neubau des Geheimen Staatsarchivs in Berlin-Dahlem', *Archivalische Zeitschrift* (1925), 35, pp. 22–40

Pospieszalski, K. M. 'Z Pamiętnika Profesors „Reichsuniversität Posen"', *Przegląd Zachodni* (1955), 11, pp. 275–99

Remer, Claus. Über die Tätigkeit der Arbeitsgemeinschaft zur Bekämpfung der westdeutschen Ostforschung', *Jahrbuch für Geschichte der UdSSR und der volksdemokratischen Länder Europas* (1963), 7, pp. 449–56

Ringer, Fritz. *The Decline of the German Mandarins. The German Academic Community, 1890–1933* (Cambridge, Mass. 1969)

Ritter, Ernst. *Das Deutsche Ausland-Institut in Stuttgart 1917–1945. Ein Beispiel deutscher Volkstumsarbeit zwischen den Weltkriegen. Frankfurter Historische Abhandlungen*, eds. W. Gembruch, P. Herde, P. Kluke *et al.* (Wiesbaden 1976)

Ronneberger, Franz. 'Zwischenbilanz der Südosteuropa-Forschung: Leistungsstand, Schwierigkeiten, Zukunftsprognosen', *Südosteuropa-Mitteilungen* (1980), 20, pp. 3–17

Rössler, Mechthild. 'Die Geographie an der Universität Freiburg 1933–1945. Ein Beitrag zur Wissenschaftsgeschichte des Faches im Dritten Reich', *Zulassungsarbeit. Universität Freiburg* (1983)

Rothbarth, Maria. 'Der Bund Deutscher Osten – Instrument des aggressiven faschistischen deutschen Imperialismus', *Wissenschaftliche Zeitschrift der Universität Rostock. Gesellschafts- und Sprachwissenschaftliche Reihe* (1972), 21, pp. 3–17

Saller, K. *Die Rassenlehre des Nationalsozialismus in Wissenschaft und Propaganda* (Darmstadt 1961)

Schabrod, Karl. *Widerstand gegen Flick und Florian. Düsseldorfer Antifaschisten über ihren Widerstand 1933–1945* (Frankfurt am Main 1976)

Scholz, Harald. 'Die NS-Ordensburgen', *VjHZG* (1967), 15, pp. 269–98

Schreiner, Klaus. 'Führertum, Rasse, Reich. Wissenschaft von der Geschichte nach der nationalsozialistischen Machtergreifung', in *Wissenschaft im Dritten Reich*, ed. Peter Lundgreen (Frankfurt am Main 1985), pp. 163–252

Schwabe, Klaus. *Wissenschaft und Kriegsmoral. Die deutschen Hochschullehrer und die politischen Grundfragen des Ersten Weltkrieges* (Göttingen 1969)

—— Sołta, Jan, Klaus Schiller, Martin Kasper and Frido Mětšk. *Geschichte der Sorben. Schriftenreihe des Instituts für sorbische Volksforschung in Bautzen*, vols. 1–4 (Bautzen 1977–9)

Spill, Ingetraud. 'Prof. Dr Harald Cosack – vom "Ostforscher" zum akademischen Lehrer an der Universität Rostock', *Staatsexamensarbeit*. Wilhelm-Pieck-Universität Rostock 1965

Stavenhagen, Kurt. 'Herders Geschichtsphilosophie und seine Geschichtsprophetic', *ZfO* (1952), 1, pp. 16–43

Stebelski, Adam. *The Fate of Polish Archives During World War II. The Central Directorate of State Archives* (Warsaw 1964)

Stern, Leo. 'Die klerikal-imperialistische Abendland-Ideologie im Dienste des deutschen Imperialismus', *ZfG* (1962), 10, pp. 286–315

Stökl, Günther. *Osteuropa und die Deutschen* (Stuttgart 1982₃)

Szarota, Tomasz. 'Poland and Poles in German Eyes during World War II', *Polish Western Affairs* (1978), 19, pp. 228–54

Szeczinowski, W. 'Die Organisation der „Ostforschung" in Westdeutschland', *ZfG* (1954), 2, pp. 288–309

Tröger, Jörg, ed. *Hochschule und Wissenschaft im Dritten Reich* (Frankfurt am Main/New York 1986)

Unger, Manfred. 'Georg Sacke – Ein Kämpfer gegen den Faschismus', *Karl-Marx-Universität Leipzig 1409–1959. Beiträge zur Universitätsgeschichte* (Leipzig 1959), 2, pp. 307ff.

—— 'Georg Sacke (1901–1945)', in *Bedeutende Gelehrte in Leipzig*, ed. M. Steinmetz (Leipzig 1965), 1, pp. 239–242

Unser, Jutta. '„Osteuropa" Biographie einer Zeitschrift', *Osteuropa* (1975), 25, pp. 555–602

Vierhaus, Rudolf. 'Walter Frank und die Geschichtswissenschaft im national-sozialistischen Deutschland', *HZ* (1968), 207, pp. 617–27

Voigt, Gerd. 'Des "Institut für deutsche Ostarbeit" in Krakau', *September 1939*, ed. Basil Spiru (Berlin 1959), pp. 109–24

—— 'Methoden der "Ostforschung"', *ZfG* (1959), 7, pp. 1781–1803

—— 'Aufgaben und Funktion der Osteuropa Studien in der Weimarer Republik', in *Studien über die deutsche Geschichtswissenschaft*, ed. Joachim Streisand, vol. 1, *Die bürgerliche deutsche Geschichtsschreibung von der Reichseinigung von oben bis zur Befreiung Deutschlands vom Faschismus* (East Berlin 1965), pp. 369–99

—— *Otto Hoetzsch 1876–1946. Wissenschaft and Politik im Leben eines deutschen Historikers. Quellen und Studien zur Geschichte Osteuropas*, eds. Eduard Winter, Heinz Lemke *et al.*, vol. 21 (East Berlin 1978)

Voigt, Gerd and J. Kalisch. ' "Reichsuniversität Posen". Zur Rolle der faschist-ischen deutschen Ostforschung im Zweiten Weltkrieg', in *Juni 1941*, ed. A. Anderle (East Berlin 1961), pp. 183–204

Voigt, Gerd, J. Kalisch and E. Wolfgramm. 'Die „Ostforschung" – ein Stosstrupp des deutschen Imperialismus', *ZfG* (1958), 6, pp. 1181–220

Wasicki, J. 'Origins of the "Grenzmark Posen-Westpreussen" Province', *Polish Western Affairs* (1965), 6, pp. 150–70

Wegner, Bernd. *Hitlers Politische Soldaten: Die Waffen-SS 1933–1945. Studien zu Leitbild, Struktur and Funktion einer nationalsozialistischen Elite* (Paderborn 1983₂)

Wehler, Hans-Ulrich. 'Die Polenpolitik im deutschen Kaiserreich 1871–1918', in *Politische Ideologien und nationalstaatliche Ordnung. Studien zur Geschichte des 19. und 20. Jahrhunderts. Festschrift für Theodor Schieder*, eds. Kurt Kluxen and Wolfgang J. Mommsen (Munich/Vienna 1968), pp. 297–316

—— 'Von den „Reichsfeinden" zur "Reichskristallnacht": Polenpolitik im

Deutschen Kaiserreich 1871–1918', in his *Krisenherde des Kaiserreich 1871–1918. Studien zur deutschen Sozial- und Verfassungsgeschichte* (Göttingen 1970), pp. 181–99

—— 'Radikaldemokratische Geschichtswissenschaft: Eckart Kehr', *ibid.*, pp. 259–79

Weissbecker, Manfred. 'Bund Deutscher Osten (BDO)', in *Lexikon zur Parteiengeschichte. Die bürgerlichen und kleinbürgerlichen Parteien und Verbände in Deutschland (1789–1945)*, vols. 1–4, eds. Dieter Fricke, Herbert Gottwald, Siegfried Schmidt and Manfred Weissbecker (Leipzig 1983), 1, pp. 308–15

Werkstatt Düsseldorf des Werkkreises Literatur der Arbeitswelt ed. *Der rote Grossvater erzählt. Berichte und Erzählungen von Veteranen der Arbeiterbewegung aus der Zeit von 1914 bis 1945* (Frankfurt am Main 1974)

Werner, Karl Ferdinand. *Das NS-Geschichtsbild und die Geschichtswissenschaft* (Stuttgart 1967)

—— 'On Some Examples of the National-Socialist View of History', *JCH* (1968), 3, pp. 193–206

—— 'Die deutsche Historiographie unter Hitler', in *Geschichtswissenschaft in Deutschland. Traditionelle Positionen und gegenwärtige Aufgaben*, ed. B. Faulenbach (Munich 1974), pp. 86–96

Wippermann, Wolfgang. 'Geschichte and Ideologie im historischen Roman des Dritten Reiches', in *Die deutsche Literatur im Dritten Reich*, eds. Horst Denkler and Karl Prümm (Stuttgart 1976), pp. 183–206

—— *Der Ordensstaat als Ideologie. Das Bild des Deutschen Ordens in der deutschen geschichtsschreibung und Publizistik. Einzelveröffentlichungen der Historischen Kommission zu Berlin*, vol. 24: *Publikationen zur Geschichte der deutsch-polnischen Beziehungen*, vol. 2 (Berlin 1979)

—— 'Die Ostsiedlung in der deutschen Historiographie und Publizistik. Probleme, Methoden and Grundlinien der Entwicklung bis zum Ersten Weltkrieg', in *Germania Slavica*, ed. Wolfgang H. Fritze (Berliner Historische Studien) (Berlin 1980), 1, pp. 41–69

—— 'Das Bild der mittelalterlichen deutsche Ostsiedlung bei Marx and Engels', *ibid.*, pp. 71–97

—— '"Gen Ostland wollen wir reiten!" Ordensstaat und Ostsiedlung in der historischen Belletristik Deutschlands', in *Germania Slavica*, ed. Wolfgang M. Fritze (Berlin 1981), 2, pp. 187–235

—— *Der "Deutsche Drang nach Osten": Ideologie und Wirklichkeit eines politischen Schlagwortes. Impulse der Forschung*, vol. 35 (Darmstadt 1981)

—— 'Nationalsozialismus und Preussentum', *Aus Politik und Zeitgeschichte* (1981), B 52–53/81, pp. 13–22

—— 'Das Slawenbild der Deutschen im 19. and 20. Jahrhundert', *Slawen und Deutsche zwischen Elbe und Oder. Vor 1000 Jahren: Der Slawenaufstand von 983* (Berlin 1983), pp. 69–81

—— 'Die deutsche und polnische Frage in der deutschen Historiographie', *Aus Politik und Zeitgeschichte* (1987), B14/87, pp. 29–36

—— 'Probleme und Aufgaben der Beziehungsgeschichte zwischen Deutschen, Polen, und Juden' *Deutsche-Polen-Juden* ed. Stefi Jersch-Wenzel (Berlin 1987), pp. 1–47

—— 'Nationalsozialistische Zwangslager in Berlin III, Das „Zigeunerlager" Marzahn', *Berlin-Forschungen* ed. Wolfgang Ribbe (Berlin 1987), 2, pp. 189–201

—— 'Die Geschichte des "Reichsehrenmals Tannenberg"', *Niemandsland* (1987), 1, pp. 58–69

Wippermann, Wolfgang, ed. *Kontroversen um Hitler* (Frankfurt am Main 1986)

Wolfgramm, Eberhard. 'Kämpf für den Frieden, arbeitet für die Zukunft des deutschen Volkes! Abrechnung mit der Vergangenheit, von einem ehemaligen "Ostforscher"', *Deutscher Aussenpolitik* (1959), 9, pp. 991–1000

Wolfgramm, Eberhard and F.-H. Gentzen. *„Osforscher" – „Ostforschung"* Taschenbuch Geschichte no. 8 (Berlin 1960)

Wróblewski, Tadeusz Seweryn. *Ewolucja „Ostforschung" w Republice Federalnej Niemiec: (1969–1982) Studium Niemcoznawcze Instytutu Zachodniego* (Poznań 1986)

Zernack, Klaus. *Osteuropa. Eine Einführung in seine Geschichte* (Munich 1977)

Zientara, Benedykt. 'Zum Problem des geschichtlichen Terminus "Drang nach Osten"', *Preussen, Deutschland. Polen im Urteil polnischer Historiker*, ed. Lothar Dralle, *Einzelveröffentlichungen der Historischen Kommission zu Berlin*, vol. 37, *Reihe: Anthologien. Publikationen zur Geschichte der deutsch-polnischen Beziehungen*, vol. 4 (Berlin 1983), pp. 171–81

Zmarlik, Hans-Günther. 'Der Sozialdarwinismus in Deutschland als geschichtliches Problem', *VjHSZG* (1963), 11, pp. 246–73

INDEX

014847

THOMAS TALLIS SCHOOL LIBRARY